# MONEY,
# BANKING,
# & FINANCIAL MARKETS

CANADIAN EDITION

# MONEY, BANKING,
## & FINANCIAL MARKETS

**Stephen G. Cecchetti**

*The Bank for International Settlements*
*Basel Switzerland*

**Angela Redish**

*University of British Columbia*

McGraw-Hill Ryerson
Connect. Learn. Succeed.

**McGraw-Hill Ryerson**
Connect. Learn. Succeed.

**Money, Banking & Financial Markets**
**Canadian Edition**

Copyright © 2010 by McGraw-Hill Ryerson Limited, a Subsidiary of The McGraw-Hill Companies. Copyright © 2008, 2006 The McGraw-Hill Companies, Inc. All rights reserved. No part of this publication may be reproduced or transmitted in any form or by any means, or stored in a data base or retrieval system, without the prior written permission of McGraw-Hill Ryerson Limited, or in the case of photocopying or other reprographic copying, a license from The Canadian Copyright Licensing Agency (Access Copyright). For an Access Copyright licence, visit www.accesscopyright.ca or call toll free to 1-800-893-5777.

Statistics Canada information is used with the permission of Statistics Canada. Users are forbidden to copy the data and redisseminate them, in an original or modified form, for commercial purposes, without permission from Statistics Canada. Information on the availability of the wide range of data from Statistics Canada can be obtained from Statistics Canada's Regional Offices, its World Wide Web site at http://www.statcan.gc.ca, and its toll-free access number 1-800-263-1136.

ISBN-13: 978-0-07-098399-1
ISBN-10: 0-07-098399-2

1 2 3 4 5 6 7 8 9 10 TCP 1 9 8 7 6 5 4 3 2 1 0

Printed and bound in Canada.

Care has been taken to trace ownership of copyright material contained in this text; however, the publisher will welcome any information that enables them to rectify any reference or credit for subsequent editions.

VICE-PRESIDENT AND EDITOR-IN-CHIEF: Joanna Cotton
EXECUTIVE SPONSORING EDITOR: Leanna MacLean
SPONSORING EDITORS: Bruce McIntosh & James Booty
EXECUTIVE MARKETING MANAGER: Joy Armitage Taylor
DEVELOPMENTAL EDITORS: Daphne Scriabin & Andria Fogarty
SENIOR EDITORIAL ASSOCIATE: Stephanie Hess
SUPERVISING EDITOR: Jessica Barnoski
PHOTO/PERMISSIONS RESEARCH: Lynn McIntyre
COPY EDITOR: Karen Rolfe
PRODUCTION COORDINATOR: Sharon Stefanowicz
COVER DESIGN: Word & Image Design Studio Inc.
COVER IMAGE: artpartner-images.com/Alamy
INTERIOR DESIGN: Word & Image Design Studio Inc.
PAGE LAYOUT: Heather Brunton, Lesley Lavender/ArtPlus Limited
PRINTER: Transcontinental Printing Group

**Library and Archives Canada Cataloguing in Publication**

Cecchetti, Stephen G. (Stephen Giovanni)

Money, banking, and financial markets / Stephen G. Cecchetti, Angela Redish.—1st Canadian ed.
    Includes index.

ISBN 978-0-07-098399-1

    1. Money—Textbooks.    2. Banks and banking—Textbooks.    3. Finance—Textbooks.
4. Capital market—Textbooks.    I. Redish, Angela, 1952–    II. Title.

HG221.C386 2010              332              C2009-907018-9

# DEDICATION

*To my father, Giovanni Cecchetti, who argued tirelessly that financial markets are not efficient; and to my grandfather Albert Schwabacher, who patiently explained why inflation is destructive.*

*To Steve Elves, with thanks.*

# About the Authors

**STEPHEN G. CECCHETTI** is Economic Adviser and Head of the Monetary and Economic Department at the Bank for International Settlements in Basel Switzerland, an international organization which fosters international monetary and financial cooperation and serves as a bank for central banks. Prior to joining the BIS, Dr. Cecchetti was the Barbara and Richard M. Rosenberg Professor of Global Finance at the International Business School. He also taught at the New York University Stern School of Business and, for approximately 15 years, was a member of the Department of Economics at The Ohio State University. He has been a Visiting Professor of Economics at Princeton University, Oxford University, the University of Melbourne, and Boston College.

In addition to his current position at the BIS and his academic appointments, Cecchetti's background includes serving as Executive Vice President and Director of Research, Federal Reserve Bank of New York (1997–1999); Editor, *Journal of Money, Credit, and Banking* (1992–2001); Research Associate, National Bureau of Economic Research (1989–present); Research Fellow, Centre for Economic Policy Research (2008–present); Board of Editors, American Economic Review (1992–1998), and the *Journal of Economic Literature* (1993–2005), among others.

He has consulted for various central banks around the world, including the European Central Bank, the Bank of England, the Central Bank of Bolivia, the Bank of Israel, and the Reserve Bank of Australia.

Cecchetti's research interests include inflation and price measurement, monetary policy, macroeconomic theory, economics of the Great Depression, and financial economics. His initial work concentrated on the theoretical basis and empirical plausibility of new Keynesian models of the business cycle that are based on nominal rigidities. More recently, he has developed new measures of core inflation and examined how monetary policy can be used to control aggregate price movements.

He has published over 75 articles in academic and policy journals and from 2000 to 2008 was a regular contributor to the *Financial Times*.

Cecchetti received an SB in Economics from MIT in 1977 and a Ph.D. in Economics from the University of California at Berkeley in 1982.

**ANGELA REDISH** is a Professor of Economics at the University of British Columbia where she has taught since 1982. She served as Special Advisor to the Bank of Canada in 2000–1 and was Head of the Economics Department at UBC from 2001 to 2006. She has been a visiting scholar at the University of Toronto and Oxford University. As a CUSO volunteer, she worked as an economist at the Papua New Guinea Development Bank from 1978 to 1980.

She is the author of a book on the history of monetary standards before the 19th century, *Bimetallism: An Economic and Social Analysis* (Cambridge University Press, 2000) and numerous scholarly articles on the history of money and banking. These include historical comparisons of the stability of the U.S. and Canadian banking systems, and an analysis of the role of the Canadian banking system in Canada's economic growth. She has served on the Editorial Board of the *Journal of Economic History* (1997–2000) and the *Financial History Review* (2006–present), and is currently a Trustee of the Economic History Association and a member of the C.D. Howe Monetary Policy Council.

Redish received her Ph.D. in Economics from the University of Western Ontario after completing her M.A. there, and has a B.A. (Hons.) from Wilfrid Laurier University.

# BRIEF CONTENTS

# CONTENTS

## Part V    Modern Monetary Economics  454

# PREFACE

For most of the 20th century, defining money and banks was straightforward. Money was currency or a chequing account balance; banks were institutions that took deposits and made loans. Then the invention of computers and the resulting revolution in information technology changed everything. Paying bills used to require sending cheques to each of your utilities; buying dinner used to require cash in your hand. Now bills can be paid online and diners can pick up the tab for a restaurant meal with a plastic card for which they earn points for travel or even discounts on future purchases. The changes have been so sweeping that if a banker of the 1960s or 1970s were transported to the present day, he or she would hardly recognize our current financial system. The way we use money, financial instruments, financial markets, and financial institutions is completely different from the way our grandparents' generation used them.

Not only do today's money and banks differ from yesterday's, but tomorrow's financial system will surely differ from the current one in ways that are difficult to predict. Thus, students who memorize the operational details of today's financial system are investing in a short-lived asset. Our purpose in writing this book is to focus on the basic functions served by the financial system, while de-emphasizing its current structure and rules. Learning the economic rationale behind financial tools, rules, and structures is much more valuable than concentrating on the tools, rules, and structures themselves. It is an approach designed to give students the lifelong ability to understand and evaluate whatever financial innovations they may one day confront.

## The Core Principles Approach

Toward that end, the entire content of this book is based on five *core principles*. Knowledge of these principles is the basis for learning what the financial system does, how it is organized, and how it is linked to the real economy.

1. Time has value.
2. Risk requires compensation.
3. Information is the basis for decisions.
4. Markets determine prices and allocate resources.
5. Stability improves welfare.

These five core principles serve as a framework through which to view the history, current status, and future development of money and banking. They are discussed in detail in Chapter 1; throughout the rest of the text, marginal icons remind students of the principles that underlie particular discussions.

Focusing on core principles has created a book that is both concise and logically organized. This approach does require some adjustments to the traditional methodology used to teach money and banking, but for the most part they are changes in emphasis only. That said, some of these changes have greatly improved both the ease of teaching and the value students draw from the course. Among them are the emphasis on risk; use of the term "financial instrument"; parallel presentation of the Bank of Canada, the Federal Reserve System (Fed), and the European Central Bank (ECB); a streamlined, updated section on monetary economics; and the adoption of an integrated global perspective.

## Innovations in This Text

In addition to the focus on core principles, this book introduces a series of innovations designed to foster coherence and relevance in the study of money and banking, in both today's financial world and tomorrow's.

### Early Introduction of Risk

It is impossible to appreciate how the financial system works without understanding risk. In the modern financial world, virtually all transactions transfer some degree of risk between two or more parties. These risk trades can be extremely beneficial, as they are in the case of insurance markets. But there is still potential for disaster. In 2008, risk taking in the (particularly U.S.) financial system threatened the stability of the international financial system.

Even though risk is absolutely central to an understanding of the financial system, most money and banking books give very little space to the topic. In contrast, this book devotes an entire chapter to defining and measuring risk. Chapter 5 introduces the concept of a risk premium as compensation for risk and shows how diversification can reduce risk. Because risk is central to explaining the valuation of financial instruments, the role of financial intermediaries, and the job of central bankers, the book returns to this concept throughout the chapters.

### Emphasis on Financial Instruments

Financial instruments are introduced early in the book, where they are defined based on their economic function. This perspective leads naturally to a discussion of the uses of various instruments and the determinants of their value. Bonds, stocks, and derivatives all fit neatly into this framework, so they are all discussed together.

This approach solves one of the problems with existing texts, use of the term "financial market" to refer to bonds, interest rates, and foreign exchange. In its conventional microeconomic sense, the term market signifies a place where trade occurs, not the instruments that are traded. This book follows standard usage of the term "market" to mean a place for trade. It uses the term "financial instruments" to describe virtually all financial arrangements, including loans, bonds, stocks, futures, options, and insurance contracts. Doing so clears up the confusion that can arise when students arrive in a money and banking class fresh from a course in the principles of economics.

### Parallel Presentation of the Bank of Canada with the Federal Reserve and the European Central Bank

To foster a deeper understanding of central banking and monetary policy, the presentation of this material begins with a discussion of the central bank's role and objectives. Descriptions of the Bank of Canada, the Fed, and the ECB follow. By starting on a theoretical plane, students gain the tools they need to understand how all central banks work. This avoids focusing on institutional details that may quickly become obsolete. Armed with a basic understanding of what central banks do and how they do it, students will be prepared to grasp the meaning of future changes in institutional structure.

Another important innovation is the integrated discussion of central banks other than the Bank of Canada, especially the Fed and the ECB. Students of the 21st century are ill-served by books that focus entirely on the Canadian financial system. They need a global perspective on central banking, the starting point for which is a detailed knowledge of the Fed and the ECB.

## Modern Treatment of Monetary Economics

The discussion of central banking is followed by a simple framework for understanding the impact of monetary policy on the real economy. Modern central bankers think and talk about changing the interest rate when inflation and output deviate from their target objectives. Yet traditional treatments of monetary economics employ aggregate demand and aggregate supply diagrams, which relate output to the price level, and discuss inflation in terms of shifts in the AD and AS curves. The resulting development is lengthy and difficult. Because this book skips the ISLM framework, its presentation of monetary economics is several chapters shorter. Only those topics that are most important in a monetary economics course are covered: long-run money growth and inflation and short-run monetary policy and business cycles. This streamlined treatment of monetary theory is not only concise, but also more modern and more relevant than the traditional approach. Moreover, it gives students a sound framework for understanding business-cycle fluctuations.

## Integrated Global Perspective

Recent technological advances have dramatically reduced the importance of a bank's physical location, producing a truly global financial system. Twenty years ago, money and banking books could afford to focus primarily on the domestic financial system, relegating international topics to a separate chapter that could be considered optional. But in today's financial world, no country can be treated in isolation. The global financial system is truly an integrated one, rendering separate discussion of a single country's institutions, markets, or policies impossible. This book incorporates the discussion of international issues throughout the text, emphasizing when national borders are important to bankers and when they are not. For example, the Balance Sheet of the Bank of China is compared to that of the Bank of Canada and the Fed; the principles of Islamic banking and of microfinance (such as the Grameen Bank) are described; and global imbalances are explored in the context of the financial crisis of 2008–9.

# Organization

This book is organized to help students understand both the financial system and its economic effects on their lives. That means surveying a broad series of topics, including what money is and how it is used; what a financial instrument is and how it is valued; what a financial market is and how it works; what a financial institution is and why we need it; and what a central bank is and how it operates. More importantly, it means showing students how to apply the five core principles of money and banking to the evolving financial and economic arrangements that they inevitably will confront during their lifetimes.

**Part I: Money and the Financial System.** Chapter 1 introduces the core principles of money and banking, which serve as touchstones throughout the book. Chapter 2 examines money both in theory and in practice. Chapter 3 follows with a bird's-eye view of financial instruments, financial markets, and financial institutions. (Instructors who prefer to discuss the financial system first can cover Chapters 2 and 3 in reverse order.)

### Part II: Interest Rates, Financial Instruments, and Financial Markets.

Part II contains a detailed description of financial instruments and the financial theory required to understand them. It begins with an explanation of present value and risk, followed by specific discussions of bonds, stocks, derivatives, and foreign exchange. Students benefit from concrete examples of these concepts. In Chapter 7 (The Risk and Term Structure of Interest Rates), for example, students learn how the information contained in the risk and term structure of interest rates can be useful in forecasting. In Chapter 8 (Stocks, Stock Markets, and Market Efficiency), they learn about stock bubbles and how those anomalies influence the economy. And in Chapter 10 (Foreign Exchange), they study the Big Mac index to understand the concept of purchasing power parity. Throughout this section, two ideas are emphasized: that financial instruments transfer resources from savers to investors, and that in doing so, they transfer risk to those best equipped to bear it.

### Part III: Financial Institutions.

In the next section, the focus shifts to financial institutions. Chapter 11 introduces the economic theory that is the basis for our understanding of the role of financial intermediaries. Through a series of examples, students see the problems created by asymmetric information as well as how financial intermediaries can mitigate those problems. The remaining chapters in Part III put theory into practice. Chapter 12 presents a detailed discussion of banking, the bank balance sheet, and the risk that banks must manage. Chapter 13 provides a brief overview of the financial industry's structure, and Chapter 14 explains financial regulation.

### Part IV: Central Banks, Monetary Policy, and Financial Stability.

Chapters 15 through 19 survey what central banks do, how they do it and why they do it. This part of the book begins with a discussion of the role and objectives of central banks, which leads naturally to the principles that guide central bank design. Chapter 16 applies those principles to the Bank of Canada, the Federal Reserve, and the European Central Bank. Chapter 17 presents the central bank balance sheet, and explains how the central bank can set the overnight interest rate. The next two chapters show how that interest rate affects the real economy. Chapter 18 presents a complete macroeconomic model complete with a dynamic aggregate demand that integrates monetary policy directly into the presentation, along with short- and long-run aggregate supply curves. In Chapter 19, the model is used to help understand the sources of business cycles and to demonstrate how monetary policy can be used to stabilize the economy.

### Part V: Modern Monetary Economics.

The last part of the book returns to a focus on the money stock. Chapter 20 begins with the empirical relationship between inflation and the money stock and then develops the theoretical relationship showing how the central bank influences money supply and discussing factors influencing money demand. Chapter 21 starts by reminding students that there are many open questions in monetary economics and then examines issues such as the transmission mechanism and the measurement of potential output. Chapter 22 turns to the relationship between monetary policy and the exchange rate system, looking at the pros and cons of alternative exchange rate regimes. The book culminates, in Chapter 23, by using the knowledge of institutions, markets, and instruments learned through the course of the text to understand the causes of the financial crisis of 2008–9 and the policy responses to it.

For those instructors who have the time, we recommend closing the course with a rereading of the first chapter and a review of the core principles. What is the future likely to hold for the five parts of the financial system: money, financial instruments, financial markets, financial institutions, and central banks? How do students envision each of these parts of the system 20 or even 50 years from now?

## Learning Tools

In a sense, this book is a guide to the principles students will need to critically evaluate and use what they read in the financial press. Reading the newspaper and applying the information it contains require some basic knowledge. Supplying that knowledge is the purpose of the four types of inserts that complement the chapters, providing a break from the more technical material in the body of the text:

**Your Financial World**    inserts provide students with practical information that is based on lessons covered in the chapter. Most chapters contain two of these boxes, each of which examines a personal finance problem that everyone faces. These boxes show students that the concepts taught in the money and banking course are relevant to their everyday lives. Among the topics covered are how to get a credit rating, the cost of using payday loans, how deposit insurance works, and techniques for getting the most out of the financial news.

**Applying the Concept** sections show how ideas introduced in the chapter can be applied to the world around us. Most describe historical episodes or examine issues relevant to the public policy debate. Subjects include how the Canadian Asset-Backed Commercial Paper market developed and then cratered in August 2007; why investors flocked to hold U.S. Treasury Bills in late 2008; how the price of a Big Mac can tell you whether the Canadian dollar is overvalued; and why economists think the gold standard should not be reinstated. Most chapters contain two of these applications.

**In the News** boxes present articles drawn from the *Financial Post*, *The New York Times*, the *Wall Street Journal*, and *The Economist*. These readings show how concepts introduced in the chapter are applied in the financial press. Each article is accompanied by a brief analysis that reinforces key concepts. One In the News box appears in nearly every chapter.

**Tools of the Trade** boxes teach useful skills, including how to read bond and stock tables, how to read charts, and how to do some simple algebraic calculations. Some provide further detail on technical operations such as how the clearing and settlement system works, or emphasize key concepts such as the distinction between causation and correlation. Most chapters contain one of these boxes.

Finally, the end-of-chapter material is divided into three sections:

**Key Terms**    A listing of all the technical terms introduced and defined in the chapter. The key terms are defined in full in the glossary at the end of the book.

**Chapter Summary**    A list of the key lessons in the chapter. Other texts summarize a small number of points at length. This book summarizes a larger number of points, each short, clear, and couched in the form of an outline that matches the chapter headings—a format designed to aid student comprehension and retention.

**Problems**   Each chapter contains 18 problems, ten conceptual and eight analytical, of varying levels of difficulty. These problems are designed to reinforce the lessons in the chapter.

## Organizational Alternatives

While this book greatly streamlines the traditional approach to money and banking, it remains flexible enough to be used in a broad variety of courses. Sixteen to 19 of the book's 23 chapters can be assigned in the following courses:

*General Money and Banking Course*. Chapters 1–8, 11, 12, 15–19, 20
This course covers the primary material needed to appreciate the connections between the financial system and the economy.

*General Money and Banking Course with International Emphasis*. Chapters 1–8, 10–12, 15–17, 20, 22
This alternative to the general money and banking course substitutes chapters on foreign exchange and exchange-rate policy for the macroeconomic model included in courses with less international emphasis.

*Financial Markets and Institutions*. Chapters 1–9, 11–17, 23.
The traditional financial markets and institutions course covers money, financial instruments and markets, financial institutions, and central banking. The focus is on Parts II and III of the book.

*Monetary Economics and Monetary Policy*. Chapters 1–7, 10–12, 15–23
A course called monetary economics and monetary policy uses the material in Parts II and III as a foundation for understanding the material in Parts IV and V. A half-semester course for students with a background in financial instruments and institutions might cover only Chapters 1–3 and 15–23

## What's New in the Canadian Edition?

This edition has been thoroughly revised for Canadian students and has been updated to reflect recent events in financial markets and monetary policy. Importantly, the framework, based on the five core principles, continues to provide the underpinnings for our analysis. To fit the needs of Canadian students, we have added Canadian content, and changed the order of some of the discussion to reflect the structure of the Canadian financial system. We have updated material throughout the book and have also added a final chapter that uses the knowledge of financial instruments, markets, and institutions built up throughout the text to analyze the causes of the financial crisis of 2008–9 and the policy responses that have been used (through 2009). All of the figures and data have been updated to reflect the most recent available information. In addition, Appendices have been added that give algebraic versions of some of the models for those who prefer a more formal treatment.

### Focus on Canada

The authors have included new material on:

- The regulation of Canadian financial institutions;
- The structure of Canadian financial markets

- The conduct of Canadian monetary policy
- The history of Canadian banks and monetary system.

The material has been reorganized so that:

- Students learn about the use of interest rates to implement monetary policy;
- The macro model is taught immediately after the discussion of how monetary policy is done so that students—having learnt how monetary policy can be conducted—learn why it is done.
- The discussion of the deposit expansion multiplier (which largely relies on required reserves that are not a feature of the Canadian banking system) is moved to later in the book.

## Technical Supplements

Some students may prefer a more analytical treatment of the topics; the technical appendices support the discussion in the text with algebraic models that may provide greater clarity for interested students.

www.mcgrawhill.ca/olc/
cecchetti

- Consumption smoothing (Chapter 3): Shows how the welfare benefits of the possibility of saving for retirement depend on the interest rate.
- The algebra of Present Value formulas (Chapter 4): Derives some formulas that were asserted in the text and—in the online learning centre—relates them to the built-in spreadsheet formulas.
- Moral hazard (Chapter 11): Algebraic analysis illustrates what factors determine the extent of the consequences of moral hazard in debt and equity markets.
- The algebra of the macro model (Chapter 18): Algebraic analysis permits comparative statics analysis and clarifies the mechanics of the model.

In addition to the technical appendix, the online centre has material to supplement the presentation on present values in Chapter 4. The Online Learning Centre page shows how the formulas used in Chapter 4 can be used in a spreadsheet, either by using a built-in formula or by working from first principles.

## Relevant and Timely News Coverage

The news articles included in each chapter examine

- Changes in technology, such as the use of mobile phones to make payments
- The declining importance of monetary aggregates in the operation policy of the vast majority of the world's central banks
- The challenges facing Bank of Canada policymakers.

Here are some examples of the new and/or significantly revised features:

**Your Financial World**
Paper Cheques Become Digital Images (Chapter 2)
Should You Own Stocks? (Chapter 8)
The Cost of Payday Loans (Chapter 12)
Are Your Deposits Insured? (Chapter 14)
The Production of Money (Chapter 16)
The Financial Crisis Hits Students (Chapter 23)

**Apply the Concept**
The Pros and Cons of VaR Models (Chapter 5)
The Flight to Quality (Chapter 7)
Purchasing Power Parity and Cross-Country GDP Comparisons (Chapter 10)
Public Pensions and the Social Insurance System (Chapter 13)
Financial Innovation and the Shifting Definition of Money (Chapter 21)
The Balance of Payments and "Global Imbalances" (Chapter 22)

**In the News**
Canada Edges Towards M-Payments (Chapter 2)
A Poor Retirement (Chapter 5)
Bre-X and the Golden Fleece (Chapter 8)
Canada on the Sidelines of CDS Regulation (Chapter 9)
BMO Trader Pleads Guilty (Chapter 12)
Bizarre World of Bank Mergers (Chapter 14)
Bank of Canada Needs More Power of Oversight (Chapter 16)
Making Sense of Currency Union with the United States (Chapter 22)

**Tools of the Trade**
Trading in Financial Markets (Chapter 3)
Reading Stock Indexes (Chapter 8)
The Bank of Canada Announcement Statement (Chapter 16)
Clearing and Settling (Chapter 17)
Defining a Recession (Chapter 19)
The Remarkable Expanding Balance Sheet (Chapter 23)

# Supplements for Students

## Online Learning Centre

The Online Learning Centre, located at www.mcgrawhill.ca/olc/cecchetti, contains a variety of content for students, including chapter quizzes, interactive graphs with related exercises, and true/false quizzes to give students added variety and practice.

# Supplements for Instructors

## Online Learning Centre

The Online Learning Centre, located at www.mcgrawhill.ca/olc/cecchetti, contains downloadable instructor resources:

## Instructor's Manual and Solutions

This manual includes chapter overviews, outlines, and a discussion of how the core principles apply to each chapter. It also addresses concepts students often find difficult, including suggestions for alleviating confusion. Solutions to the problems are given at the end of each chapter.

## Test Bank

The test bank includes approximately 2,500 multiple-choice and 600 short-answer and essay questions.

## PowerPoint Slides

The slides outline the main points in each chapter and reproduce major graphs and charts.

## WebCT and Blackboard

In addition, content cartridges are available for the course management systems **WebCT** and **Blackboard**. These platforms provide instructors with user-friendly, flexible teaching tools. Please contact your local McGraw-Hill Ryerson *i*Learning Sales Specialist for details.

## E-STAT

**E-STAT** is an educational resource designed by Statistics Canada and made available to Canadian educational institutions. Using 450,000 current CANSIM (Canadian Socioeconomic Information Management System) Time Series and the most recent—as well as historical—census data, E-STAT lets you bring data to life in colourful graphs and maps. Access to E-STAT is made available to purchasers of this book by special agreement between McGraw-Hill Ryerson and Statistics Canada.

## CourseSmart

**CourseSmart** brings together thousands of textbooks across hundreds of courses in an e-textbook format providing unique benefits to students and faculty. By purchasing an e-textbook, students can save up to 50 percent off the cost of a print textbook, reduce their impact on the environment, and gain access to powerful Web tools for learning including full-text search, notes and highlighting, and e-mail tools for sharing notes between classmates. For faculty, CourseSmart provides instant access to review and compare textbooks and course materials in their discipline area without the time, cost, and environmental impact of mailing print exam copies. For further details, contact your *i*Learning Sales Specialist or go to www.coursesmart.com.

## Create Online

McGraw-Hill's **Create Online** gives you access to the most abundant resource at your fingertips—literally. With a few mouse clicks, you can create customized learning tools simply and affordably. McGraw-Hill Ryerson has included many of our market-leading textbooks within Create Online for e-book and print customization as well as many licensed readings and cases. For more information, go to www.mcgrawhillcreate.com.

# FEATURE WALKTHROUGH

| Table 4.4 | Number of Months to Pay Off a $2,000 Credit Card Debt | |
| --- | --- | --- |
| **Annual Interest Rate** | **Monthly Payment** | |
| | **$50** | **$60** |
| 10% | 48.4 | 38.9 |
| 13% | 51.7 | 41.0 |
| 15% | 54.3 | 42.5 |
| 20% | 62.4 | 47.0 |

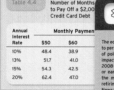

For a complete listing of titles of chapter features and their page references, refer to the information found on the inside front cover of this text.

## Your Financial World

These boxes show students that the concepts taught in the text are relevant to their everyday lives. Among the topics covered are the costs of payday loans, the coverage of deposit insurance, the desirability of owning stocks, and techniques for getting the most out of the financial news.

## Applying the Concept

These sections showcase history and examine issues relevant to the public policy debate. Subjects include how asset-backed commercial paper imperiled the financial system, how purchasing power parity exchange rates are used to make cross-country comparisons, and the problems of the Japanese economy in the 1990s.

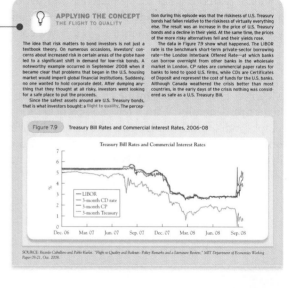

### U.S. prosecutors probe cozy dealing with broker that cost bank $853M

Eoin Callan, Financial Post

PUBLISHED: Wednesday, November 19, 2008

When David Lee walked into the Borgata Spa on this day two years ago, he was greeted by a tranquil oasis of soothing aromas and warm hands trained to knead stresses from the muscles of Wall Street bankers.

Amid chauffeured limousine trips to casinos in Atlantic City, the trader and his boss at Bank of Montreal, Robert Moore, ran up a bill at the spa that was not excessive by the standards of bankers at the peak of a bull-market run, $1,218.46.

It was not the price of the indulgence that piqued the interest of U.S. federal investigators, but the name that appeared on the bill: Kevin Cassidy, an executive at New Jersey-based Optionable, a brokerage that handled billions in transactions for Bank of Montreal's natural-gas derivatives trading operation in New York.

After a lengthy investigation, U.S. prosecutors yesterday unsealed a raft of suits and criminal charges against the two former BMO officers and executives at the brokerage alleging collusion in a scheme to conceal losses on natural gas trades.

Mr. Lee is pleading guilty, and has admitted overvaluing the bank's gas-options portfolio by inflating the worth of trading positions.

The illegal activity first came to light last year after disclosures by the Bay Street bank and enquiries by *The Financial Post*, and prompted BMO to record related losses of $853-million.

The trader has admitted he would regularly sit at his desk in BMO's Times Square office in Manhattan and create flattering values for his "book" of trading positions by using his own mathematical model, when market prices were difficult to ascertain or unavailable.

These generous calculations made the performance of the New York unit look better than it was in reality and allowed Mr. Lee to collect bigger bonuses.

"Lee inflated the value of his book so that it would appear to BMO that his trading was more," investigators said.

To help cover up the distortions and meet his bank's requirement for independent verification of the value of his portfolio, the trader would then e-mail the figures to his personal e-mail address.

After arriving home from the office, the 37-year-old would then forward the over-inflated estimates by e-mail in a spreadsheet to brokers at Optionable, with whom a close relationship had been developed, according to investigators who pieced together a trail of electronic communications that Mr. Lee had attempted to destroy.

The next morning, brokers at Optionable, including Mr. Cassidy, would forward the numbers fabricated by BMO's own trader to BMO's compliance office, prosecutors alleged yesterday.

The "brokers knowingly deceived and defrauded BMO" by passing the falsified figures off as independent estimates, federal officials said in court documents.

The motive of Mr. Lee was to maintain his high-living lifestyle, inflate his performance and conceal losses, according to investigators who accused his supervisor, Mr. Moore, of looking the other way.

The investigators found a lengthy list of "gambling vacations" and visits to men's grooming clubs by Mr. Moore, the BMO executive, sometimes accompanied by Mr. Lee, that were paid for by executives at Optionable and appear to form a pattern of expensive gifts that violated the bank's policy.

A person close to the investigation said there were indications Mr. Lee had sought a seat on the board of the brokerage, though the complaints and indictments unsealed yesterday focused on the cozy relationship that existed between traders at BMO and its broker.

The person pointed out that BMO was Optionable's biggest customer and that this gave the broker an interest in maintaining a good working relationship with the Canadian bank.

In turn, it was trades executed by Mr. Lee that accounted for the bulk of the fees collected by Optionable, which prosecutors allege showered the trader with gifts and helped cover up losses.

The scheme operated successfully for years, but came undone when BMO insisted multiple outside brokers periodically value trading portfolios.

Mr. Cassidy, 49, a founder of Optionable, faces sentences of up to 70 years, on charges of wire fraud, securities fraud and false bank entry.

"We are pleased with the actions taken today by the authorities to bring proceedings against those involved with the commodities trading losses," said a spokesperson for BMO.

**Back Story**

May 5, 2007 BMO's explanation for $450-million in losses is questioned widely. BMO had claimed it was left with a bunch of bad trades when the demand for natural gas options dried up and there was a sharp decline in price volatility, claims that turned out to be false.

May 10, 2007 *The Financial Post* discovers the existence of a Deloitte and Touche report identifying irregularities in the company's New York natural gas trading book. BMO confirms that David Lee, the BMO trader blamed for the losses, is on a leave of absence.

May 11, 2007 *The Financial Post* reports that three senior executives had cashed in US$27-million before the company received

the Deloitte and Touche report. David Lee is found to have a close personal relationship with executives at Optionable.

May 17, 2007 BMO reports further losses from natural gas trades, bringing the total to $680-million.

May 25, 2007 *The New York Post* reports that the U.S. Securities and Exchange Commission is investigating Optionable Inc.

Nov. 18, 2008 David Lee pleads guilty to hiding trading losses from BMO

## In the News

One article per chapter from major media such as the *Financial Post*, *The New York Times*, *The Economist*, and the *Wall Street Journal* is featured. These readings show how concepts introduced in the chapter are applied in the financial press. A brief analysis of the article, called "Lessons," reinforces key concepts.

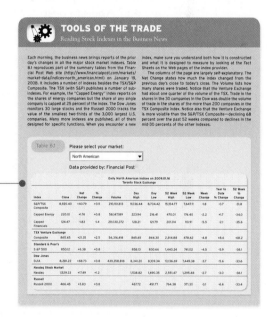

## Tools of the Trade

These boxes teach useful skills, including how to read bond and stock tables, how to read charts, and how to do some simple algebraic calculations. Some provide brief reviews of material from the principles of economics course, or explain technical terms.

## Financial Markets

Financial markets are the plac
They are the economy's central
quickly, allocating resources, an
enable both firms and individu
are working well, new firms can
don't have sufficient savings car
resources are available to those
costs of transactions as low as
When financial markets cease
nelled to their best possible use

## Core Principle Marginal Icons

The entire text discussion is organized around the following five core principles: time has value, risk requires compensation, information is the basis for decisions, markets set prices and allocate resources, and stability improves welfare. Exploring these principles is the basis for learning what the financial system does, how it is organized, and how it is linked to the real economy. They are discussed in detail in Chapter 1; throughout the rest of the text, marginal icons remind students of the principles that underlie particular discussions.

# Acknowledgments

I would like to thank Knick Harley, David Laidler, and Peter Howitt, who nourished my interest in monetary economics—and challenged me to think ever more carefully about the nature of money—as I wrote my dissertation at the University of Western Ontario on monetary problems in 19th-century Ontario. I would also like to thank my colleagues and the graduate and undergraduate students at the University of British Columbia who, for more than two decades, have asked questions and provided answers as we all learn about the role of money and financial institutions. I would also like to thank my many colleagues at the Bank of Canada from whom I have learned so much about the challenges of monetary policy making. My frequent co-authors Michael Bordo and Warren Weber have taught me more than they probably imagine as we sought to learn from the vast laboratory of history about the power of money for better and worse.

At McGraw-Hill Ryerson, I have been supported by an outstanding team: from the ever-cheerful Daphne Scriabin who supported me when the project seemed overwhelming, to the remarkably creative and careful freelance copy editor Karen Rolfe, the patient permissions editor Lynn McIntyre, the thoughtful reader Helen Prankie, and Andria Fogarty, who pulled it all together. I have been amazed and grateful for the care they have taken with this work.

Finally, I would like to thank my family. Steve, Jeff, and Ben have, as usual, surrounded me with a warm and happy home. They have supported my preoccupation with things monetary, and reminded me that there's more to life when I got too preoccupied with the minutiae of yet another financial institution.

**Angela Redish**
University of British Columbia

# Reviewers

Thank you to the following contributing reviewers

George Chuchman, *University of Manitoba*
Yolina Denchev, *Camosun College*
Frank Ingold, *George Brown College*
Eric Kam, *Ryerson University*
Amir Kia, *Carleton University*
Jean-Paul Lam, *University of Waterloo*
Michael Leonard, *Kwantlen Polytechnic University*
Horatio Morgan, *York University*
Goeffrey Newman, *University of British Columbia*
Dan Otchere, *Concordia University*
Marc Prud'homme, *University of Ottawa*
Gary Riser, *Memorial University*
Lance Shandler, *Kwantlen Polytechnic University*
Brenda Spotton, *York University*
Thomas Velk, *McGill University*

# MONEY,
# BANKING,
# & FINANCIAL MARKETS

# CHAPTER 1

## An Introduction to Money and the Financial System

This morning, a typical Canadian student bought coffee at the local coffee shop, paying for it with a debit card. Then she jumped into her insured car, and drove to the university, which she attends thanks to her student loan. She may have left her parents' home, which is mortgaged, a few minutes early to avoid construction work on a new dormitory, financed by bonds issued by the university. Or perhaps she needed to stop at the bookstore to purchase this book, using her credit card, before her first money and banking class began.

Beneath the surface, each financial transaction in this story—even the seemingly simple ones—is quite complicated. If the coffee shop owner and the student use different banks, paying for the coffee will require an interbank funds transfer. The company that insures the student's car has to invest the premiums she pays until they are needed to pay off claims. The student's parents almost surely obtained their home mortgage through a bank or credit union. And the bonds the university issued to finance construction of the new dormitory were created with the aid of an investment bank.

This brief example hints at the complex web of interdependent institutions and markets that is the foundation for our daily financial transactions. The system is so large, so efficient, and, generally speaking, so well run that most of us rarely take note of it. But a financial system is like the operating system of a computer: if it breaks down suddenly, the economy stops running smoothly. And in 2008 that's what happened. Problems in the United States became visible in 2007 when the fall in house prices led financial institutions to fear that borrowers would default on their mortgages. In Canada, borrowers who relied on the short-term loan market (the commercial paper market) were suddenly unable to borrow as lenders feared that the collateral they were offering included (perhaps worthless) U.S. mortgages. In 2008, the crisis gradually worsened as U.S. banks

declared significant losses, and in September 2008 the crisis became a rout. The Canadian banks were relatively unscathed but the Canadian economy too went into a deep recession. In 2009, it was clear that the financial crisis had spread around the globe and had caused a recession more serious than any since the Great Depression in the 1930s.

How did this happen? What should governments and central banks do to ease the way out of the recession? How can financial markets be improved so that it doesn't happen again? These are the very difficult questions that policy makers around the globe are addressing. In this book we cannot give you the answers! However, we will give you an introduction to the structure of financial markets in Canada and globally so that you can get a better understanding of the source of the crisis and of the policy options being proposed. We begin by describing the components and the operation of the financial system and then discuss the tools of monetary policy and financial market regulation. The final chapter brings all this together to analyze the financial crisis and the future of the financial system.

## The Five Parts of the Financial System

The financial system has five parts, each of which plays a fundamental role in our economy. Those parts are money, financial instruments, financial markets, financial institutions, and central banks.

We use the first part of the system, money, to pay for our purchases and to store our wealth. We use the second part, financial instruments, to transfer resources from savers to investors and to transfer risk to those who are best equipped to bear it. Stocks, mortgages, and insurance policies are examples of financial instruments. The third part of our financial system, financial markets, allows us to buy and sell financial instruments quickly and cheaply. The Toronto Stock Exchange is an example of a financial market. Financial institutions, the fourth part of the financial system, provide a myriad of services, including access to the financial markets and collection of information about prospective borrowers to ensure they are creditworthy. Banks, securities firms, and insurance companies are examples of financial institutions. Finally, central banks, the fifth part of the system, monitor and stabilize the economy. The Bank of Canada is the central bank of Canada.

While the essential functions that define these five categories endure, their physical form is constantly evolving. *Money* once consisted of gold and silver coins, which were eventually replaced by paper currency, which today is being eclipsed by electronic funds transfers. Methods of accessing means of payment have changed dramatically as well. As recently as 1970, people customarily obtained currency from bank tellers when they cashed their paycheques or withdrew their savings from the bank. Today, they can get cash from practically any ATM anywhere in the world. To pay their bills, people once wrote cheques and put them in the mail, then waited for their monthly bank statements to ensure the transactions had been processed correctly. Today, payments can be made automatically, and account holders can check the transactions at any time on their bank's Web site.

*Financial instruments* (or securities, as they are often called) have evolved just as much as currency. In the last few centuries, investors could buy individual stocks through stockbrokers, but the transactions were costly. Furthermore, putting together a portfolio of even a small number of stocks and bonds was extremely time consuming; just collecting the information necessary to evaluate a potential investment was a daunting task. As a result, investing was an activity reserved for the wealthy. Today, financial institutions offer people with as little as $1,000 to invest the ability to purchase shares in mutual funds, which pool the savings of a large number of investors. Because of their size, mutual funds can construct portfolios of hundreds or even thousands of different stocks and/or bonds.

The markets where stocks and bonds are sold have undergone a similar transformation. Originally, *financial markets* were located in coffeehouses and taverns where individuals met to exchange financial instruments. The next step was to create organized markets, like the Toronto Stock Exchange—trading places specifically dedicated to the buying and selling of stocks and bonds. Today, much of the activity that once occurred at these big-city financial exchanges is handled by electronic networks. Buyers and sellers obtain price information and initiate transactions from their desktop computers or from handheld devices. Because electronic networks have reduced the cost of processing financial transactions, even small investors can afford to participate in them. Just as important, today's financial markets offer a much broader array of financial instruments than those available even 50 years ago.

"This is Fluffy, my pet money."

*Financial institutions* have changed, as well. Banks began as vaults where people could store their valuables. Gradually, they developed into institutions that accepted deposits and made loans. For hundreds of years, in fact, that was what bankers did. Today, a bank is more like a financial supermarket. Walk in and you will discover a huge assortment of financial products and services for sale, from access to the financial markets to insurance policies, mortgages, consumer credit, and even investment advice.

Finally, *central banks* have changed a great deal. They began as large private banks founded by monarchs to finance wars. For instance, King William of Orange created the Bank of England in 1694 for the express purpose of raising taxes and borrowing to finance a war between Austria, England, and the Netherlands on one side and Louis XIV's France on the other. Eventually, these government treasuries grew into the modern central banks we know today. While only a few central banks existed in 1900, now nearly every country in the world has one, and they have become one of the most important institutions in government. Central banks control the availability of money and credit to ensure low inflation, high growth, and the stability of the financial system. Because their current mission is to serve the public at large rather than land-hungry monarchs, their operating methods have changed as well. Once the central bank's decisions were shrouded in mystery, but today's policymakers strive for transparency in their operations. Officials at the Bank of Canada, and those of the other important central banks, go out of their way to explain the rationale for their decisions.

Though the changing nature of our financial system is a fascinating topic, it poses challenges for both students and instructors. How can we teach and learn about money and banking in a way that will stand the test of time, so that the knowledge we gain won't become outmoded? The answer is that we must develop a way to understand and adapt to the evolutionary structure of the financial system. That means discussing money and banking within a framework of core principles that do not change over time. The next section introduces the five core principles that will guide our studies throughout this book.

# The Five Core Principles of Money and Banking

Five core principles will inform our analysis of the financial system and its interaction with the real economy. Once you have grasped these principles, you will have a better understanding not only of what is happening in the financial world today but of changes that will undoubtedly occur in the future. The five principles are based on **time**, **risk**, **information**, **markets**, and **stability**.

## Core Principle 1: Time Has Value

The first principle of money and banking is that *time has value*. At some very basic level, everyone knows this. If you take a job at the local supermarket, you will almost surely be paid by the hour. An hour's worth of work equals a certain number of dollars. Literally, your time has a price.

On a more sophisticated level, time affects the value of financial transactions. Most loan contracts allow the borrower to spread out the payments over time. If you take out an auto loan, for example, the lender will allow you to make a series of monthly payments over three, four, or even five years. If you add up the payments, you'll discover that the total exceeds the amount of the loan. At an interest rate of 6 percent, a four-year, $10,000 car loan will require 48 monthly payments of $235 each. That means you will repay a total of $11,280 (48 × $235). The reason your repayments total more than the loan amount is that you are paying interest to compensate the lender for the time during which you use the funds. That is, the resources you borrowed have an opportunity cost to the lender so you have to pay rent on them.

Interest payments are fundamental to a market economy. In Chapter 4, we will develop an understanding of interest rates and how to use them. Then, throughout the remainder of Part II, we will apply the principle that time has value in our discussion of the valuation of bonds, stocks, and other financial instruments involving future payments. How much should you be willing to pay for a particular stock or bond? Figuring out what alternative investments are worth, and comparing them, means valuing payments made on different future dates. The same principle applies to the question of how much you must invest today to achieve a particular financial objective in the future. How much of your salary, for example, do you need to save each month to meet your goal of buying a house? The length of time your savings will be earning interest is a key to answering this question.

## Core Principle 2: Risk Requires Compensation

The world is filled with uncertainty. More events, both good and bad, *can* happen than *will* happen. Some of the possibilities, such as the likelihood of your home doubling in value after you buy it, are welcome. Other possibilities, such as the chance that you might lose your job and not be able to make your car payments, are distinctly unwelcome. Dealing effectively with risk requires that you consider the full range of possibilities in order to eliminate some risks, reduce others, pay someone to assume particularly onerous risks, and just live with what's left. Needless to say, no one will assume your risks for free, which brings us to the second core principle of money and banking: *Risk requires compensation*. In the financial world, compensation is made in the form of explicit payments. That is, investors must be paid to assume risk; the higher the risk, the bigger the required payment.

Car insurance is a common example of paying someone else to shoulder a risk you don't want to take. If your car is wrecked in an accident, you will want to be able to repair it. But beyond that, auto insurance shelters drivers from the possibility of losing all their wealth in the event that they cause an accident in which someone is seriously injured. Although the chances of causing such an accident are quite small, the results can be so serious that, even if the government didn't require it, most of us would voluntarily purchase auto insurance. Driving without it just isn't worth the risk. The insurance company pools the premiums that policyholders pay and invests them. Even though some of the premiums will be spent to settle claims when cars are stolen or damaged by collisions, the chance to make a profit is good. So both the insurance company and the drivers who buy policies are ultimately better off.

Bearing in mind that time has value and risk requires compensation, we can begin to see the rationale behind the valuation of a broad set of financial instruments. For example, a lender will charge a higher interest rate on a loan if there is a chance that the borrower will not repay. In Chapters 6 and 7, we will use this principle when we examine the interest rates on bonds. As we will see, a company that is on the verge of bankruptcy may still be able to issue bonds (called *junk bonds*), but it will have to pay an extremely high interest rate to do so. The reason is that the lender must be compensated for the substantial risk that the company will not repay the loan. Risk requires compensation.

## Core Principle 3: Information Is the Basis for Decisions

Most of us collect information before making decisions. The more important the decision, the more information we gather. Think of the difference between buying a $5 sandwich and a $10,000 car. You will surely spend more time comparing cars than comparing sandwiches.

What's true for sandwiches and cars is true for finance as well. That is, *information is the basis for decisions*. In fact, the collection and processing of information is the foundation of the financial system. In Chapter 11, we will learn how financial institutions such as banks funnel resources from savers to investors. Before a bank makes a loan, a loan officer will investigate the financial condition of the individual or firm seeking it. Banks want to provide loans only to the highest-quality borrowers. Thus, they spend a great deal of time gathering the information needed to evaluate the creditworthiness of loan applicants.

To understand the problem faced by the two parties to any financial transaction, think about a home mortgage. Before making the loan, the mortgage lender examines the applicant's finances and researches the home's value to make sure the applicant can afford the monthly payments and the property is more valuable than the loan.

Before the lender transfers the funds to the seller, the new homeowner must purchase fire insurance. All these requirements arise from the fact that the lender doesn't know much about the borrower and wants to ensure the loan will be repaid.

Information plays a key role in other parts of the financial system as well. In Chapters 2 and 3, we'll see that many types of transactions are arranged so that the buyer doesn't need to know anything about the seller. When merchants accept cash, they don't need to worry about the customer's identity. When stocks change hands, the buyer doesn't need to know anything about the seller, or vice versa. Stock exchanges are organized to eliminate the need for costly information gathering, facilitating the exchange of securities. In one way or another, information is the key to the financial system.

## Core Principle 4: Markets Determine Prices and Allocate Resources

Markets are the core of the economic system. They are the place, physical or virtual, where buyers and sellers meet, where firms go to issue stocks and bonds, and where individuals go to purchase assets. Financial markets are essential to the economy, channelling its resources and minimizing the cost of gathering information and making transactions. In fact, well-developed financial markets are a necessary precondition for healthy economic growth. The better developed a country's financial markets, the faster the country will grow.

The reason for this connection between markets and growth is that *markets determine prices and allocate resources*. Financial markets gather information from a large number of individual participants and aggregate it into a set of prices that signal what is valuable and what is not. Thus, markets are sources of information. By attaching prices to different stocks or bonds, they provide a basis for the allocation of capital.

To see how prices in the financial markets allocate capital, think about a large firm wishing to finance the construction of a new factory costing several hundred million dollars. To raise the funds, the firm can go directly into the financial markets and issue stocks or bonds. The higher the price investors are willing to pay in the market, the more appealing the idea will be, and the more likely it is that the firm will issue securities to raise the capital for the investment.

We will refer to the financial markets throughout much of this book. While our primary focus in Part II will be the nature of financial instruments, we will also study the markets in which those instruments are traded. Chapters 6 through 10 describe the markets for bonds, stocks, derivatives, and foreign currencies.

Importantly, financial markets do not arise by themselves—at least, not the large, well-oiled ones we see operating today. Markets such as the Toronto Stock Exchange, where hundreds of millions of shares change hands every day, require rules in order to work properly, as well as authorities to police them. Otherwise, they will not function. For people to be willing to participate in a market, they must perceive it as fair. As we will see, this creates an important role for the government. Regulators and supervisors of the financial system make and enforce the rules, punishing people who violate them. When the government protects investors, financial markets work well; otherwise, they don't.

## Core Principle 5: Stability Improves Welfare

Most of us prefer stable to variable incomes. We like a steady income more than one that is highly variable even if it works out to the same amount over a year. This brings us to the fifth core principle of money and banking: *Stability improves welfare*. Stability is a desirable quality, not also in our personal lives but also in the financial system as a whole.

If you are wondering whether this principle is related to Core Principle 2 (risk requires compensation), you are right. Because volatility creates risk, reducing volatility reduces risk. But while individuals can eliminate many risks on their own (we'll see how when we study financial instruments in Part II), some risks can be reduced only by government policy makers. Business cycle fluctuations are an example of the sort of instability individuals can't eliminate on their own. And though "automatic stabilizers" such as unemployment insurance and the income tax system reduce the burden of recessions on individuals, they cannot eliminate an economic slowdown. Monetary policy makers can moderate these downswings by carefully adjusting interest rates. In stabilizing the economy as a whole, they lessen risks that individuals can't eliminate, improving everyone's welfare in the process.

As we will learn in Part IV of this book, stabilizing the economy is a primary function of central banks such as the Bank of Canada and the Federal Reserve, the central bank of the United States. Officials of these institutions are charged with controlling inflation and reducing business cycle fluctuations. That is, they work to keep inflation low and stable and to keep growth high and stable. When they are successful, they reduce both the risk that individuals will lose their jobs and the uncertainty that firms face in making investment decisions. Not surprisingly, a stable economy grows faster than an unstable economy. Stability improves welfare.

Throughout the book you will notice icons like this in the margin at various points. These will guide you to the core principle that provides the foundation for what is being discussed at that point in the text.

## Special Features of This Book

Every chapter of this book contains a series of important elements, beginning with an introduction. The introduction presents real-world examples that lead to the big questions the chapter is designed to answer: What is money? What do banks do? How does the bond market work? What does the Bank of Canada do to prevent financial crises?

The text of each chapter presents the economic and financial theory you need to understand the topics covered. Each chapter also contains a series of inserts that apply the theory. There are four types of inserts: Your Financial World, Applying the Concept, In the News, and Tools of the Trade. Here are some guidelines for using them.

### Your Financial World

When most people decide to make a major purchase, they begin by collecting information. If they are considering buying a car, they will first try to decide which model is best for them and then work hard to pay the lowest price possible. Even for smaller purchases, like clothes or groceries, people first gather information and then buy.

Financial transactions should be no different from consumer purchases. Become informed first, and then buy. If you're thinking, "That's easier said than done," you're right. The problem is that most people have very little knowledge of the financial system, so they don't know how to start or what kind of information to collect.

That's where Your Financial World comes in. These inserts provide basic guidelines for applying economic theory to the bread-and-butter financial decisions you make nearly every day. Your Financial World answers questions about:

- Banking and Payments
  - What's the difference between credit and debit cards?
  - How should you pick a bank?
- Investments
  - Should you own stocks or bonds or gold?
  - Should you invest in the company you work for?
- Credit, Loans, and Mortgages
  - What do you need to know when you shop for a mortgage?
  - What is your credit score and why is it important?
- Insurance
  - How much life insurance do you need?
  - How much car insurance do you need?
- Saving and Retirement
  - How big an emergency saving reserve should you have?
  - Is your retirement savings insured?

## YOUR FINANCIAL WORLD
### Guard Your Identity

There is a television commercial in which a middle-aged man is sitting in his living room drinking a beer. Out of the man's mouth comes the voice of a woman describing some very expensive clothing she just bought. She didn't care how much the clothes cost because she wasn't paying—she used a credit card that was in the man's name. The ad catches viewers' attention because it is funny. But its primary purpose is to serve as a warning about identity theft, in which one person takes on the identity of another to do things such as make credit card purchases.

It is important to realize that someone who has a few pieces of key information about you can get a credit card in your name. To prevent this, you need to protect personal information. Do your best to never tell anyone your birth date and birthplace, your address, or your mother's maiden name. Most importantly, guard your social insurance number. Since it is unique, it is the key to identity

theft. Give out your social insurance number only when absolutely necessary—on tax forms, for employment records, and to open bank accounts. If you get a telephone call or an email from someone you don't know asking for personal data, don't provide it.

Beyond protecting access to personal information, you need to monitor your financial statements closely, looking for things that shouldn't be there. Be on the lookout for unauthorized charges. This means maintaining careful records so that you know what should be on your bank and credit card statements.

Identity theft is a crime, and governments work hard to find and prosecute the offenders. Even so, millions of people are victims each year. Don't be one of them. For more information about identity theft and how to avoid being a victim, see the RCMP Web site: www.rcmp-grc.ca and follow the link for "Scams."

## Applying the Concept

Each chapter in this book contains a series of applications called Applying the Concept, which show how to put theory into practice. These inserts provide real-world examples of the ideas introduced in the chapter, drawn primarily from history or from relevant public policy debates. Here are some of the questions examined in Applying the Concept:

- Why do interest rates rise when inflation goes up?
- Why can a country's exchange rate suddenly plummet?
- Why does the government restrict bank mergers?
- Why is it important for central banks to be free of political influence?
- Can monetary policy be used to stabilize the economy?
- What determines inflation?

## In the News

One of the primary purposes of this textbook is to help you understand the business and financial news. Critically evaluating what you read, hear, and see means developing a clear understanding of how the financial system works, as well as reading the news regularly. Like many other skills, critical reading of newspapers and magazines takes practice. You can't just pick up a newspaper and skim through it quickly and efficiently; you need to learn how. Your instructor will make suggestions about what you should read. See Table 1.1 for a list of reliable sources of information on the economy and the financial system.

| Table 1.1 | Sources of Economic and Financial News and Data |
|-----------|--------------------------------------------------|

**Sources of Daily News**

*The Globe and Mail* and **www.globeinvestor.com**

*The Financial Post* **(published with the** *National Post***)** and **www.financialpost.com**

Two Canadian newspapers with business sections published six days a week.
Their Web sites have up-to-the-minute news and sections on market data.

*The Wall Street Journal* and **www.wsj.com**

Published six days a week, and available both in print and on the Internet, *The Wall Street Journal* provides news, as well as comprehensive coverage of business and finance.

*The Financial Times* and **www.ft.com**

The Financial Times offers reporting, analysis, and commentary on major business, political, financial, and economic events. The *FT* is written from a distinctly European perspective, and includes detailed coverage of non-U.S. business and financial news.

**www.Bloomberg.com** and **www.bnn.ca**

Both sites offer a wide range of financial market services, including news and data.

**Sources of Weekly News**

*The Economist Magazine* and **www.economist.com**

*The Economist* covers global politics, economics, business, finance, and science. It not only reports the facts, but also analyzes them and draws policy conclusions. The Finance and Economics section, located roughly three-quarters of the way into each issue, is of particular interest.

**Economic and Financial Data**

The Bank of Canada Web site www.bankofcanada.ca provides a variety of banking, monetary, interest rate, and exchange rate data.

The Statistics Canada Web site www.statscan.gc.ca provides information on gross domestic product, consumption, investment, and other macroeconomic data.

**Personal Finance Information**

Many financial Web sites offer a variety of personal finance resources, including financial calculators to help you with mortgages, auto loans, and insurance. For example,

- www.fcac-acfc.gc.ca
- www.wsj.com (look at the money section of the personal journal)

Given your need to become a skilled consumer of financial information, each chapter in this book includes an article drawn from the financial press. These stories from *The Wall Street Journal*, the *Financial Times*, the *Financial Post*, and *The Economist*, are reproduced under the heading In the News. Each provides an example of how the concepts introduced in the chapter are discussed in the real world, and each is followed by a brief summary.

## Tools of the Trade

Many chapters in this book include an insert called Tools of the Trade that concentrates on practical knowledge relevant to the chapter. Some of these inserts cover basic skills, including how to read bond and stock tables, how to read charts, and how to do some simple algebraic calculations. Others provide brief reviews of material from principles of economics classes, such as how you compute the Consumer Price Index. Still other Tools of the Trade inserts address questions such as

- What is leverage, and how does it affect risk?
- What are hedge funds?
- What is the difference between causation and correlation?

# The Organization of This Book

This book is organized into five parts. Each one employs core principles to illuminate a particular part of the financial system and applies economic theory to the world around us. The next two chapters will continue our overview of the financial system. First, we'll study money—what it is and how it is used. We'll see that currency allows transactions to be made anonymously, which reduces the need to gather information. This advantage of currency is related to Core Principle 3: Information is the basis for decisions. In Chapter 3, we'll take a bird's-eye view of financial instruments, financial markets, and financial institutions. At various points in that chapter, we'll refer to the first four core principles.

Part II includes detailed descriptions of financial instruments. We'll study bonds, stocks, and derivatives, as well as exchange rates for foreign currency. The valuation of financial instruments requires a comparison of payments made on different dates as well as an estimate of the risk involved in each instrument. Thus, these chapters focus on Core Principles 1 and 2: Time has value and Risk requires compensation.

Throughout Part II and continuing in Part III, we'll discuss financial markets, whose purpose is to facilitate the buying and selling of financial instruments. No one would buy stocks or bonds if they could not be resold cheaply and easily. Financial markets also provide the information necessary to understand the value and risk that are associated with particular financial instruments. Core Principles 3 and 4 (Information is the basis for decisions and Markets determine prices and allocate resources) are both relevant to our discussion of markets.

Part III covers financial institutions, especially banks. Earlier in this chapter (pages 2–3), we emphasized that financial institutions spend a great deal of time collecting and processing information. Without that information, many financial transactions could not take place. This dependence of banks on information is an example of Core Principle 3: Information is the basis for decisions.

Part IV describes central banks, especially the Bank of Canada and the Federal Reserve. These institutions exist to stabilize the real economy as well as the financial system. Thus, they embody Core Principle 5: Stability improves welfare. We'll see how central banks can influence interest rates, and use a macroeconomic model to analyze how those interest rates can stabilize the economy. Finally, Part V brings together material covered in the first four parts to explain the connections between money, interest rates, and inflation. In the final chapter, we use the understanding of financial institutions, markets, and instruments developed throughout the book to look at the financial crisis of 2007–08: its causes, how monetary policies have been used to mitigate its impact, and proposals for reforming the financial system to reduce the likelihood of a recurrence.

Learning money and banking is going to be hard work. Reading and working through the remaining 22 chapters of this book will take lots of time and energy. But when you are done, you will be armed with the tools you need to understand how the financial system works and why it changes as it does. You will know how to be an informed reader of the financial and economic news and how to put the financial system to use for you. You will understand the various ways that you can pay for your morning coffee and how each one of them works. You will understand the usefulness of bonds and stocks as well as what financial institutions do and how central banks work. You will know how to make sound financial decisions for the rest of your life. Regardless of the career you choose to follow, a solid background in money, banking, and financial markets will help you make sound financial decisions from now on.

## Terms

Bank of Canada, 3
central bank, 2
financial institution, 2
financial instrument, 2
financial market, 2
financial system, 2

information, 5
markets, 5
money, 2
risk, 4
stability, 6
time, 4

## Chapter Summary

1. A healthy and constantly evolving financial system is the foundation for economic efficiency and economic growth. It has five parts:
   a. Money is used to pay for purchases and to store wealth.
   b. Financial instruments are used to transfer resources and risk.
   c. Financial markets allow people to buy and sell financial instruments.
   d. Financial institutions provide access to the financial markets, collect information, and provide a variety of other services.
   e. Central banks stabilize the economy.

2. The core principles of money and banking are useful in understanding all five parts of the financial system.
   a. Core Principle 1: Time has value.
   b. Core Principle 2: Risk requires compensation.
   c. Core Principle 3: Information is the basis for decisions.
   d. Core Principle 4: Markets determine prices and allocate resources.
   e. Core Principle 5: Stability improves welfare.

## Conceptual Problems

1. Try to list the financial transactions you have engaged in over the past week. How might each one have been carried out 50 years ago?

2. Describe the links among the five components of the financial system and the five core principles of money and banking.

3. Socialists argue that, to reduce the power exerted by the owners of capital, the state should control the allocation of resources. Thus, in a socialist system, the state allocates investment resources. In a market-based capitalist system, financial markets do that job. Which approach do you think works better, and why? Relate your answer to the core principle that markets determine prices and allocate resources.

4. Financial innovation has reduced individuals' need to carry cash. Explain how.

5.* Many people believe that, despite ongoing financial innovations, cash will always be with us to some degree as a form of money. What core principle could justify this view?

* Indicates more difficult problems.

www.mcgrawhill.ca/olc/cecchetti

6. When you apply for a loan, you are required to answer a lot of questions. Why? Why is the set of questions you must answer standardized?

7. Merchants that accept VISA or MasterCard pay the issuer of the card a percentage of the transaction. For example, for each $100 charged on VISA cards, a merchant might receive only $98. Explain why VISA charges the fee and why the merchant pays it. (You should be able to use at least two core principles in your answer.)

8. Suppose central bankers have figured out a way to eliminate recessions. What financial and economic changes would you expect to see? Relate these changes to the core principle that stability improves welfare.

9.* Why do you think the global financial system has become more integrated over time?

10. The government is heavily involved in the financial system. Explain why.

## Analytical Problems

11. If offered the choice of receiving $1,000 today or $1,000 in one year's time, why would you choose the first option?

12. If time has value, why are financial institutions sometimes willing to extend you a five-year mortgage at a lower annual interest rate than they would charge for a one-year loan?

13. Using Core Principle 2, under what circumstances would you expect a job applicant to accept an offer of a low base salary and an opportunity to earn commission over one with a higher base salary and no commission potential?

14. Suppose medical research confirms earlier speculation that red wine is good for you. Why would banks be willing to lend to vineyards that produce red wine at a lower interest rate than before?

15.* If the Ontario Securities Commission eliminated its requirement for public companies to disclose information about their finances, what would you expect to happen to the stock prices for these companies?

16. If you require 2 percent growth to undertake an investment project, under which outlook for the economy would you be more inclined to go ahead with the investment: (1) a forecast for economic growth that ranges from 0–4 percent, or (2) a forecast of 2 percent growth for sure, assuming the forecasts are equally reliable? What core principle does this illustrate?

17.* Why are large, publicly listed companies much more likely than small businesses to sell financial instruments such as bonds directly to the market, while small businesses get their financing from financial institutions such as banks?

18. Suppose financial institutions didn't exist but you urgently needed a loan. Where would you most likely get this loan? Using core principles, identify an advantage and a disadvantage this arrangement might have over borrowing from a financial institution.

## CHAPTER 2

## Money and the Payments System

The makers of the board game Monopoly print about 50 billion dollars' worth of Monopoly money every year—coincidentally about the same as the amount of Canadian currency outstanding in 2007. Every game has bills totalling 15,140 Monopoly dollars. At a cost of about 12 U.S. dollars per set, this "money" would be a good deal if you could buy things other than Boardwalk and Park Place with it. Unfortunately, attempts to pay for groceries, books, or rent with this particular form of money have been unsuccessful. And that's probably a good thing. Since the mid-1930s, Parker Brothers has sold over 200 million Monopoly games, containing more than 3 trillion Monopoly dollars.[1]

Parker Brothers' bestselling board game.

SOURCE: © *Nancy P. Alexander/PhotoEdit*

When we pay for our purchases in the real world, we have lots of choices: crisp new $20 bills, credit cards, debit cards, cheques, or more complicated electronic methods. Regardless of the choice we make, we are using *money* to buy our food and clothes and pay our bills. To make sure we can do it, thousands of people work through every night, because the payments system really never sleeps. And the volume of payments is astounding. The Bank of International Settlements (BIS) reports that in 2007 there were over 8.7 billion non-cash payments made in Canada. That means that 24 million payments were processed every day. Canadians (and the Swedish) are the world leaders in the use of debit cards, using them for roughly 40 percent of non-cash payments. By contrast, in the United States only 28 percent of non-cash payments were made with a debit card. Regardless of how you choose to pay, the path that the payment follows is pretty complicated.

To understand why money is so important to the smooth functioning of the economy and how it improves everyone's well-being, we need to understand exactly what money is. Just why is a $20 bill issued by the Bank of Canada much more useful than $20 in Monopoly money? Furthermore, to quantify the impact of money on the economy, we need to be able to measure it. Those are the goals of this chapter: to understand what money is, how we use it, and how we measure it.

## Money and How We Use It

When people use the word **money** in conversation, they mean many different things. Someone who "makes lots of money" has a high income; a person who "has lots of money" is wealthy. We will use the word *money* in a narrower, specialized sense to mean anything that can readily be used to make economic transactions. Formally defined,

[1] For more fun facts about Monopoly, see www.monopoly.com.

**money** is *an asset that is generally accepted as payment for goods and services or repayment of debt*. Income, in contrast, is a flow of earnings over time. **Wealth** is the value of assets minus liabilities. Money is one of those assets, albeit a very minor one.

Money, in the sense we are talking about, has three functions. It is (1) a means of payment, (2) a unit of account, and (3) a store of value. The first of these functions is the most important. Anything that is used as a means of payment must be a store of value and thus is very likely to become a unit of account. Let's see why this is so.

## Means of Payment

The primary use of money is as a **means of payment**. Most people insist on payment in money at the time a good or service is supplied because the alternatives just don't work very well. Barter, in which a good or service is exchanged directly for another good or service, requires that a plumber who needs food find a grocer who needs a plumbing repair. Relying on this "double coincidence of wants" surely causes the economy to run less smoothly. The plumber could pay for his breakfast cereal with a "promise" of plumbing services, which the grocer could then transfer to someone else. But while it would be possible to certify the plumber's trustworthiness, certainly taking payment in money is easier. Money finalizes payments so that buyers and sellers have no further claim on each other. That is money's special role. In fact, so long as a buyer has money, there is nothing more the seller needs to know.

As economies have become more complex and physically dispersed, reducing the likelihood that a seller will have good information about a buyer, the need for money has grown. The increase in both the number of transactions and the number of potential buyers and sellers (the vast majority of whom may never even have seen one another) argues for something that makes payment final and whose value is easily verified. That something is money.

## Unit of Account

Just as we measure length using feet and inches, we measure value using dollars and cents. Money is the **unit of account** that we use to quote prices and record debts. We could also refer to it as a standard of value.

Having a unit of account is an incredible convenience. Remember from microeconomics that prices provide the information consumers and producers use to ensure that resources are allocated to their best uses. What matters are the *relative* prices of goods and services. When the price of one product is higher than the price of another, that product is worth more to both producers and consumers. Using dollars makes these comparisons easy. Imagine what would happen if we needed to compute relative prices for each pair of goods. With two goods, we would need only one price. With three goods, we would need three prices. But with 100 goods, we would need 4,950 prices, and with 10,000 goods (substantially less than the 70,000 products in a typical supermarket), we would need nearly 50 million prices.[2] Using money as a yardstick and quoting all prices in dollars certainly is easier.

"*I suppose mere promises would not suffice.*"

[2] The general formula is that for $n$ goods we need $n(n-1)/2$ prices, so for 10,000 goods, the number would be $10,000 (9,999)/2 = 49,995,000$.

# YOUR FINANCIAL WORLD
Debit Cards versus Credit Cards

When you go shopping, should you pay with a credit card or a debit card? To decide, you need to understand the difference between the two. First, make sure you know which one of your cards is which. Usually an ATM card (the one that you got from the bank when you opened your chequing account) is a debit card. But check to make sure.

What's the real difference, from the shopper's point of view? A debit card works just like a cheque, only faster. When you write a paper cheque, it usually takes a day or two to go through the system. A debit card transaction goes through right away. The electronic message gets to your bank on the same day, and your account is debited immediately. So, if you want to use your debit card, your account balance has to be higher than the payment you want to make.

A credit card creates a deferred payment. The issuer agrees to make the payment for you, and you repay the debt later. That sounds good, but there's a catch. If you're late paying, there's a late fee. And if you don't pay the entire debt every month, you pay interest on the balance—at what is usually a very high interest rate. If you do pay the entire debt every month, however, there is no late fee and no interest charge. And since you don't pay right away, you get an interest-free loan from the time you make the purchase to the time you pay the balance. If you can pay off your credit cards in full and on time, it's to your advantage to use them.

Credit cards have another advantage over debit cards. They help you to build a credit history, which you'll need when the time comes to buy a car or a house. Because debit cards are just extensions of your bank account, they don't show potential lenders that you are creditworthy. In fact, some businesses, like car rental companies, require their customers to use credit cards for this reason.

## Store of Value

For money to function as a means of payment, it has to be a store of value, too. That is, if we are going to use money to pay for goods and services, then it must retain its worth from day to day. Sellers are much less likely to accept things that are perishable, like milk or lettuce. So the means of payment has to be durable and capable of transferring purchasing power from one day to the next. Paper currency does degrade with use ($5 bills have an average lifetime of one to two years in circulation) but regardless of its physical condition, it is usually accepted at face value in transactions.

Of course, money is not the only store of value. We hold our wealth in lots of other forms—stocks, bonds, houses, even cars. Many of these are actually preferable to money as stores of value. Some, like bonds, pay higher interest rates than money. Others, like stocks, offer the potential for appreciation in nominal value, which money does not. Still others, like houses, deliver other services over time. Yet we all hold money because money is liquid. Liquidity *is a measure of the ease with which an asset can be turned into a means of payment,* namely money. For example, a bond is much more liquid than a house because it is so much easier and cheaper to sell. The more costly it is to convert an asset into money, the less liquid it is. Because constantly transforming assets into money every time we wished to make a purchase would be extremely costly, we keep some money around.

**Table 2.1**   The Functions of Money

1. **Means of payment:** Used in exchange for goods and services.
2. **Unit of account:** Used to quote prices.
3. **Store of value:** Used to move purchasing power into the future.

## The Payments System

The **payments system** is the web of arrangements that allow for the exchange of goods and services, as well as assets, among different people. Because the efficient operation of our economy depends on the payments system, a critical public policy concern is that it functions well. As we will see in Part IV, that is why central banks are directly involved.

Money is at the heart of the payments system. Whether we realize it or not, virtually every transaction we engage in involves the use of money, whether directly or indirectly. Let's go through all the possible methods of payment to see how the system works.

## Commodity and Fiat Monies

The first means of payment were things with intrinsic value. These **commodity monies** included everything from silk in China to butter in Norway, whale teeth in Fiji, and salt in Venice. All these things had value even if they were not used as money. The worth of a block of salt, for instance, came from its value as a preservative. But successful commodity monies had other characteristics: They were usable in some form by most people; they could be made into standardized quantities; they were durable; they had high value relative to their weight and size so that they were easily transportable; and they were divisible into small units so that they were easy to trade. Gold and silver were frequently used for commodity money. Both metals could be purified and their purity easily ascertained. They could be cut into different-sized pieces without losing their value and were extremely durable. Moveover, they were relatively rare, giving them—especially gold—high value to weight. (Today there is only enough gold in existence to cover a Canadian football field 1.5 meters deep with solid gold—without the end zones.)

In 1656, a Swede named Johan Palmstruck founded the Stockholm Banco. Five years later he issued Europe's first paper money.[3] At the time, the Swedish currency was copper ingots, which worked poorly as money because of its low value per unit of weight. (Today, copper is worth only about 18 cents per ounce, or roughly 1/80 the value of silver and 1/5,000 the value of gold.) Thus, easy-to-handle paper was welcomed, at least at first.

After a few years of printing paper currency, Palmstruck and his sponsor, the King of Sweden, became overly enamored of the new money. The king needed to finance some wars he was fighting, so he convinced Palmstruck to print more and more notes. Since the bills were redeemable on demand for metal, the system worked only as long as people believed there was enough metal sitting in Palmstruck's vaults. As the number of notes increased, Swedes lost confidence in them and started to redeem them for the metal they supposedly stood for. But Palmstruck had issued too many notes, and his bank failed.

"French Regime, playing card money, 50 livres, 1714 (reproduction). Playing cards inscribed with a value and signed by the governor of New France were Canada's first paper currency and circulated from 1685 to 1714. No genuine examples are known to exist.

SOURCE: *Powell, James. A History of the Canadian Dollar. (Ottawa: Bank of Canada, 2005), p. 6. Photo courtesy of the Bank of Canada.*

---

[3] The Chinese were the real monetary pioneers, issuing their first paper currency in the 9th or 10th century, long before the Europeans.

A Canadian experiment with paper money ended like Palmstruck's. The French Intendant of Quebec wrote IOUs on playing cards in 1684 and declared that they were legal tender, which meant that citizens had to take them in payment. As in Sweden, at first only a small amount was issued and the Intendant ensured that the cards were convertible into coins so people took them willingly. But over time the government issued many cards, and people lost confidence that they would remain convertible into coin and so would take them in payment only if they charged very high prices for goods (as we will see, there is a direct link between the quantity of money and the rate of inflation). Experience in the United States during the Revolutionary War (1775–1783) and in France during the French Revolution (also at the end of the 18th century) had the same result. Both governments issued huge quantities of the currencies, and both currencies eventually became worthless. The reaction was predictable: People became suspicious of government-issued paper money. For the next several decades, governments didn't issue paper money, or if they did it was made legal tender only during wartimes. In Canada, gold coins were made legal tender in the 19th century, although during World War I and II the government issued notes that were also legal tender. Both gold coins and notes backed by gold circulated well into the 20th century.

Today, we use paper money—high-quality paper, nicely engraved, with lots of special security features, and not convertible into gold coins. This type of currency is called **fiat money**, because its value comes from government decree, or *fiat*. Some countries print notes that are durable and attractive, bearing famous works of art in multiple colours. The Australians make their notes out of plastic. But in all cases the money has very little intrinsic worth, and the cost of production is only a small fraction of the face value. The Bank of Canada pays less than 6 cents to print a note, regardless of whether it's a $5 or a $100 bill.

Why are we willing to accept these bills as payment for goods or in settlement of debts? There are two reasons. First, we take them because we believe we can use them in the future; someone else will take them from us. Second, the law says we must accept them. That is, the Canadian government stands behind its paper money. More importantly, the Canadian government is committed to accepting the currency it has issued in settlement of debts. We will always be able to pay our taxes in dollars. As long as the government stands behind its paper money and doesn't issue too much of it, we will use it. In the end, money is about trust.

## Cheques

**Cheques** are another way of paying for things. Unlike currency, the cheques you use to pay your rent and electric bill are not legal tender. A cheque is just an instruction to the bank to take funds from your account and transfer them to the person or firm whose name you have written in the "Pay to the order of" line. Thus, when you give someone a cheque in exchange for a good or service, it is not a final payment—at least, not in the same sense as currency. Instead, your cheque sets in motion a series of transactions that eventually lead to the final payment.

Here are the steps. Suppose you live in Vancouver and receive a cheque from your aunt in Toronto. You take the cheque to your bank (Bank of Montreal) and deposit it in your account. In this example, your aunt is called the drawer because she drew the cheque on her bank account (say at Scotiabank); you are the payee. Depending on the arrangement, the Bank of Montreal will credit the amount of the cheque to your account (although you may not have access to the funds for up to 10 days). At the end of the day, the Bank of Montreal sends the cheque (and all the other cheques

Figure 2.1   The Path of a Paper Cheque: Toronto–Vancouver–Toronto

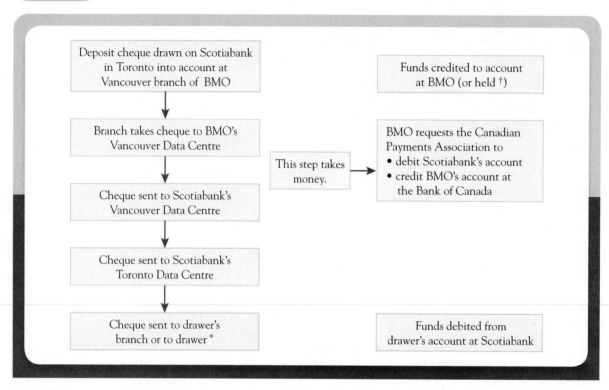

* If the drawer has no funds then the cheque goes all the way back.
† BMO may wait to receive funds from Scotiabank before crediting the depositor's account.

that it has received as deposits) to its Vancouver data centre (see Figure 2.1). There it is put with cheques drawn on Scotiabank deposited at all the other BC branches. The totals are calculated and then they are sent to the Scotiabank regional data centre in Vancouver. (The first cheque clearinghouses were pubs where bank employees met to have a drink and exchange cheques.)

Large financial institutions that process many items each day, such as the big banks and the Alberta Treasury Branches, operate as **direct clearers**.[4] That means that they have a clearing account at the Bank of Canada and that they operate a regional data centre at each of six locations across Canada. Smaller financial institutions operate as **indirect clearers**, and use one of the direct clearers as their clearing agent. When banks send the cheques they have received to the data centre of the direct clearer on which they are drawn on, they enter the total amount into the **Automated Cheque Clearing and Settlement System (ACSS)**, which is the accounting system run by the Canadian Payments Association. The same entries are done at each regional data centre by each direct clearer, so that the ACSS has a record of the amount each direct clearer owes the others. Rather than transfer the funds back and forth, the system determines the net balance of each bank and then the net funds are transferred from one direct clearer to another on the books of the Bank of Canada. (In Chapter 17 we discuss the settlement system in more detail.)

[4] Direct clearers include (Bank of Montreal, Scotiabank, CIBC, National Bank, Royal Bank, and TD Canada Trust, as well as the Alberta Treasury Branch, Caisses Desjardins, HSBC, Laurentian Bank, and Credit Union Central of Canada.

# YOUR FINANCIAL WORLD
## Paper Cheques Become Digital Images

For at least 30 years, there have been predictions that paper cheques would disappear. Credit cards, ATM machines, debit cards, automatic bill payment, and Internet banking were all supposed to get rid of them. Instead, each month millions of people receive thick envelopes from their banks that include cancelled cheques along with their monthly statements.

The cheque verification and payment process requires financial institutions to transport all paper cheques to a payments centre, and they need to be sorted and verified three times as well as possibly shipped across the country before eventually returning to the people who wrote them. Paper cheques were legal proof of payment, so customers wanted them back. But transporting tons and tons of cheques around the country was an expensive headache for banks.

Now many banks process cheques electronically. Instead of shipping paper across the country, the bank creates a digital image of each written cheque when the cheque first arrives at the bank's regional data centre. These images create "substitute cheques," and have the same legal standing as the original cheques. The image is then transmitted to the drawer's bank and is available to the drawer.

Payments in long-distance transactions are now much less complicated. A cheque processing system that used to take a few days now takes a few hours. Processing cheques electronically is definitely cheaper. Experts estimate that by scanning cheques and transmitting the images, the banks will save millions of dollars a year. The banks not only no longer have to pay for the couriers, but also reduce the risks of physically transporting cheques, including theft and weather-related delays.

Speeding up paper cheque processing does have one downside: People can't write cheques with the expectation that they will have a day or two to make a deposit to cover it. There is no more float. The new rules shrink the time between when a cheque is written and when the account is debited, especially for out-of-town cheques.*

* Just because banks are able to move cheques through the clearing system more quickly doesn't mean that they offer the depositor more timely access to the funds. Banks still place holds on funds but they are required to tell you their maximum hold time for cheques drawn on Canadian financial institutions, and an estimate of the maximum time for cheques drawn on foreign institutions. If you have to deposit a cheque and use the funds quickly, it is important to find out the policies of your financial institution.

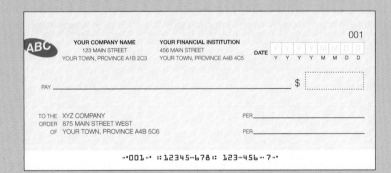

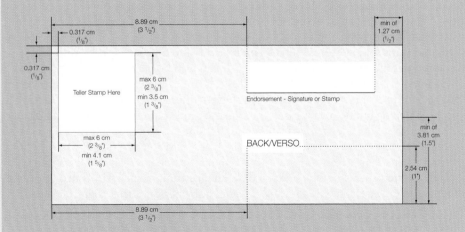

*Not to scale. Front and reverse of this cheque have been reproduced from CPA Standard 006 with the permission of the Canadian Payments Association.*

Meanwhile at the Scotiabank data centre in Vancouver the cheques are sorted so that all those drawn on branches near Toronto are sent to Scotiabank's Toronto data centre. From there, your aunt's cheque is sent to her branch, and finally her account is debited and she receives the cheque back. If the balance in her account is insufficient to cover the cheque, her bank has a few days to return it to your bank, so the transaction isn't actually final until that period has passed. In the past, all paper cheques were returned to the people who originally wrote them. Today, they are often scanned when they arrive at the data centre and then they are destroyed. Customers can view electronic images on their bank's Web sites. (See Your Financial World: Paper Cheques Become Digital Images.)

As more Canadians use electronic banking, cheque volumes have begun to fall, but paper cheques are still with us: in 2008, nearly one billion cheques were processed by the ACSS. That's down from 1.36 billion in 2000, but still a vast number of pieces of paper. Cheques are still used because, unlike cash, a cancelled cheque or its digital image gives legal proof of payment. Also, anyone can take a cheque. To receive a payment by credit or debit card or to pay a bill electronically, you need specialized hardware. Then there is force of habit.

## Electronic Payments

We are all familiar with credit cards and debit cards (see Your Financial World: Debit Cards versus Credit Cards on page 15). A less well known form of payment is electronic funds transfers, although electronic funds transfers account for the bulk of the $10 trillion worth of non-cash retail payments made each year in Canada.

Electronic funds transfers are movements of funds directly from one account to another. These transactions are used extensively by banks and are becoming increasingly popular for individuals as well. For individuals, the most common form is the preauthorized debit (PAD), which is generally used for recurring payments such as paycheques and utility bills. PAD transactions are just like cheques except that they are entirely electronic. Your bank account is debited or credited automatically, and you receive periodic notifications of the activity in your account.

Retail businesses, together with their banks, are experimenting with a variety of new methods of electronic payment. One is the stored-value card, which looks like a credit or debit card except that it doesn't bear your name. Some allow you to load them at the store at which them will be used; others require you to go online and transfer funds from your credit card account to your card. Still others allow you to buy a gift card at a grocery store, then take the card to a merchant that has a reader that deducts funds from the balance on the card. So far, these cards have limited usefulness. Some city transit systems sell stored-value cards, but it's hard to buy anything with them other than subway and bus rides. The same is true of long-distance phone cards and cards sold by stores such as Tim Hortons and Starbucks. In addition to being a convenient means of payment, these cards can also be part of a loyalty program.

E-money is another new method of payment. It can be used to pay for purchases on the Internet. You open an account by transferring funds to the issuer of the e-money. Then, when you are shopping online, you instruct the issuer to send your e-money to the merchant.

E-money is really a form of private money. It is not issued or guaranteed by the government, so you can't use it to pay your taxes. It's hard to even define what the term *e-money* means. One definition that seems helpful is "monetary value, as represented by a claim on the issuer, which is (a) stored on an electronic device, (b) issued on receipt of funds, and (c) accepted as a means of payment by persons other than the issuer."[5]

---

[5] This definition comes from Directive 2000/46 of the European Parliament and the Council of September 18, 2000, "On the Taking Up, Pursuit and Prudential Supervision of the Business of Electronic Money Institutions," *Official Journal of the European Communities*, 275/39, October 27, 2000.

But at this point, e-money is questionable at best. Will individuals develop enough trust in e-money to be willing to use it? Will merchants install the expensive equipment to handle it? Who will be allowed to issue e-money? Still, the day may come when you can park your car and pay the parking meter by simply waving your cell phone at the meter to transfer funds from your credit card to the city government that owns the parking meter. (See In the News: Canada Edges toward M-Payments on page 22.)

## The Future of Money

Let's speculate about what might happen to money and each of its three functions in the future. As a *means of payment*, it has already undergone big changes. The time is rapidly approaching when safe and secure systems for payment will use virtually no money at all.

We will always need money as a *unit of account* in which to quote values and prices; the efficiency of quoting prices in commonly understood terms won't change. But the question is, how many units of account will we need? Today, many countries have their own currencies, which give rise to their own units of account. In the future, though, there will be little reason to maintain different units of account across different countries. Price systems will be more like systems of weights and measures. Today, there are two commonly used systems of weights and measures: English ounces and yards and metric grams and metres. In the future we might see a similar sort of standardization of money and a dramatic reduction in the number of units of account.

Finally, money as a *store of value* is clearly on the way out. With the advances in financial markets, many financial instruments have become highly liquid. They are easily bought and sold, and can be converted into a means of payment quickly and cheaply. These instruments and the financial markets in which they trade are the subject of the next chapter. For now, though, we can conclude that in the future, there will almost surely be less and less money.

One caution is in order. As we look into the future and try to discern what will happen to money, we should remember that 200 years ago there was virtually no paper currency in circulation; money was coins. The first credit card was issued in the early 1950s; the first ATM was installed around 1970. Not until the mid-1990s could we shop via the Internet. Forecasting most of these developments, as well as any other trend in technology, is nearly impossible. After all, who could have predicted even 10 years ago that today we would be able to check our bank balances, buy and sell stocks, and pay our utility bills 24 hours a day, seven days a week from the comfort of our homes?

## Measuring Money

Changes in the amount of money in the economy are related to changes in interest rates, economic growth, and most directly, inflation. Inflation is the rate at which prices in general are increasing over time—and the inflation rate is a measure of that process.[6] With inflation, you need more units of money to buy the same basket of goods you bought a month or a year ago. Put another way, inflation makes money less valuable. And the primary cause of inflation is the issuance of too much money. When the Intendant of Quebec issued too many playing cards to finance military expenditures, the number of playing cards people needed to purchase food and shelter rose dramatically. Playing cards became less valuable. So the value of the means of payment depends on how much of it is circulating.

---

[6] The terms "inflation" and "inflation rate" are often used interchangeably. We will refer to inflation as the process of prices rising, and inflation rate as the measurement of the process. The relationship between these terms is analogous to that between heat and temperature. The second is the measure of the first.

## IN THE NEWS
### Canada Edges toward M-Payments

# Electronic Payments International

## By Robin Arnfield

### October 27, 2008

Canadians and their mobile phones are by and large inseparable, providing what Visa Canada and MasterCard Canada see as an opportunity for mobile phones equipped with near-field communication (NFC) to become mobile wallets; replacing plastic cards and cash, particularly for small-value purchases.

Will Giles, MasterCard Canada's vice-president, Acceptance, told EPI the ability to make payments by waving a NFC phone at a contactless card reader might particularly appeal to younger consumers.

"The fact consumers are increasingly using their cell phones for more than just calls, for example music downloads and photos, is an encouraging sign for m-payments," added Zack Fuerstenberg, Visa Canada's director of new channels.

However, m-commerce has had a bumpy ride in Canada since national banks first became interested in wireless technology around 2000. This makes it hard to predict how readily consumers and banks will adopt NFC. American Express Canada, Bank of Montreal (BMO), CIBC, TD Canada Trust and Scotiabank, have yet to make any announcements about NFC. As of October 2008, only Royal Bank of Canada (RBC) and Citibank Canada are involved in NFC trials. "We are working on NFC, but there is nothing to announce now," said TD spokeswoman Kelly Hechler. In similar vein, BMO spokesman Ralph Marranca said: "NFC is something we are investigating, but we are not currently involved in trials."

At the moment, Canadian banks' focus is ensuring that migration to EMV goes smoothly. An EMV trial is taking place in Kitchener-Waterloo, Ontario, with financial institutions aiming to have migrated the majority of Canada's cards, ATMs and POS terminals to EMV by 2012. Concurrently, many issuers plan to offer a contactless capability on their EMV cards.

Issuance of Visa PayWave and MasterCard PayPass contactless cards and readers is a necessary first step before merchants can accept NFC payments. Eight out of the 12 Canadian MasterCard credit card issuers have already started issuing PayPass cards and 20 nationwide retailers have deployed PayPass readers, Giles said. There is a lack of PayWave readers in Canada, although Visa will start rolling them out in the next few months. So far, only TD is testing PayWave readers and contactless cards, in a small pilot in Ontario. RBC also plans to start testing contactless cards. Both RBC and TD intend to issue PayWave cards, said Fuerstenberg.

### M-banking

The first Canadian mobile banking services were launched in the early part of this decade. "Canadian banks were very excited about m-commerce in 2000," said TowerGroup analyst Virginia Garcia. "But the market was not ready; handsets were inadequate, and mobile browser and text messaging speeds were too slow. Now the market is much readier for m-commerce, handsets are better and network speeds are faster."

Currently, among Canada's top banks, only RBC and TD offer mobile banking services. These enable customers to transfer funds between accounts, pay bills, and check balances. "A large number of RBC customers use m-banking," said RBC head of payments innovation Anne Koski. "M-banking is an extension, not a replacement, for our other channels. For example, it lets people pay bills on the bus."

To use the insight that money growth is somehow related to inflation, we must be able to measure how much money is circulating. This is no easy task. Let's start with money's primary function, as a means of payment. There are many means of payment so this won't provide a unique definition of money. Indeed, there is no unique definition of money. Rather, we consider a broad category of financial assets and sort them by the ease with which they can be converted into a means of payment, arranging them along a spectrum from the most liquid (currency) to the least liquid (art, antique cars, and the like). Figure 2.2 on page 24 shows what our liquidity spectrum would look like.

RBC is involved in three m-commerce projects. It is lab-testing NFC phone payments in a trial with Visa Canada, which will shortly move to an RBC staff trial in Toronto, followed by a consumer pilot, explained Fuerstenberg. With Vancouver credit union Vancity and TD, RBC is trialling a service which sends Visa card transaction alerts to participants' cell phones. "Mobile alerts help to build the connection in consumers' minds between mobile phones and their Visa cards," said Richard Robins, director, marketing and business development at Vancity's Visa card division. "In the future, we will have NFC transactions with cell phones."

...

## Mobile carriers

Apart from merchants, mobile carriers are essential for NFC to become a reality. The carriers provide the over-the-air activation facility enabling subscribers to download their payment cards to their handsets. In 2005, Canada's three main carriers, Bell Mobility, Rogers Wireless and Telus Mobility, launched a joint m-payments initiative. They initially wanted to develop remote m-payment services using short message service (SMS) texting but have refocused on NFC. Bell is participating in MasterCard's Canadian NFC trial with Citibank Canada and Citi credit cardholders, while Rogers is involved in the GSM Association's Pay-Buy-Mobile global NFC initiative. An informed source told EPI that Rogers is currently talking to a Canadian bank about an NFC trial.

...

## Encouraging results

"MasterCard Canada is very encouraged by the results of its NFC pilot so far, and plans to expand its NFC activities in the next year or so," Giles said. "When our issuers feel the time is right to roll out NFC, we will work with them on this, using the PayPass infrastructure in place." "Our tests have shown that NFC works," said Koski. "Now we need to find out if consumers want to use NFC, as this would be a change in their payments behaviour. Will they be willing to activate the NFC application on their phone and download their cards, or is this too much hassle?" "Activating an NFC phone's m-wallet takes 90 seconds, and people often do this when they first get the phone and are activating the voice capability," said Mohammad Khan, president of US contactless payments specialist VivoTech. "In the 25 NFC trials worldwide we have been involved in, we have seen that consumers really like NFC."

> ### LESSONS OF THE ARTICLE
>
> Technological advances are constantly creating new methods of payment. (EMV refers to the global protocol for debit and credit cards to have chips with a PIN number, rather than a magnetic stripe authenticated by signature). While their adoption depends on many things, one thing is for certain: Someone will always be searching for easier and cheaper ways for us to pay for things. And as the payments system evolves, so will the assets that we need to hold. As our cell phones transform into a part of the payments system, we will need to carry less and less cash.

SOURCE: "Canada Edges towards M-Payments," by Robin Arnfield. Electronic Payments International, (EPI), 27 October 2008. At: www.electronicpayments international.com/getasp?script=article& ID=34198.

Once we have our list, we could draw a line and include everything on one side of the line in our measure of money. Over the years, figuring out just where to draw the line has proven very difficult, especially since the introduction of new types of chequing accounts. There really is no perfect solution, nor a permanent solution. Instead, we have drawn the line in a number of different places and computed several measures of money. The most commonly used measures, called the monetary aggregates, are measures of transactions balances (M1 measures) and measures of broad money (M2 measures).

Table 2.2 on page 25 shows the components of the two monetary aggregates along with the size of each as of June 2008. Let's go through each one to understand how it is constructed. M1+, the narrower definition of money, includes only currency and

**Figure 2.2**   The Liquidity Spectrum

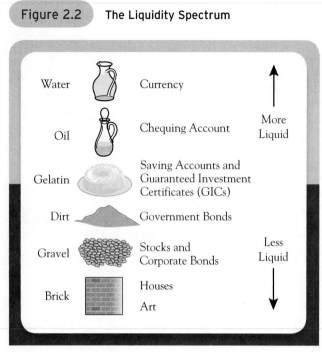

| | |
|---|---|
| Water | Currency |
| Oil | Chequing Account |
| Gelatin | Saving Accounts and Guaranteed Investment Certificates (GICs) |
| Dirt | Government Bonds |
| Gravel | Stocks and Corporate Bonds |
| Brick | Houses Art |

More Liquid

Less Liquid

Liquidity is the ease with which you can turn an asset into a means of payment without loss of value.

various deposit accounts on which people can write cheques. These are the most liquid assets in the financial system. The components of M1 include *currency outside banks*, which is the quantity of dollar bills outstanding excluding the ones in the vaults of banks and **chequable deposits** at chartered banks, trust companies, and credit unions. M1 originally included only chequing accounts at chartered banks, but now chequing accounts at the other institutions are nearly perfect substitutes for chequing accounts at banks, so the Bank of Canada considers **M1+ gross**—a measure that includes those accounts—as its measure of transactions money.

**M2++ gross** equals all of M1+ plus assets that cannot be used directly as a means of payment and are more difficult to turn into currency quickly. These include non-chequing accounts at the banks and other financial institutions as well as money market mutual funds. **Money market mutual funds** are funds that collect relatively small sums from individuals, pool them together, and invest them in short-term marketable debt issued by large corporations or governments. *Money market mutual fund shares* can be issued by non-bank financial intermediaries, such as brokerage firms, and usually carry cheque-writing privileges. Finally, because all mutual funds and Canada Savings Bonds can be turned into cash almost as easily as the accounts at the financial intermediaries, they are incorporated into M2++.

Notice that Table 2.2 refers to all the aggregates as "gross." When monetary aggregates were first used, cheques were a sizable part of the monetary base, and also took several days to go between the bank at which they were deposited and the bank from which the funds were to be withdrawn. During that time, the person depositing the cheque counted it in his or her account, and so did the person who had written the cheque. That meant the amount was double counted, so after counting up the value of deposit accounts the value of cheques in transit was subtracted; that is, the aggregates were net of "in transit" items. Now many payments by cheque have been replaced with electronic transactions, and cheques clear very quickly so that the difference between gross and net is small and the Bank of Canada reports and uses "gross" values.

To clarify what the monetary aggregates mean, let's compare their size to the size of the economy. In 2008, nominal Canadian **gross domestic product (GDP)** was $1.6 trillion. Putting that number into the same units as those in Table 2.2, that's $1,600,081 million. So M1+ is about one-quarter the size of GDP and M2++ is about the same amount as GDP.

What is the relationship between the two monetary aggregates? Figure 2.3 on page 28 shows that the growth rate of M1+ is more volatile than that of M2++. But remember that M2++ is roughly four times as large as M1+. A given increase in demand deposits will cause a much larger percentage increase in M1+ than in M2++. Before 1990, the two growth rates behaved quite differently. In the early 1980s, M1+ shrank while M2++ was growing. All the components of M1+ are in M2++, so if M1+ decreased while M2++ grew, it meant that people moved funds out of their chequing accounts and into their savings accounts. This made sense in the late 1970s and early 1980s because

**Table 2.2**   The Monetary Aggregates

| Monetary Aggregates | June 2008 ($ millions) |
|---|---|
| Currency outside banks | 50,047 |
| Chequable deposits at banks | 349,232 |
| Chequable deposits at other FIs | 47,766 |
| M1+gross | 447,045 |
| Other deposits at banks | 422,867 |
| Other deposits at other FIs | 204,783 |
| Money Market MFs | 71,435 |
| M2+ gross | 1,146,130 |
| CSBs | 13,125 |
| Other MFs | 524,372 |
| M2++ gross | 1,683,627 |

SOURCE: *Bank of Canada, Banking and Financial Statistics; December 2008–Table E1.*

NOTES: MF—mutual funds; CSBs—Canada Savings Bonds; "other FIs" include trust and loan companies, Alberta Treasury branches, caisse populaires, and credit unions, life insurance companies individual annuities are included in M2++. Other deposits at banks do not include nonpersonal term deposits.

high interest rates raised the opportunity cost of funds in low-interest-paying chequing accounts. In the mid-1980s (and in early 2009) M1+ grew more rapidly than M2++. This means that money holders substituted out of an asset that is in only M2++ into assets that are in M1+ as well as in M2++; for example, moving funds out of money market mutual funds and into chequing accounts. From 1991 up to 2008, the growth rates of the two aggregates behaved quite similarly, although M1+ continues to be more volatile than M2++.

What is the relationship between money growth and inflation? To answer this question we will distinguish between high rates of inflation and moderate rates of inflation. We already know that when the quantity of money grows quickly, it produces very high inflation. A cross-country analysis of money growth supports this conclusion. In Turkey, Venezuela, and Ukraine, where in the last half of the 1990s the inflation rate ranged from 30 to 75 percent per year, the money supply grew at comparable rates.[7] Similarly, in Zimbabwe, where the inflation rate in 2008 was over 165,000 percent, the growth rate of M1 was nearly 100,000 percent. By contrast, in the United States, Canada, and Europe, the inflation rate averaged only about 2 percent, and the money growth rate stayed in the range of 6 to 7 percent. Because high money growth means high inflation, controlling inflation means controlling the money supply. Imagine how much inflation there would be if people could spend the 3 trillion in Monopoly dollars Parker Brothers has printed over the last seven decades!

[7] From 1995 to 2000, inflation averaged 74 percent, 42 percent, and 30 percent, respectively, in Turkey, Venezuela, and Ukraine. At the same time, the money stock (the countries' equivalent to M2) grew at 86, 33, and 36 percent per year. respectively. Data for these comparisons come from the International Monetary Fund's *International Financial Statistics.*

# TOOLS OF THE TRADE
## The Consumer Price Index

Understanding how to measure inflation is central to understanding economics and finance. Most of us keep a close eye on measures like the Consumer Price Index (CPI) to help gauge the value of our salary increases or the purchasing power of the money we hold. And adjusting interest rates for inflation is critical for making investment decisions. (See Chapter 4.)

The CPI is designed to answer the following question: How much more would it cost for people to purchase today the same basket of goods and services that they actually bought at some fixed time in the past?

To calculate the CPI, every few years statisticians at Statistics Canada survey people to find out what they bought. This gives us the basket of goods and services bought by the typical consumer. Next, every month Statistics Canada collects information on the prices of the hundreds of goods and services in the basket—everything from breakfast cereal to gasoline to washing machines to the cost of cable television. Combining the expenditure and price surveys allows statisticians to compute the current cost of the basket. Finally, this current cost is compared to a benchmark to yield an index. The percentage change in this index is a measure of inflation.

To see how this works, let's look at an example. Assume people spend 25 percent of their income on food, 50 percent on housing, and 25 percent on transportation. That's the survey information. Examples of the prices are in Table 2.3. Importantly, these are the prices of exactly the same bundle of food, the same size and quality of housing, and the same transportation for each year.

Using the numbers in Table 2.2, we can compute the cost of the basket of goods in each year:

Cost of the basket in 2007

$= 0.25 \times$ Price of food $+ 0.5 \times$ Price of housing

$\quad + 0.25 \times$ Price of transportation

$= 0.25 \times \$100 + 0.5 \times \$200 + 0.25 \times \$100$

$= \$150$

And for 2008, we get \$165. Choosing 2007 as the base year, the index level in each year equals

$$\text{CPI} = \frac{\text{Cost of the basket in current year}}{\text{Cost of the basket in base year}} \times 100$$

The result of this computation is the fifth column of the table.

Finally, we can use the index number to compute the inflation rate from the previous year. From 2006 to 2007, this means that

$$\text{Inflation Rate 2008} = \frac{\text{CPI in 2008} - \text{CPI in 2007}}{\text{CPI in 2007}} \times 100.$$

Using the numbers from Table 2.2 to compute the inflation rate in 2008, we get that

$$\frac{110 - 100}{100} \times 100 = 10\%,$$

How useful is money growth in helping us to control moderate inflation? We will address this question in detail in Chapter 20 of this book. For now, though, let's look at whether money growth helps to forecast inflation.

Figure 2.4 on page 28 shows the M2++ growth rate on the horizontal axis and the inflation rate *two years later* on the vertical axis, both for Canada. The solid red diamonds represent data from 1969 to 1975, the triangles show data from 1976 to 1981, and the squares show data for 1991 to 2007. Overall, as we might expect, high money growth is associated with high inflation, but the relationship varied over time. During the period 1969–1975, M1 and M2 behaved very similarly and the correlation between M2 and inflation was high.[8] Then from 1975 to 1981, the Bank of Canada attempted to use this correlation to reduce inflation by reducing the growth rate of M1. Money holders responded by switching their funds out of assets in only M1 into assets included in M2 and M2++. The result was high inflation and high growth rates of M2. But look at what happened to the relationship more recently. The hollow blue

---

[8] Correlation is a measure of how closely two quantities are related, or change together. The numerical value ranges from +1 to −1. A positive correlation signifies that the two variables move up and down together, while a negative correlation means that they move in opposite directions.

and for 2009 the result is

$$\frac{120 - 110}{110} \times 100 = 9.1\%.$$

(These numbers are just for illustration. The Canadian inflation rate is closer to 2 percent.)

Inflation measured using the CPI tells us how much more money we need to give someone to restore the purchasing power he or she had in the earlier period when the survey was done. But adjustments in wages based on fixed-basket-weight inflation indices like the CPI are known to overcompensate people in an unintended way. This overstatement of inflation comes from what is known as substitution bias. Since inflation is not uniform, the prices of some products will increase by more than the prices of others. People can escape some of the inflation by substituting goods and services that have sustained less inflation for those that have sustained more. By assuming that any substitution makes people worse off, the index overstates the impact of price changes. To address this problem, and take into account changes in spending patterns, Statistics Canada now changes the weights every four years.

**Table 2.3**   Computing the Consumer Price Index

| Year | Price of Food | Price of Housing | Price of Transportation | Cost of the Basket | Consumer Price Index |
|------|---------------|------------------|-------------------------|--------------------|----------------------|
| 2007 | $100 | $200 | $100 | $150 | 100 |
| 2008 | $110 | $205 | $140 | $165 | 110 |
| 2009 | $120 | $210 | $180 | $180 | 120 |

dots represent data from 1991 to 2007, when there was virtually no relationship at all between the two measures. (The correlation was slightly negative.) Growth in M2++ stopped being a useful tool for forecasting inflation.

There are many possible explanations for the fact that M2++ no longer predicts inflation. One is that the relationship between the two applies only at high levels of inflation. Figure 2.4 on page 28 shows that during the period 1969–1981, the inflation rate was usually higher than 5 percent, but from 1991 to 2007, it was rarely that high. Maybe the relationship between money growth and inflation doesn't exist at low levels of inflation, or it shows up only over longer periods of time. An alternative explanation is that 1991 is the year that the Bank of Canada began setting policy so as to achieve a pre-announced inflation rate—this is called an inflation-targeting policy and we discuss it in detail in Part IV. Finally, it could be that we need a new measure of money that takes into account recent changes in the way we make payments and use money. Once economists have identified the right measure, we'll be able to predict inflation again.

Figure 2.3    Growth Rates of Monetary Aggregates, 1969–2009

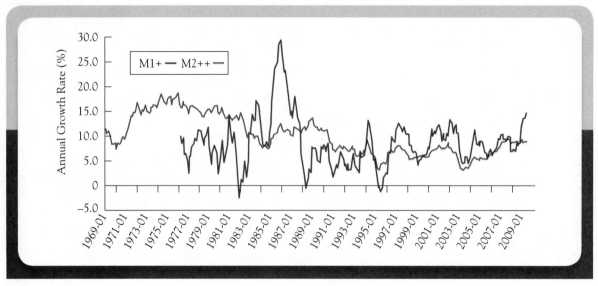

SOURCE: *Bank of Canada Banking and Financial Statistics, accessed June 2009, Table 176-0020. M1+ v37258: M2++ v41552790.*

Figure 2.4    Money Growth and Inflation, 1969–2009

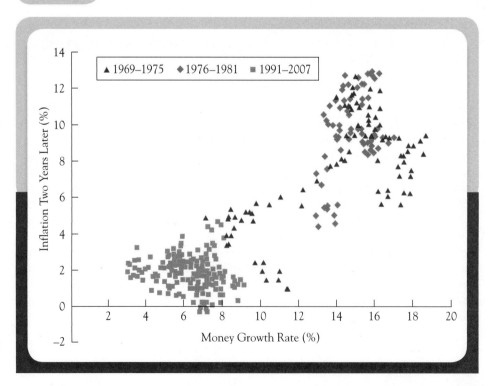

**Money growth measured as the 12-month change in M2++, and inflation measured as the 12-month change in the Consumer Price Index.**

SOURCE: *Bank of Canada Banking and Financial Statistics, accessed June 2009 Table 176-0020. M2++ (v41552790); Statistics Canada, Consumer Price Index Table 326-0020 (v41690973), accessed June 2009.*

## APPLYING THE CONCEPT
### WHERE ARE ALL THOSE $100 BILLS?

A quick look at the Annual Report of the Bank of Canada at www.bankofcanada.ca, tells us that during the winter of 2007, the public held about $50 billion in Canadian currency. That's a huge amount. To get some sense of the size of this number, you can divide it by the Canadian population, 33 million, to get roughly $1,500 per person. For a household of four, that's an average of $6,000 in cash. What's even more amazing is that about 50 percent of the $50 billion is held in the form of $100 bills, meaning that there must be seven $100 bills for each Canadian resident. In the United States, there are even more $100 bills around, an average of 18 per resident! Clearly, we do not hold all this cash in our wallets or our homes, nor does it fill the cash registers of local businesses. Where are all those $100 bills?

In many countries, people do not trust their governments to protect the value of the currency they print. They fear the authorities will print too much, creating inflation. And since money is all about trust, if you don't have confidence in your government, you don't want to hold your wealth in the government's money. In many cases, the lack of faith has been warranted. When the Soviet Union collapsed in the early 1990s, the currency issued by the old regime became nearly worthless. The same thing happened in Argentina in the 1980s.

When people stop trusting the local currency, they look for substitutes. The most sought-after is the U.S. dollar bill. With the stability of the constant addition of new security features, and the stability of the government, it is in high demand.* The U.S. Treasury estimates that between two-thirds and three-quarters of U.S. currency is held outside the United States. That's more than $500 billion—and most of it is in hundreds! The same calculation would suggest that up to half of the Canadian cash may be outside the country.

*Money issuers spend a lot of time and money developing security features to reduce counterfeiting. The measures taken by the Bank of Canada are described at www.bankofcanada.ca/en/banknotes/counterfeit/security_features.html.

## Terms

## Chapter Summary

1. Money is an asset that is generally accepted in payment for goods and services or repayment of debts.
   a. Money has three basic uses:
      i. Means of payment
      ii. Unit of account
      iii. Store of value
   b. Money is liquid. Liquidity is the ease with which an asset can be turned into a means of payment.
2. Money makes the payments system work. The payments system is the web of arrangements that allows people to exchange goods and services. There are three broad categories of payments, all of which use money at some stage:
   a. Cash
   b. Cheques
   c. Electronic payments
3. In the future, money will be used less and less as a means of payment.

www.mcgrawhill.ca/olc/cecchetti

4. There is no unique measure of money. Two commonly used measures in Canada are
   a. M1+, a narrow measure, including only the most liquid assets
   b. M2++, a broader measure, including assets not as easily usable as means of payment

5. Countries with high money growth have high inflation, but in countries with low inflation, money growth is a poor forecaster of inflation.

## Conceptual Problems

1. The country of Brieonia has an economy that is based largely on farming and agricultural products. The inhabitants of Brieonia use cheese as their money.
   a. Not surprisingly, the Brieonians complain bitterly about the problems that their commodity money creates. What are those problems?
   b. Modern medical science arrives in Brieonia, and doctors begin giving the Brieonians cholesterol tests. The results lead to the recommendation that the Brieonians reduce the amount of cheese they eat. What is the impact of this recommendation on their economy?
   c. As the economy of Brieonia becomes industrialized, what changes in the monetary system would you expect to see, and why?

2. Describe at least three ways you could pay for your morning cup of coffee. What are the advantages and disadvantages of each?

3. Explain how money encourages specialization, and how specialization improves everyone's standard of living.

4.* Could the dollar still function as the unit of account in a totally cashless society?

5. As of March 2007, 13 of the 27 countries of the European Union have adopted the euro. The remaining 14 countries, including Great Britain, Denmark, and Sweden, have retained their own currencies. What are the advantages of a common currency for someone who is travelling through Europe?

6. Using the current level of M2++ from the Bank of Canada's Web site, compute the quantity of money divided by the (approximate) population of Canada. Do you think that your answer is large? Why or why not?

7. Using data from the Bank of Canada's Web site, compute the annual percentage change in M1+ gross and M2++ gross since 1980. Use the data to reproduce Figure 2.3 on page 28. Comment on the pattern over the last five years. Would it matter which of the two monetary aggregates you looked at?

8. Despite the efforts of the Bank of Canada, someone discovers a cheap way to counterfeit $100 bills. What will be the impact of this discovery on the economy?

9.* You have decided to issue your own currency and use your computer to produce some impressive-looking notes. What could you do to increase the chances of these notes being accepted as a means of payment?

10. Over a nine-year period in the 16th century, King Henry VIII reduced the silver content of the British pound to one-sixth its initial value. Why do you think he did so? What do you think happened to the use of pounds as a means of payment? If you held both the old and new pounds, which would you use first, and why?

## Analytical Problems

11. Under what circumstances might you expect barter to reemerge in an economy that has fiat money as a means of payment?

12. You visit a tropical island that has only four goods in its economy—oranges, pineapples, coconuts, and bananas. There is no money in this economy.
    a. Draw a grid showing all the prices for this economy. (You should check your answer using the $n(n-1)/2$ formula where n is the number of goods.)

* Indicates more difficult problems.

b. An islander suggests designating oranges as the means of payment and unit of account for the economy. How many prices would there be if her suggestion was followed?

c. Do you think the change suggested in part (b) is worth implementing? Why or why not?

13. Consider again the tropical island described in question 12. Under what circumstances would you recommend the issue of a paper currency by the government of the island? What advantages might this strategy have over the use of oranges as money?

14. What factors should you take into account when considering using the following assets as stores of value?
a. Real estate
b. Stocks
c. Government bonds

15.* Under what circumstances might money in the form of currency be the best option as a store of value?

16.* The Bank of Canada sets monetary policy to try to achieve an annual 2 percent increase in the Consumer Price Index. Is the CPI a good index of your cost of living? Why or why not? Is there a better measure of the cost of living?

17. Assuming no interest is paid on chequing accounts, what would you expect to see happen to the relative growth rates of M1+ and M2++ if interest rates rose significantly?

18. If money growth is related to inflation, what would you expect to happen to the inflation rates of countries that join a monetary union and adopt a common currency such as the euro?

www.mcgrawhill.ca/olc/cecchetti

# CHAPTER 3

## Financial Instruments, Financial Markets, and Financial Institutions

Long before formal financial institutions and instruments became common, there were times when people lacked the resources to meet their immediate needs. In the terminology of introductory economics, people's incomes were exceeded by their necessary consumption. When a harvest was poor, they would dip into the reserves stored from previous years or exchange assets like land and livestock for food. But often those measures were insufficient, so communities developed informal financial arrangements that allowed people to borrow or lend among themselves. After a poor harvest, those people with relatively good yields would help those with relatively poor ones. When the tables were turned, help would flow the other way. In some societies, families spread out geographically to facilitate these arrangements. For example, in rural Indian communities, households deliberately married off their daughters to families in different regions to increase the chance that their in-laws would be able to respond in a time of crisis.[1] These informal insurance arrangements ensured that everyone had enough to eat.

While family members and friends still make loans among themselves, the informal arrangements that were the mainstay of the financial system centuries ago have given way to the formal financial instruments of the modern world. Today, the international financial system exists to facilitate the design, sale, and exchange of a broad set of contracts that mobilize and pool savings and transfer risks. As shown in Figure 3.1, we obtain the financial resources we need through this system in two ways: directly from markets and indirectly through institutions.

In indirect finance, an institution like a bank stands between the lender and the borrower, borrowing from the lender and then providing the funds to the borrower. Most of us do our borrowing and lending indirectly. If we need a loan to buy a car, we get it from a bank or finance company—that's indirect finance. Once we get the loan, the car becomes one of our assets, and the loan becomes our liability. We all have assets and liabilities. Your assets probably include financial assets, such as a bank account, as well as real assets such as a computer. If you have a student loan or credit card debt, those are your liabilities.

In direct finance, borrowers sell securities directly to lenders in the financial markets. Governments and corporations finance their activities in this way. These securities become assets for the lenders who buy them and liabilities to the government or corporation that initially sells them.

Financial development is inextricably linked to economic growth. A country's financial system has to grow as its level of economic activity rises, or the country will stagnate. The role of the financial system is to channel savings efficiently so that they facilitate production and employment, and help to smooth consumption. Savings finance the investment that allows the economy to grow, and finance consumption during periods of low income, allowing people to go to school or to retire.

In this chapter, we will survey the financial system in three steps. First, we'll study financial instruments, or *securities*, as they are often called. Stocks, bonds, and loans of all types are

[1] See M.R. Rosenzweig, "Risk, Implicit Contracts, and the Family in Rural Areas of Low-Income Countries," *Economic Journal* 98 (December 1988).

**Figure 3.1**  Funds Flowing through the Financial System

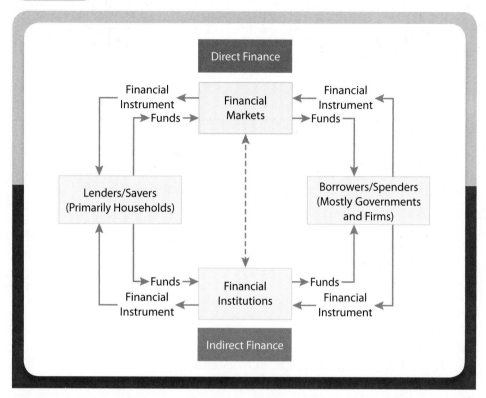

The financial system channels funds from lenders to borrowers in two ways: directly and indirectly. In direct finance, borrowers obtain resources by selling financial instruments such as bonds and stocks in financial markets directly to lenders. In indirect finance, a financial institution such as a bank takes the resources from the lender in the form of a deposit (or something like it) and then provides them to the borrower in the form of a loan (or the equivalent). Financial institutions both obtain funds from, and inject funds into, financial markets.

financial instruments, as are more exotic agreements such as options and insurance. Exactly what are these financial instruments, and what is their role in our economy? Second, we'll look at **financial markets**, such as the Toronto Stock Exchange and the Montreal Exchange, where investors can buy and sell stocks, bonds, and various other instruments. And finally, we'll look at **financial institutions**—what they are and what they do.

# Financial Instruments

A **financial instrument** is the *written legal obligation of one party to transfer something of value, usually money, to another party at some future date, under certain conditions.* Let's dissect this definition to understand it better. First, a financial instrument is a written legal obligation that is subject to government enforcement. That is, a person can be compelled to take the action specified in the agreement. The enforceability of the obligation is an important feature of a financial instrument. Without enforcement of the specified terms, financial instruments would not exist.[2]

---

[2] Myriad financial arrangements that exist outside the legal system, such as loan sharking, are also enforced, but those sorts of obligations are not part of the formal financial system.

Second, a financial instrument obligates *one party to transfer something of value, usually money, to another party*. By *party*, we mean a person, company, or government. Usually the financial instrument specifies that payments will be made. For example, if you get a car loan, you are obligated to make monthly payments of a particular amount to the lender. And if you have an accident, your insurance company is obligated to fix your car, though the cost of the repair is left unspecified.

Third, a financial instrument specifies that payment will be made *at some future date*. In some cases, such as a car loan that requires payments, the dates may be very specific. In others, such as car insurance, the payment is triggered when something specific happens, such as an accident.

Finally, a financial instrument *specifies certain conditions* under which a payment will be made. Some agreements specify payments only when certain events happen. That is clearly the case with car insurance and with stocks as well. The holder of a stock owns a small part of a firm and so can expect to receive occasional cash payments, called *dividends*, when the company is profitable. There is no way to know in advance, however, exactly when such payments will be made. In general, financial instruments specify a number of possible contingencies under which one party is required to make a payment to another.

## Uses of Financial Instruments

Stocks, loans, and insurance are all examples of financial instruments. The primary functions of financial instruments are acting as a store of value and allowing the transfer of risk. Because financial instruments are stores of value and have many of the characteristics of money (portability, durability, negotiability), they are also sometimes used as a means of payment.

Having a store of value means that your consumption doesn't need to exactly match your income. For days, months, and years, if necessary, you can spend more than you make, repaying the difference later, a process economists call **consumption smoothing**. (See the appendix to this chapter for a formal economic model of consumption smoothing.) Student loans, retirement savings, and employment insurance are all examples of consumption smoothing and all use financial instruments. As stores of value, financial instruments like stocks and bonds are thought to be better than money. Over time, they generate increases in wealth that are bigger than those we can obtain from holding money in most of its forms. These higher payoffs are compensation for higher levels of risk, because the payoffs from holding most financial instruments are generally more uncertain than those that arise from holding money. Nevertheless, many financial instruments can be used to transfer purchasing power into the future.

In addition to consumption smoothing, financial instruments allow savings to be pooled. Many investment opportunities require investments that are larger than (almost) any one person's savings. Using financial instruments, many people can combine their savings and invest in one project. Alternatively, even if someone could save enough to finance one project, he or she might prefer to invest in multiple projects to reduce risk.

The second use of a financial instrument lies in its ability to *transfer risk* between the buyer and the seller. Most financial instruments involve some sort of risk transfer. For example, think of wheat farmers. If one farm has a huge harvest, that farmer does very well. But if everyone's harvest is huge, then prices can plummet and individual farms can lose money. The risk that the harvest will be too good, resulting in low grain prices, is a risk that most individual farmers do not want to take. A *wheat futures contract* allows the farmer to transfer that risk to someone else. A wheat futures contract is a financial instrument in which two parties agree to exchange a fixed quantity of wheat on a prearranged future date at a specified price. By fixing the price at which the crop will be sold well in advance of the harvest, the farmer can forget about what happens in the wheat market because the risk has been transferred to someone else.

Insurance contracts are another example of a financial instrument that transfers risk—in this case, from individuals to an insurance company. Because a car accident can be financially catastrophic, we buy car insurance and transfer the risk to an insurance company. Because insurance companies make similar guarantees to a large group of people, they have the capacity to shoulder the risk. While the timing of an individual automobile accident is impossible to forecast, a predictable percentage of a large group of drivers will experience accidents over a given period.

Financial instruments can also be used as a means of payment. Recall that a means of payment is something that is generally accepted as payment for goods and services or repayment of a debt. It is possible to pay for purchases with financial instruments, even if they don't look much like money. An example is the willingness of employees to accept a company's stock as payment for working. (This means of payment was very popular in the late 1990s, when the stock market was booming.) While we cannot yet pay for groceries with shares of stock, the time may come when we can. For now, although some financial instruments may function as means of payment, they aren't terribly good ones.

**Table 3.1**   Uses of Financial Instruments

**Store of Value:** Transfer of purchasing power into the future.

**Transfer of Risk:** Transfer of risk from one person or company to another.

**Means of Payment:** Purchase of goods or services.

## Characteristics of Financial Instruments: Standardization and Information

As is obvious from the definition of a financial instrument, these sorts of contracts can be very complex. If you don't believe it, take a look at the fine print in a car insurance policy, a student loan, or even a credit card agreement. Complexity is costly. The more complicated something is, the more it costs to create and the more difficult it is to understand. As a rule, people do not want to bear these costs. Yes, the owner of an oil tanker may be willing to go to the expense of negotiating a specific insurance contract for each voyage a ship makes. The same owner may agree to make premium payments based on the load carried, the distance travelled, the route taken, and the weather expected. But for most of us, the cost of such custom contracts is simply too high.

In fact, people on both sides of financial contracts shy away from specialized agreements. Instead, they use standardized financial instruments to overcome the potential costs of complexity. Because of *standardization*, most of the financial instruments that we encounter on a day-to-day basis are very homogeneous. For example, most mortgages feature a standard application process and offer standardized terms. Automobile insurance contracts generally offer only certain standard options.

Standardization of terms makes sense. If all financial instruments differed in critical ways, most of us would not be able to understand them, and their usefulness would be severely limited. If the shares of Microsoft stock sold to one person differed in a crucial way from the shares sold to someone else, for instance, potential investors might not understand what they were buying. Even more important, the resale and trading of the shares would become virtually impossible, which would certainly discourage anyone from purchasing them in the first place. From this, we conclude that arrangements that obligate people to make payments to one another cannot all be one-of-a-kind arrangements.

Another characteristic of financial instruments is that they communicate *information*, summarizing certain essential details about the issuer. How much do you really want to learn about the original issuer of a financial instrument? Or if you are purchasing an existing instrument, how much do you want to have to know about the person who is selling it to you? Surely, the less you feel you need to know to feel secure about the transaction, the better. Regardless of whether the instrument is a stock, a bond, a futures contract, or an insurance contract, the holder does not want to have to watch the issuer too closely; continuous monitoring is costly and difficult. Thus, financial instruments are designed to eliminate the expensive and time-consuming process of collecting such information.

A number of mechanisms exist to reduce the cost of monitoring the behaviour of the counterparties to a financial arrangement. A counterparty is the person or institution on the other side of a contract. If you obtain a car loan from your local bank, then you are the bank's counterparty and the bank is yours. In the case of a stock or bond, the issuing firm and the investors who hold the instrument are counterparties.

### APPLYING THE CONCEPT
#### INVESTOR INFORMATION AND CONFLICTS OF INTEREST

In 2003, the Ontario Securities Commission (OSC) investigated the behaviour of CIBC World Markets, which had been lead underwriter for an Initial Public Offering (IPO) for Shoppers Drug Mart. CIBC World Markets had written five equity research reports in which it recommended the purchase of shares of Shoppers. The OSC found that CIBC World Markets had not adequately disclosed that it held 7.45 million shares of Shoppers, and that Shoppers was indebted to CIBC. In approving the settlement, Commissioner Theresa McLeod emphasized that disclosures should be in type large enough to read and it is not sufficient to "bury them in the middle of dense paragraphs" of boilerplate text. A conflict of interest arose because demand for shares in Shoppers would benefit CIBC.

The dot-com boom of the 1990s made Henry Blodget a star. After a failed career as a journalist, Blodget had turned to Wall Street. From 1994 to 1999, working for the brokerage giant Merrill Lynch, he built a reputation as one of the best stock analysts in the business. People hung on the words he was paid millions of dollars to utter. By the end of 2001, however, Blodget was banned from the financial industry, accused of misleading investors with overly optimistic recommendations

that he himself did not believe. The dot-com boom was over, and gone with it was investors' confidence in the information they received from their brokers. Stock analysts everywhere, it seemed, had been less interested in providing accurate information to their retail clients than in pumping up the value of their corporate customers' stocks, especially the dot-coms. A serious conflict of interest arose because the analysts worked for the same financial institutions that served the needs of the companies whose stock they were evaluating. On one side, equity research analysts such as Blodget were providing research information on firms' prospects. Meanwhile, the same firms were doing business with the analysts' banking colleagues, buying and selling various financial instruments, including stocks and bonds. So, rather than provide accurate information to their retail clients, the stock analysts had an incentive to publish positive assessments to ensure their firms kept the lucrative banking business.

In both Canada and the United States, new laws were introduced to reduce the conflict of interest, and to ensure that conflicts are disclosed. Today research analysts are required to be independent of their banking colleagues. The point is to improve the quality of information in the system. When investors make their decisions on the basis of bad information, savings don't flow to the most promising investments. For the financial system to work and make us all better off, investors must have good information.

The solution to the high cost of obtaining information on the parties to a financial instrument is to standardize both the instrument and the information provided about the issuer. We can also hire a specialist whom we all trust to do the monitoring. The institutions that have arisen over the years to support the existence of financial instruments provide an environment in which everyone can feel secure about the behaviour of the counterparties to an agreement.

In addition to simply summarizing information, financial instruments are designed to handle the problem of *asymmetric information*, which comes from the fact that borrowers have some information they don't disclose to lenders. Instead of buying new ovens, will a bread baker use a $50,000 loan to take an extended vacation in Tahiti? The lender wants to make sure the borrower is not misrepresenting what he or she will do with borrowed funds. Thus, the financial system is set up to gather information on borrowers before giving them resources and to monitor their use of the resources afterward. These specialized mechanisms were developed to handle the problem of asymmetric information.

## Underlying versus Derivative Instruments

There are two fundamental classes of financial instruments. The first, underlying instruments (sometimes called *primitive securities*), are used by savers/lenders to transfer resources directly to investors/borrowers. Through these instruments, the financial system improves the efficient allocation of resources in the real economy.

The primary examples of underlying securities or instruments are stocks and bonds that offer payments based solely on the issuer's status. Bonds, for example, make payments depending on the solvency of the firm that issued them. Stocks sometimes pay dividends when the issuing corporation's profits are sufficient.

The second class of financial instruments is known as derivative instruments. Their value and payoffs are "derived" from the behaviour of the underlying instruments. The most common examples of derivatives are futures and options. In general, derivatives specify a payment to be made between the person who sells the instrument and the person who buys it. The amount of the payment depends on various factors associated with the price of the underlying asset. The primary use of derivatives is to shift risk among investors. We will see some examples in a moment; Chapter 9 discusses derivatives in detail.

## A Primer for Valuing Financial Instruments

Why are some financial instruments more valuable than others? If you look at the Web site of *The Globe and Mail* or *The Financial Post*, you'll see the prices of many bonds and stocks. They are quite different from each other. Not only that, but from day to day, the prices of an individual bond or stock can vary quite a bit. What characteristics affect the price someone will pay to buy or sell a financial instrument?

Four fundamental characteristics influence the value of a financial instrument: (1) the *size* of the payment that is promised, (2) *when* the promised payment is to be made, (3) the *likelihood* that the payment will be made, and (4) the *circumstances* under which the payment is to be made. Let's look at each one of these traits.

First, people will pay more for an instrument that obligates the issuer to pay the holder $1,000 than for one that offers a payment of $100. Regardless of any other conditions, this simply must be true: *The bigger the promised payment, the more valuable the financial instrument.*

Second, if you are promised a payment of $100 sometime in the future, you will want to know when you will receive it. Receiving $100 tomorrow is different from receiving $100

| Table 3.2 | What Makes a Financial Instrument Valuable? |
| --- | --- |

**Size:** Payments that are larger are more valuable.
**Timing:** Payments that are made sooner are more valuable.
**Likelihood:** Payments that are more likely to be made are more valuable.
**Circumstances:** Payments that are made when we need them most are more valuable.

next year. This simple example illustrates a very general proposition: *The sooner the payment is made, the more valuable is the promise to make it.* Time has value because of opportunity cost. If you receive a payment immediately, you have an opportunity to invest or consume it right away. If you don't receive the payment until later, you lose that opportunity.

The third factor that affects the value of a financial instrument is the odds that the issuer will meet the obligation to make the payment. Regardless of how conscientious and diligent the party who made the promise is, there remains some possibility that the payment will not be made. Since risk requires compensation, the impact of this uncertainty on the value of a financial instrument is clear: *The more likely it is that the payment will be made, the more valuable the financial instrument.*

Finally, the value of a financial instrument is affected by the conditions under which a promised payment is to be made. Insurance is the best example. We buy car insurance to receive a payment if we have an accident, so we can repair the car. No one buys insurance that pays off when good things happen. *Payments that are made when we need them most are more valuable than other payments.*[3]

## Examples of Financial Instruments

We'll have quite a bit to say about financial instruments in Part II of the book. For now, let's take a look at some of the most common varieties. The best way to organize them is by whether they are used primarily as stores of value or for trading risk.

### Financial Instruments Used Primarily as Stores of Value

1. **Bank loans.** A borrower obtains resources from a lender immediately in exchange for a promised set of payments in the future. The borrower, who can be either an individual or a firm, needs funds to make an investment or purchase, while the lender is looking for a way to store value into the future.
2. **Bonds.** Bonds are a form of loan. In exchange for obtaining funds today, a corporation or government promises to make payments in the future. While bond payments are often stated in fixed dollars, they need not be. Unlike most bank loans, most bonds can be bought and sold in financial markets. Like bank loans, bonds are used by the borrower to finance current operations and by the lender to store value.

[3] This conclusion is related to the principle of declining marginal utility, which you may recall from your study of microeconomics. The idea is that the satisfaction obtained from consumption declines as the level of consumption increases. Each succeeding candy bar brings less pleasure than the last one. Thus, a financial instrument that pays off when marginal utility is high is worth more than one that pays off when marginal utility is low. This means that payoffs that are made when income and wealth are low are more valuable than payoffs that are made when income and wealth are high.

**APPLYING THE CONCEPT**
ASSET-BACKED SECURITIES

By mid-2009, asset-backed securities (ABS) had lost much of their appeal as they were blamed for causing or at least seriously exacerbating the financial and economic crisis. We will discuss how this might have happened as we go through the book, but as a first step we need to describe what they are. Suppose a bank holds a group of loans, which could be student loans, mortgages, commercial loans, or credit card debts. The bank can pool together a set of similar loans and sell them to an investor. Usually this is done by selling the loans to a trust and then selling shares in the trust. The investor gives the money to the trust upfront and is repaid his or her principal and interest by the repayments on the original loan. The collateral for the investor is whatever collateralized the original loans.

Mortgage-backed securities (MBS) are the prototypical version of ABS. The owners of mortgage-backed securities receive a share of the mortgage payments made by the homeowners who borrowed the funds, and in case of default are reimbursed by the sale of the house. In Canada, mortgage-backed securities are almost all insured by the government of Canada, through CMHC, and they are therefore very safe assets. As securitization (the process of selling loans) developed, institutions began selling asset-backed commercial paper (ABCP). These were short-term loans (three to nine months) backed by long-term assets. Every three to nine months the trust would "roll over" the commercial paper—that is, would repay the expiring commercial paper with the proceeds of reselling it. In Chapter 6 we discuss the consequences of this maturity mismatch.

Why issue asset-backed securities? There are many different reasons. ABCP permits firms to finance long-term debts with short-term funding, which is often cheaper. We will see later that banks are required to hold capital to back their risky loan portfolios, and that securitization allows the banks to get the loans off their balance sheet, reducing their capital requirements. In general, securitization allows issuers to spread risk but it reduces transparency as holders often don't know what assets were actually backing a product and, in the case of ABCP, creates a maturity mismatch. When the financial crisis began, these two features interacted to amplify the market breakdown.

3. **Home mortgages.** Most people who wish to purchase a home need to borrow some portion of the funds. A mortgage is a loan that is used to purchase real estate. In exchange for the funds, the borrower promises to make a series of payments. The house is collateral for the loan. Collateral is the term used to describe specific assets a borrower pledges to protect the lender's interests in the event of nonpayment. If the payments aren't made, the lender can take the house, a process called *foreclosure*.

4. **Stocks.** The holder of a share of a company's stock owns a small piece of the firm and is entitled to part of its profits. The owner of a firm sells stock as a way of raising funds to enlarge operations as well as a way of transferring the risk of ownership to someone else. Buyers of stocks use them primarily as stores of wealth.[4]

5. **Asset-backed securities.** Asset-backed securities are shares in the returns or payments arising from specific assets, such as home mortgages, student loans, credit card debt, or even movie box-office receipts. Investors purchase shares in the revenue that comes from these underlying assets (see Applying the Concept: Asset-backed Securities, above).

## Financial Instruments Used Primarily to Transfer Risk

1. **Insurance contracts.** The primary purpose of insurance policies is to assure that payments will be made under particular, and often rare, circumstances. These instruments exist expressly to transfer risk from one party to another.

---

[4] Stocks can be purchased individually, or you could buy a share in a mutual fund, which holds shares of many different companies. Slightly different are exchange-traded funds (ETFs) which also provide a means of holding a diversified portfolio. Mutual fund shares are bought and sold by brokers while ETFs (such as iShares) are traded on stock exchanges.

2. **Futures contracts.** A futures contract is an agreement between two parties to exchange a fixed quantity of a commodity (such as wheat or corn) or an asset (such as a bond) at a fixed price on a set future date. A futures contract always specifies the *price* at which the transaction will take place. A futures contract is a type of derivative instrument, since its value is based on the price of some other asset. It is used to transfer the risk of price fluctuations from one party to another.

3. **Options.** Like futures contracts, options are derivative instruments whose prices are based on the value of some underlying asset. Options give the holder the right, but not the obligation, to buy or sell a fixed quantity of the underlying asset at a predetermined price either on a specified date or at any time during a specified period.

These are just a few examples of the most prominent financial instruments. Together, they allow people to buy and sell almost any sort of payment on any date under any circumstances. Thus, they offer the opportunity to store value and trade risk in almost any way that one might want. When you encounter a financial instrument for the first time, try to figure out whether it is used primarily for storing value or for transferring risk. Then try to identify which characteristics determine its value.

## Financial Markets

Financial markets are the places where financial instruments are bought and sold. They are the economy's central nervous system, relaying and reacting to information quickly, allocating resources, and determining prices. In doing so, financial markets enable both firms and individuals to find financing for their activities. When they are working well, new firms can start up and existing firms can grow; individuals who don't have sufficient savings can borrow to purchase cars and houses. By ensuring that resources are available to those who can put them to the best use, and by keeping the costs of transactions as low as possible, these markets promote economic efficiency. When financial markets cease to function properly, resources are no longer channelled to their best possible use, and we all suffer.

In this section, we will look at the role of financial markets and the economic justification for their existence. Next, we will examine the structure of the markets and how they are organized. Finally, we will look at the characteristics that are essential for the markets to work smoothly.

### The Role of Financial Markets

Financial markets serve three roles in our economic system. They offer savers and borrowers *liquidity*; they pool and communicate *information*; and they allow *risk sharing*. We encountered the concept of liquidity in our discussion of money, where we defined liquidity as the ease with which an asset can be turned into money without loss of value. Without financial markets and the institutional structure that supports them, selling the assets we own would be extremely difficult. Thus, we cannot overstate the importance of liquidity for the smooth operation of an economy. Just think what would happen if the stock market were open only one day a month. Stocks would surely become less attractive investments. If you had an emergency and needed money immediately, you probably would not be able to sell your stocks in time. Liquidity is a crucial characteristic of financial markets.

Related to liquidity is the fact that financial markets need to be designed in a way that keeps transactions costs—the cost of buying and selling—low. If you want to buy

## YOUR FINANCIAL WORLD
### Disability Income Insurance

People insure their houses so they can rebuild them if they burn down. They insure their cars so they can repair them if they have an accident. And they insure their lives so their families will be financially secure if they die prematurely. But few people insure their most important asset: their ability to produce an income. The biggest risk all of us face is that we will become disabled and lose our earning capacity. Insuring it should be one of our highest priorities.

If you think this advice is alarmist, just look at a few numbers. The odds of a man becoming disabled for 90 days or longer between the ages of 20 and 60 are one in five. For women they're somewhat lower, more like one in seven. In fact, the chance you'll become disabled during your working life is far higher than the chance of your house burning down—which over 40 years is about one in 30.*

Fortunately, you may already have some disability insurance. The Canada Pension Plan provides some insur-

ance; your employer may insure you; and if you're injured on the job and can't work, there is always workers' compensation insurance. But is that enough? Most people spend a maximum of one quarter of their time working so most of their time isn't insured through workers' compensation. You should evaluate what your needs are likely to be. If the disability insurance you already have is not enough, you should buy more. While it isn't very pleasant to think about what would happen if you became disabled, you need to do it. Surely this is one risk you should transfer to someone else.

* The chance of any particular house burning down is 1 in 1,200 in a given year. So there is a 1,199 chance in 1,200 of a house not burning down in a particular year. This means that the probability of a house *not* burning down in 40 years is $(1,199/1,200)^{40} = 0.967$. So the probability of the house burning down is 0.033, which is 1 in 30.

or sell a stock, you have to hire someone to do it for you. The process is complex, and we need not go into it in detail, but you must pay a broker to complete the purchase or sale on your behalf. While this service can't be free, it is important to keep its cost relatively low. The very high trading volumes that we see in the stock market—several hundred million shares per day in Canada—is evidence that Canadian stock markets have low transactions costs as well as being liquid. (One market in which transactions costs are high is the market for housing. Once you add together everything you pay agents, bankers, and lawyers, you have spent almost 10 percent of the sale price of the house to complete the transaction. The housing market is not very liquid.)

Financial markets pool and communicate information about the issuers of financial instruments, summarizing it in the form of a price. Does a company have good prospects for future growth and profits? If so, its stock price will be high; if not, its stock price will be low. Is a borrower likely to repay a bond? The more likely repayment is, the higher the price of the bond. Obtaining the answers to these questions is time consuming and costly. Most of us just don't have the resources or know-how to do it. Instead, we turn to the financial markets to summarize the information for us so that we can look it up in the newspaper or on the Internet.

Finally, while financial instruments are the means for transferring risk, financial markets are the place where we can do it. The markets allow us to buy and sell risks, holding the ones we want and getting rid of the ones we don't want. As we will see in Chapter 5, a prudent investor holds a collection of assets called a portfolio, which includes a number of stocks and bonds

**Table 3.3**   The Role of Financial Markets

**Liquidity:** Ensure that owners of financial instruments can buy and sell them cheaply and easily.

**Information:** Pool and communicate information about the issuer of a financial instrument.

**Risk Sharing:** Provide individuals with a place to buy and sell risks, sharing them with others.

as well as various forms of money. A well-designed portfolio has a lower overall risk than any individual stock or bond. An investor constructs it by buying and selling financial instruments in the marketplace. Without the market, we wouldn't be able to share risk.

## The Structure of Financial Markets

There are lots of financial markets and many ways to categorize them. Just take a look at any source of business news. You will see charts and tables for domestic stocks, global stocks, bonds and interest rates, the dollar exchange rate, commodities, and more. Keep going and you will find references to stock markets, bond markets, credit markets, currency trading, options, futures, new securities, and on and on. Grasping the overall structure of all of these financial markets requires grouping them in some sort of meaningful way—but how?

There are three possibilities. First, we can distinguish between markets where new financial instruments are sold and those where they are resold, or traded. Second, we can categorize the markets by the way they trade financial instruments—whether on a centralized exchange or not. And third, we can group them based on the type of instrument they trade—those that are used primarily as a store of value or those that are used to transfer risk.

### Primary versus Secondary Markets

A **primary financial market** is one in which a borrower obtains funds from a lender or investor by selling newly issued securities. Businesses use primary markets to raise the resources they need to grow. Governments use them to finance ongoing operations. Most of the action in primary markets occurs out of public view. While some companies that want to raise funds go directly to the financial markets themselves, most use an investment dealer as an underwriter. The bank's analysts examine the company's financial health to determine whether the proposed issue is sound. Assuming that it is, the bank will determine a price and then purchase the securities in preparation for resale to clients.

To access the market, you will need to use a broker—either real or virtual. For example, you could use QTrade, which enables you to place orders for shares listed on the TSX. Everyone knows about **secondary financial markets**. Those are the markets where people can buy and sell existing securities. If you want to buy a share of stock in RIM or Microsoft, you won't get it from the company itself. Instead, you'll buy it in a secondary market from another investor. The prices in the secondary markets are the ones we hear about in the news. The stock of outstanding securities is much larger than the number of new issues in any month, and there is much more activity in the secondary markets than purchases of new issues.

### Centralized Exchanges, Over-the-Counter Markets, and Electronic Networks

Buying a stock or bond is not like buying a new pair of shoes. You can't just go into a store, ask for the stock you want, pay for it with your credit card, and walk out with it in a bag. Instead, you can either ask a broker to buy the stock for you or you can do it yourself on an electronic exchange. In both cases, the transaction is in a secondary market. The organization of secondary financial markets is changing rapidly. Historically, there have been two types. Some, such as the Toronto Stock Exchange and the large exchanges in New York and Tokyo, are **centralized exchanges**. Others, such as the NASDAQ, are electronic networks of dealers who trade with one another from wherever they are sitting. Today, we can add **electronic communication networks (ECNs)** to the list—Pure Trading and Alpha Group are the biggest in Canada.

# TOOLS OF THE TRADE
Trading in Financial Markets

Trading is what makes financial markets work. No one would ever buy a stock or bond if he or she couldn't sell it. Let's take a brief look at how trading works. For this example, we will focus on the stock market.

Placing an order in a stock market is a bit like going to a fast-food restaurant or a coffee shop. You have to enter your order and wait to be served. Not only that, but the order can be very complicated, and how long you wait depends on both what you ordered and on how many other people are waiting to be served.

If you place an order, it will have a number of important characteristics:

- The stock you wish to trade
- Whether you wish to buy or sell
- The size of the order—how many shares you wish to trade
- The price at which you would like to trade

You can place either a *market order*, in which case your order is executed at the most favourable price currently available on the other side, or a *limit order*, which places a maximum on the price you wish to pay to buy or a minimum on the price you will accept to sell. Placing a market order means you value speed over price; you want the trade to occur as soon as possible and are willing to pay for the privilege. By contrast, you can specify a time at which the limit order is cancelled if it hasn't been filled.

Executing the trade requires finding someone to take the other side. To do this, you can ask a broker to do it, or you can do it yourself. Even though Bell Canada (BCE) is traded on the Toronto Stock Exchange, you are not required to send an order to buy 100 shares of BCE to the floor of the exchange. Instead, you can use one of the electronic networks (ECNs) such as Pure Trading or Alpha Group.

Electronic networks operate in a very simple way. If you want to buy, you enter a bid. If your bid is better than everyone else's, and there is someone willing to sell at or below the price you bid, then you trade immediately. Otherwise, your bid goes into an order book to wait for a seller. On a network such as Pure Trading or Alpha Group, customer orders interact automatically, following a set of priority rules established by the network, but with no one acting as an intermediary in the transaction. The liquidity in the market is provided by the customers.

The Toronto Stock Exchange is an alternative place to send the order. At the TSX, any trade over 3000 shares will go through a registered trader. The registered trader is the person charged with making a market for that stock, ensuring that it is liquid so that people can both buy and sell and that prices aren't overly volatile. The registered trader matches the orders as they come in, keeping track of orders that are outstanding. (This is all done electronically.) To make the system work, registered traders often buy and sell on their own account.

**Equity Order Entry**

| | Cash | $ 773,951.17 |
| | Portfolio Value | $ 3,910,921.17 |
| | Buying Power | $ 2,870,710.49 |
| | (Consolidated) | |

Help: For useful comments on the terms used on this page (e.g. "Order Type"), place your mouse over the term in question to produce the desired explanation.

| Account | $CDN Account |
| Action | Buy |
| Quantity | 1,000 |
| Symbol | PCA    Symbol Search |
| Market | Canada    Real-time Quote |
| Order Type | Trailing Stop Limit    Trigger Rule $ _____ or 10 % |
| Good Through | August 21, Friday    Limit Rule $ 1.00 |
| Phone Contact | 000.123.4567 |
| | (Format: 111.111.1111) |

Clear    Review Order

**Real-time Quote - PETRO CANADA COM NPV(PCA)**    Last Trade: Jul 21, 2010 15:10 (EST)    Currency: CDN

| Size | Bid | Ask | Size | Last | Chg | % Chg | Volume | Open | High | Low |
|------|-----|-----|------|------|-----|-------|--------|------|------|-----|
| 7 | 46.07 | 46.15 | 57 | 46.15 | 1.25 | 2.78 | 2,855,264 | 45.20 | 46.19 | 44.63 |

SOURCE: *Qtrade Financial Group.*

The dominant Canadian exchange for trading equities is still the Toronto Stock Exchange (TSX). Trading used to take place in person on the floor of the exchange, as it still does on the New York Stock Exchange, but in 1997 the TSX became the first North American exchange to move to an electronic platform, and today the trading is all done electronically. Each stock listed on the TSX is assigned a *registered trader* who is responsible to reduce volatility and enhance liquidity by buying or selling that stock against the market.

In the past, the only alternative to a centralized exchange was an **over-the-counter (OTC)** market. These markets are best thought of as networks of dealers connected together electronically. The dealers buy and sell various securities both for themselves

SOURCE: *TMX Group.*

and for their customers. With the exception of stocks that are sold on organized exchanges, financial instruments are sold in dealer-based markets. The biggest is the NASDAQ, which trades the stocks of roughly 4,000 companies, most of them small. You can think of NASDAQ as a large network of dealers, each with a computer screen on which buy and sell orders are posted. The dealers use their computers to match the orders and execute the trades.

Compared with a physically centralized exchange, such as the NYSE, a financial market that is organized as an electronic network has both advantages and disadvantages. On the plus side, customers can see the orders (look at the Tools of the Trade: Trading in Financial Markets on page 43), orders are executed quickly, costs are low, and trading is 24 hours a day. But electronic networks are not perfect. When dealers are in a hurry or simply get tired, they can push the wrong button, turning a $3 million trade into a $30 million or $300 million trade. On the morning of December 8, 2005, an unlucky clerk for the Japanese firm Mizuho Securities discovered the risks. Instead of entering an order to sell one single share of J-Com, a small Japanese recruiting firm, at a price of ¥610,000 (about $5,200), the clerk placed an order to sell 610,000 shares at ¥1 (less than $0.01) apiece. The sell order was for 40 times the number of J-Com shares in existence! Since Mizuho was acting as a broker for a client, the mistake was the firm's and it was financially responsible. What became known as the "fat-finger incident" eventually cost Mizuho $US340 million. Such mistakes cannot occur on the floor of centralized exchanges where trades are executed face to face between two people who write them down for verification later.

On the other side, a clear advantage of electronic networks was evident on September 11, 2001. The NYSE building stands only a few blocks from the site of the World Trade Center. When the twin towers fell, the floor of the Exchange became inaccessible. Since its operation depends on the ability of people to gather there, trading stopped and did not restart until Monday, September 17, 2001. Meanwhile, the NASDAQ could have continued functioning. The New York dealers shut down, but those located elsewhere in the country were able to continue. Networks are designed so that if one section shuts down, the rest can continue working, and that is what happened. In a dealer-based market, when one dealer can't trade, someone else is usually waiting to step in.

Innovations in communications continue to drive the evolution of the stock markets. Today, speed is critical, and the new electronic trading systems have been able to execute trades for program traders' "algorithmic trading" across multiple exchanges very quickly (see In the News: Point of Sale: The Stock Exchange on page 46).

The rationale for having registered traders is that they are necessary to maintain liquidity in the market—especially for small stocks that trade infrequently. But today, individuals can enter and execute trades on their own, so one has to wonder if registered traders are still necessary. We'll have to wait and see.

**Debt and Equity versus Derivative Markets** A useful way to think of the structure of financial markets is to distinguish between markets where debt and equity are traded and those where *derivative instruments* are traded. **Debt markets** are the markets for loans, mortgages, and bonds—the instruments that allow for the transfer of resources from lenders to borrowers and at the same time give investors a store of value for their wealth. **Equity markets** are the markets for stocks. For the most part, stocks are traded in the countries in which the companies are based. U.S. companies' stocks are traded in

| Table 3.4 | The Structure of Financial Markets |
|---|---|

**Primary versus Secondary Markets**

| Primary markets: | Markets where newly issued securities are sold. |
|---|---|
| **Secondary markets:** | Markets where existing securities are traded. |

**Centralized Exchanges versus Over-the-Counter Markets**

| Centralized exchanges: | Secondary markets where buyers and sellers meet in a central, physical location. |
|---|---|
| Over-the-counter markets: | Decentralized secondary markets where dealers stand ready to buy and sell securities electronically. |
| Electronic Communication Networks (ECNs): | Electronic systems that bring buyers and sellers together for electronic execution of trades without the use of a broker or dealer. |

**Debt and Equity versus Derivatives Markets**

| Debt and equity markets: | Markets where financial claims are bought and sold for immediate cash payment. |
|---|---|
| Derivatives markets: | Markets where claims based on an underlying asset are traded. |

the United States, Japanese stocks in Japan, Chinese stocks in China, and so on. Derivative markets are the markets where investors trade instruments such as futures and options, which are designed primarily to transfer risk. To put it another way, in debt and equity markets, actual claims are bought and sold for immediate cash payment; in derivative markets, investors make agreements that are settled later. In Canada, financial futures and options are traded on the Montreal Exchange while commodity futures and options are traded on the ICE in Winnipeg.

Looking at debt instruments in more detail, we can place them in one of two categories, depending on the length of time until the final payment, called the loan's maturity. Debt instruments that are completely repaid in a year or less (from their original issue date) are traded in **money markets**, while those with a maturity of more than a year are traded in **bond markets**. *Money market instruments* have different names and are treated somewhat differently from *bond market instruments*. For example, the federal government issues Treasury bills, which have a maturity of one year or less when they are issued and are traded in the money market. Government of Canada bonds, which have a maturity of more than one year, are traded in the bond markets. The same distinction can be made for large private corporations, which issue commercial paper when borrowing for short periods and corporate bonds when borrowing for long periods.

## Characteristics of a Well-Run Financial Market

Well-run financial markets exhibit a few essential characteristics that are related to the role we ask them to play in our economies. First, these markets must be designed to keep transaction costs low. Second, the information the market pools and communicates must be both accurate and widely available. If analysts do not communicate accurate assessments of the firms they follow, the markets will not generate the correct

INFORMATION

## IN THE NEWS

### Point of Sale: The Stock Exchange

# Financial Post

### By John Greenwood

#### June 2, 2009

Trading floors are out. Computers are in. Here comes the competition.

Once stocks were traded by men in garish jackets who bellowed orders across massive trading floors, like the one at the old Toronto stock exchange. Then along came electronic trading, and the people disappeared. Exchanges became little boxes with the ability to process transactions in nanoseconds. Technology sparked another change: competition. Today, the TSX competes for business with new alternative trading systems—known as ATSs—all fighting for your business on speed and price.

TSX industry ranking: largest stock exchange in Canada and among the world's top 10 by market value.

First ATS competitor to TSX: Pure Trading ... which launched in 2003 as Canadian trading and quotation system.

TSX's share of Canadian stock trades in March 2008: 98%.

In March 2009: 90%

Projected share in 2012: 70%; number of ATSs in Canada today: 7

Main drivers of ATS growth: greater anonymity for investors; less strict listing requirements; regulatory changes

Most successful new ATS: Alpha Trading Systems, launched in November 2008.

Alpha's share of the non-TSX market in March: 40%.

Biggest impact of ATS arrival: significantly lower trading fees for investors.

Average daily volume of shares traded by TSX and TSX venture in 2009: six billion.

In 2006: 3.75 billion.

Reason for increase: rise of computer trading has increased exchange volumes overall

Future of stock trading: experts predict growing market share for ATSs, thanks to improving technology and industry regulation that favours competition. But historic market leaders, such as the TSX, are expected to be dominant players in the future.

### LESSONS OF THE ARTICLE

The stock exchange operates to match buyers and sellers and as in other parts of the financial services sector, information flows are fundamental. Innovation in the Information and Communications Technology (ICT) sector is rapidly changing the role of financial intermediaries. If you go to the Web site of Alpha Trading Systems of Pure Trading you can see what their current share is. It has probably grown from the 11% that ATSs had in July 2009.

SOURCE: *"Point of Sale: The Stock Exchange"* by John Greenwood. Financial Post Business Magazine, June 2, 2009. Material reprinted with the express permission of *"The National Post Company,"* a CanWest Partnership.

prices for the firms' stocks. The prices of financial instruments reflect all the information that is available to market participants. Those prices are the link between the financial markets and the real economy, ensuring that resources are allocated to their most efficient uses. If the information that goes into the market is wrong, then the prices will be wrong, and the economy will not operate as effectively as it could.

Finally, investors need protection. For the financial system to work at all, borrowers' promises to pay lenders must be credible. Individuals must be assured that their investments will not simply be stolen. In countries that have weak investor protections, firms can behave deceptively, borrowing when they have no intention of repaying the funds and going unpunished. The lack of proper safeguards dampens people's willingness to invest. Thus, governments are an essential part of financial markets, since they set and enforce the rules of the game. While informal lending networks do develop

**APPLYING THE CONCEPT**
FINANCIAL DEVELOPMENT
REQUIRES INVESTOR PROTECTION

Investors will provide capital to firms only if they expect to get their money back. For equity holders, this requires that they must be able to vote out directors and managers who do not pay them. For creditors, it means that they must have the authority to repossess collateral. In addition to having these legal rights, investors must also have confidence that the laws will be enforced.

Disparities in investor protections help us to understand the differences in financial market development around the world. The better a country's investors are protected, the bigger that country's stock market. For example, the United Kingdom has the largest stock market—roughly three times the size of its GDP—and its investor protection is second only to Norway's. In contrast, Greece, a country that offers investors very poor protection, has a stock market that is only one-third the size of its GDP. Not surprisingly, where

markets flourish, firms have no trouble raising the funds they need to grow; it pays to protect investors. In countries that do a poor job of protecting stock and bondholders, banks take up much of the slack. Lacking access to primary financing, everyone is forced to go to financial intermediaries for secondary financing.

Combining this with the fact that economic and financial development are closely linked means that in order for countries to improve the general welfare of their citizenry they need to create a system that gives investors enforceable legal rights.

It is interesting to consider the case of China. During the quarter century beginning in 1980, China grew at an average annual rate of 9.5 percent. And China has achieved this growth without a set of formal investor safeguards. As China becomes more prosperous, firms in the country will naturally become larger. Without legal protections, will investors be willing to finance these growing companies? If not, what will happen to Chinese growth? This will be a test of the conclusion that financial and economic development require a formal legal system.

and flourish spontaneously, they can accommodate only simple, small-scale transactions. Because modern financial markets require a legal structure that is designed and enforced by the government, countries with better investor protections have bigger and deeper financial markets than other countries.

# Financial Institutions

Financial institutions are the firms that provide access to the financial markets, both to savers who wish to purchase financial instruments directly and to borrowers who want to issue them. Because financial institutions sit between savers and borrowers, they are also known as *financial intermediaries*, and what they do is known as intermediation. Banks, insurance companies, securities firms, and pension funds are all financial intermediaries. These institutions are essential; any disturbance to the services they provide will have severe adverse effects on the economy.

To understand the importance of financial institutions, think what the world would be like if they didn't exist. Without a bank, individuals and households wishing to save would either have to hold their wealth in cash or figure out some way to funnel it directly to companies that could put it to use. The assets of these household savers would be some combination of government liabilities and the equity and debt issued by corporations. All finance would be direct, with borrowers obtaining funds straight from the lenders.

Such a system would be unlikely to work very well, for a number of reasons. First, individual transactions between saver-lenders and spender-borrowers would likely be extremely expensive. Not only would the two sides have difficulty finding each other but, even if they did, writing the contract to effect the transaction would be very costly. Second, lenders need to evaluate the creditworthiness of borrowers and then monitor them to ensure that they don't abscond with the funds. Individuals are not specialists in monitoring. Third, most borrowers want to borrow for the long term, while lenders favour more liquid short-term loans. Lenders would surely require compensation for the illiquidity of long-term loans, driving up the price of borrowing.

A financial market could be created in which the loans and other securities could be resold, but that would create the risk of price fluctuations. All these problems would restrict the flow of resources through the economy. Financial institutions open up the flow, ensuring that it goes to the most productive investments and increasing the system's efficiency.

## The Role of Financial Institutions

Financial institutions reduce transactions costs by specializing in the issuance of standardized securities. They reduce the information costs, the cost of screening and monitoring borrowers to make sure they are creditworthy and that they use the proceeds of a loan or security issue properly. In other words, financial institutions curb information asymmetries and the problems that go along with them, helping resources flow to their most productive uses.

The relative scale of some financial institutions is shown in Table 3.5. The banking system is by far the largest type of financial intermediary, while life insurance companies are the next largest.

## The Structure of the Financial Industry

In analyzing the structure of the financial industry, we can start by dividing intermediaries into two broad categories called depository and nondepository institutions. *Depository institutions* take deposits and make loans; they are what most people think of as banks, whether they are commercial banks, savings banks, credit unions, or caisses populaires. *Nondepository institutions* include insurance companies, securities firms, mutual fund companies, finance companies, and pension funds. Each of these serves a very different function from a bank. Some screen and monitor borrowers; others transfer and reduce risk. Still others are primarily brokers. Here is a list of the major groups of financial institutions, together with a brief description of what they do.

1. **Depository institutions** (chartered banks, trust and loan companies, Alberta Treasury Branch, and credit unions and caisses populaires) take deposits and make loans. Banks alone hold 55 percent of the assets of the financial sector.

2. **Insurance companies** accept premiums, which they invest in securities and real estate (their assets) in return for promising compensation to policyholders should certain events occur (their liabilities). Life insurers protect against the risk of untimely death. Property and casualty insurers protect against personal injury loss and losses from theft, accidents, and fire.

3. **Pension funds** invest individual and company contributions in stocks, bonds, and real estate (their assets) in order to provide payments to retired workers (their liabilities).

4. **Securities firms** include brokers, investment dealers, underwriters, and mutual fund companies. Brokers and investment banks issue stocks and bonds to corporate customers, trade them, and advise customers. All these activities give customers access to the financial markets. Mutual fund companies pool the resources of individuals and companies and invest them in portfolios of bonds, stocks, and real estate. Customers own shares of the portfolios, so they face

**Table 3.5**   Canadian Financial Institutions

| | Number[1] | Assets[2,3] ($ Millions) |
|---|---|---|
| **Banks** | | |
| Domestic | 20 | 2,596,712 |
| Foreign Bank Subsidiaries | 24 | 139,523 |
| Foreign Bank Branches | 29 | 79,191 |
| **Trust and Loan Companies** | | |
| Bank-owned | 31 | 243,163 |
| Other | 39 | 23,292 |
| **Cooperative Credit Associations** | 7 | 17,877 |
| **Cooperative Retail Association** | 1 | 3,275 |
| **Life Insurance Companies** | | |
| Canadian-incorporated | 46 | 456,440 |
| Foreign Branches | 48 | 15,275 |
| **Fraternal Benefit Societies** | | |
| Canadian-incorporated | 10 | 5,809 |
| Foreign Branches | 8 | 1,775 |
| **Property and Casualty Insurance Companies** | | |
| Canadian-incorporated | 96 | 78,256 |
| Foreign Branches | 100 | 30,873 |

[1] *Number of OSFI regulated companies as at March 31, 2008. Includes institutions in the process of liquidation or termination and institutions limited to servicing existing business.*

[2] *As at January 31 or March 31, 2008 (depending on fiscal year-end) where available, otherwise December 31, 2007.*

[3] *Total assets of the industries regulated by OSFI are not the simple sum of the above-noted figures. The figures for entities that report on a consolidated basis include subsidiaries whose assets may also be included in a different category.*

SOURCE: *Office of the Superintendent of Financial Institutions Canada, Annual Report, 2007–8. Reproduced with the permission of the Minister of Public Works and Government Services, 2009.*

the risk that the assets will change in value. But portfolios are less risky than individual securities, and individual savers can purchase smaller units than they could if they went directly to the financial markets.

5. **Finance companies** raise funds directly in the financial markets in order to make loans to individuals and firms. Finance companies tend to specialize in particular types of loans, such as mortgage, automobile, or certain types of business equipment. While their assets are similar to a bank's, their liabilities are debt instruments that are traded in financial markets, not deposits.

6. **Government-sponsored enterprises** such as CMHC, are active in financial markets; for example, by ensuring mortgage loans (CMHC) or making small business loans (Atlantic Canada Opportunities Fund).

As we continue our study of the relationship between the financial system and the real economy, we will return to the importance of financial institutions, the conduits that channel resources from savers to investors. These intermediaries are absolutely essential to the operation of any economy. When they cease to function, so does everything else. Recall from Chapter 2 that the measures of money (M1+ and M2++) include chequing deposits, savings deposits, and certificates of deposit, among other things. These are all important liabilities of banks. Because they are very liquid, they are accepted as a means of payment. Clearly, the financial structure is tied to the availability of money and credit. But we are getting ahead of ourselves. Before we study financial institutions, we need to look more closely at financial instruments and financial markets, the subjects of Part II of this book.

## Terms

asset, 32
asset-backed security, 39
bond market, 45
centralized exchange, 42
collateral, 39
consumption smoothing, 34
counterparty, 36
debt market, 44
derivative instrument, 37
direct finance, 32
electronic communications networks (ECNs), 42
equity market, 44

financial institutions, 47
financial instrument, 33
financial markets, 40
indirect finance, 32
information costs, 48
liability, 32
money market, 45
over-the-counter (OTC) market, 43
portfolio, 41
primary financial market, 42
secondary financial market, 42
transaction costs, 40
underlying instrument, 37

## Chapter Summary

1. Financial instruments are crucial to the operation of the economy.
   a. Financial arrangements can be either formal or informal. Industrial economies are dominated by formal arrangements.
   b. A financial instrument is the written legal obligation of one party to transfer something of value, usually money, to another party at some future date, under certain conditions.
   c. Financial instruments are used primarily as stores of value and means of trading risk. They are less likely to be used as means of payment, although many of them can be.
   d. Financial instruments are most useful when they are simple and standardized.
   e. There are two basic classes of financial instruments: underlying and derivative.
      i. Underlying instruments are used to transfer resources directly from one party to another.
      ii. Derivative instruments derive their value from the behaviour of an underlying instrument.
   f. The payments promised by a financial instrument are more valuable
      i. The larger they are.
      ii. The sooner they are made.
      iii. The more likely they are to be made.
      iv. If they are made when they are needed most.
   g. Common examples of financial instruments include
      i. Those that serve primarily as stores of value, including bank loans, bonds, mortgages, stocks, and asset-backed securities.
      ii. Those that are used primarily to transfer risk, including futures and options.

2. Financial markets are essential to the operation of our economic system.
   a. Financial markets
      i. Offer savers and borrowers liquidity so that they can buy and sell financial instruments easily.
      ii. Pool and communicate information through prices.
      iii. Allow for the sharing of risk.
   b. There are several ways to categorize financial markets.
      i. Primary markets that issue new securities versus secondary markets, where existing securities are bought and sold.
      ii. Physically centralized exchanges, dealer-based electronic systems (over-the-counter markets), or electronic network.
      iii. Debt and equity markets (where instruments that are used primarily for financing are traded) versus derivative markets (where instruments that are used to transfer risk are traded).
   c. A well-functioning financial market is characterized by
      i. Low transactions costs and sufficient liquidity.
      ii. Accurate and widely available information.
      iii. Legal protection of investors against the arbitrary seizure of their property.
3. Financial institutions perform brokerage and asset transformation functions.
   a. In their role as brokers, they provide access to financial markets.
   b. In transforming assets, they provide indirect finance.
   c. Indirect finance reduces transaction and information costs.
   d. Financial institutions, also known as financial intermediaries, help individuals and firms to transfer and reduce risk.

## Conceptual Problems

1. As the end of the month approaches, you realize that you probably will not be able to pay the next month's rent. Describe both an informal and a formal financial instrument that you might use to solve your dilemma.

2.* While we often associate informal financial arrangements with poorer countries where financial systems are less developed, informal arrangements often co-exist with even the most developed financial systems. What advantages might there be to engaging in informal arrangements rather than utilizing the formal financial sector?

3. The Montreal Exchange has announced the introduction of a financial instrument that is based on rainfall in Ontario. The standard agreement states that for each inch of rain over and above the average rainfall for a particular month, the seller will pay the buyer $1,000. Who could benefit from buying such a contract? Who could benefit from selling it?

4. An annuity is a promise to pay someone a fixed amount regularly (often monthly) for the rest of their life. Describe what happens to the purchase price of the annuity as (1) the age of the purchaser goes up, (2) the size of the monthly payment rises, and (3) the health of the purchaser improves.

5. Consider the investment returns to holding stock. Which of the following would be more valuable to you: Stocks that rise in value when your income rises or stocks that rise in value when your income falls? Why?

6. The *Financial Post* (http://www.financialpost.com/markets/market_data/index.html) has a daily listing of what are called "Money Rates" or interest rates on short-term securities. Find data on the chartered banks' prime rate, the overnight money market rate, and the Treasury bill rate. Describe the instruments each of these rates relates to and report the current rate quoted in the paper.

7. Trading on private information is illegal. Why? What would happen to the financial markets if you could trade on information that is not public?

8. You are asked for advice by the government of a small developing country interested in increasing its rate of economic growth. You notice that the country has no financial markets. What advice would you give?

\* Indicates more difficult problems.

9. The design and function of financial instruments, markets, and institutions are tied to the importance of information. Describe the role of information in each of these three parts of the financial system.

10.* Advances in technology have facilitated the widespread use of credit scoring by financial institutions in making their lending decisions. Credit scoring can be defined broadly as the use of historical data and statistical techniques to rank the attractiveness of potential borrowers and guide lending decisions. In what ways might this practice enhance the efficiency of the financial system?

## Analytical Problems

11. For each pair of instruments below, use the criteria for valuing a financial instrument to choose the one with the highest value.
    a. A Treasury bill that pays $1,000 in six months or a Treasury bill that pays $1,000 in three months.
    b. A Treasury bill that pays $1,000 in three months or commercial paper issued by a private corporation that pays $1,000 in three months.
    c. An insurance policy that pays out in the event of serious illness or one that pays out when you are healthy.
    Explain each of your choices briefly.

12. Suppose there is a huge influx of inexperienced, reckless drivers into the area where you live. Assuming this increase is large enough to influence the market in which your insurance company operates, explain why the price of your car insurance policy will go up even though your driving record hasn't changed.

13.* Everything else being equal, which would be more valuable to you—a derivative instrument whose value is derived from an underlying instrument with a very volatile price history or one derived from an underlying instrument with a very stable price history? Explain your choice.

14. Explain why a person starting up a small business is more likely to take out a bank loan than to issue bonds.

15. Splitland is a developing economy with two distinct regions. The northern region has great investment opportunities, but the people who live there need to consume all of their income to survive. Those living in the south are better off than their northern counterparts and save a significant portion of their income. The southern region, however, has few profitable investment opportunities and so most of the savings remain in shoeboxes and under mattresses. Explain how the development of the financial sector could benefit both regions and promote economic growth in Splitland.

16. Suppose the government decided to abolish the Ontario Securities Commission. What would you expect to happen to investment and growth in the economy?

17. What risks might financial institutions face by funding long-term loans such as mortgages to borrowers (often at fixed interest rates) with short-term deposits from savers?

18.* As the manager of a financial institution, what steps could you take to reduce the risks referred to in question 17?

# APPENDIX 3

## Consumption Smoothing

A crucial function of financial markets is to enable households to move funds across time, for example, from working age to retirement. The benefits of financial markets can be illustrated by a basic model that captures the essence of the issue. For simplicity, let's break the lifetime of a household into two periods, young and old. The household members want to consume when both young and old, but gets most of their income when young. We'll make two further assumptions: (1) members of the household have a slight preference for consuming when young rather than when old, and (2) the amount of consumption they would be willing to give up to get a unit of consumption when old is higher when they have less old consumption.[5] In Figure 3A.a, consumption when young ($C_1$) is measured on the horizontal axis, and consumption when old ($C_2$) is measured on the vertical axis. Every point in the figure represents a combination of consumption when old and young. We can illustrate the household's preferences by drawing a line connecting all the points that the household would be equally satisfied with. For example, the curve IC is one set of such points. (IC stands for "indifference curve" because the household is indifferent among the points on the curve.) The household doesn't care which combination on the curve it has, but prefers any point *on* the curve to all the points *below* the curve and would be even happier with a point *above* the curve. It's important to realize that every point in Panel (a) of Figure 3A.a is on an indifference curve; we just chose one for illustration.

Let's assume that when young the household earns $\$Y_1$ and when old $\$Y_2$, and we'll assume that $Y_1$ is a lot more than $Y_2$. We will look at three possible situations. In the first case, the income can't be carried over from one period to the next. That means that the set of possible combinations of consumption is given by $C_1 \le Y_1$ and $C_2 \le Y_2$ (this is the shaded area in the figure). Given our assumptions, the household would consume all its income each period, which is represented by point $E_0$ in Figure 3A.a.

The scenario that the income disappears is quite extreme—it could capture the possibility that rats ate any money that was stored in the mattress—so we will look at the household's behaviour when it is possible to carry over income. Let's suppose the household carries over $\$S$, where $S \ge 0$. The budget constraint for the household is now

$$C_1 + S \le Y_1$$
$$C_2 \le Y_2 + S$$

By rewriting the second equation and then substituting for S in the first equation, we can combine these two equations to get what is called the intertemporal budget constraint: $C_1 + C_2 \le Y_1 + Y_2$, and $C_1 \le Y_1$. We can write the first half of this

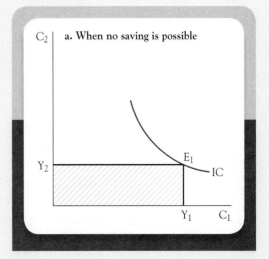

**Figure 3A**   **Consumption Smoothing**

a. When no saving is possible

[5] This is the principle of diminishing marginal utility: the more you have of something, the less benefit you get from an additional unit of it.

www.mcgrawhill.ca/olc/cecchetti

Figure 3A    Consumption Smoothing (continued)

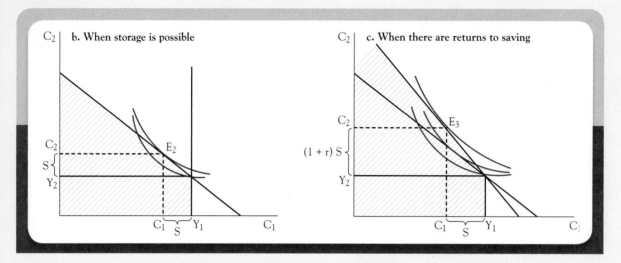

as $C_2 \leq Y_1 + Y_2 - C_1$. Figure 3A.b shows that this possibility allows the household to save and therefore to consume more when old, so the household's satisfaction level is higher: point $E_2$.

Now, let's suppose that the household could invest its income and receive a return of $r$ percent. Then the budget constraint would be

$$C_1 + S \leq Y_1$$
$$C_2 \leq Y_2 + S(1 + r).$$

Here $S$ can be positive or negative; that is, the household could save or lend when young. Again we can combine the two-period budget constraints to get the intertemporal budget constraint:

$$C_2 \leq Y_1(1 + r) + Y_2 - C_1(1 + r)$$

This budget line is drawn in Figure 3A.c and now the household can attain a higher indifference curve and consume at point $E_3$. Under the assumptions we have made, the household will now (1) have more equal consumption in the two periods and (2) be happier. Notice that it is not clear whether the household will save more, as now members don't need to save as much to raise second-period consumption.

Saving for retirement is a large component of the supply of savings. But if everyone were a lender, there would be no one willing to pay to use those savings. Luckily, there are plenty of borrowers:

- Businesses—They borrow to undertake investment projects that take time to pay off, or that need to pool the savings of many people.
- Young people—Our example of the household above assumed that young households were all the same. In fact, very young households often borrow to finance their education or a house purchase.
- The government—Governments borrow to finance their infrastructure spending or stabilization policy.
- Foreigners—With global capital markets, savings could come from overseas. Most recently, for example, much of U.S. investment has been financed by China (of course, foreigners could use savings as well).

# CHAPTER 4

## Future Value, Present Value, and Interest Rates

Lenders have been despised for most of history. They make borrowers pay for loans, while just sitting around doing nothing. No wonder people have been vilified for charging interest. No wonder that for centuries, clerics pointed to biblical passages damning interest. Even philosophers such as Aristotle weighed in against the practice, calling the "breeding of money from money" unnatural.

After scorning lenders for millennia, today we recognize their service as a fundamental building block of civilization. Credit is one of the critical mechanisms we have for allocating resources. Without it, our market-based economy would grind to a halt. Even the simplest financial transaction, such as saving some of your paycheque each month to buy a car, would be difficult, if not impossible. And corporations, most of which survive from day to day by borrowing to finance their activities, would not be able to function. Credit is so basic that we can find records of people lending grain and metal from 5,000 years ago. Credit probably existed before common measures of value, and it predates coinage by 2,000 years.

Despite its early existence and its central role in economic transactions, credit was hard to come by until the Protestant Reformation. By the 16th century, views had changed, and interest payments were tolerated if not encouraged, so long as the rate charged was thought to be reasonable. Some historians even point to this shift as a key to the development of capitalism and its institutions. Protestant European countries did develop faster than Catholic ones, at least at first.[1] Since then, credit has exploded, facilitating extraordinary increases in general economic well-being. Yet even so, most people still take a dim view of the fact that lenders charge interest. Why?

The main reason for the enduring unpopularity of interest comes from the failure to appreciate the fact that lending has an opportunity cost. Think of it from the point of view of the lender. People who offer credit don't need to make loans. They have alternatives, and extending a loan means giving them up. While lenders can eventually recoup the sum they lend, neither the time that the loan was outstanding nor the opportunities missed during that time can be gotten back. So interest isn't really "the breeding of money from money," as Aristotle put it; it's more like a rental fee that borrowers must pay lenders to compensate them for lost opportunities.

It's no surprise that in today's world, interest rates are of enormous importance to virtually everyone—individuals, businesses, and governments. Quoted as a percentage of the amount borrowed, interest rates link the present to the future, allowing us to compare payments made on different dates. Interest rates also tell us the future reward for lending today, as well as the cost of borrowing now and repaying later. To make sound financial decisions, we must learn how to calculate and compare different rates on various financial instruments. In this chapter, we'll explore interest rates using the concepts of future value and present value and then apply those concepts to the valuation of bonds. Finally, we'll look at the relationship between interest rates and inflation.

## Valuing Monetary Payments Now and in the Future

To compare the value of payments made on different dates, we need a set of tools called *future value* and *present value*. We'll use them to see how and why the promise to make a payment on one date is more or less valuable than the promise to make a payment on a different date. For example, we already know that if you want to borrow $100 today, your repayment needs to be bigger if you promise to make it in a year than if you promise to make it in a month. But how much more will you have to pay? The answer depends on both the date of payment and the interest rate. For the time being, we're going to assume that we know for sure that you will repay the loan. We'll get to the possibility of default when we study risk in the next chapter.

### Future Value and Compound Interest

What is the future value of one dollar deposited in an interest-bearing account today? To answer this question, let's start with a definition: **Future value** *is the value on some future date of an investment made today.* Say that today you invest $100 in a savings account that guarantees 5 percent interest per year. After one year, you'll have $105 (the investment at its present value of $100 plus $5 in interest). So the future value of $100 one year from now at an interest rate of 5 percent is $105. We could also say that the $100 investment yields $5, which explains why an interest rate is sometimes called a **yield**. Notice that the same calculation works for a simple loan in which you borrow $100 for one year at 5 percent interest. The amount you will need to repay is $105. Remember Core Principle 1: Time has value.

[1] Max Weber makes this argument in his classic work *The Protestant Ethic and the Spirit of Capitalism*, first published in 1905.

To generalize this concept so that we can handle different interest rates and initial investments of any size, we can express it mathematically. First we need to convert the percentage interest rate into a decimal, so that 5 percent becomes 0.05. It is essential to convert all interest rates to decimals before doing any computation. This is consistent with the fact that we quote interest rates as "parts per 100," so 5 percent means 5 parts per 100, or 0.05.

Now we can express future value as an equation. If the present value of your initial investment is $100 and the interest rate is 5 percent, then the *future value* one year from now is

$$\$100 + \$100 \times (0.05) = \$105$$

Present value of the investment + Interest = Future value in one year

Or in the notation we will use in this chapter,

$$FV = PV + PV \times i$$
$$= PV \times (1 + i) \tag{1}$$

This expression shows us immediately that the higher the interest rate, the higher the future value.

But this example is too simple. Most financial instruments don't make single payments in exactly one year, so we need to figure out what happens when the time to repayment varies. Computing the future value of an investment to be repaid two years from now is straightforward, so let's do that first. But since we quote interest rates on a yearly basis, we need to be careful. Using one-year interest rates to compute the value of an investment that will be repaid more than one year from now requires applying the concept of compound interest, *which is interest on the interest.* If you leave an investment in an interest-bearing account for two years, during the second year you will receive interest not only on your initial investment but also on the interest you earned for the first year (since they both have an opportunity cost).

Getting back to our example, let's say that you leave your $100 deposit in the bank for two years at 5 percent interest per year. The future value of this investment has four parts. The first three are straightforward. They are the initial investment of $100, the interest on that investment in the first year, and the interest on it in the second year. But because you left the interest from the first year in the bank during the second year, it is as if you made a new deposit at the beginning of the second year, and that earns interest too. So the fourth part of the future value is the interest you receive during the second year on the interest you received in the first year. That's compounding. With an initial deposit of $100 and an interest rate of 5 percent, we can add up these four parts to compute your investment's future value in two years.

$$\$100 + \$100(0.05) + \$100(0.05) + \$5(0.05) = \$110.25$$

Present value of the initial investment

+ Interest on the initial investment in first year

+ Interest on the initial investment in second year

+ Interest on the interest from first year in second year

= Future value in two years

We can use a small amount of algebra to show that this equals

$$\$100(1.05)(1.05) = \$100(1.05)^2.$$

| Table 4.1 | Computing the Future Value of $100 at 5 Percent Annual Interest | |
|---|---|---|

| Years into Future | Computation | Future Value |
|:---:|:---:|:---:|
| 1 | $100(1.05) | $105.00 |
| 2 | $100(1.05)$^2$ | $110.25 |
| 3 | $100(1.05)$^3$ | $115.76 |
| 4 | $100(1.05)$^4$ | $121.55 |
| 5 | $100(1.05)$^5$ | $127.63 |
| 10 | $100(1.05)$^{10}$ | $162.89 |

Extending it to three years, four years, or more just means multiplying by (1.05) over and over again. The multiplication takes care of the compounding. Table 4.1 shows the calculations. The final line shows that after 10 years, a deposit with a present value of $100 becomes $162.89. That is, it earns $62.89 in interest. If we had ignored compounding and just multiplied 5 percent by 10 years to get 50 percent, the answer would have been $150. Compounding produced an additional $12.89 in interest over 10 years. To put it as clearly as possible, multiplying the number of years times the annual interest rate gives the *wrong* answer!

Using the computations in Table 4.1, we can derive a general formula for future value.

$$FV_n = PV \times (1 + i)^n \qquad (2)$$

Future value in $n$ years = Present value of the investment

$\times$ (One plus the interest rate) raised to $n$

*So to compute future value, all we need to do is calculate one plus the interest rate (measured as a decimal) raised to the nth power and multiply it by the present value.*

Before we go any further, we should stop to consider an important problem. What if you want to put your $100 into a bank for six months, or 2½ years, or any amount of time that is not a round number of years? The answer is that the formula still works. You can compute the future value using equation (2) regardless of whether $n$ is a whole number. There is one pitfall, however. *In computing future value, both the interest rate and* n *must be measured in the same time units.* We have been measuring interest rates as the percentage per year, so we were careful to measure $n$ in years as well. So, if we want the future value in half of one year, $n$ would be ½; if we wanted it in one month, $n$ would be 1/12; and if we wanted the future value in one day, $n$ would be 1/365.

As you can see, taking advantage of the future-value formula requires an understanding of the transformations needed to convert time from years to months or vice versa. Converting $n$ from years to months is easy—everyone knows there are 12 months in a year—but converting the interest rate is harder. If the annual interest rate is 5 percent, what is the interest rate for one month? To figure out the answer, we'll start with the future-value formula, but in months. Remember that compounding means you *cannot* just multiply the monthly interest rate by 12 to get the annual interest rate. Instead, if $i^m$ is the one-month interest rate and $n$ is the number of months, then a deposit made for one year will have a future value of $100(1 + i_m)^{12}$.

# TOOLS OF THE TRADE
Computing Compound Annual Rates

Comparing changes over days, months, years, and decades can be very confusing, but the formula for compounding can help you find answers, as we show in these two examples.

If someone tells you that an investment grew at a rate of 1/2 percent last month, what should you think? You're used to thinking about growth in terms of years, not months. The way to deal with such problems is to turn the monthly growth rate into a *compound annual rate*. Here's how you do it.

An investment whose value grows 1/2 percent per month goes from 100 at the beginning of the month to 100.5 at the end of the month. To convert this monthly rate to an annual rate, we need to figure out what would happen if the investment's value continued to grow at a rate of 1/2 percent per month for the next 12 months. We can't just multiply 0.5 times 12. Instead, we need to compute a 12-month compound rate by raising the one-month rate to the 12th power. Assuming that our index starts at 100 and increases by 1/2 percent per month, we can use the expression for a compound future value to compute the index level 12 months later. Remembering to convert percentages to their decimal form, so that 0.5 percent is 0.005, we find the result is

$$FV_n = PV(1 + i_s)^n = 100(1.005)^{12} = 106.17,$$

an increase of 6.17 percent. That's the compound annual rate, and it's obviously bigger than the 6 percent result we get from just multiplying 0.5 by 12. The difference between the two answers—the one you get by multiplying by 12 and the one you get by compounding—grows as the interest rate grows. At a 1 percent monthly rate, the compounded annual rate is 12.68 percent.

We can use this logic to find a general solution. Let's first rewrite the solution as

$$FV_n = PV(1 + i_s)^n = 100(1.005)^{12} = 106.17 = PV(1 + i_l)$$

so that $i_l = 1.0617 - 1 = .0617$ or 6.17 percent. Now notice that from the second and last terms we can write

$$(1 + i_s)^n = (1 + i_l)$$

This is the general rule that will let you either convert a monthly rate to a compound annual rate or vice versa. In that case, $i_s$ is the shorter interest rate and $i_l$ is the longer one and $n$ represents the number of shorter periods there are in the longer period.

Suppose you want to compute the percentage change per year when you know how much an investment has grown over a number of years. This rate is sometimes referred to as the *average annual rate*. Say that over five years an investment has increased 20 percent, from 100 to 120. What annual increase will give us a 20 percent increase over five years? Dividing by 5 gives the wrong answer because it ignores compounding; the increase in the second year must be calculated as a percentage of the index level at the end of the first year.

Because we want to find the interest for the shorter period ($i_s$) in our formula, we need to invert the equation to get:

$$i_s = \sqrt[n]{(1 + i_l)} - 1$$

Now we have $n = 5$ and since the return over the long period is 20%, $i_l = 0.2$, so

$$i_s = \sqrt[5]{(1 + .2)} - 1 = 0.0371$$

This tells us that five consecutive annual increases of 3.71 percent will result in an overall increase of 20 percent. (Just to check, we can compute $(1.0371)^5 = 1.20 = 120/100$.)

We know that this amount equals $100(1.05)$, so figuring out the answer means equating the two amounts,

$$(1 + i_m)^{12} = (1.05),$$

and raising each side to the one-twelfth power:

$$(1 + i_m) = (1.05)^{1/12} = 1.0041.$$

Converting from decimals to a percentage, the one-month interest rate is 0.41 percent. We can handle any mismatch between the time units of $i$ and $n$ in a similar way (see Tools of the Trade: Computing Compound Annual Rates above).

These fractions of percentage points, such as 0.41 percent, are so important in discussing interest rates that they have their own name, basis points. A **basis point**—sometimes referred to as a bp or "beep"—is one one-hundredth of a percentage point. That is, one basis point equals 0.01 percent.

You're probably wondering how useful all this discussion of future value really is. To see, consider the following question: If you put $1,000 per year into the bank at 4 percent interest, how much would you have saved after 40 years? The answer is $98,826—more than twice the $40,000 you deposited. The practical implication of this calculation is that buying one fewer soft drink or candy bar per day isn't just good for your physical health; it's good for your financial health too. Figuring out the exact answer is complicated since we need to add up the future values of forty $1,000 deposits, each made in a different year, but doing so uses the concept of future value. The first $1,000 is deposited for 40 years, so its future value is

$$\$1,000(1.04)^{40} = \$4,801.02;$$

the second $1,000 is deposited for 39 years, so its future value is

$$\$1,000(1.04)^{39} = \$4,616.37;$$

and so on. In the appendix to this chapter (and on the spreadsheet link) we show how to derive the formula to solve this problem. Then you will have the tools to calculate the future value of any series of payments, for any period, at any interest rate.

www.mcgrawhill.ca/olc/
cecchetti

## Present Value

It's easy to see why future value is important. We often want to know what savings and investments will be worth in the future. But that isn't the only thing we need to know. There is another, somewhat different task that we face with some regularity. We need to be able to figure out how much a payment promised in the future is worth today. Say you agree to make a $225 loan, and the borrower offers to repay you either $100 a year for three years or $125 a year for two years. Which offer should you take? Answering this question means figuring out the current value of the promised payments on the dates when they will be made. To do that, we'll use the concept of present value, sometimes referred to as *present discounted value*.

**The Definition**   In our discussion of future value, we used the term *present value* to mean the initial amount invested or deposited. The way we used the term suggests its technical definition: **Present value** *is the value today (in the present) of a payment that is promised to be made in the future*. Put another way, present value is the amount that must be invested today in order to realize a specific amount on a given future date. Financial instruments promise future cash payments, so we need to know how to value those payments. Present value is an integral component of the computation of the price of all financial instruments.

To understand the calculation of present value, go back to future value. Remember that at a 5 percent interest rate, the future value one year from now of a $100 investment today is $105. It follows that at this same 5 percent interest rate, the present value of $105 one year from now is $100. *All we did was invert the future value calculation.*

Reversing the calculation in general terms is just as easy. We can invert equation (1) to get

$$PV = \frac{FV}{(1 + i)} \times 100 \tag{3}$$

Present value = Future value of the payment divided by (One plus the interest rate)

## APPLYING THE CONCEPT
### ISLAMIC BANKING

More than one-fifth of the world's 6.8 billion inhabitants are Muslims. That's about 1.5 billion people. And, like all religions, there are vast differences in the way the religion is practised. The most observant adhere closely to Islamic Law, or *Shari'a*. This divine law, revealed in the holy book of the Islamic religion called the *Qur'an*, forbids a number of activities including gambling, smoking, drinking of alcoholic beverages, eating pork, and paying of interest.

The challenge is that interest payments are the foundation of the modern financial system. Interest is the price the borrower pays for the credit extended by the lender. And financial development and economic development go hand in hand. Without interest payments, it is difficult to imagine the modern economy we see around us.

Because they are prohibited from paying or receiving interest, people in the Islamic world have found alternative mechanisms for promoting the flow of funds from savers to investors. They have developed banks that engage in financial transactions that are in compliance with *Shari'a*. In place of interest payments on deposits and interest charges on loans, Islamic banks enter into an alternative set of agreements with their customers. On the liability side, banks accept transaction and investment deposits. The former are available on demand, have a guaranteed nominal value, pay no interest, and may require the depositor to pay a maintenance fee. Investment deposits, which are the principle source of Islamic bank funding, carry no guarantees and do not pay fixed returns. Instead, investment deposits represent shares in the profits or losses of the bank. In servicing its investment accounts, an Islamic bank operates much like traditional mutual fund managers, distributing profits that are proportional to the size of the investment deposits.

Lending from Islamic banks is governed by the same principles of risk sharing. The two most important types of loans are called *mudarabah* and *murabaha*. Mudarabah is a profit-sharing agreement in which, in exchange for lent funds, the bank receives a previously agreed upon fraction of the gains from the borrowers' activities, in much the same way that a stockholder receives dividends. In a murabaha contract, the bank purchases goods on behalf of a customer and then resells them on a deferred basis, adding a profit margin. That is, the bank is making the purchase on behalf of the customer, and then the customer pays for the goods in a series of instalments.

Today a growing system of financial institutions is engaging in transactions that comply with Islamic Law. While they may be different in character, these banks serve the same basic functions that traditional banks do: They channel funds from savers to investors.

In our example, we see that

$$\frac{FV}{(1 + i)} = \frac{\$105}{(1.05)} = \$100$$

so the present value of $105 one year from now, at a 5 percent interest rate, is indeed $100.

While future value tells us what today's investment will be worth in the future, present value tells us what promised future payments are worth today. This means that the properties of present value mirror those of future value. In the same way that future value *rises* as the interest rate rises, present value *falls* as the interest rate rises. To see this, first look at the calculation of the present value of $105 in one year at an interest rate of 6 percent. The answer is

$$\frac{\$105}{1.06} = \$99.06$$

less than the $100 needed when the interest rate is only 5 percent. *Present value falls as the interest rate rises.*

What happens if the payment will be made in two years instead of one? What is the present value of $105 in two years at an interest rate of 5 percent? Again, we can compute the answer using the future-value formula by asking what present value has a future value of $105 in two years at an interest rate of 5 percent. This is the solution to

$$\$105 = PV(1.05)^2.$$

The answer is

$$PV = \frac{\$105}{1.05^2} = \$95.24$$

We can generalize this process by looking at the future value in $n$ years of an investment today: $FV_n = PV(1 + i)^n$. Dividing both sides of this expression by $(1 + i)^n$, we get the general formula for present value:

$$PV = \frac{FV_n}{(1 + i)^n} \qquad (4)$$

Present value = Future value of a payment made in $n$ years divided
by (One plus the interest rate) raised to $n$

From this simple expression, we can deduce three important properties of present value. Present value is higher

1. The higher the future value of the payment, $FV_n$.
2. The shorter the time until the payment, $n$.
3. The lower the interest rate, $i$.

We'll use equation (4) over and over again. *It is the single most important relationship in our study of financial instruments.* Once we can figure out the present value of any future payment, then we understand the fundamentals of mortgages, credit cards, car loans, and even stocks.

We will spend the rest of this chapter looking at how present value changes when we change the various components of the formula, and how to use it more generally. But before we do, it is important to note one final similarity between present value and future value. Recall that to calculate future value, $n$ need not be measured in years. We can do the computation even when $n$ is the number of months, so long as the interest rate is measured in months as well. The same is true of present value. So long as we measure $n$ and $i$ in the same time unit, and the interest rate is expressed as a decimal, the formula works.

**How Present Value Changes**  It is useful to go through each of the three properties of present value, looking at the impact of changing each one: the size of the future payment ($FV_n$), the time until the payment is made ($n$), and the interest rate ($i$). Starting with $FV_n$, we see that *doubling the future value of the payment, without changing the time of the payment or the interest rate, doubles the present value.* For example, at a 5 percent interest rate, a $100 payment made in two years has a present value of $90.70. Doubling the payment to $200 doubles the present value to $181.40. In fact, increasing or decreasing $FV_n$ by any percentage will change $PV$ by the same percentage, in the same direction.

We have already seen that *the sooner a payment is to be made, the more it is worth.* How much more? To see, let's return to the example of a $100 payment at 5 percent interest. How sensitive is the present value of this payment to the time until it is made? Plugging some numbers into the general present-value formula (equation 4), and allowing the time to go from 0 to 30 years, we can construct

"I'm just glad we got out before interest rates went up again."

Figure 4.1, which shows that the present value of the payment is worth $100 if it is made immediately but declines gradually to $23 for a payment made in 30 years.

The rate of decline in the present value is related to the same phenomenon that gives us the rule of 72 (described in Your Financial World: How Long Does Your Investment Take to Double? on page 64). Consider this question: At a 5 percent interest rate, how long into the future must a payment of $100 be received for it to be worth the same as $50 received today? The answer is 14.4 years. That is, at 5 percent interest, the present value of $100 paid in 14.4 years is $50. Note that 14.4 equals 72 divided by 5, so it is also the number of years an investment takes to double in value when the return is 5 percent per year. We can repeat the computation to see that the investment takes 28.8 years to double twice, which tells us that the present value of $100 paid 28.8 years from now is $25. These two points are highlighted in Figure 4.1.

The interest rate is the third important determinant of the present value of a future payment. To see how important it is, let's look at the present value of a $100 payment made 1, 5, 10, and 20 years from now at various interest rates. The general formula (equation 4) allows us to do this series of computations. Table 4.2 shows the numerical results. Note what happens as the interest rate increases—that is, as you read down a column in the table. You can see immediately that *higher interest rates are associated with lower present values, no matter what the size or timing of the payment.* Conversely, lower interest rates are associated with higher present values.

Note, too, that *at any fixed interest rate, an increase in the time until a payment is made reduces its present value.* Read across any row of the table and you will see that as the time increases from 1 to 5 to 10 to 20 years, the present value goes down.

The final lesson to take away from these calculations has to do with how present value changes with both time and the interest rate. Table 4.2 shows what happens to the present value of a payment as the interest rate increases.

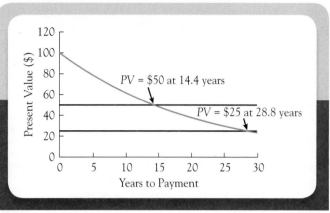

**Figure 4.1**   Present Value of $100 to Be Paid in *n* Years at 5 Percent Interest

**Table 4.2**   Present Value of a $100 Payment

| Interest Rate | Payment due in | | | |
|---|---|---|---|---|
| | 1 Year | 5 Years | 10 Years | 20 Years |
| 1% | $99.01 | $95.15 | $90.53 | $81.95 |
| 2% | $98.04 | $90.57 | $82.03 | $67.30 |
| 3% | $97.09 | $86.26 | $74.41 | $55.37 |
| 4% | $96.15 | $82.19 | $67.56 | $45.64 |
| 5% | $95.24 | $78.35 | $61.39 | $37.69 |
| 6% | $94.34 | $74.73 | $55.84 | $31.18 |
| 7% | $93.46 | $71.30 | $50.83 | $25.84 |
| 8% | $92.59 | $68.06 | $46.32 | $21.45 |
| 9% | $91.74 | $64.99 | $42.24 | $17.84 |
| 10% | $90.91 | $62.09 | $38.55 | $14.86 |
| 11% | $90.09 | $59.35 | $35.22 | $12.40 |
| 12% | $89.29 | $56.74 | $32.20 | $10.37 |
| 13% | $88.50 | $54.28 | $29.46 | $8.68 |
| 14% | $87.72 | $51.94 | $26.97 | $7.28 |
| 15% | $86.96 | $49.72 | $24.72 | $6.11 |

## YOUR FINANCIAL WORLD
How Long Does Your Investment Take to Double?

You invest $100 at 5 percent interest. How long will you need to wait until you have $200? That may seem like a simple question, but compounding makes it difficult. The straightforward (some people would call it "brute force") way to find the answer is to take out your calculator and multiply $100 times 1.05 over and over again counting how many times it takes to get to an answer that is close to $200. If you did that, you would find that after the 14th time, you had reached $197.99. And multiplying once more, you would have $207.89. You would conclude that, at 5 percent interest, your investment takes between 14 and 15 years to double.

While the brute force technique works—you can multiply over and over again—it's clumsy. Fortunately, there is a simpler way called the Rule of 72. If you want to compute the number of years it takes an investment to double, divide the annual interest rate measured as an integer into 72.* So at an interest rate of 5 percent, we would expect an investment to double in 72/5 = 14.4 years (we can check and see that $1.05^{14.4} = 2.02$). If the interest rate were 8 percent, we would estimate 9 years ($1.08^9 = 2.00$).

The rule of 72 shows the power of compounding. It shows that when the interest rate doubles, the time a

$100 investment takes to become $200 is cut in half. That is, while it takes 14.4 years to double at 5 percent interest, it takes only 7.2 years at 10 percent (72/10 = 7.2 and $1.10^{7.2} = 1.99$). This rule works for anything that is growing at a constant rate. So, if you want to estimate how long it will take a country's population or company's sales to double, just divide the annual growth rate measured as a percentage per year into 72.

Why does the Rule of 72 work?

The rule of 72 is an approximation of the solution to an algebraic problem that requires the use of logarithms. Consider the formula for compound interest, in which the future value after $n$ years is equal to $FV = PV (1 + i)^n$. Setting the present value $PV$ equal to 1 and the future value $i$ equal to 2 and taking logarithms, we get $n = ln(2)/ln(1 + i)$. This formula is exact. Next, we use the approximation that $ln(1 + i) \approx i$ for small $i$. Substituting this into the equation gives us $n = ln(2)/i$. The $ln(2) = 0.693$, so it might seem that we should be using the rule of 69.3. For very low interest rates, we should, but that approximation isn't that useful with real world interest rates. In the range of interest rates that we normally see (2 to 15 percent), 72 works better.

You can see that if the payment is to be made in one year (column 2), as the interest rate increases from 1 percent to 5 percent, the present value falls from $99.01 to $95.24. This is a drop of $3.77, or just under 4 percent. In fact, for the single payment made in one year, the percentage change in the present value is approximately equal to the percentage point change in the interest rate: A rise of 4 percentage points in the interest rate has caused a decline in present value of 4 percent.

Now look at the present value of a payment that will be made in 10 years (column 4 of Table 4.2 on page 63). As the interest rate goes from 1 to 5 percent, the present value of a $100 payment 10 years from now falls from $90.53 to $61.39. This is a decline of $29.14, or more than 30 percent. *Not only does the present value of a future payment fall with the interest rate; the further in the future the promised payment is to be made, the more the present value falls.* As a result, a change in interest rates has a much greater impact on the present value of a payment made far in the future than it has on one to be made soon. Remember this principle because it will be extremely important when we discuss bonds in the next section.

## Applying Present Value

All of our examples thus far have focused on computing the present value of a single payment on a given future date. Thinking of present value in this way gives us enormous flexibility. It means that we can compute the present value not just of a single payment but also of any group of payments made on any number of dates. As we saw earlier, to use present value in practice, we need to look at sequences, or streams of payments. And valuing a stream of payments means summing their present values. That is, the value of the whole is the sum of the value of its parts. *Present value is additive*. To see how present value is applied to a stream of payments, we will look at two applications: internal rate of return and the valuation of bonds.

## Internal Rate of Return

Imagine that you run a sports equipment factory. As part of your strategic planning, you are considering buying a new machine that makes tennis racquets. The machine costs $1 million and can produce 3,000 racquets a year. If you can sell the racquets for $50 apiece (wholesale), the machine will generate $150,000 in revenue each year. To simplify the analysis, we will assume that the machine is the only necessary input in the production of tennis racquets; that we know the exact amount of revenue it will produce (in reality, that has to be estimated); and that the machine will last for exactly 10 years, during which time it will work perfectly, without requiring any maintenance. At the end of the 10 years, the machine will abruptly cease to operate and will have no resale value. Should you buy the machine?

# YOUR FINANCIAL WORLD
### Should You Buy a New Car Now or Wait?

For a long time you've wanted to buy a new car and you know you'll need a loan to do it. You have $4,000 in savings and figure you can afford a monthly payment of $300. A quick check on the Internet tells you that you can get a four-year loan at $6\frac{3}{4}$ percent interest. Payments are $237 a month for each $10,000 you borrow. That is, $10,000 is the present value of $237 per month for 48 months at a monthly interest rate of 0.54581 percent (the monthly rate that equals $6\frac{3}{4}$ percent per year). Since you can afford a $300 payment, you can get a loan of up to $12,658, or (300/237) × $10,000. With a $4,000 down payment, you can afford a car that costs $16,658.

You don't have to buy the car right away, however. You could wait and drive your old car a while longer. What if you wait a year to buy the car? Waiting means you should put $300 per month into the bank along with the $4,000 you already have. At 4 percent interest, at the end of a year you will have $7,838—the future value of the $4,000 plus 12 monthly contributions of $300 each.

For the sake of comparison, let's keep the out-of-pocket cost at $300 per month for 4 years, so that at the end of the year you look for a three-year loan with a $300

payment. At $6\frac{3}{4}$ percent interest, you can now afford to borrow $9,781. Adding this amount to your savings, you can spend a total of $7,837 + $9,781, or $17,618. So by waiting a year, you'll be able to afford a car that costs about $1,000 more. (That's approximately the 4 percent interest you earned on your $4,000 down payment plus the $6\frac{3}{4}$ percent interest you didn't pay on a $12,658 loan: $160 + $854 = $1,014.)

Should you buy the new car now or wait? It depends on how you feel about the extra $1,000 you will have available to spend if you wait and how much you'll have to pay to repair your old car in the meantime.[*]

[*] In addition, there is always the possibility that the price of the car will change. It could go up because of general inflation or down as a result of increases in the efficiency of production. If you have reason to believe that the price may change in a particular direction, factor that into your computation.

The answer is: It depends. If you borrow the $1 million to pay for the machine, will the revenue from the machine, $150,000 per year, be enough to cover the payments on the loan? If so, and you have something left over, then buying the machine may be a good idea. But if you can't make the payments, then buying the machine is a losing proposition. So you need to figure out whether the machine's revenue will be high enough to cover the payments on the loan you would need to buy it. We'll do this in two steps: First, we'll compute the internal rate of return on your investment in the machine, and second, we'll compare that return to the cost of buying the machine. If the cost is less than the return, then you should buy the machine.

The **internal rate of return** is *the interest rate that equates the present value of an investment with its cost.* For the tennis racquet machine, it is the interest rate at which the present value of the revenue from the tennis racquets, $150,000 per year for 10 years, equals the $1 million cost of the machine. To find the internal rate of return, we take the sum of the present value of each of the yearly revenues (we can't take the present value of the total revenue) and equate it with the machine's cost. Then we solve for the interest rate, $i$:

$$\$1,000,000 = \frac{\$150,000}{(1 + i)^1} + \frac{\$150,000}{(1 + i)^2} + \ldots + \frac{\$150,000}{(1 + i)^{10}} \quad (5)$$

You can solve this equation using a financial calculator or spreadsheet. The answer, 8.14 percent, is the internal rate of return on your investment. That is, the annual rate of return for investing $1 million in the machine is 8.14 percent. But is that rate of return high enough to justify your investment? That depends on the cost of the $1 million you need to buy the machine.

There are two ways you can come up with the $1 million. You can use your company's retained earnings—the funds you've saved from your past profits. Or you can borrow. In the first case, you need to figure out if the machine is more profitable than other ways you might use the funds, just as you might compare interest-bearing investments. The other main use for the retained earnings is to lend it to someone at the same rate at which you could borrow. That is the opportunity cost of your investment. If you borrow the money to buy the machine, you need to know whether you will have a profit left after paying off the loan. Let's assume you're considering borrowing.

Table 4.3 shows the payments you will have to make if you borrow $1 million at various interest rates. To keep the example fairly simple, we'll assume that the loan requires 10 equal payments, one for each year. This type of loan is called a fixed-payment loan, and it is exactly the same as a car loan or a mortgage. Using the present-value formula (equation 4), we know that the amount of the loan must equal the present value of the 10 payments. If the interest rate is $i$, then

| Table 4.3 | Fixed Annual Payments on a 10-Year, $1 Million Loan |
|---|---|

| Interest Rate | Payment |
|---|---|
| 5% | $129,505 |
| 6% | $135,868 |
| 7% | $142,378 |
| 8% | $149,030 |
| 9% | $155,820 |
| 10% | $162,745 |

$$\$1,000,000 = \frac{\textit{Fixed payment}}{(1 + i)} + \frac{\textit{Fixed payment}}{(1 + i)^2} + \ldots + \frac{\textit{Fixed payment}}{(1 + i)^{10}} \quad (6)$$

$1,000,000 = Present value of 10 equal annual payments at interest rate $i$.

Using this relationship (and the methods described in the Appendix to this chapter), we can compute your loan payment at various interest rates, as shown in Table 4.3. As we would expect, when the interest rate rises, the payments rise too.

### APPLYING THE CONCEPT
#### EARLY RETIREMENT

Many people want to retire early. They would love to quit work when they turn 40 (that's less than 20 years of work after college or university) and spend the next 40 years doing whatever they want. In fact, few Canadians save enough to reach such a goal, and the financial crisis in 2007–09, which reduced interest rates and drastically lowered the value of savings in the stock market, wiped out many dreams of early retirement. Some early retirees discovered that they really couldn't afford retirement. Some had to go back to work.

How expensive is early retirement anyway? The answer is, very expensive. Here's the problem. Assume that you'll live to be exactly 85 years old. Though you're rich, you are willing to live modestly (for a rich person) and spend only $100,000 a year. Remember that you'll be on vacation 365 days a year and you'll want to put your kids through college or university, buy new cars, and so on. And you'll still need to pay income taxes, so you won't see all of your income. Assuming you have no other retirement plan, and no Canada Pension Plan payments (you can't get those for at least 20 years anyway), you'll need $100,000 a year for 45 years.

To figure out how much you need to save by age 40, you can use the present value concept. Think of the amount you need to invest today to have $100,000 in five years. That is:

$$\$100,000 = PV(1 + i)^5$$

Assuming a 4 percent interest rate on your investment (that may seem conservative, but you can't count on much more than that*), the answer is

$$PV = \frac{\$100,000}{(1.04)^5} = \$82,193$$

To retire at 40, you need to do this for *each* of the 45 years of your retirement. That is, you need a sequence of $100,000 payments:

$$\frac{\$100,000}{(1.04)^1} + \frac{\$100,000}{(1.04)^2} + \cdots + \frac{\$100,000}{(1.04)^{44}} + \frac{\$100,000}{(1.04)^{45}} = \$2,072,004$$

Retiring at 40 with an income of $100,000 a year means accumulating about $2 million in assets (not counting your house). You can see how someone who retired at age 40 with a few million dollars worth of Internet stocks might have had to go back to work when the bubble burst, reducing his or her wealth by 75 percent or more.

The point of this discussion is that retirement, especially early retirement, is expensive. Even if you are willing to work until you are 65, and live on only $50,000 a year (plus your CPP pension), you'll need to amass around $700,000. As a rule of thumb, people in their mid-20s should be putting away 10 percent of their income toward retirement in order to retire at the same preretirement standard of living by age 65. It takes significant savings to live without a paycheque.

\* Later in the chapter we explain that to adjust for inflation you need to subtract the expected inflation rate from the interest rate. Here we assume you expect to earn 6 percent but have subtracted 2 percent because you expect an inflation rate of 2 percent.

At what interest rate can you afford a loan to buy the tennis racquet machine? Recall that you have $150,000 a year in revenue, and your internal rate of return is 8.14 percent. So as long as the interest rate is 8.14 percent or less, you know you can cover the payments. But we can answer this question with more precision. To see why, notice that the internal rate of return equation 5 is virtually identical to the loan equation 6. In fact, the internal rate of return is the interest rate at which $150,000 a year for 10 years will exactly cover the loan. So we really needed to do this computation only once to answer the question. You should buy the tennis racquet machine if its internal rate of return exceeds the interest rate on the loan you would need to finance it. In general, *an investment will be profitable if its internal rate of return exceeds the cost of borrowing.*

Before we go on, we can use the concept of internal rate of return to answer the question at the beginning of the present-value section on page 60: If you agree to make a $225 loan, and the borrower offers to repay either $100 a year for three years or $125 a year for two years, which should you take? The first step in figuring out what

## IN THE NEWS

### Economic Scene: Pentagon Shows That It Doesn't Always Pay to Take the Money and Run

# The New York Times

**Alan B. Krueger**

May 24, 2001

Suppose your employer hands you a pink slip and offers you a choice: an annual payment of $8,000 a year for 30 years or a lump sum of $50,000 today. Which would you choose?

This is not just a hypothetical exercise. When it downsized in the early 1990s, the Defense Department offered many military personnel a similar choice. The military also provided pamphlets and counseling to explain how to make the choice wisely. To the surprise of most economists, the affected personnel rarely followed the military's sound advice.

The decision should depend, of course, on how much one values money received today versus tomorrow. A bird in the hand is worth more today than tomorrow, but how much more? The difference between the value an individual places on a dollar received today as opposed to a year from now is called the discount rate.*

Standard economic theory says that if capital markets work perfectly, people will borrow or lend until their discount rate equals the market rate for borrowing or lending. Someone with a low discount rate will save and accumulate interest; someone with a high discount rate will borrow and accumulate debt. This should continue to the point where their personal discount rates equal the market rate.

Thus, with some justification, the military's pamphlet provided calculations of the present value of the annuity payment using a 7 percent discount rate, the interest rate on money-market funds at the time. If the annuity's present value exceeds the value of the lump sum, the annual payment is a better deal.

Mounting evidence indicates that most people put excessive weight on a bird in the hand. That $8,000 annual payment is worth more than $106,000 if future income is discounted at 7 percent a year—more than double the value of the lump sum. If the discount rate is 10 percent, as high as the interest rate on 30-year fixed-rate mortgages has been the last decade, the promised $8,000 payment is still worth $83,000. The annual payment is a better deal for anyone who can borrow from a bank.

---

* The author is using the term "discount rate" in the same way that we used the term "interest rate" in the present value calculation.

---

to do is to compute the internal rate of return of the two payment streams. For the series of three $100 payments, we need to find the interest rate $i$ that solves

$$\$225 = \frac{\$100}{(1 + i)} + \frac{\$100}{(1 + i)^2} + \frac{\$100}{(1 + i)^3}$$

The answer is $i = 0.159$, or 15.9 percent.

Turning to the alternative, we need to calculate the interest rate that solves

$$\$225 = \frac{\$125}{(1 + i)} + \frac{\$125}{(1 + i)^2}$$

The answer here is $i = 0.073$, or 7.3 percent.

This means that if you choose the three $100 payments, you will earn 15.9 percent interest on the loan, while if you accept the two $125 payments, the interest rate will be 7.3 percent. Clearly, the three payments are better for you as the lender, but we had to do quite a bit of work to figure it out.

Yet when the military offered essentially this package, three-quarters of enlisted personnel selected the lump sum, according to an article by John Warner of Clemson University and Saul Pleeter of the Defense Department in *The American Economic Review*. The authors also examined a number of other separation packages. The break-even discount rate—or rate that makes the lump sum and annuity payment equivalent—varied from 17 to 20 percent, depending on years of service and salary. Overall, 92 percent of enlisted personnel and 51 percent of officers chose the lump sum.

Because the government could borrow at 7 percent at the time, Mr. Warner and Mr. Pleeter calculate that the Treasury saved $1.7 billion by offering the lump-sum option.

Using a sample of 65,000 departing members of the armed forces, they estimate that the average personal discount rate, taking taxes into account, exceeded 25 percent. Discount rates were higher for the less educated, the young, minorities, and those with dependants; they were lower for officers.

Recognition of this fact helps to explain a number of other phenomena. For instance, the public's penchant for holding high credit card debt—more than $6,000 per household with a credit card—at interest rates near 15 percent a year is also consistent with high discount rates, as are low savings rates. (Indeed, one wonders why the government, which borrows at 5 percent, doesn't offer a credit card to every man, woman, and child at an interest rate of, say, 10 percent. This would help reduce the debt and quench individuals' thirst for fast cash.)

### LESSONS OF THE ARTICLE

This article examines a common problem faced by people who are retiring. Should they take a single lump-sum payment or a series of annual payments? Answering this question requires using the concept of present value. The article also describes how most people are extremely impatient, behaving as if their own personal discount rate is extraordinarily high, and how that explains the willingness to borrow at very high interest rates.

## Bonds: The Basics

One of the most common uses of the concept of present value is in the valuation of bonds. A bond is a promise to make a series of payments on specific future dates. It is issued as part of an arrangement to borrow. In essence, the borrower, or seller, gives an IOU to the lender, or buyer, in return for some amount of money. Both governments and corporations need to borrow, so both issue bonds. Because bonds create obligations, they are best thought of as legal contracts that (1) require the borrower to make payments to the lender and (2) specify what happens if the borrower fails to do so.

Because there are many different kinds of bonds, to focus our discussion, we'll look at the most common type, a coupon bond. Say a borrower who needs $100 "issues," or sells, a $100 coupon bond to a lender. The bond issuer is required to make annual payments, called coupon payments. The annual amount of those payments (expressed as a percentage of the amount borrowed) is called the coupon rate. If the coupon rate is 5 percent, then the borrower/issuer pays the lender/bondholder $5 per year per $100 borrowed. The yearly coupon payment equals the coupon rate times the amount

A coupon bond issued in 1918 by the Canadian Northern Railway Company.

SOURCE: *Scripophily.com, The Gift of History.*

borrowed. The bond also specifies when the issuer will repay the initial $100 and the payments will stop, called the **maturity date** or *term to maturity*. The final payment, a repayment of the initial $100 loan, is often referred to as the **principal**, **face value**, or **par value** of the bond.

Before the advent of computers, an investor buying a bond would receive a certificate with a number of dated coupons attached. To claim the coupon payments, the investor would cut off the coupons and mail them to the bond issuer. At maturity, the investor would redeem the certificate for the final payment. The Canadian Northern Railway Company bond pictured above still has its coupons attached.

You can see that the borrower that issues a bond is promising to make a series of regular interest payments over the life of the bond, plus a final payment on the maturity date. How much should someone be willing to pay for such a contract? The answer comes directly from present value: *The price of a bond is the present value of its payments.* To see how to value a bond, we'll start with repayment of the principal; then we'll add the coupon payments.

### Valuing the Principal Payment

Valuing the bond's principal, or final payment, is a straightforward application of present value. Let's look at a bond that promises a principal payment of $100 on its maturity date $n$ years in the future. The present value of this payment is

$$P_{BP} = \frac{F}{(1 + i)^n} = \frac{S100}{(1 + i)^n} \qquad (7)$$

Present value of bond principal ($P_{BP}$) =
    Principal payment ($F$) divided by (One plus the interest rate) raised to $n$.

We can see immediately that the value of the principal payment varies with both the time to maturity and the interest rate. The longer the time until the payment is made—the higher the $n$—the lower the value of the payment. And the higher the interest rate, $i$, the lower the value of the payment.

To see how this works, let's start with an interest rate of 6 percent and a final payment of $1,000 to be made in 30 years. If the interest rate is 6 percent, the present value of the final payment is

$$P_{BP} = \frac{\$1000}{(1.06)^{30}} = \$174.11$$

Not surprisingly, this promise to make a payment that far in the future is worth only a fraction of the $1,000 principal. Lowering the interest rate, say to 4 percent, would increase the present value of the principal payment to $308.32, but it would still be much less than half of the payment itself.

**Valuing the Coupon Payments**   What about the coupon payments? This series of equal payments resembles the loan payments we examined in our discussion of internal rate of return. There, we computed the sum of a series of equal payments by adding up the present value of each payment. Let's look at this process in more detail, starting with two $10 payments made in consecutive years. Assuming an interest rate of 6 percent, the value of these two payments is

$$\frac{\$10}{1.06} + \frac{\$10}{1.06^2} = \$9.43 + \$8.90 = \$18.33$$

Adding additional payments simply means adding more terms. So for five $10 payments made over five consecutive years, the present value is

$$\frac{\$10}{1.06} + \frac{\$10}{1.06^2} + \frac{\$10}{1.06^3} + \frac{\$10}{1.06^4} + \frac{\$10}{1.06^5} = \$9.43 + \$8.90 + \$8.40 + \$7.92 + \$7.47$$
$$= \$42.12$$

This example highlights two important properties of periodic fixed payments. First, the longer the payments go on—the more of them there are—the higher their total value. Even though the additional payments fall further into the future, the overall present value still grows. Since a long-term bond (one that lasts for 30 years, for instance) has more payments than a short-term maturity bond (one whose final payment is made, say, in five years) the coupon payments on the long-term bond will be worth more than the coupon payments on the short-term bond.

Second, as is always the case in present-value calculations, the higher the interest rate, the lower the present value. Raising the interest rate from 6 to 7 percent, for example, lowers the total value of the five future payments on our short-term bond from $42.12 to $41.00.

We can use the present-value expression to write a general formula for a string of yearly coupon payments made over $n$ years. It is simply the sum of the present value of the payments for each year from one to $n$ years:

$$P_{CP} = \frac{C}{(1 + i)^1} + \frac{C}{(1 + i)^2} + \frac{C}{(1 + i)^3} + \ldots + \frac{C}{(1 + i)^n} \qquad (8)$$

Present value of a series of bond coupon payments ($P_{CP}$) = Sum of yearly coupon payments (C) divided by (one plus the interest rate) raised to the power equal to the number of years from now. This formula is messy, but that's why we have calculators and spreadsheets. (For a derivation of a simpler version of this formula, see the appendix to this chapter.)

**Valuing the Coupon Payments plus Principal**   To value the yearly coupon payments plus the principal, we can combine equations (7) and (8) as follows:

$$P_{CB} = P_{CP} + P_{BP} = \left[\frac{C}{(1 + i)^1} + \frac{C}{(1 + i)^2} + \frac{C}{(1 + i)^3} + \ldots + \frac{C}{(1 + i)^n}\right] + \frac{F}{(1 + i)^n} \quad (9)$$

Present value of coupon bond ($P_{CB}$)

$$= \text{Present value of yearly coupon payments } (P_{CP})$$

$$+ \text{Present value of principal payment } (P_{BP})$$

This formula looks complicated because it is. But we can learn two simple facts just by looking at its parts. The value of the coupon bond, $P_{CB}$, rises when (1) the yearly coupon payments, C, rise, and (2) the interest rate, $i$, falls. The first of these conclusions follows from the fact that a higher coupon rate means larger payments, and the present value of a larger payment is larger. The second follows directly from the present-value relationship: the lower the interest rate, the higher the present value of any and all future payments.

The fact that lower interest rates mean higher bond prices—and higher interest rates mean lower bond prices—is extremely important. Since bonds promise fixed payments on future dates, the higher the interest rate, the lower their present value. It follows that the *value of a bond varies inversely with the interest rate used to calculate the present value of the promised payment.*

## Real and Nominal Interest Rates

In calculating present value, our goal has been to assess the number of dollars you would pay today for fixed dollar payments in the future. To do this, we used the **nominal interest rate**, which is the interest rate expressed in current-dollar terms. We did not worry about the possibility that inflation might change the purchasing power of the dollars. However, since borrowers and lenders care about the purchasing power of the money they pay out and receive, they do care about inflation. So we need to adjust the return on a loan, looking at not only the nominal interest rate but also the inflation-adjusted interest rate, called the **real interest rate**.

Think about a $100 loan made at 5 percent interest rate for one year. The borrower receives $100 at the beginning of the year and repays $105 at the end of the year. If prices go up 5 percent during the year—that is, if the inflation rate is 5 percent—then the $105 returned to the lender at the end of the year will buy exactly what $100 did at the beginning of the year. The lender's inflation-adjusted return is zero. No lender would be happy with a zero return, so no lender is likely to make a loan at a 5 percent nominal interest rate if expected inflation is 5 percent. (Since the inflation rate can exceed the nominal interest rate, the real interest rate can be negative.)

# YOUR FINANCIAL WORLD
## Pay Off Your Credit Card Debt as Fast as You Can

Credit cards are extremely useful. They make buying things easy—sometimes too easy. While we all plan to pay off our credit card balances every month, sometimes we just don't have the resources. So we take advantage of the loans the card issuers offer and pay off only part of what we owe. Suddenly we find ourselves deeply in debt.

How fast should you pay off your credit card balance? All the bank or finance company that issued the card will tell you is the minimum you have to pay. You get to decide whether to pay more, and your decision makes a big difference. We can use the present-value concept to figure out your alternatives.

Let's take a typical example. You have a balance of $2,000 and can afford to pay at least $50 per month. How many monthly payments will you need to make to pay off the full debt? What if you paid $60 or $75 per month? To find the answer, use equation (8) for the present value of a fixed series of payments. In this case, the present value is the loan amount, $2,000; the fixed monthly payment is $50, $60, or $75; and the interest rate is whatever your credit card company charges per month—10 to 20 percent a year. (The average rate is around 15 percent.) We need to figure out the number of payments, or $n$ in equation (8).[*]

Table 4.4 shows the number of months needed to pay off your $2,000 balance at various interest rates and payment amounts. The first entry tells you that if your credit card company is charging a 10 percent annual interest rate (which is comparatively low), and you pay $50 per month, then you will need to make payments for 48.4 months—just over four years.

Looking at the entire table, you can see the advantage of making big payments. Assume you're paying 15 percent, which is realistic. The table shows that increasing your payment from $50 to $60 will allow you to finish paying off your debt in 42.5 months rather than 54.3 months. In other words, paying $10 more a month will allow you to finish paying off the loan one full year sooner. And if you can manage to pay $75 a month, you'll be finished 10 months before that.

How fast should you pay off your credit card balance?

SOURCE: © Masterfile

Looking more closely, you can see that making large payments is much more important than getting a low interest rate. The lesson is: Pay off your debts as fast as you possibly can. Procrastination is expensive.

[*] The most straightforward way to do this is to use a spreadsheet to add up the payments until their present value equals the credit card balance. In the Appendix to this chapter, we show you how to use logarithms to find the number of payments.

| Table 4.4 | Number of Months to Pay Off a $2,000 Credit Card Debt | | |

| Annual Interest Rate | Monthly Payment | | |
|---|---|---|---|
| | $50 | $60 | $75 |
| 10% | 48.4 | 38.9 | 30.1 |
| 13% | 51.7 | 41.0 | 31.3 |
| 15% | 54.3 | 42.5 | 32.2 |
| 20% | 62.4 | 47.0 | 34.5 |

The point of this example is that borrowers look at the inflation-adjusted cost of borrowing, while lenders focus on the inflation-adjusted return. *No one cares only about the number of dollars. People also care about what those dollars can buy. In other words, everyone cares about real interest rates.* This is why economists think of the nominal interest rate as having two parts, the real interest rate and expected inflation.

Say that you want to borrow $100 for one year. You find a lender who is willing to give you a loan, but the two of you need to agree on the interest rate. Both of you care about the inflation rate over the coming year, which will affect the purchasing power of the dollars you will use to repay the loan. But neither of you knows what that rate will be, so you need to forecast it to conclude your agreement. That is, the nominal interest rate you agree on must be based on *expected inflation* over the term of the loan, plus the real interest rate you agree on.

Writing this statement in the form of an equation is helpful. The nominal interest rate, $i$, equals the real interest rate, $r$, plus expected inflation, $\pi^e$:[2]

$$i = r + \pi^e \tag{10}$$

This is called the *Fisher equation* after the early 20th-century economist Irving Fisher. It shows that in general, the nominal interest rate is positively related to expected inflation. The higher expected inflation, the higher the nominal interest rate. As we can see in Figure 4.2, the data bear this out. While the relationship is not a tight one, higher nominal interest rates are usually associated with higher inflation rates.

**Figure 4.2    The Nominal Interest Rate, the Inflation Rate, and the Real Interest Rate**

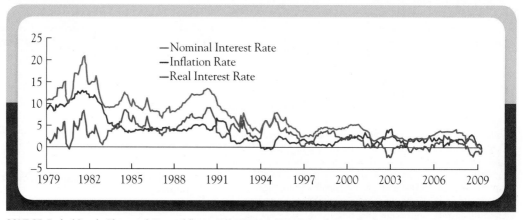

SOURCE: *Bank of Canada. Three-month Treasury bill rates, Table 176-0043 (V122531) and 12-month inflation rates (based on CPI–V41690973) are from CANSIM. The real interest rate is the Tbill rate minus the inflation rate over the previous 12 months; Statistics Canada, Consumer Price Index Table 326-0020 (V41690973), accessed June 2009.*

[2] This equation is an approximation that works only at low levels of inflation and the real interest rate. The exact relationship among the nominal interest rate, real interest rate, and the inflation rate is $(1 + i) = (1 + r)(1 + \pi^e)$, which equals $(1 + i) = 1 + r + \pi^i + r\pi^e$. The approximation, $i = r + \pi^e$, ignores the cross-term $r\pi^e$, which is usually small. For example, if the real interest rate and the inflation rate are both 5 percent, then $r\pi^e = 0.05 \times 0.05 = 0.0025$, or 0.25 percent. But when inflation is very high, this cross-term becomes important. If the real interest rate is 5 percent, at zero inflation, a nominal interest rate of 5 percent means that a $100 investment yields $105. But if the inflation rate rises to 100 percent, an investor will require $210 to make the same investment a year later, so the nominal interest rate that results in a 5 percent real return at 100 percent inflation is $(1 + i) = (1 + 0.05)(1 + 1) = 2.1$, which implies an interest rate of 110 percent, not 105 percent. The 5 percent difference comes from the part of the equation that we ignore in the approximation.

# APPLYING THE CONCEPT
## HIGH INTEREST RATES, LOW INTEREST RATES

Once we realize that the nominal interest rate moves with the expected inflation, big swings in interest rates become less of a mystery. And the fact that the Canadian interest rate is about 3 percent when the Japanese interest rate is less than 1 percent, and the Icelandic interest rate is over 15 percent, is easier to understand. All we need to do is look at differences in inflation. In 2008, for example, Canadian prices were rising at about 2 percent per year, while Japanese prices were rising at about 1 percent. The Icelandic inflation rate had risen to 12 percent per year. A lot of the differences in nominal interest rates are explained by the differences in inflation.

Figure 4.3 shows the nominal interest rate and the inflation rate in the OECD countries in mid-2008. Note first that high inflation is associated with high nominal interest rates (as in Iceland) and low inflation with low nominal interest rates (as in Japan). Second, the vast majority of the points lie above the 45-degree line, meaning that in these countries, the nominal interest rate is higher than the inflation rate. So the real interest rate is positive at an average of 1 3/4 percent. Note also that the distance of these points from the 45-degree line, which represents the real interest rate, does not vary nearly as much as their distance from the horizontal axis, which represents the nominal interest rate.

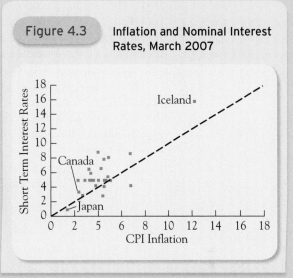

**Figure 4.3**    Inflation and Nominal Interest Rates, March 2007

SOURCE: *Inflation rate data based on Main Economic Indicators under Monthly Economic Indicators, OECD. Stat Extracts, http://stats.oecd.org/index.aspx. Interest rate data based on Financial Indicators (MEI), under Finance, OECD. Stat Extracts, http://stats.oecd.org/index.aspx. OECD, www.oecd.org.*

In 1981, for example, Canadian interest rates were sky high; the Canadian government had to pay over 18 percent for its short-term borrowing. By 1986, interest rates had dropped to more reasonable levels, close to 8 percent. That's a 10-percentage point move in just five years! The figure shows that as inflation fell, nominal interest rates also fell. In fact, the declines were almost identical. The real interest rate didn't change much.

The term *"real interest rate"* can cause confusion. The financial markets quote nominal interest rates, the ones that appear in the newspaper and on bank statements.[3] They are "real" in the sense that they are real-life interest rates. When people use the term *"interest rate"* without qualification, they are referring to the *nominal* interest rate, the one they see every day. We will follow this convention, using the term *"interest rate"* to mean the nominal rate and the term *"real interest rate"* to refer to the nominal rate less expected inflation.

Unlike the nominal rates, we cannot directly observe the real interest rate; we have to estimate it. The easiest way to do that is to turn the Fisher equation around, rewriting it as

$$r = i - \pi^e \qquad\qquad (11)$$

---

[3] One exception is certain bonds whose interest rates are quoted in real, inflation-adjusted terms. We will examine these *inflation-indexed* bonds in detail in Chapter 6.

Since we know the nominal interest rate, $i$, measuring the real interest rate means subtracting forecasted inflation. There are a number of sources for these forecasts. The Bank of Canada Web site (http://www.bankofcanada.ca/en/rates/indinf.html) has CPI forecasts by the Conference Board of Canada and Consensus Economics.

But since forecasts are often wrong, our estimate will usually differ from the real interest rate that occurs. Someone who is making an economically important decision will do so based on the expected real interest rate. Some time later, that person will look back and compute the real interest rate actually paid or received. The first of these is known as the *ex ante* real interest rate, meaning "before the fact." The second, or realized rate, is the *ex post* real interest rate, meaning "after the fact." We can always compute the *ex post* real interest rate, since we know the nominal interest rate and the actual inflation rate. But it is the *ex ante* real interest rate that we really want to know.

## Terms

## Chapter Summary

1. The value of a payment depends on when it is made.
   a. Future value is the present value of an initial investment times one plus the interest rate for each year you hold it. The higher the interest rate, the higher the future value.
   b. Present value is equal to the value today of a payment made on a future date.

   $$PV = \frac{FV_n}{(1 + i)^n}$$

   i. The higher the payment, the higher the present value at a given interest rate.
   ii. The higher the interest rate, the lower the present value of a given payment.
   iii. The longer the time until the payment is made, the lower the present value of a given payment at a given interest rate.
   iv. For a given increase in the interest rate, the present value of a promised payment falls more the farther into the future the payment is to be made.
   v. When computing present value, the interest rate and the time until the payment is to be made must be measured in the same time units.

2. Present value can be used to value any stream of future payments.
   a. The internal rate of return is the interest rate that equates the present value of the future payments or profits from an investment with its current cost. *An investment will be profitable if its internal rate of return exceeds the cost of borrowing.*
   b. A coupon bond is a promise to make periodic interest payments and a final principal payment on specific future dates.
      i. The present value of a bond depends on its coupon rate, date of maturity, and the current interest rate.
      ii. The higher the coupon rate, given the maturity and the interest rate, the higher the present value of the bond.
      iii. The price of a bond is inversely related to the interest rate. The higher the price, the lower the interest rate that equates the price with the present value of the promised payments.

3. The real interest rate is the nominal interest rate minus expected inflation. It expresses the interest rate in terms of purchasing power rather than current dollars.

# Conceptual Problems

1. Compute the future value of $100 at an 8 percent interest rate 5, 10, and 15 years into the future.

2. Compute the present value of a $100 investment made six months, five years, and ten years from now at 4 percent interest.

3. Assuming that the current interest rate is 3 percent, compute the value of a five-year, 5 percent coupon bond with a face value of $1,000. What happens when the interest rate rises to 4 percent?

4.* Given a choice of two investments, would you choose one that pays a total return of 30 percent over five years or one that pays 0.5 percent per month for five years?

5. A financial institution offers you a one-year certificate of deposit with an interest rate of 5 percent. You expect the inflation rate to be 3 percent. What is the real return on your deposit?

6. You decide you would like to retire at age 65, and expect to live until you are 85 (assume there is no chance you will die younger or live longer). You figure that you can live nicely on $50,000 per year.
   a. Describe the calculation you need to make to determine how much you must save to purchase an annuity paying $50,000 per year for the rest of your life. Assume the interest rate is 7 percent.
   b. How would your calculation change if you expected inflation to average 2 percent for the rest of your life?

7. Most businesses replace their computers every two to three years. Assume that a computer costs $2,000 and that it fully depreciates in three years, at which point it has no resale value whatsoever and is thrown away.
   a. If the interest rate for financing the equipment is equal to $i$, show how to compute the minimum cash flow that a computer must generate to be worth the purchase. Your answer will depend on $i$.
   b. How much difference would it make if the computer did not fully depreciate, but still had some value at the time it was replaced? Assuming its resale value is $250, recompute your answer to part a.

   c. What if financing can be had only at a 10 percent interest rate? Recompute your answer to part a.

8. Some friends of yours have just had a child. Thinking ahead, and realizing the power of compound interest, they are considering investing for their child's college or university education, which will begin in 18 years. Assume that the cost of a university education today is $125,000; there is no inflation; and there are no taxes on interest income that is used to pay tuition and expenses.
   a. If the interest rate is 5 percent, how much will your friends need to put into their savings account today to have $125,000 in 18 years?
   b. What if the interest rate is 10 percent?
   c. The chance that the price of a university education will be the same 18 years from now as it is today seems remote. Assuming that the price will rise 3 percent per year, and that today's interest rate is 8 percent, what will your friends' investment need to be?
   d. Return to part a, the case with a 5 percent interest rate and no inflation. Assume that your friends don't have enough financial resources to make the entire investment at the beginning. Instead, they think they will be able to split their investment into two equal parts, one invested immediately and the second invested in five years. Describe how you would compute the required size of the two equal investments, made five years apart.

9. You are considering buying a new house, and have found that a 30-year fixed-rate mortgage for $100,000 is available with an interest rate of 7 percent. This mortgage requires 360 monthly payments of approximately $651 each. If the interest rate rises to 8 percent, what will happen to your monthly payment? Compare the percentage change in the monthly payment with the percentage change in the interest rate.

10.* Use the Fisher equation to explain in detail what a borrower is compensating a lender for when he pays her a nominal rate of interest.

* Indicates more difficult problems.

## Analytical Problems

11. If the current interest rate increases, what would you expect to happen to bond prices? Explain.

12. Which would be most affected in the event of an interest rate increase—the price of a five-year coupon bond that paid coupons only in years 3, 4 and 5 or the price of a five-year coupon bond that paid coupons only in years 1, 2 and 3, everything else being equal? Explain.

13. Under what circumstances might you be willing to pay more than $1,000 for a coupon bond that matures in three years, has a coupon rate of 10 percent and a face value of $1,000?

14.* Approximately how long would it take for an investment of $100 to reach $800 if you earned 5 percent? What if the interest rate were 10 percent? How long would it take an investment of $200 to reach $800 at an interest rate of 5 percent? Why is there a difference between doubling the interest rate and doubling the initial investment?

15. Recently, some lucky person won the lottery in the United States. The lottery winnings were reported to be $85.5 million. In reality, the winner got a choice of $2.85 million per year for 30 years or $46 million today.
    a. Explain briefly why winning $2.85 million per year for 30 years is not equivalent to winning $85.5 million.
    b. The evening news interviews a group of people the day after the winner was announced. When asked, most of them responded that, if they were the lucky winner, they would take the $46 million upfront payment. Suppose that you were that lucky winner. How would you decide between the annual instalments or the upfront payment?

16. You are considering going to graduate school for a one-year master's program. Your research indicates that the master's degree will add $5,000 per year to your salary for the next 10 years of your working life, starting at the end of this year. After the next 10 years, it makes no difference. Completing the master's program will cost you $35,000, which you would have to borrow at an interest rate of 6 percent. How would you decide if this investment in your education is profitable?

17. Assuming the chances of being paid back are the same, would a nominal interest rate of 10 percent always be more attractive to a lender than a nominal rate of 5 percent? Explain.

18.* Suppose two parties agree that the expected inflation rate for the next year is 3 percent. Based on this, they enter into a loan agreement where the nominal interest rate to be charged is 7 percent. If the inflation rate for the year turns out to be 2 percent, who gains and who loses?

# APPENDIX 4

## The Algebra of Present-Value Formulas

In this appendix, we will derive a formula for computing present value. To do it, we need to use some algebra, but the result is worth the trouble. The formula is useful in computing the present value of any series of payments, such as a car loan, a mortgage, or a coupon bond, or for figuring out how long it will take you to pay off a loan. In the spreadsheets, we show you how to do these calculations using the formulas here or by using the built-in formulas.

Imagine that you will buy a house. You would like to borrow $PV$ dollars at interest rate $i$ and agree to make $n$ equal mortgage payments. How large will your payment be? It will be just big enough so that the present value of all your payments, discounted at interest rate $i$, equals the amount of the loan.

To compute the payment, we will use the present-value formula. If we call the size of the monthly payments C, then we need to solve the following formula:

$$PV = \frac{C}{(1+i)^1} + \frac{C}{(1+i)^2} + \frac{C}{(1+i)^3} + \ldots + \frac{C}{(1+i)^n} \qquad \text{(A-1)}$$

Each term in equation (A-1) is the present value of a payment C made on a future date. To simplify (A-1), we multiply it by $[1/(1+i)]$ to get

$$\frac{1}{(1+i)}PV = \frac{1}{(1+i)}\left[\frac{C}{(1+i)^1} + \frac{C}{(1+i)^2} + \frac{C}{(1+i)^3} + \ldots + \frac{C}{(1+i)^n}\right] \text{(A-2)}$$

$$= \frac{C}{(1+i)^2} + \frac{C}{(1+i)^3} + \frac{C}{(1+i)^4} + \ldots + \frac{C}{(1+i)^n} + \frac{C}{(1+i)^{n+1}}$$

Now subtract (A-2) from (A-1):

$$PV - \frac{1}{(1+i)}PV = \frac{C}{(1+i)^1} + \frac{C}{(1+i)^2} + \frac{C}{(1+i)^3} + \ldots + \frac{C}{(1+i)^n} \qquad \text{(A-3)}$$

$$- \frac{C}{(1+i)^2} + \frac{C}{(1+i)^3} + \frac{C}{(1+i)^4} + \ldots + \frac{C}{(1+i)^n} + \frac{C}{(1+i)^{n+1}}$$

to get

$$\frac{i}{(1+i)}PV = \frac{C}{(1+i)^1} - \frac{C}{(1+i)^{n+1}} \qquad \text{(A-4)}$$

Simplifying this result yields the following formula:

$$PV = \left(\frac{C}{i}\right)\left[1 - \frac{1}{(1+i)^n}\right] \qquad \text{(A-5)}$$

www.mcgrawhill.ca/olc/cecchetti

Notice that as the number of payments increases (as $n$ gets bigger), the term $[1/(1 + i)^n]$ grows smaller. If the payments never end, so that $n$ represents infinity, then $[1/(1 + i)^n]$ shrinks to zero. Thus, the present value of a stream of fixed payments that never ends is $[C/i]$.

To see how to use equation (A-5), suppose you're taking out a $100,000 loan that you agree to repay over 30 years at an interest rate of 8 percent. To figure out your annual payment just solve the following equation for C:

$$\$100{,}000 = \left(\frac{C}{.08}\right)\left[1 - \frac{1}{(1 + .08)^{30}}\right] \qquad \text{(A-6)}$$

Simplifying the right-hand side gives us

$$\$100{,}000 = 11.258C \qquad \text{(A-7)}$$

So your annual payment will be $8,882.57. (In reality you would probably be making monthly payments so we can do the same calculation for 360 monthly payments using a monthly interest rate of 0.6434 percent, which annualizes to 8 percent.)

To show how useful equation (A-5) is, we can use it to derive three of the results in this chapter:

**a: Determining the annual payments on a loan (as in Table 4.3 on page 66):**

This just means rearranging equation (A-5) to solve for C given that you know *PV*.

$$C = \frac{PV \times i}{1 - \dfrac{1}{(1 + i)^n}}$$

$$= \frac{PV \times i(1 + i)^n}{(1 + i)^n - 1} \qquad \text{(A-8)}$$

Plugging in the values of $1,000,000 for *PV*, $n = 10$ and $i = 0.05$, you can find that the annual payment would be $129,505. But now you can see exactly how the payment changes if you change the length of time, or the interest rate, or the amount of the loan.

**b: Determining how long it takes to pay off a loan (as in Table 4.4 on page 73):**

This is a little more complex as we need to use logarithms to solve equation (A-5) for *n*. So, first we rearrange equation (A-5) to isolate the term with *n*:

$$\frac{PV \times i}{C} = 1 - \frac{1}{(1 + i)^n}$$

$$\frac{1}{(1 + i)^n} = 1 - \frac{PV \times i}{C}$$

Now invert both sides of this formula:

$$(1 + i)^n = \frac{C}{C - (PV \times i)}$$

And taking logs of both sides:

$$n \log (1 + i) = \log \left[\frac{C}{C - i \times PV}\right]$$

So that finally,

$$n = \frac{log \dfrac{C}{C - i \times PV}}{log(1 + i)} \tag{A-9}$$

Now to see how long it will take you to pay off that credit card debt or student loan, plug in the amount you owe ($PV$) the interest rate, and the amount of each payment (be careful to match the interest rate (annual or monthly) to the payment frequency (annual or monthly).

**c: Determining the amount you will have if you save annually (as on page 60):**

We can combine equation (A-5) with equation (4) to find the expression for future values:

$$FV = \left(\frac{C}{i}\right)[(1 + i)^n - 1] \tag{A-10}$$

When using this equation, it is very important that you know whether the monthly payments are being made at the beginning or end of the month.[4] In our present value examples, we assumed that payments were made at the end of the month. Now we want to assume that payments are made on the first of the month. So we need to add that first payment (with its $n$ years of interest) and then subtract the last payment. Call $FV_b$ the future value when payments are made at the beginning of the period, then

$$FV_b = \left(\frac{C}{i}\right)[(1 + i)^n - 1] + C(1 + i)^n - C$$

$$= \left(\frac{C}{i}\right)[(1 + i)^{n+1} - 1] - C \tag{A-11}$$

So, in the example on page 60, $1,000 put away each year for 40 years and earning 8 percent yields,

$$FV_b = \frac{1000}{.08}\{1.08^{41} - 1\} - 1000$$

$$= \$98,826$$

---

[4] If you use a formula in a spreadsheet program you will have to state whether the payment is at the beginning of the period (the usual default) or the end.

# CHAPTER 5

## Understanding Risk

Risk may be a four-letter word, but it's one we can't avoid. Every day we make decisions that involve financial and economic risk. How much car insurance should we buy? Should we refinance the mortgage now or a year from now? Should we save more for retirement, or spend the extra money on a new car? Making any decision that has more than one possible outcome is similar to gambling: We put the money on the roulette table and take our chances.

Interestingly enough, the tools we use today to measure and analyze risk were first developed to help players analyze games of chance such as roulette and blackjack. For thousands of years, people have played games based on a throw of the dice, but they had little understanding of how those games actually worked. In ancient times, dice of various sorts were used to consult the gods, so any effort to analyze the odds was thought improper. But even those who ignored religious concerns could not correctly analyze a single throw of a die because they did not understand the concept of zero. That meant that the complex computations necessary to develop a theory of probability were impossible.[1]

By the mid-17th century, the power of religion had waned and mathematical tools had developed to the point that people could begin to make sense out of cards, dice, and other games. Since the invention of probability theory, we have come to realize that many everyday events, including those in economics, finance, and even weather forecasting, are best thought of as analogous to the flip of a coin or the throw of a die. For better or worse, we no longer treat these random events as if they were divinely ordained.

Still, while experts can make educated guesses about the future path of interest rates, inflation, or the stock market, their predictions are really only that—guesses. And while meteorologists are fairly good at forecasting the weather a day or two ahead, economists, financial advisors, and business gurus have dismal records. So understanding the possibility of various occurrences should allow everyone to make better choices. While risk cannot be eliminated, it can often be managed effectively.

Finally, while most people view risk as a curse to be avoided whenever possible, risk also creates opportunities. The payoff from a winning bet on one hand of cards can often erase the losses on a losing hand. Thus, the importance of probability theory to the development of modern financial markets is hard to overemphasize. People require compensation for taking risks. Without the capacity to measure risk, we could not calculate a fair price for transferring risk from one person to another, nor could we price stocks and bonds, much less sell insurance. The market for options didn't exist until economists learned how to compute the price of an option using probability theory.

In this chapter, we will learn how to measure risk and assess whether it will increase or decrease. We will also come to understand why changes in risk lead to changes in the demand for particular financial instruments and to corresponding changes in the price of those instruments.

---

[1] For further details on this history, see the extended discussion on the book's Web site at www.mcgrawhill.ca/olc/cecchetti.

# Defining Risk

The dictionary definition of *"risk,"* the "possibility of loss or injury," highlights the perils of putting oneself in a situation in which the outcome is unknown. But this common use of the word doesn't quite fit our purposes because we care about gains as well as losses. We need a definition of risk that focuses on the fact that the outcomes of financial and economic decisions are almost always unknown at the time the decisions are made. Here is the definition we will use:

Risk is a measure of uncertainty about the future payoff to an investment, measured over some time horizon and relative to a benchmark.

This definition has several important elements. First, risk is a *measure* that can be quantified. In comparing two potential investments, we want to know which one is riskier and by how much. All other things held equal, we expect a riskier investment to be less desirable than others and to command a lower price. Uncertainties that are not quantifiable cannot be priced.

Second, risk arises from *uncertainty about the future*. We know that the future will follow one and only one of many possible courses, but we don't know which one. This statement is true of even the simplest random event—more things can happen than will happen. If you flip a coin, it can come up either heads or tails. It cannot come up both heads and tails or neither heads nor tails; only one of two possibilities will occur.

Third, risk has to do with the *future payoff* of an investment, which is unknown. Though we do not know for certain what will happen to our investment, we must be able to list all the possibilities. Imagining all the possible payoffs and the likelihood of each one is a difficult but indispensable part of computing risk.

Fourth, our definition of risk refers to an *investment* or group of investments. We can use the term "investment" very broadly here to include everything from the balance in a bank account to shares of a mutual fund to lottery tickets and real estate.

Fifth, risk must be measured over some *time horizon*. Every investment has a time horizon. We hold some investments for a day or two and others for many years. In most cases, the risk of holding an investment over a short period is smaller than the risk of holding it over a long one, but there are important exceptions to the rule that we will discuss later.[2]

Finally, risk must be measured *relative to a benchmark* rather than in isolation. If someone tells you that an investment is risky, you should immediately ask, "Relative to what?" The simplest answer is "Relative to an investment with no risk at all," called a *risk-free investment*. But there are other possibilities, often more appropriate. For example, in considering the performance of a particular investment advisor or money manager, a good benchmark is the performance of a group of experienced investment advisors or money managers. If you want to know the risk associated with a specific investment strategy, the most appropriate benchmark would be the risk associated with other strategies.

Now that we know what risk is, how do we measure it? We use some rudimentary tools of probability theory, as we will see in the next section.

# Measuring Risk

Armed with our definition of risk, we are now ready to quantify and measure it. In this section we will become familiar with the mathematical concepts useful in thinking about random events. We have already used some of these concepts. Recall from the last chapter that the *real* interest rate equals the *nominal* interest rate minus *expected* inflation. Without the proper tools, we weren't able to be explicit about what the

---

[2] In Chapter 8, we will consider evidence that holding stock for one year is riskier than holding it for 20 years.

term "expected inflation" means. The same is true of the term "expected return." Now we will propose that the best way to think about expected inflation and expected return is as the average or best guess—the *expected value*—of inflation, or the investment's return out of all the possible values.

## Possibilities, Probabilities, and Expected Value

Probability theory tells us that in considering any uncertainty, the first thing we must do is to *list all the possible outcomes* and then *figure out the chance of each one occurring*. When you toss a coin, what are all the *possible* outcomes? There are two and only two. The coin can come down either heads or tails. What is the *chance* of each one of these two outcomes occurring? If the coin is fair, it will come down heads half the time and tails the other half; that's what we mean by *fair*. If we tossed a fair coin over and over again, thousands of times, it would come down heads half the time and tails the other half. But for any individual toss, the coin has an equal chance of coming down heads or tails. To quantify this statement, we can say that the *probability* that the coin will come up heads is one-half.

Probability is a measure of the likelihood that an event will occur. It is always expressed as a number between zero and one. The closer the probability is to zero, the *less* likely it is that an event will occur. If the probability is exactly zero, we are sure that the event will *not* happen. The closer the probability is to one, the *more* likely it is that an event will occur. If the probability is exactly one, the event *will* definitely occur.

Some people prefer to think of random outcomes in terms of frequencies rather than probabilities. Instead of saying that the probability of a coin coming down heads is one-half, we could say that the coin will come down heads once every two tosses on average. Probabilities can always be converted into frequencies in this way.

To grasp these concepts, it is helpful to construct a table. The table lists everything that can happen (all the possibilities) together with their chances of occurring (their probabilities). Let's start with a single coin toss. Table 5.1 lists the possibilities—heads or tails—and the probabilities, both equal to one-half.

In constructing a table like this one, we must be careful to list *all* possible outcomes. In the case of a coin toss, we know that the coin can come down only two ways, heads or tails. We know that one of these outcomes *must* occur. We just don't know which one.

One important property of probabilities is that we can compute the chance that one *or* the other event will happen by adding the probabilities together. In the case of the coin flip there are only two possibilities; the probability that the coin will come up either heads or tails must be one. If the table is constructed correctly, then, *the values in the probabilities column will sum to one.*

Let's move from a coin toss to something a bit more complicated: an investment that can rise or fall in value. Assume that for $1,000 you can purchase a stock whose value is equally likely to fall to $700 or rise to $1,400. We'll refer to the amount you could get back as the investment's **payoff**. Following the procedure we used to analyze the coin toss, we can construct Table 5.2. Again we list the possibilities and the probability that each will occur, but we add their payoffs (column 3).[3]

**Table 5.1** A Simple Example: All Possible Outcomes of a Single Coin Toss

| Possibilities | Probability | Outcome |
|---|---|---|
| #1 | $\frac{1}{2}$ | Heads |
| #2 | $\frac{1}{2}$ | Tails |

[3] As you go through the examples in the chapter, be aware that it is often very difficult to estimate the probabilities needed to do the risk computations. The best way to do it is often to look at history. Investment analysts usually estimate the possibilities and probabilities from what happened in the past.

## APPLYING THE CONCEPT
### IT'S NOT JUST EXPECTED RETURN THAT MATTERS

Your life seems to be going well. You enjoy your job, and it pays enough that you can put a little aside each month. You can't resist the dollar-for-dollar match your employer is offering on contributions to your retirement account, so you're slowly building up some long-term savings. But every so often, you wonder if you're saving enough. One day you go home and fire up the financial planning program on your computer, just to check.

Going through the retirement planner, you enter all the standard information: your age now and when you hope to retire; your salary and the value of all your assets; the monthly contribution to your retirement account; and the monthly income you want at retirement. When you finish, the program asks what rate of return to assume. That is, how fast do you expect your savings to grow from now until your retirement? Following the suggestion on the screen and adjusting for inflation, you enter 7 percent.* The light flashes green, signalling that you're on track to meet your financial goals. But are you?

Maybe. The program did a series of future- and present-value calculations like the ones described in Applying the Concept: Early Retirement on page 67. The green light means that if the assumptions you entered are valid, your saving rate is sufficient. That is, *if* your savings grow at 7 percent (adjusted for inflation), you'll be okay. So you need to decide whether you think 7 percent is a reasonable number. The program suggested 7 percent because it was the average real rate of return in the stock market from 1930 to 2006. But between 2006 and 2009 the stock market fell by about 30 percent. If you had been saving for your retirement from 1980 to 2009 (like so many of the baby boomers) your real rate of return would have been closer to 4 percent. What if your investment return is only 4 percent per year? Over 40 years that's an enormous difference. At 7 percent annual growth, one dollar today is worth nearly $15 in 40 years, and if you can save $1,000 per year you'll have over $200,000 saved up. Reducing the growth rate to 4 percent means that the future value of one dollar today 40 years from now falls to less than $5. The lower return means that with the same $1,000 per year savings, you're left with less than $100,000 after 40 years.† You'll have to save twice as much to meet the same goal. Now that's risk!

You need to know what the possibilities are and how likely each one is. Only then can you assess whether your retirement savings plan is risky or not.

* Inflation complicates computations over very long time periods. Price increases of 2 or 3 percent per year may not seem like much, but over 40 years they add up. At 2 percent inflation, prices double every 36 years. The simplest approach is to ignore inflation and measure income, wealth, and savings in current dollars. Then use a real rate of interest to compute future and present value.

† These numbers are based on future-value calculations. If you save $1,000 per year, after 40 years you will have $1,000 \times (1.07)^{40} + $1,000 \times (1.07)^{39} + \ldots + $1,000 \times (1.07)^{2} + $1,000 \times (1.07) = $213,610. Or you can use the formula in the appendix of Chapter 4 (for $FV_b$).

We can now go a step further and compute what is called the expected value of the investment. We are familiar with the idea of expected value as the average or most likely outcome. The expected value is also known as the mean. After listing all of the possible outcomes and the probabilities that they will occur, we compute the expected value as the sum of their probabilities times their payoffs. (Another way to say this is that the expected value is the probability-weighted sum of the possible outcomes.)

Computing the expected value of the investment is straightforward. In Table 5.2, the first step is to take the probabilities in the second column and multiply them by their associated payoffs in the third column. The results are in the fourth column.

**Table 5.2**  Investing $1,000: Case 1

| Possibilities | Probability | Payoff | Payoff × Probability |
|---|---|---|---|
| #1 | $\frac{1}{2}$ | $700 | $350 |
| #2 | $\frac{1}{2}$ | $1,400 | $700 |

Expected Value = Sum of (Probability times Payoff) = $1,050

Summing them, we get

$$\text{Expected value} = \frac{1}{2}\,(\$700) + \frac{1}{2}\,(\$1{,}400) = \$1{,}050$$

which appears at the bottom of the table.

The expected value of an investment is a very useful concept, but it can be difficult at first. The problem is that if we make this investment only once, we will obtain either $700 or $1,400, not $1,050. In fact, regardless of the number of times we make this particular investment, the payoff will *never* be $1,050. But what would happen if we were to make this investment 1 million times? About 500,000 of those times the investment would pay off $1,400 and the other 500,000 times it would pay off $700. (Notice that we just converted the probabilities into frequencies.) So the *average* pay-off from the 1 million investments would be

$$\frac{1}{1{,}000{,}000}\,[(500{,}000 \times \$700) + (500{,}000 \times \$1{,}400)] = \$1{,}050\ (\textit{the expected value})$$

While the world of casino gambling may offer simple bets with just two outcomes, the financial world rarely does. To make the example more realistic, let's double the number of possibilities and look at a case in which the $1,000 investment might pay off $100 or $2,000 in addition to $700 or $1,400. Table 5.3 shows the possibilities, probabilities, and payoffs. We'll assume that the two original possibilities are the most likely; the two new possibilities are much less likely to occur. Note that the probabilities, as always, sum to one: $0.1 + 0.4 + 0.4 + 0.1 = 1$. Again, we could convert the probabilities to frequencies, so that 0.4 means 4 out of 10. And again, we can compute the expected value by multiplying each probability times its associated payoff and then summing them. So the expected value is

$$\text{Expected value} = \frac{1}{10}\,\$100 + \frac{4}{10}\,\$700 + \frac{4}{10}\,\$1{,}400 + \frac{1}{10}\,\$2{,}000 = \$1{,}050$$

Once again the expected value is $1,050.

We can generalize the calculation of expected value using some algebra, which will help you to calculate the expected value of more complex investments, and will be helpful as we develop measures of risk. We'll denote the investment payoff by y and allow for the possibility of n different payoffs. The probability of each $y_i$ is $p_i$. So we can write

$$E(y) = p_1 y_1 + p_2 y_2 + \ldots + p_n y_n$$

$$= \sum_{i=1}^{n} p_i y_i \qquad\qquad (1)$$

**Table 5.3**  Investing $1,000: Case 2

| Possibilities | Probability | Payoff | Payoff × Probability |
|:---:|:---:|:---:|:---:|
| #1 | 0.1 | $100 | 10 |
| #2 | 0.4 | $700 | 280 |
| #3 | 0.4 | $1,400 | 560 |
| #4 | 0.1 | $2,000 | 200 |
| Expected Value = Sum of (Probability times Payoff) = $1,050 | | | |

Because the expected value of this $1,000 investment is $1,050, the expected gain is $50. But most people don't discuss investment payoffs in terms of dollars; instead, they talk about the percentage return. Expressing the return as a percentage allows investors to compute the gain or loss on the investment regardless of the size of the initial investment. In this case, the expected return is $50 on a $1,000 investment, or 5 percent. Note that the two $1,000 investments we just discussed are not distinguishable by their expected return, which is 5 percent in both cases. Does that mean an investor would be indifferent between them? Even a casual glance suggests that the answer is no because the second investment has a wider range of payoffs than the first. The highest payoff is higher and the lowest payoff lower than for the first investment. So the two investments carry different levels of risk. The next section discusses measures of risk.

One last word on expected values. Recall from the last chapter that to compute the real interest rate, we need a measure of *expected inflation*. One way to calculate expected inflation is to use the technique we just learned. That is, list all the possibilities for inflation, assign each one a probability, and then calculate the expected value of inflation.

## Measures of Risk

Most of us have an intuitive sense of risk and its measurement. For example, we know that walking on a sidewalk is usually a safe activity. But imagine that one day as you are strolling along, you come upon a three-foot hole in the sidewalk. The only way across is to jump over it. If the hole is just a few inches deep, it won't stop you. But the deeper it is, the greater the risk of jumping across because the greater the range of injuries you could sustain. We all have an intuitive sense that the wider the range of outcomes, the greater the risk. That's why the investment that has four possible payoffs (Table 5.3) seems riskier than the one with two possible payoffs (Table 5.2).

Thinking about risk in terms of the range of possible outcomes is straightforward. The best way to do it is to start with something that has no risk at all—a sidewalk without a hole in it or an investment with only one possible payoff. We will refer to a financial instrument with no risk at all as a risk-free investment or risk-free asset. A **risk-free asset** *is an investment whose future value is known with certainty and whose return is the* **risk-free rate of return**.[4] The payoff that you will receive from such an investment is guaranteed and cannot vary. For instance, if the risk-free return is 5 percent, a $1,000 risk-free investment will pay $1,050, its expected value, with certainty. If there is a chance that the payoff will be either more or less than $1,050, the investment is risky.

Let's compare this risk-free investment with the first investment we looked at, the one in which $1,000 had an equal chance of turning into $1,400 or $700 (see Table 5.2). That investment had the same expected return as the risk-free investment, 5 percent. The difference is that the payoff wasn't certain, so risk was involved. What caused the risk was the increase in the spread of the potential payoffs. The larger the spread, the higher the risk.

*"Come on, Louis. No risk, no reward."*

---

[4] In most financial markets, no truly risk-free asset exists, so the risk-free rate of return is not directly observable. Regardless of our inability to measure it exactly, the risk-free rate of return remains a useful concept.

These examples suggest that we can measure risk by quantifying the spread among an investment's possible outcomes. We will look at two such measures. The first is based on a statistical concept called the *standard deviation* and is strictly a measure of spread. The second, called *value at risk*, is a measure of the riskiness of the worst case. When the hole in the sidewalk gets deep enough, you risk being killed if you fall in.

### Variance and Standard Deviation

The **variance** is defined as the sum of the squared deviations of the possible outcomes from their expected value, weighted by their probabilities. We square the differences from the expected value so that high and low payoffs don't cancel each other out and we get a measure of how spread out they are. After calculating the variance we can derive the **standard deviation**, which is the (positive) square root of the variance. The standard deviation is more useful than the variance because it is measured in the same unit as the payoffs: dollars. (Variance is measured in dollars squared.)

It takes several steps to compute the variance and standard deviation of an investment. First, compute the expected value. Then find the Variance by (a) subtracting the expected value from each of the possible payoffs, (b) squaring each one of the results, and (c) multiplying each result by its probability and adding up the results. Finally, compute the standard deviation by taking the square root of the variance.

In the example of the $1,000 investment that pays either $700 or $1,400, the steps are:

1. Compute the expected value: $\frac{1}{2}$ ($1,400) + $\frac{1}{2}$ ($700) = $1,050
2. Compute the variance:
   (a) subtract the expected value from each of the possible payoffs;
   $1,400 − $1,050 = +$350
   $700 − $1,050 = −$350
   (b) square the results:
   $350^2 = 122,500(\text{dollars})^2$ and $(−$350)^2 = 122,500(\text{dollars})^2$
   (c) multiply each result times its probability and add up the results:

   $$\frac{1}{2} [122,500(\text{dollars})^2] + \frac{1}{2} [122,500(\text{dollars})^2] = 122,500(\text{dollars})^2$$

   We can write our procedure more compactly as

   $$\text{Variance} = \frac{1}{2}(\$1,400 − \$1,050)^2 + \frac{1}{2}(\$700 − \$1,050)^2 = 122,500(\text{dollars})^2$$

3. Compute the standard deviation, which is the (positive) square root of the variance:

   $$\text{Standard deviation} = \sqrt{\text{Variance}} = \sqrt{122,500 \text{ dollars}^2} = \$350$$

We can convert the standard deviation into a percentage of the initial investment of $1,000, or 35 percent. This calculation provides a baseline against which we can measure the risk of alternative investments. Given a choice between two investments with the same expected payoff, most people would choose the one with the lower standard deviation. A higher-risk investment would be less desirable.

Let's compare this two-payoff investment with the one that has four possible payoffs. We already concluded that the second investment is riskier, since the payoffs are more spread out. But how much riskier is it? To answer this question, we can compute the standard deviation. That means following the four steps to calculate the variance,

# YOUR FINANCIAL WORLD
Choosing the Right Amount of Car Insurance

Car insurance is expensive, especially for young drivers. That should be no surprise, since the younger you are, the more likely you are to have an accident. Only about one in seven drivers is under 25 years old, but more than one quarter of the 10 million accidents that happen each year involve a driver between 16 and 24. Men are worse risks than women. It's hard to fault insurance companies for charging higher premiums to drivers who are more likely than others to file claims.

While you must have some insurance—most provinces require that you have *liability insurance*, to pay for damage and injuries to others if you cause an accident—you do have some choices. The most important choice is whether or not to buy collision insurance, which pays for damage to your car when the accident is your fault. If you go without it, you'll have to pay for the repairs if you cause a crash.

There is no easy way to figure out how much collision insurance to buy, but there are a few things to think about when you make your decision. First, how much is your car worth? If you do have an accident, the insurance company doesn't promise to fix your car regardless of the costs. Instead, the company will pay you what it is worth.

So if your car is old and you crash, the odds are you'll get a cheque, not a repaired car. Buying collision insurance on old cars is rarely worth it.

What should you do if you have a new car? Here the question is not whether to buy collision insurance but how much. The choice is in something called a *deductible*, the amount you pay for the repair after a crash. If you have a $250 deductible, you'll pay the first $250 and the insurance company will pay the rest. The higher your deductible is, the lower your insurance premium will be.

To see how much your premium can vary, let's look at an example: a 19-year-old male British Columbian driving a new Mazda (a four-door sedan that cost around $15,000 in 2009). A college student living away from home, he has a good driving record and a good student discount. With a $300 collision deductible, his insurance costs about $3,200 per year. Raising the deductible to $1,000 would lower the premium by $500 per year, to around $2,700. Can $700 worth of extra insurance possibly be worth paying an extra $500 a year? Only if the driver expects to have an accident once every 17 months. Ideally he won't, so the extra insurance isn't worth paying for.

and then taking the square root. From the detailed computation in Table 5.4 on page 90 you can see the standard deviation is $528. This is one and one-half times the $350 standard deviation of the first investment, with only two possible payoffs. Since the two investments have the same expected value, the vast majority of people would prefer the first. The greater the standard deviation, the higher the risk.

To see this conclusion graphically, start with Case 1 from Table 5.2 on page 85 where a $1,000 investment is equally likely to rise in value to $1,400 or fall in value to $700. That is, there are two possibilities, each with probability ½: $700 and $1,400. We can plot this on a bar graph, where the horizontal axis has the payoffs $700 or $1,400 and the height of each bar is the probability (in this case 0.5 for both). The result is in the left panel of Figure 5.1 on page 91. Recall from Table 5.2 that the expected value of this investment is $1,050, the vertical line in the figure.

Compare this to Case 2 from Table 5.3. Recall that in this case, the $1,000 investment has four possible payoffs, $100, $700, $1,400 and $2,000; and these occur with probability 0.1, 0.4, 0.4, and 0.1. As in Case 1, the expected value continues to be $1,050. Using the same method as before, where the height of each bar represents the probability of each outcome, we can plot the right-hand panel of Figure 5.1. Comparing the two figures, we can see that in Case 2, where the investment has four possible payoffs, the distribution is more spread out. This matches the result from computing the standard deviation. *The more spread out the distribution of possible payoffs from an investment, the higher the standard deviation and the bigger the risk.*

| **Table 5.4** | Expected Value, Variance, and Standard Deviation |

Again we can use algebra to define the variance and standard deviation more generally. Using the notation in the text for the case where there are $n$ possible payoffs of $y_i$ each with probability $p_i$,

$$E(y) = \sum_{i=1}^{n} p_i y_i$$

Our definition of variance is

$$Var(y) = p_1(y_1 - E(y))^{2+} p_2(y_2 - E(y))^2 + \dots + p_n(y_n - E(y))^2$$
$$= \sum_{i=1}^{n} p_i(y_i - E(y))^2 \tag{2}$$

And the standard deviation of $y$ is

$$sd(y) = \sqrt{Var(y)}$$

We can use these formulas to compute the expected value, variance, and standard deviation of the four-payoff investment in Table 5.3:

Here's the information we need:

| Probability | Payoff | Payoff − Expected Value | (Payoff − Expected Value)$^2$ |
|---|---|---|---|
| 0.1 | $100 | ($100 − $1,050) = −$950 | 902,500 (dollars)$^2$ |
| 0.4 | $700 | ($700 − $1,050) = −$350 | 122,500 (dollars)$^2$ |
| 0.4 | $1,400 | ($1,400 − $1,050) = +$350 | 122,500 (dollars)$^2$ |
| 0.1 | $2,000 | ($2,000 − $1,050) = +$950 | 902,500 (dollars)$^2$ |

1. Using columns 1 and 2, we can compute the expected value:

   Expected Value = Sum of (Probability times Payoff)

   = 0.1 × $100 + 0.4 × $700 + 0.4 × $1,400 + 0.1 × $2,000

   = $10 + $280 + $560 + $200

   = $1,050

2. Using column 4, we can compute the variance:

   Variance = Sum of (Probability × Squared Difference between the Payoff and Expected Value)

   = 0.1 × 902,500 + 0.4 × 122,500 + 0.4 × 122,500 + 0.1 × 902,500

   = 278,500 (dollars)$^2$

3. Finally, using this result, we can compute the standard deviation:

   Standard deviation = $\sqrt{\text{Variance}}$

   = $\sqrt{278,500 \text{ dollars}^2}$

   = $528

**Value at Risk**   Standard deviation is the most common measure of financial risk, and for most purposes it is adequate. But in some circumstances we need to take a different approach to the measurement of risk. Sometimes we are less concerned with the spread of possible outcomes than with the value of the worst outcome. For example, no one wants a bank to close its doors. Nor is anyone interested in a discount price for a life insurance policy from an insurance company that is in poor financial condition. Neither the customers nor the government regulators care how well or how badly a financial

**Figure 5.1**   Investing $1,000

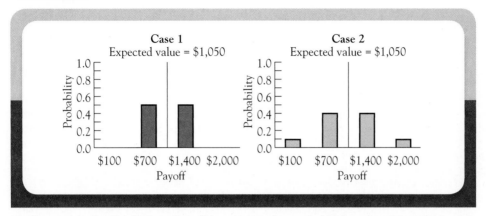

The figure plots the distribution of possible outcomes from a $1,000 investment from Tables 5.2 and 5.3 on pages 85 and 86. In each case, the payoff is on the horizontal axis and the height of each bar equals the probability that outcome will occur.

institution's shareholders fare, so long as they do well enough to keep the doors open. The concept used to assess this sort of risk is called **value at risk (VaR).**

To understand how value at risk works, let's look at an example. Assume you are considering buying a house. In going through your finances, you conclude that you can afford a monthly mortgage payment of $1,400 and no more. You find a nice house and a mortgage lender that will lend you $200,000 to buy it. But you need to decide on the type of mortgage to get. One of your choices is how long to lock in your payments. Should it have a short or long term? The answer is different for different people. But let's see if we can organize our thinking.

Assume that the current interest rate on a 5-year fixed-rate mortgage with a 25-year amortization (the most popular kind) is 6.75 percent, so it has monthly payments around $1,370, which is within your budget. One alternative is a mortgage with the same 25-year amortization period but that fixes the payments for only one year. The one-year mortgage rate is 5.6 percent and so your monthly payment would be $1,230.

Remember Core Principle 2: Risk requires compensation. By taking the one-year mortgage, you can save nearly $150 per month. But after one year, rates could go up or down. That's a risk. Which mortgage should you sign up for?

The lower initial monthly payments do seem to come with higher risk. Without doing any computations, we know that the standard deviation of monthly payments for a 6½ percent five-year mortgage is zero, and that the standard deviation of the payment for the one-year mortgage is greater than zero. Let's just suppose that there is an equal probability of interest rates going up and down, so the expected value of the monthly payments in the second circumstance is still $1,230. But what does that tell us?

The computation of the expected value and standard deviation does not seem to get at the heart of the problem. The reason is that it doesn't take proper account of the worst case. Interest rates could rise a lot during the year and when you have to renew the mortgage your monthly payments might have shot up. How can we get an estimate of that risk? Since 1992, interest rates have been above 9.7% about 10% of the time. So, if history is our guide (we'll develop some other guides later in the book) there is a 10% chance that after one year rates will rise to a level where the monthly payment is $1,750. You wouldn't be able to afford the payment. That's the risk.

# TOOLS OF THE TRADE
The Impact of Leverage on Risk

"Leverage not so sweet on the downside" read a headline in *The Globe and Mail* in October 2008 as the financial world reeled during the liquidity crisis. What is leverage, and how does it affect risk and return? **Leverage** is the practice of borrowing to finance part of an investment. Common examples of leverage are borrowing to buy stock (through what is called *margin loans*), corporate borrowing (using bonds), and borrowing to acquire a house (by obtaining a mortgage). In the case of a margin loan, an investor borrows from a brokerage firm to increase the quantity of stock purchased.

To understand the effects of leverage, let's look at an investment of $1,000 with an expected return of 5 percent (a gain of $50) and a standard deviation of 35 percent ($350). That's the example in Table 5.2 on page 85. What if in addition to investing $1,000 of your own, you borrow $1,000 and invest a total of $2,000? This investment strategy changes the risk involved. The reason is that the lender wants to be repaid the $1,000 loan regardless of how much your investment returns. If the investment's payoff is high, your $2,000 investment will increase in value to $2,800. After repaying the $1,000 loan, you will be left with $1,800—an increase of $800 over your initial investment of $1,000. If your investment falls in value, the $2,000 will become $1,400. After repaying the $1,000 loan, you will be left with $400—a loss of $600.

Since these two results are equally likely, the expected value of your leveraged investment is $\frac{1}{2}(\$1,800) + \frac{1}{2}(\$400) = \$1,100$. Your expected gain—the difference between your investment of $1,000 and its expected value of $1,100—is now $100 and your expected return is 10 percent. That's double the expected return from your investment of $1,000 without any borrowing—double what it would be without leverage. So we have part of the answer to our question: *Leverage increases the expected return.*

But what about risk? To figure it out, let's calculate the standard deviation of your leveraged investment.

$$\text{St.dev.} = \sqrt{\tfrac{1}{2}(1,800 - 1,100)^2 + \tfrac{1}{2}(400 - 1,100)^2} = \$700$$

The standard deviation has doubled: *twice the expected return at twice the risk!*

We can repeat these calculations for any amount of leverage we want. For example, homebuyers commonly pay 20 percent of the price of a house with their savings and borrow the remaining 80 percent. Since mortgage lenders expect to be repaid, changes in the price of the house become gains or losses to the owner. Say you buy a $100,000 house by borrowing $80,000 and paying $20,000 from your savings, often called your *equity*. A 10 percent increase in your home's value would raise the price to $110,000. Subtracting the $80,000 you borrowed, your $20,000 down payment would become $30,000, a 50 percent increase. On the other hand, if your home's value fell by 10 percent, you would *lose* half your $20,000 down payment. *Leverage magnifies the effect of price changes* (see Figure 5.2).

| Figure 5.2 | The Effect of Leverage on Risk and Return |
|---|---|

To understand leverage, picture a set of two gears, one large and one small. The movement in the price of the leveraged investment is measured by the number of revolutions in the big gear. The investor's risk and return are measured by the number of revolutions in the small gear. The bigger the big gear, the more times the small gear goes around with each revolution of the big gear. That's leverage.

This mortgage example highlights the fact that sometimes risk should be measured by the value of the worst case rather than by expected value and standard deviation. Value at risk, which measures risk as the maximum potential loss, is more appropriate in the example we just studied. VaR is the answer to the question, How much will I lose if the worst possible scenario occurs? In the example of the $1,000 investment, summarized in Table 5.2 on page 85, the worst case was a loss of $300. In

## The Impact of Leverage

| | No Leverage | Leverage Ratio = 2 |
|---|---|---|
| Your Investment | $1,000 | $1,000 |
| + Amount Borrowed | 0 | $1,000 |
| = Total Invested | $1,000 | $2,000 |
| Possible Payoffs | $1,400 or $700 | $2,800 or $1,400 |
| Net of repayment | $1,400 or $700 | $1,800 or $400 |
| Expected Value (net of repayment) | $1,050 (5%) | $1,100 (10%) |
| Standard Deviation | $350 (35%) | $700 (70%) |

The example uses the information from Table 5.2 where a $1,000 investment has an equal probability of a $1,400 and a $700 payoff. In the example with leverage on the right, the investor borrows $1,000, invests a total of $2,000, obtains a payoff of either $2,800 or $1,400, and must repay the $1,000 loan for a net payoff $1,800 or $400.

We can use these examples to develop a formula for the impact of leverage on the expected return and standard deviation of an investment. If you borrow to purchase an asset, you increase both the expected return and the standard deviation by a leverage ratio of

$$\text{Leverage ratio} = \frac{\text{Cost of investment}}{\text{Owner's contribution to the purchase}}$$

where the "Owner's contribution to the purchase" in the denominator is just the cost of investment minus the amount borrowed. If the expected return and standard deviation of the unleveraged investment are 5 percent and 35 percent (as in our first example), then borrowing half and contributing half means that for each dollar invested, the buyer is contributing 50 cents. The formula tells us that the leverage ratio is 1/0.5, which equals 2. Thus the investment's expected return is 2 × 5 percent = 10 percent, and its standard deviation is 2 × 35 percent = 70 percent. (See the tabular presentation above.) And if the homeowner borrows 80 percent of the purchase price of the house, his or her contribution is 20 percent, so the leverage ratio is 1/(1 − 80/100) = 1/0.2 = 5 times what it would be for someone who could buy the house outright, with no mortgage.*

We have focused on the impact of leverage on risk, but leverage has at least as big an impact on value at risk. Note that for the $1,000 investment without leverage in Table 5.2, the worst case was a loss of $300, or 30 percent, half the time. If an investor borrowed 90 percent of the funds needed to make the investment, half the time the investor would lose not only the entire $100 invested but an additional $200 of borrowed funds as well. *Leverage compounds the worst possible outcome.*

As *The Globe and Mail* headline pointed out, leverage is great when returns are positive, but "not so sweet" when they are negative. As we will see in later chapters, bank regulators restrict the amount of leverage that banks can have, but in 2007-08, many non-bank financial institutions were highly leveraged; the bad outcome was very bad for them as well as for many others.

* The leverage ratio is very closely related to the debt–equity ratio. Using balance-sheet language, the cost of investment is the Assets, the Owner's contribution is Equity, and Assets minus equity is Debt. So, the debt-equity ratio is the leverage ratio −1.

the more complex $1,000 investment, summarized in Table 5.3 on page 86, the VaR was $900—the most you could possibly lose. In the mortgage example, the VaR is the house: If the payment increases to $1,750 a month, you can't make the payments on your loan and you will be forced to sell the house. There are surely cases where the lower payments of a short-term mortgage are worth the risk, but this may not be one of them.

## APPLYING THE CONCEPT
### THE PROS AND CONS OF VaR MODELS

Value at risk (VaR) models were first popularized in the early 1990s as a tool to help management of financial firms understand and manage risk. An $x million VaR tells management that there is a 95 percent (or sometimes 99 percent) probability that losses will be less than $x million over a period of time, such as a month. The models have a number of advantages: first, because the answer is a given number of dollars, they quantify risk, and that quantity can then be compared to the capital of the firm. Second, they also can be used at many levels—an individual trader is given a VaR, but so is the overall firm. The firm's VaR incorporates all the risk spreading and hedging by the different traders.

However, VaR models also have their limitations. First, they don't capture the extent of the bad event that occurs 5 percent or 1 percent of the time. For a monthly VaR model with a 95 percent probability, the bad event will likely occur every 20 months. Suppose you have a $100 million monthly VaR at 95 percent. Then you are likely to lose more than $100 million every 20 months. The model doesn't say whether you are likely to lose $101 million or $1 billion, yet surely that is important. Even more challenging is that if traders are rewarded on the basis of their returns for a given VaR, they can "game" the VaR. An asset with a less than 1 percent (for a 99 percent VaR) loss doesn't hurt the VaR even though it could add to the portfolio's risk, so traders would invest in assets such as credit default swaps.

A second limitation of VaR models is their use of only a short span of data to condition the model (this is a limitation of how they are used rather than of VaR models per se). For example, mortgage-backed securities risks were often measured over only the most recent two or five years, years when house prices were rising. When U.S. house prices began to fall, the VaR suddenly shot up. In addition, in 2007–08 the correlation between the values of different assets turned out to be much higher than the models had predicted, so that spreading the risk had not reduced variance or VaR as much as expected. When asset holders realized how risky their portfolios were, the risk premium on financial assets went up, and (since yields and prices are the inverse of each other) asset prices went down.*

*To learn more about VaR models and the financial crisis read Joe Nocera, "Risk Mismanagement," The New York Times Magazine, January 2, 2009.

A more sophisticated VaR analysis would include a time horizon and probabilities. In fact, the formal definition of VaR is *the worst possible loss over a specific time horizon, at a given probability*. For the mortgage example, the time horizon is the one year over which the interest rate can move, and the probability that the worst case will actually occur is 10 percent. VaR is a measure of risk that we will find very useful in discussing the management and regulation of financial institutions. By restricting the sorts of financial instruments banks can hold, bank managers and financial regulators ensure that financial collapse is an extremely remote possibility, and to do it they employ the concept of VaR.

## Risk Aversion, the Risk Premium, and the Risk–Return Tradeoff

The implication of our discussion so far is that most people don't like risk and will pay to avoid it. While some people enjoy risky activities like skydiving and car racing, most of us are more careful. And while some people gamble large sums, most of us don't because we can't sustain large losses comfortably. In fact, the reason we buy insurance is that we want someone else to take the risk. Insurance is an interesting case; remember, for an insurance company to make a profit, it must charge more than it expects to pay out. Thus, insurance premiums are higher than the expected value of the policyholder's losses. We pay to avoid risks because most of us are *risk averse*.

Basic economic theory can help us understand the concept and measurement of risk aversion. In your first Economics course you probably learned that economists use utility theory and the principle of diminishing marginal utility to capture how consumers make choices. The principle of **diminishing marginal utility** says that while a consumer may get more satisfaction ("utility") from having more of a good, the extra satisfaction from consuming another unit is smaller the more units you already have. We can use this principle to understand how investors choose which assets to buy and how much to pay for them.

Figure 5.3 shows the utility or satisfaction that an investor gets from a given level of wealth; the upward slope says more wealth is better than less, but the gradually decreasing slope reflects the smaller gain in utility from an extra dollar of wealth if you are already wealthy. Now, suppose that our investor

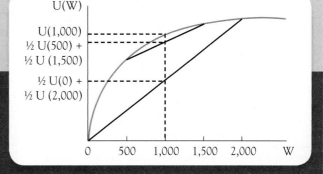

**Figure 5.3**   The Cost of Risk

When investors maximize expected utility they prefer a safe investment to a risky one.

wants to maximize the expected utility of wealth. The principle of diminishing marginal utility implies that he or she will be risk averse. Why? Let's define a **risk-averse investor** as one who prefers a given amount for sure over an uncertain amount with the same expected value. (A **risk-neutral investor** is someone who cares only about the expected returns and doesn't mind if there is risk—he or she would have a linear utility of wealth curve).

Suppose that an investor is offered a choice between (1) $1,000 for sure or (2) a coin toss where if the coin comes up tails they get $1,500 and if it comes up heads they get $500. In expected value terms the two choices are the same. Which would our investor prefer? The expected utility from the coin toss is [0.5U(500) + 0.5U(1500)], and looking at Figure 5.3 we can see that this is less than U(1,000). If the consumer is maximizing her expected utility, she will be risk averse.[5]

We can define the **risk premium** as the amount that you would have to pay an investor to make her equally content between the risky and the risk-free option. In Figure 5.3, this would be {U(1,000) − [0.5U(500) +.5U(1,500)]}. Notice what happens if we increase the risk by changing the bet from 500 or 1,500 to 0 to 2,000. You would have to pay the consumer more to take this riskier bet. In general, the riskier the investment, the higher the risk premium. By extension, if riskier investments have higher risk premiums, they must have higher expected returns. Thus, there is a tradeoff between risk and expected return; you can't get a high return without taking considerable risk. So if someone tells you he or she made a big return on an investment, you should suspect that it was a very risky investment. No risk, no reward!

To see how the idea of a risk premium works, take the case of a bond. We will study this in much more detail in chapters 6 and 7, but for now let's compare bonds issued by DaimlerChrysler Financing Company with those of Scotiabank. Scotiabank is in very good financial condition, while DaimlerChrysler is not. That leads us to expect that the return to holding Chrysler's bonds will contain a higher risk premium. And

---

[5] You will probably notice that this simple model implies that no one would buy a lottery ticket as the risk premium is negative for a lottery ticket. Some economists argue that the return to buying lottery tickets includes entertainment value. Others, that individual preferences are somewhat asymmetric and that a small negative can be more than offset by a small chance of a very large positive event. Behavioural models, described in Chapter 9, try to capture both the frequently observed purchases of insurance and risk premiums, and the demand for gambling.

**"I'm sorry, but you don't get frequent flyer miles for regularly investing in high risk securities."**

it does. In the fall of 2008, the two companies had coupon bonds with one year to maturity. Scotiabank's bond paid 2.6 percent while Daimler Chrysler's paid 11.50 percent. Meanwhile, a Canadian Treasury bill of the same maturity had an interest rate of 1.3% percent. Since the Treasury bill is certain to pay, we'll use that as our estimate of the risk-free rate. So, to get an estimate of the risk premium for the Scotiabank and Chrysler bonds, we need to subtract 1.3 from each: For Scotiabank, the result is 2.6 − 1.3 = 1.3 percent; for DaimlerChrysler, we get 11.5 − 1.3 = 10.2 percent. Not surprisingly, the risk premium on the relatively risky company is much bigger—in this case, eight times bigger!

## Sources of Risk: Idiosyncratic and Systematic Risk

Risk is everywhere. It comes in many forms and from almost every imaginable place. In most circumstances the sources of risk are obvious. For drivers, it's the risk of an accident; for farmers, the risk of bad weather; for investors, the risk of fluctuating stock prices. Regardless of the source, however, we can classify all risks into one of two groups: (1) those affecting a small number of people but no one else and (2) those affecting everyone. We'll call the first of these idiosyncratic or unique risks and the second systematic or economywide risks.[6]

To understand the difference between idiosyncratic and systematic risk, think about the risks facing WestJet stockholders. Why would the value of WestJet's stock go up or down? There are two main reasons. First, there is the risk that WestJet will lose sales to other airlines. Air Canada and new airlines such as Porter Air are working every day to take away some of WestJet's business. So WestJet may do poorly compared to its competition, and its market share may shrink (see Figure 5.4). This risk is unique to WestJet because if WestJet does poorly, another company must be doing better than usual. Idiosyncratic risk affects specific firms, not everyone.

The second risk WestJet's stockholders face is that the entire airline industry will do poorly (see Figure 5.4). This is systematic, economy-wide risk. If we think of idiosyncratic risk as a change in the *share* of the airline pie, systematic risk is a change in the *size* of the pie. In other words, systematic risk is the risk that everyone will do poorly at the same time. The entire economy could slow for reasons that are completely unrelated to any individual company's performance. Macroeconomic factors, such as swings in consumer and business confidence brought on by global economic conditions or changes in the political climate, are the source of systematic risks that affect *all* firms and individuals in the entire economy.

Idiosyncratic risks come in two types. In the first, one set of firms is affected in one way and other firms

**Figure 5.4**    **Idiosyncratic and Systematic Risk**

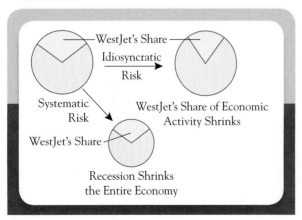

[6] These are also sometimes referred to as *specific* and *common risks*.

in another way. An example would be a change in the price of oil. History tells us that when oil prices rise, airline profits fall, and the airline suffers. But higher oil prices improve the profits of firms that supply energy, such as Petro-Canada and Suncor. An oil price change that is bad for WestJet is good for the oil companies. Looking at the economy as a whole, this is an idiosyncratic risk.

Not all idiosyncratic risks are balanced by opposing risks to other firms or industries. Some unique risks are specific to one person or company and no one else. The risk that two people have an automobile accident is unrelated to whether anyone else has one. We will include these completely independent risks in the category of idiosyncratic risks.

## Reducing Risk through Diversification

When George T. Shaheen left his $4 million-a-year job overseeing 65,000 employees of a large management consulting firm to become chief executive of the Webvan Group, he may not have realized how much of a risk he was taking. He thought Webvan would change the way people bought their groceries. Consumers would order their cereal, milk, apples, and ice cream over the Internet, and Webvan would deliver to their door. In November 1999, just a few months after Mr. Shaheen joined the company, his stock in Webvan was worth more than $280 million. But by April 2001, his shares were worth a paltry $150,000 and Mr. Shaheen had left the company. On July 10, 2001, Webvan collapsed and stockholders were left with nothing.

What happened to Webvan and its plan to change the way people shop? Maybe people actually like getting out of the house and going to the grocery store. But this story is about more than shopping; it's also about risk. Shaheen took on so much risk that a single big loss wiped him out. Traders in the financial markets call this experience "blowing up." Surely Shaheen could have done something to protect at least a portion of his phenomenal wealth from the risk that it would suddenly disappear. But what?

Cervantes answered this question in *Don Quixote* in 1605: "It is the part of a wise man to keep himself today for tomorrow, and *not to venture all his eggs in one basket* [emphasis added]." In today's terminology, risk can be reduced through diversification, the principle of holding more than one risk at a time. Though it may seem counterintuitive, holding several different investments can reduce the idiosyncratic risk an investor bears. A combination of risky investments is often less risky than any one individual investment. There are two ways to diversify your investments. You can *hedge* risks or you can *spread* them among many investments. Let's discuss hedging first.

## Hedging Risk

Hedging is the strategy of reducing idiosyncratic risk by making two investments with opposing risks. When one does poorly, the other does well, and vice versa. So while the payoff from each investment is volatile, together their payoffs are stable.

Consider the risk an investor faces from a potential change in the price of oil. Increases in the price of oil are bad for most of the economy, but they are good for oil companies. So an investor might buy stock in both Bombardier, a manufacturer of aircraft and rail equipment, and Husky, a large oil company. For the sake of our example, let's assume that oil prices have an equal chance of rising or falling. When they rise, owners of Husky stock receive a payoff of $120 for each $100 they invested. When oil prices fall, Husky's shareholders just get their $100 investment back. The reverse is true for Bombardier. When oil prices fall, owners of Bombardier stock get $120 for each $100 they invested; when oil prices rise, they get $100.

| Table 5.5 | Payoffs on Two Separate Investments of $100 |
| --- | --- |

| | Payoff from Owning Only | | |
| Possibility | Bombardier | Husky | Probability |
| --- | --- | --- | --- |
| Oil prices rise | $100 | $120 | $\frac{1}{2}$ |
| Oil prices fall | $120 | $100 | $\frac{1}{2}$ |

Table 5.5 summarizes these relationships.

Let's compare three strategies for investing $100, given the relationships shown in the table:

1. Invest $100 in Bombardier.

2. Invest $100 in Husky.

3. Invest half in each company: $50 in Bombardier and $50 in Husky.

Regardless of whether you invest $100 in Bombardier or Husky, the expected payoff is ½($120) + ½($100) = $110; and

$$\text{Var}(Y_B) = \text{Var}(Y_H) = \frac{1}{2}(\$120 - \$110)^2 + \frac{1}{2}(\$100 - \$110)^2 = \$100$$

$$sd(Y_B) = sd(Y_B) = \sqrt{\$100} = \$10$$

But what about the third option? What if you split your $100 and put half in Bombardier and half in Husky? The expected value of your investment is the weighted sum of the expected value of each investment, where the weights are the shares in your portfolio. So using the notation of $Y_B$ and $Y_H$ for the payoff to the investments, and $Y_{BH}$ for the payoff to option 3,

$$E(Y_{BH}) = 0.5 \times E(Y_B) + 0.5 \times E(Y_H)$$

And we know that $E(Y_B) = E(Y_H) = 110$, so that $E(Y_{BH}) = 110$. What about the standard deviation of the third option? Intuitively you can see that when oil prices go up, Husky does well but Bombardier does badly. When oil prices fall, the reverse happens. We can calculate the variance precisely but again we need some algebra. To calculate the standard deviation of option three, we use the formula for the variance of a weighted sum. That is,

$$\text{Var}(ax + by) = a^2\text{Var}(x) + b^2\text{Var}(y) + 2ab\text{Cov}(x, y) \qquad (3)$$

where

$$\text{Cov}(x, y) = p_1(x_1 - E(x))(y_1 - E(y)) + p_2(x_2 - E(x))(y_2 - E(y)) + \ldots$$
$$+ p_n(x_n - E(x))(y_n - E(y))$$
$$= \Sigma_i p_i(x_i - E(x))(y_i - E(y))$$

This formula looks complicated but we already know most of it. Start with equation (3): In our example $a$ and $b$ are the portfolio weights, so both are 0.5. $(x,y)$ refer to the payoffs to the Husky investment and the Bombardier investment, and we know $\text{Var}(Y_H) = 100$ as is $\text{Var}(Y_B)$. We just need to calculate the covariance between the returns to the two investments. Using the formula for covariance[7]

$$\text{Cov}(Y_B, Y_H) = 0.5(120 - 110)(100 - 110) + 0.5(100 - 110)(120 - 110)$$
$$= 0.5 \times (-100) + 0.5 \times (-100) = -100.$$

[7] In our simple example we have used one-half both for the share of the portfolio and for the probability that each payoff happens (i.e., that oil prices rise). Be careful to notice that in the formula for covariance $p_i$ is the probability that oil prices rise, while a and b are the portfolio shares.

Now, using the variances of each investment and their covariance, we can find the variance of option 3:

$$\text{Var}(Y_{BH}) = \frac{1}{2}^2 \text{Var}(Y_B) + \frac{1}{2}^2 \text{Var}(Y_H) + 2\left(\frac{1}{2} \times \frac{1}{2}\right)$$

$$\text{Cov}(Y_B, Y_H)$$

$$= \frac{1}{4} \times 100 + \frac{1}{4} \times 100 - \frac{1}{2} \times (-100)$$

$$= 0.$$

| Table 5.6 | Results of Possible Investment Strategies: Hedging Risk |
|---|---|

Initial Investment = $100

| Investment Strategy | Expected Payoff | Standard Deviation |
|---|---|---|
| Bombardier only | $110 | $10 |
| Husky only | $110 | $10 |
| $\frac{1}{2}$ and $\frac{1}{2}$ | $110 | $0 |

Option 3 has zero variance! Regardless of whether oil prices go up or down, you will get back $110 on your $100 investment. Investing $50 in each stock ensures your payoff. Hedging—splitting your investment between two stocks with different payoff patterns—has eliminated your risk entirely. Table 5.6 summarizes the returns to the three options.

Could George Shaheen have hedged the risk of owning so much Webvan stock? To do it, he would have had to find a company whose stock price would rise when Webvan's fell. That would have been difficult, since Webvan's business concept was new and untested. But Shaheen did have another option.

## Spreading Risk

Because investments don't always move predictably in opposite directions, you can't always reduce risk through hedging. Fortunately, there is another way. You can simply spread risk around—and that's what George Shaheen should have done. To spread your risk, all you need to do is find investments whose payoffs are unrelated. Let's replace Husky with Sears Canada and assume that Bombardier and Sears's payoffs are independent of each other.[8] So we toss a coin once to see if Bombardier does well or badly, and then we toss it a second time to see how Sears does. As before, a $100 investment in either company pays off either $120 or $100 with equal probability.

Again, we'll consider three investment strategies: (1) Bombardier only, (2) Sears only, and (3) half in Bombardier and half in Sears. The expected payoff on each of these strategies is the same: $110. For the first two strategies, $100 in either company, the standard deviation is still $10, just as it was before. But for the third strategy, $50 in Bombardier and $50 in Sears, the analysis is more complicated. There are four possible outcomes, two for each stock.

To solve the problem, we need to create a table showing all the possibilities, their probabilities, and the associated payoffs (see Table 5.7 on page 101). We're familiar with possibilities 2 and 3, in which one stock pays off but the other one doesn't, just as in the Bombardier/Husky example.

Remember that the standard deviation is the square root of the sum of the squared deviations from the expected value, weighted by the probabilities. Using the information in Table 5.7, and our formula from Table 5.4 on page 90, we can calculate the standard deviation.

$$E(Y_{BS}) = \frac{1}{4} \times 120 + \frac{1}{2} \times 110 + \frac{1}{4} \times 100 = 110.$$

---

[8] The assumption of independence makes the calculations easier but is not essential. All we need to know is that the two payoffs, Bombardier and Sears, are not perfectly correlated so they do not move in lock-step.

## IN THE NEWS
### A Poor Retirement

# Financial Post

**Derek DeCloet**

**July 5, 2002, page FP1**

A retirement plan for employees of Nortel Networks Corp. lost US $1-billion last year investing in the company's shares, documents show.

Nortel's plunging stock price wiped out one-third of the assets in its long-term investment plan, which the company offers to its non-unionized workers in the United States.

The plan's assets shrank to US$2-billion from US $3-billion in 2001. Nortel's Canadian employees are enrolled in a similar plan, the financial performance of which has not been disclosed. Nortel, led by Frank Dunn, chief executive, is already facing a U.S. lawsuit over the investment losses. The suit, filed last year, alleges Nortel engaged in "material misrepresentations and omissions" to entice employees into investing.

Tina Warren, a Nortel spokeswoman, said those enrolled in the plan have options on where their money is invested. Employees can choose from a number of mutual funds (including some that invest exclusively in bonds) or company stock, or a combination of the two.

They're not obligated to place their money in Nortel shares," she said. "It's totally up to them."

The company kicks in between 50% and 100% of each employee's contribution, up to a certain limit.

While the losses will affect thousands of Nortel employees, they are not expected to hurt the company's bottom line because they occurred in a defined-contribution plan, in which employees have not been promised a specific payout when they retire. (However, the company also has a separate defined-benefit plan, which was underfunded by US$1.02-billion as of the end of 2001, a gap analysts say will have to be repaired.)

Pension experts said Nortel's disclosure shows the hazards of investing too much of your retirement savings in your employer's stock.

Peter Hallett, an investment consultant with Towers Perrin in Calgary, said he often advises companies not to offer their employees shares through a pension plan, but rather through a savings plan that is separate from their retirement funds.

"In my experience, there aren't too many pension plans sponsors that do that" the way Nortel did, said Mr. Hallett.

It is likely Nortel's Canadian employees would have fared better than their U.S. colleagues because the rules governing employee retirement plans are more restrictive here. Registered pension plans in Canada cannot invest more than 10% of the plan's assets in one company.

A recent survey of large U.S. employee-directed retirement plans found that, on average, they have 30% of their assets in company stock, said Keith Ambachtsheer, president

$$\text{Var}(Y_{BS}) = \frac{1}{4}(120 - 110)^2 + \frac{1}{4}(110 - 110)^2 + \frac{1}{4}(110 - 110)^2 + \frac{1}{4}(100 - 110)^2$$

$$= 50$$

$$sd\,(Y_{BS}) = \sqrt{\text{Var}(y)} = \sqrt{50} = 7.1$$

Notice that we could also have calculated the variance using the formula for the variance of a weighted sum in equation (3) on page 98:

$$\text{Var}(ax + by) = a^2\text{Var}(x) + b^2\text{Var}(y) + 2ab\text{Cov}(x, y)$$

Here we have assumed that the covariance between the returns to the two investments is zero, so

$$\text{Var}(Y_{BS}) = \left(\frac{1}{2}\right)^2\text{Var}(Y_B) + \left(\frac{1}{2}\right)^2\text{Var}(Y_S) = \frac{1}{4} \times 100 + \frac{1}{4} \times 100 = 50$$

of KPA Advisory Services, a Toronto-based consultant to the pension industry.

"In a lot of these cases, the employees want to hold their company's stock, because it's the company they know best," said Mr. Ambachtsheer. "And they think it's a good investment."

The figures re-open the debate about whether there should be stricter regulations of employee pensions and retirement schemes. At a minimum, employees should be given more warning about the risks of concentrating their investments, Mr. Ambachtsheer suggested.

"Should you drum into people's minds that a very fundamental diversification rule is have at least 10 [stocks], instead of one? That clearly is a good idea, and it would have saved a lot of people a lot of grief," he said.

Employee pensions became an issue last year during the collapse of Enron Corp. Employees of the ill-fated energy trading firm lost at least US $1-billion from their retirement plans when the company went bankrupt, in part because they were prohibited from selling their shares during a critical period as Enron was imploding in an accounting scandal.

Nortel shares fell 75% last year and have lost 98% of their value since hitting a record high two years ago.

In addition to the hit it took on Nortel shares, the Nortel investment plan lost US$120-million because of the poor performance of the equity markets. The losses were slightly offset by interest and dividend payments. For its pension beneficiaries, the financial carnage might not be over.

As of the start of this year, employees enrolled in the plan still had US$400-million invested in Nortel shares, which have declined another 78% since then. Nortel stock closed at $2.57 yesterday on the Toronto Stock Exchange.

## LESSON OF THE ARTICLE

Don't put all of your eggs in one basket; diversify. Diversification is especially important for retirement savings. But Nortel employees lost more than just their investment in Nortel stock. Many of them lost their jobs, too. Almost every aspect of their financial well-being was tied up in the same company. The real lesson is that it is very risky to invest in stock of the company you work for. If the company runs into difficulties, as Nortel did, you're in bad enough shape. You don't want your savings to go down the drain along with your job.

SOURCE: "A Poor Retirement," by Derek DeCloet, Financial Post, July 5, 2002. Material reprinted with the express permission of "The National Post Company," a CanWest Partnership.

**Table 5.7**    Payoffs from Investing $50 in Each of Two Stocks
Initial Investment = $100

| Possibilities | Bombardier | Sears | Total Payoff | Probability |
|---|---|---|---|---|
| #1 | $60 | $60 | $120 | $\frac{1}{4}$ |
| #2 | $60 | $50 | $110 | $\frac{1}{4}$ |
| #3 | $50 | $60 | $110 | $\frac{1}{4}$ |
| #4 | $50 | $50 | $100 | $\frac{1}{4}$ |

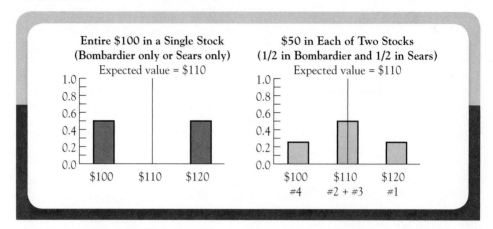

**Figure 5.5** Spreading Risk Payoffs from Two Investment Strategies

The left panel shows the distribution of payoffs from investing all $100 in either Bombardier or Sears where each pays off either $100 or $110 with probability 1/2. The right panel shows the distribution of payoffs from investing $50 each in Bombardier and Sears where each pays off either $50 or $60 with probability 1/2 and are independent (see Table 5.7 on page 101).

Figure 5.5 shows the distribution of outcomes from the possible investment strategies. The left-hand panel plots the payoffs from investing the entire $100 in one stock, either Bombardier or Sears. The right-hand panel has the distribution of the payoffs from investing $50 in each of two stocks (from Table 5.7). The figure makes clear that by spreading your investment among independently risky investments you lower the spread of the outcomes, and lower the risk.

Measures of risk other than standard deviation will give us the same result. When you split your investment between the two stocks, 75 percent of the time the payoff is $110 or higher; only 25 percent of the time is the payoff $100. For most people, that prospect is more appealing than a 50 percent probability of getting $100 and a 50 percent probability of getting $120, the odds an investor faces in holding only one stock.

In the real world, there is no reason for an investor to stop diversifying at two stocks. The more independent sources of risk you hold in your portfolio, the lower your overall risk. Using the same numbers in this example—a payoff of either $100 or $120 per $100 investment, with equal probability—we can increase the number of stocks from two to three to four, and the standard deviation of a $100 investment will fall from $7.1 to $5.8 to $5.0. If we use equation (3) on page 98 we can see that if we add more and more independent sources of risk, the standard deviation becomes negligible.

Suppose that you invest equal amounts of your portfolio in n different stocks, and that the returns to the stocks are uncorrelated. For simplicity we'll assume that each share is equally risky, they all have the variance $\sigma^2$.[9] Then equation (3) says the variance of your portfolio is

$$\text{Var(portfolio)} = \left(\frac{1}{n}\right)^2 \sigma^2 + \left(\frac{1}{n}\right)^2 \sigma^2 + \dots + \left(\frac{1}{n}\right)^2 \sigma^2$$

$$\text{Var(portfolio)} = \left(\frac{1}{n}\right)^2 n\sigma^2 = \frac{\sigma^2}{n}$$

[9] $\sigma^2$ (pronounced sigma squared) is the term economists most frequently use for variance, and they represent the standard deviation by $\sigma$ (sigma).

That is, the variance of the payoff on a portfolio of *n* independent stocks is the variance divided by *n*. Most important, as *n* increases, the variance declines, so when the value of *n* is very large, the variance is essentially zero. In summary, spreading exposure to risk among a wide range of independent risks reduces the overall risk of a portfolio.

Spreading the risk is a fundamental investment strategy. As Cervantes put it (and George Shaheen learned), never put all your eggs in one basket. If Shaheen had sold his Webvan stock and invested the proceeds in a portfolio composed of many stocks representative of the stock market as a whole, he would probably still have most of his $280 million. Diversification really reduces risk.

Diversification through the spreading of risk is the basis for the insurance business. A large automobile insurer writes millions of policies. It counts on the fact that not everyone will have accidents at the same time, for the risk of any one policy holder crashing is independent of the risk of another policy holder crashing. If it writes enough policies, the company can expect a predictable number of accident claims each year. Just as when you toss a coin a million times, you know it will turn up heads 500,000 times and tails 500,000 times, assembling a large enough pool of independent risks isn't risky.

Now that we understand both what risk is and how to measure it, we can move on to study the impact of risk on the value of bonds, stocks, and other financial instruments. Using the tools from this chapter, we will see how risk affects decisions by individual investors, managers of financial institutions, and officials who make public policy decisions. As we do, always remember Core Principle 2: Risk requires compensation.

## Terms

| | |
|---|---|
| average, 85 | risk, 83 |
| benchmark, 83 | risk-averse investor, 95 |
| diminishing marginal utility 95 | risk-neutral investor, 95 |
| | risk-free asset, 87 |
| diversification, 97 | risk-free rate of return, 87 |
| expected return, 87 | |
| expected value, 85 | risk premium, 95 |
| hedging, 97 | spreading risk, 99 |
| idiosyncratic risk, 96 | standard deviation, 88 |
| leverage, 92 | systematic risk, 96 |
| mean, 85 | value at risk (VaR), 91 |
| payoff, 84 | variance, 88 |
| probability, 84 | |

## Chapter Summary

1. Risk is a measure of uncertainty about the possible future payoffs of an investment. It is measured over some time horizon, relative to a benchmark.

2. Measuring risk is crucial to understanding the financial system.

   a. To study random future events, start by listing all the possibilities and assign a probability to each. Be sure the probabilities add to one.
   b. The expected value is the probability-weighted sum of all possible future outcomes.
   c. A risk-free asset is an investment whose future value, or payoff, is known with certainty.
   d. Risk increases when the spread (or range) of possible outcomes widens but the expected value stays the same.
   e. One measure of risk is the standard deviation of the possible payoffs.
   f. A second measure of risk is value at risk (VaR), the worst possible loss over a specific time horizon, at a given probability.

3. A risk-averse investor
   a. Always prefers a certain return to an uncertain one with the same expected return.
   b. Requires compensation in the form of a risk premium in order to take risk.
   c. Trades off between risk and expected return: the higher the risk, the higher the expected return risk-averse investors will require for holding an investment.

www.mcgrawhill.ca/olc/cecchetti

4. Risk can be divided into idiosyncratic risk, which is specific to a particular business or circumstance, and systematic risk, which is common to everyone.

5. There are two types of diversification:
   a. Hedging, in which investors reduce idiosyncratic risk by making investments with offsetting payoff patterns.
   b. Spreading, in which investors reduce idiosyncratic risk by making investments with independent payoff patterns.

## Conceptual Problems

1. Consider a game in which a six sided die is tossed three times. For each time the "6" comes up you will be paid $100.
   a. Construct a table of the possibilities and probabilities in this game.
   b. Compute the expected value of the game.
   c. How much would you be willing to pay to play this game?
   d. Consider the effect of a change in the game so that if the "6" comes up two times in a row, you get nothing. How would your answers to the first three parts of this question change?

2.* Why is it important to be able to quantify risk?

3. You are the founder of IGRO, an Internet firm that delivers groceries.
   a. Describe the idiosyncratic and systematic risks your company faces.
   b. As founder of the company, you own a significant portion of the firm, and your personal wealth is highly concentrated in IGRO shares. What risks do you face, and how should you try to reduce them?

4. Assume that the economy can experience high growth, normal growth, or recession. Under these conditions, you expect the following stock market returns for the coming year.

| State of the Economy | Probability | Return |
|---|---|---|
| High Growth | 0.2 | +30% |
| Normal Growth | 0.7 | +12% |
| Recession | 0.1 | -15% |

a. Compute the expected value of a $1,000 investment both in dollars and as a percentage over the coming year.
b. Compute the standard deviation of the return as a percentage over the coming year.
c. If the risk-free return is 7 percent, what is the risk premium for a stock market investment?

5. You are a typical Canadian investor. An insurance broker calls and asks if you would be interested in an investment with a high payoff if the annual Indian monsoons are less damaging than normal. If damage is high, you will lose your investment. On calculating the expected return, you realize that it is roughly the same as that of the stock market. Is this opportunity valuable to you? Why or why not?

6. Among the many consequences of Enron's bankruptcy in 2001 was the loss of savings Enron employees suffered. Roughly 47 percent of employee pension funds were invested in Enron stock. Why was this investment so risky? How could the risk have been reduced?

7. Car insurance companies eliminate risk (or come close) by selling a large number of policies. Explain how they eliminate risk in this way.

8. Mortgages increase the risk faced by homeowners.
   a. Explain how.
   b. What happens to the homeowner's risk as the down payment on the house rises from 10 percent to 50 percent?

9. Banks pay substantial amounts to monitor the risks that they take. One of the primary concerns of a bank's risk managers is to compute the value at risk (VaR). Why is VaR so important for a bank (or any financial institution)?

10.* Give an example of how you might reduce your exposure to a risk that is systematic to the Canadian economy.

* Indicates more difficult problems.

# Analytical Problems

11. Which of the investments in the table below would be most attractive to a risk-averse investor? How would your answer differ if the investor was described as risk neutral?

| Investment | Expected Value | Standard Deviation |
|---|---|---|
| A | 75 | 10 |
| B | 100 | 10 |
| C | 100 | 20 |

12.* In a graph, plot the risk–return combinations in the table below with the expected return measured on the vertical axis and the risk on the horizontal axis. If an investor claimed to be indifferent between these four investments, how would you classify his attitude toward risk? If he was a risk-averse investor, how would you expect a plot of equally attractive investments to be sloped?

| Investment | Expected Return | Risk |
|---|---|---|
| A | 5 | 8 |
| B | 10 | 4 |
| C | 20 | 2 |
| D | 40 | 1 |

13. Consider two possible investments whose payoffs are completely independent of one another. Both investments have the same expected value and standard deviation. If you have $1,000 to invest, could you benefit from dividing your funds between these investments? Explain your answer.

14.* Suppose, as in question 13, you considered only investments that had the same expected value and standard deviation and whose payoffs were independent of each other. Would it matter if you spread your $1,000 across 10 of these investments rather than two?

15. You are considering three investments, each with the same expected value and each with two possible payoffs. The investments are sold only in increments of $500. You have $1,000 to invest so you have the option of either splitting your money equally between two of the investments or placing all $1,000 in one of the investments. If the payoffs from investment A are independent of the payoffs from investments B and C and the payoffs from B and C are perfectly negatively correlated with each other (meaning when B pays off, C doesn't and vice versa), which investment strategy will minimize your risk?

16. In which of the following cases would you be more likely to decide whether to take on the risk involved by looking at a measure of the value at risk? Explain your reasoning.
   a. You are unemployed and are considering investing your life savings of $10,000 to start up a new business.
   b. You have a full-time job paying $100,000 a year and are considering making a $1,000 investment in stock of a well-established, stable company.

17. Consider an investment that pays off $800 or $1,400 per $1,000 invested with equal probability. Suppose you have $1,000 but are willing to borrow to increase your expected return. What would happen to the expected value and standard deviation of the investment if you borrowed an additional $1,000 and invested a total of $2,000? What if you borrowed $2,000 to invest a total of $3,000?

18. Looking again at the investment described in question 17, what is the maximum leverage ratio you could have and still have enough to repay the loan in the event the bad outcome occurred?

# CHAPTER 6

## Bonds, Bond Prices, and the Determination of Interest Rates

Virtually any financial arrangement involving the current transfer of resources from a lender to a borrower, with a transfer back at some time in the future, is a form of bond. Car loans, home mortgages, even credit card balances all create a loan from a financial intermediary to an individual making a purchase—just like the bonds governments and large corporations sell when they need to borrow.

When companies like Bell Canada, or Canadian Tire need to finance their operations, they sell bonds. When the Canadian government or a provincial government needs to borrow, it sells bonds. And they do it billions of dollars at a time. In 2008 alone, Canadian corporations raised nearly $100 billion through bonds, adding to the nearly $500 billion they had already borrowed. Federal, provincial, and local Canadian governments have nearly $700 billion in outstanding debt as well.[1] The ease with which individuals, corporations, and governments borrow is essential to the functioning of our economic system. Without this free flow of resources through the bond markets, the economy would grind to a halt.

Historically, we can trace the concept of using bonds to borrow to monarchs' almost insatiable appetite for resources. To maintain lavish lifestyles, fight wars, and explore the globe, kings, princes, and other rulers drew on every available source of financing. Even with these incentives, after thousands of years of civilization only a few possibilities had been developed: outright confiscation; taxation, which is a mild form of confiscation; debasement of currency, in which people are required to exchange their coins for ones that weigh less—in effect, a tax on currency; and borrowing. Monarchs who borrowed directly from international bankers frequently defaulted or failed to make the loan payments they had promised.

Between 1557 and 1696, the various kings of Spain defaulted 14 times. With that track record, it's no wonder they had to pay interest rates close to 40 percent. The Dutch invented modern bonds to finance their lengthy war of independence against those same Spanish kings who defaulted on loans in the 16th and 17th centuries. Over the next two centuries, the British refined the use of bonds to finance government activities. The practice then spread to other countries. The U.S. government borrowed in Europe to pay for the War of Independence, and then refinanced domestically, creating the first U.S. government bonds. In Canada, government-guaranteed bonds sold in England paid for the construction of the CP Railway, and then the domestic bond market became thoroughly established in the early 20th century when the Canadian government needed to raise money to pay for World War I. While the depth and complexity of bond markets have increased in modern times, many of their original features remain.

If we want to understand the financial system, particularly the bond market, we must understand three things. The first is the relationship between bond prices and interest rates (yet another application of present value). The second is that supply and demand in the bond market determine bond prices. The third is why bonds are risky. Let's get started.

[1] These numbers come from the Bank of Canada's Banking and Financial Statistics, March 2009, Table K8. The Canadian government debt is almost all in Canadian dollars, but the corporations and the provinces borrow about a third of their funds in foreign currency, mostly U.S. dollars.

# Bond Prices

A standard bond specifies the fixed amounts to be paid and the exact dates of the payments. *How much should you be willing to pay for a bond?* The answer depends on the bond's characteristics. We will look at four basic types:

1. *Discount bonds*, which promise a single future payment, such as a Canadian Treasury bill.
2. *Fixed-payment loans*, such as conventional mortgages.
3. *Coupon bonds*, which make periodic interest payments and repay the principal at maturity. Canadian government bonds and most corporate bonds are coupon bonds.
4. *Consols*, which make periodic interest payments forever, never repaying the principal that was borrowed. (There aren't many examples of these.)

"The name's Bond. Duane Bond."

SOURCE: © The New Yorker Collection 2000. Michael Crawford from cartoonbank.com. All Rights Reserved.

Let's see how each of these bonds is priced. To keep the analysis simple, we'll ignore risk for now.

## Discount Bonds

Treasury bills (commonly known as T-bills) are the most straightforward type of bond. Each T-bill represents a promise by the Canadian government to pay $100 on a fixed future date. There are no coupon payments. They are called discount bonds, since the price is less than their face value—they sell at a discount. This isn't a discount in the sense of a markdown at a clothing store, however. If a $100 face value T-bill sells for $96, the $4 difference is the interest, the payment to the lender for making the loan.

Since a Treasury bill makes a single payment on a future date, its price is just the present value of that payment:

$$\text{Price of \$100 face value zero-coupon bond} = \frac{\$100}{(1+i)^n} \qquad (1)$$

where $i$ is the interest rate expressed in decimal form and $n$ is the time until the payment is made, measured in the same time units as the interest rate. Suppose the annual interest rate is 5 percent. What is the price of a one-year T-bill? To figure out the answer, set $i$ at 0.05 and $n$ at 1, and then compute the price:

$$\text{Price of one-year Treasury bill} = \frac{\$100}{(1+0.05)} = \$95.24$$

The Canadian government doesn't issue T-bills with a maturity of more than one year; six-month T-bills are much more common. At an annual interest rate of 5 percent, what is the price of a six-month discount bond? We can use the present-value formula, again, but this time we have to be careful. Recall that we need to measure $i$ and $n$ in the same time units. Since $i$ is the interest rate for one year, we need to measure $n$ in years, and since six months is half a year,

$$\text{Price of a six-month Treasury bill} = \frac{\$100}{(1+0.05)^{1/2}} = \$97.59$$

As you can see, the price of a six-month Treasury bill is higher than that of a one-year T-bill. The shorter the time until the payment is made, the more we are willing to pay for it now. If we go on to compute the price of a three-month T-bill, setting $n$ at 0.25 (one-fourth of a year), we find the answer is $99.02.

Equation (1) on page 107 shows that for a discount bond, the relationship between the price and the interest rate is the same as the one we saw in our discussion of present value. When the price moves, the interest rate moves with it, albeit in the opposite direction. Thus we can compute the interest rate from the price using the present-value formula. For example, if the price of a one-year T-bill is $95, then the interest rate is $i = (\$100/\$95) - 1 = 0.0526$, or 5.26 percent.

## Fixed-Payment Loans

Home mortgages and car loans are called *fixed-payment loans* because they promise a fixed number of equal payments at regular intervals. These loans are *amortized*, meaning that the borrower pays off the principal along with the interest over the life of the loan. Each payment includes both interest and a portion of the principal. Pricing these sorts of loans is straightforward using the present-value formula: The value of the loan today is the present value of all the payments. If we assume that the annual interest rate is $i$ (measured as a decimal) and that the loan specifies $n$ payments, then

$$\text{Value of a fixed payment loan} = \frac{\text{Fixed payment}}{(1 + i)} + \frac{\text{Fixed payment}}{(1 + i)^2} + \ldots + \frac{\text{Fixed payment}}{(1 + i)^n} \quad (2)$$

This formula looks complicated, but in the Appendix to Chapter 4 we showed that it has a simple solution:

$$\text{Value of a fixed payment loan} = \left(\frac{\text{Fixed payment}}{(1 + i)}\right)\left(1 - \frac{1}{(1 + i)^n}\right)$$

When lenders figure out your monthly payment for a car loan or home mortgage, this is how they do it.

## Coupon Bonds

Recall from Chapter 4 that the issuer of a coupon bond promises to make a series of periodic interest payments called coupon payments, plus a principal payment at maturity. So we can value a coupon bond using (you guessed it) the present-value formula. The price of the coupon bond is

$$P_{CB} = \left[\frac{\text{Coupon payment}}{(1 + i)^1} + \frac{\text{Coupon payment}}{(1 + i)^2} + \ldots + \frac{\text{Coupon payment}}{(1 + i)^n}\right] + \frac{\text{Face value}}{(1 + i)^n} \quad (3)$$

The right side of this equation has two parts. The first part, in brackets, looks just like the fixed-payment loan—and it is, with the important exception that it represents only the interest. The second part, on the far right, looks just like a discount bond, and it is. It represents the value of the promise to repay the principal at maturity.

## Consols

Another type of bond offers only periodic payments. That is, the borrower pays only interest, never repaying the principal. These loans, called consols or perpetuities, are like coupon bonds whose payments last forever. The British government has a

## YOUR FINANCIAL WORLD

### Fixed versus Variable Mortgages

Choosing a mortgage can be confusing. First there is the term of the mortgage. Remember, the amortization period is the overall length of time you will agree to repay the loan over; the term of the mortgage refers to how long until you renegotiate the rate. Then, you can choose open or closed—depending on whether you think you might have to pay your mortgage off early or not. Finally, you can choose a variable rate or a fixed rate mortgage. When you take a variable rate mortgage, your mortgage rate changes every time the bank's prime rate changes, but that doesn't mean your monthly payment changes. Instead, if the interest rate goes down, you make the same monthly payment but a greater proportion of it goes to repaying the principal and that means that you can repay your loan more quickly. Of course, the opposite is true too. If the rate goes up, more of your payment has to go to paying the interest costs and less to paying down the principal, which means you'll be paying your mortgage off for longer.

Suppose that you took out a variable rate mortgage at 4.6 percent for $200,000 with a fixed term of 5 years and plan to amortize the loan over 25 years. Then your monthly payment would be about $1,120 of which $766 would be interest in the first month. (By the last year, most of your payment goes to principal, but initially most of it goes to interest costs.) But suppose that before you even made your first payment the prime rate went up 50 basis points, so now your interest rate is 5.1 percent. Your monthly payment stays at $1,120 for the 5 years, but now $935 goes towards interest and it will take you 32 years to pay off the mortgage. At the end of 5 years you will have paid off only $12,750 of your mortgage even though your payments add up to $67,000.

Most financial institutions have calculators that will help you determine the monthly payment for a mortgage of a particular type. For example, go to the Alberta Credit Union Web site (http://albertacreditunions.com/public/bins/index.asp) and look under calculators for a mortgage calculator.

number of consols currently outstanding, the oldest of which was issued in 1853. Historically, railroad companies such as the CP Rail Company and the Grand Trunk issued perpetual bonds.

You won't be surprised to learn that the price of a consol is the present value of all the future interest payments. The fact that the number of payments is infinite complicates things. But we can derive a formula for the price of a consol that makes a coupon payment every year forever.[2] At interest rate $i$,

$$P_{Consol} = \frac{\text{Yearly coupon payment}}{i} \qquad (4)$$

The price of a consol equals the annual coupon payment divided by the interest rate. So at an interest rate of 5 percent, a consol that promises $1 per year forever would sell for $20. If the interest rate changes to 4 percent, the price rises to $25. Again, the interest rate and the price move in opposite directions.

## Bond Yields

Now that we know how to calculate a bond price given the interest rate, we need to move in the other direction and calculate the interest rate, or the return to an investor, implicit in the bond's price. Doing so means combining information about the promised payments with the price to obtain what is called the *yield*—a measure of the cost of borrowing and the reward for lending. When people talk about bonds, they use the terms "yield" and "interest rate" interchangeably, so we will too.

[2] This equation is derived in the Appendix to Chapter 4.

## Yield to Maturity

The most useful measure of the return on holding a bond is called the **yield to maturity**, or the yield bondholders receive if they hold the bond to its maturity when the final principal payment is made. Take a $100 face value 5 percent coupon bond with one year to maturity. At maturity, the owner of this bond receives a coupon payment of $5 plus a principal payment of $100.[3] Using the formula from equation (3) on page 108, we know that the price of the bond is

$$\text{Price of one-year 5\% coupon bond} = \frac{\$5}{(1 + i)} + \frac{\$100}{(1 + i)} \qquad (5)$$

The value of $i$ that solves this equation is the *yield to maturity*. Remembering that present value and interest rates move in opposite directions, we can conclude the following:

1. If the price of the bond is $100, then the yield to maturity equals the coupon rate. (Recall from Chapter 4 that the coupon rate is the ratio of the annual coupon payments to the face value of the bond.)
2. Since the price rises as the yield falls, when the price is *above* $100, the yield to maturity must be *below* the coupon rate.
3. Since the price falls as the yield rises, when the price is *below* $100, the yield to maturity must be *above* the coupon rate.

Looking at the one-year 5 percent coupon bond, we can see right away that if the yield to maturity is 5 percent, then

$$\text{Price of one-year 5\% coupon bond} = \frac{\$5}{(1 + 0.05)} + \frac{\$100}{(1 + 0.05)} = \frac{\$105}{1.05} = \$100$$

That's the first point. Now look at what happens when yield to maturity falls to 4 percent. The price becomes

$$\text{Price of one-year 5\% coupon bond} = \frac{\$5}{(1 + 0.04)} + \frac{\$100}{(1 + 0.04)} = \frac{\$105}{1.04} = \$100.96$$

That's the second point. If the yield to maturity rises to 6 percent, then the price falls to

$$\text{Price of one-year 5\% coupon bond} = \frac{\$5}{(1 + 0.06)} + \frac{\$100}{(1 + 0.06)} = \frac{\$100}{1.06} = \$99.06$$

That's the third point. You can try this process with a more complicated bond—say, one with 10 years to maturity that makes more than just one coupon payment—and get exactly the same results.

The fact that the return on a bond depends on the price you pay for it really isn't that mysterious. If you pay $95 for a $100 face value bond, for example, you will receive both the interest payments and the increase in value from $95 to $100. This rise in value, referred to as a **capital gain**, is part of the return on your investment. So when the price of the bond is below the face value, the return is above the coupon rate. When the price is above the face value, the bondholder incurs a **capital loss** and the bond's yield to maturity falls below its coupon rate.

---

[3] Most bonds offer two semiannual payments, each equal to half the annual coupon. We will ignore this complication.

## Current Yield

Current yield is a commonly used, easy-to-compute measure of the proceeds the bondholder receives for making a loan. It is the yearly coupon payment divided by the price:

$$\text{Current yield} = \frac{\text{Yearly coupon payment}}{\text{Price paid}} \tag{6}$$

Looking at this expression, we can see that the current yield measures that part of the return from buying the bond that arises solely from the coupon payments. It ignores the capital gain or loss that arises when the price at which the bond is purchased differs from its face value. So if the price is below par, the current yield will be below the yield to maturity.

Let's return to the one-year 5 percent coupon bond and assume that it is selling for $99. The current yield is easy to calculate as

$$\frac{5}{99} = 0.0505,$$

or 5.05 percent. The yield to maturity for this bond is the solution to

$$\frac{\$5}{(1 + i)} + \frac{\$100}{(1 + i)} = \$99,$$

which is 6.06 percent. The yield to maturity is higher because, if you buy the bond for $99, one year later you get not only the $5 coupon payment but also a guaranteed $1 capital gain for a total of $6.

We can repeat these calculations for a case in which the bond is selling for $101. Then the current yield is

$$\frac{5}{101} = 0.0495,$$

or 4.95 percent, and the yield to maturity is

$$\frac{\$5}{(1 + i)} + \frac{\$100}{(1 + i)} = \$101,$$

or 3.96 percent.

Putting all this together, we see the relationship between the current yield and the coupon rate. Again, it comes from the fact that current yield moves in the opposite direction from the price: it falls when the bond's price goes up and rises when the price goes down. So when the price equals the face value of the bond, the current yield and coupon rate are equal. When the price rises above the face value, the current yield falls below the coupon rate. And when the price falls below the face value, the current yield rises above the coupon rate.

Table 6.1 on page 112 summarizes the relationships among the price, coupon rate, current yield, and yield to maturity. We know that when the bond price is less than face value, the current yield and the yield to maturity are both higher than the coupon rate. But since the yield to maturity takes account of the capital gain the bondholder receives, while the current yield does not, the yield to maturity must be even higher than the current yield. When the price is above the face value, the yield to maturity is lower than the current yield, which is lower than the coupon rate.

| Table 6.1 | Relationship among a Bond's Price and Its Coupon Rate, Current Yield, and Yield to Maturity |
|---|---|

Bond price < Face value: Coupon rate < Current yield < Yield to maturity
Bond price = Face value: Coupon rate = Current yield = Yield to maturity
Bond price > Face value: Coupon rate > Current yield > Yield to maturity

## Holding Period Returns

We have emphasized that if you buy a bond whose yield to maturity deviates from the coupon rate, the price will not be the face value. Similarly, the return from holding a bond need not be the coupon rate. For example, if you pay $95 for a one-year 6 percent coupon bond, one year later you will get both the $6 coupon payment and the $5 difference between the purchase price and the $100 face value at maturity. But this example is really too simple, since it assumes that the investor holds the bond to maturity. Most holders of long-term bonds plan to sell them well before they mature. And since the price of the bond may change between the time of the purchase and the time of the sale, the return to buying a bond and selling it before it matures—the holding period return—can differ from the yield to maturity.

Take an example in which you pay $100 for a 10-year, 6 percent coupon bond with a face value of $100. You intend to hold the bond for one year. That is, you are going to buy a 10-year bond and then a year later, you'll sell a 9-year bond. What is your return from holding this bond? If the interest rate doesn't change (that is, it stays at 6 percent) your return will be $6/$100 = 0.06, or 6 percent. But if the interest rate changes, calculating your return becomes more complicated. Say that over the year you hold the bond, the interest rate falls from 6 to 5 percent. That is, the yield to maturity falls to 5 percent. Using equation (3) on page 108, we can figure out that you have bought a 10-year bond for $100 and sold a 9-year bond for $107.11. What is your one-year holding period return on the initial $100 investment? It has two parts: the $6 coupon payment and the $7.11 capital gain (the difference between the price at which you bought the bond and the price at which you sold it). So the holding period return is

$$\text{One-year holding period return} = \frac{\$6}{\$100} + \frac{\$107.11 - \$100}{\$100} = \frac{\$13.11}{\$100} = 0.1311$$
$$= 13.11\%$$

Obviously, bond prices can go down as well as up. Consider what happens if the yield to maturity rises to 7 percent so that the price falls to $93.48. Now the one-year holding period return is

$$\text{One-year holding period return} = \frac{\$6}{\$100} + \frac{\$93.48 - \$100}{\$100} = \frac{\$.52}{\$100} = 0.0052$$
$$= -0.52\%$$

The coupon payment still represents a 6 percent return, but the capital loss from the price movement is 6.52 percent. The one-year holding period return is negative, as overall there is a small loss.[4]

To generalize these examples, notice that the one-year holding period return is the sum of the yearly coupon payment divided by the price paid for the bond, and the change in the price (price sold minus price paid) divided by the price paid:

$$\text{Holding period return} = \frac{\text{Yearly coupon payment}}{\text{Price paid}} + \frac{\text{Change in price of bond}}{\text{Price paid}} \qquad (7)$$

The first part on the right-hand side of this equation is the current yield (equation (6) on page 111). The second part is the capital gain. So the holding period return is

$$\text{Holding period return} = \text{Current yield} + \text{Capital gain} \qquad (8)$$

Whenever the price of a bond changes, there is a capital gain or loss. The greater the price change, the more important a part of the holding period return the capital gain or loss becomes. The potential for interest rate movements and changes in bond prices creates risk. The longer the term of the bond, the greater those price movements and the associated risk can be, as we'll see in more detail in the last section of this chapter.

## The Bond Market and the Determination of Interest Rates

Now that we understand the relationship between bond prices and various measures of interest rates, we need to figure out how bond prices are determined and why they change. The best way to do that is to look at bond supply, bond demand, and equilibrium prices in the bond market. Once we understand how the bond market determines bond prices, we can figure out why the prices change.

To keep the analysis simple, we need to make a few choices about how to proceed. First we'll consider the market for a one-year discount bond (one that makes no coupon payments) with a face value of $100. Second, we'll discuss bond prices rather than interest rates. Remember, since a bond's price, together with its various characteristics, determines its yield, it really doesn't matter whether we talk about yields (interest rates) or bond prices. Once we know the price, we know the yield.

"Your pot o' gold is doing nothing for you sitting at the end of the rainbow. At the very least, you should put it in a no-risk interest-bearing account."

---

[4] The multi-year case is somewhat more complex. Say that an investor purchased the same 10-year 6 percent coupon bond at par, and then held it for *two* years. If the interest rate were to rise from 7 percent, the price of the now 8-year bond would fall to $94.03 per $100 of face value. This means that the investor would receive $6 in coupon payments after year 1 (which would be worth $6 × 1.07 at the end of year 2), $6 in coupon payments at the end of year 2, plus a capital loss of $5.97, for a total payoff over two years of $106.45. Using the methods described in the Tools of the Trade: Computing Compound Annual Rates on page 64, we can compute the annual rate of return as

$\left[\left(\frac{106.45}{100}\right)^{1/2} - 1 = .0317\right]$ or 3.17 percent.

# TOOLS OF THE TRADE
Reading the Bond Page

Every day Web sites for *The Globe and Mail* and *National Post* list the previous day's closing prices and yields for a wide variety of bonds, including Canadian and U.S. government bills and bonds and corporate bonds. Representative data are in Table 6.2. Let's see how to read this information.

Government securities with a year or less maturity are issued as Treasury Bills or notes, and are listed separately. The table shows only a few of the 32 Canada issues listed on January 16, and in addition to the direct liabilities of the federal government, bonds issued by the Canada Mortgage and Housing Corporation (CMHC) and Export Development Corporation (EDC) are also listed under "Federal" because they are backed by the federal government.

We'll read across the table from left to right:

*Coupon.* Column 2 reports the coupon rate. The rate of 3.75 for the bond listed in the first row means that the holder will receive $3.75 a year (split into two semiannual payments of $1.875) for each $100 of face value held.

*Maturity.* Column 3 shows the date on which the principal and final interest payment are paid. The Canadian government makes payments on the 1st and 15th of the month, so the owner of a June 01/10 bond will receive payment on June 1, 2010.

*Bid.* Column 4 shows the price dealers are willing to pay to buy the bond. Notice that the bid price depends on the issuer (federal/provincial/corporate) the maturity date, and the coupon rate. Because interest rates on treasury bills were less than 1%, a federal government bond that would pay 3.75% was very valuable.

*Yield.* Column 5 reports the yield to maturity computed using the asked price. That is, if investors purchased the bond at the asked price, this is the yield to maturity they would receive. Notice that in January 2009 yields on government securities were very low by historic standards.

| Table 6.2 | Canadian Bonds on 2009.01.16 | | | |
|---|---|---|---|---|
| | **Coupon** | **Maturity Date** | **Bid $** | **Yield %** |
| **FEDERAL** | | | | |
| Canada | 3.750 | Jun 01/10 | 103.93 | 0.84 |
| Canada | 9.500 | Jun 01/10 | 111.70 | 0.84 |
| Canada | 5.500 | Jun 01/10 | 106.30 | 0.84 |
| Canada | 4.000 | Sep 01/10 | 104.93 | 0.91 |
| Canada | 2.750 | Dec 01/10 | 103.30 | 0.96 |
| Canada | 9.000 | Mar 01/11 | 116.46 | 1.09 |
| Canada | 8.500 | Jun 01/11 | 117.22 | 1.10 |
| Canada | 6.000 | Jun 01/11 | 111.40 | 1.10 |
| Canada | 3.750 | Sep 01/11 | 106.53 | 1.20 |

(continued)

If we assume the investor is planning to purchase a one-year bond and hold it to maturity—he has a one-year investment horizon—then the holding period return equals the bond's yield to maturity, and both are determined directly from the price.

Notice that the first three bonds listed all have the same maturity date, but have different coupons, likely reflecting when they were issued. The bid price is highest (of course) for the bond with the highest coupon, and the bid prices are such that the yield on each of the bonds is the same. Since they are all issued by the same issuer and have the same maturity date there would be an arbitrage opportunity if they didn't have the same yield.

The *Financial Post* also lists bid prices for provincial securities and corporate securities. The BC government bond with maturity in August 2010 has roughly the same time to mature as the federal government bond that matures in September 2010, but notice that the provincial bond yields 1.35 percent compared to the federal bond yielding 0.91 percent. The corporate bonds have higher yields still. Look at the Bank of Montreal bonds (BMO) that mature in June 2010 and December 2010: their yields are 6.34 percent and 6.41 percent respectively. The higher yield is necessary to compensate the bondholders for the higher risk.

| | Coupon | Maturity Date | Bid $ | Yield % |
|---|---|---|---|---|
| **PROVINCIAL** | | | | |
| BC | 6.375 | Aug 23/10 | 107.87 | 1.35 |
| BC | 8.500 | Aug 23/13 | 125.08 | 2.66 |
| BC | 6.150 | Nov 19/27 | 114.92 | 4.92 |
| BC | 5.700 | Jun 18/29 | 110.18 | 4.90 |
| BC | 4.700 | Jun 18/37 | 99.93 | 4.70 |
| BCMF | 5.900 | Jun 01/11 | 108.81 | 2.05 |
| HydQue | 6.500 | Feb 15/11 | 109.89 | 1.62 |
| HydQue | 10.250 | Jul 16/12 | 126.46 | 2.31 |
| HydQue | 11.000 | Aug 15/20 | 156.59 | 4.63 |
| **CORPORATE** | | | | |
| AGT Lt | 8.800 | Sep 22/25 | 108.10 | 7.91 |
| Bell | 6.550 | May 01/29 | 78.06 | 8.90 |
| BMO | 6.903 | Jun 30/10 | 100.76 | 6.34 |
| BMO | 6.647 | Dec 31/10 | 100.42 | 6.41 |
| BMO | 6.685 | Dec 31/11 | 98.65 | 7.20 |
| BMO | 5.200 | Jun 21/12 | 98.96 | 5.54 |
| BMO | 5.040 | Sep 04/12 | 104.36 | 3.74 |
| BMO | 5.180 | Jun 10/15 | 102.92 | |

SOURCE: *Financial Post*, retrieved January 19, 2009, from http://www.financialpost.com/markets/market-data/bonds-canadian.html.

The present-value formula shows that the relationship between the price and the yield on such a bond is simply

$$P = \$100/(1 + i), \text{ so } i = [(\$100 - P)/P]$$

For example, if a bond sells for $95, then the yield is $i = \$5/\$95 = 0.0526$, or 5.26 percent.

## Bond Supply, Bond Demand, and Equilibrium in the Bond Market

How are bond prices (and bond yields) determined? We will think about that question at two different levels. The fundamental forces driving bond prices and yields are the supply and demand for loanable funds; that is, how much people want to save and how much they want to invest. But, we can also look at the narrower forces, those that determine whether that savings and investment is done through the bond market. The supply and demand curves for bonds reflect both these factors.

The *bond supply curve* is the relationship between the price and the quantity of bonds people are willing to sell, all other things being equal. The higher the price of a bond, the larger the quantity supplied will be for two reasons. From investors' point of view, the higher the price, the more tempting it is to sell a bond they currently hold. From the point of view of companies seeking finance for new projects, the higher the price at which they can sell bonds, the better. Taking our example of a $100 one-year discount bond, the quantity supplied will be higher at $95 per bond than it will be at $90 per bond, all other things being equal. This means that *the bond supply curve slopes upward.*

The *bond demand curve* is the relationship between the price and quantity of bonds that investors demand, all other things being equal. As the price falls, the reward for holding the bond rises, so the demand goes up. That is, the lower the price potential bondholders must pay for a fixed-dollar payment on a future date, the more likely they are to buy a bond. Again, think of the discount bond promising to pay $100 in one year. That bond will attract more demand at $90 than it will at $95 per bond, all other things being equal. Thus, *the bond demand curve slopes downward.* Since the price of bonds is inversely related to the yield, the demand curve implies that the higher the demand for bonds, the higher the yield.

Equilibrium in the bond market is the point at which quantity supplied equals quantity demanded—point $E$ in Figure 6.1. As is always the case with supply and demand analysis, we need to explain how the market adjusts when the price deviates from the price that equates quantity supplied and quantity demanded—point $P_0$ in Figure 6.1. Let's look briefly at the two possibilities: either the price is too high or the price is too low. If bond prices start out above the equilibrium point, somewhere greater than $P_0$, quantity supplied will exceed quantity demanded. That is, excess supply means that suppliers cannot sell the bonds they want to at the current price. To make the sale, they will start cutting the price. The excess supply will put downward pressure on the price until supply equals demand.

When the price is below the equilibrium point, quantity demanded will exceed quantity supplied. Those people who wish to buy bonds cannot get all they want at the prevailing price. Their reaction is to start bidding up the price. Excess demand continues to put upward pressure on the price until the market reaches equilibrium.

So far, so good. But to really understand how bond prices (and bond yields) change over time, we need to learn what determines the location of the supply and demand curves. Over time they shift around, leading to changes in the equilibrium prices.

**MARKETS**

**Figure 6.1** **Supply, Demand, and Equilibrium in the Bond Market**

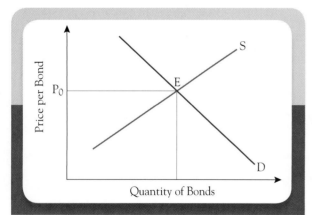

The supply of bonds from borrowers slopes up and the demand for bonds from lenders slopes down. Equilibrium in the bond market is determined by the intersection of supply and demand.

As we discuss the causes of such shifts in the following section, make sure you remember the distinction between moving *along* a supply or demand curve and *shifting* a curve. When the quantity demanded or quantity supplied changes because of a change in the price, it produces a movement along the curve. But when the quantity demanded or supplied at a given price changes, it shifts the entire curve. More importantly, in the bond market, a shift in either the supply or the demand curve changes the price of bonds, so it changes the yield as well.

## Factors That Shift Bond Supply

What changes the quantity of bonds *supplied* at a given price, shifting the supply curve? Broadly speaking, there are two sources of changes: factors that influence the amount that individuals, corporations, or governments want to borrow at a given real rate of interest, and (since the bond price is a function of the nominal interest rate) changes in the relationship between the nominal and real interest rate. Let's highlight two of the leading examples of the first source and then at changes in the expected inflation rate, which is an example of the second.

### Changes in Government Borrowing
The government's need to issue bonds affects the supply of bonds outstanding. Both changes in tax policy and adjustments in fixed spending can affect a government's need to borrow. Regardless of the reason, any increase in the government's borrowing needs increases the quantity of bonds outstanding, shifting the bond supply curve to the right. The result is an increase in quantity of the bonds supplied at every price (see Figure 6.2). Since the demand curve stays where it is (remember, we're holding everything else constant), the increase in supply drives the price down. The added supply of government bonds has reduced prices, raising interest rates.

### Changes in General Business Conditions
During business-cycle expansions, when general business conditions are good, investment opportunities abound, prompting firms to increase their borrowing. As the amount of debt in the economy rises, the quantity of bonds outstanding goes up. So as business conditions improve, the bond supply curve shifts to the right, forcing bond prices down and interest rates up. Again, Figure 6.2 shows what happens. This connection between general business conditions and the supply of bonds also helps explain how weak economic growth can lead to rising bond prices and lower interest rates.

### Changes in Expected Inflation
Bond issuers care about the real cost of borrowing—the cost of the loan taking inflation into account. At a given nominal interest rate, higher expected inflation means a lower real interest rate. And at a lower real interest rate, fewer real resources are required to make the payments promised by a bond. So when expected inflation rises, the cost of borrowing falls and the desire to borrow rises. As in Figure 6.2, an

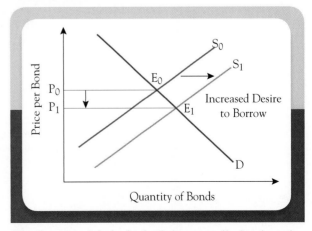

**Figure 6.2**   **A Shift in the Supply of Bonds**

When borrowers' desire for funds increases, the bond supply curve shifts to the right, lowering bond prices and raising interest rates.

increase in expected inflation shifts the bond supply curve to the right. Higher expected inflation increases the bond supply, reducing bond prices and raising the nominal interest rate.

Table 6.3 summarizes the factors that increase the quantity of bonds supplied at every price, shifting the bond supply curve to the right. Before moving on to shifts in the demand for bonds, we should mention that there is one other factor that shifts the bond supply: changes in corporate taxation. Because such changes in the tax code require government legislation, they don't occur very often. But when they do, they can affect the economy-wide supply of bonds. Corporations pay taxes on their profits, just as individuals pay taxes on their income, so they are concerned with after-tax profits. Governments often create special tax subsidies that make corporate investments less costly. These tax incentives increase the supply of bonds because they raise the after-tax profitability of investing in new equipment purchased with funds raised from selling bonds. Like the other three factors we have considered, government tax incentives increase bond supply, shift the supply curve to the right, and lower the price of bonds.

**Table 6.3** Factors That Shift Bond Supply to the Right, Lower Bond Prices, and Raise Interest Rates

| Change | Effect on Bond Supply, Bond Prices, and Interest Rates | Shift in Bond Supply |
|---|---|---|
| An increase in the government's desired expenditure relative to its revenue | Bond supply shifts to the right, Bond prices ↓, and interest rates ↑ | |
| An improvement in general business conditions | Bond supply shifts to the right, Bond prices ↓, and interest rates ↑ | |
| An increase in expected inflation, reducing the real cost of repayment | Bond supply shifts to the right, Bond prices ↓, and interest rates ↑ | |

## Factors That Shift Bond Demand

Now we move on to bond demand. Again, we can separate the factors into those that affect the *demand* for bonds at a given real interest rate and changes in expected inflation. We can further divide factors influencing the demand for bonds into those that affect total savings in the economy and those that affect the share of that savings that goes into the bond market. In the first group are wealth and demography; the second group includes the expected return on stocks and other assets, risk, and the liquidity of bonds.[5] We'll look at examples of each.

**Figure 6.3**   **Shift in Bond Demand**

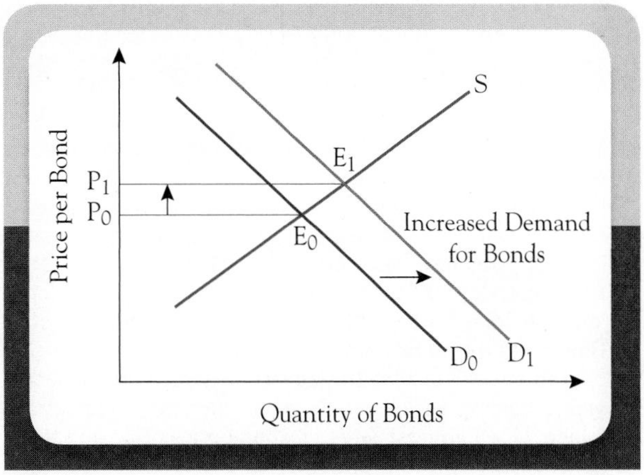

When there is an increase in investors' willingness to hold bonds, the bond demand curve shifts to the right, increasing bond prices and reducing interest rates.

**Wealth**   The more rapidly the economy grows, the wealthier individuals become. As their wealth increases, they increase their investment in stocks, bonds, real estate, and art. Thus, increases in wealth shift the demand for bonds to the right, raising bond prices and lowering yields (see Figure 6.3). This is what happens in a business-cycle expansion. In a recession, as wealth falls, the demand for bonds falls with it, lowering bond prices and raising interest rates.

**Demography**   As we discussed in Chapter 4, if you want to live well after you retire you need to save when you are young. That means that the changing age structure of the population will change the savings rate, and that will affect the demand for bonds. When the baby boom generation was working, they were saving (though perhaps not as much as necessary for a comfortable retirement) and now that they are retiring we would expect the amount of savings to decline.

**Expected Inflation**   Changes in expected inflation alter investors' willingness to purchase bonds promising fixed-dollar payments. A decline in expected inflation means that the payments promised by the bond's issuer have a higher value than borrowers originally thought, so the bond will become more attractive. This fall in expected inflation shifts the bond demand curve to the right, increasing demand at each price and lowering the yield, as shown in Figure 6.3. In short, the higher real return on the bond increases the willingness of would-be lenders to buy it at any given price. Note that the decline in expected inflation has reduced the nominal interest rate that investors require in order to make a loan.

**Expected Returns and Expected Interest Rates**   An investor's desire to hold any particular financial instrument depends on how its return compares to those of alternative instruments. Bonds are no different. *If the return on bonds rises relative to the return on alternative investments, the quantity of bonds demanded at every price will rise, shifting the bond demand curve to the right.* This leads us to conclude that bond prices are

---

[5] We are discussing the bond market as though Canada didn't supply savings to other countries, and didn't receive savings from other countries, whereas in fact both of these forces are very important. One way to deepen the discussion is to think of our model as a model of global bond prices and yields. (Real) global interest rates tend to move together and all the factors that we have listed are the forces that determine the level of global interest rates. In Chapter 10 we discuss the global capital market.

# YOUR FINANCIAL WORLD
Understanding the Ads in the Newspaper

You're drinking your coffee and as you read the business news, something catches your eye. An investment company is advertising that its bond mutual funds returned 13½ percent over the last year. But you remember that interest rates have been pretty low—7 percent at most. And a quick check of the numbers in the business section you're holding tells you that your recollection is correct. How could the ad be right?

The answer is that the advertisement is about last year's holding period return, when interest rates were falling. When interest rates fall, bond prices rise and the holding period return is higher than the interest rate. And the longer the term of the bond, the bigger the price movements for a given interest rate change. To see what can happen, take an example of a 20-year, 7 percent

coupon bond with a face value $100. If the interest rate is initially 7 percent, this bond sells for $100. But if the interest rate falls by even one-half of one percentage point to 6½ percent, the price will rise to about $106.50, giving the owner a 6½ percent capital gain. Adding this to the 7 percent coupon payments, we get a one-year holding period return of 13½ percent.

So the ad isn't really much of a mystery once you think about it. But the implication of the ad, that these are great investments, is something you ought to think about. Remember, if interest rates go back up, things won't be so pretty. When it says at the bottom of the ad that "Past Performance Is No Indication of Future Returns" you should take the statement very seriously.

connected to the stock market. Investors see bonds as an alternative to stocks, so when the stock market drops, they shift their portfolios into bonds, increasing demand, driving prices up and interest rates down.

Similarly, when interest rates are expected to change in the future, bond prices adjust immediately. Recall that the holding period return on a bond depends on the coupon payment plus the capital gain or loss. When interest rates fall, bond prices rise, creating a capital gain. Whenever interest rates are expected to fall, then bond prices are expected to rise, creating an expectation of a capital gain. This makes bonds more attractive. Knowing that bonds are a good investment, investors increase their demand immediately, driving bond prices up. So *an increase in the expected return on a bond, relative to the return on alternatives, shifts bond demand to the right*.

### Default Risk Relative to Alternatives
On May 13, 2002, a headline in The Wall Street Journal read "Japan Gets Irate at Having Its Risk Compared to Botswana." What's going on here? Japan is the second largest economy in the world, with a population of more than 125 million and a GDP of $3.5 trillion. Botswana is a country in Southern Africa with a population of 1.5 million people and a GDP of $13.5 billion.

The problem was that investors had two reasons to question Japan's budget outlook. First, the current fiscal deficit was a very high 7 percent of GDP. Second, over the next few decades, the Japanese government would have to find a way to meet its promises to make pension payments to the growing number of retirees. Together these created the perception that Japan's bonds were risky, which meant that investors would be less interested in holding them.

Remember that investors require compensation for risk, which means that when a bond becomes more or less risky, the demand for the bond changes. The less risky the bond, the higher the price investors are willing to pay for it, all other things being equal. From this, we can conclude that *if a bond becomes less risky relative to alternative investments, the demand for the bond shifts to the right*. The reason Japan was irate was because the price of its bonds would be lower, so its borrowing costs would be higher.

**Table 6.4**   Factors That Shift Bond Demand to the Right, Raise Bond Prices, and Lower Interest Rates

| Change | Effect on Bond Demand | Shift in Bond Demand |
|---|---|---|
| An increase in wealth or an increase in the share of young workers in the economy increases demand for all assets including bonds. | Bond demand shifts to the right, bond prices $\uparrow$, and interest rates $\downarrow$ | |
| A reduction in expected inflation makes bonds with fixed nominal payments more desirable. | Bond demand shifts to the right, bond prices $\uparrow$, and interest rates $\downarrow$ | |
| A decrease in the expected future interest rate makes bonds more attractive. | Bond demand shifts to the right, bond prices $\uparrow$, and interest rates $\downarrow$ | |
| An increase in the expected return on the bond relative to the expected return on alternatives makes bonds more attractive. | Bond demand shifts to the right, bond prices $\uparrow$, and interest rates $\downarrow$ | |
| A fall in the riskiness of the bond relative to the riskiness of alternatives makes bonds more attractive. | Bond demand shifts to the right, bond prices $\uparrow$, and interest rates $\downarrow$ | |
| An increase in the liquidity of the bond relative to the liquidity of alternatives makes bonds more attractive. | Bond demand shifts to the right, bond prices $\uparrow$, and interest rates $\downarrow$ | |

**Liquidity Relative to Alternatives** Liquidity measures how easily and cheaply investors can convert one financial instrument into another. A liquid asset is something investors can sell without a large loss in value. Investors like liquidity; the more liquid a bond, the higher the demand for it, all other things being equal. So if a bond's liquidity changes, demand for it changes, too.

During the financial crisis in the fall of 1998, for example, the bonds issued by emerging-market governments in Latin America and Eastern Europe became virtually impossible to sell. For all practical purposes, the market for them disappeared. When a buyer could be found, prices were severely depressed. Who wants to buy a bond that is difficult to sell? Liquidity matters. The less liquid a bond is, the lower the demand for it, and the lower the price. So *when a bond becomes more liquid relative to alternatives, the demand curve shifts to the right*.

## Understanding Changes in Equilibrium Bond Prices and Interest Rates

Before we continue, let's look again at how bond prices and interest rates move in response to changes in expected inflation and a change in general business conditions. Recall that expected inflation affects both bond supply and bond demand. An increase in expected inflation reduces the real cost of borrowing, shifting bond *supply* to the *right*. But at the same time, this increase in expected inflation lowers the real return on lending, shifting bond *demand* to the *left*. These two effects reinforce each other, lowering the price of the bond and raising the interest rate (see Figure 6.4).

But we can say more than that. Notice that in Figure 6.4, point $E_1$ is directly below $E_0$. When the expected inflation rate rises, the shifts exactly offset each other, so that the equilibrium bond price falls but the quantity traded doesn't change. Is this always the case? To answer that, we can use the concept of real interest rates. If the quantity of bonds demanded and the quantity supplied are functions of the real rate of return, then the shifts will be offsetting and the new price level $P_1$ will imply the same real rate of return as the old price level $P_0$. Remember, the lower price of bonds implies a higher nominal rate of return.

We also saw that changes in business conditions affect both the supply and the demand for bonds. A business-cycle downturn reduces business investment opportunities, shifting the bond *supply* to the left, and reduces wealth, shifting bond *demand* in the same direction. When both curves shift in the same direction, the price can rise or fall. The theory does not give us an unambiguous prediction. In cases like this, we can look for regular movements in the data to help resolve the question. In this case we know that in recessions, interest rates tend to fall, so prices should increase (see Figure 6.5).

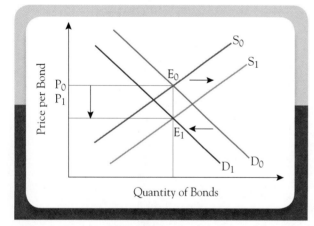

**Figure 6.4** **Equilibrium in the Bond Market: The Effect of an Increase in Expected Inflation**

An increase in expected inflation increases bond supply from $S_0$ to $S_1$ by lowering the real cost of borrowing. At the same time, it reduces bond demand from $D_0$ to $D_1$ by reducing the real interest rate bondholders receive. These two effects reinforce each other, lowering the bond's price from $P_0$ to $P_1$ and increasing the interest rate.

# Why Bonds Are Risky

"Bonds Look Attractive Now but They
Come with Risks"
—*The Wall Street Journal*, July 26, 2002

How can bonds be risky? They are promises to make
fixed payments on future dates. Where is the risk in
that? The fact is that the return an investor receives
for holding a bond is far from riskless. Bondholders
face three major risks. **Default risk** is the chance that
the bond's issuer may fail to make the promised payment. **Liquidity risk** means that when an investor
wants to sell a bond there may not be anyone who
wants to buy it. **Inflation risk** means an investor
can't be sure of what the real value of the payments
will be, even if they are made. And **interest rate
risk** arises from a bondholder's investment horizon,
which may be shorter than the maturity of the bond.
If, for example, the interest rate were to rise between
the time the bond is purchased and the time it is
sold, the investor would suffer a capital loss.[6]

We'll look at each of these sources of risk separately, using the tools for understanding risk intro-

**Figure 6.5**   Equilibrium in the Bond Market: The Effect of a Business-Cycle Downturn

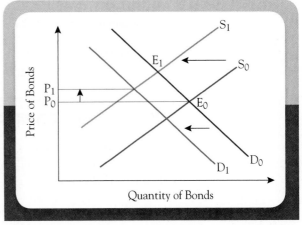

Interest rates tend to fall during business-cycle downturns.
The combination of reduced investment opportunities for
businesses, which shifts the bond supply curve to the left
from $S_0$ to $S_1$, and a decline in household wealth, which shifts
the bond demand curve to the left from $D_0$ to $D_1$, may cause
an increase in bond prices and a drop in the interest rate.

duced in Chapter 5. Remember that risk arises from the fact that an investment has
many possible payoffs during the horizon for which it is held. So, in looking at the risk a
bondholder faces, we need to ask what the possible payoffs are and how likely each one is
to occur. As we do, we will be looking at the impact of risk on the bond's return relative
to the risk-free rate. That is, we will try to figure out how certain risks affect the premium
investors require over the risk-free return. Once again, *risk requires compensation*.

## Default Risk

Default risk, sometimes termed "credit risk," is the risk that a bond issuer will fail to
make the promised payments. While we might ignore default risk in thinking about
Canadian government bonds, we cannot do so when discussing bonds issued by private corporations. When corporations fail to meet their payments, what happens to
the price of their bonds?

To figure out the answer, let's list all the possibilities and payoffs that might occur,
along with their probabilities. We can then calculate the expected value of the promised payments, from which we can compute the bond's price and yield. Suppose, for
example, that the one-year risk-free interest rate is 5 percent. Flim.com, an Internet
firm hoping to market its own brand of e-cash called "Flam,"[7] has issued one-year, 5
percent coupon bonds with a face value of $100. This represents a promise to pay
$105 in one year. What is the price of this bond?

---

[6] Beyond these primary sources of risk, the buyer of a bond faces a number of more subtle risks. For example,
downgrade risk means that a bond may be downgraded and if the investor wants to sell it before maturity the
price will have decreased. An investor who buys a bond denominated in a foreign currency faces the risk of
changes in the exchange rate. A bond may promise payments in euros, say, which must be converted into
dollars before they can be used or reinvested.

[7] This example is not farfetched. In the 1990s a company called flooz.com tried to issue e-money called "flooz."

| Table 6.5 | Expected Value of Flim.com Bond Payment | | |

| Possibilities | Payoff | Probability | Payoff Probabilities |
| --- | --- | --- | --- |
| Full Payment | $105 | 0.90 | $94.50 |
| Default | $0 | 0.10 | $0 |
| Expected Value = Sum of Payoffs times Probabilities = $94.50 | | | |

If Flim.com were risk free, and lenders were certain they would be paid back, the price of the bond would be computed as the present value of the $105 payment, calculated using the 5 percent risk-free interest rate.

$$\text{Price of Flim.com bond if it is risk free} = \frac{\$100 + \$5}{1.05} = \$100.00$$

But unlike the Canadian government, Flim.com may not make the payments. People might be unwilling to use Flam, so Flim.com could default. Suppose there is a 0.10 probability (one chance in ten) that Flim.com will go bankrupt before paying bondholders their $105. To simplify the example, we will assume that in the case of default, the bondholders get nothing. This means that there are two possible payoffs, $105 and $0 (see Table 6.5).

Table 6.5 shows that the expected value of the payment on this bond is $94.50. But even if the payment is made, it will be made one year from now, which means that the price we would be willing to pay for the bond today must be the present value of the future payment. Using the risk-free interest rate for this computation, we find that

$$\text{Expected present value of Flim.com bond payment} = \frac{\$94.50}{1.05} = \$90$$

So the bond will sell for $90. What yield to maturity does this price imply? If the promised payment is $105, the promised yield to maturity is

$$\text{Promised yield on Flim.com bond} = \frac{\$105}{\$90} - 1 = 0.1667$$

Converting the decimal to a percentage, we get an interest rate of 16.67 percent.[8] Since the default-risk premium is the promised yield to maturity minus the risk-free rate, it is 16.67 percent – 5 percent = 11.67 percent.

In calculating the default-risk premium on Flim.com's bond, we computed the expected value of holding the bond—the yield at which the bond is a fair bet. But we know that risk-averse investors require some compensation for bearing risk. The more risk, the greater the compensation they demand. Only a risk-neutral investor would be willing to pay $90 for this bond. Any risk premium will drive the price down below $90 and push the yield to maturity above 16.67 percent.

This example shows that the higher the default risk, the higher the probability that the bondholders will not receive the promised payments. Risk reduces the expected value of a given promise, lowering the price an investor is willing to pay and raising the yield. The higher the default risk, the higher the yield.

---

[8] This set of calculations could have been done in reverse. Given the yield of 16.67 percent and the characteristics of the bond, it is straightforward to compute the probability of default as 10 percent.

## APPLYING THE CONCEPT
### RISKY TRUCK-SCHOOL STUDENT LOANS

You can find default risk in some strange places. On November 11, 2002, the Credit Markets column of *The Wall Street Journal* told the story of 90,000 student loans valued at more than $500 million.[*] The loans, made to students at truck-driving schools, had been bundled together and bonds had been issued, backed by payments on the loans. These are *asset-backed securities*, as described in Chapter 3. Unfortunately, by 2002, a staggering 70 percent of the student loans included in this investment were in default, guarantee-ing that someone involved in this particular investment was going to take a hit. Interestingly, that someone turned out not to be the people who bought the securities backed by the loans, but the company that had insured the loans.

What is surprising is that anyone was willing to insure these loans in the first place. Think about it: How do you find a truck driver who stops paying you back in order to demand repayment? Most of the time truck drivers are on the road. Sometimes you don't need mathematical formulas to see risk. You just need a bit of common sense.

[*] See Christine Richard and David Feldheim, "Truck-School Loans Get Lost as Royal Indemnity Files Suit," *The Wall Street Journal*, November 11, 2002, C13.

## Liquidity Risk

Many bondholders expect that they will be able to sell their bonds on the secondary market if they need to have cash. For government securities this expectation is almost always realized and government securities have little liquidity risk. But the market for corporate bonds is a lot thinner; even in good times there may not be anyone wanting to hold a particular corporate bond when you want to sell it. In bad times, it is a lot worse. For example, the spread between AAA corporate bonds and U.S. Treasury bonds in mid-2007 was about 60 basis points. In March 2009, it peaked at 300 bps. If you wanted to sell a good corporate bond in early 2009, you would have taken a significant capital loss; the potential for that kind of loss is liquidity risk.[9]

## Inflation Risk

With few exceptions, bonds promise to make fixed-dollar payments. That is, a $100 face value, one-year bond at 5 percent is a promise to make a $105 payment in one year. If this promise comes from the government (and therefore is free of default risk), the bondholder can be sure of receiving the $105 payment. Still, there is a risk of inflation. Remember that what you care about is the purchasing power of the money, not the number of dollars. In other words, bondholders are interested in the *real interest rate*, not just the nominal interest rate. And they don't know what the inflation rate will be.

Let's look at an example that shows how inflation risk affects the interest rate. To begin with, think about the interest rate as having three components: the real interest rate, expected inflation, and a compensation for inflation risk. Suppose the real interest rate is 3 percent but we are unsure what the inflation rate will be. It could be either 1 percent or 3 percent with equal probability (see case I in Table 6.6 on page 126). Expected inflation is 2 percent, with a standard deviation of 1.0 percent. This means the nominal interest rate should equal the 3 percent real interest rate plus the 2 percent expected inflation plus the compensation for inflation risk. The greater the inflation risk, the larger the compensation for it will be.

[9] If there is a maturity mismatch (for example, the issue of corporate paper to finance long-term debts) then liquidity risk can be extreme. The inability of ABCP issuers to roll over their commercial paper in August 2007, and the resulting Montreal Accord that froze the issues, meant that holders could not get cash for what they had thought were short-term liquid assets. See Applying the Concept: The ABCP Debacle in Chapter 7 on page 137.

# YOUR FINANCIAL WORLD
## Bonds Guaranteed to Beat Inflation

Inflation creates risk that the nominal return you receive on a bond won't be worth as much as you expected. If a bond pays a 6 percent yield but the inflation rate is also 6 percent, then the real return is zero! What can you do? You could accept the inflation risk, buy a regular bond, and hope for the best. But that's not always appealing.

Fortunately, there are alternatives. One is to buy a type of Canadian government bond that compensates you for inflation, a real return bond (RRB). This inflation-indexed bond is structured so that the government promises to pay you a fixed interest rate on the principal adjusted for the change in the consumer price index (the CPI). Interest is paid semi-annually so, for instance, if you buy a $1,000 bond with an interest rate of 3 percent, and the CPI rises by 1 percent in the first six months, you will get a payment of half of 3 percent of $1,010 ($1,000 plus 1 percent). If the CPI increased by 5 percent, then you'll get half of 3 percent of $1,050 for your first interest payment. And at maturity you receive the inflation-adjusted principal so

there is no inflation risk. And since the Canadian government issues these bonds, there is no default risk.

The Government of Canada real return bonds are available through financial institutions or an online brokerage in denominations of $1,000 or more. You could also buy real return bonds issued by a provincial government, or shares in an ETF (Exchange Traded Fund) such as iShares™ XRB, which holds a range of federal and provincial real return bonds. In either case, remember that the holding period return has two components, the current yield and the capital gain or loss. If the current inflation rate falls, the current yield will fall. If the expected future inflation rate falls, then the price will fall and you will experience a capital loss. Of course, it works the other way if the inflation rate rises.

In general, the RRBs trade in a relatively thin market and so are not as liquid as other government securities, which we have seen reduces their price relative to similar (not inflation-protected) bonds.

In cases II and III, expected inflation is the same (2 percent) but the standard deviation is lower, since we are more certain that the inflation rate will be close to its expected value. That is, case III is less risky than case II, which is less risky than case I. Since risk requires compensation, we would expect the interest rate to be highest in case I and lowest in case III. While we may not see this distinction much in Canada or the United States, where inflation is stable, emerging-market countries can go through periods when increases in inflation risk substantially drive up nominal interest rates.

Table 6.6    Inflation Risk

| Inflation Rate | Probabilities | | |
|---|---|---|---|
| | Case I | Case II | Case III |
| 1 percent | 0.50 | 0.25 | 0.10 |
| 2 percent | – | 0.50 | 0.80 |
| 3 percent | 0.50 | 0.25 | 0.10 |
| Expected inflation | 2 percent | 2 percent | 2 percent |
| Standard deviation | 1.0 percent | 0.71 percent | 0.45 percent |

## Interest Rate Risk

To explain interest rate risk, we'll focus on a government bond and assume that we know how much inflation there will be, so there is no default or inflation risk. Interest rate risk arises from the fact that investors don't know the holding period return of a long-term bond. Remember that when interest rates change, bond prices move; the longer the term of the bond, the larger the price change for a given change in the interest rate. Now think about what happens if you have a short investment horizon. If you buy a long-term bond, you will need to sell the bond before it matures, so you have to worry about what will happen if the interest rate changes.

Whenever there is a mismatch between your investment horizon and a bond's maturity, there is interest rate risk. Because the prices of long-term bonds can change dramatically, this can be an important source of risk. Looking at Table 6.2, you can see that in January 2009, the Canada bond maturing on June 1, 2010 with a 9.5 percent coupon, traded for $111.70 per $100 face value. But between January and June 2009, interest rates had fallen across the board, and the price of this bond fell to $108.78. An investor who bought the bond in January and sold it only five months later would have experienced a roughly 2 percent capital loss.

The lesson is that any move in interest rates changes the price of a bond. For investors with holding periods shorter than the maturity of the bond, the potential for a change in interest rates creates risk. The more likely interest rates are to change during the bondholder's investment horizon, the larger the risk of holding a bond.

Table 6.7 summarizes the main sources of risk in bond holding. (For investors holding foreign currency–denominated bonds we would need to include currency risk.) Although investing in a bond is less risky than, say, investing in an equity, it is not risk-free. To minimize risk, an investor can buy a bond that will mature when the funds are needed, so that any illiquidity or interest rate risk is not important or can buy a government bond to eliminate default risk and a real return bond to eliminate inflation risk. Of course, such a bond has the lowest rate of return.

**Table 6.7**   **What Makes Bonds Risky?**

| | |
|---|---|
| *Default risk* | The issuer may not make the promised payments. |
| *Liquidity risk* | The investor may not be able to sell the bond when she would like. |
| *Inflation risk* | Inflation may turn out to be higher than expected, reducing the real return on holding the bond. |
| *Interest rate risk* | Interest rates may rise between the time a bond is purchased and the time it is sold, reducing the bond's price. |

## IN THE NEWS
### Bowie Bonds May Make a Comeback

## The Wall Street Journal

### By Karen Richardson

#### August 23, 2005

The boom in digital downloads is music to the ears of bankers and others hoping to start selling "Bowie bonds" again.

These bonds give investors a piece of future earnings by a musician or other notable artist. The original bond sold in 1997 raised $55 million for musician David Bowie, whose album sales created the revenue stream for the securities. Other bonds followed, securitizing the tuneful takings of James Brown, Ashford & Simpson and the Isley Brothers.

Then the recording industry skidded into an extended downturn, and the Bowie bond structure lost much of its glamour. Last year, Mr. Bowie's bonds fell to Earth when Moody's Investors Service lowered its rating* citing lower-than-expected revenue "due to weakness in sales for recorded music." Few Bowie bonds have been sold since 2001, and music-backed bonds today represent less than 1 percent of the so-called asset-backed securities market.

Now, with iTunes and other online platforms showing promise in selling songs again, bankers and others are hoping for an encore performance for the bonds.

The legal, paid-for downloading of tunes "definitely helps," says James Altucher, managing partner at Formula Capital LLC, a hedge fund in New York. Mr. Altucher says he would be interested in buying new Bowie bonds.

"Technology is bad for us in terms of illegal file-sharing, but it's positive in terms of 500 cable-TV channels, iTunes and online ads," says David Pullman, head of Pullman Group LLC, who created and launched the Bowie bond in 1997. "Technology is disruptive for a short time, but the volume of sales is going to be so much greater."

Mr. Pullman's firm has had a sometimes-contentious relationship with other banks over the creation of new Bowie bonds, but Pullman Group is now in talks with heirs of Bob Marley to create bonds based on the deceased reggae artist's song catalog. The firm also has copyrights from several dozen artists and songwriters for songs from the 1940s to the 1980s with an eye toward more bonds.

Of course, digital technology and the Internet continue to pose huge risks to the music industry and have hurt royalty streams, which for decades were based on multisong recordings (Frank Sinatra helped usher in the "long-play" format in the 1950s with his theme albums). The International Federation of the Phonographic Industry estimates about 870 million music files are offered illegally online.

## Terms

## Chapter Summary

1. Valuing bonds is an application of present value.
   a. Discount bonds promise to make a single payment on a pre-determined future date.
   b. Fixed-payment loans promise to make a fixed number of equal payments at regular intervals.
   c. Coupon bonds promise to make periodic interest payments and repay the principal at maturity.
   d. Consols (perpetuities) promise to make periodic coupon payments forever.

"Pirates will always find new ways of challenging copyright lawyers," says Alan Dalinka, a partner in Chicago law firm DLA Piper Rudnick Gray Cary US LLP.

But while royalties from new sources such as digital downloads, satellite radio, and cell phone ring tones are small relative to the industry's lost revenue, they are growing fast. "If more people figure out how to make money from music digitally, then you have a new, predictable revenue stream that you can securitize," Mr. Dalinka says.

Consider: Apple Computer Inc.'s iTunes Web-based music store has already sold more than 500 million songs since it was launched in 2003, and song sales now account for a big chunk of Apple's revenue.

And while the Internet has in one sense taken consumers back to the days of the 45-rpm record, buying just one song at a time, it has also opened up other potential revenue streams that can be turned into bonds. For example, ring tones—snippets of original recordings that announce an incoming call on a cell phone—"are growing exponentially" as a royalty stream, says Mark Friesen, founder of market-research firm Consect.

Meanwhile, the price competition already affecting the music-download business may squeeze profit margins for record companies, but it doesn't cut the artists' payday: Every single downloaded to burn a new CD, "ring" a cell phone or serve as fodder for spirited karaoke fans by law pays the musician about 8.5 U.S. cents.

### LESSONS OF THE ARTICLE

Virtually anything can be turned into a bond, even the future revenues from the sale of rock music. Here, the revenue from the retail sales of David Bowie's music in all its forms has been turned into an asset-backed security. The benefit to Bowie is that he received a cash payment immediately, and shifted the risk that future revenue would be low to the bondholders. Thus buyers of Bowie bonds must have believed that his music will continue to sell well, maintaining the revenue needed to make the promised payments.

* Ratings provide investors with an estimate of a bond's default risk; the lower the rating, the higher the risk of default. See the discussion in Chapter 7.

2. Yields are measures of the return on holding a bond.
   a. The yield to maturity is a measure of the interest rate on a bond. To compute it, set the price of the bond equal to the present value of the payments.
   b. The current yield on a bond is equal to the coupon rate divided by the price.
   c. When the price of a bond is above its face value, the coupon rate is greater than the current yield, which is higher than the yield to maturity.
   d. One-year holding period returns are equal to the sum of the current yield and any capital gain or loss arising from a change in a bond's price.

3. Bond prices (and bond yields) are determined by supply and demand in the bond market.
   a. The higher the price, the larger the quantity of bonds supplied.
   b. The higher the price, the smaller the quantity of bonds demanded.
   c. The supply of bonds rises when
      i. Governments need to borrow more.
      ii. General business conditions improve.
      iii. Expected inflation rises.
   d. The demand for bonds rises when
      i. Wealth increases.
      ii. The population is younger.
      iii. Expected inflation falls.

iv. The expected return, relative to other investments, rises.

v. The expected future interest rate falls.

vi. Bonds become less risky relative to other investments.

vii. Bonds become more liquid relative to other investments.

4. Bonds are risky because of

a. Default risk: the risk that the issuer may fail to pay.

b. Liquidity risk: the risk that you can't sell the bond when you want.

b. Inflation risk: the risk that the inflation rate may be more or less than expected, affecting the real value of the promised nominal payments.

c. Interest rate risk: the risk that the interest rate may change, causing the bond's price to change.

## Conceptual Problems

1. Consider a Canadian government Treasury bill with 270 days to maturity. If the annual yield is 3.8 percent, what is the price?

2. Which of these $100 face value bonds will have a higher yield to maturity and why?

a. 6 percent coupon bond selling for $85

b. 7 percent coupon bond selling for $100

c. 8 percent coupon bond selling for $115

3. You are considering purchasing a consol that promises annual payments of $4.

a. If the current interest rate is 5 percent, what is the price of the consol?

b. You are concerned that the interest rate may rise to 6 percent. Compute the percentage change in the price of the consol and the percentage change in the interest rate. Compare them.

c. Your investment horizon is one year. You purchase the consol when the interest rate is 5 percent and sell it a year later, following a rise in the interest rate to 6 percent. What is your holding period return?

4.* Suppose you purchase a three-year, 5 percent coupon bond at par and hold it for two years. During that time, the interest rate falls to 4 percent. Calculate your annual holding-period return.

5. Go to the Bank of Canada website and find the data on yields on two-year Government of Canada bonds over the last five years. Use the supply and demand model to explain the changes you see.

6. A 10-year discount bond has a yield of 6 percent. Through a series of unfortunate circumstances, expected inflation rises from 2 percent to 3 percent.

a. Compute the change in the price of the bond.

b. Suppose that expected inflation is still 2 percent, but the probability that it will move to 3 percent has risen. Describe the consequences for the price of the bond.

7. Other musicians, among them Rod Stewart, James Brown, and Dusty Springfield, have issued bonds similar to the Bowie bonds described in In the News: Bowie Bonds May Make a Comeback on page 128. What is likely to make such bond issues successful?

8. As you read the business news, you come across an ad for a bond mutual fund, a fund that pools the investments from a large number of people and then purchases bonds, giving the individuals "shares" in the fund. The company claims its fund has had a return of 13½ percent over the last year. But you remember that interest rates have been pretty low—5 percent at most. A quick check of the numbers in the business section you're holding tells you that your recollection is correct. Explain the logic behind the mutual fund's claim in the ad.

9. At the dinner table, your father is extolling the benefits of investing in bonds. He insists that as a conservative investor he will make only investments that are safe, and what could be safer than a bond, especially a Canadian government bond? What accounts for his view of bonds? Explain why you think he is right or wrong.

10.* Consider a one-year, 10 percent coupon bond with a face value of $1,000 issued by a private corporation. The one-year risk-free rate is 10 percent. The corporation has hit hard times, and the consensus is that there is a 20 percent probability that it will default on its bonds. If an investor were willing to pay $775 for the bond, is that investor risk neutral or risk averse?

* Indicates more difficult problems.

# Analytical Problems

11. After one year, if the yield to maturity on a multi-year coupon bond issued at par is higher than the coupon rate, what happened to the price of the bond during that first year?

12. Use your knowledge of bond pricing to explain under what circumstances you would be willing to pay the same price for a consol that pays $5 a year forever and a 5 percent, 10-year coupon bond with a face value of $100 that makes annual coupon payments for only 10 years.

13.* You are about to purchase your first home and read an ad regarding mortgage rates. What factors would you consider in deciding whether to buy a fixed- or variable-rate mortgage? A five-year mortgage or a one-year mortgage?

14. Use the model of supply and demand for bonds to illustrate and explain the impact of each of the following on the equilibrium quantity of bonds outstanding and on equilibrium bond prices and yields:
    a. A new Web site is launched, facilitating the trading of corporate bonds with much more ease than before.
    b. Expected inflation falls, evoking a much stronger response from issuers of bonds than investors in bonds.

c. The government removes tax incentives for investment and spends additional funds on a new education program. Overall, the changes have no affect on the government's financing requirements.
d. All leading indicators point to stronger economic growth in the near future. The response of bond issuers dominates that of bond purchasers.

15. Suppose the Canadian government decides to finance a deficit by increasing the amount of government debt outstanding. How would you expect this development to affect the Canadian bond market?

16. The real estate market is expected to weaken. Using the model of supply and demand for bonds, determine the impact on bond prices and yields.

17.* Suppose there is an increase in investors' willingness to hold bonds at a given price. Use the model for the demand and supply of bonds to show that the impact on the equilibrium bond price depends on how sensitive the quantity supplied of bonds is to the bond price.

18. Under what circumstances would purchasing a real return bond be virtually risk free?

# CHAPTER 7

## The Risk and Term Structure of Interest Rates

Borrowing is fundamental to the structure of capitalist economies: firms rely on borrowing to finance investments in plant and equipment and to finance working capital; households rely on borrowing to buy houses, cars, and other durable goods. Governments borrow to finance infrastructure development or cyclical deficits. The instruments that are used differ—bonds, commercial paper, credit cards, mortgages—but crucial to each is the interest rate and the risk attached to the loan.

Risk is endemic to financial markets. In December 2008, *The New York Times* declared that "the credit crunch has ballooned into Wall Street's biggest crisis since the Great Depression," and Mark Carney, the Governor of the Bank of Canada began a speech noting that "the turmoil has deteriorated into a full blown financial crisis."[1] A financial crisis affects investors in different ways, as the value of financial assets changes dramatically. The lucky few who predicted the crisis (and acted on that prediction!) did well, but the majority of investors were made much worse off. But while prices for many assets fell, there were also tremendous changes in relative asset prices. In the bond market, some interest rates plummeted while others soared. This simultaneous increase in some interest rates and decline in others—a rise in what are called interest rate spreads—was a clear sign that the substantial stress the financial markets were experiencing could easily spread to the wider economy, affecting everyone.

Changing bond prices have a pronounced effect on the borrowing costs that corporations and governments face. After World War II, Canadian government debt was approximately 150 percent of GDP, but interest rates were about 1 percent, so the amount of taxes that had to be raised to service that debt was about 1.5 percent of GDP. Contrast that with the situation in the mid-1990s when the government's debt was less than 100 percent of GDP but interest rates were above 6 percent. Then, debt service cost 8 percent of GDP a year, which was nearly 20 percent of government expenditures. To reduce the burden of that debt, the government cut back services in many areas for many years. The long-term impact of the dramatic increases in government expenditures in 2009–10 will depend a lot on what happens to interest rates over the next few years.

These examples highlight the need to understand the differences among the many types of bonds that are sold and traded in financial markets. We will study the differences among the multitude of bonds issued by governments and private corporations. As we will see, these bonds differ in two crucial respects: the identity of the issuer and the time to maturity. The purpose of this chapter is to examine how each of these affects the price of a bond, and then to use our knowledge to interpret fluctuations in a broad variety of bond prices.

## Ratings and the Risk Structure of Interest Rates

Default is one of the most important risks a bondholder faces. Not surprisingly, the risk that an issuer will fail to make a bond's promised payments varies substantially from one borrower to another. The risk of default is so important to potential investors that

[1] Mark Carney, Speech to "Women in Capital Markets," December 17, 2008, http://www.bankofcanada.ca/en/speeches/2008/sp08-16.htm, retrieved August 5, 2009.

independent companies have come into existence to evaluate the creditworthiness of potential borrowers. These rating agencies estimate the likelihood that a corporate or government borrower will make a bond's promised payments. Let's look at these companies and the information that they produce.

## Bond Ratings

Two of the frequently used rating agencies in Canada are DBRS (Dominion Bond Rating Service Limited) and Standard & Poor's.[2] These companies monitor the status of individual bond issuers and individual bond issues, and assess the likelihood that a lender/bondholder will be repaid by a borrower/ bond issuer. Companies with good credit—those with low levels of debt, high profitability, and sizable amounts of cash assets—earn high bond ratings. A high rating suggests that a bond issuer will have little problem meeting a bond's payment obligations.

SOURCE: *Courtesy of Standard & Poor's.*

Table 7.1 on page 134 reports the rating systems of DBRS and Standard & Poor's. As you can see, they are very similar. Both systems are based on letters and bear a broad similarity to the rankings in minor-league baseball. Firms or governments with an exceptionally strong financial position carry the highest ratings and are able to issue the highest-rated bonds, Triple A. The Canadian federal government and Imperial Oil are both examples of entities that S&P has given AAA bond ratings.

The top four categories, AAA down to BBB, are considered investment-grade bonds, meaning they have a very low risk of default. These ratings are reserved for most government issuers as well as corporations that are among the most financially sound.[3] The distinction between investment-grade and speculative, noninvestment-grade bonds is an important one. A number of regulated institutional investors, among them some insurance companies, pension funds, and commercial banks, are not allowed to invest in bonds that are rated below BBB.[4]

Bonds issued by Sears Canada, and (the foreign currency debt of) Argentina are in the next two rating categories, BB and B. These companies and countries may have difficulty meeting their bond payments but are not at risk of immediate default. The final categories in Table 7.1, highly speculative bonds, include debts that are in serious risk of default (Category C bonds) or are already in default (Category D bonds).

Bonds rated in the speculative grades, those below BBB, are often referred to as junk bonds or sometimes more politely as *high-yield bonds* (a reminder that to obtain a high yield, investors must take a large risk).[5] There are two types of junk bonds. The first type, called fallen angels, were once investment-grade bonds, but their issuers fell on hard times. The second are cases in which little is known about the risk of the issuer.

Material changes in a firm's or government's financial conditions precipitate changes in its debt ratings. The rating services are constantly monitoring events and announcing modifications to their views on the creditworthiness of borrowers. If a particular

---

[2] The rating agencies recognized by Canadian securities regulators also include Moody's Investors Service, and Fitch Ratings.

[3] Government debt ratings are important, as they generally create a ceiling on the ratings for private companies in that country.

[4] Restrictions on the investments of financial intermediaries, such as insurance companies, are a matter for provincial regulators. There is no comprehensive reference for all of the legal restrictions that force financial firms to sell bonds whose ratings fall below BBB. In many cases, such as those of bond mutual funds, the restrictions are self-imposed.

[5] "Junk bond" is an informal term used to mean a highly speculative security that has a low rating; it has no exact or formal definition. For a history of junk bonds, see the book's Web site at www.mcgrawhill.ca/olc/cecchetti.

**Table 7.1**    A Guide to Bond Ratings

| | DBRS | Standard & Poor's | Description | Examples of Issuers with Bonds Outstanding in 2008 (S&P Ratings) |
|---|---|---|---|---|
| Investment Grade | AAA | AAA | Bonds of the best quality with the smallest risk of default. Issuers are exceptionally stable and dependable. | Government of Canada<br>Imperial Oil |
| | AA | AA | Superior credit quality with slightly higher degree of long-term risk than AAA. | Canadian Wheat Board<br>University of British Columbia |
| | A | A | Satisfactory quality, but somewhat vulnerable to changing economic conditions. | Potash Corp of Saskatchewan<br>Barrick Gold<br>Hydro One<br>Botswana |
| | BBB | BBB | Adequate credit quality, but vulnerable to changing economic conditions. | Rona<br>Republic of Colombia |
| Noninvestment, Speculative Grade | BB | BB | Some speculative element, with moderate security but not well safeguarded. | Cogeco Cable<br>Teck Cominco<br>Sears Canada |
| | B | B | Able to pay now but at risk of default in the future. | Mitel Networks<br>Argentina |
| Highly Speculative | CCC | CCC | Highly speculative quality; danger of default. | Air Canada<br>Mega Brands |
| | CC | CC | Poor quality, clear danger of default. | |
| | C | C | Lowest-rated, poor prospects of repayment. | |
| | D | D | In default. | Nortel Networks |

*For a more detailed definition of ratings, see DBRS' Web site, http://www.dbrs.com or Standard and Poor's Web site, http://www.standardandpoors.com. The example companies' ratings are S&P ratings as of June 5, 2009. Ratings must be construed solely as statements of opinion and not statements of fact as to creditworthiness or recommendations to purchase, sell, or hold any securities.*

*Institutions are reported here by whole rating category; there are subcategories, e.g., AA+, AA, AA– in S&P ratings. Remember that ratings are always subject to change and if you are interested in a particular company you should get updated rating information from S&P or one of the other ratings agencies.*

business or country encounters problems (as occurs with some frequency), the rating agencies will lower that issuer's bond rating in what is called a **ratings downgrade**. **Ratings upgrades** occur as well. Roughly 7 percent of AA-rated bonds are upgraded to AAA each year.[6] In 2005, Standard and Poor's upgraded 13 Canadian bonds and downgraded 24.

---

[6] On the Web sites of the rating agencies you can find the current and past ratings of particular issuers and of particular issues. The sites also include research papers on the frequency of downgrades and upgrades (http://www.dbrs.com; http://www.standardandpoors.com; http://www.moodys.com, or http://www.fitchrating.com.

## Commercial Paper Ratings

Commercial paper is a short-term version of a bond. Both corporations and governments issue commercial paper. Traditional commercial paper offers no collateral, or is *unsecured*, so only the most creditworthy companies can issue it.[7] Since 2000, asset-backed commercial paper (ABCP), which is secured by such assets as auto loans and credit card receivables—see Applying the Concept: The ABCP Debacle on page 137—has taken an increasing share of the commercial paper market. In 2007, there was over $100 billion of commercial paper outstanding in the Canada, mostly issued by financial institutions, about a third of which was ABCP.

Like a Treasury bill, commercial paper is issued on a discount basis, as a zero-coupon bond that specifies a single future payment with no associated coupon payments. For legal reasons, commercial paper usually has a maturity of less than a year, and often between 5 and 45 days.[8] Roughly one-third of all commercial paper is held by money market mutual funds (MMMFs), which require very short-term assets with immediate liquidity.

The rating agencies rate the creditworthiness of commercial paper issuers in the same way as they do bond issuers. Again, DBRS and Standard & Poor's have parallel rating schemes that differ primarily in their labelling (see Table 7.2). By some estimates,

**Table 7.2**   Commercial Paper Ratings

| | DBRS | Standard & Poor's | Description | Examples of Issuers with Commercial Paper Outstanding in 2009 (DBRS Ratings) |
|---|---|---|---|---|
| Investment or Prime Grade | R-1 high R-1 middle R-1 low | A-1+, A-1 | Considered very strong to strong credits, and exemplify above-average strength for the timely repayment of short-term liabilities. | ATB Financial Société de Transport de Montréal |
| | R-2 | A-2 | The ability to repay obligations as they mature remains acceptable; ratings in this category would be more vulnerable to adverse changes in financial and economic conditions. | Canada Safeway Magna International Ltd. |
| | R-3 | A-3 | Repayment is still expected, but the certainty of repayment could be affected by a variety of possible adverse developments. | Textron Financial Corp. |
| Speculative, below Prime Grade | R-4, R-5 | B, C | Capacity for repayment is small relative to higher-rated issuers. | GM Canada Ltd. E*Trade Financial Corp. |
| Defaulted | | D | | |

SOURCE: *For definitions of ratings see http://www.standardandpoors.com and http://www.dbrs.com Sample ratings are of DBRS ratings as of June 8, 2009. Remember that ratings are always subject to change and if you are interested in a particular company you should get updated rating information from DBRS or one of the other ratings agencies. Ratings must be construed solely as statements of opinion and not statements of fact as to creditworthiness or recommendations to purchase, sell or hold any securities.*

[7] Recall that collateral is something of value pledged by the borrower that the lender could sell if the loan is not repaid.

[8] Securities that have less than a year to maturity typically have much less costly requirements with respect to registration and issue of a prospectus.

Figure 7.1    **The Effect of an Increase in Risk on Equilibrium in the Bond Market**

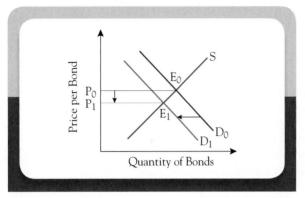

Increased risk reduces the demand for the bond at every price, shifting the demand curve to the left from $D_0$ to $D_1$. The result is a decline in the equilibrium price and quantity in the market. Importantly, the price falls from $P_0$ to $P_1$, so the yield on the bond must rise.

90 percent of issuers carry Standard and Poor's A-1 rating and another 9 percent are rated A-2. Speculative-grade commercial paper does exist, but not because it was originally issued as such.

## The Impact of Ratings on Yields

Bond ratings are designed to reflect default risk: The lower the rating, the higher the risk of default. We know investors require compensation for risk, so everything else held equal, the lower a bond's rating, the lower its price and the higher its yield. From Chapter 6, we know that we can think about changes in risk as shifts in the demand for bonds. Increases in risk will reduce investor demand for bonds at every price, shifting the demand curve to the left, decreasing the equilibrium price and increasing the yield (see Figure 7.1).

The easiest way to understand the quantitative impact of ratings on bond yields is to compare different bonds that are identical in every way except for the issuer's credit rating. Government of Canada bonds are the natural standard of comparison because they are the closest to being risk free. The yields on other bonds are measured in terms of the spread over Government of Canadas. (Remember from the definition in Chapter 5: Risk is measured relative to a benchmark. For bonds, the benchmark is Government of Canada bonds.[9])

We can think of any bond yield as the sum of two parts: the yield on the benchmark Government bond plus a default-risk premium, sometimes called a risk spread.

$$\text{Bond yield} = \text{Government of Canada yield} + \text{Default risk premium} \quad (1)$$

If bond ratings properly reflect the probability of default, then the lower the rating of the issuer, the higher the default-risk premium in equation (1). This way of thinking about bond yields provides us with a second insight: When Government bond yields move, all other yields move with them.

These two predictions—that interest rates on a variety of bonds will move together and that lower-rated bonds will have higher yields—are both borne out by the data. To see this, let's look at a plot of the risk structure of interest rates. Panel A of Figure 7.2 on page 138 shows the yield to maturity for 10-year government bonds and long-term corporate bonds. As you can see from the figure, the yields move together. When the government yield goes up or down, the corporate yield does too. While the default-risk premiums do fluctuate, changes in the Government of Canada yield accounts for most of the movement in the bond yields. Furthermore, the yield on the higher-rated government bond is consistently the lowest. In fact, over the 30 years from 1977 to 2007, the long-term government bond yield has averaged a full percentage point below the average yield on corporate bonds.

---

[9] Because having a benchmark is so important, and because there are so many different issues of Government of Canada bonds, particular Government of Canada bonds are designated "benchmark bonds" for each of the major maturities: 2 year, 3 year, 5 year, 7 year, and long term.

## APPLYING THE CONCEPT
### THE ABCP DEBACLE

In August 2007, the *Financial Post* headlined screamed "ABCP debacle"—and a year later the problems in the ABCP market were still making headlines. Investors who had bought $32 billion in short-term assets still had not received any return. The ABCP "debacle" illustrates the complexities of the financial markets and also many of the features that underlie the financial crisis that peaked in October 2008.

Let's begin with some basics. In Chapter 3, we described the process of securitization where a bank could bundle some loans together (for example, auto loans or credit card receivables) and sell them as a financial instrument—an asset backed security (ABS). The proceeds of the sale would give the bank funds for more lending and the buyer (termed a conduit) would be repaid when the loans came due. A conduit that bought the ABS could in turn finance that purchase by borrowing. For example, the firm could sell commercial paper using the ABS as collateral. That paper is Asset-Backed Commercial Paper (ABCP), which, in 2007, represented about one-third of the short-term assets in the Canadian capital market.

Firms, businesses, and crown corporations, even universities, frequently invest their working capital in commercial paper, which has a higher return than, say, putting the money in the bank, but is still highly liquid. ABCP has both default risk and liquidity risk. Default risk reflects the possibility that the underlying assets (the loans) may not repay when they come due. Liquidity risk arises because the ABCP has a fundamental maturity mismatch: The underlying loans were long term, but commercial paper is short term. So, if you held ABCP, the issuer typically got the funds to return your investment by rolling over the ABCP—when your commercial paper comes due, the issuer repaid you by selling it to another buyer.

Two factors mitigated these risks: commercial paper ratings and liquidity protection. Almost all the ABCP in the Canadian market was rated R-1 by DBRS, so that lenders were reassured that the underlying assets had relatively low default risk. To mitigate liquidity risk, all issuers of ABCP bought liquidity protection from a financial institution that committed to provide funds to issuers that could not roll over their ABCP under specific circumstances. Crucial to this story is that Canadian ABCP often had what was termed Canadian-type liquidity protection rather than global-style liquidity protection. Canadian-type liquidity protection required the insuring institution to buy the ABCP in the event of a general market disruption, something such as the market chaos following 9/11. In contrast, global-style protection covered any mismatch in asset and liability term, whether due to credit deterioration or market disruption. While DBRS did not reduce the rating of the ABCP with Canadian-style liquidity, Standard and Poor's declined to rate such assets. In 2002 the organization wrote, "Without liquidity lines .... [there are some sources of liquidity but] each of these avenues requires a leap of faith that liquidity relief will actually be available, which is insufficient as a primary response to liquidity risk for a conduit to achieve an investment grade CP rating."* But the investor might have looked to the market to see how much of a risk premium was included in the price of the ABCP with Canadian-style liquidity. In fact, the risk premium was low, less than 10 basis points, suggesting that the majority of investors did not see much risk.

Since 2000 the ABCP market had grown dramatically and had become more complex. The underlying assets were not only auto loans or credit card receivables, but also included complex derivatives, and derivatives of derivatives. While much of the ABCP was sponsored by Canadian banks, about one-third was sponsored by non-bank "third-party" institutions, and for those the liquidity protection was typically Canadian-style liquidity provided by offshore financial institutions.

Through 2007, the U.S. housing market had begun to cool, and the possibility of significant numbers of defaults loomed. Potential buyers of Canadian ABCP worried that these securities contained exposure to U.S. mortgages. Suddenly, it became hard, then impossible, to roll over the ABCP. Nobody wanted to buy it. Canadian banks provided liquidity support to ABCP they had sponsored, but while some institutions providing liquidity protection to the non-bank-sponsored ABCP funded when called upon, others argued that there had been no "general market disruption" and so they were not required to step in.

On August 16, 2007, the largest holders of third-party ABCP met and agreed to a standstill—rather than sell the ABCP at fire-sale prices, they would extend the loan and work out a longer-term strategy. Few realized how long that process would take. The holders of ABCP ranged from nearly 2,000 retail investors with less than $1 million each, to the large investors such as the Caisse de dépôt et placements du Québec—the manager of public-sector pensions in Quebec—which held $13 billion. The total value of non-bank-sponsored ABCP was $32 billion, about 9 percent of the short-term capital market assets in Canada. The restructuring took until March 2008. The large holders agreed that they would accept long-term notes, and that retail investors would get their money back immediately, and the holders agreed that they would not take legal action against any parties involved in the issuance and marketing of the ABCP. (Some holders believed that they had been misinformed about the riskiness of non-bank-sponsored ABCP by the institution that had sold it to them; agreeing not to take legal action was a difficult pill for them to swallow.) By August 2008, court challenges to the restructuring had been resolved and it seemed that the restructuring would occur. But, in the meantime, credit markets had seized up more widely, and so the deal struck in March was no longer viable. At the end of 2008, the Pan Canadian committee that had worked out the restructuring received guarantees totalling $3.15 billion from the governments of Canada, Quebec, Ontario, and Alberta to support the restructuring. Finally, in January 2009 the restructuring took place. Small investors got their investment back and the larger investors received long-term notes.

* "Regulatory Study, Review and Recommendations Concerning the Manufacture and Distribution by IIROC Member Firms of Third Party ABCP in Canada," October 2008, Investment Industry Regulatory Organization of Canada. Available at http://www.iiroc.ca.

Figure 7.2    The Risk Structure of Interest Rates

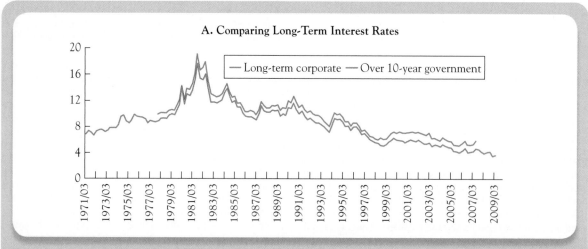

SOURCE: *Bank of Canada. CANSIM data, Table 176-0043, Government of Canada over 10 years, v122487; Corporate long term yields, v122518.*

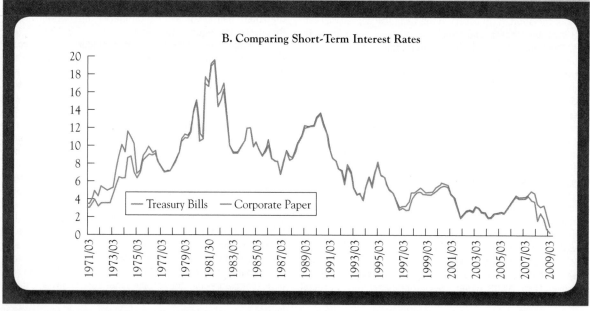

SOURCE: *Bank of Canada. CANSIM data, Table 176-0043, 3 month treasury bill yields, v122531; 3 month corporate paper yields, v122491.*

How important is one or two percentage points in yield? To see, we can do a simple computation. At an interest rate of 5 percent, the present value of a $100 payment made 10 years from now is $61.39. If the interest rate rose to 7 percent, the value of this same promise would decline to $50.83. So a two-percentage point increase in the yield, from 5 percent to 7 percent, lowers the value of the promise of $100 in 10 years by $10.56, or 17 percent!

## YOUR FINANCIAL WORLD
### Your Credit Rating

Companies aren't the only ones with credit ratings; you have one, too. Have you ever wondered how someone decides whether to give you a loan or a credit card? The answer is that there are companies keeping track of your financial information. They rate your creditworthiness, and they know more about you than you might think. Credit-rating companies know all about your credit cards, your car loan or mortgage (if you have one), and whether you pay your bills on time. All of this information is combined in something called a credit score. If you have low levels of debt and pay your bills on time, you have a high credit score.

You should care about your credit score; here's why. Lenders use credit scores to calculate the interest rate they charge on a loan. With a top credit score, a four-year, $10,000 car loan might have an interest rate of 6¾ percent and monthly payments of $237. But if your credit score was low, because you missed a payment on a credit card or paid your utility bill late, then the interest rate could be as high as 16 percent, which would mean monthly payments as much as $50 higher. The same principle applies to home mortgages; the better your credit score, the lower the interest rate. It pays to pay all your bills on time.

Ironically, someone who has never had a credit card and never owed anyone any money has no credit history at all and so will have a low credit score. You cannot start too soon in creating a record as a good credit risk. And you are entitled to a free annual credit report from each of the credit-rating companies. To find out how to get it, go to http://www.ic.gc.ca/eic/site/oca-bc.nsf/eng/ca02197.html.

From the viewpoint of the borrower, an increase in the interest rate from 5 percent to 7 percent means paying $7 rather than $5 per year for each $100 borrowed. That is a 40 percent difference. Clearly, ratings are crucial to corporations' ability to raise financing. Whenever a company's bond rating declines, the cost of funds goes up, impairing the company's ability to finance new ventures.[10]

What is true for long-term bond yields is true for short-term bond yields; they move together, and lower ratings imply higher yields. Compare the yields on three-month Treasury bills with those on corporate paper of the same maturity (see Panel B of Figure 7.2). The two yields clearly move together, and the Treasury bill yield is always lower than the yield on corporate paper. From 1971 to 2008, the spread of corporate paper over Canadian Treasury bills averaged about half of one percentage point, or roughly 50 basis points. (Recall from Chapter 4 that a basis point is one one-hundredth of a percentage point, or 0.01 percent.)

The lesson is clear; investors must be compensated for assuming risk. The less creditworthy the borrower, the higher the risk of default, the lower the borrower's rating, and the higher the cost of borrowing. And the lower the rating of the bond or commercial paper, the higher the yield.

## The Term Structure of Interest Rates

A bond's rating isn't the only factor that affects its yield. In fact, bonds with the same default rate but different maturity dates usually have different yields. Why? The answer is that long-term bonds are like a composite of a series of short-term bonds, so their yield depends on what people expect to happen in years to come. In this section, we will develop a framework for thinking about *future interest rates*.

---

[10] The same is true for individuals. Consider the impact on the monthly payments required to service a 30-year, $100,000 mortgage. At an interest rate of 5 percent, payments would be approximately $530 per month. If the interest rate were to increase to 7 percent, the required monthly payments would rise to more than $650. You can compute these amounts using the formulas in the Appendix to Chapter 4.

| Figure 7.3 | The Term Structure of Government of Canada Interest Rates |

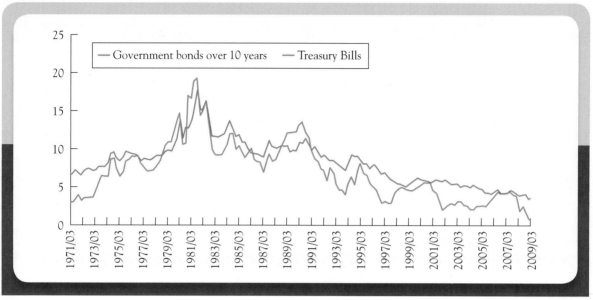

SOURCE: *Cansim data, Table 176-0043 Government of Canada long-term bonds v122544, 3-month treasury bill yields v122531.*

The relationship among bonds with the same risk characteristics but different maturities is called the **term structure of interest rates**.

In studying the term structure of interest rates, we will focus our attention on Government of Canada yields; see Figure 7.3. Comparing information on 3-month (the green line) and 10-year (the red line) Treasury issues, we can draw three conclusions:

1. *Interest rates of different maturities tend to move together.* The bulk of the variation in short- and long-term interest rates is in the same direction. That is, the green and red lines clearly move together.

2. *Yields on short-term bonds are more volatile than yields on long-term bonds.* The green line moves over a much broader range than the red line.

3. *Long-term yields tend to be higher than short-term yields.* The red line usually, but not always, falls above the green line.

Since the bonds are all AAA and issued by the same issuer, default risk cannot explain these relationships. What can? We will begin by examining a theory called the expectations hypothesis and show that alone it cannot explain all three relationships. Then we will augment the expectations hypothesis with an assumption about a liquidity premium and show that the augmented expectations hypothesis can explain all three.

## The Expectations Hypothesis

If we think about yields as the sum of a risk-free interest rate and a risk premium, the **expectations hypothesis** focuses on the first of those elements. It begins with the assumption that there is no uncertainty about the future. That is, we know not just the yield on bonds available today but the yields that will be available on bonds next year, the year after that, and so on.

Figure 7.4      The Canadian Government Bond Yield Curve

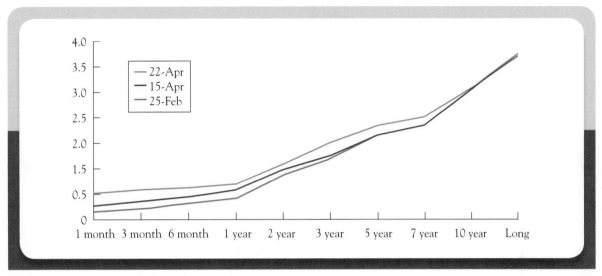

The Figure plots the yields on Treasury bills and bonds for January 8, 2009.

SOURCE: *Bank of Canada data Treasury bills and benchmark bonds, Table F1, Bank of Canada Banking and Financial Statistics, May 2009.*

To understand the implications of this statement, think about an investor who wishes to purchase a bond and hold it for two years. Since there is no uncertainty, the investor knows the yield today on a bond with two years to maturity, as well as the yields on a one-year bond purchased today and on a second one-year bond purchased one year from now. Being sure about all of these, the investor will be indifferent between holding the two-year bond and holding a series of two one-year bonds. *Certainty means that bonds of different maturities are perfect substitutes for each other.* This is the essence of the expectations hypothesis.

To see how this works, assume that the current one-year interest rate is 5 percent. The expectations hypothesis implies that the current two-year interest rate should equal the average of 5 percent and the one-year interest rate one year in the future. If that future interest rate is 7 percent, then the current two-year interest rate will be $(5 + 7)/2 = 6$ percent.

According to the expectations hypothesis, then, when interest rates are expected to rise in the future, long-term interest rates will be higher than short-term interest rates. This means that the **yield curve**, which plots the yield to maturity on the vertical axis and the time to maturity on the horizontal axis, will slope up. (*The Globe and Mail's Report on Business* frequently includes a plot like the one shown in Figure 7.4.) Analogously, the expectations hypothesis implies that if interest rates are expected to fall, the yield curve will slope down. And if interest rates are expected to remain unchanged, the yield curve will be flat. (See Figure 7.5 on page 142.)

If bonds of different maturities are perfect substitutes for each other, then we can construct investment strategies that must have the same yields. Let's look at the investor with a two-year horizon. Two possible strategies are available to this investor:

A.  Invest in a two-year bond and hold it to maturity. We will call the interest rate associated with this investment $i_{2t}$ (*i* stands for the interest rate, "2" for two years, and *t* for the time period, which is today). Investing one dollar in this bond will yield $(1 + i_{2t})(1 + i_{2t})$ two years later.

Figure 7.5    The Expectations Hypothesis and Expectations of Future Short-term Interest Rates

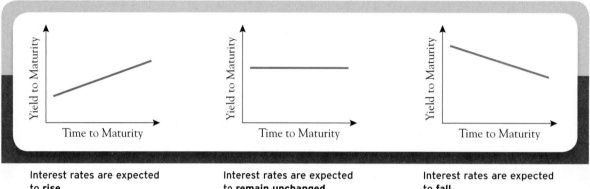

Interest rates are expected    Interest rates are expected    Interest rates are expected
to **rise**.                   to **remain unchanged**.       to **fall**.

B. Invest in two one-year bonds, one today and a second when the first one matures. The one-year bond purchased today has an interest rate of $i_{1t}$ ("1" stands for one year). The one-year bond purchased one year from now has an interest rate of $i^e_{1t+1}$, where the "$t+1$" stands for one time period past period $t$, or next year. The $e$, which stands for *expected*, indicates that this is the one-year interest rate investors *expect* to obtain one year ahead. Since we are assuming that the future is known, this expectation is certain to be correct. A dollar invested using this strategy will return $(1 + i_{1t})(1 + i^e_{1t+1})$ in two years.

The expectations hypothesis tells us that investors will be indifferent between these two strategies. (Remember, the bonds are perfect substitutes for each other.) Indifference between strategies A and B means that they must have the same return, so

$$(1 + i_{2t})(1 + i_{2t}) = (1 + i_{1t})(1 + i^e_{1t+1}), \qquad (2)$$

Expanding (3) and taking an approximation that is very accurate, we can write the two-year interest rate as the average of the current and future expected one-year interest rates:[11]

$$i_{2t} = \frac{i_{1t} + i^e_{1t+1}}{2} \qquad (3)$$

For a comparison between a three-year bond and three one-year bonds, we get

$$i_{3t} = \frac{i_{1t} + i^e_{1t+1} + i^e_{1t+2}}{3} \qquad (4)$$

where the notation $i_{3t}$ stands for a three-year interest rate and $i^e_{1t+2}$ for the expected one-year interest rate two years from now.

The general statement of the expectations hypothesis is that the interest rate on a bond with $n$ years to maturity is the average of $n$ expected future one-year interest rates:

$$i_{nt} = \frac{i_{1t} + i^e_{1t+1} + i^e_{1t+2} + \ldots + i^e_{1t+n-1}}{n} \qquad (5)$$

[11] Expanding equation (2) gives us $1 + 2i_{2t} + i^2_{2t} = 1 + i_{1t} + i^e_{1t} + 1 + (i_{1t})(i^e_{1t+1})$. The squared term on the left-hand side and the product term on the right-hand side of this equation are small, and their difference is even smaller. Using the example of 5 percent and 7 percent for the one-year interest rates, we can see that ignoring the two product terms means ignoring $((.06)2 - (.05*.07))/2 = (0.0036 - 0.0035)/2 = 0.00005$, an error of 0.005 percentage points.

Figure 7.6    The Expectations Hypothesis of the Term Structure

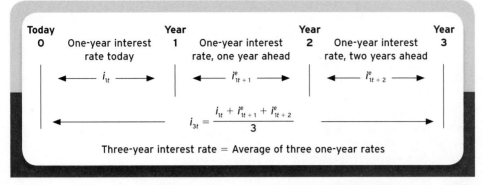

If the one-year interest rate today is $i_{1t}$ = 5%, one-year interest rate, one year ahead is $i^e_{1t+1}$ = 6%, and the one-year interest rate two years ahead, $i^e_{1t+2}$ = 7%, then the expectation hypothesis tells us that the three-year interest rate will be $i_{3t}$ = (5% + 6% + 7%)/3 = 6%.

What are the implications of this mathematical expression? Does the *expectations hypothesis of the term structure of interest rates* explain the three observations we started with? Let's look at each one.

1. The expectations hypothesis tells us that long-term bond yields are all averages of expected future short-term yields—the same set of short-term interest rates—so *interest rates of different maturities will move together.* From equation (5) we see that if the current one-year interest rate, $i_{1t}$, changes, all the yields at higher maturities will change with it.

2. The expectations hypothesis implies that *yields on short-term bonds will be more volatile than yields on long-term bonds.* Because long-term interest rates are averages of a sequence of expected future short-term rates, if the current 3-month interest rate moves, it will have only a small impact on the 10-year interest rate. Again, look at equation (5).[12]

3. The expectations hypothesis *cannot* explain why *long-term yields are normally higher than short-term yields,* since it implies that the yield curve slopes upward only when interest rates are expected to rise. To explain why the yield curve normally slopes upward, the expectations hypothesis would suggest that interest rates are normally expected to rise. But as the data in Figure 7.3 show, interest rates have been trending downward for the past 20 years, so anyone constantly forecasting interest rate increases would have been sorely disappointed.

The expectations hypothesis has gotten us two-thirds of the way toward understanding the term structure of interest rates. By ignoring risk and assuming that investors view short- and long-term bonds as perfect substitutes, we have explained why yields at different maturities move together and why short-term interest rates are more volatile than long-term rates. But we have failed to explain why the yield curve normally slopes upward. To understand this, we need to extend the expectations hypothesis to include risk. After all, we all know that long-term bonds are riskier than short-term bonds. Integrating this observation into our analysis will give us the *augmented expectations theory* of the term structure of interest rates.

---

[12] Take a simple example in which the one-year and two-year interest rates, $i_{1t}$ and $i_{2t}$, are both 5 percent. If the one-year interest rate increases to 7 percent, then the two-year interest rate will rise to 6 percent. The two move together, and the short-term rate is more volatile than the long-term rate.

# TOOLS OF THE TRADE
## Reading Charts

A picture can be worth a thousand words, but only if you know what it represents. To decode charts and graphs, use these strategies:

1. *Read the title of the chart.* This point may seem trivial, but titles are often very descriptive and can give you a good start in understanding a chart.

2. *Read the label on the horizontal axis.* Does the chart show the movements in a stock price or in the interest rate over minutes, hours, days, weeks, months, or years? Are the numbers spaced evenly?

Look at Figure 7.7, a sample of the Treasury yield curve similar to that which appears in *The Globe and Mail* every day. The horizontal axis extends from three months to 30 years, but the increments are not evenly spaced. In fact, a distance that starts out as three months on the left-hand corner becomes over 10 years at the far right. The axis is drawn in this way for two reasons. First, it focuses the reader's eye on the shorter end of the yield curve. Second, the telescoped axis narrows so that it takes up less space.

Interestingly, this particular yield curve shows a slight downward slope from three months to one year, followed by a steep upward slope. This pattern suggests that investors expected interest rates to decline sharply for the next year and then rise after that, which is exactly what happened.

3. *Read the label on the vertical axis.* What is the range of the data? This is a crucial piece of information, since most charts are made to fill the space available. As a result, small movements can appear to be very large. Compare Panel A and Panel B of Figure 7.8. The first shows the behaviour of U.S. house prices from 2000–2006; the second shows the same data starting in 2006.

In Panel A, the vertical axis ranges from $0 to $300; in Panel B, it covers only $150 to $290. To fill the second panel visually, the artist changed the vertical scale.

### Figure 7.7 Treasury Yield Curve

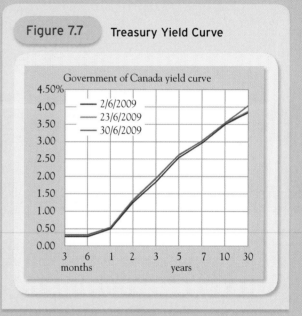

SOURCE: Bank of Canada, at http://www.bankofcanada.ca/en/rates/yield_curve.html, accessed October 12, 2009.

Looking quickly at these two charts can be misleading. Without noticing the difference in their vertical scale, we might conclude that the fall in house prices after May 2007 erased all the gains since 2000. But on closer inspection, we see that from January 2006 to July 2008 house prices in L.A., for example, fell to their level in mid-2004. (Notice also that the units on the axis are $. Your understanding of index numbers should tell you that because this is an index of house prices it should have no units. It does have a base year, which in this case is 2000.)

## The Augmented Expectations Hypothesis

Throughout our discussion of bonds, we emphasized that even default-free bonds are risky because of uncertainty about inflation and future interest rates. What are the implications of these risks for our understanding of the term structure of interest rates? The answer is that risk is the key to understanding the *slope* of the yield curve. The

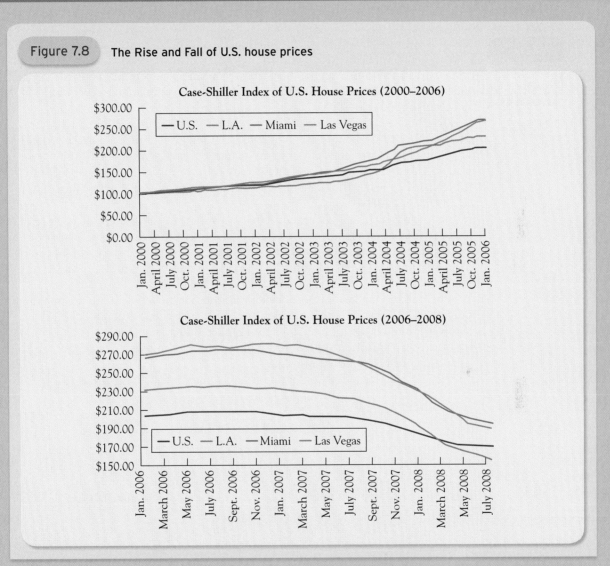

**Figure 7.8**   **The Rise and Fall of U.S. house prices**

Case-Shiller Index of U.S. House Prices (2000–2006)

Case-Shiller Index of U.S. House Prices (2006–2008)

SOURCE: *Standard and Poor's Global Index Client Services. Cited in Canadian Investment Review, Winter 2008 p.13.*

yield curve's upward slope (the fact that long-term interest rates are usually higher than short-term interest rates) is explained by the fact that long-term bonds are riskier than short-term bonds. Bondholders face both inflation and interest rate risk. The longer the term of the bond, the greater both types of risk.

The reason for the increase in inflation risk over time is clear-cut. Remember that bondholders care about the purchasing power of the return—the *real* return—they receive from a bond, not just the nominal dollar value of the coupon payments. Computing the real return from the nominal return requires a forecast of future inflation, or *expected* future inflation. For a three-month bond, an investor need be concerned with inflation only over the next three months. For a 10-year bond, however, computation of the real return requires a forecast of inflation over the next decade.

In summary, uncertainty about inflation creates uncertainty about a bond's real return, making the bond a risky investment. The further we look into the future, the greater the uncertainty about inflation. We are more uncertain about the level of inflation several years from now than about the level of inflation a few months from now, which implies that *a bond's inflation risk increases with its time to maturity.*

What about interest rate risk? Interest rate risk arises from a mismatch between the investor's investment horizon and a bond's time to maturity. Remember that if a bondholder plans to sell a bond prior to maturity, changes in the interest rate (which cause bond prices to move) generate capital gains or losses. The longer the term of the bond, the greater the price changes for a given change in interest rates and the larger the potential for capital losses.

Since some holders of long-term bonds will want to sell their bonds before they mature, interest rate risk concerns them. These investors require compensation for the risk they take in buying long-term bonds. As in the case of inflation, the risk increases with the term to maturity, so the compensation must increase with it: Investors require a **liquidity premium** to hold longer-term bonds.

What are the implications of including risk in our model of the term structure of interest rates? To answer this question, we can think about a bond yield as having two parts, one that is risk free and another that is a risk premium. The expectations hypothesis explains the risk-free part, and inflation and interest rate risk explain the risk premium. Together they form the **augmented expectations hypothesis of the term structure** of interest rates. Adding the risk premium to equation (5) on page 142, we can express this theory mathematically as

$$i_{nt} = rp_n + \frac{i_{1t} + i^e_{1t+1} + i^e_{1t+2} + \dots + i^e_{1t+n-1}}{n} \tag{6}$$

where $rp_n$ is the risk premium associated with an $n$-year bond. The larger the risk, the higher the risk premium, $rp_n$, is. Since risk rises with maturity, and $rp_n$ increases with $n$, the yield on a long-term bond includes a larger risk premium than the yield on a short-term bond.

To get some idea of the size of the risk premium $rp_n$, we can look at the average slope of the term structure over a long period. From 1971 to 2008, the difference between the interest rate on a long-term government bond and that on a three-month Treasury bill averaged 1¼ percentage points. It is important to keep in mind that this risk premium will vary over time. For example, if inflation is very stable or the variability of the real interest rate were to fall, then the 10-year bond risk premium could easily fall below one percentage point.

Can the augmented expectations hypothesis explain all three of our conclusions about the term structure of interest rates? The answer is yes. Like the expectations hypothesis, the augmented expectations hypothesis predicts that *interest rates of different maturities will move together* and that *yields on short-term bonds will be more volatile*

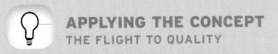

**APPLYING THE CONCEPT**
THE FLIGHT TO QUALITY

The idea that risk matters to bond investors is not just a textbook theory. On numerous occasions, investors' concerns about increased risk in certain areas of the globe have led to a significant shift in demand for low-risk bonds. A noteworthy example occurred in September 2008 when it became clear that problems that began in the U.S. housing market would imperil global financial institutions. Suddenly, no one wanted to hold corporate debt. After dumping anything that they thought at all risky, investors went looking for a safe place to put the proceeds.

Since the safest assets around are U.S. Treasury bonds, that is what investors bought: a flight to quality. The percep-

tion during this episode was that the riskiness of U.S. Treasury bonds had fallen relative to the riskiness of virtually everything else. The result was an increase in the price of U.S. Treasury bonds and a decline in their yield. At the same time, the prices of the more risky alternatives fell and their yields rose.

The data in Figure 7.9 show what happened. The LIBOR rate is the benchmark short-term private-sector borrowing rate—the London Interbank Offered Rate—at which banks can borrow overnight from other banks in the wholesale market in London. CP rates are commercial paper rates for banks to lend to good U.S. firms, while CDs are Certificates of Deposit and represent the cost of funds for the U.S. banks. Although Canada weathered the crisis better than most countries, in the early days of the crisis nothing was considered as safe as a U.S. Treasury Bill.

**Figure 7.9**   Treasury Bill Rates and Commercial Interest Rates, 2006-08

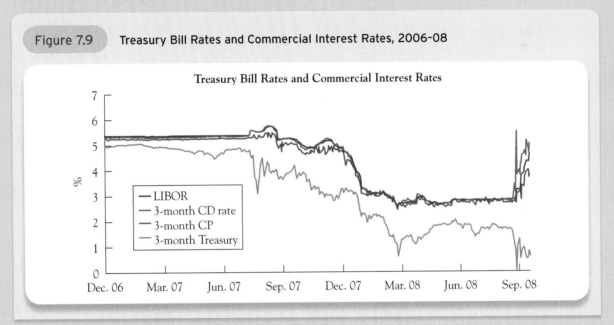

SOURCE: *Ricardo Caballero and Pablo Kurlat. "Flight to Quality and Bailouts: Policy Remarks and a Literature Review," MIT Department of Economics Working Paper 08-21, Oct. 2008.*

*than yields on long-term bonds.* And by adding a risk premium that grows with time to maturity, it explains why *long-term yields are higher than short-term yields.* Since the risk premium increases with time to maturity, the augmented expectations hypothesis tells us that the yield curve will normally slope upward; only rarely will it lie flat or slope downward. (A flat yield curve means that interest rates are expected to fall; a downward-sloping yield curve suggests that the financial markets are expecting a significant decline in interest rates.)

# The Information Content of Interest Rates

The risk and term structure of interest rates contain useful information about overall economic conditions. These indicators are helpful in evaluating both the present health of the economy and its likely future course. Risk spreads provide one type of information, the term structure another. In the following sections we will apply what we have just learned about interest rates to recent Canadian economic history and show how forecasters use these tools.

## Information in the Risk Structure of Interest Rates

When the overall growth rate of the economy slows or turns negative, it strains private businesses, increasing the risk that corporations will be unable to meet their financial obligations. The immediate impact of an impending recession, then, is to raise the risk premium on privately issued bonds. Importantly, though, an economic slowdown or recession does not affect the risk of holding government bonds.

The increased risk of default is not the same for all firms. The impact of a recession on companies with high bond ratings is usually small, so the spread between government bonds and AAA-rated bonds of the same maturity is not likely to move by much. But for issuers whose finances were precarious prior to the downturn, the effect is quite different. Those borrowers who were least likely to meet their payment obligations when times were good are even less likely to meet them when times turn bad. There is a real chance that they will fail to make interest payments. Of course, firms for whom even the slightest negative development might mean disaster are the ones that issue low-grade bonds. The lower the initial grade of the bond, the more the default-risk premium rises as general economic conditions deteriorate. The spread between government bonds and junk bonds widens the most.

Panel A of Figure 7.10 shows annual GDP growth over nearly four decades superimposed on shading that shows the dates of recessions.[13] In Panel B of Figure 7.10, GDP growth is drawn as the green line, and the red line is the spread between yields on government and corporate bonds. Note that the two lines move in opposite directions. (The correlation between the two series is $-0.34$.) That is, when the risk spread rises, output falls. The risk spread provides a good measure of general economic activity, and since financial markets operate every day, this information is available well before GDP data, which is published only once every three months.

## Information in the Term Structure of Interest Rates

Like information on the risk structure of interest rates, information on the term structure—particularly the slope of the yield curve—helps us to forecast general economic conditions. Recall that according to the expectations hypothesis, the long-term interest rates contain information about expected future short-term interest rates. And according to the augmented expectations hypothesis, the yield curve usually slopes upward. The key term in this statement is *usually*. On rare occasions, short-term interest rates exceed long-term yields. When they do, the term structure is said to be *inverted*, and the yield curve slopes downward.

An inverted yield curve is a valuable forecasting tool because it predicts a general economic slowdown. Since the yield curve slopes upward even when short-term yields are expected to remain constant—it's the average of expected future short-term

---

[13] We use Statistics Canada's definition of a recession. See Philip Cross, "The Impact of Recessions in the United States in Canada," *Canadian Economic Observer* (March 2009) Section 3 for exact dates.

**Figure 7.10**    The Risk Spread and GDP Growth

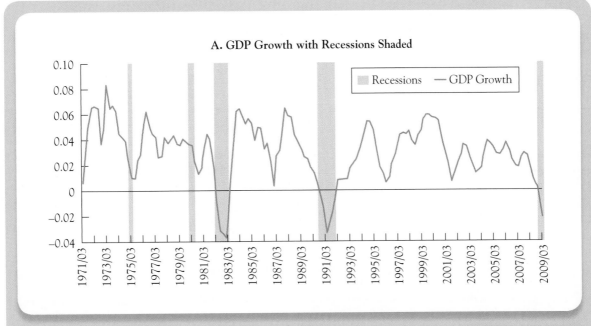

SOURCE: *Statistics Canada CANSIM database, http://www.cansim2.statcan.ca, Table 380-0002, GDP Growth v19920637, accessed 17 June 2009.*

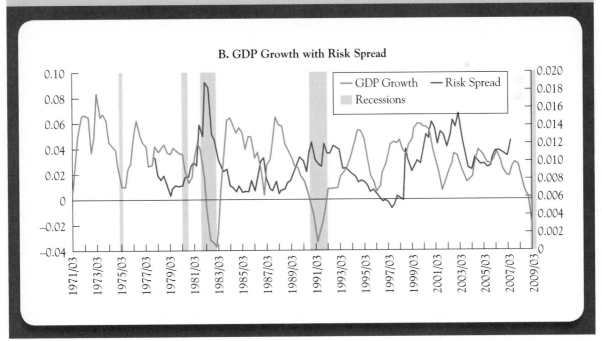

SOURCE: *Bank of Canada. Risk spread is Average yield on Government of Canada bonds over 10 year (v122487) minus average yield on 3 month Treasury bills (v122531) Table 176-0043; Statistics Canada CANSIM database, http://cansim2.statcan.ca, GDP Growth, Table 380-0002, accessed 17 June 2009.*

# IN THE NEWS
## The Long and the Short of It

# The Economist

January 5, 2006

### America's bond market is upside down.
### Is the economy about to capsize as well?

Shortly before America's last recession, which began in March 2001, something odd happened to interest rates. Short-term rates rose above long. The same thing happened before the recessions of 1990, 1981, 1980, 1973, 1969, and 1960. A dark omen, then, but why worry about it now? In recent months, yields on short-term securities have crept up on those offered by longer-dated instruments. In the last week of December, it was (slightly) cheaper for the American government to borrow for ten years than for two.

This is unusual. Normally, the longer the maturity, the higher the yield a security must offer: the "yield curve" slopes upwards. Markets take this to be the natural state of affairs.

When things are upended, the yield curve is said to be "inverted", a condition now exciting much chatter among analysts. Despite all this talk, the yield curve is not yet inverted across its full length. The yield on two-year Treasuries may have risen above that on ten-year bonds, but the rate on three-month bills still falls short by about 0.4 percentage

points. The spread between ten-year and three-month securities has been this narrow twice before (in 1998 and 1995) without a recession ensuing. Nonetheless, the ironing-out of the yield curve is not normally welcome news. According to a statistical model estimated by Arturo Estrella[*], an economist at the Federal Reserve Bank of New York, a spread of 0.4 points, averaged over a month, has historically signaled an 18 percent chance of recession within a year.

What gives the yield curve its predictive power? Long-term rates represent, in part, the market's expectations for future short-term rates. An inverted yield curve, then, suggests that short-term rates are higher today than they will be in the future. But why should this necessarily spell recession? Normally, it is because the Federal Reserve is in the midst of a campaign against inflation. To win this battle, short-term rates are sometimes raised high enough to induce a recession, which squeezes inflation out of the system. In due course, lower inflation will pave the way for lower short-term rates. But before this happens, long-term bond yields fall in anticipation of the future victory. [Remember, long-term interest rates are an average of future short-term interest rates.] In this case, an inverted yield curve is just a measure of the Fed's power.

In contrast to previous inversions, this time the yield curve is flat not because short rates are unusually high, but because long rates are unusually low. Yields on ten-year Treasuries have hovered around 4–4.5 percent, even as the Fed has

interest rates plus a risk premium—an inverted yield curve signals an expected fall in short-term interest rates. If interest rates are comparatively high, they serve as a brake on real economic activity. As we will see in Part IV, monetary policy makers adjust short-term interest rates in order to influence real economic growth and inflation. When the yield curve slopes downward, it indicates that policy is *tight* because policy makers are attempting to slow economic growth and inflation.

Careful statistical analysis confirms the value of the yield curve as a forecasting tool.[14] Figure 7.11 on page 152 shows GDP growth and the slope of the yield curve, measured as the difference between the 10-year and 3-month yields—what is called a term spread. Panel A of Figure 7.11 shows GDP growth (as in Figure 7.9 on page 147) together with the contemporaneous term spread (the growth and the term spread at the same time). Notice that when the term spread falls, GDP growth tends

[14] For a detailed recent discussion of the effectiveness of the yield curve as a predictor see "The Yield Curve, April 2009" by Joseph H. Haubrich and Kent Cherny, Federal Reserve Bank of Cleveland, retrieved July 30, 2009, from http://www.clevelandfed.org/research/trends/2009/0509/01monpol.cfm.

hoisted short-term rates 13 times. Federal Reserve officials do not fully understand why this is so—no doubt it has much to do with foreign purchases of long-dated American securities by oil producers and Asian central banks. Nonetheless, on this reading, the bond market offers a puzzle more than a worrying omen. Optimists find comforting parallels in the events of 1966. In the last few months of that year, the interest rate on three-month bills edged above that on ten-year bonds, but no recession followed—the only time a fully inverted yield curve has cried wolf. Then, as now, long-term rates were unusually low, averaging under 5 percent.

The pessimists, however, look back five years, not 40. In the second half of 2000 the yield curve inverted, and then, as now, the vast majority of commentators dismissed it, arguing that the old portent had nothing to say about the new economy. Three months into 2001, the economy slipped into recession.

Although monetary policy may not be that tight as yet, the economy's strength may rely, more than most realize, on interest rates remaining low. To a disturbing degree, America's economy is still debt-led. Can this borrowing continue to drive growth now that interest rates are no longer "accommodative" and house prices are starting to cool? The answer is not easy to find in the bond market. But it will decide whether America's economy is as flat in the year ahead as the yield curve is today.

> ### LESSONS OF THE ARTICLE
>
> The yield curve predicts changes in the economy. At the beginning of 2006 the yield curve was usually flat, and occasionally downward-sloping. But Figure 7.11 on page 152 shows that it was nowhere near as inverted as in 1981 and 1991. As we discuss in Chapter 19, the recessions of those years were in part triggered by tight monetary policy as the Bank of Canada attempted to reduce the inflation rate. In 2008, the recession was triggered by the financial crisis so the risk spread (shown in Figure 7.2 on page 138) is a more accurate harbinger of the recession of 2008 than the term spread.

\* "The Yield Curve as a Leading Indicator: Frequently Asked Questions," October 2005. Available at www.newyorkfed.org/research/capital_markets/ycfaq.pdf.

to fall somewhat later. In fact, when the yield curve becomes inverted, the economy tends to go into a recession roughly a year later. Panel B of Figure 7.10 on page 149 makes this clear. At each point, GDP growth in the current year (e.g., 1990) is plotted against the slope of the yield curve *one year earlier* (e.g., 1989). The two lines clearly move together; their correlation is +0.60. What the data show is that when the term spread falls, GDP growth tends to fall one year later. The yield curve is a valuable forecasting tool.

We started this chapter by asking why different types of bonds have different yields and what we can learn from those differences. After a bit of work, we can now see that differences in both risk and time to maturity affect bond yields. The less likely the issuer is to repay or the longer the time to maturity, the riskier a bond and the higher its yield. Even more importantly, both increases in the risk spread and an inverted yield curve suggest troubled economic times ahead.

**Figure 7.11** The Term Spread and GDP Growth

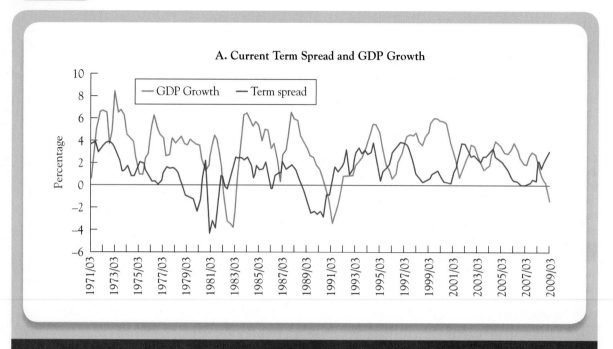

A. Current Term Spread and GDP Growth

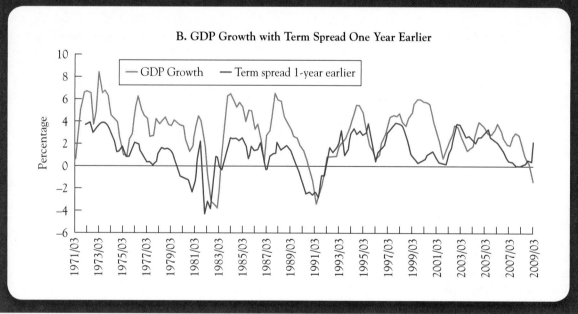

B. GDP Growth with Term Spread One Year Earlier

SOURCE: Bank of Canada. *Term spread is average yield on Government of Canada bonds over 10 year (v122487) minus average yield on 3 month Treasury bills (v122531). Both Table 176-0043, accessed April 2009. GDP growth based on Statistics Canada, GDP (v19920637) Table 380-0002, CANSIM database, http:// cansim2.statcan.ca, data Table 380-0002, GDP Growth, V19920637, accessed 17 June 2009.*

# Terms

## Chapter Summary

1. Bond ratings summarize the likelihood that a bond issuer will meet its payment obligations.
   a. Highly rated investment-grade bonds are those with the lowest risk of default.
   b. If a firm encounters financial difficulties, its bond rating may be downgraded.
   c. Commercial paper is the short-term version of a privately issued bond.
   d. Junk bonds are high-risk bonds with very low ratings.
   e. Investors demand compensation for default risk in the form of a risk premium. The higher the risk of default, the lower a bond's rating, the higher its risk premium, and the higher its yield.

2. The term structure of interest rates is the relationship between yield to maturity and time to maturity. A graph with the yield to maturity on the vertical axis and the time to maturity on the horizontal axis is called the yield curve.
   a. Any theory of the term structure of interest rates must explain three facts:
      i. Interest rates of different maturities move together.
      ii. The yields on short-term bonds are more volatile than the yields on long-term bonds.
      iii. Long-term yields are usually higher than short-term yields.
   b. The expectations hypothesis of the term structure of interest rates states that long-term interest rates are the average of expected future short-term interest rates. This hypothesis explains only the first two facts about the term structure of interest rates.
   c. The augmented expectations hypothesis of the term structure of interest rates, which is based on the fact that long-term bonds are riskier than short-term bonds, explains all three facts in 2a.

3. The risk structure and the term structure of interest rates both signal financial markets' expectations of future economic activity. Specifically, the likelihood of a recession will be higher when
   a. The risk spread, or the range between low- and high-grade bond yields, is growing.
   b. The yield curve slopes downward, or is inverted, so that short-term interest rates are higher than long-term interest rates.

## Conceptual Problems

1. Suppose the risk premium on bonds increases. How would the change affect your forecast of future economic activity, and why?

2. Several years ago, as a result of problems with the tires on Ford Explorers (a sport-utility vehicle), Ford faced the possibility of a downgrade in its commercial paper rating, from A1-R1 to A2-R2. The spread between the two ratings is roughly ½ percentage point. If Ford needed to issue $1 billion of commercial paper in order to maintain its operations, how much would this ratings downgrade cost the company?

3. If regulations restricting institutional investors to investment grade bonds were lifted, what do you think would happen to the spreads between yields on investment grade and speculative grade bonds?

4. Go to the Bank of Canada's Web site (http://www.bankofcanada.ca), and click first on *Rates and Statistics*, then on *Canadian bonds* and then on *Money Market Yields*. Compute the spread between the yield on three-month corporate paper and three-month Treasury bills. Now use the previous data button to find the data for a year ago. What can you infer from the movements in the spread?

5. Suppose that the interest rate on one-year bonds is 4 percent today, and is expected to be 5 percent

www.mcgrawhill.ca/olc/cecchetti

one year from now and 6 percent two years from now. Using the expectations hypothesis, compute the yield curve for the next three years.

6.* According to the augmented expectations hypothesis, if the yield on both one-year bonds and two-year bonds are the same, would you expect the one-year yield in one year's time to be higher, lower, or the same? Explain your answer.

7. You have $1,000 to invest over an investment horizon of three years. The bond market offers various options. You can buy (a) a sequence of three one-year bonds; (b) a three-year bond; or (c) a two-year bond followed by a one-year bond. The current yield curve tells you that the one-year, two-year, and three-year yields to maturity are 3.5 percent, 4.0 percent, and 4.5 percent, respectively. You expect that one-year interest rates will be 4 percent next year and 5 percent the year after that. Assuming annual compounding, compute the return on each of the three investments, and discuss which one you would choose.

8.* If inflation and interest rates become more volatile, what would you expect to happen to the slope of the yield curve?

9. As economic conditions improve in countries with emerging markets, the cost of borrowing funds there tends to fall. Explain why.

10. When countries with emerging markets have financial problems, the yields on U.S. Treasury issues tend to fall. Can you explain this phenomenon? What would happen to the risk spread under such circumstances, and how would you use that information?

## Analytical Problems

11. After years of responsible financial behaviour, you give into temptation and go on a spending spree using your credit cards. You exceed some credit limits and then go on to carry unpaid balances for months. In addition to the fees and charges associated with your credit card debt, how might this episode turn out to be an even costlier indulgence in the long run?

12. Some economists argue that the term spread is becoming less useful as a forecaster of recessions. Using data from the Bank of Canada's Web site (http://www.bankofcanada.ca), collect monthly data on the yield on 10-year government bonds and 3-month Treasury bills. Use these data to compute the term spread over the last five years. Compare these data to those in Figure 7.11 on page 152. Give your opinion on whether or not the term spread is still a useful predictor.

13. Suppose a country with a struggling economy suddenly discovered vast quantities of valuable minerals under government-owned land. How might the government's bond rating be affected? Using the model of demand and supply for bonds, what would you expect to happen to the bond yields of that country's government bonds?

14. How do you think the abolition of investor protection laws would affect the risk spread between corporate and government bonds?

15. You and a friend are reading *The Globe and Mail* and notice that the government of Canada yield curve is slightly upward sloping. Your friend comments that all looks well for the economy but you are concerned that the economy is heading for trouble. Assuming you are both believers in the augmented expectations hypothesis, what might account for your difference of opinion?

16.* Given the data in the table below, would you say that this economy is heading for a boom or for a recession? Explain your choice.

| | 3-month Treasury-Bill | 10-year Government of Canada Bond | Long-Term Corporate Bond |
|---|---|---|---|
| January | 1.0 percent | 3 percent | 7 percent |
| February | 1.05 | 3.5 | 7.2 |
| March | 1.1 | 4 | 7.6 |
| April | 1.2 | 4.6 | 8 |
| May | 1.25 | 5 | 8.2 |

* Indicates more difficult problems.

## CHAPTER 8

# Stocks, Stock Markets, and Market Efficiency

Stocks play a prominent role in our financial and economic lives. For individuals, they provide a key instrument for holding personal wealth as well as a way to diversify, spreading and reducing the risks that we face. Importantly, diversifiable risks are risks that are more likely to be taken. By giving individuals a way to transfer risk, stocks supply a type of insurance, enhancing our ability to take risk.[1]

For companies, they are one of several ways to obtain financing. Beyond that, though, stocks and **stock markets** are a central link between the financial world and the real economy. Stock prices are fundamental to the functioning of a market-based economy. They tell us the value of the companies that issued the stocks and, like all other prices, they allocate scarce investment resources. The firms deemed most valuable in the marketplace for stocks are the ones that will be able to obtain financing for growth. When resources flow to their most valued uses, the economy operates more efficiently.

Mention of the stock market provokes an emotional reaction in many people. They see it as a place where fortunes are easily made or lost, and they recoil at its unfathomable booms and busts. In three weeks in the fall of 2008, the TSX lost 30 percent of its value. That wasn't quite as dramatic as the infamous time in October 1929, when the New York Stock Exchange lost over 25 percent of its value in one week, but it represented a huge loss of wealth for shareholders. Even worse, the Crash in October 1929 marked the beginning of the Great Depression—so there was widespread fear in 2009 that we were on the verge of a recurrence of the Great Depression. Optimists noted that in October 1987, share prices fell nearly 30 percent in one week, including a record decline of 20 percent in a single day, without resulting in even a recession. Others argued that both in 1929 and in 2008, the stock market crash was primarily a symptom of the economic problem rather than the cause; however, stock markets are an important tool for allocating investment resources, and stock market declines have real economic effects that exacerbate these economic problems.

Stock market collapses are dramatic when you live through them, but over the long term, stock prices tend to rise steadily and slowly, collapsing only on those rare occasions when normal market mechanisms are out of alignment. For most people, the experience of losing or gaining wealth suddenly is more memorable than the experience of making it gradually. By being preoccupied with the potential short-term losses associated with crashes, we lose sight of the gains we could realize if we took a longer-term view. The goal of this chapter is to try to make sense of the stock market—to show what fluctuations in stock value mean for individuals and for the economy as a whole and look at a critical connection between the financial system and the real economy. We will also explain how it is that things sometimes go awry, resulting in bubbles and crashes. First, however, we need to define the basics: what stocks are, how they originated, and how they are valued.

---

[1] This point was central to our discussions of risk in Chapter 5. Our ability to diversify risk either through the explicit purchase of insurance or through investment strategies means that we do risky things that we otherwise would not do.

# The Essential Characteristics of Common Stock

Stocks, also known as common stock or equity, are shares in a firm's ownership. A firm that issues stock sells part of itself, so that the buyer becomes a part owner. Stocks as we know them first appeared in the 16th century. They were created to raise funds for global exploration. Means had to be found to finance the dangerous voyages of explorers such as Sir Francis Drake, Henry Hudson, and Vasco de Gama. Aside from kings and queens, no one was wealthy enough to finance these risky ventures alone.

The solution was to spread the risk through joint-stock companies, organizations that issued stock and used the proceeds to finance several expeditions at once. In exchange for investing, shareholders received a share of the company's profits. In Canada, the Montreal Stock Exchange and the Toronto Stock Exchange began operating in the 1860s somewhat informally, and were incorporated in the 1870s.

The stocks traded in those early markets had two important characteristics that we take for granted today. First, the shares were issued in small denominations, allowing investors to buy as little or as much of the company as they wanted; and second, the shares were transferable, meaning that an owner could sell them to someone else. Today, the vast majority of large companies issue stock that investors buy and sell regularly. The shares normally are quite numerous, each one representing only a small fraction of a company's total value. The large number and small size of individual shares—prices are usually below $100 per share—make the purchase and sale of stocks relatively easy.

Until recently, all stockowners received a certificate from the issuing company. Figure 8.1, shows a stock certificate issued by the John Labatt Brewing Company. The right-hand side of the figure shows a certificate issued by the Canadian Pacific Railway. Today, most shareholders no longer receive certificates; the odds are that you will never hold one. Instead, the information they bear is computerized, and the shares are registered in the names of brokerage firms that hold them on investors' behalf. This procedure is safer, since computerized certificates can't be stolen. It also makes the process of selling the shares much easier.

**Figure 8.1**  **Examples of Stock Certificates**

SOURCES: *Left: Scripophily.com, The Gift of History. Right: Canadian Pacific Railway Archives, Image No.: A.37475.*

The ownership of common stock conveys a number of rights. First and most importantly, a shareholder is entitled to participate in the profits of the enterprise. Importantly, however, the shareholder is merely a **residual claimant**. If the company runs into financial trouble, only after all other creditors have been paid what they are owed will the shareholders receive what is left, if anything. Shareholders get the leftovers!

To understand what being the residual claimant means, let's look at the case of a software manufacturer. The company needs a number of things to make it run. The list might include rented office space, computers, programmers, and some cash balances for day-to-day operations. These are the inputs into the production of the company's software output. If we took a snapshot of the company's finances on any given day, we would see that the firm owes payments to a large number of people, including the owner of the office space it rents, the programmers who work for it, the supplier of its computers, and the bondholders and bankers that have lent the firm resources. The company uses the revenue from selling its software to pay these people. After everyone has been paid, the shareholders get the rest of the revenue. In some years, the company does well and there are funds left over, so the shareholders do well. But when the firm does poorly, the shareholders may get nothing. If the firm performs really poorly, failing to sell enough software to cover its obligations, it can go bankrupt and cease operating entirely. In that case, the shareholders lose their entire investment.

The possibility of bankruptcy brings up an interesting question. What happens if a company's revenue is insufficient to cover its obligations to non-shareholders? What if its revenue is too small to pay the landlord, the programmers, the supplier of the computers, and the bondholders and other lenders? It would appear that the shareholders' promised participation in the firm's profits would yield a liability rather than a payment. If the company does very poorly, will the shareholders have to pay the firm's creditors?

An arrangement in which the shareholders are held liable for the firm's losses is very unappealing and would surely discourage people from buying stock. Shareholders bore that risk until the early 19th century. It ended with the introduction of the legal concept of limited liability. **Limited liability** means that, even if a company fails completely, the maximum amount that shareholders can lose is their initial investment. Liability for the company's losses is limited at zero, meaning that investors can never lose more than they have invested. Clearly, buying stock is much more attractive if you know that your maximum potential loss is the price you pay for the stock in the first place.

Beyond participating in the firm's profits, owners of common stock are entitled to vote at the firm's annual meeting. Though managers supervise a firm's day-to-day activities, the shareholders elect the board of directors, which meets several times per year to oversee management. Ultimately, the shareholders' ability to dislodge directors and managers who are performing poorly is crucial to their willingness to purchase shares.[2] This ability to elect and remove directors and managers varies with a country's legal structure. In places where shareholders' legal rights are weak, stock ownership is less appealing, and equities are a less important form of corporate financing.

Today, stock ownership is immensely popular. Investors want to own stocks and companies want to issue them. Buying and selling newly issued shares is referred to as the **primary market**, but the majority of share trading happens on **secondary markets**, such as the Toronto Stock Exchange (TSX), where existing shares are traded. The attraction of stock ownership is closely tied to the liquidity of shares—the fact that

---

[2] Managers and directors may have different priorities and objectives from shareholders. While the firm's owners would like to see the value of their investment increase, managers may be more interested in ensuring that they retain their jobs.

## YOUR FINANCIAL WORLD
A Home Is a Place to Live

A home is a place to live; it is very different from a stock or a bond. When you own a stock, the issuing firm either pays you dividends or reinvests its profits to make the business grow. Bonds pay interest, that's how you are compensated for lending. In either case, you receive an explicit financial return on your investment.

When you buy a house and move in, what you get is a roof over your head. And you do it without paying rent to someone else. That means that you are consuming the dividend or interest payments in the form of what economists call housing services. So, if you buy a house, live in it for a while, and then sell it, you should expect to get back the original purchase price. It is as if you bought a bond and used the coupon payments to live on. What's left at the end is the principal amount, no more.

Data on the long-run real (inflation-adjusted) change in the price of housing are consistent with this. Canadian data don't go back very far, but data for the United States show that over the 20th century, from 1900 to 2000, the average annual real increase in the value of housing in the United States was less than 0.20 percent. Let's make the (heroic) assumption it was the same in Canada. That means that if you were to purchase a house for $100,000, live in it for 25 years (the time it takes to completely pay off a conventional fixed-rate mortgage), you could expect to sell it for around $105,122 plus any adjustment for inflation.

Like stocks, houses are a very volatile investment. Vancouver house prices rose rapidly in 1981 and then fell sharply. It wasn't until 1989 that house prices got back to that 1981 level. If you take account of inflation, then it wasn't until 2005 that prices exceeded their 1981 level. To put it another way, if you invested in a house in Vancouver in 1989 and then sold it in 2005, your real return would have been zero. If you sold it before 2005, your real return would have been negative. From 2005 to 2008 there were double-digit increases in house prices in many Western cities, but house prices fell by 15 percent between June 2008 and June 2009. Real estate is a risky investment.

To see the contrast with a financial investment, compare the purchase of the home to the purchase of $100,000 worth of stock. If stocks have an annual average real return of 4 percent, then after 25 years you will have accumulated over $265,000. But, unlike the house, this financial investment does not provide you with a place to live. So, when you think about the return to owning a house, remember that you get a place to live—that's the return on your investment.

you can sell your shares in the secondary market means that you don't have to lock your money up for a fixed time when you invest in shares. Over the past century, markets have developed in which people buy and sell billions of shares every day. This thriving financial trade is possible because

- An individual share represents only a small fraction of the value of the company that issued it.

- A large number of shares are outstanding.

- Prices of individual shares are low, allowing individuals to make relatively small investments.

- As residual claimants, shareholders receive the proceeds of a firm's activities only after all other creditors have been paid.

- Because of limited liability, investors' losses cannot exceed the price they paid for the stock.

- Shareholders can replace managers who are doing a bad job.

# Measuring the Level of the Stock Market

Stocks are one way in which we choose to hold our wealth. When stock values rise, we get richer; when they fall, we get poorer. These changes affect our consumption and saving patterns, causing general economic activity to fluctuate. We need to understand the dynamics of the stock market, both to manage our personal finances and to see the connections between stock values and economic conditions. From a macroeconomic point of view, we need to be able to measure the level of fluctuation in all stock values. We will refer to this concept as the value of the stock market and to its measures as **stock market indexes**.

In Chapter 2 we introduced the consumer price index as a measure of the purchasing power of money. The purpose of an **index** number is to give a measure of scale so that we can compute percentage changes. The consumer price index, for example, is not measured in dollars. Instead, it is a pure number. In April 2009, the value of the Consumer Price Index for Canada was 113.9, which isn't very interesting on its own. If, however, you know that 12 months earlier, in April 2008, the same CPI index was 113.5, then you can figure out that prices rose by 0.35 percent over a 12-month period—that's the percentage change in the index.

Stock-market indexes are the same. They are designed to give us a sense of the extent to which things are going up or down. Saying that the S&P/TSX Composite index is at 10,000 doesn't mean anything on its own. But if you know that the index rose from 10,000 to 11,000, that tells you that stock prices (by this measure) went up 10 percent. As we will see, stock indexes can tell us both how much the value of an average stock has changed and how much total wealth has gone up or down. Beyond that, stock indexes provide benchmarks for performance of money managers, allowing us to measure whether a particular manager has done better or worse than "the market" as a whole.

A quick look at the financial news reveals a number of stock market indexes, covering both domestic stocks and stocks issued by firms in foreign countries. Our goal in this section is to learn what these are and, more importantly, what question each is designed to answer. We will start with a detailed discussion of three important indexes, the S&P/TSX Composite Index, which measures the performance of the TSX, and the Dow Jones Industrial Average and S&P 500 index, which measure the performance of companies traded on the New York Stock Exchange (NYSE). A brief description of other indexes and a short history of the performance of the stock market will follow.

## The S&P/TSX Composite Index

The **S&P/TSX composite index** is a measure of the value of shares of companies listed on the TSX. The index is considered broad-based as it reflects the value of about 220 of the largest firms listed, which together account for about 70 percent of the value of shares listed, so it is called a **value-weighted index**. The shares are weighted in the index by their **market capitalization**. As at December 31, 2008, the largest single company weight is the Royal Bank, which has a weight of 5.36 percent of the entire index. The 10 companies with the highest weights make up 36 percent of the index, and include 4 financials (banks and insurance) as well as Research in Motion (2.6 percent weight) and the Potash Corporation of Saskatchewan (2.87 percent). The components of the index are reevaluated quarterly by **Standard and Poor's**.

To see how the index works, consider two companies: Company A has 10 million shares valued at $100 each while Company B has 100 million shares valued at $50 each. The total market capitalization is $6 billion. Now suppose that the shares of company A rose by 10 percent. The market capitalization of Company A would now be $1.1 billion and the total market capitalization would be $6.1 billion, a rise of 1.6 percent, so the index would rise by 1.6 percent. If instead the shares of Company B had risen by 10 percent the market capitalization would have risen to $6.5 billion, a rise of 8.3 percent. Note that the index averages out the performance of individual companies, and that it weights the increases by the size of the company.

## U.S. Market Indexes: The Dow Jones Industrial Average and the S&P 500

The Dow Jones Industrial Average (DJIA) is one of the best known indexes in the world. Created by Charles Dow in 1884, it began as an average of the prices of 11 stocks.[3] Today, the index is based on the stock prices of 30 of the largest companies in the United States. The DJIA is a price-weighted average, meaning that it measures the value of purchasing a single share of each of the stocks in the index. Originally, this meant adding up the per-share prices of all 30 stocks and dividing by 30 to calculate the yield of the index. Now, the index incorporates adjustments for changing components and stock splits so it is proportional to the prices of all 30 stocks.[4] The percentage change in the DJIA over time is the percentage change in the sum of the 30 prices. Thus, the DJIA measures the return to holding a portfolio of a single share of each stock included in the average.

Since Charles Dow first created his index of 11 stocks, nine of which were railroad stocks, the structure of the U.S. economy has changed markedly. At various times, steel, chemical, and automobile stocks have dominated the DJIA. The index now includes the stocks of information technology firms, such as Microsoft and Intel, as well as of retailing firms, such as Walmart and Home Depot. General Electric is the only one of the original 11 stocks that remains in the index.

The S&P 500 is an alternative index for shares listed in U.S. stock exchanges and, like the TSX/S&P composite, it is a value-weighted index, based on the value of the 500 largest firms listed on the NYSE. Because there are only 30 stocks in the DJIA, some have very large weights—for example, (in June 2009) IBM has the highest weight in the Dow, 9.27 percent, while the highest single weight in the S&P 500 is Exxon Mobil with 4.38 percent. The price weighting implies that the relative weights of companies are different in the two indexes: IBM has a weight of only 1.76 percent in the S&P 500. In the broad index, most companies have a smaller weight than they do in the DJIA, but GE, which has a weight of only 1.17 percent in the DJIA, has a weight of 1.74 percent in the S&P 500 based on the size of its market capitalization.

The use of price weights also makes the performance of the DJIA different from the S&P indexes. Price-weighted averages give greater weight to shares with higher prices. Using our earlier example, when Company A's shares cost $100 and Company B's shares cost $50 the index total for a price weighted index is $150. Now if the price of Company A's shares rise by 10 percent, the index rises to $160, a 6.7 percent increase, compared to

---

[3] A detailed description of the history and current composition of the DJIA is at http://www.djindexes.com.

[4] This explains how the DJIA climbed to over 10,000 when it is the average of 30 stock prices, all less than $200 per share. There is a simple way to compute the change in the index level: (1) Take the list of 30 stocks in the DJIA and add up the changes from the previous day's close, so if each stock rose by $1, that's $30. (2) Go to page C2 of *The Wall Street Journal* and locate something called the "divisor." It's usually near the top of the page above the plot of the recent performance of the index and is a number like 0. 0.125552709000 (that was the value for December 17, 2008). (3) Divide the sum of changes in the prices of the DJIA stocks by the divisor and add that to the previous day's close. The result is the current level of the DJIA.

the 1.6 percent increase in the value-weighted index. In contrast, if Company B's shares rose by 10 percent, the index would rise to $155, an increase of 3.33 percent, compared to the 8.3 percent increase in the value-weighted index. The behaviour of higher-priced stocks, then, dominates the movement of a price-weighted index such as the DJIA.

Neither price weighting nor value weighting is necessarily the best approach to constructing a stock price index. The S&P 500 is neither better nor worse than the DJIA. Rather, the two types of index simply answer different questions. Changes in a price-weighted index such as the DJIA tell us the change in the value of a portfolio composed of a single share of each of the stocks in the index. Changes in a value-weighted index tell us the return to holding a portfolio of stocks weighted in proportion to the size of the firms. Thus, they more accurately mirror changes in the economy's overall wealth.

## Other U.S. and Canadian Stock Market Indexes

The TSX Venture Exchange is Canada's junior equity exchange; the exchange is very active with volume about one-third of the TSX, but the shares have much lower value than those on the senior exchange—in May 2009, the value of shares traded was only 1 percent of that of the TSX. The Venture Exchange lists many new companies (the listing requirements are less stringent than those of the senior exchange) and also many natural resource stocks, and tends to be much more volatile than the TSX. Compare the 52-week high and 52-week low for the two exchanges in Table 8.1: the low on the TSX was about half the high; on the Venture Exchange it was roughly one quarter.

Besides the S&P 500 and the DJIA, the prominent indexes in the United States include the Nasdaq Composite index, or Nasdaq for short, and the Russell 2000. The Nasdaq is a value-weighted index of over 5,000 companies traded on the over-the-counter (OTC) market through the National Association of Securities Dealers Automatic Quotations (Nasdaq) service. The Nasdaq Composite is composed mainly of smaller, newer firms and in recent years has been dominated by technology and Internet companies. The Russell 2000 is a value-weighted index of publicly traded "small cap" companies. Companies included in the S&P 500 have a median market capitalization (value of outstanding shares) of over $5 billion. In contrast, the companies in the Russell 2000 have a median market capitalization of about $300 million. The Wilshire 5000 is the most broadly based U.S. index. It covers all publicly traded stocks in the United States, including all the stocks on the New York Stock Exchange, the American Stock Exchange, and the OTC, which together total more than 6,500 (contrary to the index's name). Like the Nasdaq and the S&P 500, the Wilshire 5000 is value weighted. Because of its great breadth, this index is the best measure of overall market wealth.

## Performance of the Stock Market

Figure 8.2 on page 163 illustrates the performance of the S&P/TSX Composite for the last 50 years with data on the U.S. stock markets for comparison. Notice that the vertical axis is what is called a logarithmic or log scale. This scale has the property that when two lines have the same slope they have the same growth rate. Log scales are useful when (1) we are primarily interested in the growth rate of the series and (2) the series is growing over time. If this is the case then a regular linear axis may make changes late in the series (which are large in absolute size but not as a percentage) look larger than the same percentage change earlier in the series. When the TSX was at 1,000, a 10 percent increase was 100 points; at a level of 10,000 a 1,000 point change is a 10 percent increase. On normal linear graph paper that 1000 points would be a steeper line than the 100 point increase. Using a log axis, the slope of the two segments would be the same.

# TOOLS OF THE TRADE
## Reading Stock Indexes in the Business News

Each morning, the business news brings reports of the prior day's changes in all the major stock market indexes. Table 8.1 reproduces part of the summary tables from the Financial Post Web site (http://www.financialpost.com/markets/market-data/indices-north_american.html) on January 19, 2008. It includes a number of indexes besides the TSX/S&P Composite. The TSX (with S&P) publishes a number of subindexes. For example, the "Capped Energy" index reports on the shares of energy companies but the share of any single company is capped at 25 percent of the index. The Dow Jones monitors 30 large stocks and the Russell 2000 tracks the value of the smallest two-thirds of the 3,000 largest U.S. companies. Many more indexes are published, all of them designed for specific functions. When you encounter a new

index, make sure you understand both how it is constructed and what it is designed to measure by looking at the Fact Sheets on the Web pages of the index provider.

The columns of the page are largely self-explanatory. The Net Change states how much the index changed from the previous day's close to today's close. The Volume lists how many shares were traded. Notice that the Venture Exchange had about one quarter of the volume of the TSX. Trade in the shares in the 30 companies in the Dow was double the volume of trade in the shares of the more than 200 companies in the TSX Composite index. Notice also that the Venture Exchange is more volatile than the S&P/TSX Composite—declining 68 percent over the past 52 weeks compared to declines in the mid-30 percents of the other indexes.

### Table 8.1

**Please select your market:**

| North American ▼ |

**Data provided by: Financial Post**

**Daily North American Indices on 2009.01.16**
**Toronto Stock Exchange**

| Index | Close | Net Change | % Change | Volume | Day High | Day Low | 52 Week High | 52 Week Low | Week Change | Year to Date % Change | 52 Week % Change |
|---|---|---|---|---|---|---|---|---|---|---|---|
| S&P/TSX Composite | 8,920.40 | +40.79 | +0.5 | 210,110,813 | 9,036.44 | 8,734.42 | 15,154.77 | 7,647.11 | -1.8 | -0.7 | -31.8 |
| Capped Energy | 220.10 | +1.76 | +0.8 | 58,147,189 | 223.94 | 216.41 | 470.01 | 176.40 | -2.2 | +1.7 | -34.0 |
| Capped Financials | 124.47 | -1.83 | -1.4 | 29,030,372 | 128.21 | 121.79 | 201.04 | 110.91 | -5.5 | -2.1 | -35.6 |
| **TSX Venture Exchange** | | | | | | | | | | | |
| Composite | 865.65 | +21.35 | +2.5 | 56,316,418 | 865.65 | 844.30 | 2,814.88 | 678.62 | -4.8 | +8.6 | -68.2 |
| **Standard & Poor's** | | | | | | | | | | | |
| S&P 500 | 850.12 | +6.38 | +0.8 | | 858.13 | 830.66 | 1,440.24 | 741.02 | -4.5 | -5.9 | -38.1 |
| **Dow Jones** | | | | | | | | | | | |
| DJIA | 8,281.22 | +68.73 | +0.8 | 439,358,818 | 8,341.20 | 8,109.34 | 13,136.69 | 7,449.38 | -3.7 | -5.6 | -33.6 |
| **Nasdaq Stock Market** | | | | | | | | | | | |
| Nasdaq | 1,529.33 | +17.49 | +1.2 | | 1,538.82 | 1,490.35 | 2,551.47 | 1,295.48 | -2.7 | -3.0 | -36.1 |
| **Russell** | | | | | | | | | | | |
| Russell 2000 | 466.45 | +3.83 | +0.8 | | 467.72 | 451.77 | 764.38 | 371.30 | -3.1 | -6.6 | -33.4 |

| Figure 8.2 | Performance of North American Stock Markets, 1956–2009 |

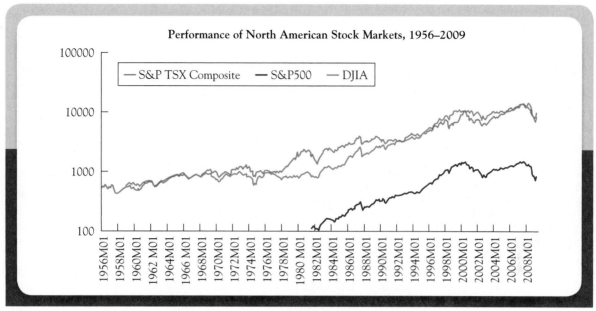

SOURCE: *Bank of Canada CANSIM data: TSX, v122620, Table 176-0047; S&P 500 v37425, Table 176-0046; DJIA v37416, Table 176-0046.*

A number of features stand out in the figure. First, the volatility. The fall in prices in late 2008 was one of the most dramatic over the entire period, but there have been several sharp market declines. Notice also that the volatility has many components: there are sharp rises and falls, there are a lot of small movements, and then there are long cycles. Between 1966 and 1982, returns in the stock market were relatively low. Then from the mid-1970s in Canada and the early 1980s in the United States, the stock markets grew more rapidly. Finally, notice that the overall time paths of the Dow and the TSX are very similar, despite being different types of indexes for different countries. This is because while individual stocks have different degrees of success, over the long run the stock market reflects the state of the economy, and the two economies have performed relatively similarly.

## Valuing Stocks

People differ on how stocks should be valued. Some believe they can predict changes in a stock's price by looking at patterns in its past price movements. Because these people study charts of stock prices, they are called chartists. Other investors, known as behaviouralists, estimate the value of stocks based on their perceptions of investor psychology and behaviour. Still others estimate stock values based on a detailed study of companies' financial statements. In their view, the value of a firm's stock depends both on its current assets and on estimates of its future profitability—what they call the fundamentals. Thus, the **fundamental value** of a stock is based on the timing and uncertainty of the returns it brings.

We can use our toolbox for valuing financial instruments to compute the fundamental value of stocks. Based on the size and timing of the promised payments, we can use the present-value formula to assess how much a stock is worth in the absence of any risk. Then, realizing that the payments are uncertain in both their size and timing, we can adjust our estimate of the stock's value to accommodate those risks. Together, these two steps give us the fundamental value.

The chartists and behavioralists question the usefulness of fundamentals in understanding the level and movement of stock prices. They focus instead on estimates of the deviation of stock prices from those fundamental values. These deviations can create short-term bubbles and crashes, which we'll take up later in the chapter. First, though, let's use some familiar techniques to develop an understanding of basic stock valuation.

## Fundamental Value and the Dividend-Discount Model

Like all financial instruments, a stock represents a promise to make monetary payments on future dates, under certain circumstances. With stocks, the payments are usually in the form of **dividends**, or distributions made to the owners of a company when the company makes a profit.[5] If the firm is sold, the shareholders receive a final distribution that represents their share of the purchase price.

Let's begin with an investor who plans to buy a stock today and sell it in one year. The principle of present value tells us that the price of the stock today should equal the present value of the payments the investor will receive from holding the stock. This is equal to the selling price of the stock in one year's time plus the dividend payments received in the interim. Thus, the current price is the present value of next year's price plus the dividend. If $P_{\text{today}}$ is the purchase price of the stock, $P_{\text{next year}}$ is the sale price one year later, and $D_{\text{next year}}$ is the size of the dividend payment, we can write this expression as

$$P_{\text{today}} = \frac{D_{\text{next year}}}{(1 + i)} + \frac{P_{\text{next year}}}{(1 + i)} \qquad (1)$$

where $i$ is the interest rate used to compute the present value (measured as a decimal).

What if the investor plans to hold the stock for two years? To figure out the answer, start by using present value to calculate that the price next year equals the value next year of the price in two years plus next year's dividend payment. Using the logic and notation from equation (1), this is

$$P_{\text{next year}} = \frac{D_{\text{in two years}}}{(1 + i)} + \frac{P_{\text{in two years}}}{(1 + i)} \qquad (2)$$

Substituting equation (2) into equation (1), we get that the current price is the present value of the price in two years plus two dividend payments, one each year, or

$$P_{\text{today}} = \frac{D_{\text{next year}}}{(1 + i)} + \frac{D_{\text{in two years}}}{(1 + i)^2} + \frac{P_{\text{in two years}}}{(1 + i)^2} \qquad (3)$$

Extending this formula over an investment horizon of $n$ years, the result is

$$P_{\text{today}} = \frac{D_{\text{next year}}}{(1 + i)} + \frac{D_{\text{in two years}}}{(1 + i)^2} + \ldots + \frac{D_{n \text{ years from now}}}{(1 + i)^n} + \frac{P_{n \text{ years from now}}}{(1 + i)^n} \qquad (4)$$

---

[5] To be precise, not all profits are distributed to shareholders. As we will see in Chapter 11, some of these "earnings" are retained by the firm and used to increase its size. A firm may also use profits to buy back its own stock, thereby increasing the value of the remaining shares. We will discuss these complications later.

That is, the price today is the present value of the sum of the dividends plus the present value of the price at the time the stock is sold $n$ years from now. (Notice that this equation is the same as the expression for the price of a coupon bond on page 108.)

At this point, you may be asking: What about companies that do not pay dividends? How do we figure out their stock price? The answer is that we estimate when they will start paying dividends and then use the present-value framework. From equation (4) you can see that there is no reason all of the dividends need to be positive. Some of them can be zero, and we can still do the calculation. So if we figure that the company will start paying dividends in 10 years, we just set the first 9 years' worth of dividends equal to zero, and compute the present discounted value of dividend payments starting in year 10.

Returning to our baseline case, looking at the messy equation (4) we can see that unless we know something more about the annual dividend payments, we are stuck. We can proceed in the case where dividends grow at a constant rate of $g$ per year. That is, the dividend next year will equal the dividend today multiplied by one plus the growth rate:

$$D_{\text{next year}} = D_{\text{today}} (1 + g) \tag{5}$$

As long as the growth rate remains constant, all we need to do is multiply by $(1 + g)$ to compute future dividends. Following the procedure for computing present value in $n$ years, we can see that the dividend $n$ years from now will be

$$D_{n \text{ years from now}} = D_{\text{today}} (1 + g)^n \tag{6}$$

Using equation (6), we can rewrite the price equation (4) as

$$P_{\text{today}} = \frac{D_{\text{today}}(1 + g)}{(1 + i)} + \frac{D_{\text{today}}(1 + g)^2}{(1 + i)^2} + \ldots + \frac{D_{\text{today}}(1 + g)^n}{(1 + i)^n} + \frac{P_{n \text{ years from now}}}{(1 + i)^n} \tag{7}$$

Even if we know the dividend today, $D_{\text{today}}$, and the interest rate, $i$, as well as an estimate of the dividend growth rate, $g$, we still can't compute the current price, $P_{\text{today}}$, unless we know the future price, $P_{n \text{ years from now}}$. We can solve this problem by assuming the firm pays dividends forever and noting that as $n$ gets big, $[1/(1 + i)^n]$ approaches zero until it finally disappears. This assumption turns the stock into something like a consol—the strange bond that makes fixed coupon payments forever and never repays the principal.[6] It allows us to convert equation (6) into the following simple formula:[7]

$$P_{\text{today}} = \frac{D_{\text{today}} (1 + g)}{i - g} \tag{8}$$

This relationship is the **dividend-discount model**. Using the concept of present value, we have discovered that if a firm's dividends grow at a constant rate $g$, the "fundamental" price of a stock is simply the current dividend divided by the interest rate, minus the

---

[6] Since neither the consol nor the stock has a maturity date, it makes sense that they would be formally the same.

[7] To compute equation (8), let $D_0$ represent $D_{\text{today}}$, and $P_0$ represent $P_{\text{today}}$. Then we can rewrite equation (7) as

$$P_0 = D_0 \sum_{t=1}^{\infty} \frac{(1 + g)^t}{(1 + i)^t}$$

This expression looks exactly like the one for a consol, with the current dividend in place of the coupon payment and an interest rate equivalent to $(1 + i^*) = (1 + i)/(1 + g)$. That is, we can write it as

$P_0 = \sum_{t=1}^{\infty} \frac{D_0}{(1 + i^*)^t}$. Using the techniques in the Appendix to Chapter 4, we can simplify this to $\frac{D_0}{i^*}$.

Rewriting $i^* = \frac{i - g}{1 + g}$ and substituting, we get equation (8).

dividend growth rate. The model tells us that stock prices should be high when dividends ($D_{today}$) are high, when dividend growth ($g$) is rapid (that is, when g is large), or when the interest rate ($i$) is low. (In using the dividend-discount model, we will need to remember to write both $i$ and $g$ as decimals—numbers such as 0.03 and 0.05.)

The dividend-discount model is simple and elegant, but we have ignored risk in deriving it. Stock prices change constantly, making investors' returns uncertain. Where does this risk come from, and how does it affect a stock's valuation? We turn now to an analysis of risk.

## Why Stocks Are Risky

Recall that shareholders are the firm's owners, so they receive the firm's profits. But their profits come only after the firm has paid everyone else, including bondholders. It is as if the shareholders bought the firm by putting up some of their own wealth and borrowing the rest. This borrowing creates leverage, and leverage creates risk. (See the Tools of the Trade: The Impact of Leverage on Risk on page 92.)

A simple example will show what happens. Imagine a software business that needs only one computer. Say the computer costs $1,000 and the purchase can be financed by any combination of stock (equity) and bonds (debt). If the interest rate on bonds is 10 percent, for each $100 borrowed the firm must pay $10 in interest. Finally, assume that the company, which produces software, earns $160 in good years and $80 in bad years, with equal probability.

Table 8.2 shows what happens to the company's equity returns as its level of debt changes. The more debt, the more leverage and the greater the owners' risk (as measured by the standard deviation of the equity return). As the proportion of the firm financed by equity falls from 100 percent to 20 percent, the expected return to the equity holders rises from 12 percent to 20 percent, but the associated risk rises substantially as well.

If the firm were only 10 percent equity financed, the shareholders' limited liability could come into play. Issuing $900 worth of bonds would mean incurring an obligation to make $90 in interest payments. If business turned out to be bad, the firm's revenue would be only $80—not enough to pay the interest. Without their limited liability, the common shareholders, who are the firm's legal owners, would be liable for the $10 shortfall. Instead, the shareholders would lose only their initial $100 investment, and no more, and the firm goes bankrupt.

Stocks are risky, then, because the shareholders are residual claimants. Because they are paid last, they never know for sure how much their return will be. Any variation in the firm's revenue flows through to them dollar for dollar, making their returns highly volatile. In contrast, bondholders receive fixed nominal payments and are paid before the shareholders in the event of a bankruptcy. To be clear, as we have seen, bonds are still risky because a bankrupt firm may not have sufficient funds to repay its debts; but the shares of a bankrupt firm are worth zero, while bondholders usually get some repayment.

## Risk and the Value of Stocks

Shareholders require compensation for the risk they face; the higher the risk, the greater the compensation. To integrate risk into stock valuation, we will return to the simple question we asked earlier: How will investors with a one-year investment horizon value a stock? Our initial answer was that the stock price equals the present value of the price of the stock in one year's time plus the dividend payments received in the interim. From this statement, we derived the dividend-discount model. But

| | | Required | Payment | | Expected | Standard |
| Percent | Percent | Payments on | to Equity | Equity | Equity | Deviation of |
| Equity (%) | Debt (%) | 10% Bonds ($) | Holders ($) | Return (%) | Return (%) | Equity Return |
|---|---|---|---|---|---|---|
| 100% | 0 | 0 | $80–$160 | 8-16% | 12% | 4% |
| 50% | 50% | $50 | $30–$110 | 6-22% | 14% | 8% |
| 30% | 70% | $70 | $10–$90 | $3\frac{1}{3}$-30% | $16\frac{2}{3}$% | $13\frac{1}{3}$% |
| 20% | 80% | $80 | $0–$80 | 0-40% | 20% | 20% |

**Table 8.2**  Returns Distributed to Debt and Equity Holders under Different Financing Assumptions

A firm requires a $1,000 capital investment that can be financed by either stock (equity) or 10 percent bonds (debt). Revenue is either $80 or $160, with equal probability.

once we recognize the risk involved in buying stock, the answer to our question must change. The new answer is that an investor will buy a stock with the idea of obtaining a return that includes compensation for the stock's risk.

Here is how the process works. Buying the stock for an initial price $P_{today}$ entitles the investor to a dividend $D_{next\ year}$ plus the proceeds from the sale of the stock one year later, at price $P_{next\ year}$. The return from the purchase and subsequent sale of the stock equals the dividend plus the difference in the price, both divided by the initial price:

$$\text{Return to holding stock for one year} = \frac{D_{next\ year}}{P_{today}} + \frac{P_{next\ year} - P_{today}}{P_{today}} \quad (9)$$

Since the ultimate future sale price is unknown, the stock is risky and the investor will require compensation in the form of a risk premium. We will think of the required return as the sum of the risk-free interest rate and the risk premium (sometimes called the equity risk premium). Recall from earlier chapters that we can think of the risk-free rate as the interest rate on a government bond with a maturity of several months. Such an instrument has virtually no default risk, since the government isn't going to collapse, and it has almost no inflation risk, since inflation is highly persistent and so is unlikely to change over a year or so. In addition, there is very little price risk, since interest rates normally don't move quickly and suddenly either. Dividing the required stock return into its two components, we can write

Required stock return ($i$) = Risk-free return ($rf$) + Risk premium ($rp$)     (10)

Combining this equation with our earlier analysis is straightforward. All we need to do is recognize that the interest rate used for the present-value calculation in the dividend-discount model, equation (8), is the sum of the risk-free return and a risk premium. Using this insight, we can rewrite equation (8) as

$$P_{today} = \frac{D_{today}(1+g)}{rf + rp - g} \quad (11)$$

Looking at equation (11), we can see that the higher the risk premium investors demand to hold a stock, the lower its price. Similarly, the higher the risk-free return, the lower the stock's price. (See Table 8.3 on page 168 for a summary.)

# YOUR FINANCIAL WORLD

Beware Percentage Change

On Friday, April 20, 2001, an article titled "Will Beaten-Up Funds Rise Again?" appeared in *The Wall Street Journal*. The story noted that money managers whose funds had lost significant value during the market declines of the early 1970s went on to become the stars of the next decade. One fund, called the American Heritage Fund, declined in value more than 75 percent during the 21 months from December 1972 through September 1974. Over the next 10 years, from the end of 1974 to the end of 1984, the same fund rose 250 percent. The implication of the story was that, while the fund was hard hit in 1973 and 1974, it later recouped its losses and went on to post large gains. But did it really?

To see how well the fund actually did, imagine that you made a $100 investment in American Heritage in December 1972 and sold it in December 1984. What kind of return would you have realized? First, by September 1974, your $100 would have shrunk to $23.20. Over the next 10 years, you would have received a cumulative return of 250 percent on this sum, or a total of $58. When you sold your shares in the American Heritage Fund at the end of 1984, you would have realized $81.20. That is, over the 12 years beginning at the end of 1972, you would have lost $18.80! In comparison, if you had invested $100 in the S&P 500 Index in December 1972, you would have sustained a loss of 42.6 percent followed by a gain of 298 percent. At the end of 1984, you would have had $228.45.

Sometimes investment reports imply that it is possible to evaluate a fund's overall performance simply by adding the percentage loss over one period to a subsequent percentage gain. But, as this example suggests, nothing could be further from the truth.

What percentage increase will bring an investment in the American Heritage Fund back to its original level following the loss of 75 percent? The easiest way to answer this question is to compute a general formula for percentage increase required to bring a losing investment back to its original value. If $d$ is the initial decline in the value of a $100 investment, then $(100 - d)$ is left. What percentage increase in $(100 - d)$ will return the investment to a value of 100? Recall that the percentage change is just the end value, which is $100 minus the initial value $(100 - d)$, divided by the initial value, and multiplied by 100 (so that the answer is a percentage). Putting this all together, we get the formula we are looking for:

$$\text{Percentage increase required to return to original value} = 100 \times \frac{100 - (100 - d)}{(100 - d)}$$

$$= 100 \times \frac{d}{(100 - d)}$$

What happens to this formula as $d$ increases? For very small losses, such as 1 percent to 5 percent, the percentage increase needed is nearly the same as the loss. But as $d$ increases, the required percentage increase climbs rapidly. While a 10 percent decline requires an 11.1 percent increase to return to the initial level, a 75 percent decline requires a 300 percent increase. Beware percentage change!

**Table 8.3** Implications of the Dividend-Discount Model with Risk

**Stock Prices Are High When**
1. Current dividends are high ($D_{today}$ is high).
2. Dividends are expected to grow quickly ($g$ is high).
3. The risk-free rate is low ($rf$ is low).
4. The risk premium on equity is low ($rp$ is low).

We can use equation (11) to see why the stock market is so volatile. Between December 2007 and December 2008, the TSX/S&P composite fell from 13,833 to 8,988, a decline of 35 percent! Equation (11) shows that stock prices are very sensitive to changes in the expected growth of the economy. Historical information suggests values for $rf$ and $rp$ of 2 percent and 4 percent respectively. Over the long term, dividends on average should grow as fast as the economy. Suppose the economy, and

## APPLYING THE CONCEPT
### THE CHINESE STOCK MARKET

After being closed for more than half a century, China reopened its stock market in the early 1990s. Since then the market has grown rapidly, so that today there are over 1,500 Chinese companies with market capitalization of more than $1 trillion.

There are two stock exchanges in China, one in Shanghai (on the east coast) and one in Shenzhen (near Hong Kong). When they were started in the early 1990s, the idea was to transfer the ownership of state-owned enterprises into private hands. For ideological reasons at the time, government officials wanted to retain control of these companies, so they created a system of restricted share ownership. Two types of shares were issued: A shares, priced in Chinese yuan (China's currency unit), and B shares, denominated in either U.S. or Hong Kong dollars. To maintain control, the state retained two-thirds of the A shares.

Until 2001, domestic Chinese investors could hold only A shares while foreigners could purchase only B shares. Despite the fact that the two classes of shares gave owners the same rights, A shares prices were on average more than four times that of the otherwise identical B shares. This is strange. Two things that are the same should sell for the same price.

Some observers suggested that the premium resulted from a combination of the lack of Chinese investor sophistication, a shortage of information, and euphoria at being able to purchase common stock. But a critical piece of evidence suggests prices were high because there weren't enough shares to go around. A few years ago, as the Chinese government loosened its grip on the economy, officials decided to reduce their stock holdings and announced a plan to sell the government's A shares into the market. Prices collapsed, falling by more than 50 percent from their peak. Elementary supply and demand analysis teaches us that when supply is low, prices are likely to be high, and that when supply increases, prices fall.

The lesson is that price differences can be a consequence of institutional constraints. And if they are, when institutional constraints are relaxed, prices change.

dividends, are expected to grow at 3 percent; then, equation (11) says that the price would be 34 times the level of dividends; If the expected growth rate fell to 1 percent, then the price would fall to 20 times the level of dividends. You can see that a change in the expected growth rate would lead to a 40 percent decline in the stock market. More generally, the calculation shows that stock prices are very sensitive to expected future growth rates. When the expected growth rate moves around a lot, as in 2009, then stock prices will be very volatile.

## The Theory of Efficient Markets

Stock prices change nearly continuously. Why? One explanation starts in the same place as the dividend-discount model and is based on the concept of fundamental value. When fundamentals change, prices must change with them.

This line of reasoning gives rise to what is commonly called the theory of efficient markets. The basis for the theory of efficient markets is the notion that the prices of all financial instruments, including stocks, reflect all available information. As a result, markets adjust immediately and continuously to changes in fundamental values. If the theory of efficient markets is correct, the chartists are doomed to failure.

The theory of efficient markets implies that stock price movements are unpredictable. If they weren't—if you could accurately forecast that the price of a stock was going to rise tomorrow—you would immediately buy as many shares of the stock as possible. Your action would increase demand for the stock, driving its price up today. In other words, the fact that you think a stock's price will rise tomorrow makes it rise today.[8] When markets are efficient, the prices at which stocks currently trade reflect all available information, so future price movements are unpredictable.

---

[8] If you felt sure that a stock's price was going to fall, you could take advantage of your forecast by using a strategy called short selling. You would borrow shares and sell them with the idea of buying them back at a lower price in the future. This tactic increases the supply of shares for sale, driving the stock's price down.

If no one can predict stock price movements, then what good is investment advice? Not much! If the theory of efficient markets is correct, no one can consistently beat the market average. This means that active portfolio management—buying and selling stocks based on someone's advice—will not yield a higher return than that of a broad stock-market index—the market average—year after year.

There is quite a bit of evidence to support the view that stock price changes are unpredictable and that professional money managers cannot beat an index such as the S&P 500 with regularity. On average, the return on managed portfolios is about 2 percent less than average stock-market returns. But we do see managers who at least claim to exceed the market average year after year.[9] How can this be? There are four possibilities: (1) They have private information, which is illegal; (2) they are taking on risk, which brings added compensation but means that at times, returns will be extremely poor; (3) they are lucky; or (4) markets are not efficient.

It is intriguing to think that high (or low) investment returns could simply be the result of chance. To understand why this is so, consider the following parable, which appears in Peter Bernstein's book *Capital Ideas*.[10] Suppose that 300 million people all join in a coin-tossing contest. On the first day, each person finds a partner and they each bet a dollar on the coin toss. The winner gets $2 and the loser leaves the game. Each day the coin toss is repeated, with the losers turning their dollars over to the winners, who then stake their winnings on the next day's toss. The laws of chance tell us that, after 10 flips on 10 consecutive mornings, only 220,000 people will still be in the contest, and each will have won a little more than $1,000. Then the game heats up. Ten days later, after 20 tosses, only 286 people will still be playing, and each will have nearly $1,050,000. These winners had no special knowledge. No skill was involved in their accumulation of high returns, just pure chance.

You may be asking what this has to do with investment and efficient markets. The answer is that when there are lots of people placing bets—and there surely are a large number of investors trying to gain advantages in the stock market—there will be a fair number of people who do well just by pure chance. And the problem with the stock market is that the number of people who "win" is about the same as the number we would expect to be lucky.

## Behavioural Finance

While many economists believe that the professed ability of some money managers to "beat the market" reflects luck, advocates of behavioural finance models argue that (1) arbitrage does not always rule out violations of the efficient-market hypothesis and (2) that investments are made by human beings, not automatons. These economists draw on research by psychologists into human decision making to explain the violations.[11] Psychologists have found that individuals deviate from what economists would call "rational" decision making in systematic ways. For example, there is a framing effect that occurs when an individual's choice depends on the context in

---

[9] Remember that someone owns every share in the stock market, so above-average returns to one person must be matched by below-average returns to someone else.

[10] Peter Bernstein. *Capital Ideas: The Improbable Origins of Modern Wall Street* (New York: Free Press, 1993).

[11] See N. Barberis, and R. Thaler (2002) "A Survey of Behavioural Finance" for an introduction to behavioural finance models and further references. http://badger.som.yale.edu/faculty/ncb25/ch18_6.pdf.

which it is presented[12]; also, individuals tend to be overconfident and overoptimistic. Loss aversion refers to the observation that individuals appear to be risk averse when offered potential gains but risk seeking when offered losses. People behave particularly "irrationally" when it comes to measuring and dealing with uncertainty and probabilities.

Advocates of behavioural models argue that incorporating these biases into models of investor decision making can explain some of the violations of the efficient-markets theory. Many of these violations of the theory take the form of predictable high returns: the January effect says that equity investments make high returns between December and January; the small-firm effect observes that small cap stocks do better than large cap; the mean reversal effect shows that stocks that have overperformed in the past do worse than recent poor performers. A second set of violations are at the macro level. For example, economists have long been puzzled that the returns to equities are higher than can be justified by reasonable estimates of the risk premium, the so-called equity-premium puzzle. Home bias refers to the fact that investors typically do not diversify across international equity markets as much as economic models predict. Other examples include overtrading—investors actively managing portfolios rather than investing in index funds, which on average do better—and the existence of bubbles discussed in the next section.

Behavioural models have explanations for all of these. For example, biases can explain overtrading: it is due to the overconfidence of investors who believe that they can beat the market. The mean reversal of stock prices is explained by a model in which investors overreact to news either positive or negative. Home bias is explained by a preference for the familiar. Barberis and Thaler (2003; see footnote 12 below) show how each violation has been explained by relying on deviations from "rational" behaviour.

Many economists argue that the behavioural models are vague enough to explain anything and therefore have no predictive power (one of the strengths of economics is that by using simple models that abstract from many secondary factors the models yield clear predictions that can be falsified). These economists believe that the observed "violations" of the efficient market hypothesis are not true violations because some institutional factor (say, taxes or the inability to short sell) means that there it would not be possible to turn the observation into a profit opportunity. Despite the award of a Nobel Prize in Economics to Daniel Kahneman for his use of psychological evidence to improve economic modelling, the verdict as to how much behavioural finance models will become the standard models of financial markets is still undetermined.

## Investing in Stocks for the Long Run

Stocks appear to be risky, yet many people hold a substantial proportion of their wealth in the form of stock. We can reconcile our perception of risk with observed behaviour in two ways. Either stocks are not that risky, or people are not that averse to the risk and so do not require a large risk premium to hold stocks. Which of these explanations is more plausible?

---

[12] The framing effect is neatly illustrated by Barberis and Thaler: "In one experiment, subjects were asked to estimate the percentage of African countries belonging to the United Nations. More specifically, before giving a percentage, they were asked whether their guess was higher or lower than a randomly generated number between 0 and 100. Their subsequent estimates were significantly affected by the initial random number. Those who were asked to compare their estimate to 10, subsequently estimated 25 percent, while those who compared to 60, estimated 45 percent".

| Figure 8.3 | S&P 1-Year and 25-Year Stock Returns, 1871-2004 |

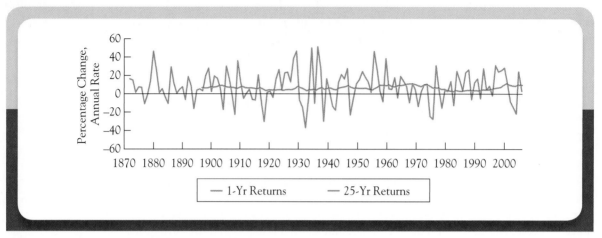

(Returns are Real, Adjusted for Inflation Using the CPI.)

SOURCE: *From Irrational Exuberance, 2e, Princeton 2005. Reprinted with permission by Robert J. Shiller.*

To get a sense of the risk in holding stock, we can look at the one-year return on the S&P 500 Index for each of the past 130 years. The red line in Figure 8.3 plots the one-year real return to holding this portfolio (including dividend payments and adjusted for inflation using the consumer price index). The average real return over 130 years exceeded 8.5 percent per year.

In looking at the figure, remember to check the axis labels. Start by noting that the scale on the vertical axis goes from −60 percent to +60 percent, a huge range. The minimum return was nearly −40 percent (in 1932), and the maximum was more than +50 percent (in 1936). Over the last 50 years the range has narrowed, to a maximum annual return of 46 percent (in 1955) and a minimum of −27 percent (in 1975). Nearly half the time, the return on holding stocks has been either less than zero (negative) or above 25 percent (substantially positive). The graph certainly gives the impression that prices fluctuate wildly and that holding stocks is extremely risky.

In 1994 though, Professor Jeremy Siegel of the University of Pennsylvania's Wharton School published a book titled *Stocks for the Long Run*,[13] in which he suggested that investing in stocks is risky only if you hold them for a short time. If you buy stocks and hold them for long enough, they really are not very risky.

To see Professor Siegel's point, we can look at the return to holding stocks for 25 years instead of one. The smooth green line in Figure 8.3 shows the average annual return from investing in the S&P 500 for a 25-year period. We can see immediately that the green line is much smoother and fluctuates over a much smaller range than the red line—and it never dips below zero. In fact, the *minimum average* annual return over 25 years is a substantial 4.7 percent, while the maximum is 16.6 percent. Changing these nominal rates to real, inflation-adjusted rates simply lowers their level by about 2 percent. Siegel's point is that if you buy stocks and hold them for the long run—25 years or so—your investment is not very risky.

That was not the end of Professor Siegel's analysis. His next step was to compare the returns from holding bonds with those from holding stock. The results were star-

[13] Jeremy J. Siegel. *Stocks for the Long Run: A Guide to Selecting Markets for Long-Term Growth* (Chicago: Richard D. Irwin, 1994).

# YOUR FINANCIAL WORLD
## Should You Own Stocks?

Should you own stocks? The answer is yes, especially if you are young! Many people shy away from stocks and invest in bonds (or other interest-bearing assets). But remember that bonds are risky, too—even government bonds carry interest rate risk and inflation risk. Though stocks may look risky, history suggests that a well-diversified portfolio of stocks held over the long term is not. The real question is how to buy stock.

There are five issues to think about when buying stock: affordability, liquidity, diversification, management, and cost. Prepackaged portfolios called mutual funds address all these issues in one way or another as do exchange traded funds (ETFs). The problem is that there are literally thousands of mutual funds and quite a few ETFs to choose from. So, how do we choose? Here are some points to keep in mind:

1. *Affordability*. Most mutual funds allow a small initial investment. You can start with as little as $500.

2. *Liquidity*. In an emergency, you may need to withdraw resources quickly. ETFs can be sold through a broker (such as Qtrade or iTrade) while mutual funds are redeemed.

3. *Diversification*. The vast majority of mutual funds are much more diversified than any individual portfolio of stocks. Even so, it is important to check before you buy.

4. *Management*. Mutual funds offer the advantage of professional management. You do need to be careful, as funds in which people make the decisions, so-called managed funds, tend to perform worse than index funds, which are designed to mimic stock market indexes like the S&P 500.

5. *Cost*. Mutual fund managers charge fees for their services. The fees for managed funds often run over 2 percent per year, compared to 1 percent or less for index funds. This is a significant difference. Over 20 years, an investment of $10,000 with an average annual net return of 7 percent will amount to $38,697. If your net return averages only 6 percent, the value of the investment drops to $32,071, or $6,626 less. Investing in index ETFs (such as XIC-TSX) gives you access to a lower management fee although you have to pay a broker to trade the shares and will lose the bid-ask spread when you buy and then sell.

Taken together, these considerations persuade many people to invest in either index funds or index ETFs. Index funds are affordable and liquid, they offer excellent diversification, and they tend to be cheap. Don't take my word for it; always ask before you invest.

tling. Siegel reported that, between 1871 and 1992, there was no 30-year period when bonds outperformed stocks. In other words, when held for the long term, stocks are less risky than bonds!

For many people, investing in stock is a way of saving for retirement, so their investment horizon is very long. Professor Siegel's calculations tell us that our retirement savings should be invested in stock and that we shouldn't worry about year-to-year fluctuations in their value.[14]

# The Stock Market's Role in the Economy

The stock market plays a crucial role in every modern capitalist economy. The prices determined there tell us the market value of companies, which guides the allocation of resources. Firms with a high stock market value are the ones investors prize, so they have an easier time garnering the resources they need to grow. In contrast, firms whose stock value is low have difficulty financing their operations.

[14] For a more sobering view of the stock market rise of the late 1990s, see Robert J. Shiller, *Irrational Exuberance* (Princeton, NJ: Princeton University Press, 2000).

# IN THE NEWS

## Bre-X and the Golden Fleece:
## The Biggest Mining Scam in History
## Is Now the Stuff of Legends and Lawsuits

**Peter Kennedy**

**February 2, 1998**

Proving that truth can sometimes be stranger than fiction, Bre-X Minerals Ltd.'s Indonesian gold scam has become the blockbuster business story of the decade.

Who would have thought that a bunch of prospectors working in the Borneo jungle could have fooled almost the entire mining industry into thinking they had found a motherlode of gold?

Certainly not the mining analysts whose glowing reports about the so-called Busang find sent the stock soaring over $280 on a pre-split basis.

Far from questioning Bre-X's numbers, major North American gold producers like Barrick Gold Corp. and Placer Dome Inc. were tripping over themselves to curry favor with Indonesian President Suharto and get control of Busang.

A 55 percent stake in the site was eventually awarded to Freeport McMoRan Copper & Gold Inc. of New Orleans, which didn't have to pay Bre-X any compensation.

Reporters working on the story weren't able to say for sure that Bre-X's Busang find was a scam until consultant Strathcona Mineral Services Ltd. provided confirmation on May 4, 1997.

Strathcona found that the magnitude of the tampering with core samples and falsification of assay values was, to its knowledge, of a scale and precision without precedent in the history of mining anywhere in the world.

For much of last year this was also a human interest story centred on the apparent suicide of Bre-X geologist Michael de Guzman. This year it becomes a high-profile courtroom drama, with an emphasis on who knew what and when.

Investors, who saw about $ 3-billion worth of value wiped out when the scandal was revealed, have launched multibillion-dollar class action law suits in the U.S. and Canada in a bid to recover their money.

So long as stock prices accurately reflect fundamental values, this resource allocation mechanism works well. The signals are accurate, and investment resources flow to their most socially beneficial uses. But at times, stock prices deviate significantly from the fundamentals and move in ways that are difficult to attribute to changes in the real interest rate, the risk premium, or the growth rate of future dividends.

While many economists believe that markets are always efficient and that prices never deviate from fundamental values, it is worth entertaining the possibility that shifts in investor psychology may distort prices. The fact is, both euphoria and depression are contagious, so when investors become unjustifiably exuberant about the market's future prospects, prices rise regardless of the fundamentals. Such mass enthusiasm creates bubbles, persistent and expanding gaps between actual stock prices and those warranted by the fundamentals. These bubbles inevitably burst, creating crashes. This phenomenon is one explanation for the very jagged pattern in annual stock returns—the large gains followed by equally large losses—shown in Figure 8.3 on page 172.[15]

Investors surely care about the large gains and losses they see when stock prices rise or fall serendipitously. But they are not the only ones who should be concerned. Bubbles affect all of us because they distort the economic decisions companies and

---

[15] The fact that large declines tend to be followed by equally large increases is what makes stocks less risky when held over a long period, as Professor Siegel noticed.

## LESSONS OF THE ARTICLE

Investing in stocks can bring high returns, but investing in a single company is very, very risky. The Bre-X scam cost investors over $3 billion. While many investors had only a few shares as part of a diversified portfolio, some Albertans had put all of their savings into Bre-X when the gold discoveries were first announced. In November 1995 shares were trading at $45, and by May 1997 they had risen (including the impact of a 10:1 split) to over $200. Days later they were worth zero. Investors argued that brokerage houses that promoted the stock, and the TSX, which listed the stock, should bear some responsibility for the losses, but up to July 2009 no compensation had been paid.

The damage went beyond the losses to individual investors as it made it harder for honest mining and exploration companies to raise money. Traditionally, the strict listing requirements of the Toronto Stock Exchange meant that a TSX listing was seen as a signal of quality. The Bre-X scam damaged that signal, hurting the investment industry more broadly.

SOURCE: *The Financial Post*, February 2, 1998. Section 1, Special Report: *The Financial Post: 1988-1998*, p. 41, 1997. Peter Kennedy.

consumers make. Here is what happens to companies. When their stock prices rise, financing becomes easier to obtain. They can sell shares and use the proceeds to fund new business opportunities. In the feeding frenzy of a bubble, companies can sell shares for prices that are too high, so financing new investments becomes too easy. It is not much of a challenge to identify high-technology companies that raised staggering sums in the equity markets in the late 1990s, only to crash and burn several years later. They spent the funds they raised on investments in equipment and buildings that turned out later to be worth nothing, to them or anyone else.[16]

The consequences of such a bubble are not innocuous. The companies whose stock prices rise the most can raise financing the most easily. The result is that they invest too much. Meanwhile, firms in businesses that are not the objects of investor euphoria have a more difficult time raising financing, so they invest too little. The distortions can be large, and recovery can be slow, especially since companies find it almost impossible to find financing for new projects after the bubble bursts.

The impact of stock price bubbles on consumer behaviour is equally damaging. Rising equity prices increase individual wealth. The richer we become, the more income we spend and the less we save. Unjustifiably high stock prices lead us to buy luxury cars, large houses, and extravagant vacations, which fuels a boom in economic activity.

[16] Stories about the Internet boom of the late 1990s, together with data on stock prices and market values of firms, are collected in John Cassidy's *Dot.con: How America Lost Its Mind and Money in the Internet Era* (New York: HarperCollins, 2002).

People begin to think they will not need to work as long before they retire. After all, the stock market has made them wealthy, and rich people don't need to work.

The euphoria can't last. When the bubble eventually bursts, individuals are forced to reevaluate their wealth. People discover that their houses and mortgages are too large for their paycheques and their investment accounts are only a shadow of what they once were. Now they need to work harder than ever just to keep up, and their plans for an early retirement are a distant memory. That's not all. Firms that geared up to produce luxury goods for rich shoppers are in trouble. Their wealthy customers disappeared when the bubble burst, and now they are stuck with products people can't afford to buy.

If bubbles result in real investment that is both excessive and inefficiently distributed, crashes do the opposite. The shift from overoptimism to excessive pessimism causes a collapse in investment and economic growth. Normally, the stock market works well and investment funds flow to their most beneficial uses. Occasionally the process goes awry and stock prices move far from any reasonable notion of fundamental value. When these bubbles grow large enough, especially when they lead to crashes, the stock market can destabilize the real economy.

## Terms

bubble, 174
common stock, 156
dividend-discount model, 165
dividends, 164
Dow Jones Industrial Average (DJIA), 160
equity premium puzzle, 171
equity, 156
exchanged traded funds (ETFs), 173
fundamental value, 163
index, 159
January effect, 171
limited liability, 157
market capitalization, 159
mean reversal effect, 171
mutual fund, 173

Nasdaq Composite Index, 161
price-weighted average, 160
primary market, 157
residual claimant, 157
Russell 2000, 161
S&P 500, 160
secondary market, 157
small firm effect, 171
Standard & Poor's, 159
stock market, 155
stock-market indexes, 159
theory of efficient markets, 169
S&P/TSX composite index, 159
value-weighted index, 159
Wilshire 5000, 161

## Chapter Summary

1. Shareholders own the firms in which they hold shares.
   a. They are residual claimants, which means they are last in line after all other creditors.
   b. They have limited liability, so their losses cannot exceed their initial investments.

2. There are two basic types of stock-market index.
   a. The S&P/TSX is a value-weighted index.
   b. The Dow Jones Industrial Average is a price-weighted index.
   c. For every stock market in the world, there is a comprehensive index that is used to measure overall performance.

3. There are several ways to value stocks.
   a. Some analysts examine patterns of past performance; others follow investor psychology.
   b. The fundamental value of a stock depends on expectations for a firm's future profitability.
   c. To compensate for the fact that stocks are risky investments, investors in stock require a risk premium.
   d. The dividend-discount model is a simple way to assess fundamental value. According to this model, stock prices depend on the current level of dividends, the growth rate of dividends, the risk-free interest rate, and the equity risk premium.
   e. According to the theory of efficient markets, stock prices reflect all available information.
   f. If markets are efficient, then stock price movements are unpredictable, and investors cannot systematically outperform a comprehensive stock market index such as the S&P/TSX Composite.

g. According to behavioural finance models, deviations from efficient markets are observed and can be explained by incorporating a richer model of investor decision making.

4. Stock investments are much less risky when they are held for long periods than when they are held for short periods.

5. Stock prices are a central element in a market economy, because they ensure that investment resources flow to their most profitable uses. When occasional bubbles and crashes distort stock prices, they can destabilize the economy.

## Conceptual Problems

1. Explain why being a residual claimant makes stock ownership risky.

2. Check the business section of a recent newspaper (or a financial Web site) to find the current level of each of the following indexes, along with their change over the last 12 months:
   a. S&P/TSX Composite Index
   b. S&P/Venture Index
   c. S&P 500
   d. Dow Jones Industrial Average
   Comment on what you found, including the differences among the indexes.

3. A stock that sells for $100 entitles you to a dividend payment of $4. You estimate that the growth rate of the firm's dividends is about 2 percent per year, and that the risk-free rate is 3½ percent. What is the risk premium suggested by the price of this stock? Does it strike you as high or low? How would your answer change if the stock price were $150 instead of $100?

4. As you flip through *Financial Post* you notice advertisements by investment firms wanting to sell you their products. Common among all of the ads is the claim that the firm has a track record of above-average performance. Explain how they can all be above average. Is this inconsistent with the efficient markets theory?

5. Explain why an investment portfolio composed of all the stocks in the S&P/TSX Composite Index is less risky than an investment portfolio composed of 20 stocks chosen randomly.

6.* What are the advantages of holding stock in a company versus holding bonds issued by the same company?

7. Return to the example summarized in Table 8.2 on page 167, in which a firm purchases a $1,000 computer. Assume that the firm has only 20 percent equity outstanding, so it needs an $800 loan. Managers expect revenue of $200 in good times and $100 in bad times. Compute the percentage change in revenue and profits (revenue minus interest payments) if revenue is $200 in the first year and $100 in the second year. Then compute the return to the shareholders in each year.

8. Do you think a proposal to abolish limited liability for shareholders would be supported by companies issuing stock?

9.* Why is a booming stock market not always a good thing for the economy?

10. The financial press tends to become excited when the S&P/TSX Composite Index rises or falls sharply. After a particularly steep rise or fall, newspapers may publish tables ranking the day's results with other large advances or declines. What do you think of such reporting? If you were asked to construct a table of the best and worst days in stock market history, how would you do it, and why?

## Analytical Problems

11. You are thinking about investing in stock in a company that paid a dividend of $10 this year and whose dividends you expect to grow at 4 percent a year. The risk-free rate is 3 percent and you require a risk premium of 5 percent. If the price of the stock in the market is $200 a share, should you buy it?

12.* Consider again the stock described in question 11. What might account for the difference in the market price of the stock and the price you are willing to pay for the stock?

13. You are trying to decide whether to buy stock in Company X or Company Y. Both companies need $1,000 capital investment and will earn $200 in good years (with probability 0.5)

* Indicates more difficult problems.

and $60 in bad years. The only difference between the companies is that Company X is planning to raise all of the $1,000 needed by issuing equity while Company Y plans to finance $500 through equity and $500 through bonds on which 10 percent interest must be paid. Construct a table showing the expected value and standard deviation of the equity return for each of the companies. (You could use Table 8.2 on page 167 as a guide.) Based on your table, in which company would you buy stock? Explain your choice.

14. Your brother has $1,000 and a one-year investment horizon and asks your advice about whether he should invest in a particular company's stock. What information would you suggest he analyze when making his decision?

Is there an alternative investment strategy you might suggest to him to gain exposure to the stock market?

15. Your friend's sister brags that she consistently gains higher returns on her stock portfolio than the market average. As a believer in efficient markets, what explanation for these rates of returns would seem most likely to you?

16. Based on the dividend-discount model, what do you think would happen to stock prices if there were an increase in the perceived riskiness of bonds?

17.* Use the dividend-discount model to explain why an increase in stock prices is often a good indication that the economy is expected to do well.

## CHAPTER 9

# Derivatives: Futures, Options, and Swaps

In the credit crisis that began in the fall of 2007, derivatives were frequently identified as a leading culprit. Warren Buffett had described derivatives as "financial weapons of mass destruction" in 2003, and it seemed that the crisis proved his point, as headlines blamed esoteric financial instruments such as credit default swaps (CDS) for the collapse of large U.S. financial institutions. Derivatives were also at the core of the scandal that engulfed Enron immediately after it declared bankruptcy in November 2001, the largest bankruptcy to date in the United States.

Financial derivatives were also linked to the collapse of Long-Term Capital Management (LTCM), a Connecticut-based hedge fund, in fall 1998. On a single day in August 1998, LTCM lost an astounding $553 million. By late September, the fund had lost another $2 billion. That left LTCM with over $99 billion in debt and $100 billion in assets. With loans accounting for 99 percent of total assets, repayment was nearly impossible. LTCM also had significant derivatives positions that did not show up on the balance sheet as assets or liabilities. These off-balance-sheet arrangements, which carried even more risk, were the primary cause of the fund's stunningly swift losses.

If derivatives are open to abuse, why do they exist? The answer is that, when used properly, derivatives are extremely helpful financial instruments. They can be used to reduce risk, allowing firms and individuals to enter into agreements that they otherwise wouldn't be willing to accept. Derivatives can also be used as insurance. For example, in winter 1998, snowmobile manufacturer Bombardier offered a $1,000 rebate to buyers should snowfall in 44 cities total less than half what it had averaged over the preceding three years. Sales rose 38 percent. The existence of "weather derivatives" enabled Bombardier to undertake this risky marketing strategy. Paying the rebates would have bankrupted the company, but Bombardier purchased derivatives that would pay off if snowfall were low. By using this unorthodox form of insurance, Bombardier transferred the risk to someone else.

What exactly are derivatives, and why are they so important? Though they play a critical role in our financial well-being, most people barely know what they are. This chapter will provide an introduction to the uses and abuses of derivatives.

## The Basics: Defining Derivatives

To understand what derivatives are, let's begin with the basics. A derivative is a financial instrument whose value depends on—is *derived* from—the value of some other financial instrument, called the *underlying asset*. Some common examples of underlying assets are stocks, bonds, wheat, snowfall, and stock market indexes such as the S&P/TSX Composite.

A simple example of a derivative is a contractual agreement between two investors that obligates one to make a payment to the other, depending on the movement in interest rates over the next year. This type of derivative is called an interest-rate *futures contract*. Such an arrangement is quite different from the outright purchase of a bond for two reasons. First, derivatives provide an easy way for investors to profit from price declines. The purchase of a bond, in contrast, is a bet that its price will rise.[1] Second,

---

[1] Investors can bet that prices will fall using a technique called short selling. The investor borrows an asset from its owner for a fee, sells it at the current market price, and then repurchases it later. The short seller is betting that the price of the asset will fall between the time it is sold and the time it is repurchased.

*"At the Hawescroft School we've de-emphasized singing and drawing and emphasized stocks and derivatives."*

and more important, in a derivatives transaction, one person's loss is always another person's gain. Buyer and seller are like two people playing poker. How much each player wins or loses depends on how the game progresses, but the total amount on the table doesn't change.

While derivatives can be used to *speculate*, or gamble on future price movements, the fact that they allow investors to manage and reduce risk makes them indispensable to a modern economy. Bombardier used a derivative to hedge the risk of having to pay rebates in the event of low snowfall (we discussed hedging in Chapter 5). As we will see, farmers use derivatives regularly, to insure themselves against fluctuations in the market prices of their crops. Risk can be bought and sold using derivatives. Thus, *the purpose of derivatives is to transfer risk from one person or firm to another.*

When people have the ability to transfer risks, they will do things that they wouldn't do otherwise. Think of a wheat farmer and a bread baker. If the farmer cannot insure against a decline in the price of wheat, the farmer will plant fewer acres of wheat. And without a guarantee that the price of flour will not rise, the baker will build a smaller bakery. Those are prudent responses to the risks created by price fluctuations.

Now introduce a mechanism through which the farmer and the baker can guarantee the price of wheat. As a result, the farmer will plant more and the baker will build a bigger bakery. Insurance is what allows them to proceed. Derivatives provide that insurance. In fact, by shifting risk to those willing and able to bear it, derivatives increase the risk-carrying capacity of the economy as a whole, improving the allocation of resources and increasing the level of output.

Derivatives allow individuals and firms to not only manage risk, but also conceal the true nature of certain financial transactions. In the same way that stripping a coupon bond separates the coupons from the principal payment, buying and selling derivatives can unbundle virtually any group of future payments and risks. A company that hesitates to issue a coupon bond for fear analysts will frown on the extra debt can instead issue the coupon payments and the principal payment as individual zero-coupon bonds, using derivative transactions to label them something other than borrowing. Thus, if stock market analysts penalize companies for obtaining funding in certain ways, derivatives (as we will see) allow the companies to get exactly the same resources at the same risk but under a different name.

Derivatives may be divided into three major categories: forwards and futures, options, and swaps. Let's look at each one.

## Forwards and Futures

Of all derivative financial instruments, forwards and futures are the simplest to understand and the easiest to use. A **forward**, or **forward contract**, is an agreement between a buyer and a seller to exchange a commodity or financial instrument for a specified amount of cash on a prearranged future date. Forward contracts are private agreements between two parties. Because they are customized, forward contracts are very difficult to resell to someone else.

To see why forward contracts are difficult to resell, consider the example of a yearlong apartment lease, in which the tenant agrees to make a series of monthly payments to the landlord in exchange for the right to live in the apartment. Such a lease is a sequence of 12 forward contracts. Rent is paid in predetermined amounts on prearranged future dates in exchange for housing. While there is some standardization of leases, a contract between a specific tenant and a specific landlord is unlike any other rental contract. Thus, there is no market for the resale or reassignment of apartment rental contracts. The most common forward contracts in Canada are for foreign exchange. Wholesale importers and exporters frequently buy or sell forward contracts for U.S. dollars in one month, three months, and six months.

Trading pit at the New York Mercantile Exchange in New York City.

SOURCE: © *Reuters/CORBIS*.

*In contrast, a* **future**, *or* **futures contract**, *is a forward contract that has been standardized and sold through an organized exchange.* A futures contract specifies that the seller—who has the short position—will deliver some quantity of a commodity or financial instrument to the buyer—who has the long position—on a specific date, called the *settlement* or *delivery* date, for a predetermined price. No payments are made initially when the contract is agreed to. The seller/short position benefits from declines in the price of the underlying asset, while the buyer/long position benefits from increases.[2]

The Montreal Exchange (MX) is the Canadian derivatives exchange where interest rate futures, and equity and equity index futures are traded. Futures and options on canola and barley are traded on ICE Futures Canada (the successor company to the Winnipeg Commodity Exchange). U.S. markets, such as the Chicago Mercantile Exchange (CME) provide platforms to trade many more futures contracts such as metals, weather, government bonds, or exchange rates. For example, let's look at the Canadian dollar contracts traded at the CME. Table 9.1 on page 182 shows the prices and trading activity for this contract on June 1, 2009. There are contracts that specify delivery of C$100,000 in June 2009 and every three months after that until September 2010. Notice that the volume of trade is highest for the near-term contracts and for the electronic rather than regular-hour trading.

The existence of the exchange creates a natural place for people who are interested in a particular futures contract to meet and trade. Historically, exchanges have been physical locations, but with the Internet came online trading of futures. Now trading can happen 24/7 and anyone on the planet with an Internet connection can take part.

One more thing is needed before anyone will actually buy or sell futures contracts: assurance that the buyer and seller will meet their obligations. In the case of the Canadian dollar futures contract, the buyer must be sure the seller will deliver the currency, and the seller must believe that the buyer will pay for it. Market participants have found an ingenious solution to this problem. Instead of making a bilateral arrangement, the two parties to a futures contract each make an agreement with a *clearing corporation*. The clearing corporation, which operates like a large insurance company, is the counterparty to both sides of a transaction, guaranteeing that they will meet their obligations. This arrangement reduces the risk buyers and sellers face.

## Margin Accounts and Marking to Market

To reduce the risk it faces, the clearing corporation requires both parties to a futures contract to place a deposit with the corporation itself. This practice is called posting

[2] The term "short" refers to the fact that one party to the agreement is obligated to deliver something, whether or not he or she currently owns it. The term "long" signifies that the other party is obligated to buy something at a future date.

| Table 9.1 | Interest Rate Futures |
|---|---|

| (1) | (2) Open Range | (3) High | (4) Low | (5) Closing Range | (6) Set Price & Pt. Chg | (7) RTH Volume | (8) Global Volume | (9) Open Interest | (10) Contract High | (11) Contract Low |
|---|---|---|---|---|---|---|---|---|---|---|
| **Canada DLR Futures** | | | | | | | | | | |
| JUNE09 | 0.9244 | .9244 | .9204 | 0.9204 | .9180 (1.0893) + 37 | 1672 | 72767 | 84157 - 1356 | 1.0173B | .7666 |
| SEP09 | 0.9265 | .9265 | .9265 | 0.9265 | .9186 (1.0886) + 38 | 41 | 2325 | 5669 + 574 | 1.0145B | .7699A |
| DEC09 | 0.9240 | .9250 | .9240 | 0.9250 | .9194 (1.0877) + 40 | 6 | 54 | 1523 - 5 | .9937 | .7712A |
| MAR10 | - | - | - | 0.9161N | .9200 (1.0870) + 39 | - | 2 | 439 + 2 | .9370 | .7731A |
| JUN10 | - | - | - | 0.9169N | .9208 (1.0860) + 39 | - | 1 | 81 + 1 | .9279B | .7875 |
| SEP10 | - | - | - | 0.9177N | .9216 (1.0851) + 39 | - | - | 130 UNCH | - | - |
| TOTAL CANADA DLR FUTURES | | | | | | 1719 | 75149 | 92359 - 784 | | |

This table reports information on a contract for delivery of C$100,000.

*Column 1* reports the month when the contract requires delivery from the short position/seller to the long position/buyer.

*Column 2.* "Open" is the price quoted when the exchange opened on the morning of June 1, 2009. This need not be the same as the price at the preceding afternoon's close. The price is U.S. dollars per Canadian dollar. The noon spot price for Canadian dollars on June 1 was $0.9198.

*Columns 3 and 4.* "High" and "Low" are the highest and lowest prices posted during the trading day.

*Column 5.* "Close" is the end of day price

*Column 6.* "Settlement price" is the settlement price at the end of the trading day, and the reciprocal shows its equivalent in Canadian dollars per U.S. dollar. This is the price used for marking to market. "Pt change" is the percentage change since the previous day's settlement price.

*Column 7.* "RTH volume" is the number of trades that day in regular trading hours.

*Column 8.* "Globex volume" is the number of electronic trades after regular hours.

*Column 9.* "Open interest" is the number of contracts outstanding, or open. For contracts near expiration, this number is often quite large. Often contract sellers repurchase their positions rather than delivering the currency, a procedure called *settlement by offset.*

*Columns 10 and 11.* "Contract: High and low" state the highest and lowest price respectively of this contract over the months it has been traded.

*N shows the price is nominal because there were no trades.*

SOURCE: *Prices provided by CME Group Daily Bulletin for Trade Date June 1, 2009.*

margin in a *margin account.* The margin deposits guarantee that when the contract comes due, the parties will be able to meet their obligations. But the clearing corporation does more than collect the *initial margin* when a contract is signed. It also posts daily gains and losses on the contract to the margin accounts of the parties involved.[3] This process is called **marking to market.**

Marking to market is analogous to what happens during a poker game. At the end of each hand, the amount wagered is transferred from the losers to the winner. In financial parlance, the account of each player is marked to market. Alternative methods of accounting are too complicated, making it difficult to identify players who should be

---

[3] On June 1, 2009 the March Canadian dollar futures contract in Table 9.1 rose by .0037%. A single contract covers $100,000, so the value of each contract would have fallen by ($100,000 × .0037) = $370. Marking to market means that, at the end of the day for each outstanding contract, the clearing corporation would credit the long position/seller and debit the short position/buyer $370.

excused from the game because they have run out of resources. For similar reasons, the clearing corporation marks futures accounts to market every day. Doing so ensures that sellers always have the resources to make delivery and that buyers always can pay. As in poker, if someone's margin account falls below the minimum, the clearing corporation will sell the contracts, ending the person's participation in the market.

An example will help. Take the case of a futures contract for the purchase of 5,000 ounces of silver at $10 per ounce. The contract specifies that the buyer of the contract, the long position, will pay $50,000 in exchange for 5,000 ounces of silver. The seller of the contract, the short position, will receive the $50,000 and will deliver the 5,000 ounces of silver. We can think about this contract as guaranteeing the long position the ability to buy 5,000 ounces of silver for $50,000 and guaranteeing the short position the ability to sell 5,000 ounces of silver for $50,000. Now consider what happens when the price of silver changes. If the price rises to $11 per ounce, the seller needs to give the buyer $5,000 so that the buyer pays only $50,000 for the 5,000 ounces of silver. By contrast, if the price falls to $9 an ounce, the buyer of the futures contract needs to pay $5,000 to the seller to make sure that the seller receives $50,000 for selling the 5,000 ounces of silver. Marking to market is the transfer of funds at the end of each day that ensures the buyers and sellers get what the contract promises.

## Hedging and Speculating with Futures

Futures contracts allow the transfer of risk between buyer and seller. This transfer can be accomplished through hedging or speculation. Let's look at *hedging* first. Say a government securities dealer wishes to insure against declines in the value of an inventory of bonds. Recall from Chapter 5 that this type of risk can be reduced by finding another financial instrument that delivers a high payoff when bond prices fall. That is exactly what happens with the sale of a Government of Canada bond futures contract: the seller/short position benefits from price declines.[4] Put differently, the seller of a futures contract—the securities dealer, in this case—can guarantee the price at which the bonds are sold. The other party to this transaction might be a pension fund manager who is planning to purchase bonds in the future and wishes to insure against possible price increases. Buying a futures contract fixes the price that the fund will need to pay. In this example, *both sides use the futures contract as a hedge*. They are both *hedgers*.[5]

Producers and users of commodities employ futures markets to hedge their risks as well. Farmers, mining companies, oil drillers, and the like are sellers of futures, taking short positions. After all, they own the commodities outright, so they want to stabilize the revenue they receive when they sell. In contrast, millers, jewellers, and oil distributors want to buy futures to take long positions. They require the commodity to do business, so they buy the futures contract to reduce risk arising from fluctuations in the cost of essential inputs. (See Applying the Concept: Who Can Use Commodity Futures Markets? on page 184 for a detailed example of this process.)

What about *speculators*? Their objective is simple: They are trying to make a profit. To do so, they bet on price movements. Sellers of futures are betting that prices will fall, while buyers are betting that prices will rise. Futures contracts are popular tools for speculation because they are cheap. An investor needs only a relatively small amount of investment—the margin—to purchase a futures contract that is worth a great deal. Margin requirements of 10 percent or less are common. In the case of

---

[4] Recall from Chapters 4 and 6 that bond prices and interest rates move in opposite directions. That means the bond dealer who sells the futures contract is insuring against interest rate increases.

[5] Hedgers who buy futures are called "long hedgers" and hedgers who sell futures are called "short hedgers."

## APPLYING THE CONCEPT
### WHO CAN USE COMMODITY FUTURES MARKETS?

Commodity prices are notoriously volatile, a fact that makes farming a risky business. In the industrialized world, farmers use futures contracts to hedge the risk arising from price fluctuations. For instance, I have a friend who owns a 2,500 hectare wheat farm. Wheat farming is risky because the farmer's profits depend on the price of wheat at harvest time. To guarantee the price of the wheat he grows, my friend relies on wheat futures. As he plants, investing heavily in his crop, he simultaneously sells futures contracts. The contracts obligate the farmer to deliver the wheat when it is ripe, and fix the price he will receive when he does. Wheat futures are a hedge against the risk of price fluctuations.

Imagine what would happen without this kind of insurance. If prices collapsed, in the absence of insurance the farmer could go bankrupt. Unable to guarantee the harvest price, the farmer would surely plant a smaller, less risky crop. Thus, the ability of people to buy insurance increases their willingness to take risks.

But who has access to commodity futures markets? Remember that trading in futures markets requires the posting of margin; poor farmers need not apply. This hard fact is particularly unfortunate for people in less-developed countries. Growth is the way out of poverty, and risk taking increases growth. But without insurance, farmers in poor countries, such as coffee growers in Latin America, cannot risk planting large crops. So they remain poor.

Futures markets, and derivatives in general, allow people to transfer risk to those who are equipped to handle it. They increase the risk-taking capacity of the economy, making everyone better off. In parts of the world where people do not have access to futures markets, the economy suffers.

a futures contract for the delivery of C\$100,000, the Chicago Board of Trade (the clearing corporation that guarantees the contract) requires an initial margin of only \$4,400 per contract. That is, an investment of only \$4,400 gives the investor the same returns as the purchase of \$100,000 worth of currency. It is as if the investor borrowed the remaining \$95,600 without having to pay any interest.[6]

To see the impact of this kind of leverage on the return to the buyer and seller of a futures contract, notice that an increase of .0037% in the price of the Canadian dollar futures contract meant that the long position/seller gained \$370, while the short position/buyer lost \$370. With a minimum initial investment of \$4,400 for each contract, this represents an 8.4 percent gain to the futures contract buyer and an 8.4 percent loss to the futures contract seller. In contrast, the owner of the Canadian dollars would have gained \$370 on an approximately \$100,000 investment, which is a gain of less than 1 percent! *Speculators, then, can use futures to obtain very large amounts of leverage at a very low cost.*

## Arbitrage and the Determinants of Futures Prices

To understand how the price of a futures contract is determined, let's start at the settlement date and work backward. On the settlement or delivery date, we know that the price of the futures contract must equal the price of the underlying asset the seller is obligated to deliver. The reason is simple: If, at expiration, the futures price were to deviate from the asset's price, then it would be possible to make a risk-free profit by engaging in offsetting cash and futures transactions. If the current market price of a bond were below the futures contract price, someone could buy a bond at the low price and simultaneously sell a futures contract (take a short position and promise to deliver the bond on a future date). Immediate exercise of the futures contract and delivery of the bond would yield a profit equal to the difference between the market price and the futures price. Thinking about this example carefully, we can see that the investor who engages in these transactions has been able to make a profit without taking on any risk or making any investment.

[6] It is even possible to arrange a margin account so that the balance earns interest.

The practice of simultaneously buying and selling financial instruments in order to benefit from temporary price differences is called **arbitrage**, and the people who engage in it are called *arbitrageurs*. Arbitrage means that two financial instruments with the same risk and promised future payments will sell for the same price. If, for example, the price of a specific bond is higher in one market than in another, an arbitrageur can buy at the low price and sell at the high price. The increase in demand in the market where the price is low drives the price up there, while the increase in supply in the market where the price is high drives the price down there, and the process continues until prices are equal in the two markets. As long as there are arbitrageurs, on the day when a futures contract is settled, the price of a futures contract will be the same as the market price—what is called the *spot price*—of the underlying asset. This is an example of a **no-arbitrage condition**.

So we know that on the settlement date, the price of a futures contract must equal the spot price of the underlying asset. But what happens before the settlement date? The principle of arbitrage still applies. The price of the futures contract depends on the fact that someone can buy a bond and sell a futures contract simultaneously. Here's how it's done. First, the arbitrageur borrows at the current market interest rate. With the funds, the arbitrageur buys a bond and sells a bond futures contract. Now the arbitrageur has a loan on which interest must be paid, a bond that pays interest, and a promise to deliver the bond for a fixed price at the expiration of the futures contract. Because the interest owed on the loan and received from the bond will cancel out, this position costs nothing to initiate.[7] As before, if the market price of the bond is below the futures contract price, this strategy will yield a profit. *Thus, the futures price must move in lockstep with the market price of the bond.*

To see how arbitrage works, consider an example of a bond futures contract. Suppose that the spot price of a 6 percent coupon 10-year bond is $100, the current interest rate on a 3-month loan is also 6 percent (quoted at an annual rate), and the futures market price for delivery of a 6 percent, 10-year bond is $101. An investor could borrow $100, purchase the 10-year bond, and sell a bond future for $101 promising delivery of the bond in three months. The investor could use the interest payment from the bond to pay the interest on the loan and deliver the bond to the buyer of the futures contract on the delivery date. This transaction is completely riskless and nets the investor a profit of $1—without even putting up any funds. A riskless profit is extremely tempting, so the investor will continue to engage in the transactions needed to generate it. Here that means continuing to buy bonds (driving the price up) and sell futures (forcing the price down) until the prices converge and no further profits are available.[8]

Table 9.2 on page 186 summarizes the positions of buyers and sellers in the futures market.

## Options

Everyone likes to have options. Having the option to go on vacation or buy a new car is nice. The alternative to having options, having our decisions made for us, is surely worse. Because options are valuable, people are willing to pay for them when they can. Financial options are no different; because they are worth having, we can put a price on them.

---

[7] Unlike you and me, the arbitrageur can borrow at an interest rate that is close to the one received from the bond. There are two reasons for this. First, the arbitrageur is likely to be a large financial intermediary with a very high credit rating; second, the loan is collateralized by the bond itself.

[8] In a commodity futures contract, the futures price will equal the present value of the expected spot price on the delivery date, discounted at the risk-free interest rate.

| Table 9.2 | Who's Who in Futures | |
|---|---|---|

| | **Buyer of a Futures Contract** | **Seller of a Futures Contract** |
|---|---|---|
| This is called the | Long position | Short position |
| Obligation of the party | Buy the commodity or asset on the settlement date | Deliver the commodity or asset on the settlement date |
| What happens to this person's margin account after a rise in the market price of the commodity or asset? | Credited | Debited |
| Who takes this position to *hedge*? | The *user* of the commodity or *buyer* of the asset who needs to insure against the price *rising* | The *producer* of the commodity or owner of the asset who needs to insure against the price *falling* |
| Who takes this position to *speculate*? | Someone who believes that the market price of the commodity or asset will *rise* | Someone who believes that the market price of the commodity or asset will *fall* |

Calculating the price of an option is incredibly complicated. In fact, no one knew how before Fischer Black and Myron Scholes figured it out in 1973. Traders immediately programmed their famous Black-Scholes formula into the computers available at the time, and the options markets took off. By June 2000, the market value of outstanding options was in the neighbourhood of $500 billion. Today, millions of options contracts are outstanding, and millions of them change hands every day.

Before we learn how to price options, we'll need to master the vocabulary used to describe them. Once we have the language, the next step is to move on to how to use options and how to value them.

## Calls, Puts, and All That: Definitions

Like futures, options are agreements between two parties. There is a seller, called an *option writer*, and a buyer, called an *option holder*. As we will see, option writers incur obligations, while option holders obtain rights. There are two basic options, *puts* and *calls*.

A **call option** is the right to buy—"call away"—a given quantity of an underlying asset at a predetermined price, called the **strike price** (or *exercise price*), on or before a specific date. For example, a January 2011 call option on 100 shares of Barrick stock at a strike price of 45 gives the option holder the right to buy 100 shares of Barrick for $45 apiece on or before the third Friday of January 2011. The writer of the call option *must* sell the shares if and when the holder chooses to use the call option. The holder of the call is *not required* to buy the shares; rather, the holder has the option to buy and will do so only if buying is beneficial. When the price of Barrick stock exceeds the option strike price of 45, the option holder can either call away the 100 shares from the option writer by *exercising* the option or sell the option to someone else at a profit. If the market price rose to $50, for example, then exercising the call would allow the holder to buy the stock from the option writer for $45 and reap a $5 per share profit. Whenever the price of the stock is above the strike price of the call option, exercising the option is profitable for the holder, and the option is said to be in the money (as in "I'm in the money!"). If the price of the stock exactly equals the strike price, the option is said to be **at the money**. If the strike price exceeds the market price of the underlying asset, it is termed out of the money.

A **put option** gives the holder the right but not the obligation to sell the underlying asset at a predetermined price on or before a fixed date. The holder can "put" the asset in the hands of the option writer. Again, the writer of the option is obliged to buy the shares should the holder choose to exercise the option. Returning to the example of Barrick stock, consider a put option with a strike price of 45. This is the right to sell 100 shares at $45 per share, which is valuable when the market price of Barrick stock falls below $45. If the price of a share of Barrick stock were $40, then exercising the put option would yield a profit of $5 per share.

The same terminology that is used to describe calls—in the money, at the money, and out of the money—applies to puts as well, but the circumstances in which it is used are reversed. Since the buyer of a put obtains the right to sell a stock, the put is *in the money* when the option's strike price is *above* the market price of the stock. It is *out of the money* when the strike price is *below* the market price.

While it is possible to customize options in the same way as forward contracts, many are standardized and traded on exchanges, just like futures contracts. The mechanics of trading are the same. A clearing corporation guarantees the obligations embodied in the option—those of the option writer. And the option writer is required to post margin. Because option holders incur no obligation, they are not required to post margin.

There are two types of calls and puts: American and European. **American options** can be exercised on any date from the time they are written until the day they expire. As a result, prior to the expiration date, the holder of an American option has three choices: (1) continue to hold the option, (2) sell the option to someone else, or (3) exercise the option immediately. **European options** can be exercised only on the day that they expire. Thus, the holder of a European option has two choices on a date prior to expiration: hold or sell. The vast majority of options traded in the Canada and the United States are American.

## Using Options

Who buys and sells options, and why? To answer this question, we need to understand how options are used. *Options transfer risk* from the buyer to the seller, so they can be used for both hedging and speculation. Let's take hedging first. Remember that a hedger is buying insurance. For someone who wants to purchase an asset such as a bond or a stock in the future, a call option ensures that the cost of buying the asset will not rise. For someone who plans to sell the asset in the future, a put option ensures that the price at which the asset can be sold will not go down.

To understand the close correspondence between options and insurance, think of the arrangement that automobile owners have with their insurance company. The owner pays an insurance premium and obtains the right to file a claim in the event of an accident. If the terms of the policy are met, the insurance company is obligated to pay the claim. If no accident occurs, then there is no claim and the insurance company makes no payment; the insurance premium is lost. In effect, the insurance company has sold an American call option to the car's owner where the underlying asset is a working car and the strike price is zero. This call option can be exercised if and only if the car is damaged in an accident on any day before the policy expires.

Options can be used for speculation as well. Say that you believe that interest rates will fall over the next few months. There are three ways to bet on this possibility. The first is to purchase a bond outright, hoping that its price will rise as interest rates fall.

This is expensive, since you will need to come up with the resources to buy the bond. A second strategy is to buy a futures contract, taking the long position. If the market price of the bond rises, you will make a profit. As we saw in the last section, this is an attractive approach, since it requires only a small investment. But it is also very risky, because the investment is highly leveraged. Both the bond purchase and the futures contract carry the risk that you will take a loss, and if interest rates rise substantially, your loss will be large.

The third strategy for betting that interest rates will fall is to buy a call option on a government bond. If you are right and interest rates fall, the value of the call option will rise. But if you are wrong and interest rates rise, the call will expire worthless and your losses will be limited to the price you paid for it. This bet is both highly leveraged and limited in its potential losses.

In the same way that purchasing a call option allows an investor to bet that the price of the underlying asset will rise, purchasing a put option allows the investor to bet that the price will fall. Again, if the investor is wrong, all that is lost is the price paid for the option. In the meantime, the option provides a cheap way to bet on the movement in the price of the underlying asset. The bet is highly leveraged, since a small initial investment creates the opportunity for a large gain. But unlike a futures contract, a put option has a limited potential loss.

So far we have discussed only the purchase of options. For every buyer there must be a seller. Who is it? After all, an option writer can take a large loss. Nevertheless, for a fee, some people are willing to take the risk and bet that prices will not move against them. These people are simply speculators. A second group of people who are willing to write options are insured against any losses that may arise. They are primarily dealers who engage in the regular purchase and sale of the underlying asset. These people are called *market makers* since they are always there to make the market. Because they are in the business of buying and selling, market markers both own the underlying asset so that they can deliver it and are willing to buy the underlying asset so that they have it ready to sell to someone else. If you own the underlying asset, writing a call option that obligates you to sell it at a fixed price is not that risky. These people write options to obtain the fee paid by the buyer.

Writing options can also generate clear benefits. To see how, think about the case of an electricity producer who has a plant that is worth operating only when electricity prices exceed a relatively high minimum level. Such peak-load plants are relatively common. They sit idle most of the time and are fired up only when demand is so high that prices spike. The problem is that when they are not operating—which is the normal state of affairs—the owner must pay maintenance charges. To cover these charges, the producer might choose to write a call option on electricity. Here's how the strategy works. For a fee, the plant owner sells a call option with a strike price that is higher than the price at which the plant will be brought on line. The buyer of the call might be someone who uses electricity and wants insurance against a spike in prices. The option fee will cover the producer's maintenance cost while the plant is shut down. And, since the producer as option writer owns the underlying asset here—electricity—he or she is hedged against the possibility that the call option will pay off. As the price of electricity rises, the plant's revenue goes up with it.

Options are very versatile and can be bought and sold in many combinations. They allow investors to get rid of the risks they do not want and keep the ones they do want. In fact, options can be used to construct synthetic instruments that mimic the payoffs of virtually any other financial instrument. For example, the purchase of an at-the-money call and simultaneous sale of an at-the-money put gives the exact same

**Table 9.3**   A Guide to Options

| | Calls | Puts |
|---|---|---|
| Buyer | *Right* to *buy* the underlying asset at the strike price prior to or on the expiration date.<br><br>"Hey, send it over!" | *Right* to *sell* the underlying asset at a fixed price prior to or on the expiration date.<br><br>"Here it is!" |
| Seller | *Obligation* to *sell* the underlying asset at the strike price prior to or on the expiration date. | *Obligation* to *buy* the underlying asset at the strike price prior to or on the expiration date. |
| Option is *in the money* when | Price of underlying asset is *above* the strike price of the call. | Price of underlying asset is *below* the strike price of the put. |
| Who buys one | Someone who<br><br>• Wants to *buy* an asset in the future and insure the price paid will not *rise*.<br><br>• Wants to bet that the price of the underlying asset will rise. | Someone who<br><br>• Wants to *sell* an asset in the future and insure the price paid will not fall.<br><br>• Wants to bet that the price of the underlying asset will fall. |
| Who *sells* one to speculate | Someone who<br><br>• Wants to bet that the market price of the underlying asset will *not* rise.<br><br>• A broker who is always willing to sell the underlying asset and is paid to take the risk. | Someone who<br><br>• Wants to bet that the market price of the underlying asset will *not* fall.<br><br>• A broker who is always willing to buy the underlying asset and is paid to take the risk. |

payoff pattern as the purchase of a futures contract. If the price of the underlying asset rises, the call's value increases just as a futures contract does, while the put remains worthless. If the price falls, the put seller loses, just as a futures contract does, while the call is out of the money. Finally, options allow investors to bet that prices will be volatile. Buy a put and a call at the same strike price, and you have a bet that pays off only if the underlying asset price moves up or down significantly.

In summary, options are extremely useful. Remember the example at the beginning of the chapter, in which snowmobile manufacturer Bombardier purchased insurance so it could offer its customers a rebate? What it bought were put options with a payoff tied to the amount of snow that fell. The puts promised payments in the event of low snowfall. This hedged the risk the company incurred when it offered rebates to the purchasers of its snowmobiles. The providers of this insurance, the sellers of the snowfall options, may have been betting that snowfall would be low. That is, they may have been speculating—but not necessarily. After all, there are many companies whose sales and profits rise during warm weather and who are well positioned to take such a risk. Insurance companies, for instance, have lower expenses during warm winters, since there are fewer accident claims when there is less snow. If there is little snow, the insurance company has the funds to make the payments, while if there is lots of snow they can use the price they were paid to write the put to help pay the cost of the claims they face.[9]

Table 9.3 provides a summary of what options are, who buys and sells them, and why they do it.

[9] Bombardier purchased its snowfall insurance from Enron (prior to that company's bankruptcy). As it turned out, there was sufficient snowfall so no payments were made either from Bombardier to the buyers of the snowmobiles or from Enron to Bombardier.

## Pricing Options: Intrinsic Value and the Time Value of the Option

An option price has two parts. The first is the value of the option if it is exercised immediately, and the second is the fee paid for the option's potential benefits. We will refer to the first of these, the value of the option if it is exercised immediately, as the *intrinsic value*. The second, the fee paid for the potential benefit from buying the option, we will call the time value of the option to emphasize its relationship to the time of the option's expiration. This means that

$$Option\ price\ =\ Intrinsic\ value\ +\ Time\ value\ of\ the\ option$$

As an example, before we launch into a discussion of option valuation in general, let's apply what we know about present value and risk analysis. Consider the example of an at-the-money European call option on the stock of XYZ Corporation that expires in one month. Recall that a European option can be exercised only at expiration and that an at-the-money option is one for which the current price of the underlying asset equals the strike price. In this case, both equal $100. So, to start with, the intrinsic value of this call option is zero. To the extent that it has any value at all, that value resides entirely in the option's time value. Assume that, over the next month, the price of XYZ Corporation's stock will either rise or fall by $10 with equal probability. That is, there is a probability of ½ the price will go up to $110, and there is a probability of ½ it will fall to $90. What is the value of this call option?

To find the answer, we can compute the expected present value of the payoff. Let's assume that the interest rate is so low that we can ignore it. (If the payoff were postponed sufficiently far into the future or the interest rate were high enough, we could not ignore the present-value calculation but would have to divide by one plus the interest rate.) Now notice that the option is worth something only if the price goes up. In the event that XYZ's stock price falls to $90, you will allow the option to expire without exercising it. For a call option, then, we need to concern ourselves with the upside, and the expected value of that payoff is the probability, ½, times the payoff, $10, which is $5. This is the time value of the option.

Now think about what happens if, instead of rising or falling by $10, XYZ's stock will rise or fall by $20. This change increases the standard deviation of the stock price. In the terminology used in options trading, the stock price volatility has increased. Doing the same calculation, we see that the expected payoff is now $10. As the volatility of the stock price rises, the option's time value rises with it.

**General Considerations**   In general, calculating the price of an option and how it might change means developing some rules for figuring out its intrinsic value and time value. We can do that using the framework from Chapter 3. Recall that the value of any financial instrument depends on four attributes: the size of the promised payment, the timing of the payment, the likelihood that the payment will be made, and the circumstances under which the payment will be made.[10] As we consider each of these, remember that the most important thing about an option is that the buyer is not obligated to exercise it. An option gives the buyer a choice! What this means is that someone holding an option will never make any additional payment to exercise it, so its value cannot be less than zero.

Since the option can either be exercised or expire worthless, we can conclude that the intrinsic value depends only on what the holder receives if the option is exercised. The intrinsic value is the difference between the price of the underlying asset and the

---

[10] Because the pricing of European options is easier to understand, we will talk about options as if they can be exercised only at the expiration date. The principles for pricing American options are the same, however.

# YOUR FINANCIAL WORLD

## Should You Accept Options as Part of Your Pay?

What if someone offers you a job in return for a salary and stock options. Should you take it? Before you do, ask questions! Let's look at what you need to know. Many firms that offer options on their own stock to employees view the options as a substitute for wages. Employees receive call options that give them the right to purchase the company's stock at a fixed price. The strike price is usually set at the current market price of the stock, so that when employees receive the options, they are at the money. Normally, the expiration date is from one to 10 years in the future. Since the options are long term, they will have substantial value, as measured by the option's time value. But there is a catch. Employees generally are not allowed to sell them and may need to remain with the firm to exercise them.

Nevertheless, the price of the company's stock could skyrocket, so the options may bring a substantial payoff. To take an extreme example, from January 1991 to January

2000, Microsoft's stock price rose from $2 to $116 per share. An employee with 1,000 options to purchase the stock at $2 would have made $114,000 by exercising them. Though Microsoft employees were winners, there are many losers in the options game. Employees holding options to purchase stock in Enron or WorldCom, both of which went bankrupt in 2001, got nothing.

So what should you do? If taking the options means accepting a lower salary, then you are paying for them, and you should think hard before you take the offer. Stock options are almost like lottery tickets, but with a drawing that may not occur for years. They give you a small chance to make a large profit. But investing in the same company that pays your salary is a risky business. If the company goes broke or you lose your job, the options will be worthless to you. So think hard before you trade a high-paying job for a lower-paying job with options.

strike price of the option. This is the *size of the payment* that the option represents, and it must be greater than or equal to zero—the intrinsic value cannot be negative. For an in-the-money call, or the option to buy, the intrinsic value to the holder (the long position) is the market price of the underlying asset minus the strike price. If the call is at the money or out of the money, it has no intrinsic value. Analogously, the intrinsic value of a put, or the option to sell, equals the strike price minus the market price of the underlying asset, or zero, whichever is greater.

At expiration, the value of an option equals its intrinsic value. But what about prior to expiration? To think about this question, consider an at-the-money option—one whose intrinsic value is zero. Prior to expiration, there is always the chance that the price of the underlying asset will move so as to make the option valuable. This potential benefit is represented by the option's time value. *The longer the time to expiration*, the bigger the likely payoff when the option does expire and, thus, the more valuable it is. Remember that the option payoff is asymmetric, so what is important is the chance of making a profit. In the last example, think about what will happen if the option expires in three months instead of one and the stock price has an equal probability of rising or falling $10 each month. The expected payoff of the call option rises from $5 after one month to $7.50 after three. (After three months, the stock can either rise by $30 with probability 1/8, rise by $10 with probability 3/8, fall by $10 with probability 3/8 or fall by $30 with probability 1/8. When the price falls, the call option is not exercised, so the expected value of the three-month call is 1/8 × $30 + 3/8 × $10 = $7.50.)

The *likelihood that an option will pay off depends on the volatility, or standard deviation, of the price of the underlying asset.* To see this, consider an option on Barrick stock that is currently at the money—one with a strike price that equals the current price of the stock. The chance of this option being in the money by the time it expires increases with the volatility of Barrick's stock price. Think about an option on an asset whose

**Table 9.4** Factors Affecting the Value of Options

*Option Value = Intrinsic Value + Time Value*

| Increase in one factor, holding all others fixed | Call (the right to buy) | Put (the right to sell) |
| --- | --- | --- |
| Increase in the strike price | Decrease (intrinsic value falls) | Increase (intrinsic value rises) |
| Increase in the market price of the underlying asset | Increase (intrinsic value rises) | Decrease (intrinsic value falls) |
| Increase in the time to expiration | Increase (time value rises) | Increase (time value rises) |
| Increase in the volatility of the underlying asset price | Increase (time value rises) | Increase (time value rises) |

price is simply fixed—that is, whose standard deviation is zero. This option will never pay off, so no one would be willing to pay for it. Add some variability to the price, however, and there is a chance that the price will rise, moving the option into the money. That is something people will pay for. Thus, the option's time value increases with the volatility of the price of the underlying asset. Taking this analysis one step further, we know that regardless of how far the price of the underlying asset falls, the holder of a call option cannot lose more. In contrast, whenever the price rises higher, the call option increases in value. Increased volatility has no cost to the option holder, only benefits.

We have emphasized that options provide insurance, allowing investors to hedge particular risks. The bigger the risk being insured, the more valuable the insurance, and the higher the price investors will pay. Thus, *the circumstances under which the payment is made* have an important impact on the option's time value. As with futures, however, both writers and holders of options may be hedging risks, so it is impossible to know exactly how risk will affect the option price. Table 9.4 summarizes the factors that affect the value of options.

## The Value of Options: Some Examples

To see how options are valued, we can examine a simple example. The daily news reports the prices of options that are traded on organized exchanges. Table 9.5 shows the prices of Barrick puts and calls on January 15, 2009, as reported on the website of the Montreal Exchange. Panel A shows the prices of options with different strike prices but the same expiration date, February 2009. Panel B shows the prices of options with different expiration dates but the same strike price. From the top of the table we can see that the price of Barrick stock, the underlying asset on which these options were written, was $42.06 per share at the close of that day.

By examining the table, we can discover the following:

- At a given price of the underlying asset and time to expiration, the higher the strike price of a call option, the lower its intrinsic value and the less expensive the option. That is, as you read down the column labelled "Strike Price" in Panel A, the intrinsic value under "Calls" (Barrick stock price minus the strike price) falls. For example, as the strike price goes from $38 to $42, the intrinsic value falls from $4.06 to $.06.

**Table 9.5**   Prices of Barrick Puts and Calls

ABX - Barrick Gold Corporation
Last Price: 42.06   Last update: Jan. 15, 2009 18:26 Montréal time (data 15 mins delayed)

**A. February Expiration**

| | Calls | | | Puts | | |
|---|---|---|---|---|---|---|
| Strike Price | Call Price | Intrinsic Value | Time Value of Call | Put Price | Intrinsic Value | Time Value of Put |
| $38 | 6.05 | 4.06 | 1.99 | 2.12 | 0.00 | 2.12 |
| 40 | 4.80 | 2.06 | 2.74 | 2.85 | 0.00 | 2.85 |
| 42 | 3.70 | 0.06 | 3.64 | 3.80 | 0.00 | 3.80 |
| 44 | 2.79 | 0.00 | 2.79 | 4.90 | 1.94 | 2.96 |
| 46 | 2.06 | 0.00 | 2.06 | 6.15 | 3.94 | 2.21 |

**B. Strike Price of 42**

| | Calls | | | Puts | | |
|---|---|---|---|---|---|---|
| Expiration Month | Call Price | Intrinsic Value | Time Value of Call | Put Price | Intrinsic Value | Time Value of Put |
| February | 3.70 | 0.06 | 3.64 | 3.80 | 0.00 | 3.80 |
| April | 5.50 | 0.06 | 5.44 | 5.55 | 0.00 | 5.55 |
| July | 7.50 | 0.06 | 7.44 | 7.50 | 0.00 | 7.50 |

Intrinsic value of a call = Stock price − Strike price, or zero, whichever is larger.
Intrinsic value of a put = Strike price − Stock price, or zero, whichever is larger.
Time value of the option = Option price − Intrinsic value.

SOURCE: *Prices of Puts and Calls. Stock price from Montreal Stock Exchange, 15 January 2009. Montreal Exchange.*

- At a given price of the underlying asset and time to expiration, the higher the strike price of a put option, the higher the intrinsic value and the more expensive the option. (See the "Intrinsic Value" column for Puts in Panel A.) As the strike price rises from $44 to $46, the intrinsic value of the Barrick put (the strike price minus the Barrick stock price) rises from $1.94 to $3.94.
- The closer the strike price is to the current price of the underlying asset, the larger the option's time value. (See the two columns in Panel A labelled "Time Value of Call" and "Time Value of Put.") For a call option with a strike price of $42 and an intrinsic value of $0.06, the time value is $3.64. As the strike price goes down to $40, the time value falls to $2.74.
- Deep in-the-money options have lower time value (see the time value of the calls in Panel A). Because a deep in-the-money call option is very likely to expire in

the money, buying one is much like buying the stock itself. Note that the call with a strike price of $38 and an intrinsic value of $4.06 has a time value of $1.99, much less than the $3.64 time value of a call with an intrinsic value of $.06.

- The longer the time to expiration at a given strike price, the higher the option price. Looking at the prices of both puts and calls in Panel B of Table 9.5, you can see that as you read down those columns and the time to expiration rises, the price goes up with it. That is because the option's time value is going up. A $42 Barrick call that expires in February sells for $3.70, while the price of one that expires five months later sells for $7.50. The same rule applies to puts.

# Swaps

Swaps are financial instruments that allow the holder of a financial instrument to keep some of its properties, but to trade away others. For example, an interest rate swap would allow the holder of a long-term floating rate bond to trade the floating interest rate for a fixed rate. The bondholder still holds the default risk on the bond and now has eliminated the interest rate risk. The other side of this transaction (the counterparty) might be a bank that has depositors with floating rate deposits so the bank doesn't worry about the interest rate risk. Alternatively, a bank might want to keep the priniipal and interest on a loan, but swap the credit risk for a monthly stable payment. Notice that this instrument—termed a credit default swap or (CDS)—is essentially the same as credit insurance. The third common type of swap is a currency swap. Currency swaps are used to swap the payments of a loan between two currencies. The first currency swap in 1981 was between the World Bank/IBM: the World Bank could borrow relatively cheaply in the United States but wanted funds in Switzerland, while the opposite was true of IBM. They each borrowed where it was cheapest and the swap enabled them to share the net benefit.

The market for interest rate swaps dwarfs the other types of swaps. In December 2008, the Bank of International Settlements estimated that the notional value of outstanding swaps was $492 trillion, of which 71 percent were interest rate swaps. Notional value is a measure of scale, but not of the liability that the swaps represent. The gross market value of swaps is a better measure of that as it measures the cost of replacing the swap in the market today. The financial turmoil of the last two years has increased the market value of CDS, which represent about 7 percent of the outstanding notional value, but 16 percent of the gross market value.

## Understanding Interest-Rate Swaps

Government debt managers—the people at the Federal Finance department who decide when and how to issue government bonds, notes, and bills—do their best to keep public borrowing costs as low as possible. That means (1) selling bonds at the lowest interest rates possible and (2) ensuring that cash will be available when payments must be made. Because of the structure of financial markets, keeping interest costs low usually is not a problem. Demand for long-term government bonds is high. (They are used as collateral in many financial transactions.) Thus, government debt managers can sell them at relatively high prices.

Managing government revenues is more of a challenge. Revenues tend to rise during economic booms and fall during recessions. Even if tax revenues fall, the government must still make its bond payments. Short-term interest rates, like tax revenues, tend to move with the business cycle, rising during booms and falling during recessions.

## Figure 9.1    An Interest-Rate Swap Agreement

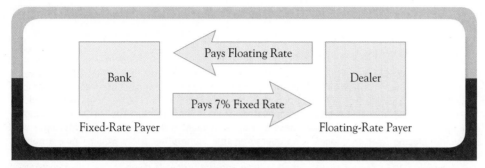

Pays Floating Rate

Bank

Dealer

Pays 7% Fixed Rate

Fixed-Rate Payer

Floating-Rate Payer

**The bank agrees to pay a fixed rate to the swap dealer in exchange for payments based on a floating rate. The fixed-rate payments match the bank's loan income, while the floating-rate payments match the payments promised to the bank's deposit holders.**

(Improvements in general business conditions raise the corporate bond supply, lowering bond prices and raising interest rates.) Ensuring that future interest expenses match future tax revenues might be easier if government borrowers issued short-term bonds.

This difficulty leaves the public debt manager in a quandary. Which is more important, keeping interest costs down by issuing long-term debt or matching costs with tax revenues by issuing short-term debt? Fortunately, derivatives allow government debt managers to meet both these goals using a tool called an interest-rate swap.

**Interest-rate swaps** are agreements between two counterparties to exchange periodic interest-rate payments over some future period, based on an agreed-upon amount of principal—what's called the **notional principal**. The term "notional" is used here because the principal of a **swap** is not borrowed, lent, or exchanged; it just serves as the basis for calculation of the periodic cash flows between the counterparties to the swap. In the simplest type of interest-rate swap, one party agrees to make payments based on a fixed interest rate, and in exchange the counterparty agrees to make payments based on a floating interest rate. The effect of this agreement is to transform fixed-rate payments into floating-rate payments and vice versa.

Figure 9.1 shows a typical interest-rate swap. A bank agrees to make payments to a swap dealer at a fixed interest rate, say 7 percent, in exchange for payments based on a floating rate determined in the market.[11] Both payments are based on the same agreed-upon principal, say $100 million. That is, the notional principal on the swap is $100 million. The bank is the **fixed-rate payer** and the swap dealer is the **floating-rate payer**. Put slightly differently, the two parties enter into a series of forward agreements in which they agree today to exchange interest payments on a series of future dates for the life of the swap. As in a futures contract, no payment is made at the outset.

Now let's return to the government debt manager's problem. Remember that the government can issue long-term debt cheaply but its revenues tend to fluctuate with the short-term interest rate, going up when short-term interest rates rise and down when they fall. The solution is to sell long-term bonds and then enter into an interest-rate swap. The government becomes the floating-rate payer for the term of the bonds.

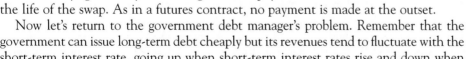

RISK

---

[11] The floating rate is the interest rate at which banks make loans to each other. Specifically, it is the London Interbank Offered Rate (LIBOR), the rate at which banks in London make loans to each other.

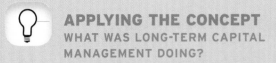

## APPLYING THE CONCEPT
### WHAT WAS LONG-TERM CAPITAL MANAGEMENT DOING?

The credit crisis that began in 2007 is too recent for detailed forensic analysis, but even now we can tell that there were many similarities with the meltdown of Long Term Capital Management (LTCM) in 1998. From mid-August to late September 1998, LTCM, a hedge fund based in Greenwich, Connecticut, lost over $2.5 billion, placing itself in danger of default. (For a detailed description of hedge funds, see Tools of the Trade: Hedge Funds on page 296.) The prospect of LTCM's failure struck fear into world financial markets, prompting the Federal Reserve Bank of New York to form a group of 14 banks and investment companies to purchase the company. How did so much wealth disappear so quickly, and why did so many people care?

The answer is that LTCM had engaged in a large number of complex speculative transactions, including interest rate swaps and options writing, which all failed simultaneously. One of the bets LTCM had made was based on the belief that interest rate spreads would shrink. Following the Russian government bond default on August 17, 1998, financial market participants' willingness to take on risk declined dramatically, so the risk premium exploded. As a result, the spread between corporate bonds and U.S. Treasury bonds grew in a way that had never before occurred. By relying on historical data, LTCM lost billions. While the interest rate spread did eventually shrink, so that the bets LTCM had made paid off in the long run, marking to market drove the fund bankrupt.

The really scary part of this episode was that many of the transactions LTCM had engaged in involved instruments that could not easily be resold. The most amazing discovery was the $1.25 trillion (yes, trillion) in interest rate swaps. Granted, this was a notional principal of all the transactions added together, but the problem is that swaps are individualized, bilateral transactions. The fact that LTCM was willing to make a swap agreement with a particular counterparty was no guarantee that some other party would. Thus, a normal bankruptcy settlement, in which assets are sold off in the marketplace and the proceeds given to the failed company's creditors, was not an option. LTCM's failure would mean it could not honour its side of the agreements, which would mean the counterparties would not be able to honour their own agreements, creating a cascade of failure. Its collapse would jeopardize the entire financial system. Large banks, insurance companies, pension funds, and mutual fund companies with which LTCM did business were at risk of being bankrupted themselves.

In short, while one person's derivatives loss is another's gain, the system works only if the winners can collect. LTCM was essentially sold to its creditors—the banks from which it had borrowed—and then closed down about a year later.*

*For a detailed history of the rise and fall of Long-Term Capital Management, see Roger Lowenstein's *When Genius Failed* (New York: Random House, 2000).

## Pricing and Using Interest-Rate Swaps

Pricing interest rate swaps means figuring out the fixed interest rate to be paid. To do so, financial firms begin by noting the market interest rate on a government bond of the same maturity as the swap, called the benchmark. The rate to be paid by the fixed-rate payer, called the *swap rate*, will be the benchmark rate plus a premium. The difference between the benchmark rate and the swap rate, called the swap spread, is a measure of risk. In recent years, the swap spread has attracted substantial attention as a measure of systematic risk, or overall risk in the economy. When it widens, it signals that general economic conditions are deteriorating.

Who uses all these interest rate swaps? Two groups have a comparative advantage in issuing bonds of a particular maturity. The first group is government debt managers, who find long-term fixed-rate bonds cheaper to issue but prefer short-term variable-rate obligations for matching revenues with expenses. The second group uses interest rate swaps to reduce the risk generated by commercial activities. The prime example is a bank that obtains funds by offering interest-bearing chequing accounts but makes mortgage loans at a fixed rate. In essence, the bank is issuing short-term variable-rate bonds (the chequing accounts) and buying long-term fixed-rate bonds (the mortgages) with the borrowed funds. The problem is, changes in the slope of the yield curve create risk. That is, the revenue from the mortgages may fall short of the payments due on the chequing accounts. Swaps insure the bank against such a shortfall.

# Credit Default Swaps (CDS)

The market for credit default swaps is just over a decade old, but it is already notorious. CDS were created as a mechanism for financial institutions that wanted to reduce the credit risk of their loan portfolio. A protection provider would agree to pay a fixed amount to the protection buyer in the event of a "credit event," such as a default on an underlying asset, over a certain horizon. In return the protection buyer would pay a regular premium. For example, a bank holding a $10 million Air Canada bond might want to buy protection against Air Canada defaulting on the bond over the next five years, and would pay a 1 percent premium (usually quarterly) to a protection seller. This might be cheaper than selling the bond in the illiquid secondary bond market. Initially, CDS were used by banks to insure their loan portfolio. If a bank was concerned about its credit risk but didn't want to break any of its ongoing relationships with customers by refusing them a loan, it could make the loan and use a CDS to protect against the default risk. The CDS had another benefit. Banks' capital requirements depended on the riskiness of their loan portfolio (we'll discuss this more in Chapter 14) so if a bank reduced its credit risk, it could reduce its (expensive) capital requirements. As with any insurance, the amount of protection offered by a CDS depended on the strength of the institution providing the protection. If the protection were provided by a firm with a AAA credit rating, bank regulators thought that it was solid; if the protector's rating declined, it would be expected to post collateral to shore up the protection.

Before the turn of the century, the issuers of a CDS were primarily holders of the underlying assets, but by 2007 CDS were commonly used to insure asset-backed securities, including mortgage-backed securities, and were issued by parties without any exposure to the underlying asset (which is rather like you buying insurance on a friend's house because you thought it was likely to catch fire). This meant that trading in CDS was essentially betting on credit risk: if you thought Air Canada might default you would buy protection and if you thought the company was sound you would sell protection. You wouldn't have to own an Air Canada bond to buy or sell this protection. Unlike insurance contracts where only interested parties can buy insurance, there was no natural limit to the amount of CDS issued. The CDS market was also different from the insurance market in that the sellers of protection did not have to demonstrate capital and reserves. Of course, a protection buyer would be unlikely to pay premiums every quarter to an institution that it doesn't believe will be able to pay off when needed, but it may not know how many CDS the protection seller is exposed to. Exposure depended not only on the volume of CDS but also correlation: if the events that will lead to a payoff are all uncorrelated, then even if the protection seller has many CDS, it may be able to meet all its obligations. If the credit events are correlated then the protection seller may not be able to cover its obligations in all cases.

The issues of CDS initially improved the efficiency of financial markets by enabling parties to hold the risk levels they wanted. But they were a significant factor in the financial crisis of 2008. The story of AIG demonstrates the problem. AIG is an insurance company with a division that sold many CDS. It was also a AAA–rated corporation. AIG was holding large amounts of mortgage-backed securities (MBS) and as defaults on MBS rose, the ratings agencies downgraded AIG.[12] In turn, that triggered a call for AIG to post collateral against its CDS, but it didn't have enough cash to do

---

[12] More specifically, AIG had to mark its MBS portfolio to market, which meant a writedown, which reduced its capital reserves, which led to a ratings downgrade.

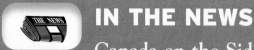

## IN THE NEWS
### Canada on the Sidelines of CDS Regulation

### Derivatives Debate: Custom Contracts Will Never Fit on Exchange: Critics

**Financial Post**

**John Greenwood**

June 8, 2009

Nearly two years after the collapse of the $35-billion of commercial paper market backed by risky credit derivatives, Canadian authorities have yet to take steps to rein in what many are calling the wild west of the investment world.

At issue is the market for credit default swaps, essentially bond insurance contracts traded on the over-the-counter market, that allow players to make massive leveraged bets and which many blame as playing a pivotal role in the global financial crisis.

While lawmakers in the United States are in the final stages of a loud public debate about over [sic] new regulations, an eerie silence prevails in Canada as regulators plan their next steps behind closed doors.

Last week Gary Gensler, chairman of the U.S. Commodity Futures Trading Commission, announced new proposals to regulate the market for derivatives—estimated to have held a global notional value of a staggering US$592-trillion at the end of 2008—that seeks to push them off the private over-the-counter market and onto a regulated exchange.

Meanwhile, the Ontario Securities Commission and the Canadian Securities Administrators are keeping a close watch on the discussion in Washington and elsewhere, said Laurie Gillett, a spokeswoman for the Ontario Securities Commission.

"The CSA has undertaken a policy review of derivatives, which is ongoing," Ms. Gillett said. "Our chair, David Wilson, is a participant on a head of agencies working group that is looking at the recommendations of the G20 and their implementation in our jurisdiction."

However, the OSC declined to talk about the matter in greater detail.

How to regulate credit default swaps "is a huge topic," agreed Connie Craddock, spokeswoman for the Investment Industry Regulatory Organization of Canada. "There is a lot of discussion underway," she said. Ms. Craddock also declined to discuss specifics.

By global standards, Canada is not a big player in CDS. Canada's big banks for the most part avoided speculating in the global US$41.9-trillion CDS market but they nonetheless employed the instruments as a hedging tool, collectively gaining more than $800-billion of exposure last year, according to RBC Capital Markets.

... the brokerage industry insists that it recognizes the need for transparency and structure in the CDS market but that process takes time.

"This is really an industry-wide initiative," said a senior official at one of the big banks. "The industry as a whole is working in conjunction with regulators."

Observers say part of the holdup for Canadian regulators is that the CDS market is global, with most of the trading taking place in the United States. The G20 countries recently agreed to regulate derivatives, but Washington is leading the push, leaving it to the rest of the world to follow its lead.

that.[13] But if AIG defaulted then, all the counterparties to its CDS would find their protection had vanished; either they would have to find new protection (unlikely) or to increase their capital (very difficult in the fall of 2008). As we describe in more detail in Chapter 23, the Federal Reserve and the Treasury decided that AIG was "too big to fail," and provided a cash injection to keep it from defaulting.

Unsurprisingly, in the aftermath of the financial crisis, regulators are exploring how the market for CDS could be regulated or monitored so that the exposures are better understood and less potentially damaging. Unlike futures and options, swaps

---

[13] A further cause of the difficulties of CDS issuers in 2008 was that they had priced their issues on the basis of correlations over the previous decade, but these correlations weren't a good guide to the correlations across markets in 2007/8.

"Everything is up in the air, everyone is waiting to see what happens in the U.S.," another industry insider said.

U.S. President Barack Obama's administration has made clear it wants to shine a light on the over-the-counter derivatives market and bring trading out in the open.

In May, Treasury Secretary Timothy Geithner unveiled a plan to push CDS trading onto exchanges so contracts can be centrally cleared. But he left out customized CDS, suggesting they are too complex to be handled by an exchange and therefore might continue to change hands privately. That prompted critics to pile on, arguing that the industry would take advantage of the loophole to keep their business private.

Last week's proposal by CFTC chairman Gensler was an attempt to deal with the criticisms.

The theory behind Washington's strategy is that by bringing the market out into the open, players would not get into a situation like one that led to the credit crunch, in which banks and hedge funds were swapping the same risk back and forth, to the point where the collapse of one party would bring down the whole system. But to bring about that kind of transparency would likely result in fundamental changes to CDS contracts that might limit their utility.

So they are pushing back against Mr. Geithner's proposals. They say custom CDS contracts will never fit on an exchange and they must be permitted to continue to trade over the counter. There are better ways to achieve transparency, they say.

Meanwhile cracks in the united front established by the G20 are starting to appear.

A senior official in the U.K. last week seemed to acknowledge that CDS aren't going to be trading on exchanges, at least in the U.K., any time soon.

"We do genuinely recognize there is a place for [the over-the-counter market]," said Alexander Justham, director of markets at the U.K. Financial Services Authority, according to Reuters. The trend ... toward greater transparency in this space is inevitable. Whether that means it's all on exchange, I don't think we are yet in that space."

The worry is that if countries can't agree on a single system, trading will simply migrate to jurisdictions with the loosest rules.

The CDS market represents a big piece of the global financial system, making this a unique and important challenge for regulators. Some observers predict that the Wall Street banks continue to make significant profits from CDS trading and they are loath to move their business onto an exchange because any competitive advantage would quickly disappear.

---

### LESSONS OF THE ARTICLE

This article highlights tensions in financial regulation between the need for transparency and the need for flexibility, and also the necessity of global coordination of financial regulation to reduce the amount of "regulatory arbitrage," that is, the search for the most permissive jurisdiction. Regulations that the authorities are seeking include ensuring that the issuers of CDS have the capital to back up their commitments.

SOURCE: By *John Greenwood, Financial Post, Monday, June 8, 2009. Material reprinted with the express permission of "The National Post Company," a CanWest Partnership.*

---

are not traded on organized exchanges; they are bilateral agreements between two financial intermediaries. Many experts are calling for a central counterparty that would make the market more transparent and more standardized (see Applying the Concept: What Was Long-Term Capital Management Doing? on page 196). When LTCM failed, the bilateral nature of its interest rate swaps made it both hard to value its positions and hard to trade them; it also meant its counterparties didn't realize how large the other exposures were. CDS have similar characteristics. As with other nuclear material, the question is whether safe handling of these potential "weapons of financial mass destruction" can enable us to benefit from them without paying too high a price.

# Terms

American option, 187
arbitrage, 185
at the money option, 187
call option, 186
credit default swap (CDS), 194
derivatives, 179
European option, 187
fixed-rate payer, 195
floating-rate payer, 195
forward contract, 180
futures contract, 181
interest rate swaps, 195
long futures position, 181

margin, 182
marking to market, 182
no-arbitrage condition, 185
notional principal, 195
put option, 187
short futures position, 181
strike price, 186
swap spread, 196
swap, 195
time value of the option, 190

# Chapter Summary

1. Derivatives transfer risk from one person or firm to another. They can be used in any combination to unbundle risks and resell them.

2. Futures contracts are standardized contracts for the delivery of a specified quantity of a commodity or financial instrument on a prearranged future date, at an agreed-upon price. They are a bet on the movement in the price of the underlying asset on which they are written, whether it is a commodity or a financial instrument.
   a. Futures contracts are used both to decrease risk, which is called hedging, and to increase risk, which is called speculating.
   b. The futures clearing corporation, as the counterparty to all futures contracts, guarantees the performance of both the buyer and the seller.
   c. Participants in the futures market must establish a margin account with the clearing corporation and make a deposit that ensures they will meet their obligations.
   d. Futures prices are marked to market daily, as if the contracts were sold and repurchased every day.
   e. Since no payment is made when a futures contract is initiated, the transaction allows an investor to create a large amount of leverage at a very low cost.

   f. The prices of futures contracts are determined by arbitrage within the market for immediate delivery of the underlying asset.

3. Options give the buyer (option holder) a right and the seller (option writer) an obligation to buy or sell an underlying asset at a predetermined price on or before a fixed future date.
   a. A call option gives the holder the right to buy the underlying asset.
   b. A put option gives the holder the right to sell the underlying asset.
   c. Options can be used both to reduce risk through hedging and to speculate.
   d. The option price equals the sum of its intrinsic value, which is the value if the option is exercised, plus the time value of the option.
   e. The intrinsic value depends on the strike price of the option and the price of the underlying asset on which the option is written.
   f. The time value of the option depends on the time to expiration and the volatility in price of the underlying asset.

4. Swaps are agreements between two parties to exchange certain features of a financial instrument, such as the interest rate sequences, the currency, or the credit risk over a future period.
   a. The fixed-rate payer in an interest rate swap pays the government bond rate plus a risk premium.
   b. The flexible-rate payer in an interest rate swap normally pays the London Interbank Offered Rate (LIBOR).
   c. Interest rate swaps are useful when a government, firm, or investment company can borrow more cheaply at one maturity but would prefer to borrow at a different maturity.
   d. Credit default swaps allow the purchase and sale of credit risk by those with or without exposure to that risk.
   e. Swaps are bilateral trades that do not trade on an exchange and have no central counterparty.

5. Derivatives allow firms to arbitrarily divide up and rename risks and future payments, making it very challenging to interpret financial statements.

# Conceptual Problems

1. An agreement to lease a car can be thought of as a set of derivative contracts. Describe them.

2. In spring 2002, an electronically traded futures contract on the stock index, called an E-mini future, was introduced. The contract was one-fifth the size of the standard futures contract, and could be traded on the 24-hour Globex electronic trading system. Why might someone introduce a futures contract with these properties?

3. A hedger has taken a long position in the wheat futures market. What is the hedger's position? What does it mean to take a "long position"? Describe the risk that is hedged in this transaction.

4. A futures contract on a payment of $200 times the Standard & Poor's TSX 60 Index is traded on the Montreal Exchange. At an index level of $500 or more, the contract calls for a payment of over $100,000. It is settled by a cash payment between the buyer and the seller. Who are the hedgers and who are the speculators in the S&P TSX 60 futures market?

5. What are the risks and rewards of writing and buying options? Are there any circumstances under which you would get involved? Why or why not? (Hint: Think of a case in which you own shares of the stock on which you are considering writing a call.)

6. A three-month at-the-money European call option on the XYZ Corporation has an expected value of $8.75. XYZ's stock rises or falls with equal probability by $10 each month, starting where it ended the previous month. When the option is purchased, the stock is priced at $100, so after three months the price could be as high as $130 or as low as $70. Derive the value of this call option.

7. Find a recent listing of stock options prices in the financial news or on a financial Web site. Pick a stock for which a large number of options are traded. Using the data you have collected, compute and comment on the following for both puts and calls:
   a. The change in the time value of the option as the strike price for options of the same expiration date changes.
   b. The change in the time value of the option as the expiration date for options of the same strike price changes.

8.* Why might a borrower who wishes to make fixed interest rate payments and who has access to both fixed- and floating-rate loans still benefit from becoming a party to a fixed-for-floating interest rate swap?

9. Concerned about possible disruptions in the oil stream coming from the Middle East, the chief financial officer (CFO) of Air Canada would like to hedge the risk of an increase in the price of jet fuel. What tools can the CFO use to hedge this risk?

10.* How does the existence of derivatives markets enhance an economy's ability to grow?

## Analytical Problems

11. Of the following options, which would you expect to have the highest option price?
   a. A European three-month put option on a stock whose market price is $90 where the strike price is $100. The standard deviation of the stock price over the past five years has been 15 percent.
   b. A European three-month put option on a stock whose market price is $110 where the strike price is $100. The standard deviation of the stock price over the past five years has been 15 percent.
   c. A European one-month put option on a stock whose market price is $90 where the strike price is $100. The standard deviation of the stock price over the past five years has been 15 percent.

12. What kind of an option should you purchase if you anticipate selling $1 million of Government of Canada bonds in one year's time and wish to hedge against the risk of interest rates rising?

13. You sell a bond futures contract and, one day later, you see that there are funds credited to your margin account. What happened to interest rates over that day?

14. You are convinced that the price of copper will rise significantly over the next year and want to take as large a position as you can in the market but have limited funds. How could you use the futures market to leverage your position?

* Indicates more difficult problems.

15. Suppose you have $8,000 to invest and you follow the strategy you devise in question 14 to leverage your exposure to the copper market. Copper is selling at $3 a pound and the margin requirement for a futures contract for 25,000 pounds of copper is $8,000.
   a. Calculate your return if copper prices rise to $3.10 a pound.
   b. How does this compare with the return you would have made if you had simply purchased $8,000 worth of copper and sold it a year later?
   c. Compare the risk involved in each of these strategies.

16.* You are given the following information on three firms. Firms A and B want to be exposed to a floating interest rate while Firm C would prefer to pay a fixed interest rate. Which pair(s) of firms (if any) should borrow in the market they do not want and then enter into a fixed-for-floating interest rate swap?

|        | Fixed Rate | Floating Rate     |
|--------|------------|-------------------|
| Firm A | 7%         | LIBOR + 50 bps    |
| Firm B | 12%        | LIBOR + 150 bps   |
| Firm C | 10%        | LIBOR + 150 bps   |

17. Suppose you were the manager of a bank that raised most of its funds from short-term variable-rate deposits and used these funds to make fixed-rate mortgage loans. Should you be more concerned about rises or falls in short-term interest rates? How could you use interest-rate swaps to hedge against the interest-rate risk you face?

18.* Basis swaps are swaps where, instead of one payment stream being based on a fixed interest rate, both payment streams are based on floating interest rates. Why might anyone be interested in entering a floating-for-floating interest rate swap? (You should assume that both payment flows are denominated in the same currency.)

# CHAPTER 10

## Foreign Exchange

Canada's economy is tightly interwoven with the international economy. More than one-third of the final goods and services produced in Canada are exported, and one-third of our expenditures on goods and services are on imported goods. Our financial sectors are equally interconnected with the rest of the world. Of the $95 billion in Canadian corporate bonds issued in 2007, nearly half ($40 billion) were issued outside Canada as Canadian corporations accessed international capital markets (predominantly in the United States) for their investment programs. All these transactions required or generated foreign currency and their profitability or benefits depend on the price of foreign currency. To understand the nature of these transactions, we must become familiar with a key tool that makes this trade possible: *exchange rates*.

Whenever you buy something that has been made overseas, whether it is an article of clothing, a car, a stock, or a bond, someone somewhere has exchanged dollars for the currency used where the item was made. The reason is simple: You want to use dollars to pay for an imported shirt that you buy in a local store, but the Malaysian producer wants to be paid in ringgit. All cross-border transactions are like this; the buyer and seller both want to use their own currency. The exchange rate, at its most basic level, is the tool we use to measure the price of one currency in terms of another.

Exchange rates have broad implications both for countries and for individuals. In December 2006, the Canadian dollar was worth US$0.87, but a year later the Canadian dollar was at par (see Figure 10.1). Canadian exports are typically priced in U.S. dollars and so this meant that exporters received 15 percent fewer Canadian dollars for every item they sold in the United States (unless its price rose, which typically didn't happen). The result was that the Canadian manufacturing sector became less competitive and employment in manufacturing fell by 3 percent. But by December 2008, the Canadian dollar had fallen back again; it cost US$0.81 to buy a Canadian dollar. Exporters were

**Figure 10.1    U.S. Dollar Exchange Rate**

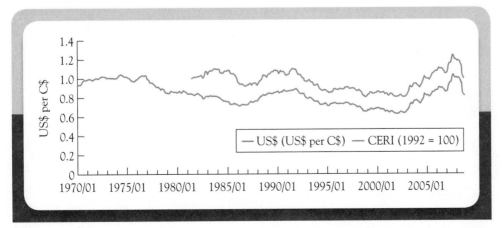

SOURCE: *Bank of Canada. CANSIM Table 176-0064. Average noon spot rates. US$ v37426, accessed June 29, 2009; CERI v41498903.*

doing well, and importers were in trouble. The Blue Jays baseball team has most of its expenses (players' salaries) fixed in U.S. dollars but most of its revenues are in Canadian dollars. A 20 percent increase in the cost of a U.S. dollar significantly affects the team's financial affairs—and will likely lead to an increase in seat prices.

Exchange rates go through long swings as well as sudden spikes. Figure 10.1 on page 203 shows that between 1977 and 2002 the Canadian dollar gradually declined from parity with the U.S. dollar to being worth only US$0.65. How are foreign exchange rates determined, and what accounts for their fluctuation over days, months, years, and decades? This chapter provides an introduction to foreign exchange rates and exchange markets.

## Foreign Exchange Basics

After graduation, you are planning to travel to Europe. You would like to see the Eiffel Tower in Paris, the Colosseum in Rome, and the Parthenon in Athens. As you pack, you worry a little about paying your hotel bills and the tab for all that great food you expect to eat. The waiters in French, Italian, and Greek restaurants aren't interested in your Canadian dollars; they want to be paid in their own currency. But you are fortunate, for while the French, Italians, and Greeks speak different languages, they all use the same coins and bills. In fact, buying anything in Europe—at least in the countries that are members of the European Monetary Union—means exchanging your dollars for **euros**. So when you get to Europe, you will care about the number of euros you can "buy" for one Canadian dollar. The price of euros in dollars is called the Canadian dollar–euro exchange rate.

### The Nominal Exchange Rate

Exchanging dollars for euros is like any other economic transaction: you are using your money to buy something—in this case, money to spend in another country. The price you pay for this currency is called the nominal exchange rate, or simply the *exchange rate*. Formally defined, the **nominal exchange rate** *is the rate at which one can exchange the currency of one country for the currency of another country*. The dollar–euro exchange rate is the number of dollars you can get for each euro. In summer 2009, one euro (the symbol for the euro is €) would buy $1.63. So a Canadian who went to Europe in the summer of 2009 paid $163 for €100.

Theoretically, exchange rates can be quoted in units of either currency—for example, as the number of Canadian dollars needed to buy one euro or as the number of euros needed to buy one Canadian dollar. The two prices are equivalent; one is simply the reciprocal of the other. In practice, however, each currency has its convention. Typically, Canadians state the exchange rate with the United States as the number of U.S. dollars to buy a Canadian dollar. But the price of the British pound and the euro are usually stated as the number of Canadian dollars that can be exchanged for one pound (£) or euro. The price of the Japanese yen (¥) is quoted as the number of yen that can be purchased with one Canadian dollar.

"When did your dad first explain foreign-currency exchange rates to you?"

A 20-euro note used in the countries that participate in the European Monetary Union.

Unfortunately, there is no simple rule for determining which way a particular exchange rate should be quoted. If you need to guess which way to quote an exchange rate, the best guess is that it is the way that yields a number larger than one though that doesn't help with the U.S. dollar exchange rate: it has generally cost fewer than 100 U.S. cents to buy a Canadian dollar. But the real solution is always to state the units explicitly, to avoid confusion.

Whichever way the exchange rate is reported, economists call a reduction in the value of one currency relative to another a depreciation of the currency. For example, a decrease in the number of U.S. dollars required to buy a Canadian dollar is a depreciation of the Canadian dollar. Conversely, when one currency buys more units of another it is called an appreciation. In 1971, the U.S. dollar was roughly at par (that means one Canadian dollar cost one U.S. dollar) but over the next 30 years the price of a Canadian dollar fell by 35 percent—the Canadian dollar depreciated relative to the U.S. dollar. But during the next eight years the Canadian dollar appreciated—rose in value—by 54 percent. Later in this chapter, we will consider the reasons for large movements in exchange rates.

Notice that the behaviour of the U.S. dollar is the mirror image of that of the Canadian dollar. When the Canadian dollar depreciated against the U.S. dollar, we could equally have said that the U.S. dollar appreciated against the Canadian dollar. When one currency goes up in value *relative to another*, the other currency must go down. But remember to be wary of percentage changes: The Canadian dollar depreciated by 35 percent (from par to US$0.65), but the U.S. dollar appreciated by 54 percent from par to C$1.54.

Since the exchange rate is the cost of foreign currency, Canada doesn't have *an* exchange rate; there is an exchange rate for each different currency. And the Canadian exchange rate could appreciate with respect to one currency, say the U.S. dollar, and depreciate with respect to another, say the euro. (What does this imply happened to the exchange rate between the euro and the U.S. dollar?) The Bank of Canada has developed an index that measures the average of the changes of the value of the Canadian dollar against our six major trading partners, called the CERI, the Canadian dollar effective exchange rate index. The CERI is plotted in Figure 10.1 on page 203 (CERI data are available only since 1980). The United States is Canada's major trading partner, and has a weight of 76 percent in the index, so the CERI behaves a lot like the Canadian dollar–U.S. dollar exchange rate, Remember that the CERI is an index number and not a price. Index numbers have no units and are useful only for measuring the amount of change between two periods.

## The Real Exchange Rate

While it may be interesting to know that one euro is worth $1.63, you are interested in more than just the rate at which one country's currency can be exchanged for another. What you really want to know when you travel to Europe is how much you can buy with that euro. When all is said and done, will you return home thinking that your trip was cheap or expensive?

Because nominal exchange rates do not provide an answer to this question, we now turn to the concept of a **real exchange rate**, *the rate at which one can exchange the goods and services from one country for the goods and services from another country.* It is the cost of a basket of goods in one country relative to the cost of the same basket of goods in another country. To grasp this concept, we will start with the real exchange rate between two cups of espresso, one Canadian and the other Italian. The local Starbucks charges $1.68 for an espresso; in Florence, Italy, a cup of espresso costs €0.80. (Yes, the Italian version is better and espresso is a luxury in Canada, but for the sake of the example, let's pretend they're the same.) At a nominal exchange rate of $1.63 per euro, this means that to buy an espresso on your European vacation, you need to spend $1.30. More importantly, you can buy 1.29 cups of Italian espresso for the same amount of Canadian dollars as one Starbucks coffee. This is the *real* exchange rate. You will return from your European vacation thinking that espresso was cheap in Italy.

There is a simple relationship between the real exchange rate and the nominal exchange rate, which we can infer from our espresso calculation. To compute the real exchange rate, we took the euro price of an espresso in Italy and multiplied it by the nominal exchange rate, the number of dollars per euro. Then we divided it into the dollar price of a cup of espresso in Canada:

$$\text{Real coffee exchange rate} = \frac{\text{Dollar price of expresso in Canada (\$1.68)}}{\text{Dollar price of expresso in Italy (€0.80)} \times (\$1.63/€)} \qquad (1)$$

$$= \frac{\$1.68}{\$1.30}$$

$$= 1.29$$

At these prices and exchange rate, one cup of Starbucks espresso buys 1.29 cups of Italian espresso. Note in equation (1) that the units of measurement cancel out. In the denominator, we multiplied the price in euros by the nominal exchange rate (measured as dollars per euro) to get an amount stated in dollars. Then we divided that number into the numerator, also expressed in dollars. The real exchange rate has no units of measurement.

We can use the same procedure to compute the real exchange rate more broadly by comparing the prices of a set of goods and services that are commonly purchased in any country. If we can transform a basket of goods and services produced in Canada into more than one basket produced in Europe, as in the coffee example, then we are likely to return from a trip to Paris, Rome, and Athens thinking that the cost of living there is relatively cheap. Using this idea, we can write the real exchange rate as

$$\text{Real exchange rate} = \frac{\text{Dollar price of domestic goods}}{\text{Dollar price of foreign goods}} \qquad (2)$$

From this definition of the real exchange rate, we can see that whenever the ratio in equation (2) is more than one, foreign products will seem cheap.

The real exchange rate, then, is much more important than the nominal exchange rate. It is the rate that measures the relative price of goods and services across countries, telling us where things are cheap and where they are expensive. The real exchange rate is the guiding force behind international transactions. When foreign goods are less expensive than domestic goods, their prices create an incentive for people to buy imports. Competing with foreign imports becomes more difficult for local producers. Think about what would happen if you could ship cups of espresso to Canada from Italy and sell them in an import shop. Starbucks would lose business.

# TOOLS OF THE TRADE

Following Exchange Rates in the News

Exchange rate data are available in many places. Newspapers, both online and in hard copy, carry exchange rates for the most popular currencies every day. The Bank of Canada Web site has data for 56 currencies. Most of these Web sites also have a currency converter that allows you to either determine the foreign currency value of a number of Canadian dollars or the Canadian dollar value of a number of units of foreign currency. Table 10.1 shows the Foreign Exchange report on the Web site of the *Financial Post*. Looking at the second column, we can see that C$1 would buy US$0.8669 or €0.6143 or £0.5231. Notice that the rows give you the amount of Canadian dollars that it takes

to buy one unit of foreign currency. For example, it takes C$1.15 to buy US$1, or C$1.91 to buy a British pound. Of course, you could compute that yourself simply by taking the inverse of the value of C$1.

Remember that these exchange rates are the prices paid by those transacting in millions of dollars, and that for consumers buying or selling small amounts of foreign currency the buy and sell spread can be as much as 5 percent. See Your Financial World: Buying Foreign Currency on page 210.

The *Financial Post* Web site also allows you to plot the performance of each exchange rate over the preceding three months, one year, or two years.

**Table 10.1**   Home/Personal Finance/Currency Converter

**Currency Calculator**

Initial Currency

Convert: [          ]   [ Canadian Dollar ▼ ]   into   [ US Dollar ▼ ]

[ Calculate ]   [ Reset ]

| CURRENCIES | | | | | | | | | |
| --- | --- | --- | --- | --- | --- | --- | --- | --- | --- |
| | US Dollar | Canadian Dollar | Euro | British Pound | Japanese Yen | Swiss Franc | Australian Dollar | Brazilian Real | Mexican Peso | Russian Ruble |
| US Dollar | 1 | 0.86690 | 1.41120 | 1.65720 | 0.01040 | 0.92490 | 0.81250 | 0.51520 | 0.07620 | 0.03220 |
| Canadian Dollar | 1.15354 | 1 | 1.62787 | 1.91164 | 0.01200 | 1.06691 | 0.93725 | 0.59430 | 0.08790 | 0.03714 |
| Euro | 0.70862 | 0.61430 | 1 | 1.17432 | 0.00737 | 0.65540 | 0.57575 | 0.36508 | 0.05400 | 0.02282 |
| British Pound | 0.60343 | 0.52311 | 0.85156 | 1 | 0.00628 | 0.55811 | 0.49028 | 0.31089 | 0.04598 | 0.01943 |
| Japanese Yen | 96.15385 | 83.35577 | 135.69231 | 159.34615 | 1 | 88.93269 | 78.12500 | 49.53846 | 7.32692 | 3.09615 |
| Swiss Franc | 1.08120 | 0.93729 | 1.52579 | 1.79176 | 0.01124 | 1 | 0.87847 | 0.55703 | 0.08239 | 0.03481 |
| Australian Dollar | 1.23077 | 1.06695 | 1.73686 | 2.03963 | 0.01280 | 1.13834 | 1 | 0.63409 | 0.09378 | 0.03963 |
| Brazilian Dollar | 1.94099 | 1.68265 | 2.73913 | 3.21661 | 0.02019 | 1.79523 | 1.57706 | 1 | 0.14790 | 0.06250 |
| Mexican Peso | 13.12336 | 11.37664 | 18.51969 | 21.74803 | 0.13648 | 12.13780 | 10.66273 | 6.76115 | 1 | 0.42257 |
| Russian Ruble | 31.05590 | 26.92236 | 43.82609 | 51.46584 | 0.32298 | 28.72360 | 25.23292 | 16.00000 | 2.36646 | 1 |

Click on a currency name to see a historical chart

SOURCE: *www.financialpost.com*, accessed June 30, 2009.

Obviously, you can't do that with freshly brewed coffee, but you can do it with clothing, electronics, cars, airplanes, and a wide variety of other goods and services. As a result, the competitiveness of Canadian exports depends on the real exchange rate. *Appreciation* of the real exchange rate makes Canadian exports more expensive to foreigners, reducing their competitiveness, while *depreciation* of the real exchange rate makes Canadian exports seem cheaper to foreigners, improving their competitiveness.

## Foreign Exchange Markets

The volume of foreign exchange transactions is enormous. On an average day in 2007, $3.2 trillion in foreign currency was traded in a market that operates 24 hours a day.[1] To get a sense of how huge this number is, compare it to world output and trade. The International Monetary Fund estimates that in 2007, world GDP (at market prices) was roughly $US54 trillion, and international trade transactions (measured as exports plus imports) totalled $34 trillion. But these are annual numbers. If there are 260 business days in a normal year, the volume of foreign exchange transactions is nearly $832 trillion per year—15 times world GDP and 25 times world trade volume.

Because of its liquidity, the U.S. dollar is one side of roughly 90 percent of these currency transactions.[2] That means that someone who wishes to exchange Thai baht for Japanese yen is likely to make two transactions, the first to convert the baht to dollars and the second to convert the dollars to yen. Most likely, these transactions will take place in London, because the United Kingdom is home to roughly one-third of foreign exchange trades—about one and one-half times the volume in New York. Other significant foreign exchange trading takes place in Tokyo (8 percent), Singapore (5 percent), Frankfurt (5 percent), and Zurich (3 percent).

# Exchange Rates in the Long Run

How are exchange rates determined? To answer this question, we will divide our discussion into two parts. This section will look at the determination of the long-run exchange rate and the forces that drive its movement over an extended period, such as a year or more. The next section will consider what causes exchange rates to vary over the short term—a few days or months.

## The Law of One Price

The starting point for understanding how long-run exchange rates are determined is *the law of one price*. The law of one price is based on the concept of *arbitrage*—the idea that identical products should sell for the same price. Recall from our discussion in Chapter 9 that two financial instruments with the same risk and promised future payments will sell for the same price. We might refer to this phenomenon as financial arbitrage. If we extend the concept of arbitrage from financial instruments to goods and services, we can conclude that identical goods and services should sell for the same price regardless of *where* they are sold. Identical televisions or cars should cost the same whether they are sold in Halifax or Toronto. When they don't, someone can make a profit.

---

[1] This estimate comes from a triennial survey by the Bank for International Settlements in Basel, Switzerland. The complete survey is available at http://www.bis.org.

[2] The liquidity of the market for dollars creates a premium, driving up the dollar's value in the same way that liquidity increases the price of a bond.

For instance, if a specific model television were cheaper in Toronto than in Halifax, someone could buy it in Toronto, drive to Halifax, and sell it at a profit. This opportunity to profit from arbitrage would increase demand for televisions in Toronto, where the price is low, and increase the supply of televisions in Halifax, where the price is high. Higher demand drives prices up, while a larger supply forces them down. The process will continue until the television sells for the same price in both cities. Of course, complete price equalization occurs only in the absence of transportation costs. If it costs $10 to transport the television 1250 kilometres from Toronto to the East Coast, then arbitrage will continue until the price in Toronto is within $10 of the price in Halifax.

We can extend the law of one price from cities in the same country to cities in different countries. Instead of Toronto and Halifax, think of Windsor, Ontario, and Detroit, Michigan—two cities separated by the Detroit River and the Canadian border. The river can be crossed by bridge or tunnel in roughly one minute. Ignoring transportation costs and any tariffs, once we have converted a price from Canadian to U.S. dollars, the cost of a television should be the same in both cities. If a TV costs C$500 in Canada, at a nominal exchange rate of US$0.87 (see Table 10.1), the U.S. price should be (C$500 × US$0.87/C$) = US$435. That is, the law of one price tells us that

$$\begin{array}{c}\text{U.S. dollar price of a}\\ \text{TV in Detroit}\end{array} = \begin{array}{c}\text{Canadian dollar price of a TV in Windsor}\\ \times \text{ U.S. dollars per Canadian dollar}\end{array} \qquad (3)$$

This example shows once again the importance of using the correct units when working with exchange rates. In converting the Canadian dollar price to U.S. dollars, we multiply by the number of U.S. dollars needed to buy one Canadian dollar. That is, we compute (Canadian dollars) times (U.S. dollars/Canadian dollar) equals U.S. dollars. This is the same calculation we did earlier to figure out the Canadian dollar price of an Italian cup of coffee. There, we multiplied (euros) times (Canadian dollars/euro) to get Canadian dollars.

Returning to the law of one price, we can see immediately that it fails almost all the time. The fact is that the same commodity or service sells for vastly different prices in different countries. Why? Transportation costs can be significant, especially for heavy items such as marble or slate. Tariffs—the taxes countries charge at their borders—are high sometimes, especially if a country is trying to protect a domestic industry. And technical specifications can differ. A television bought in Paris will not work in Toronto because it requires a different input signal. A car sold in Great Britain is difficult to use in Canada or the United States because its steering wheel is on the right. Moreover, tastes differ across countries, leading to different pricing. Finally, some things simply cannot be traded. A haircut may be cheaper in New Delhi than in Vancouver, but most Canadians simply can't take advantage of that price difference.

## Purchasing Power Parity

Since the law of one price fails so often, why do we bother with it? Because even with its obvious flaws, the law of one price is extremely useful in explaining the behaviour of exchange rates over long periods, such as 10 or 20 years. To see why, we need to extend the law from a single commodity to a basket of goods and services. The result is the theory of **purchasing power parity (PPP)**, which means that one unit of domestic currency will buy the same basket of goods and services anywhere in the world. This idea may sound absurd, but let's look at its implications.

# YOUR FINANCIAL WORLD

Buying Foreign Currency

On January 13, 2009, the *Financial Post* reported that the U.S. dollar was trading at C$1.22654. However, Scotiabank's Web site and phone information line reported a buy rate of C$1.254 and a sell rate of C$1.1945 for non-cash transactions of less than $1,000 or cash transactions up to $10,000. Why so many rates?

The difference between the buy and sell rate-the "spread"-allows a financial institution to pay for the costs of the transaction. If the transaction is not for cash, then the costs are back-office costs of accounting systems, and those costs tend to be the same whether the transactions are large or small so that there are econo-mies of scale. If the transaction is for more than $1,000 the spread would be smaller. If it is a cash transaction, then the financial institution has the additional cost of carrying an inventory of U.S. dollars, so the cost is higher. The newspaper reports the rate for transactions in the wholesale market where the amounts traded are in the millions so the spread is very thin.

Financial institutions change their buying and selling rates for cash on a daily basis and do not all have the same rates so it pays to shop around when you want to buy or sell foreign currency.

According to the theory of purchasing power parity, the dollar price of a basket of goods and services in Canada should be the same as the dollar price of a basket of goods and services in Mexico, Japan, or the United States. In the case of the United Kingdom, this statement means that

$$\text{Dollar price of basket of goods in Canada} = \text{Dollar price of basket of goods in the United Kingdom} \tag{4}$$

Rearranging this expression gives us

$$\frac{\text{Dollar price of basket of goods in Canada}}{\text{Dollar price of basket of goods in United Kingdom}} = 1 \tag{5}$$

The left-hand side of equation (5) is familiar: It is the real exchange rate (see equation (2) on page 206). Thus, *purchasing power parity implies that the real exchange rate is always equal to one.* The implication of this conclusion is straightforward: the purchasing power of a dollar is always the same, regardless of where in the world you go.

This idea must seem doubly absurd. If a dollar doesn't even buy the same number of cups of coffee in Italy and Canada, how can it have the same purchasing power all the time, everywhere in the world? On any given day, it doesn't. But over the long term, exchange rates do tend to move, so this concept helps us to understand changes that happen over years or decades. To see how, remember that the dollar price of a foreign basket of goods is just the foreign currency price of the basket of goods times the number of dollars per unit of foreign currency. This means that if we quote the price of a basket of goods in the United Kingdom in pounds instead of dollars, then

$$\frac{\text{Dollar price of basket of goods in Canada}}{(\text{Pound price of basket in the United Kingdom}) \times (\text{Dollars per pound})} = 1, \tag{6}$$

implies

$$\frac{\text{Dollar price of basket of goods in Canada}}{\text{Pound price of basket of goods in United Kingdom}} = (\text{Dollars per pound}) \tag{7}$$

That is, purchasing power parity implies that when prices change in one country but not in another, the exchange rate should change as well. If inflation occurs in one country but not in another, the change in prices creates an international inflation differential. Purchasing power parity tells us that the currency of a country with high inflation will depreciate.

To see this point, think about what would happen if there were no inflation in the United Kingdom, but prices in Canada doubled. We would not expect the dollar–pound exchange rate to stay the same. Instead, we would predict that one dollar would now buy half as many British pounds as it did before (that is, twice as many dollars would be needed to purchase one pound).[3] There is strong evidence to support this conclusion, but the data must be drawn over fairly long periods, and the relationship is not perfect.

We can look at a plot of (a) the historical difference between inflation in other countries and inflation in the United States against (b) the percentage change in the number of units of other countries' currencies required to purchase one dollar—that is, the average annual depreciation of the exchange rate.

Figure 10.2 presents data for 71 countries drawn from files maintained by the International Monetary Fund. Each point represents a country. The difference between its average annual inflation and that of the United States is on the horizontal axis, and the average annual percentage change in the exchange rate between the country's currency and the U.S. dollar is on the vertical axis. Points further to the right represent countries with higher levels of inflation, and points higher up are countries whose dollar-exchange rate experienced more depreciation over the 25-year period of the sample. The solid line is a 45-degree line that is consistent with the theoretical

**Figure 10.2**   **Exchange Rate Movements and Inflation Differentials, 1980-2005**

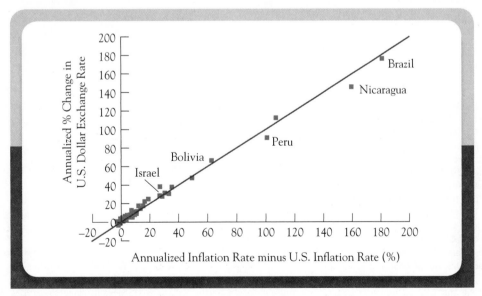

SOURCE: © *The International Monetary Fund.*

[3] It is possible to show this mathematically. If $P$ represents the domestic (Canadian) currency price of a basket of goods, $P_f$ the foreign currency price of the foreign (British) basket of goods, and e the nominal exchange rate, expressed as the domestic currency price of foreign currency (dollars per pound), then purchasing power parity tells us that $(P/eP_f) = 1$ (eq. 5), so $e = (P/P_f)$ (equation (7)). This expression immediately implies that the change in the exchange rate equals the difference between domestic and foreign inflation.

## APPLYING THE CONCEPT
### THE BIG MAC INDEX

By the close of the 20th century, the Big Mac was available to consumers in 121 countries. Regardless of where it was sold, a Big Mac was defined as "two all-beef patties, special sauce, lettuce, cheese, pickles, onions on a sesame seed bun." Needless to say, every McDonald's restaurant requires payment in the local currency. In 1986, the staff of *The Economist* magazine realized that this presented an opportunity. Together, the market exchange rate and the price of a Big Mac would allow them to estimate the extent to which a country's currency deviates from the level implied by purchasing power parity.

Every year, under headlines like "Big MacCurrencies" and "Burgernomics," *The Economist* publishes a table showing Big Mac prices in about 50 countries. The table from the February 1, 2007, edition is reprinted here. Using Big Mac prices as a basis for comparison, it shows the extent to which each country's currency was undervalued or overvalued relative to the U.S. dollar. As you look at the table, you will realize that with the exception of the pound and the euro, all exchange rates are quoted as the number of units of local currency required to purchase one dollar. The pound and the euro are exceptions—they are quoted as the number of dollars required to purchase one pound or one euro.

To see how the Big Mac index works, take the case of Canada. In February 2007, the Canadian dollar traded at C$1.181/US$1. A Big Mac cost C$3.63 in Canada while a Big Mac in the U.S. cost US$3.22. (In general, column A shows the local price of a Big Mac divided by the nominal exchange rate.) Recall that the real exchange rate is the rate at which goods cost the same price measured in the same currency. To figure out the purchasing power parity implied by Big Macs we need to determine what nominal exchange rate would mean that it would cost C$3.63 to buy a Big Mac in the United States. The answer is 3.63/3.22 = 1.13. If each U.S. dollar cost C$1.13 then a Canadian could either buy a Big Mac for C$3.63 or take the C$3.63 and buy US$3.22 and buy a Big Mac in the United States. At an exchange rate of 1.13 the Big Mac costs the same in both countries. But that would imply a 4.2 percent appreciation of the Canadian dollar. Alternatively, we could say that the Canadian dollar is undervalued by 4.2 percent against the U.S. dollar. (Indeed, over the next ten months the Canadian dollar did appreciate—to parity, C$1.00 = US$1—and since the prices of Big Macs didn't change, the Canadian dollar was overvalued by the Big Mac measure by the end of 2007.)

The Big Mac index is a clever idea, and it works remarkably well considering that it is based on a single commodity that is not tradeable, and whose local price surely depends on costs such as wages, rent, and taxes.

### Figure 10.3   A Feast of Burgernomics: The Big Mac Index

| | Big Mac Prices | | | | |
| | In Local Currency | In Dollars | Implied PPP* of the Dollar | Actual Dollar Exchange Rate Jan 31st | Under (−)/Over (+) Valuation against the Dollar, % |
|---|---|---|---|---|---|
| United States** | $3.22 | 3.22 | | | |
| Argentina | Peso 8.25 | 2.65 | 2.56 | 3.11 | −18 |
| Australia | A$3.45 | 2.67 | 1.07 | 1.29 | −17 |
| Brazil | Real 6.4 | 3.01 | 1.99 | 2.13 | −6 |
| Britain | £1.99 | 3.90 | 1.62‡ | | |
| Canada | C$3.63 | 3.08 | 1.13 | 1.18 | −4 |
| Chile | Peso 1,670 | 3.07 | 519 | 544 | −5 |
| China | Yuan 11.0 | 1.41 | 3.42 | 7.77 | −56 |
| Czech Republic | Koruna 52.1 | 2.41 | 16.2 | 21.6 | −25 |
| Denmark | DKr27.75 | 4.84 | 8.62 | 5.74 | +50 |
| Egypt | Pound 9.09 | 1.60 | 2.82 | 5.70 | −50 |
| Euro area† | €2.94 | 3.82 | 1.10‡ | 1.30‡ | +19 |
| Hong Kong | HK$12.0 | 1.54 | 3.73 | 7.81 | −52 |
| Hungary | Forint 590 | 3.00 | 183 | 197 | −7 |
| Indonesia | Rupiah 15,900 | 1.75 | 4,938 | 9.100 | −46 |
| Japan | ¥280 | 2.31 | 87.0 | 121 | −28 |
| Malaysia | Ringgit 5.50 | 1.57 | 1.71 | 3.50 | −51 |
| Mexico | Peso 29.0 | 2.66 | 9.01 | 10.9 | −17 |
| New Zealand | NZ$4.60 | 3.16 | 1.43 | 1.45 | −2 |
| Peru | New Sol 9.50 | 2.97 | 2.95 | 3.20 | −8 |
| Philippines | Peso 85.0 | 1.74 | 26.4 | 48.9 | −46 |
| Poland | Zloty 6.90 | 2.29 | 2.14 | 3.01 | −29 |
| Russia | Rouble 49.0 | 1.85 | 15.2 | 26.5 | −43 |
| Singapore | S$3.60 | 2.34 | 1.12 | 1.54 | −27 |
| Sweden | SKr32.0 | 4.59 | 9.94 | 6.97 | +43 |
| Switzerland | SFr6.30 | 5.05 | 1.96 | 1.25 | +57 |
| Taiwan | NT$75.0 | 2.28 | 23.3 | 32.9 | −29 |
| Thailand | Baht 62.0 | 1.78 | 19.3 | 34.7 | −45 |
| Turkey | Lire 4.55 | 3.22 | 1.41 | 1.41 | nil |
| Venezuela | Bolivar 6,800 | 1.58 | 2,112 | 4,307 | −51 |

*Purchasing-power parity: local price divided by price in United States
**Average of New York, Atlanta, Chicago, and
†Weighted average of prices in euro area equivalent to $4.84.
‡Dollars per euro

prediction of purchasing power parity. On the 45-degree line, exchange rate movements exactly equal differences in inflation. Granted, the points don't all lie exactly on the line, but the pattern is clearly there. The higher a country's inflation, the greater the depreciation in its exchange rate.

Take the extreme example of Bolivia. From 1980 to 2005, Bolivia's inflation minus U.S. inflation averaged 63 percent per year, and the Bolivian currency (originally the Bolivar, now the Boliviano) depreciated at an average annual rate of 66 percent. Putting that into perspective, the 2005 Bolivian price level was more than 340,000 times the 1980 Bolivian price level, and the exchange rate depreciated by roughly the same multiple. That means purchasing one dollar in the foreign exchange market required 340,000 times as many Bolivianos in 2005 as in 1980. Importantly, Figure 10.2 on page 211 shows that there are no countries with high inflation differentials and small exchange rate changes or big exchange rate changes and low inflation differentials. All of the points lie close to the 45-degree line.

The data in Figure 10.2 tell us that purchasing power parity held true over a 25-year period. Even if we look at a decade, the connection between movements in the exchange rate and differences in inflation across countries holds up to scrutiny. But the same exercise applied to periods of a few weeks, months, or even years would be a total failure. Consider the experience of the euro.

Similarly, after its inception in January 1999, the U.S. dollar–euro rate fell steadily for two years, dropping more than 25 percent. At the same time, inflation in the euro area ran a full percentage point *below* U.S. inflation. Examples like these are the norm, not the exception. Over weeks, months, and even years, nominal exchange rates can deviate substantially from the levels implied by purchasing power parity. So, while the theory can help us to understand long swings in exchange rates, it provides no explanation for the short-term movements we see all the time. Fortunately, we do have some equipment in our tool kit that we can use to explain short-term movements in exchange rates.

Before continuing, we should note the meaning of two additional terms. We often hear currencies described as **undervalued** or **overvalued**. When people use these terms, they have in mind a current market rate that deviates from what they consider to be purchasing power parity. For example, a person who thinks that one dollar should purchase one euro—that is, that one to one is somehow the "correct" long-run exchange rate—would say that if one dollar purchases only €0.90, it is *undervalued* relative to the euro, or the euro is *overvalued* relative to the dollar.

## Exchange Rates in the Short Run

While purchasing power parity helps us to understand movements in nominal exchange rates over decades, it cannot explain the weekly, monthly, or even yearly movements we see. What can? What sorts of phenomena are responsible for the nearly constant movement in exchange rates? To explain short-run changes in nominal exchange rates, we turn to an analysis of the supply of and demand for currencies. Since, in the short run, prices don't move much, these nominal exchange rate movements represent changes in the real exchange rate. That is, a 1 or 2 percent change in the *nominal* Canadian dollar–U.S. dollar exchange rate over a day or week creates a roughly equivalent change in the *real* Canadian dollar–U.S. dollar exchange rate.

## APPLYING THE CONCEPT
### PURCHASING POWER PARITY AND CROSS-COUNTRY GDP COMPARISONS

Countries often want to compare their economic standing with others, and GDP or average GDP per capita are frequently used as benchmarks for such a comparison. But how do you compare GDPs when they are measured in different currencies? In 2008, GDP per capita in the United States was US$46,859, while Canadian per capita GDP was C$48,123. Which was higher? We could use nominal exchange rates to convert the Canadian dollars to U.S dollars, but an alternative would be to compute an exchange rate by comparing the relative prices of the same basket of goods in each country. This is the PPP exchange rate. Using nominal exchange rates (C$1.06=US$1) Canadian GDP was equivalent to US$45,399, slightly less than U.S. per capita income. Using PPP exchange rates (C$1.22=US$1), Canadian incomes had the purchasing power of US$39,445—significantly less.

Figure 10.4 shows the nominal exchange rate between Canada and the United States and the PPP exchange rate between 2000 and 2008 (notice that the OECD data present the exchange rate as Canadian dollars per U.S. dollar, not vice versa). While the nominal exchange rate has gyrated, the PPP exchange rate has been relatively stable. If you compared the ratios of Canadian to U.S. GDP in 2002 with those in 2008 using nominal exchange rates, the answer would be very different depending on whether you used nominal exchange rates or PPPs. Using nominal exchange rates it would look as though Canada had closed the gap, while, using PPP exchange rates, the gap wouldn't change. Economists typically use PPP-based GDP levels to compare incomes across countries as they better represent the relative standards of living.

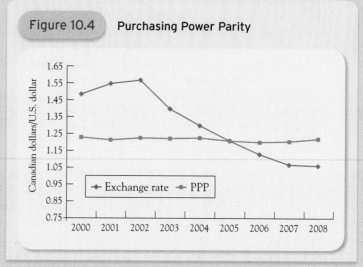

**Figure 10.4    Purchasing Power Parity**

SOURCE: *Data based on Purchasing Power Parities (PPP). Statistics under Prices and Purchasing Power Parities, from OECD.Stat Extracts, http://stats.oecd.org. OECD, www.oecd.org.*

## The Supply of Canadian Dollars

As is always the case in discussing foreign exchange, we need to pick a home country and stick to it. The most natural choice for us is Canada, so we'll use the Canadian dollar as the domestic currency. Consistent with this, we will discuss the number of units of foreign currency that it takes to purchase one Canadian dollar. For example, we will talk about the number of U.S. dollars per Canadian dollar.

Who supplies Canadian dollars to the foreign exchange markets? People who have them, of course—primarily people in Canada. There are two reasons that someone who is holding Canadian dollars would want to exchange them for U.S. dollars or yen: (1) to purchase goods and services produced abroad, such as a dinner in Hawaii or a Japanese television set; and (2) to invest in foreign assets, such as bonds issued by computer company Apple, or shares in Honda, the Japanese manufacturer of cars and motorcycles.

Figure 10.5 shows the supply of dollars in the Canadian dollar–U.S. dollar market. Just like any other supply curve, it slopes upward. The higher the price a Canadian dollar commands in the market, the more Canadian dollars are supplied. And the more valuable the Canadian dollar, the cheaper are foreign-produced goods and foreign assets *relative to domestic ones* in Canadian markets.

To see why, suppose you are planning a vacation. You have narrowed your options to trip to California or to British Columbia. Price is important to you. Since the California hotels charge prices in U.S. dollars, a change in the value of the dollar will affect your decision. As the Canadian dollar increases in value, the price of the U.S. holiday falls and you become more likely to go there. If you do, you will be supplying Canadian dollars to the foreign exchange market. What is true for your holiday is true for everything else. The more valuable the Canadian dollar, the cheaper foreign goods, services, and assets will be and the higher the supply of Canadian dollars in the Canadian dollar–U.S. dollar market. Thus, *the supply curve for Canadian dollars slopes upward*, as shown in Figure 10.5.

**Figure 10.5**    The Foreign Exchange Market

SOURCE: *The International Monetary Fund.*

## The Demand for Canadian Dollars

Foreigners who want to purchase Canadian-made goods, assets, or services need Canadian dollars to do so. Suppose a U.S. student would like to attend university in Canada. The university will accept payment only in Canadian dollars, so paying the tuition bill means exchanging U.S. dollars for Canadian dollars. The lower the Canadian dollar–U.S. dollar exchange rate—the fewer U.S. dollars needed to buy one Canadian dollar—the cheaper the tuition bill will be from the viewpoint of the U.S. student. At a given Canadian dollar price, the fewer U.S. dollars needed to purchase one Canadian dollar, the cheaper are Canadian-made goods and services. And the cheaper a good or service, the higher the demand for it. The same is true of investments. The cheaper the Canadian dollar—the lower the Canadian dollar–U.S. dollar exchange rate—the more attractive are Canadian investments and the higher is the demand for Canadian dollars with which to buy them. Thus, *the demand curve for dollars slopes downward* (see Figure 10.5).

## Equilibrium in the Market for Canadian Dollars

The equilibrium exchange rate, labelled E in Figure 10.5, equates the supply of and demand for Canadian dollars. Because the values of most of the major currencies of the world (including the dollar, the euro, the yen, and the pound) float freely, they are determined by market forces. As a result, fluctuations in their value are the consequence of shifts in supply or demand.

## Shifts in the Supply of and Demand for Canadian Dollars

Shifts in either the supply of or the demand for dollars will change the *equilibrium exchange rate*. Let's begin with *shifts in the supply of dollars*. Remember that Canadians wanting to purchase products from abroad or to buy foreign assets will supply dollars to the foreign exchange market. Anything that increases their desire to import goods and services from abroad, or their preference for foreign stocks and bonds, will increase the supply of dollars, leading to a depreciation of the dollar. Figure 10.6 shows the mechanics of this process.

What causes Canadians' preferences for foreign goods, services, and assets to increase, prompting them to supply more dollars to the foreign exchange market and shifting

## YOUR FINANCIAL WORLD
### Don't Bet on Exchange Rates

Lots of people have an opinion about the likely course of exchange rates. Should you listen to them to try to turn a profit on changes in the exchange rate? The answer is surely no. To see why, let's look at a recent episode in economic history. In 2008, the financial crisis in the United States led to a dramatic reduction in U.S. interest rates and a decision to run a sizable fiscal deficit. Anyone who followed such matters would tell you that the dollar should have depreciated. But having a good sense of what will happen over the long run doesn't help much in the short run. The U.S. dollar appreciated against the Canadian dollar and the euro and the yen. What the experts can't tell you is when the dollar will depreciate.

So how can you get a forecast of the future exchange rate? You can look at the *forward markets* for the major currencies. In these markets, foreign currency dealers agree today to a price at which they will sell euros (or yen or other major currencies) three months from now. Since they don't want to incur losses, the dealers will use all the information available to them (including interest rates) to make the most accurate forecast they can for the exchange rate on the day they agree to make the transaction. But if you look at the newspaper, you will discover that forward rates are virtually always within 1 or 2 percent of the current spot rate. In other words, the best forecast is that the exchange rate won't change much. (Take a look at the "Exchange Rates" column in the business section of a newspaper such as *The Globe and Mail* to confirm this claim.) This tendency holds true even if the Big Mac index or more sophisticated calculations based on purchasing power parity tell us that the exchange rate should move significantly in one direction or another.

The problem is that, in the short run, exchange rates are inherently unpredictable. No one has any idea what will happen over the next week, month, or even year. In short, the best forecast of the future exchange rate is usually today's exchange rate. Because you really can't do any better than that, betting on exchange rates is a bad idea.

---

**Figure 10.6**  Effect of an Increase in the Supply of Canadian Dollars in the Foreign Exchange Market

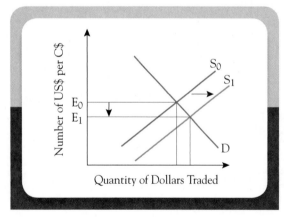

the supply of dollars to the right? This question has many answers. The list includes the following possibilities:

*A rise in the supply of dollars Canadians use to purchase foreign goods and services can be caused by*

- *An increase in Canadians' preference for foreign goods.* For instance, a successful advertising campaign might convince Canadian consumers to buy more imported orange juice. To fill the new orders, Canadian importers would exchange Canadian dollars for U.S. dollars, shifting the Canadian dollar supply curve to the right.

*A rise in the supply of dollars Canadians use to purchase foreign assets can be caused by*

- *An increase in the real interest rate on foreign bonds (relative to Canadian bonds).* With Canadian real interest rates holding steady, an increase in the return on foreign bonds would make them a more appealing investment. Since buying U.S. bonds means exchanging Canadian dollars for U.S. dollars, a rise in the desire to purchase foreign bonds shifts the supply curve for Canadian dollars to the right. (Remember that the real interest rate is the nominal interest rate minus expected inflation, so real interest rates increase either when the nominal interest rate rises and expected inflation holds steady or when expected inflation falls and the nominal interest rate remains the same.)

- *An increase in Canadian wealth*. Just as an increase in income raises consumption of everything, an increase in wealth raises investment in everything. The wealthier we are, the more foreign investments we will make, and the more dollars we will exchange for foreign currency, shifting the supply of dollars to the right.

- *A decrease in the riskiness of foreign investments relative to Canadian investments*. Lower-risk bonds are always more desirable than others, regardless of their country of origin. If the risk associated with foreign investments falls, Canadians will want more of them. To get them, they will increase the supply of dollars in the foreign exchange market.

- *An expected depreciation of the Canadian dollar*. If people think the dollar will lose value, possibly because of inflation, they will want to exchange it for foreign currency. To see why, assume that the Canadian dollar is trading at par (US\$1.00 = C\$1) and that you expect it to fall to US\$0.90 = C\$1 over the next year. If you exchange C\$100 for U.S. dollars today, you will get US\$100. Reversing the transaction a year later, you will receive C\$111: an 11 percent return. The point is simple: if investors think the Canadian dollar will decline in value—it will depreciate—they will sell Canadian dollars, increasing the supply of Canadian dollars in the foreign exchange market.

To understand *shifts in the demand for dollars*, all we need to do is review the list just presented, this time from the point of view of a foreigner. Anything that increases the desire of foreigners to buy Canadian-made goods and services, or to invest in Canadian assets, will increase the demand for dollars and shift the demand curve to the right. Increases in demand come about when foreigners prefer more Canadian-made goods, when the real yield on Canadian bonds rises (relative to the yield on foreign bonds), when foreign wealth increases, when the riskiness of Canadian investments falls, and when the dollar is expected to appreciate. All these events increase demand, shifting the demand curve to the right and causing the dollar to appreciate (see Figure 10.7). Table 10.2 on page 218 summarizes all the events that increase the supply of and demand for dollars in the foreign exchange market.

**Figure 10.7**   Effect of an Increase in the Demand for Canadian Dollars in the Foreign Exchange Market

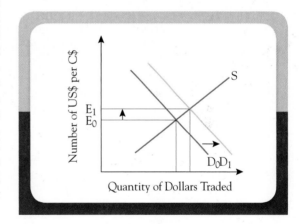

## Explaining Exchange Rate Movements

The supply and demand model of the determination of exchange rates helps to explain short-run movements in currency values. Let's return to the appreciation of the Canadian dollar relative to the U.S. dollar that occurred between 2002 and 2007 (see Figure 10.1 on page 203). Over this period, the number of U.S. dollars required to purchase one Canadian dollar increased from 0.65 to 1. Our model allows us to conclude that the cause was either a decrease in the dollars supplied by Canadians or an increase in the Canadian dollars demanded by Americans. The first would shift the supply curve to the right and the second would shift the demand curve to the left, decreasing the equilibrium exchange rate and making Canadian dollars less valuable. To figure out which of these is right, we need to look for other evidence.

| Table 10.2 | Causes of an Increase in the Supply of and Demand for Canadian Dollars |
| --- | --- |

| Increased Supply Shifts Supply Curve to the Right (Leads to a fall in the value of the dollar) | Increased Demand Shifts Demand Curve to the Right (Leads to a rise in the value of the dollar) |
| --- | --- |
| Increase in Canadian preference for foreign goods | Increase in foreign preference for Canadian goods |
| Increase in real interest rate on foreign bonds (relative to Canadian bonds) | Increase in real interest rate on Canadian. bonds (relative to foreign bonds) |
| Increase in Canadian wealth | Increase in foreign wealth |
| Reduction in riskiness of foreign investment (relative to Canadian. investment) | Reduction in riskiness of Canadian investment (relative to foreign investment) |
| Expected depreciation of the Canadian dollar | Expected future Canadian dollar appreciation |

Figure 10.8 provides part of the answer. Since 2002, the Canadian dollar has appreciated when the price of oil rose and depreciated when the price of oil fell. Since Canada is a net exporter of oil, a rise in the price of oil increases the demand for Canadian dollars. Notice, though, that the two variables were not so tightly linked prior to 2002. The high price of oil in the last few years coincided with technological breakthroughs that mean that development of the oil sands is financially viable. The result was an influx of investment into the oil sands, increasing yet further the demand for the Canadian dollar. The lesson from Figure 10.8 is that the value of the Canadian dollar depends on many variables and the relationship between those variables and the exchange rate is not fixed.

| Figure 10.8 | Oil Prices and the Canadian Dollar |
| --- | --- |

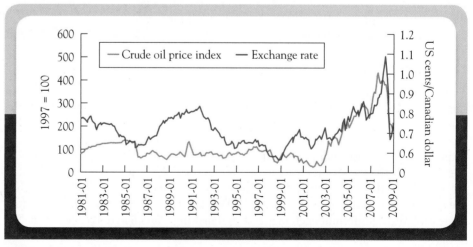

SOURCE: Bank of Canada, CANSIM Table 176-0064, exchange rate v37426. Statistics Canada, Oil Price Index, Table 330-0006, v1576530, 18 September 2009.

## Interest Rate Parity and Short-Run Exchange Rate Determination

There is another way to think about the determinants of exchange rates in the short run. Rather than focus on the supply of and demand for currency, we can look at exchange rates from an investor's point of view. If the bonds issued in different countries are perfect substitutes for one another, then arbitrage will equalize the returns on domestic and foreign bonds. And since investing abroad means exchanging currencies, the result is a relationship among domestic interest rates, foreign interest rates, and the exchange rate. From this intuition, we can develop an understanding of the short-run movements in exchange rates.

Let's take the example of a Canadian investor with a one-year investment horizon and $1,000 to invest in either a one-year Government of Canada bond or a one-year German government bond. Since the investor is from Canada, we will assume that at the end of the year when the bonds mature, she wants to receive dollars. We'll consider first the case where our investor can't hedge the foreign exchange risk in the forward market, and then we'll look at that possibility. The question is, Which investment is more attractive? To find the answer, we need to compute the dollar return on buying a one-year $1,000 Government of Canada bond and compare it to the dollar return on converting $1,000 to euros, buying a German government bond, and converting the proceeds back to dollars after one year. The value of the first investment is easy to find. If the one-year Government of Canada bond interest rate is $i$, then

$$\text{Value of \$1,000 invested in domestic bonds after one year} = \$1,000(1 + i) \quad (8)$$

Computing the return to investing $1,000 in a one-year German bond requires a series of steps. First, the investor needs to take the $1,000 and convert it to euros. If $E$ is the dollar–euro exchange rate measured as the number of euros per dollar, then $1,000 purchases $E \times 1,000$ euros. Next, the investor purchases the German bond. If the one-year German bond rate is $i^f$, a $1,000 investment yields $E \times 1,000 \times (1 + i^f)$ euros in one year. Finally, at the end of the year, the investor must exchange the euros for dollars. If we call $E^e$ the expected future exchange rate—the number of euros per dollar expected in a year's time—then the dollar return to a $1,000 investment in foreign bonds is

$$\text{Value of \$1,000 invested in foreign bonds after one year}$$

$$= \$1,000 \, \frac{E(1 + i^f)}{E^e}$$

$$= \$1,000 \, \frac{(1 + i^f)}{E^e/E} \quad (9)$$

Looking at this equation, we can see that for the Canadian investor, the return to holding the German bond has two parts: (1) the interest income and (2) the expected change in the exchange rate.

To see why the return depends on the change in the exchange rate, take an example in which the dollar–euro rate is €1/$1 at the start of the year and €1.05/$1 at the end of the year. That is, at the start of the year, you exchange one dollar for one euro, but at the end of the year the dollar is worth 1.05 euros—an appreciation of 5 percent in the value of the dollar. If the German interest rate is 6 percent, then a $1,000 investment will yield $1,000 × (1.06/1.05) = $1,010. Because the dollar has appreciated by 5 percent, the return on a 6 percent German bond is only 6 percent − 5 percent = 1 percent.

Returning to our comparison of a domestic and a foreign bond, let's assume that the investor is risk neutral and that therefore if the investor is indifferent between the two investments, their expected returns must be the same. That must be the case for the two bonds to be perfect substitutes. The implication is that

Value of $1,000 invested in Government of Canada bonds for one year
= Value of $1,000 invested in foreign bonds after one year.

This means that

$$\$1,000\,(1 + i) = \frac{\$1,000(1 + i^f)}{E^e/E} \tag{10}$$

With the notation that $\Delta E^e = E^e - E$ and using an approximation[4] we find that

$$i = i^f - \frac{\Delta E^e}{E} \tag{11}$$

This equation, called the **uncovered interest parity condition**, tells us that the Canadian interest rate equals the German interest rate minus the dollar's expected appreciation. (These calculations ignore the risk of exchange rates moving in an unexpected way.)

If the interest parity condition did not hold, people would have an incentive to shift their investments until it did. For instance, if the Canadian interest rate exceeded the German interest rate minus the expected depreciation in the dollar, then foreign and domestic investors would sell German bonds and buy Government of Canada bonds. Their action would drive down the price of German bonds and drive up the price of Canadian bonds, raising the foreign interest rate and lowering the domestic rate until the relationship held.

So far we have assumed that the investor doesn't use the forward market to hedge the exchange rate risk, but from Chapter 9 we know that many investors do just that. Suppose our investor could buy Canadian dollars (and sell euros) in the forward market; how would that change her calculation? Let $F$ represent the forward price of dollars, then equation (9) becomes

Value of $1,000 invested in foreign bonds after one year

$$= \frac{\$1,000\ E(1 + i^f)}{F}$$

$$= \frac{\$1,000(1 + i^f)}{F/E} \tag{12}$$

We will write $F$ as the product of the spot rate ($E$) and one plus the forward premium [i.e., $F = E(1 + e)$ where $e$ is the forward premium], and then substitute (12) into equation (10):

$$(1 + i) = \frac{1 + i^f}{1 + e} \tag{13}$$

Finally, using a similar approximation to that used to derive equation (11), we can simplify equation (13) to get

$$i = i^f - e \tag{14}$$

---

[4] From (10), $(1 + i) = (1 + i^f)/(1 + \frac{\Delta E^e}{E})$, so that $(1 + i)(1 + \frac{\Delta E^e}{E}) = (1 + i^f)$. The approximation $(i \times \frac{\Delta E^e}{E})= 0$ gives equation (11). This approximation is useful to show the close relationship between interest differentials and the expected change in the exchange rate. If the interest rate is 5 percent and the expected depreciation is 5 percent then this is .0025, or .025 percent. This is a small number but traders of million of dollars don't make this approximation!

That is, the interest differential equals the forward exchange premium.[5] This is known as the covered interest parity condition because the arbitrage operation that it models does not expose the investor to exchange rate risk.

If we know the current Canadian and German interest rates, the interest parity conditions tells us what the current Canadian dollar–euro exchange rate should be for a given forward or expected future Canadian dollar–euro exchange rate. The interest rate parity condition tells us that the current value of the Canadian dollar will be higher

1. The higher Canadian interest rates.
2. The lower German interest rates.
3. The higher the expected future value of the Canadian dollar.

These are the same conclusions we arrived at using supply and demand theory.

## Government Policy and Foreign Exchange Intervention

The more a country relies on exports and imports, the more important its exchange rate. Currency appreciation drives up the price foreigners pay for a country's exports as it reduces the price residents of the country pay for imports. This shift in foreign versus domestic prices hurts domestic businesses. Companies with big export businesses suffer the most, along with businesses whose products compete with imported goods. They often respond by pressuring elected officials to reduce the value of the currency. After all, government policymakers control the prices of lots of goods and services. Milk, rent, and electric power are just a few possibilities. Why not exchange rates too?

Government officials can intervene in foreign exchange markets in several ways. Some countries adopt a fixed exchange rate and act to maintain it at a level of their choosing, but what they fix is the nominal exchange rate. We will discuss the implications of this approach in Chapter 22. For now, all we need to know is that exchange rates can be controlled if policymakers have the resources available and are willing to take the necessary actions.

Figure 10.9 on page 224 shows the exchange rate between the yuan and the U.S. dollar. From January 1994 until July 2005, the Bank of China pegged the exchange rate at 8.27 yuan per U.S. dollar. During these years Chinese manufacturing boomed and so did exports, meaning the demand for Chinese yuan rose (as did the supply of U.S. dollars). We would expect that the yuan would have appreciated, but the Bank of China did not sell its U.S. dollars back to the United States; instead, it held an increasing amount of U.S. dollar reserves. But while the nominal exchange rate was fixed, the real exchange rate was appreciating. Inflation in China was approximately 70 percent over those years, while it was only 35 percent in the United States, so the real exchange rate depreciated by 35 percent. It's a lot harder to fix the nominal exchange rate than the real exchange rate.

Large industrialized countries and common currency zones generally allow currency markets to determine their exchange rate. Even so, there are occasions when officials in these countries try to influence the currency values. Sometimes they make public statements in the hope of influencing currency traders. But talk is cheap, and such statements rarely have an impact on their own. At other times, policymakers will buy or sell currency in an attempt to affect demand or supply. This approach is called a foreign exchange intervention.

---

[5] You have probably noted that combining equations (11) and (14) yields the prediction that the forward exchange premium will equal the expected future exchange rate appreciation. This prediction is explored in detail in courses in international finance.

## IN THE NEWS
### Benefits of Diversification Are Declining

## The Financial Post

**David Berman**

January 5, 2008

### Investors can't hide in one big market

Going global has long been a key mantra for investors, and for good reason: By putting money to work in, say, the United States or the United Kingdom or Japan, you can smooth out some of the bumps in your portfolio and give your overall returns a boost.

But then came the border-busting effects of globalization, and now international diversification has become a hot topic of debate. In an era when companies are straddling the globe, economies are opening up and monetary policies are increasingly integrated, the world is beginning to look like one giant market, with stocks on one side of the planet behaving a lot like stocks on the other side.

"Global diversification still makes sense from an investor's perspective, but there have been some market-wide changes that have made it slightly less attractive," said Stephen Foerster, finance professor at Richard Ivey School of Business at the University of Western Ontario.

"You get the big kicker from diversification when you can invest in markets that have low correlations. In other words, when one market is doing not so well, another market is picking up the slack."

Trouble is, non-correlated markets are no longer easy to find, especially when it comes to developed markets, such as Western Europe, the United States, Japan, Australia and Canada—the very places investors have embraced in the past because of their modern economies and stable political climates.

Admittedly, many of these markets produced returns last year that differ sharply from Canada's, especially after you factor in currency shifts. For example, in Canadian-dollar terms, the S&P 500 is down about 12%, Japan's Nikkei 225 is down about 20% and the United Kingdom's FTSE 100 is down about 10%. The S&P/TSX composite index, however, is up 3.5%.

Not only do these returns bode ill for international diversification (Canadian investors lost money), many observers will point out that international markets have tended to zig and zag together—on the same day. When the S&P 500 is up, there is a good chance that Germany's DAX index, the FTSE 100 and the Nikkei 225 are up, too; and when one index is down, they all tend to be down. This was the case yesterday.

International markets have tended to move together after key pronouncements from the U.S. Federal Reserve. And when you examine particular sectors that have performed well this year, they tend to have one thing in common: ties to China.

This summer, when U.S. sub-prime mortgages shook credit markets, the reverberations were felt around the world even though the initial splash was an entirely local concern: the U.S. housing downturn. Geographically diverse markets fell, then rebounded, then fell again more or less in unison. In other words, when investors needed diversification the most—in times of volatility—it was not there.

"The correlation among markets is becoming higher, there is no question about it," said Chen Zhao, managing editor of Global Investment Strategy at BCA Research.

An academic paper by Shalini Perumpral, a finance professor at Radford University, published by the American Society

Some countries hardly ever attempt to influence their exchange rates in this way, while others intervene in the markets frequently. Among the major industrialized countries, the Japanese are the most frequent participants in foreign exchange markets. The spring of 2002 provides a good example of their approach.

In the latter half of the 1990s, the Japanese economy was stagnant; real GDP grew at a rate of about 1 percent. In 2001, the economic situation worsened and output fell 2 percent. After trying almost every other approach imaginable to resuscitate the economy, Japanese officials decided to see if depreciating the yen would help. The idea was to help Japanese exporters increase their foreign sales by reducing the prices foreigners paid for Japanese products. In late May 2002, Japan's Ministry of Finance sold yen in exchange for dollars, hoping to drive down the price by increasing the supply of yen. While the yen did depreciate very modestly of Business and Behavioral Sciences last year, looked at correlations between 1988 and 2003 and concluded that they have picked up in the new millennium.

"Market-liberalization policies throughout the world appear to have blurred the distinctions among markets," Ms. Perumpral said in the paper, co-written with two others.

The car market is a good example. Whether you have invested in Toyota Motor Corp. in Japan, General Motors Corp. in the United States or Daimler AG in Germany, the three automotive giants move less on the changing conditions of their home bases and more on the international car market.

This can drive investors to ask an important question about international diversification: What's the point?

However flawed it may look today, most observers contend it is still the best approach. While markets tend to move in a closer formation than they have in the past, they do not yet move in lockstep—meaning that a globally diversified portfolio should still give investors a smoother ride over the longer term.

As well, the stronger correlations among markets tends to be most pronounced among developed markets, which means that investors can still tap the benefits of diversification by moving beyond the usual suspects in North America and Europe and into the woollier world of emerging markets.

"There are markets that are still not correlated with the U.S. market," Mr. Zhao said. "If you look at Russia and India, for example, they are making new highs. They have demonstrated completely different behaviour."

Don Reed, chief executive of Franklin Templeton Investments and manager of the Templeton International Stock Fund, noted as well that correlation among developed markets tends to go in waves. It was particularly strong in the

early 1990s, then fell in the mid-1990s, only to pick up again at the end of the decade and remain strong to this day.

"The correlation among global markets ebbs and flows," Mr. Reed said. "This is historical. When it gets closer, someone says there's no need for international diversification. And when it reverses itself over a period of four or five years, the people who said that are nowhere in sight."

That said, globalization—and its impact on international markets—remains alive and well, which means that even diversified investors are likely to feel some pain when stocks turn volatile. For now at least, the smooth ride is over.

### LESSONS OF THE ARTICLE

More diversification is always better. Increasing the number of independent risks in a portfolio by spreading investments across a broader set of stocks and bonds can reduce risk without decreasing the expected return. So long as the returns on stocks in other countries do not move in lockstep with the Canadian stock market, holding them will reduce the risk in your investment portfolio. But the extent of the gain is decreasing as global markets become more integrated.

SOURCE: By David Berman, Financial Post, January 5, 2008. Material reprinted with the express permission of "The National Post Company," a CanWest Partnership.

as a result of intervention, by the end of the month its price was higher than it had been before the intervention.

Why did the Japanese government's policy fail? Shouldn't an increase in the supply of yen, regardless of where it comes from, lead to a depreciation? The primary reason the intervention didn't work was that, while the Japanese Ministry of Finance was selling yen, the Bank of Japan was buying them. The Bank of Japan is in charge of monetary policy in Japan, which means controlling a particular short-term interest rate. Operationally, the result was that, within a few days, the Bank of Japan reversed the Ministry's foreign-exchange intervention. If it hadn't, the interest rate it wished to control would have changed. Thus, foreign exchange interventions will be ineffective unless they are accompanied by a change in the interest rate. That is the reason countries such as Canada rarely intervene in the foreign exchange markets.

| Figure 10.9 | Yuan–U.S. Dollar Exchange Rate |

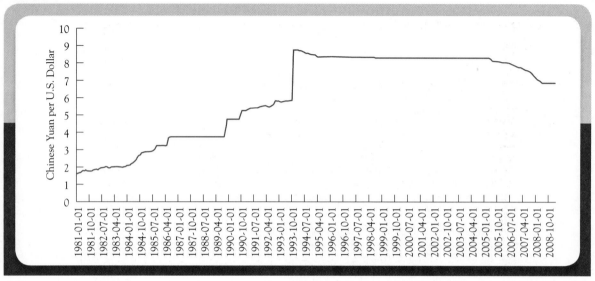

SOURCE: *FRED (Federal Reserve Economics Database), G.5 Foreign Exchange Rates. Series EXCHUS. Accessed June 29, 2009. Federal Reserve Bank of St. Louis.*

## Terms

appreciation (of a currency), 205
Canadian dollar effective exchange rate index (CERI) 205
covered interest parity condition, 221
Big Mac index, 212
demand for Canadian dollars, 215
depreciation (of a currency), 205
foreign exchange intervention, 221

euro, 204
law of one price, 208
nominal exchange rate, 204
overvalued currency, 213
purchasing power parity (PPP), 209
real exchange rate, 206
supply of dollars, 214
uncovered interest parity condition, 220
undervalued currency, 213

## Chapter Summary

1. Different areas and countries of the world use different currencies in their transactions.
   a. The nominal exchange rate is the rate at which the currency of one country can be exchanged for the currency of another.

   b. A decline in the value of one currency relative to another is called depreciation.
   c. An increase in the value of one currency relative to another is called appreciation.
   d. When the dollar appreciates relative to the euro, the euro depreciates relative to the dollar.
   e. The real exchange rate is the rate at which the goods and services of one country can be exchanged for the goods and services of another.
   f. Over $3 trillion worth of currency is traded every day in markets run by brokers and foreign exchange dealers.

2. In the long run, the value of a country's currency is tied to the price of goods and services in that country.
   a. The law of one price states that two identical goods should sell for the same price, regardless of location.
   b. The law of one price fails because of transportation costs, differences in taxation and technical specifications, and the fact that some goods cannot be moved.
   c. The theory of purchasing power parity applies the law of one price to international transactions;

it states that the real exchange rate always equals one.

d. Purchasing power parity implies that countries with higher inflation than other countries will experience exchange rate depreciation.

e. Over decades, exchange rate changes are approximately equal to differences in inflation, implying that purchasing power parity holds.

3. In the short run, the value of a country's currency depends on supply of and demand for the currency in foreign exchange markets.

a. When people in Canada wish to purchase foreign goods and services or invest in foreign assets, they must supply dollars to the foreign exchange market.

b. The more foreign currency that can be exchanged for one dollar, the greater will be the supply of dollars. That is, the supply curve for dollars slopes upward.

c. Foreigners who wish to purchase Canadian-made goods and services or invest in Canadian assets will demand dollars in the foreign exchange market.

d. The fewer units of foreign currency needed to buy one dollar, the higher the demand for dollars. That is, the demand curve for dollars slopes downward.

e. Anything that increases the desire of Canadians to buy foreign-made goods and services or invest in foreign assets will increase the supply buy Canadian-made goods and services or invest in Canadian assets will increase the demand for dollars (shift the demand curve for dollars to the right), causing the dollar to appreciate.

4. With open capital markets, interest parity conditions imply that interest rate differentials will reflect expected changes in exchange rates. If the Canadian interest rate is higher than the U.S. interest rate, the Canadian dollar is expected to depreciate versus the U.S. dollar.

5. Some governments buy and sell their own currency in an effort to fix or to influence the nominal exchange rate. Fixing the nominal exchange rate doesn't necessarily fix the real exchange rate

## Conceptual Problems

1. If the Canadian dollar–British pound exchange rate is $1.50 per pound, and the Canadian dollar–euro rate is $0.90 per euro:
   a. What is the pound per euro rate?
   b. How could you profit if the pound per euro rate were above the rate you calculated in part *a*? What if it were lower?

2. If a compact disc costs $15 in Canada and £13 in the United Kingdom, what is the real CD exchange rate? Look up the current dollar–pound exchange rate in a newspaper or an online source, and compare the two prices. What do you conclude?

3. Suppose the euro–Canadian dollar exchange rate moves from $0.90 per euro to $0.92 per euro. At the same time, the prices of European-made goods and services rise 1 percent, while prices of Canadian-made goods and services rise 3 percent. What has happened to the real exchange rate between the dollar and the euro? Assuming the same change in the nominal exchange rate, what would happen if inflation were 3 percent in Europe and 1 percent in Canada?

4. The same television set costs $500 in Canada, €450 in France, £300 in United Kingdom, and ¥100,000 in Japan. If the law of one price holds, what are the euro–dollar, pound–dollar, and yen–dollar exchange rates? Why might the law of one price fail?

5.* What does the theory of purchasing power parity predict in the long run regarding the inflation rate of a country that fixes its exchange rate to the U.S. dollar?

6.* Why is it not a good idea to speculate on short-term exchange rate movements using the predictions of purchasing power parity?

7. You need to purchase Japanese yen and have called two brokers to get quotes. The first broker offered you a rate of 125 yen per dollar. The second broker, ignoring market convention, quoted a price of 0.0084 dollars per yen. To which broker should you give your business? Why?

* Indicates more difficult problems.

www.mcgrawhill.ca/olc/cecchetti

8. Suppose you expect the euro to appreciate 5 percent relative to the dollar over the next year.

   a. Find the current value of the euro in the newspaper or on the Internet, and compute what your expectation implies about the euro-dollar exchange rate in one year's time.

   b. In the same source, find the interest rate on one-year U.S. treasury bonds. Using this value, compute the European interest rate that would make the return on a one-year domestic investment equal to the return on a foreign one. Provide an example to show your answer is correct.

9. During the 1990s, the U.S. secretary of the treasury often stated, "a strong dollar is in the interest of the United States."

   a. Is this statement true? Explain your answer.

   b. What can the secretary of the treasury actually do about the value of the dollar relative to other currencies?

10. Your investment advisor calls to suggest that you invest in Mexican bonds with a yield of 8.5 percent—3 percent above Government of Canada interest rates. Should you do it? What factors should you consider in making your decision?

## Analytical Problems

11. If the price (measured in a common currency) of a particular basket of goods is 10 percent higher in the United Kingdom than it is in Canada, which country's currency is undervalued, according to the theory of purchasing power parity?

12.* You hear an interview with a well-known economist who states that she expects the Canadian dollar to strengthen against the British pound over the next 5 to 10 years. This economist is known for her support of the theory of purchasing power parity. Using an equation to summarize the relationship predicted by purchasing power parity between exchange-rate movements and the inflation rates in the two countries, explain whether you expect inflation in Canada to be higher or lower on average compared with that in the United Kingdom over the period in question. How could interest rate data confirm or reject her view?

13. Using the model of demand and supply for Canadian dollars, what would you expect to happen to the Canadian dollar exchange rate if, in light of a worsening geopolitical situation, Canadians viewed U.S. bonds as more risky than before? (You should quote the exchange rate as number of units of foreign currency per Canadian dollar.)

14. In recent times, the Chinese central bank has been buying U.S. dollars in the market in an effort to keep its own currency, the yuan, weak. Use the model of demand and supply for dollars to show what the immediate effect would be on the yuan/dollar exchange rate of a decision by China to allow its currency to float freely.

15. In the aftermath of the World Baseball Classic, demand for U.S.–produced baseball paraphernalia skyrocketed in Italy and the Netherlands. What impact would this have on the euro–dollar exchange rate in the short run?

16. Suppose consumers across the world (including in Canada), driven by a wave of national pride, decided to buy home-produced products where possible. How would demand and supply for dollars be affected? What can you say about the impact on the equilibrium dollar exchange rate?

17. Suppose the interest rate on a one-year U.S. bond were 10 percent and the interest rate on an equivalent Canadian bond were 8 percent. If the interest rate parity condition holds, is the U.S. dollar expected to appreciate or depreciate relative to the Canadian dollar over the next year? Explain your choice.

18.* Suppose government officials in a small open economy decided they wanted their currency to weaken in order to boost exports. What kind of foreign exchange market intervention would they have to make to cause their currency to depreciate? What would happen to domestic interest rates in that country if its central bank doesn't take any action to offset the impact on interest rates of the foreign exchange intervention?

## Financial Institutions

# CHAPTER 11

## The Economics of Financial Intermediation

Economic well-being is inextricably tied to the health of the financial intermediaries that make up the financial system. From Chapter 3, we know that financial intermediaries are the businesses whose assets and liabilities are primarily financial instruments. Various sorts of banks, brokerage firms, investment companies, insurance companies, and pension funds all fall into this category. These are the institutions that pool funds from firms and people who save and lend them to firms and people who need to borrow, transforming assets and providing access to financial markets. They funnel savers' surplus resources into home mortgages, business loans, and investments. As we discussed briefly at the end of Chapter 3, financial intermediaries are involved in both direct finance—in which borrowers sell securities directly to lenders in the financial markets—and indirect finance, in which a third party stands between those who provide funds and those who use them. Intermediaries investigate the financial condition of the firms and individuals who want financing to figure out which have the best investment opportunities. As providers of indirect finance, banks want to make loans only to the highest-quality borrowers. When they do their job correctly, financial intermediaries increase investment and economic growth at the same time that they reduce investment risk and economic volatility.

Ensuring that the best investment opportunities and highest-quality borrowers are funded is extremely important. Any country that wants to grow must ensure that its financial system works. When a country's financial system crumbles, its economy fails with it. This situation threatened the United States in 2008 when the financial system came close to collapse and the government kept the system functioning by a massive injection of capital. The banking system survived (just) but the economic

| Figure 11.1 | Financial and Economic Development |

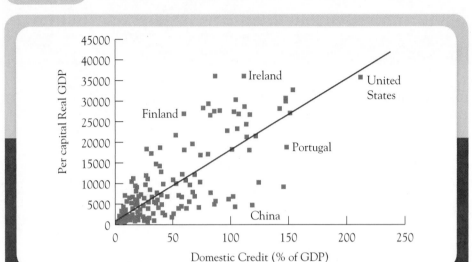

SOURCE: *Financial development is measured as total financial system credit extended to the private sector. World Development Indicators, the World Bank. All data are for 2002. Used with permission from World Bank Publications.*

consequences spread across the globe in 2009 with high unemployment, rising bankruptcy rates, and declining economic output. The Asian crisis of 1997, in which the banking systems of Thailand and Indonesia collapsed, had a similar, although less far-reaching, impact. Similarly, Russia's default on its bonds in August 1998 caused a significant deterioration in the Russian economy. Without a stable, smoothly functioning financial system, no country can prosper.

The strong relationship between financial development and economic development is clearly apparent from the data. Figure 11.1 plots a commonly used measure of financial activity—the ratio of credit extended to the private sector (both through financial intermediaries and markets) to Gross Domestic Product (GDP)—against real GDP per capita. The resulting strong correlation, nearly 0.8., is no surprise. There aren't any rich countries that have very low levels of financial development.

In theory, the market system may seem neat and simple, but the reality is that economic growth is a messy, chaotic thing. The flow of information among parties in a market system is particularly rife with problems—problems that can derail real growth unless they are addressed properly. In this chapter, we will discuss some of these information problems and learn how financial intermediaries attempt to solve them.

## The Role of Financial Intermediaries

Markets are great when they work. And financial markets are among the most important markets, pricing and allocating economic resources to their most productive uses. But while the performance of financial markets makes headlines, financial intermediaries are almost as important a source of funds for people or businesses.

Table 11.1 on page 229 illustrates the relative importance of these two types of finance. As you look at the table, note two things. First, to make comparisons across countries of vastly different size and across time we measure everything relative to GDP. Second, there is no reason that the value of a country's stock market, bonds outstanding, or bank loans cannot be bigger than its GDP. In fact, we would expect

**Table 11.1**   The Relative Importance of Direct and Indirect Finance

| | 1990 | | | |
|---|---|---|---|---|
| | **Direct Finance** | | **Indirect Finance** | |
| | **Stock Market Capitalization as Percent of GDP** | **Outstanding Domestic Debt Securities as Percent of GDP** | **Credit Extended by FIs as Percent of GDP** | **Ratio of indirect to Direct Finance C/(A+B)** |
| **Country** | **(A)** | **(B)** | **(C)** | **(D)** |
| **Industrialized Countries** | | | | |
| Canada | 47 | 13 | 88 | 1.47 |
| France | 28 | 46 | 89 | 1.20 |
| United States | 57 | 70 | 117 | 0.92 |
| **Emerging Markets Countries** | | | | |
| Argentina | 3 | 0.4 | 13 | 3.82 |
| Brazil (1992) | 11 | 1.2 | 27 | 2.21 |
| India | 10 | 0.2 | 24 | 2.35 |
| | 2007 | | | |
| | **Direct Finance** | | **Indirect Finance** | |
| | **Stock Market Capitalization as Percent of GDP** | **Outstanding Domestic Debt Securities as Percent of GDP** | **Credit Extended by FIs as Percent of GDP** | **Ratio of indirect to Direct Finance C/(A+B)** |
| **Country** | **(A)** | **(B)** | **(C)** | **(D)** |
| **Industrialized Countries** | | | | |
| Canada | 147 | 30 | 157 | 0.89 |
| France | 102 | 48 | 100 | 0.67 |
| United States | 144 | 125 | 202 | 0.75 |
| **Emerging Markets Countries** | | | | |
| Argentina | 0.3 | 6 | 12 | 1.90 |
| Brazil | 79 | 17 | 44 | 0.46 |
| India | 112 | 43 | 43 | 0.28 |

Note that numbers in columns A, B, and C are as a percentage of GDP. Since these are not components of GDP, there is no reason they should add to 100. Domestic securities include private but not public (i.e., government) bonds.

SOURCE: "A new database on financial development and structure," *World Bank Policy Paper*, by Beck, Thorsten; Demirguc-Kunt, Asli; Levine, Ross. Copyright 1999 and 2008 by World Bank. Reproduced with permission of World Bank in the format Textbook via Copyright Clearance Center.

it to be much larger, as the value of a company to its owners is normally quite a bit more than one year's sales. This means that when you add up all the types of financing, direct and indirect, the numbers will generally sum to more than 100.

To see the lessons from the data in the table, take the example of Canada in 1990 in the first row. The value of the Canadian stock market was equivalent to roughly 47 percent of Canadian GDP (column A); the value of Canadian private debt securities, about 13 percent of GDP (column B). Adding columns A and B tells us that in Canada, direct finance equalled about 60 percent of GDP. But the credit extended by Canadian banks and other financial intermediaries was equivalent to nearly 90 percent of the country's GDP (column C). The final column, D, reports the ratio of indirect to direct finance. For Canada, the result is 1.47, which means that indirect finance was roughly one and one-half times the size of direct finance. But now look at the lower half of the table. In 2007, the size of the stock market relative to the economy had tripled. (By the end of 2008, the stock market had fallen about 35 percent from the end of 2007, but if you reduced the amount of market capitalization by one-third, the stock market would still be much larger relative to GDP than it was in 1990.) Similarly, the bond market had more than doubled relative to GDP (column B), and the scale of credit provided by financial intermediaries had nearly doubled (column C). The data show that the role of both direct and indirect finance grew significantly over the last 30 years, with direct finance growing more rapidly than indirect finance.

The trends that shaped financial systems in industrialized countries also led to changes in emerging market economies. First, notice that in 1990 credit from financial institutions dominated the sources of funds, although they played a much smaller role in those economies than in the industrialized countries. But there were dramatic changes between 1990 and 2007. Most remarkable was the shift in equity finance in India, but in each country (the data for Brazil aren't available until 1992) the share of the bond market increased. As in the industrialized countries, direct and indirect finance both grew relative to the size of the economy, but direct finance grew more rapidly.

To summarize, the data show that historically businesses have received the majority of their external funds through loans from financial intermediaries rather than from direct sources such as the bond market or the stock market. Over time, and as economies develop, financial markets play a larger role, but in most industrialized economies financial intermediaries are large and growing relative to GDP. What accounts for this pattern of financing? In earlier chapters we focused on the markets, but here we ask why financial intermediaries are so important.

The answer has to do with information. To understand the importance of information in the role financial intermediaries play in the economy, consider the online company eBay. This virtual auction house may seem an unlikely place to start, but although eBay deals primarily with physical objects, it faces some of the same information problems as financial firms. As an online intermediary, eBay provides a mechanism through which almost anyone can auction off almost anything. At any time, upward of 100 million items are for sale at www.ebay.com—everything from $5 dinner plates to $3 million vacation homes. And people buy them! In a single year, eBay reports total transactions valued at over $60 billion, entered into by nearly 100 million active users worldwide.

While millions of items are for sale on eBay, if you look carefully you'll notice an absence of financial products. You can purchase collectible coins and paper currency on eBay, but you can't borrow. There are no listings for Samantha's student loan, Chad's car loan, Chloe's credit card balance, or Mike's mortgage—at least, not yet. And though you can buy defaulted bond certificates, you can't buy or sell bonds on which the issuer is still making payments. People are selling cars and even real estate on eBay, but no one

## APPLYING THE CONCEPT
### HELPING THE POOR WITH MICROFINANCE

Over 40 percent of the world's population lives in extreme poverty with income of less than $2 per day. Many of the more fortunate among us have a clear desire to help, so we have organized grants and loans to the governments in South Asia, Sub-Saharan Africa, and East Asia where these people live. This hasn't worked well. Instead of building institutions capable of supporting productive economic activity, funds have either been diverted into projects that aid very few of a country's inhabitants or are simply stolen outright by corrupt bureaucrats and leaders.

Attempts at traditional bank lending have failed as well. It cost too much to lend to poor households. They saved too little to repay loans and had no collateral to pledge in the case of default. In the end, the poor have remained very poor. In India and Bangladesh alone there are still more than 400 million people living on less than $1 per day.

Recently, a new type of financial institution has developed. Started in Bangladesh in the late 1970s, these banks lend directly to the poor in very tiny amounts. Loans as small as $75 repaid over several months or a year are made with no collateral. Borrowers use the funds to support self-employment activities for things like buying materials to produce bamboo furniture. Critically, the typical borrower is a group rather than an individual. The members of the group are collectively responsible for the repayment. Collective responsibility helps overcome the information asymmetries—adverse selection and moral hazard problems—that plague lending agreements. And while real interest rates of 20 percent plus are needed to cover the fixed costs of making and monitoring the loan, repayment rates are typically over 90 percent.

By 2005, the World Bank estimated that there were 7,000 microfinance institutions serving 16 million people. The oldest of these is the Grameen Bank in Bangladesh, which, along with its founder Professor Muhammad Yunus, was awarded the 2006 Nobel Peace Prize. In 2008, the last year for which data are available, Grameen reported making nearly $1 billion in loans to over 7 million borrowers. Repayment rates are 98 percent, and in a culturally conservative, traditionally male-dominated country, 97 percent of borrowers are women.

Some people have noted that microfinance institutions are unlikely to be profitable. In fact, the Banco Solidario in Bolivia that runs on a for-profit basis has moved away from small loans and now focuses on automobile and mortgage lending—bigger, collateralized loans. But maybe microfinance shouldn't be about turning a profit in a conventional sense. Instead it should be the focus of aid that the more fortunate among us provide to the billions of desparately poor people who do not have access to the traditional financial system. Today microfinance institutions are helping people not only in Bangladesh and Bolivia, but also in China, Ethiopia, Honduras, Thailand, and even in parts of the United States. And while it is too early to tell conclusively, there are indications that small loans have contributed to lower rates of poverty as well as healthier and better educated children.

is auctioning off chequing account services. (There are hints that this may be changing. See the In the News: Lenders, Borrowers Hook up Over the Web on page 246.)

Think for a moment about why eBay doesn't auction mortgages. First, Mike might need a $100,000 mortgage, and not many people can finance a mortgage of that size. The people who run eBay could try to establish a system in which 100 people sign up to lend Mike $1,000, but it would be extremely complex and cumbersome. Imagine collecting the payments, figuring out how to repay the lenders, and writing all the legal contracts that go with the transaction. Just as importantly, before offering to finance Mike's mortgage, lenders would want to know something about Mike and the house he's proposing to buy. Is Mike accurately representing his ability to repay the loan? Does he really intend to buy a house with the loan? The questions are nearly endless, and answering them is both difficult and time consuming.

Financial intermediaries exist so that individual lenders don't have to worry about getting answers to all of these questions. Most people take for granted the ability of the financial system to shift resources from savers to investors, but when you look closely at the details, you're struck by how complicated the task is. It's amazing the enterprise works at all. Lending and borrowing involve both *transactions costs*, like the cost of writing a loan contract, and *information costs*, like the cost of figuring out whether a borrower is trustworthy. Financial institutions exist to reduce these costs.

| Table 11.2 | A Summary of the Role of Financial Intermediaries |
|---|---|
| 1. *Pooling savings* | Accepting resources from a large number of small savers/lenders in order to provide large loans to borrowers. |
| 2. *Safekeeping and accounting* | Keeping depositors' savings safe, giving them access to the payments system, and providing them with accounting statements that help them to track their income and expenditures. |
| 3. *Providing liquidity* | Allowing depositors to transform their financial assets into money quickly, easily, and at low cost. |
| 4. *Diversifying risk* | Providing investors with the ability to diversify even small investments. |
| 5. *Collecting and processing information services* | Generating large amounts of standardized financial information. |

In their role as financial intermediaries, financial institutions perform five functions (see Table 11.2): (1) pooling the resources of small savers; (2) providing safekeeping and accounting services, as well as access to the payments system; (3) supplying liquidity by converting savers' balances directly into a means of payment whenever needed; (4) providing ways to diversify risk; and (5) collecting and processing information in ways that reduce information costs. As we go through these, you'll see that the first four have to do with lowering transactions costs. That is, by specializing and providing these services to large numbers of customers, a financial firm can reduce the cost of providing them to individual customers. As in other fields, experts can do a better job than others, and more cheaply at that. The fifth function on the list, collecting and processing information, is a category all by itself, so we'll consider it in more detail.

While we will not discuss the international role of banks in very much depth, banks also handle transactions that cross international borders. That may mean taking deposits from savers in one country and providing them to investors in another country. It may also mean converting currencies in order to facilitate transactions for customers who do business or travel abroad.

## Pooling Savings

The most straightforward economic function of a financial intermediary is to pool the resources of many small savers. By accepting many small deposits, banks empower themselves to make large loans. So, for example, Mike might get his $100,000 mortgage from a bank or finance company with access to a large group of savers, 100 of whom have $1,000 to invest (see Figure 11.2). Similarly, a government or large company that wishes to borrow billions of dollars by issuing bonds will rely on a financial intermediary to find buyers for the bonds.

To succeed in this endeavour—pooling people's savings in order to make large loans—the intermediary must attract substantial numbers of savers. This is the essence of indirect finance, and it means convincing potential depositors of the institution's soundness. Banks are particularly adept at making sure customers feel that their funds will be safe. In the past, they did so by installing large safes in imposing bank buildings. Today, they rely on their reputations, as well as on government guarantees such as deposit insurance. We'll return to this topic in Chapter 14.

**Figure 11.2**   Financial Intermediaries Pool Savings

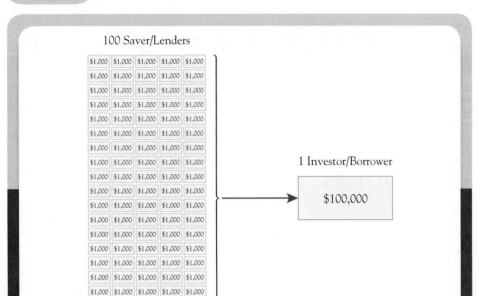

Financial intermediaries pool the funds of many small savers and lend them to one large borrower.

## Safekeeping, Payments System Access, and Accounting

Goldsmiths were the original bankers. To keep their gold and jewellery safe, they had to construct vaults. Soon people began asking the goldsmiths to store gold for them in return for a receipt to prove it was there. It didn't take long for someone to realize that trading the goldsmith's receipts was easier than trading the gold itself. The next step came when the goldsmith noticed that there was quite a bit of gold left in the vault at the end of the day, so that some of it could safely be lent to others. The goldsmiths took the resources of those with gold to spare—the savers of the day—and channelled them to individuals who were short— the borrowers. Today, banks are the places where we put things for safekeeping—not just gold and jewellery, but also our financial wealth. We deposit our paycheques and entrust our savings to a bank or other financial institution because we believe it will keep our resources safe until we need them.

When we think of banks, safekeeping is only one of several services that immediately come to mind. The others are automated teller machines, chequebooks, and monthly bank statements. In providing depositors with access to ATMs, credit and debit cards, cheques, and monthly statements, a bank gives them access to the payments system—the network that transfers funds from the account of one person or business to the account of another. The bank provides

The door to the largest gold vault in the world at the Federal Reserve Bank of New York. The only entry is through a 10-foot passageway cut into a 9-foot high, 90-ton steel cylinder that rotates 90 degrees to open and close the vault. Many governments keep their gold here.

SOURCE: © *Courtesy of the Federal Reserve Bank of New York.*

## YOUR FINANCIAL WORLD
### Your First Credit Card

Credit card interest rates are outrageous, running to over 30 percent in some cases (really)! Your Financial World: Pay Off Your Credit Card Debt as Fast as You Can on page 73 discussed how expensive borrowing can be and demonstrated why you should pay off your credit card debt as quickly as possible. The odds are, when you get your first credit card, the interest rate will be extremely high. Why?

Unless your parent signed your credit card papers (or you worked a steady job before starting college or university), as a student you have no credit history, and the company that issued the card will assume the worst. So you're lumped in with people who have very poor credit, who would rather get lower-interest loans elsewhere but can't. This is adverse selection at its worst. When you get your first credit card, the assumption is that you are in a group of people who will have a high default rate. No wonder the issuers charge high interest rates. It is compensation for the risk they are taking. And just to prove the point, this is not a very profitable business.*

You need a credit card to build up a credit history, to establish yourself as a person who repays loans promptly. After a while, you'll be able to get a new card at a lower interest rate. But in the meantime, remember that your interest rate is extremely high, so borrowing is very expensive.

*Victor Stango and Jonathan Zinman's study "What Do Consumers Really Pay on Their Checking and Credit Card Accounts? Explicit, Implicit and Avoidable Costs," *American Economic Review*, 44, No. 2 (May 2009), pp. 424–29, notes that many consumer pay unnecessary fees.

depositors a way to get cash into their wallets and to finalize payments using credit cards, debit cards, and cheques. And since banks specialize in handling payments transactions, they can offer all these services relatively cheaply. Financial intermediaries reduce the costs of financial transactions.

This is not a trivial matter. It would be a disaster if we didn't have a convenient way to pay for things. By giving us one, financial intermediaries facilitate the exchange of goods and services, promoting specialization. Remember that in efficient economies—those that manage to get the most output from a given set of inputs—people and companies concentrate on the activities at which they are best and for which their opportunity cost is lowest. This principle of comparative advantage leads to specialization so that each of us ends up doing just one job and being paid in some form of money. But as specialization increases, more and more trading must take place to ensure that most of us end up with the goods and services we need and want. The more trading, the more financial transactions, and the more financial transactions, the more important it is that those transactions be cheap. If getting hold of money and using it to make payments were costly, that would surely put a damper on people's willingness to specialize. Financial intermediaries, by providing us with a reliable and inexpensive payments system, help our economy to function more efficiently.

Beyond safekeeping and access to the payments system, financial intermediaries provide bookkeeping and accounting services. They help us to manage our finances. Just think about your financial transactions over the past few months. If you work, you were paid, probably more than once. If you rent an apartment or own a home, you paid the rent or mortgage and probably the electric and gas bills. You paid your phone bill. Then there's transportation. If you have a car, you may have made a loan payment. You surely paid for gasoline and possibly for a repair. You purchased food too, both at the grocery store and in various restaurants. And don't forget the movies and books you bought. As you get older, you may shoulder the expense of having children, along with saving for their education and your retirement. The point is, our financial lives are extraordinarily complex, and we need help keeping track of them. Financial intermediaries do the job: They provide us with bookkeeping and accounting services, noting all our transactions for us and making our lives more tolerable in the process.

Before we continue, we should note that providing safekeeping and accounting services, as well as access to the payments system, forces financial intermediaries to write legal contracts. Writing individualized contracts to ensure that each customer will maintain a chequing account balance as required, or repay a loan as promised, would be extremely costly. But a financial intermediary can hire a lawyer to write one very high-quality contract that can be used over and over again, thus reducing the cost of each use. In fact, much of what financial intermediaries do takes advantage of what are known as economies of scale, in which the average cost of producing a good or service falls as the quantity produced increases. As we will see later, information is subject to economies of scale just as other goods and services are.

## Providing Liquidity

One function that is related to access to the payments system is the provision of liquidity. Recall from Chapter 2 that liquidity is a measure of the ease and cost with which an asset can be turned into a means of payment. When a financial asset can be transformed into money quickly, easily, and at low cost, it is said to be very liquid. Financial intermediaries offer us the ability to transform assets into money at relatively low cost. That's what ATMs are all about—converting deposit balances into cash on demand.

Financial intermediaries provide liquidity in a way that is both efficient and beneficial to all of us. To understand the process, think about your bank. Two kinds of customers come through the doors: those with funds, who want to make deposits, and those in need of funds, who want to take out loans. Depositors want easy access to their funds—not just the currency they withdraw every week or so but the larger amounts they may need in an emergency. Borrowers don't want to pay the funds back for a while, and they certainly can't be expected to repay the entire amount on short notice.

In the same way that an insurance company knows that not all its policyholders will have automobile accidents on the same day, a bank knows that not all its depositors will experience an emergency and need to withdraw funds at the same time. The bank can structure its assets accordingly, keeping enough funds in short-term, liquid financial instruments to satisfy the few people who will need them and lending out the rest. And since long-term loans usually have higher interest rates than short-term money market instruments—for instance, commercial paper and Government of Canada treasury bills—the bank can offer depositors a higher interest rate than they would get otherwise.

Even the bank's short-term investments will do better than an individual depositors could, because the bank can take advantage of economies of scale to lower its transactions costs. It isn't much more expensive to buy a $1 million government of Canada treasury bill than it is to buy a Canada Savings Bond worth only $1,000. By collecting funds from a large number of small investors, the bank can reduce the cost of their combined investment, offering each individual investor both liquidity and high rates of return. Pooling large numbers of small accounts in this way is very efficient. By doing so, an intermediary offers depositors something they can't get from the financial markets on their own.

The liquidity services financial intermediaries provide go beyond fast and easy access to account balances. Intermediaries offer both individuals and businesses lines of credit, which are similar to overdraft protection for chequing accounts. A line of credit is essentially a preapproved loan that can be drawn on whenever a customer needs funds. Home equity lines of credit, credit card cash advances, and business lines of credit are examples. Like a deposit account, the line of credit provides a customer with access to liquidity, except that in this case withdrawals may exceed deposit balances. To offer this service profitably, a financial intermediary must specialize in liquidity management. That is, it must design its balance sheet so that it can sustain sudden withdrawals.

## Diversifying Risk

If you had $1,000 or $10,000 or even $100,000 to invest, would you want to keep it all in one place? Would you be willing to lend it all to a single person or firm? Since by now you have read Chapter 5, you know the answer to this question: Don't put all your eggs in one basket, it's unnecessarily risky. But even without knowing much about diversifying through hedging and spreading risk, you would sense intuitively that lending $1 to each of 1,000 borrowers is less risky than lending $1,000 to just one borrower, and putting $1 in each of 1,000 different stocks is safer than putting $1,000 in one stock. Financial institutions enable us to diversify our investments and reduce risk.

Banks mitigate risk in a straightforward way: They take deposits from thousands or even millions of individuals and make thousands of loans with them. Thus, each depositor has a very small stake in each one of the loans. For example, a bank might collect $1,000 from each of one million depositors and then use the resulting $1 billion to make 10,000 loans of $100,000 each. So each depositor has a 1/1,000,000 share in each of the 10,000 loans.

To picture this, look back at Figure 11.2 on page 233 and imagine that it shows 10,000 times as many deposits and 10,000 times as many mortgages. Next, picture each of those deposits cut up into 10,000 pieces, each assigned to a different loan. That is, each deposit contributes 10 cents to each loan. That's diversification! And since the bank specializes in taking deposits and making loans, it can minimize the cost of setting up all the necessary legal contracts to do this.

All financial intermediaries provide a low-cost way for individuals to diversify their investments. Mutual fund companies offer small investors a low-cost way to purchase a diversified portfolio of stocks and eliminate the idiosyncratic risk associated with any single investment. Many of the mutual funds based on the Standard & Poor's 500 index (described in Chapter 8) require a minimum investment of as little as a few thousand dollars. Since the average price of each stock in the index usually runs between $30 and $40, a small investor would need over $15,000 to buy even a single share of stock in each of the 500 companies in the index (not to mention the fees the investor would need to pay to a broker to do it). Thus, the mutual fund company lets a small investor buy a fraction of a share in each of the 500 companies in the fund. And since mutual fund companies specialize in this activity, the cost remains low.

## Collecting and Processing Information

One of the biggest problems individual savers face is figuring out which potential borrowers are trustworthy and which are not. Most of us do not have the time or skill to collect and process information on a wide array of potential borrowers. And we are understandably reluctant to invest in activities about which we have little reliable information. The fact that the borrower knows whether he or she is trustworthy, while the lender faces substantial costs to obtain the same information, results in an *information asymmetry*. Very simply, borrowers have information that lenders don't.

By collecting and processing standardized information, financial intermediaries reduce the problems information asymmetries create. They screen loan applicants to guarantee that they are creditworthy. They monitor loan recipients to ensure that they use the funds as they have claimed they will. To understand how this process works, and the implications it has for the financial system, we need to study information asymmetries in more detail.

## Information Asymmetries and Information Costs

Information plays a central role in the structure of financial markets and financial institutions. Markets require sophisticated information to work well; when the cost of obtaining that information is too high, markets cease to function. Information costs make the financial markets, as important as they are, among the worst functioning of all markets. The fact is, the issuers of financial instruments—borrowers who want to issue bonds and firms that want to issue stock—know much more about their business prospects and their willingness to work than potential lenders or investors—those who would buy their bonds and stocks. This asymmetric information is a serious hindrance to the operation of financial markets. Solving this problem is one key to making our financial system work as well as it does.

eBay's feedback rating system awards +1 point for each positive comment, 0 points for each neutral comment, and −1 point for each negative comment.

SOURCE: *eBay*

To understand the nature of the problem and the possible solutions, let's go back to eBay. Why are the people who win online auctions willing to send payments totalling $50 billion a year to the sellers? An amazing amount of trust is involved in these transactions. To bid at all, buyers must believe that an item has been described accurately. And winners must be sure that the seller will send the item in exchange for their payments, because the normal arrangement is for the seller to be paid first.

How can buyers be sure they won't be disappointed by their purchases when they arrive, assuming they arrive at all? The fact that sellers have much more information about the items they are selling and their own reliability creates an information asymmetry. Aware of this problem, the people who started eBay took two steps. First, they offered insurance to protect buyers who don't receive their purchases. Second, they devised a feedback forum to collect and store information about both bidders and sellers. Anyone can read the comments posted in the forum or check an overall rating that summarizes their content. Sellers who develop good reputations in the feedback forum command higher prices than others; buyers who develop bad reputations can be banned from bidding. Without this means of gathering information, eBay probably could not have been successful. Together, the buyers' insurance and the feedback forum make eBay run smoothly.[1]

---

[1] A low-cost, reliable payments system helps, too. The easier it is for buyers to pay sellers, the more likely both are to use the auction site. Realizing the need for a payments system, eBay users created *PayPal*, which allows buyers and sellers to set up electronic accounts through which to make and receive payments for their eBay transactions. Since many sellers are too small to take credit cards, this innovation greatly facilitated the online exchanges. Initially an independent concern, PayPal became so central to eBay's success that the auction site's owners bought it.

The two problems eBay faced arise in financial markets, too. In fact, information problems are the key to understanding the structure of our financial system and the central role of financial intermediaries. Asymmetric information poses two important obstacles to the smooth flow of funds from savers to investors. The first, called **adverse selection**, arises before the transaction occurs. Just as buyers on eBay need to know the relative trustworthiness of sellers, lenders need to know how to distinguish good credit risks from bad. The second problem, called moral hazard, occurs after the transaction. In the same way that buyers on eBay need reassurance that sellers will deliver their purchases after receiving payment, lenders need to find a way to tell whether borrowers will use the proceeds of a loan as they claim they will. The following sections will look at both these problems in detail to see how they affect the structure of the financial system, and how financial intermediaries help to address the problems of asymmetric information.

## Adverse Selection

Used Cars: Clean, reliable, and priced just right!

SOURCE: © *Frank Saragnese/Getty Images*

The 2001 Nobel Prize in Economics was awarded to George A. Akerlof, A. Michael Spence, and Joseph E. Stiglitz "for their analyses of markets with asymmetric information." Professor Akerlof's contribution came first, in a paper published in 1970 titled "The Market for Lemons."[2] Akerlof's paper explained why the market for used cars—some of which may be "lemons"—doesn't function very well. Here's the logic.

Suppose the used-car market has only two cars for sale, both 2004 model Honda Accords. One is immaculate, having been driven and maintained by a careful elderly woman who didn't travel much. The second car belonged to a young man who got it from his parents, loved to drive fast, and did not worry about the damage he might cause if he hit a pothole. The owners of these two cars know whether their own cars are in good repair, but used-car shoppers do not.

Let's say that potential buyers are willing to pay $15,000 for a well-maintained car, but only $7,500 for a "lemon"—a car with lots of mechanical problems. The elderly woman knows her car is a "peach." It's in good condition and she won't part with it for less than $12,500. The young man, knowing the poor condition of his car, will take $6,000 for it. But if buyers can't tell the difference between the two cars, without more information they will pay only the average price of $11,250. (A risk-averse buyer wouldn't even pay that much.) That is less than the owner of the good car will accept, so she won't sell her car and it disappears from the market. The problem is that if buyers are willing to pay only the average value of all the cars on the market, sellers with cars in above-average condition won't put their cars up for sale. Only the worst cars, the lemons, will be left on the market.

Information asymmetries aside, people like to buy new cars, and when they do, they sell their old cars. People who can't afford new cars, or who would rather not pay for them, are looking to buy good used cars. Together, these potential buyers and sellers of used cars provide a substantial incentive for creative people to solve the problem of adverse selection in the used-car market. Some companies try to help buyers separate the peaches from the lemons. For instance, *Consumer Reports* provides information

---

[2] See "The Market for 'Lemons': Quality Uncertainty and the Market Mechanism," *Quarterly Journal of Economics* (August 1970) Vol. 84, No. 3 pp. 488–500. This paper contains very little mathematics and is quite readable. You can find it through your university library using an electronic storage system called JSTOR.

about the reliability and safety of particular makes and models. Car dealers may try to maintain their reputations by refusing to pass off a clunker as a well-maintained car. For a fee, a mechanic will check out a used car for a potential buyer, and Internet services will provide a report on its accident history. Finally, many car manufacturers offer warranties on the used cars they have certified. We have found ways to overcome the information problems pointed out by Professor Akerlof, and, as a result, both good and bad used cars sell at prices much closer to their true value.

**Adverse Selection in Financial Markets**   When it comes to information costs, financial markets are not that different from the used-car market. In the same way that the seller of a used car knows more about the car than the buyer, potential borrowers know more about the projects they wish to finance than prospective lenders do. And in the same way that information asymmetries can drive good cars out of the used-car market, they can drive good stocks and bonds out of the financial market. To see why, let's start with stocks.

Think about a simple case in which there are two firms, one with good prospects and one with bad prospects. If you can't tell the difference between the two firms, you will be willing to pay a price based only on their average quality. The stock of the good company will be undervalued. Since the managers know their stock is worth more than the average price, they won't issue it in the first place. That leaves only the firm with bad prospects in the market. And since most investors aren't interested in companies with poor prospects, the market is very unlikely to get started at all.

The same thing happens in the bond market. Remember that risk requires compensation. The higher the risk, the greater the risk premium. In the bond market, this relationship between risk and return affects the cost of borrowing. The more risky the borrower, the higher the cost of borrowing. If a lender can't tell whether a borrower is a good or bad credit risk, the lender will demand a risk premium based on the average risk. Borrowers who know they are good credit risks won't want to borrow at this elevated interest rate, so they will withdraw from the market, leaving only the bad credit risks. The result is the same as for used cars and stocks: Since lenders are not eager to buy bonds issued by bad credit risks, the market will disappear.

## Solving the Adverse Selection Problem

From a social perspective, the fact that managers might avoid issuing stock or bonds because they know the market will not value their company correctly is not good. It means that the company will pass up some good investments. And since some of the best investments will not be undertaken, the economy won't grow as rapidly as it could. Thus it is extremely important to find ways for investors and lenders to distinguish well-run firms from poorly run firms. Well-run firms need to highlight their quality so they can obtain financing more cheaply. Investors need to distinguish between high- and low-risk investments so they can adjust their expected rates of return. The question is how to do it.

Recall how buyers and sellers in the used-car market developed ways to address the problem of distinguishing good from bad cars? The answer here is similar. First, since the problem is caused by a lack of information, we can create more information for investors. Second, we can provide guarantees in the form of financial contracts that can be written so a firm's owners suffer together with the people who invested in the company if the firm does poorly; requiring collateral for a loan or requiring that firms have equity in a project are examples of this approach. This type of arrangement helps to persuade investors that a firm's stocks and bonds are of high quality.

**Disclosure of Information**   One obvious way to solve the problem created by asymmetric information is to generate more information. This can be done in one of two ways, government-required disclosure and the private collection and production of information. In most industrialized countries, public companies—those that issue stocks and bonds that are bought and sold in public financial markets—are required to disclose voluminous amounts of information. For example, the Ontario Securities Commission requires firms to produce public financial statements that are prepared according to standard accounting practices. Corporations are also required to disclose, on an ongoing basis, information that could have a bearing on the value of their firms and to release to the public any information they provide to professional stock analysts.

As we learned in 2001 and 2002, however, these requirements can go only so far in assuring that investors are well informed. Despite government regulations designed to protect investors, Enron, WorldCom, Global Crossing, and numerous other companies managed to distort the profits and debt levels published in their financial statements. With the help of some unethical accountants, company executives found a broad range of ways to manipulate the statements to disguise their firms' true financial condition. As a result, most of us now suspect that public financial statements are virtually meaningless. While accounting practices have changed since then and financial statements may now convey more information than they once did, everyone remains on guard. Information problems persist.

What about the private collection and sale of information? You might think that this would provide investors with what they need to solve the adverse selection problem, but unfortunately it doesn't work. While it is in everyone's interest to produce credible proof of the quality of a company's activities, such information doesn't really exist. In a limited sense there is private information collected and sold to investors. Various research services such as Moody's, Value Line, and Dun and Bradstreet collect information directly from firms and produce evaluations.

These reports are not cheap. For example, Value Line charges $600 a year for its weekly publication. To be credible, the companies examined can't pay for the research themselves, so investors have to. And while some individuals might be willing to pay, in the end they don't have to and so they won't. Private information services face what is called a free-rider problem. A **free rider** is someone who doesn't pay the cost to get the benefit of a good or service, and free riding on stock market analysis is easy to do. Even though these publications are expensive, public libraries subscribe to some of them. Reporters for *The Wall Street Journal* and *Financial Post* and other periodicals read them and write stories publicizing crucial information. And individual investors can simply follow the lead of people they know who subscribe to the publications. Of course, all these practices reduce the ability of the producers of private information to actually profit from their hard work.

Financial intermediaries have particular abilities to obtain information. To get a loan, whether from a bank, a mortgage company, or a finance company, you must fill out an application. As part of the process, you will be asked to supply your social insurance number. The lender uses the number to identify you to a company that collects and analyzes credit information, summarizing it for potential lenders in a credit score.

Your personal credit score (described in Your Financial World: Your Credit Rating on page 139) tells a lender how likely you are to repay a loan. It is analogous to eBay's feedback forum rating or to an expert appraiser's certification of the authenticity and condition of an original painting. The credit rating company screens you and then *certifies* your credit rating. If you are a good credit risk with a high credit score, you are more likely than others to get a loan at a relatively low interest rate. Note that the company that collects your credit information and produces your credit score charges a fee each time someone wants to see it. This overcomes the free-rider problem.

Banks can collect information on a borrower that goes beyond what a loan application or credit report contains. By noting the pattern of deposits and withdrawals from your account, as well as your use of your debit card if you have one, they can learn more about you than you might like. Banks monitor both their individual and their business customers in this way. Again, the information they collect is easy to protect and use. The special information banks have puts them in an almost unique position to screen customers and reduce the costs of adverse selection. This expertise helps to explain another phenomenon, the fact that most small and medium-sized businesses depend on banks for their financing.

In the financial world, RBC Dominion and TD Securities have as much brand recognition as Coke does in the soft drink world.

SOURCE: © Michael Schwartz /The Image Works

Financial intermediaries' superior ability to screen and certify borrowers extends beyond loan making to the issuance of bonds and equity. Underwriters—such as RBC Dominion and TD Securities—screen and certify firms seeking to raise funds directly in the financial markets. Without certification by one of these firms, companies would find it difficult to raise funds. Investment banks go to great lengths to market their expertise as underwriters; they want people to recognize their names the world over, just as everyone recognizes Coca-Cola. A can of Coke, the best-selling soft drink in the world, is instantly recognizable, whether the fine print is in English, Chinese, Arabic, or Swedish. Financial institutions have applied this concept, which marketing people call branding, to their certification of financial products. If BMO Nesbitt Burns, a well-known securities firm, is willing to sell a bond or stock, the brand name suggests it must be a high-quality investment.

**Collateral and Net Worth**    Although government-required disclosure and private information collection are crucial, they haven't solved all the information problems that plague investors and the firms they invest in. Fortunately, other solutions exist. One is to make sure that lenders are compensated even if borrowers default. If a loan is insured in some way, then the borrower isn't a bad credit risk.

There are two mechanisms for ensuring that a borrower is likely to repay a lender: collateral and net worth. Recall from Chapter 3 that collateral is something of value pledged by a borrower to the lender in the event of the borrower's default. Collateral is said to back or secure a loan. Houses serve as collateral for mortgages; cars as collateral for car loans. If the borrower fails to keep up with the mortgage or car payments, the lender will take possession of the house or car and sell it to recover the borrowed funds. In circumstances like these, adverse selection is not much of a concern; that's why collateral is so prevalent in loan agreements. Loans that are made without collateral—unsecured loans, such as credit card debt—generally involve very high interest rates. Adverse selection is the reason.

Net worth is the owner's stake in a firm, the value of the firm's assets minus the value of its liabilities. Under many circumstances, net worth serves the same purpose as collateral. If a firm defaults on a loan, the lender can make a claim against the firm's net worth. Consider what would happen if a firm with a high net worth borrowed to undertake a project that turned out to be unsuccessful. If the firm had no net worth, the lender would be out of luck. Instead, the firm's owners can use their net worth to repay the lender.

The same is true of a home mortgage. A mortgage is much easier and cheaper to get when a homebuyer makes a substantial down payment. For the lender, the risk is that the price of the home will fall, in which case its value will be insufficient to fully compensate the lender in the event of a default. But with a large down payment, the homeowner has a substantial stake in the house, so even if the price falls, the mortgage can likely be repaid even if the borrower defaults. From the perspective of the mortgage lender, the homeowner's equity serves exactly the same function as net worth in a business loan.

The importance of net worth in reducing adverse selection is the reason owners of new businesses have so much difficulty borrowing money. If you want to start a bakery, for example, you will need financing to buy equipment and cover the rent and payroll for the first few months. Such seed money is very hard to get. Most small business owners must put up their homes and other property as collateral for their business loans. Only after they have managed to establish a successful business, and have built up some net worth in it, can they borrow without pledging their personal property.

## Moral Hazard

The phrase **moral hazard** originated when economists who were studying insurance noted that an insurance policy changes the behaviour of the person who is insured. Examples are everywhere. A fire insurance policy written for more than the value of the property might induce the owner to arson; a generous automobile insurance policy might encourage reckless driving. Employment arrangements suffer from moral hazard, too. How can your boss be sure you are working as hard as you can if you'll get your paycheque at the end of the week whether you do or not? Moral hazard arises when we cannot observe people's actions and so cannot judge whether a poor outcome was intentional or just a result of bad luck.

Thus, a lender's or investor's information problems do not end with adverse selection. A second information asymmetry arises because the borrower knows more than the lender about the way borrowed funds will be used and the effort that will go into a project. Moral hazard plagues both equity and bond financing, making it difficult for all but the biggest, best-known companies to issue either stocks or bonds successfully. Let's look at each type of financing and examine the ways people have tried to solve the problem of moral hazard.

**Moral Hazard in Equity Financing**  If you buy a stock, how do you know the company that issued it will use the funds you have invested in the way that is best for you? The answer is that it almost surely will not. You have given your funds to managers, who will tend to run the company in the way most advantageous to them. The separation of your ownership from their control creates what is called a *principal–agent problem*, which can be more than a little costly to stockholders. Witness the luxurious offices, corporate jets, limousines, and artwork that executives surround themselves with, not to mention the millions of dollars in salary they pay themselves. Managers gain all these personal benefits at the expense of stockholders.

A simple example will illustrate this point. Let's say that your cousin Ina, who is a whiz at writing software, has an idea for a program to speed up wireless Internet access. Together, the two of you estimate she needs $10,000 to write the program and sell it to an interested buyer. But

*"It's been moved and seconded that we fly the company plane to Zurich, split the bank accounts, and go our merry ways."*

Ina has only $1,000 in savings, so you will have to contribute $9,000. Family etiquette dictates that once you've made the investment, you won't be able to monitor Ina's progress—to tell whether she is working hard or even if she is working at all. If everything goes well, you think you can sell the program to Microsoft for $100,000, which is ten times the initial investment. But Ina had better work quickly or someone else may make it to market first and Ina's program won't be worth nearly as much, for example, just $10,000.

The difficulty in this arrangement is immediately apparent. If Ina works hard and all goes according to plan, she will get 10 percent of the $100,000 (that's $10,000) and you will get the rest, a whopping $90,000. But if Ina runs into programming problems or spends part of the time surfing instead of working, someone else may develop the product first, reducing the value of Ina's software to $10,000. The problem is, Ina's decision to go surfing would cost her only $9,000, but it would cost you $81,000! And since you wouldn't be able to tell why the venture failed, you're unlikely to part with your $9,000 in the first place.

**Solving the Moral Hazard Problem in Equity Financing**   Solutions to the moral hazard problem in equity finance are hard to come by. Information on the quality of management can be useful, but only if owners have the power to fire managers—and that can be extremely difficult. Requiring managers to own a significant stake in their own firm is another possibility. If Ina comes up with the entire $10,000, then there is no separation between ownership and control and no question whether Ina will behave in the owner's interest—she is the owner. But people who have good ideas don't always have the resources to pursue them. Ina doesn't have the $10,000 she needs.

During the 1990s, a concerted attempt was made to align managers' interests with those of stockholders. Executives were given stock options that provided lucrative payoffs if a firm's stock price rose above a certain level. This approach worked until managers found ways to misrepresent their companies' profitability, driving up stock prices temporarily so they could cash in their options. In 2008, many policymakers believed that the close tie between salaries and share prices gave U.S. bank CEOs the incentive to take short-term gains at the expense of long-term risks. Accounting methods have been reformed in an attempt to reduce such abuses, but, at this writing, no one has devised a foolproof way of writing contracts that ensure that managers will behave in the owners' interest instead of their own.

Monitoring provides an alternative mechanism to reduce moral hazard. Many financial intermediaries (other than banks) hold significant numbers of shares in individual firms. When they do, they find ways to monitor the companies' activities. For example, the Ontario Municipal Employees Retirement System (OMERS) manages over $50 billion in assets, the income from which is used to pay retired employees' pensions. About 380,000 members of OMERS depend on the fund's managers to carefully monitor its investments. Before buying a company's stock, OMERS managers do a significant amount of research on the firm; once they have purchased the shares, they monitor the firm's activities very closely and sometimes they take a direct role in overseeing management to monitor and protect their investment.

In the case of some new companies, a financial intermediary called a *venture capital firm* does the monitoring. Venture capital firms specialize in investing in risky new ventures in return for a stake in the ownership and a share of the profits. To guard against moral hazard and ensure that

Moral hazard: How can you be sure that your investment isn't being used to buy one of these vacation homes in Tahiti?

SOURCE: © RubberBall Productions

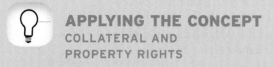

## APPLYING THE CONCEPT
### COLLATERAL AND PROPERTY RIGHTS

Having legal title to physical assets such as land, homes, businesses, and cars is not just about peace of mind. Simple and binding property rights are very important for a healthy financial system. Physical assets can act as collateral for mortgages, auto loans, or business lines of credit.

If you live in a developed country, such as Canada, the United States, or Germany, you take property rights for granted. Most of us assume that every piece of land and building has an owner, and that somewhere there exists a governmental record of who that owner is. Just as importantly, we know that there are clear laws that allow for the sale and transfer of property from one owner to another.

As hard as it may be to imagine, this is not the norm. Much of the world's population lives on land and inside structures that they do not legally own, and to which they have no legal rights. People do this because it is so time consuming and expensive to make their ownership legal. In Haiti, for example, it takes 176 bureaucratic steps over 19 years to gain legal title to a piece of land owned by the government. That's once the Haitian government has decided to sell it. In Egypt it takes 14 years, with visits to 31 public and private agencies. And in Peru, it takes 7 years and 207 steps involving 52 government offices for a private individual to get legal permission to build a house on state-owned land.*

It is fairly obvious that in order to pledge something as collateral, you have to both legally own it and have the ability to transfer that ownership to someone else. So if a person cannot obtain legal title, then the property cannot be used as collateral. Since lenders insist on collateral as insurance in case a borrower defaults, the lack of collateral greatly curtails lending in these countries. Without loans, the financial system cannot do its job of allocating resources to the best possible uses. So, before a country can develop economically, its people need to have property rights.

*These examples are from Hernando De Soto, *The Mystery of Capital: Why Capitalism Triumphs in the West and Fails Everywhere Else* (New York: Basic Books, 2000).

the new company has the best possible chance of success, the venture capitalist keeps a close watch on the managers' actions.

Finally, the threat of a takeover helps to persuade managers to act in the interest of the stockholders. If managers don't do a good job of watching out for shareholders' interests, another company can always buy the firm and replace them. In the 1980s, some firms specialized in such tactics. When the new owners put their own people in charge of the firm, they eliminate the moral hazard problem.

**Moral Hazard in Debt Finance**   When the managers of a company are the owners, the problem of moral hazard in equity financing disappears. This suggests that investors should prefer debt financing to equity financing. But debt financing has its problems, too. Imagine that instead of buying a 90 percent share in your cousin Ina's software venture, you lend her $9,000 at an 11 percent annual interest rate. The debt contract specifies that she will repay you $9,990 in one year's time. This arrangement dramatically changes Ina's incentives. Now, if she works hard, she gets $90,010, but if she goes surfing, she still has to repay the $9,990, leaving her nothing at the end of the year. Surely this solves your problem.

Debt does go a long way toward eliminating the moral hazard problem inherent in equity finance, but it doesn't finish the job. Because debt contracts allow owners to keep all the profits in excess of the loan payments, they encourage risk taking. Suppose Ina decides to use some or all of the $10,000 to buy lottery tickets. That's an extremely risky thing to do. The problem is, if her lottery number comes up, she gets the winnings, but if she loses, you pay the cost. That's not a very desirable outcome for you, the lender. While in the real world the danger isn't quite that extreme, the problem still exists. Lenders need to find ways to make sure borrowers don't take too many risks. Unfortunately, borrowers' limited liability has the same effect that an insurance policy has on the insured. People with risky projects are attracted to debt finance because they get the full benefit of the upside, while the downside is limited to their collateral, if any.

**Solving the Moral Hazard Problem in Debt Finance**   To some degree, a good legal contract can solve the moral hazard problem that is inherent in debt finance. Bonds and loans often carry *restrictive covenants* that limit the amount of risk a borrower can assume. For example, a covenant may restrict the nature of the goods or services the borrower can purchase. It may require the firm to maintain a certain level of net worth, a minimum balance in a bank account, or a minimum credit rating. Home mortgages often come with restrictive covenants requiring the homeowners to purchase fire insurance or to make monthly deposits toward payment of their property taxes. (Failure to pay property taxes can lead the government to seize the borrower's house, complicating the mortgage company's attempt to recover its principal.)

Again, monitoring can reduce the problem of moral hazard. Car dealers provide an interesting example of how monitoring works. Dealers have to finance all those shiny new cars that sit on the lot, waiting for buyers to show up. One way to do this is with a bank loan that is collateralized by the cars themselves. But the bank doesn't completely trust the dealer to use the loan proceeds properly. Every so often, the bank manager will send an associate to count the number of cars on the lot. The count tells the manager whether the dealer is using the borrowed funds properly. In monitoring the dealer this way, the bank is enforcing the restrictive covenants contained in the loan contract. Because banks specialize in this type of monitoring, they can do it more cheaply than individual borrowers and lenders.

Table 11.3 summarizes this section's discussion of how financial relationships are affected by information problems, together with a list of the various solutions used to address the information costs create.

**Table 11.3   The Negative Consequences of Information Costs**

1. Adverse selection. Lenders can't distinguish good from bad credit risks, which discourages transactions from taking place.

*Solutions include*

Government-required information disclosure

Private collection of information

Pledging of collateral to insure lenders against the borrower's default

Requiring borrowers to invest substantial resources of their own

2. Moral hazard. Lenders can't tell whether borrowers will do what they claim they will do with the borrowed resources; borrowers may take too many risks.

*Solutions include*

Requiring managers to report to owners

Requiring managers to invest substantial resources of their own

Covenants that restrict what borrowers can do with borrowed funds

Monitoring the behaviour of the owners

## IN THE NEWS
### Lenders, Borrowers Hook up Over the Web

# Looking to become "an eBay for loans"

**John Greenwood**

**Financial Post**

**April 7, 2007, FP1**

There used to be a joke that bankers operate on the 3-6-3 rule: They pay depositors 3%, lend the money at 6% and get to the golf course by 3 in the afternoon. Now a new company is betting it can shake things up in the banking sector by offering depositors the same rate as borrowers.

CommunityLend is the brainchild of a group of Toronto-based entrepreneurs, including Colin Henderson, the former head of Internet banking at Bank of Montreal, and Michael Garrity, previously vice-president of marketing and sales at Canada Post's online bill-payment division.

"We're just taking advantage of technology that already exists," Mr. Henderson said in a telephone interview. "We think we can be successful."

The idea is that instead of using its own capital like a conventional bank, the company will act as an online marketplace, matching people who need money with others who have excess cash. Borrowers list their requests along with credit information on the CommunityLend Web site and lenders will make bids for the business as part of a competitive auction. "It's an eBay for loans," Mr. Henderson said.

Because CommunityLend has only a small infrastructure—fewer than 20 employees, a Web site and a call centre—its costs are tiny compared with what banks must pay. Those costs will be covered by a small fee on each transaction, Mr. Henderson said. If it all works out as planned, borrowers and lenders will end up with a better deal than they would by going to a bank.

Mr. Henderson and his partners are busy getting the necessary regulatory approvals, but they hope to launch their business by the end of the year. They're hunting for funding from venture capitalists.

In fact, CommunityLend is modelled after two recent startups that are already making waves in other countries. In the United Kingdom, Zopa.com, backed by some of the same investors who funded eBay, has signed up more than 140,000 users after less than two years in business. According to the company, the average interest rate is about 7% and fewer than 1% of borrowers have defaulted, well below the industry norm. Zopa is now laying the groundwork for a U.S. expansion.

The other site is Prosper.com, based in San Francisco. Prosper is similar to Zopa in many respects, except for its focus on borrowers with poor credit, sometimes known as the subprime market. Interest rates range from about 8% to a

## Financial Intermediaries and Information Costs

The problems of adverse selection and moral hazard are particular challenging for direct finance, with the result that it is expensive and difficult to get. These drawbacks lead us immediately to indirect finance and the role of financial institutions. Much of the information that financial intermediaries collect is used to reduce information costs and minimize the effects of adverse selection and moral hazard. To reduce the potential costs of adverse selection, intermediaries screen loan applicants. To minimize moral hazard, they monitor borrowers. And when borrowers fail to live up to their contracts with lenders, financial intermediaries penalize them by enforcing the contracts.

## How Companies Finance Growth and Investment

Before concluding, let's pause and take stock. We began this chapter by noting three things: (1) wealthy countries all have high levels of financial development; (2) indirect finance, through financial intermediaries, is much more important than hefty 29%, and a quick tour of the Web site suggests most of the borrowers may be at the high end.

For instance, Burnelm, 34, is a single mother whose job in real estate has not been going that well. She has set a goal for herself of being debt-free, but before that can happen she needs to borrow $US,4000 for pool repairs. Several lenders have teamed up to do the deal at 22% annual interest.

"Prosper is a marketplace brimming with woe," according to the popular online journal Salon.com, which goes on to liken it to a dating site, where lovelorn singles lay bare their hearts in a bid to generate some attention.

Still, like its U.K. clone, Prosper appears to be flourishing. Launched in February, 2006, the privately held company already has 240,000 users and $US50 million in loans transacted. Both Prosper and Zopa vet borrowers, checking credit ratings and identities. Those who don't pay up must deal with collection agencies.

Mr. Henderson said CommunityLend is modelling itself after Prosper, though he disagrees with the notion he is targeting the subprime market. "Our borrowers will be just normal Canadians looking for an opportunity to get lower rates," he said.

Analysts said it's too early to say whether the company will turn out to be the eBay of the financial services sector, though they concede it is a promising concept.

Darko Mihelic, an analyst at CIBC World Markets, warns that Canadians are conservative in their habits, and are reluctant to switch banks even if they can get a lower rate. That could be a problem for CommunityLend. On the other hand, if the target market is people who get rejected by the big banks for loans then it might be a different story. "In that case, they just might succeed," he said.

## LESSONS OF THE ARTICLE

Will this really work? Will CommunityLend find ways to overcome the adverse selection and moral hazard problems inherent in individual lending arrangements, and replace financial intermediaries? The answer hinges on a number of things. Do credit scores allow lenders to predict default rates accurately enough? Will lenders be able to diversify sufficiently? And finally, is this really more efficient and cheaper than a bank? To take over from financial intermediaries, the answer to all these questions will have to be yes. Check online to see if www.communitylend.com is still around; if it is, determine who the borrowers and lenders are.

SOURCE: *John Greenwood, Financial Post, April 7, 2007. Material reprinted with the express permission of "The National Post Company," a CanWest Partnership.*

direct finance, through financial markets and (3) over time direct finance has grown relative to indirect finance. The first is explained by the fact that the financial system improves the efficient operation of the economy, helping to channel resources to their most productive uses. Our discussion suggests that information problems are the primary explanation for the second. The final feature is explained by the broad decrease in information costs, which erases some of the advantages of indirect finance.

To this point we have focused on the external sources of funding for a business, but a corporation that wants to undertake an investment project can obtain financing not only directly from financial markets, through the issuance of stocks or bonds, or indirectly from a financial intermediary, in the form of a loan but also from its own profits. That is, instead of distributing profits to shareholders in the form of dividends, the firm can retain the earnings and use them as a source of investment financing.

You may be surprised to learn that the vast majority of investment financing comes from internal sources. Looking at Figure 11.3 on page 248, notice that in Canada, (as in other large economies) most of the funds for investment come

Figure 11.3    Sources of Funds for Non-Financial Canadian Corporations.

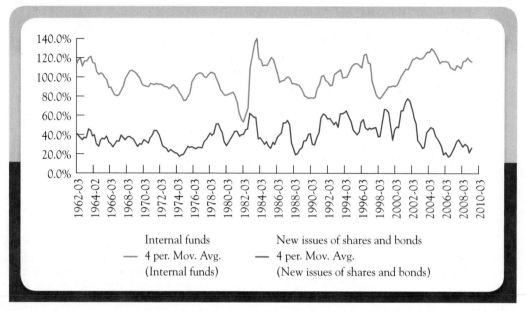

Internal funds
— 4 per. Mov. Avg.
(Internal funds)

New issues of shares and bonds
— 4 per. Mov. Avg.
(New issues of shares and bonds)

SOURCE: *Statistics Canada. Internal funds: v31778/v31782, New issues: (v31815+v31807+v31808)/v31782. Both series are quarterly, plotted as the 4 period moving average. All five series from CANSIM Table 378-0001, accessed 27 July 2009.*

from internal sources.[3] The only possible explanation for this fact is that information problems make external financing—obtained either directly from markets or indirectly from financial institutions—prohibitively expensive and difficult to get. It's not just individuals who have to finance their activities without any help—businesses do, too. The fact that managers have superior information about the way in which their firms are and should be run makes internal finance the rational choice.

[3] Since 2000, corporate profits have been sufficiently high that corporations supplied funds to the rest of the economy.

## Terms

## Chapter Summary

1. The financial sector has the following characteristics:

   a. Wealthy countries have high levels of financial development.

   b. Direct finance and indirect finance have both grown over the last 30 years relative to GDP.

   c. Direct finance has grown more rapidly than indirect finance.

   d. Internal sources of funds continue to be the main source of funding for businesses.

2. Financial intermediaries specialize in reducing costs by

   a. Pooling the resources of small savers and lending them to large borrowers.

   b. Providing safekeeping, accounting services, and access to the payments system.

c. Providing liquidity services.

d. Providing the ability to diversify small investments.

e. Providing information services.

3. For potential lenders, investigating borrowers' trustworthiness is costly. This problem, known as asymmetric information, occurs both before and after a transaction.

a. Before a transaction, the least creditworthy borrowers are the ones most likely to apply for funds. This problem is known as adverse selection.

b. Lenders and investors can reduce adverse selection by
   i. Collecting and disclosing information on borrowers.
   ii. Requiring borrowers to post collateral and show sufficient net worth.

c. After a transaction, a borrower may not use the borrowed funds as productively as possible. This problem is known as moral hazard.
   i. In equity markets, moral hazard exists when the managers' interests diverge from the owners' interests.
   ii. Finding solutions to the moral hazard problem in equity financing is difficult.
   iii. In debt markets, moral hazard exists because borrowers have limited liability. They get the benefits when a risky bet pays off, but they don't suffer a loss when it doesn't.
   iv. The fact that debt financing gives managers/ borrowers an incentive to take too many risks gives rise to restrictive covenants, which require borrowers to use funds in specific ways.

4. Financial intermediaries can reduce the problems of adverse selection and moral hazard.

a. They can reduce adverse selection by collecting information on borrowers and screening them to check their creditworthiness.

b. They can reduce moral hazard by monitoring what borrowers are doing with borrowed funds.

c. The fact that the vast majority of firms' finance comes from internal sources, suggests that information problems are too big for even financial intermediaries to solve.

## Conceptual Problems

1. Describe the problem of asymmetric information that an employer faces in hiring a new employee. What solutions can you think of? Does the problem persist after the person has been hired? If so, how and what can be done about it? Is the problem more or less severe for employees on a fixed salary? Why or why not?

2. In some cities, newspapers publish a weekly list of restaurants that have been cited for health code violations by local health inspectors. What information problem is this feature designed to solve? How?

3.* Indirect finance is important because of information costs associated with lending. Why are financial intermediaries relatively more effective at reducing these costs?

4. In some countries it is very difficult for shareholders to fire managers when they do a poor job. What type of financing would you expect to find in those countries?

5. Define the term "economies of scale" and explain how a financial intermediary can take advantage of such economies.

6. Explain how the Internet can reduce asymmetric information problems.
   a. How can the Internet help to solve information problems?
   b. Can the Internet compound some information problems?
   c. On which problem would the Internet have a greater impact: adverse selection or moral hazard?

7. The financial sector is heavily regulated. Explain how government regulations help to solve information problems, increasing the effectiveness of financial markets and institutions.

8.* How does the existence of well-defined property rights help to overcome information problems in financial markets?

9. Deflation causes the value of a borrower's collateral to drop. Define deflation and explain how it reduces the value of a borrower's collateral. What is the effect on the information problems a borrower faces?

* Indicates more difficult problems.

www.mcgrawhill.ca/olc/cecchetti

10. In 2002, the trustworthiness of corporate financial reporting was called into question when a number of companies corrected their financial statements for past years. What impact did their action have on the financial markets?

## Analytical Problems

11. Your parents give you $2,000 as a graduation gift and you decide to invest the money in the stock market. If you are risk averse, should you purchase some stock in a few different companies through a Web site with low transaction fees or put the entire $2,000 into a mutual fund? Explain your answer.

12. Historically it was argued that banks did mortgage lending because they had an information advantage. But in the early 2000s, most mortgages in the United States were securitized. Similarly, Canadian banks issue MBS (secured by NHA loans), which are insured by the CMHC. What information problems would have had to be addressed for this market to emerge and how could they be overcome?

13. Suppose two types of firms wish to borrow in the bond market. Firms of type A are in good financial health and are relatively low risk. The appropriate premium over the risk-free rate of lending to these firms is 2 percent. Firms of type B are in poor financial health and are relatively high risk. The appropriate premium over the risk-free rate of lending to these firms is 6 percent. As an investor, you have no other information about these firms except that type A and type B firms exist in equal numbers.
    a. At what interest rate would you be willing to lend if the risk-free rate were 5 percent?
    b. Would this market function well? What type of asymmetric information problem does this example illustrate?

14. Consider again the low-risk type A firm described in question 13. If you were the financial advisor to such a firm, what suggestions would you make to the firm's management about obtaining borrowed funds?

15. Consider a small company run by a manager who is also the owner. If this company borrows funds, why might a moral hazard problem still exist?

16.* The island of Utopia has a very unusual economy. Everyone on Utopia knows everyone else and knows all about the firms they own and operate. The financial system is well developed on Utopia. How would you expect the mix between direct and indirect finance on Utopia to compare with other countries? What role would financial intermediaries play in this economy?

17. You and a friend visit the headquarters of a company and are awestruck by the expensive artwork and designer furniture that grace every office. Your friend is very impressed and encourages you to consider buying stock in the company, arguing that it must be really successful to afford such elegant surroundings. Would you agree with your friend's assessment? What further information (other than the usual financial data) would you obtain before making an investment decision?

18.* Why do you think microfinance organizations have succeeded in providing lending services in poor countries where traditional financial institutions have failed?

www.mcgrawhill.ca/olc/cecchetti

# APPENDIX 11

## Moral Hazard

In the text we gave some examples of moral hazard but writing the problem more formally gives more precision to the concept and also clarifies circumstances under which moral hazard arises. We will look separately at the case of debt and equity. In both cases the person who receives the funds has an incentive to behave differently than if they used their own funds.

### Moral Hazard in Debt Financing

Consider the case where a lender is considering lending $P$ at a rate of interest $r_0$ to a borrower so that he can undertake a project that we will call project A, which has a (known and certain) rate of return $r_a$. Now suppose the borrower has an alternative opportunity that we will call project B. There is a 50:50 chance that project B will return $r_b$, but it may return zero in which case the lender will only return the borrowed principal.[4] We can calculate the expected net returns to the borrower:

$$E^b(A) = (1 + r_a)P - (1 + r_0)P = (r_a - r_0)P$$

$$E^b(B) = 0.5((1 + r_b)P - (1 + r_0)P) + 0.5\ (P - P) = .5(r_b - r_0)P$$

The borrower will have a higher expected return from project B if

$$.5(r_b - r_0) > (r_a - r_0) \tag{A1}$$

that is, if the return from project B is sufficiently high. For example, if $r_0 = 6\%$ and $r_a = 8\%$ then if $r_b > 10\%$ project B has a higher expected return. Now look at the expected returns to the lender:

$$E^l(A) = (1 + r_0)P - P = (r_0)P$$

$$E^l(B) = 0.5((1 + r_0)P - P) + 0.5 \times (P - P) = .5(r_0)P$$

The lender would always want the borrower to undertake the safe project.

If the borrower were using his own funds the expected return to projects A and B would be

$$E^0(A) = (1 + r_a)P - P = (r_a)P$$

$$E^0(B) = 0.5((1 + r_b)P - P) + 0.5 \times (P - P) = .5(r_b)P$$

So the expected return to project B is higher only if

$$.5r_b > r_a \tag{A2}$$

---

[4] Of course, we could have assumed that the principal was spent and would not be repaid, which would have exacerbated the problem.

This condition is more restrictive than equation (A.1). If $r_a$ equalled 8 percent, then project B would have to pay more than 16 percent to yield a higher expected rate of return. Here we have assumed that the lender funds all or none of the project. You should be able to calculate how the degree of moral hazard changes as the extent of leverage increases.

## Moral Hazard in Equity Financing

Now suppose that the investor decided to take an equity position in a firm, and to buy ρ percent of the firm. The profits of the firm $\pi(e)$ will be split between the manager (who gets $(1 - \rho)\pi$) and the investor (who gets $\rho\pi$). We will also assume that the profits of the firm are proportional to the effort that the manager puts in, but that the effort is costly to the manager. Figure A.1 illustrates the situation. $\pi(e)$ is linear, showing the profits rising with effort $(e)$, and $C(e)$ is increasing more rapidly. If the manager was to receive all the profits he would choose an effort level that maximized the net return. The net return is shown by the distance between $\pi(e)$ and $C(e)$ which is maximized where the two lines have the same slope, at effort level $e_0$. If the manager only receives $(1 - \rho)\pi$, then the manager will choose an effort level to maximize his/her net return, which is the distance between $(1 - \rho)\pi$ and $C(e)$. Now the effort level is given by $e_1$, where the curve $C(e)$ is parallel to $(1 - \rho)\pi$. If the investor expected to receive $\rho \pi (e_0)$, then he would be disappointed to receive the smaller amount $\rho \pi (e_1)$. You can use the figure to illustrate how the return to the investor varies with the size of his share of the firm $(1 - \rho)(\pi(e))$.

### Figure 11A.1   Moral Hazard and Equity Finance

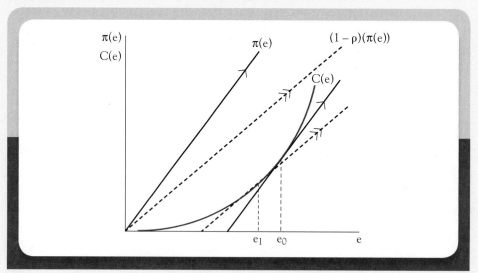

Managers have less incentive to put in effort if they get only a fraction of the returns to that effort.

# CHAPTER 12

## Depository Institutions: Banks and Bank Management

Banks are the most visible financial intermediaries in the economy. Most of us use the word "*bank*" to describe what people in the financial world call depository institutions. These are the financial institutions that accept deposits from savers and make loans to borrowers. What distinguishes depository institutions from nondepository institutions is their primary source of funds—that is, the liability side of their balance sheets. Depository institutions include chartered banks, trust and mortgage loan companies, and caisse populaires and credit unions—the financial intermediaries most of us encounter in the course of our day-to-day lives.

Banking is a business. Actually, it's a combination of businesses designed to deliver the services discussed in Chapter 11. One business provides the accounting and record-keeping services that track the balances in your accounts. Another grants you access to the payments system, allowing you to convert your account balances into cash or transfer them to someone else. Yet a third business pools the savings of many small depositors and uses them to make large loans to trustworthy borrowers. A fourth business offers customers diversification services, buying and selling financial instruments in the financial markets in an effort to make a profit. Banks trade in the financial markets not only as a service to their customers but also in an effort to earn a profit for their shareholders as well. The intent of banks, of course, is to profit from each of these lines of business. Our objective in this chapter is to see how they do it.

There are 21 domestic banks in Canada, but the 6 largest banks—Bank of Montreal, CIBC, National Bank of Canada, Royal Bank, Scotiabank, and TD Canada Trust—hold more than 90 percent of the assets of the system. Over the last 20 years the banks have grown at roughly twice the rate of economic growth. In part, this reflects growth in their core business operations, but it also reflects an expansion into activities outside the traditional banking area. The banks' expansion has not reduced their profitability: from 2001 to 2008 the average return on equity was 16 percent. But as we saw in 2009, those returns did not come without risk.

In this chapter, we will examine the business of banking. We will see where depository institutions get their funds and what they do with them. That is, we will study the sources of banks' liabilities and learn how they manage their assets. We will see how they make profits and examine the sources of risk that bankers face, as well as how those risks can be managed. In the following chapters we will look at the history of the banks and how they are regulated.

## The Balance Sheet of Chartered Banks

To focus our discussion of depository institutions, we will concentrate on what are called *chartered banks*.[1] These institutions were established to provide banking services to businesses, allowing them to deposit funds safely and borrow them when necessary.

---

[1] There are actually three classes of chartered banks. What you probably think of as traditional banks are domestic banks, which are classified as Schedule 1 banks. Subsidiaries of foreign banks that are authorized to accept deposits in Canada are classified as Schedule 2 banks, while foreign bank branches authorized to operate in limited ways in Canada are referred to as Schedule 3 banks.

Today, chartered banks offer accounts and loans to individuals as well. To understand the business of banking, we'll start by examining the chartered bank's balance sheet. A **balance sheet** is a list of a household or firm's assets and liabilities: the sources of its funds (liabilities) and the uses to which those funds are put (assets). A bank's balance sheet says that

$$\text{Total bank assets} = \text{Total bank liabilities} + \text{Bank capital} \qquad (1)$$

Banks obtain their funds from individual depositors and businesses, as well as by borrowing from other financial institutions and through the financial markets. They use these funds to make loans, purchase marketable securities, and hold cash. The difference between a bank's assets and liabilities is the bank's capital, or *net worth*—the value of the bank to its shareholders. The bank's profits come both from service fees and from the difference between what the bank pays for its liabilities and the return it receives on its assets (a topic we'll return to later).

Table 12.1 shows a consolidated balance sheet for all the chartered banks in Canada in June 2008. It reports the sum of all the items on all the balance sheets of the chartered banks that existed in Canada at the time. The government collects these statistics in the course of supervising and regulating the financial system, to ensure bank safety and soundness. The numbers in the table are also related to the measures of money discussed in Chapter 2. Recall that measures such as M1 and M2 include chequing account balances, which are liabilities of the banking system.

## Assets: Uses of Funds

Let's start with the asset side of the balance sheet—what banks do with the funds they raise. The first thing to notice in Table 12.1 is that Canadian banks hold very little of their assets in the form of Bank of Canada notes and deposits. Historically, chartered banks were required to hold Bank of Canada notes or to have deposits at the Bank of Canada as reserves against the deposits that customers held with them. Non-bank depository institutions did not face the same required reserve requirements and the banks argued that they were unfairly penalized in competing with credit unions and trust companies. In 1991, the government removed the reserve requirement. Figure 12.1 on page 256 shows the steady decline of Bank of Canada notes and deposits in the portfolio of the banks. Of course, banks still must be able to give customers cash if they want to withdraw their deposits, so the banks continue to hold some cash as well as other liquid assets.

Table 12.1 shows that assets are divided into three broad categories: Canadian dollar liquid assets, Canadian dollar less liquid assets, and foreign currency assets. Roughly 10 percent of Canadian dollar assets, or $160 billion, is held in the form of liquid assets and $1.5 trillion in the other assets. The foreign currency assets make up 38 percent of the total assets of the banks. In looking at consolidated figures such as the ones in Table 12.1, we can get some sense of their scale by comparing them to *nominal GDP*. In the second quarter of 2008, Canadian nominal GDP was roughly $1.6 trillion, so total Canadian dollar bank assets were equivalent to about one year's GDP.

**Canadian Dollar Liquid Assets**   Remember that **liquidity** measures how easily assets can be turned into means of payment. Of course, Bank of Canada notes and deposits are means of payment. Most of the Bank of Canada notes held by the banks are actually sitting in ATMs rather than in the vaults of the banks. In fact, when the use of ATMs became widespread the banks had to increase their inventories of cash. The next most liquid assets are short-term liabilities of the government of Canada,

Table 12.1   Balance Sheet of Canadian Chartered Banks, June 30, 2008

| Assets (C$millions)* | | | |
|---|---|---:|---:|
| Canadian dollar liquid assets | | | |
| Bank of Canada notes and deposits | | 5,519 | 0.3 percent |
| Government of Canada securities: | T-bills | 27,095 | 1.6 percent |
| | Bonds | 127,175 | 7.5 percent |
| Canadian dollar less liquid assets | | | |
| Securities | | 223,951 | 13.2 percent |
| Residential mortgages | | 477,420 | 28.2 percent |
| Other loans | | 614,357 | 36.3 percent |
| Other assets | | 216,213 | 12.8 percent |
| Total Canadian dollar assets | | 1,691,730 | 100.0 percent |
| Foreign currency assets | | 1,054,507 | 62.3 percent |
| Total assets | | 2,746,237 | |

| Liabilities and Shareholders Equity Deposits | | |
|---|---:|---:|
| Gross demand deposits | 195,131 | 11.6 percent |
| Personal savings | 507,891 | 30.3 percent |
| Non personal time and notice deposits | 384,161 | 22.9 percent |
| Government of Canada deposits | 2,588 | 0.2 percent |
| Advances from the Bank of Canada | 72 | 0.0 percent |
| Banker's acceptances | 60,504 | 3.6 percent |
| Other liabilities | 361,386 | 21.6 percent |
| Subordinated debt | 37,043 | 2.2 percent |
| Shareholder equity (incl. retained earnings) | 128,105 | 7.6 percent |
| Total Canadian dollar liabilities | 1,676,881 | 100.0 percent |
| Foreign currency liabilities | 1,069,356 | 63.8 percent |
| Total liabilities | 2,746,237 | |

\* Numbers in the right-hand column are the proportion of Canadian dollar assets or liabilities.

SOURCE: Bank of Canada Banking and Financial Statistics, *December 2008*, at *www.bankofcanada.ca/en/bfsgen.html*, *June 2008. Assets are from section C-3; pp. s20-1; Liabilities are from C-4 pp. s22-3.*

i.e., Treasury bills. Longer-term government bonds are also highly liquid as they carry no default risk and they can be used as collateral by the banks for advances from the Bank of Canada if necessary.

Banks hold less than 10 percent of their assets in liquid form, and it's easy to understand why. Bank of Canada notes pay no interest. Deposits at the Bank of Canada pay the lowest interest rate available, and government T bills and bonds only slightly

| Figure 12.1 | Chartered Bank Assets, 1954–2008 |

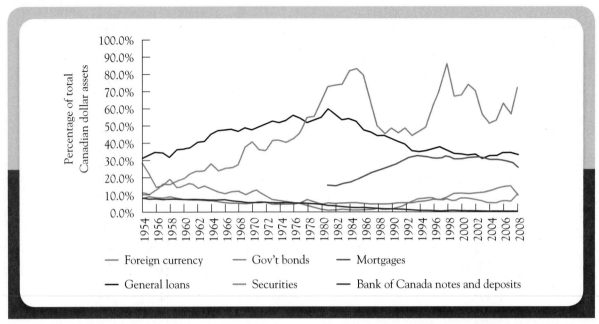

— Foreign currency     — Gov't bonds     — Mortgages

— General loans     — Securities     — Bank of Canada notes and deposits

SOURCE: *Trends in Chartered Bank Assets 1954–2008. Bank of Canada, Monthly data, CANSIM Table 176-0015. Chartered bank assets and liabilities. Accessed January 21, 2009.*

more. Holding liquid assets has a high opportunity cost. That's why banks work hard to minimize the amount of cash they hold, turning as many of their assets as possible into profitable loans and securities.

**Canadian Dollar Less Liquid Assets** The other Canadian dollar assets can be grouped into four broad categories. Securities are bonds and shares held by the banks, and may include shares of related companies. Figure 12.1 shows that the banks tripled the share of securities in their Canadian dollar portfolio since the early 1990s. The growth of securities in part reflects the process of securitization we discussed in Chapter 3. Notice that the figure suggests that the increase in securities was accompanied by a decrease in the share of holdings of government securities. (Don't be tempted to assume that the value of holdings of government securities declined! Figure 12.1 shows the *shares* of each type of asset. For example, from 2000 to 2001 the share of government securities in the Canadian dollar portfolio fell from 10.2 percent to 7.1 percent, but the value of government securities the banks held rose from $100 billion to $127 billion.)

The traditional business of banking was making loans. In the early days of Canadian banking, regulations required that most loans were for commercial businesses. By the mid-20th century, banks had expanded into consumer and industrial lending. Figure 12.1 shows that in the early 1980s more than half the banks' assets were in loans, not including residential mortgages. Loans include both personal loans (for example, car loans) and commercial and industrial loans. By the 1990s the share of loans had fallen to less than 40 percent, and residential mortgages were almost as important a component of the balance sheet. Finally, other assets includes the value of buildings owned by the banks as well as the value of derivative holdings.

Foreign Currency Assets    The first thing to notice about foreign currency asset holdings is that they are very close in magnitude to foreign currency liabilities. Figure 12.1 and Figure 12.2 on page 259 show that this is not just a happenstance event; historically, the levels of foreign currency assets and liabilities have always been roughly the same. Matching foreign currency assets and liabilities reduces the risk from swings in foreign exchange rates. The second thing to notice is that they are very large. Canadian banks have very sizable operations outside Canada. Finally, notice that the banks' foreign currency holdings have gone through dramatic swings, increasing to 83 percent of the value of the Canadian dollar assets in 1985 and then falling to about 45 percent in 1989. A similar swing occurred as holdings increased to 87 percent in 1998 before again falling. The figures show the average share for all the banks together, but individual banks have different extents of exposure to foreign currency holdings. In 2008, CIBC held 27 percent foreign assets and the Royal Bank 48 percent.[2]

The banks' foreign currency assets include a range of different assets: about one-third loans, one-third securities, and one-third "other assets," which includes gold and foreign currency.

The primary difference among various kinds of depository institutions is in the composition of their loan portfolios. Chartered banks make loans to businesses as well as consumers; trust and mortgage companies provide mortgages to individuals; credit unions specialize in consumer loans. See the Tools of the Trade: A Catalogue of Depository Institutions on page 261 for a more detailed description of the various types.

## Liabilities: Sources of Funds

To finance their operations, banks need funds. They get them from savers and from borrowing in the financial markets. To entice individuals and businesses to place their funds in the bank, institutions offer a range of deposit accounts that provide safekeeping and accounting services, access to the payments system, liquidity, and diversification of risk (see Chapter 11), as well as interest payments on the balance. Broadly speaking, there are two types of deposit accounts, transaction and nontransaction accounts. Transaction accounts are known as demand deposits (which is what they are called in Table 12.1 on page 255). Looking back at the table, you can see that banks obtain about 10 percent of their funds from demand deposits. Most of their funds come from nontransaction deposits, which account for over 50 percent of chartered bank liabilities, and from borrowings, which make up an additional 22 percent.

Demand Deposits    Demand deposits are accounts that are primarily used for transactions. Banks pay little or no interest on the funds in demand accounts, but they charge lower fees (than on savings accounts) for withdrawals, and may not charge for some Internet transactions. In addition to the names created by banks' marketing departments, economists use various other terms in speaking of chequable deposits. For example, some economists call them "sight deposits," since a depositor can show up to withdraw them when the bank is in sight. Historically, the distinction between demand accounts and savings accounts was quite significant. You could not write a cheque on a savings account, and you could be required to give notice of your intention to withdraw any amount from the account. But banks often did not enforce the notice requirement, fearing that asking people to wait seven days for their funds might send a very bad signal about their solvency.

[2] Data from the Web site of the Superintendent of Financial Institutions, retrieved January 5, 2009, from http://www.osfi-bsif.gc.ca/osfi/index_e.aspx?ArticleID=554.

## YOUR FINANCIAL WORLD
Choosing the Right Bank for You

It used to be that there were only a few banks in Canada and choosing the right bank was fairly straightforward. Now there are more options—you can bank with Canadian Tire or President's Choice, or with a credit union or trust company. This is generally a good thing but it means that it takes some work to choose a financial institution. First, you should decide exactly why you need a bank and whether a particular bank will serve your needs conveniently and cheaply. Shop around for the best deal. Ensure the bank will pay a competitive interest rate on your deposit balance and you won't be paying for services you don't use. You may want to make sure the bank will give you immediate access to your deposits. The ability to reach someone either in person or on the phone during hours that are convenient for you is also important. And be sure the bank has a reputation for courteous, efficient service. Because service isn't cheap, ask what it will cost you. Will you have to pay a fee to see a teller in person? Will you have to pay a fee to cash a cheque? If you have friends with needs similar to yours,

find out where they bank and ask whether they're happy with the cost and service.

The Internet has revolutionized banking. Traditional "bricks-and-mortar" banks now provide many of their services on the Internet. Using your computer, you can access your account, review and pay your bills, or transfer funds. In fact, when you decide to open a bank account, you may be tempted to give your business to an Internet bank—one without any local branches. If you do, be careful. Looking at your computer screen, you may not be able to tell where the Web site you are viewing is physically located. Canadian banks are members of the Canadian Deposit Insurance Corporation, which ensures deposits up to $100,000. You can check the CDIC Web site (http://www.cdic.ca) to see whether your financial institution is a member of CDIC. Credit unions and Caisse Populaires are provincially regulated, and deposits at those institutions are insured by provincial governments. Check the institution's documents to learn about the coverage.

In the 1970s, when monetary policy aimed at a particular growth rate for M1, the distinction between demand deposits and other deposits was important because demand deposits are part of M1 and other deposits are not. One of the contributors to the failure of M1 targeting was the emergence of technologies that made it easy to switch funds between accounts. As interest rates rose in the late 1970s, the opportunity cost of holding demand deposits rather than savings deposits rose so people switched out of demand deposits into savings accounts. Figure 12.2 does not include the breakdown of deposits before 1981 because the data collection method has changed, but "Public demand deposits" (which are very similar to the "Gross demand deposits" shown in Table 12.1 on page 255) fell from 18 percent of liabilities in 1975 to 11 percent in 1981. People began using their savings accounts as transactions accounts, making the targeting of M1 irrelevant.

**Nontransaction Deposits**    In 2007, nontransaction deposits, including personal savings and notice and time deposits, accounted for about half of all chartered bank liabilities. Savings deposits, commonly known as *passbook savings* accounts, were popular for many decades, though they are less so today. The major share of both personal savings deposits and nonpersonal time and notice deposits are term deposits (mostly in the form of Guaranteed Investment Certificates or GICs). The banks issue a wide variety of GICs, both short term and long term; some promise low returns while others have returns based on a stock market index (their average returns are higher but there is also a higher risk of a low return). Savers like them because the bank promises that there will not be a loss of principal, and investors like the higher returns than a savings account would pay.[3]

---

[3] Banks and other depository institutions sell a wide variety of GIC products and the details of each product are complex and important. For example, those linked to a stock index pay in proportion to how the market does, not the entire market return. (This is in a sense the price you pay for the guarantee of no loss of principal). Many have high penalties for early withdrawal of funds. Check whether the "guarantee" in GIC, is offered by the bank or by CDIC. While the government backs the CDIC guarantee, the bank's guarantee is backed by the assets of the bank so would not protect you if the bank failed.

**Other liabilities**    The "other liabilities" line includes both borrowing by banks and derivative positions, which Figure 12.2 shows have become increasingly important over the past quarter-century, today accounting for over 20 percent of bank liabilities. Banks often borrow using an instrument called a repurchase agreement, or repo, a short-term collateralized loan in which a security is exchanged for cash, with the agreement that the parties will reverse the transaction on a specific future date, as soon as the next day. For example, a bank that has a Treasury bill might need cash, while a pension fund might have cash that it doesn't need overnight. Through a repo, the bank would give the T-bill to the pension fund in exchange for cash, agreeing to buy it back—repurchase it—with interest the next day. In short, the bank gets an overnight loan and the pension fund gets some extra interest. The details are shown in Figure 12.3 on page 260.

Although banks can also borrow by obtaining a loan or an advance from the Bank of Canada, they rarely do so. We'll have much more to say about such advances in Part IV.

## Bank Capital and Profitability

Net worth equals assets minus liabilities, whether we are talking about an individual's net worth or a bank's. In the case of banks, however, net worth is referred to as bank capital, or *equity capital*. If the bank's shareholders sold all its assets (without taking a loss) and used the proceeds to repay all the liabilities, capital is what would be left. We can think of capital as the shareholders' stake in the bank.

Capital is the cushion banks have against a sudden drop in the value of their assets or an unexpected withdrawal of liabilities. It provides some insurance against

**Figure 12.2**    **Chartered Bank Liabilities**

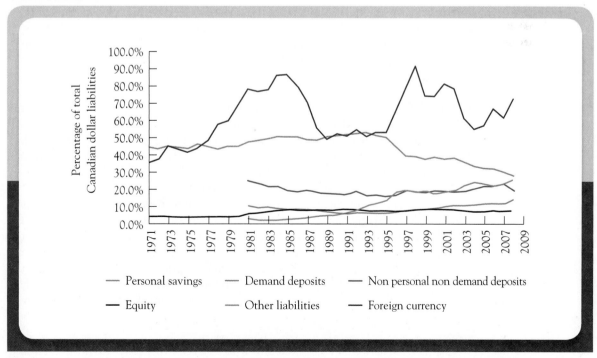

SOURCE: *Trends in Liabilities of Chartered Banks. Bank of Canada, Monthly data, CANSIM Table 176-0015; Chartered bank assets and liabilities. Accessed January 21, 2009.*

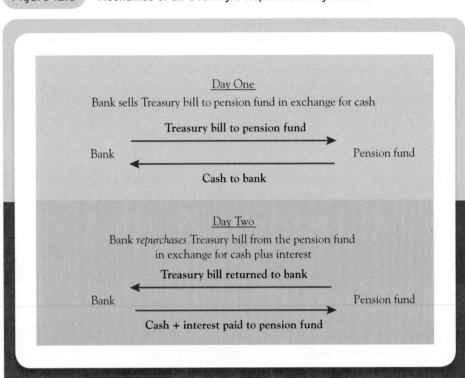

Figure 12.3  Mechanics of an Overnight Repurchase Agreement

Day One

Bank sells Treasury bill to pension fund in exchange for cash

**Treasury bill to pension fund**

Bank ──────────────────────────────▶ Pension fund

◀────────────────────────────────

**Cash to bank**

Day Two

Bank *repurchases* Treasury bill from the pension fund
in exchange for cash plus interest

**Treasury bill returned to bank**

◀────────────────────────────────

Bank                                  Pension fund

──────────────────────────────▶

**Cash + interest paid to pension fund**

insolvency (the inability to repay debts when a firm's liabilities exceed its assets). An important component of bank capital is **loan loss reserves**, an amount the bank sets aside to cover potential losses from defaulted loans. At some point a bank gives up hope that a loan will be repaid and the loan is *written off*, or erased from the bank's balance sheet. At that point the loan loss reserve is reduced by the amount of the loan that has defaulted.

Looking once again at the balance sheet in Table 12.1 on page 255, we can see that in June 2008, shareholder's equity (i.e., bank capital) in the Canadian commercial banking system totalled a bit over $125 billion. That $125 billion was combined with $2.6 trillion worth of liabilities to purchase $2.75 trillion in assets. So the ratio of debt to equity in the Canadian banking system was slightly more than 20 to 1. That's a substantial amount of leverage. (Recall that the term "leverage" refers to the portion of an asset that is purchased using borrowed funds.)

To put this ratio of slightly more than 20 to 1 into perspective, we can compare it to the debt-to-equity ratio for nonfinancial businesses, which is approximately 0.5 to 1. Household leverage is even lower, less than 0.25 to 1.[4] Recall from Tools of the Trade: The Impact of Leverage on Risk on page 92 that leverage increases both risk and expected return. If you contribute half the purchase price of a house and borrow the other half, both your risk and your expected return double. If you contribute one-fifth of the purchase price and borrow the other four-fifths, your risk and expected return go

---

[4] Statistics Canada, The Daily, Monday, March 16, 2009. These data are for the end of 2008. The household leverage ratio rose through the last quarter of 2008 as the value of the stock market, and to a lesser extent housing, fell.

# TOOLS OF THE TRADE
## A Catalogue of Depository Institutions

Traditionally, regulators saw the Canadian financial sector as comprising four separate pillars: banking, insurance, trust companies, and investment dealers. But in the second half of the 20th century the lines between the pillars blurred. Today the domestic banks own all the major securities dealers as well as some insurance companies. They also own trust companies, mutual fund companies, and electronic trading platforms. While some fear that the concentration of ownership in the financial sector is bad for consumers, others argue that economies of scale and scope are passed on to consumers. There are quite a few government agencies that help to protect and inform consumers: The Ombudsman for Banking Services and Investments assists in resolving disputes between banks and their customers. The Competition Bureau addresses complaints of unfair business practices. The Financial Consumer Agency ensures compliance with federal consumer protection laws. The Office of the Superintendent of Financial Institutions supervises federally regulated financial institutions in Canada.

There are three basic types of depository institutions: banks, trust and loan companies, and credit unions and caisse populaires.

### Banks

The Canadian banking sector includes 20 domestic banks, 24 foreign bank subsidiaries, and 29 foreign bank branches. In addition to the traditional commercial banking business of taking deposits and making loans, the large Canadian banks play a significant role in the insurance and securities markets. While there are few banks in Canada relative to the U.S. banking sector, the banks operate a large network of bank branches, with over 9,000 branches in 2008.

### Trust and Loan Companies

Trust and loan companies conduct similar retail business to that of the banks but put more emphasis on administering estates, trusts, and pension plans. Trust companies may be federally or provincially incorporated.

### Credit Unions and Caisses Populaires

Credit unions and caisses populaires are nonprofit depository institutions that are owned by people with a common bond that may be employment-related or geographical. While there has been consolidation in the credit union sector, credit unions are more numerous but much smaller than the large banks. In 2008 there were about 1,000 institutions with assets of $221 billion. That is, the sector had assets about 13 percent of the size of the Canadian dollar assets of the banking system. Over half of the institutions, and nearly half of the assets, are in Quebec. Credit unions specialize in making small consumer loans. They originated in the 19th century to meet the needs of people who could not borrow from traditional lenders. Before credit unions existed, many ordinary people had nowhere to turn when they faced unexpected home repairs or medical emergencies

---

up by a factor of 5 (see Tools of the Trade: The Impact of Leverage on Risk on page 92). So if a bank borrows $20 for each $1 in capital, its risk and expected return increase a whopping 20 times! Banking, it seems, is a very risky business. As we will see in Chapter 14, one of the explanations for the relatively high degree of leverage in banking is the existence of government guarantees such as deposit insurance, which allow banks to capture the benefits of risk taking without subjecting depositors to potential losses.

There are several basic measures of bank profitability. The first is called **return on assets (ROA)**. Return on assets equals a bank's net profit after taxes divided by the bank's total assets:

$$ROA = \frac{\text{Net profit after taxes}}{\text{Total bank assets}} \qquad (2)$$

ROA is an important measure of how efficiently a particular bank uses its assets. By looking at the different units' ROAs, for example, the manager of a bank can also compare the performance of the bank's various lines of business. But for the bank's shareholders, return on assets is less important than the return on their own investment, which is leveraged at an average ratio of 20 to 1. The bank's return to

## APPLYING THE CONCEPT
### GROWTH AND BANKING IN CHINA AND INDIA

China and India are experiencing phenomenal annual economic growth rates of 8 to 10 percent. As high as that is, some people think growth could be even higher if the banks in the two countries worked properly.

While the Chinese financial system is large overall, banks account for a disproportionate share of intermediation there. In 2004, 75 percent of all China's capital—190 percent of GDP—was channelled through banks.[*] That's twice the amount in South Korea, relative to its GDP, and three times what goes through Chile's banking system. This heavy reliance on banks for financing is a sign of inadequate financial development. The solution is to encourage the development of debt and equity markets, with broad participation by small savers.

In addition to accounting for too large a proportion of China's financial system, Chinese banks are directing resources inefficiently. State-owned enterprises that account for 48 percent of China's GDP receive 73 percent of the credit. That is, banks are directing funds to government-favoured firms. This fact should not be surprising given that the government implicitly backs loans made to the companies it owns. Improvement will require both that the government stop providing the guarantees (probably by selling the companies) and that banks learn to evaluate the creditworthiness of borrowers.

Turning to India, instead of attracting too many deposits, there banks attract too few. Overall, the Indian financial system is 1.4 times the country's GDP, half that of China, and banks attract deposits equal to only 60 percent of GDP. The problem is that the Indian people mistrust banks, holding more than half of their wealth in physical assets such as land, houses, cattle, and especially gold. Solving this problem requires finding a way to lure savers to make deposits in banks.

While private Indian firms have more access to bank financing than their Chinese counterparts, it could be better. First, Indian banks need to stop holding so many Indian government bonds—currently an amount equal to 46 percent of deposits. And second, the government has to stop directing banks to make at least 40 percent of loans to small borrowers in favoured sectors. Reforms are needed to free banks to lend where the resources can be best used.

If Chinese and Indian banks are given the proper incentives to direct financial resources to their most economically efficient uses, living standards in those two countries will be advanced. Without well-functioning financial system, growth will not be as high as it could be.

[*]These estimates, along with the information that follows, are from the McKinsey Global Institute, "Putting China's Capital to Work: The Value of Financial System Reform," May 2006; and Diana Farrell and Susan Lund, "Reforming India's Financial System," *The McKinsey Quarterly Report*, June 5, 2005, retrieved from http://www.mckinseyquarterly.com.

its shareholders is measured by the **return on equity (ROE)**, which equals the bank's net profit after taxes divided by the bank's capital:

$$ROE = \frac{\text{Net profit after taxes}}{\text{Bank capital}} \tag{3}$$

Not surprisingly, ROA and ROE are related to leverage. One measure of leverage is the ratio of bank assets to bank capital. Multiplying ROA by this ratio yields ROE:

$$ROA \times \frac{\text{Bank assets}}{\text{Bank capital}} = \frac{\text{Net profit after taxes}}{\text{Total bank assets}} \times \frac{\text{Bank assets}}{\text{Bank capital}}$$

$$= \frac{\text{Net profit after taxes}}{\text{Bank capital}}$$

$$= ROE \tag{4}$$

For large banks, the return on equity tends to be higher than for small banks, which suggests the existence of economies of scale in banking. The differential is one possible explanation for the current trend toward bank mergers and ever-larger banks.

## YOUR FINANCIAL WORLD
### The Cost of Payday Loans

If you drive through the streets of most cities, you will eventually pass a store with a sign saying "Cheques Cashed." These financial intermediaries provide loans to people who cannot borrow from mainstream financial institutions such as banks. In addition to their cheque-cashing business— they charge about 3 percent to cash a payroll or government cheque, more if the bearer can't produce acceptable identification—these firms offer small loans.

The most common type of loan these stores offer is a *payday loan*. To get one, you just walk into the store with an ID card, a utility or phone bill, a chequebook, and some pay stubs; you come out with cash. Why do you need all these documents? The utility bill proves where you live; the pay stubs establish that you are employed, how much you make, and when you are paid. You need the chequebook so you can write a cheque that the store will hold until your next payday, when it will send your cheque to the bank. With just these few requirements, the store will lend you up to $500 for the week or two weeks until you are paid.

The catch is that there is a fee, and it's huge. Payday lenders charge a fee equal to 15 or 20 percent of the loan's principal. So if you borrow $500, you will have to repay a minimum of $575. That's the size of the cheque you will need to write to get the loan and at an annual rate that would be nearly 400 percent. What if you can't repay the loan? The government has prohibited the rolling over of payday loans because then your $500 loan would become a $2,500 loan; if you can't repay $500 how could you repay $2,500? But the payday loan company will send the debt to a collection company to be sure that you repay the loan.

Payday loans should be a last resort. How will you repay the loan? Can you get the funds in a cheaper way by getting an overdraft at your bank (ask there); by using a credit card? By asking friends or family? Do you really need to spend the money?

Before continuing, it is important to introduce one more measure of bank profitability: net interest income. This measure is related to the fact that banks pay interest on their liabilities, creating interest expenses, and receive interest on their assets, creating interest income. Deposits and bank borrowing create interest expenses; securities and loans generate interest income. The difference between the two is the bank's *net interest income*.

Net interest income can also be expressed as a percentage of total assets to yield a quantity called **net interest margin**. This is the bank's **interest rate spread**, which is the (weighted) average difference between the interest rate received on assets and the interest rate paid for liabilities. A bank's net interest margin is closely related to its return on assets. Just take the bank's fee income minus its operating costs, divide by total assets, add the result to the net interest margin, and you get its ROA. Roughly equivalent to a manufacturer or retailer's gross profits and gross profit margin, net interest income and net interest margin reveal a great deal about a bank's business.

Well-run banks have high net interest income and a high net interest margin. And since we would expect most of a bank's loans to be repaid, net interest margin tells us not just current profitability but also future profitability; it is a forward-looking measure. If a bank's net interest margin is currently improving, its profitability is likely to improve in the future. Data on the net interest margin of individual Canadian banks is available in the financial statements of each bank and on the Web site of the Canadian Bankers' Association at http://www.cba.ca.

## Off-Balance-Sheet Activities

A financial firm's balance sheet provides only so much information. To generate fees, banks engage in numerous **off-balance-sheet activities**. Recall that banks exist to

# TOOLS OF THE TRADE
Income of the Big 6 Canadian Banks

**Table 12.2** Income of the Big 6 Canadian Banks

| $bn; fiscal year ended October 31, 2008 | | | | |
|---|---|---|---|---|
| Interest income | 100.4 | Total assets (annual average) | 2471 | |
| Less Interest expense | 62.8 | Total equity (annual average) | 84 | |
| Net interest income | 37.6 | Liabilities (annual average) | 2387 | |
| Plus Other income | 28.4 | | | |
| Less provision for loan loss | 5.5 | | | |
| Net interest and other income | 60.5 | Debt: equity ratio | 28.35 (2471 − 84)/84 | |
| Salaries and expenses | 26.2 | Leverage ratio (Assets: Capital) | 29.35 (2471/84) | |
| Premises and equipment | 7.9 | | | |
| Other expenses | 13.4 | | | |
| Net income before taxes | 12.9 | Return on equity: (Income/Equity) | 12.2/84.2 | 14.5 percent |
| Less minority interest | 0.5 | | | |
| Less Taxes | 0.2 | Return on assets: | 12.2/2471 | 0.49 percent |
| Net income after taxes | 12.2 | Return on equity: | .49 percent*29.35 | 14.5 percent |

SOURCE: *Canadian Bankers Association.*

Data on the performance of the Canadian banks (both individual banks and aggregate results as presented here) are available on the Web site of the Canadian Bankers Association. The banks make about 60 percent of their income from the interest rate spread between borrowing and lending and the remainder from their other activities. Although Canadian banks are less leveraged than banks in most other countries, they are still highly leveraged. You can see that the amount of leverage means that a rather low return on assets becomes a much larger return on equity.

reduce transactions costs and information costs as well as to transfer risks. When they perform these services, bankers expect to be compensated. Yet many of these activities do not appear as either assets or liabilities on the bank's balance sheet, even though they may represent an important part of a bank's profits.

For example, banks often provide trusted customers with lines of credit, which are similar to the credit limits on credit cards. The firm pays the bank a fee in return for the ability to borrow whenever necessary. When the agreement is signed, the bank receives the payment and the firm receives a *loan commitment*. However, not until a loan has actually been made—until the firm has *drawn down* the credit line—does the transaction appear on the bank's balance sheet.

In the meantime, the bank is compensated for reducing both transactions and information costs. Without the loan commitment, the firm would find credit difficult and potentially expensive to obtain on short notice (a transactions cost). And since the bank usually knows the firms to which it grants lines of credit, the cost of establishing their creditworthiness (an information cost) is negligible.

*Letters of credit* are another important off-balance-sheet item for banks. These letters guarantee that a customer of the bank will be able to make a promised payment. For example, a Canadian importer of television sets may need to reassure a Chinese exporter that the firm will be able to pay for the imported goods when they arrive. This customer might request that the bank send a *commercial letter of credit* to the Chinese exporter guaranteeing payment for the goods on receipt. By issuing the letter of credit, the bank substitutes its own guarantee for the Canadian importer's credit risk, enabling the transaction to go forward. In return for taking this risk, the bank receives a fee.

A related form of the letter of credit is called a *standby letter of credit*. These letters, which are issued to firms and governments that wish to borrow in the financial markets, are a form of insurance. Commercial paper, even when it is issued by a large, well-known firm, must be backed by a standby letter of credit that promises the bank will repay the lender should the issuer default. What is true for large corporations is true for the public sector as well: in most cases, they need a bank guarantee to issue debt. As with loan commitments, letters of credit expose the bank to risk in a way that is not readily apparent on the bank's balance sheet.

"*What I'd like, basically, is a temporary line of credit just to tide me over the rest of my life.*"

The financial crisis in 2007–08 brought home to many the dangers of off-balance-sheet exposures. Many U.S. banks had created subsidiaries (special investment vehicles or SIV) to hold securitized loans. There were two kinds of exposures: in some cases the banks had explicitly promised liquidity support to their vehicles; in other (more dangerous) cases there was no explicit promise but a concern with their reputation (see the discussion of reputational risk below) led the banks to provide liquidity support. In Canada, the banks had far less exposure to SIV. In fall 2007 when the nonbank ABCP market froze, the market for bank-supported ABCP also got tighter, meaning that some paper that the issuers thought they could roll over could not be sold. When a bank had promised liquidity support to the issuer, the bank had to buy the maturing commercial paper. In 2008–09, the Bank of Montreal had promised liquidity support of nearly $10 billion to an SIV operating in London. If the SIV ran into liquidity problems then the Bank of Montreal would have to extend them credit. The Bank of Montreal would then have a senior claim on the assets of the SIV—in this case almost all A-rated or higher financial assets.

Recall the case of Long-Term Capital Management (LTCM), which we discussed in Chapter 9. While LTCM's balance sheet carried assets worth over $100 billion when the firm got into trouble, the risky instruments that did *not* appear on its balance sheet—the $1.25 trillion in interest rate swaps—were what scared everyone. By allowing for the transfer of risk, modern financial instruments enable individual institutions to concentrate risk in ways that are very difficult for outsiders to discern. Ironically, following the failure of LTCM, regulators declared that they would monitor off-balance-sheet exposures more rigorously. After 2008, maybe they will.

# Bank Risk: Where It Comes From and What to Do About It

Banking is risky both because depository institutions are highly leveraged and because of what they do. The bank's goal is to make a profit in each of its lines of business. Some of these are simply fee-for-service activities. For example, a financial institution might act as a broker, buying and selling stocks and bonds on a customer's behalf and charging a fee in return. Banks also transform deposit liabilities into assets such as loans and securities. In the process, they pool savings, provide liquidity services, allow for diversification of risk, and capitalize on the advantages they have in producing information. All along, the goal is to pay less for the deposits the bank receives than for the loans it makes and the securities it buys. That is, the interest rate the bank pays to attract liabilities must be lower than the return it receives on assets.

In the process of all these activities, the bank is exposed to a host of risks. They include the chance that depositors will suddenly withdraw their balances, that borrowers will not repay their loans, that interest rates will change, and that the bank's securities trading operation will do poorly. Each of these risks has a name: *liquidity risk, credit risk, interest rate risk*, and *trading risk*. To understand how these risks arise and what can be done about them, we will look at each in detail.

## Liquidity Risk

All financial institutions face the risk that their liabilities holders (depositors) will seek to cash in their claims. The holder of a chequing account can always walk into the bank and ask for the balance in cash. This risk of a sudden demand for liquid funds is called liquidity risk. Banks face liquidity risk on both sides of their balance sheets. Deposit withdrawal is a liability-side risk, but there is an asset-side risk as well. Recall from our discussion of off-balance-sheet activities that banks provide firms with lines of credit—promises to make loans on demand. When this type of loan commitment is claimed, or *taken down*, the bank must find the liquidity to cover it.

If the bank cannot meet customers' requests for immediate funds, it runs the risk of failure. Even if a bank has a positive net worth, illiquidity can still drive it out of business. Who would put their funds in a bank that can't always provide cash on demand? For this reason, bankers are extremely serious about managing liquidity risk.

To fully understand liquidity risk and how banks manage it, let's look at a simplified balance sheet. Figure 12.4 shows a stripped-down version of the balance sheet of a hypothetical bank. Keep in mind that the two sides of a balance sheet must always balance. Any change in the level of assets must be mirrored by an equal change in the level of liabilities.

**Figure 12.4**  Sample Balance Sheet of a Bank ($million)

| Assets | | Liabilities | |
|---|---|---|---|
| Liquid assets | $500 | Deposits | $9,000 |
| Loans | $8,000 | Securities lent under repo | $500 |
| Securities | $1,500 | Bank capital | $500 |

In Figure 12.4, bank liabilities are composed primarily of deposits, along with some borrowing and $500 million of bank capital. Liabilities plus capital total $10,000 million. To assess liquidity risk, we need to ask how the bank will handle a customer's demand for funds. What happens if a corporate customer writes a cheque on his account for $100 million, reducing deposits by that amount?

Let's assume that the bank is in equilibrium, meaning that the banker believes that the share of each asset and liability in the overall portfolio of the bank is appropriate. Those shares (for example, the ratio of liquid to less liquid assets, the capital asset ratio) are chosen depending on such things as the interest rate spread and the general riskiness of the external environment.

This bank has two choices in responding to the shortfall created by the $100 million withdrawal: It can adjust either its assets or its liabilities. On the asset side, the bank has several options. The quickest and easiest one is to sell a portion of its liquid assets portfolio. Treasury bills can be sold quickly and easily at relatively low cost. The result of this action is shown in the top panel of Figure 12.5. Note that assets and liabilities are both $100 million lower than they were prior to the withdrawal (compare to Figure 12.4). Banks that are particularly concerned about liquidity risk can structure their securities holdings to facilitate such sales. But now the bank's portfolio is significantly less liquid than it wants to hold.

A second possibility is for the bank to refuse to renew a customer loan that has come due. Corporate customers have short-term loans that are periodically renewed, so the bank always has the option of refusing to extend the loan again for another week, month, or year. The result of that action is shown in the bottom panel of Figure 12.5. But this course of action is not very appealing either. Failing to renew a loan is guaranteed to alienate the customer and could well drive the customer to another bank. Recall from Chapter 11 that banks specialize in solving information problems by screening to find customers who are creditworthy and then monitoring them to ensure they repay their loans. The idea is to separate good customers from bad ones and develop long-term relationships with the good ones. The last thing a bank wants to do is to refuse a loan to a creditworthy customer it has gone to some trouble and expense to find.

**Figure 12.5**   Balance Sheet of a Bank Following a $100 Million Withdrawal and Asset Adjustment

**Withdrawal Is Met by Selling Treasury Bills**

| Assets | | Liabilities | |
|---|---|---|---|
| Liquid assets | $400 | Deposits | $8,900 |
| Loans | $8,000 | Securities lent under repo | $500 |
| Securities | $1,500 | Bank capital | $500 |

**Withdrawal Is Met by Reducing Loans**

| Assets | | Liabilities | |
|---|---|---|---|
| Liquid assets | $500 | Deposits | $8,900 |
| Loans | $7,900 | Securities lent under repo | $500 |
| Securities | $1,500 | Bank capital | $500 |

**Figure 12.6** Balance Sheet of a Bank Following a $100 Million Withdrawal and Liability Adjustment

**Withdrawal Is Met by Borrowing**

| Assets | | Liabilities | |
|---|---|---|---|
| Liquid assets | $500 | Deposits | $8,900 |
| Loans | $8,000 | Securities lent under repo | $600 |
| Securities | $1,500 | Bank capital | $500 |

**Withdrawal Is Met by Attracting Deposits**

| Assets | | Liabilities | |
|---|---|---|---|
| Liquid assets | $500 | Deposits | $9,000 |
| Loans | $8,000 | Securities lent under repo | $500 |
| Securities | $1,500 | Bank capital | $500 |

Moreover, bankers do not like to meet their deposit outflows by contracting the asset side of the balance sheet because doing so shrinks the size of the bank. And since banks make a profit by turning liabilities into assets, the smaller their balance sheets, the lower their profits. For this reason alone, today's bankers prefer to use liability management to address liquidity risk. That is, instead of selling assets in response to a deposit withdrawal, they find other sources of funds.

There are two ways for banks to obtain additional funds. First, they can borrow to meet the shortfall, either from the Bank of Canada or more likely by using a repo agreement from another financial institution. The result of such an action is shown in the top panel of Figure 12.6. As you can see, while deposits have fallen by $100 million, borrowing has made up the difference.

A second way to adjust liabilities in response to a deposit outflow is to attract additional deposits. The most common way to do so is to issue large-denomination term deposits. This is shown in the bottom panel of Figure 12.6. As we saw earlier, term deposits have become an increasingly important source of funds for banks. Now we know why: It is because they allow banks to manage their liquidity risk without changing the asset side of their balance sheets.

## Credit Risk

Banks profit from the difference between the interest rate they pay to depositors and the interest rate they receive from borrowers. That is, the return on their assets exceeds the cost of their liabilities. At least, that's the idea. But to ensure that this profit-making process works, for the bank to make a profit, borrowers must repay their loans. There is always some risk that they won't. The risk that a bank's loans will not be repaid is called credit risk. To manage their credit risk, banks use a variety of tools. The most basic are diversification, in which the bank makes a variety of different loans to spread the risk, and credit risk analysis, in which the bank examines the borrower's credit history to determine the appropriate interest rate to charge.

Diversification means spreading risk, which can be difficult for banks, especially those that focus on certain kinds of lending. Since banks specialize in information gathering, it is tempting to try to gain a competitive advantage in a narrow line of business. The problem is, if a bank lends in only one geographic area or only one industry, it exposes itself to economic downturns that are local or industry-specific. It is important that banks find a way to hedge such risks.

Credit risk analysis produces information that is very similar to the bond rating systems discussed in Chapter 7. There we saw that rating agencies such as Moody's and Standard & Poor's produce letter ratings for large corporations wishing to issue bonds. Banks do the same for small firms wishing to borrow, and credit rating agencies perform the service for individual borrowers (see Your Financial World: Your Credit Rating on page 139). Credit risk analysis uses a combination of statistical models and information that is specific to the loan applicant. The result is an assessment of the likelihood that a particular borrower will default. When the bank's loan officers decide to make a loan, they use the customer's credit rating to determine how high an interest rate to charge. To the interest rate they must pay on their liabilities, they add a markup that will allow them to make a profit. The poorer a borrower's credit rating, the higher the interest rate they will charge.[5]

## Interest Rate Risk

Because banks are in the business of turning deposit liabilities into loan assets, the two sides of their balance sheet do not match up. One important difference is that a bank's liabilities tend to be short term, while its assets tend to be long term. This mismatch between the maturities of the two sides of the balance sheet creates interest rate risk.

To understand the problem, think of both the bank's assets and its liabilities as bonds. That is, the bank's deposit liabilities are just like bonds, as are its loan assets. (The bank must be holding some capital as well.) We know that a change in interest rates will affect the value of a bond; when interest rates rise, the price of a bond falls. More important, the longer the term of the bond is, the greater the change in the bond's price at any given change in the interest rate. (Refer back to Chapter 4 to refresh your memory.) Thus, when interest rates rise, banks face the risk that the value of their assets will fall more than the value of their liabilities (reducing the bank's capital). Put another way, if a bank makes long-term loans, it receives payments from borrowers that do not vary with the interest rate. But its short-term liabilities—those with variable interest rates—require the bank to make larger payments when interest rates rise. So rising interest rates reduce revenues relative to expenses, directly lowering the bank's profits.

The best way to see this point is to focus on a bank's revenue and expenses. Let's start by dividing the bank's assets and liabilities into two categories, those that are interest-rate sensitive and those that are not. The term "interest rate sensitive" means that a change in interest rates will change the revenue produced by an asset. Since newly purchased short-term bonds always reflect a change in interest rates, short-term bonds that are constantly maturing and being replaced with new ones produce interest rate–sensitive revenue. In contrast, when the bank purchases long-term bonds, it receives a fixed stream of revenue. Purchasing a 5 percent, 10-year bond means getting $5 per

---

[5] Banks can also manage their credit risk by selling *credit derivatives,* a type of option (discussed in Chapter 9) that allows lenders to insure themselves against changes in borrowers' credit ratings. For example, a bank could buy insurance that a particular borrower will not default on a specific loan. For a detailed discussion, see José Lopez, "Financial Instruments for Mitigating Credit Risk," *Federal Reserve Bank of San Francisco Economic Letter,* no. 2001–34, November 23, 2001; retrieved August 25, 2009, from http://www.frbsf.org/ publications/economics/letter/2001/el2001-34.html.

$100 of face value for 10 years, regardless of what happens to interest rates in the meantime. So the revenue stream from a long-term bond is not interest rate sensitive.

Suppose that 20 percent of a bank's assets fall into the first category, those that are sensitive to changes in the interest rate. Another 80 percent fall into the second category, those that are not sensitive to changes in the interest rate. If the interest rate has been stable at 5 percent for some time, then for each $100 in assets, the bank receives $5 in interest.

The bank's liabilities tend to have a different structure. Let's assume that half the bank's deposits are interest rate sensitive and half are not. In other words, half the bank's liabilities are deposits that earn variable interest rates, so the costs associated with them move with the market rate. Interest-bearing chequing accounts fall into this category. The remainder of the bank's liabilities are time deposits such as guaranteed investment certificates, which have fixed interest rates. The payment a bank makes to the holder of existing GICs does not change with the interest rate.

For the bank to make a profit, the interest rate on its liabilities must be lower than the interest rate on its assets. The difference between the two rates is the bank's net interest margin. Assuming that the interest rate on its liabilities has been 3 percent, the bank has been paying out $3 per $100 in liabilities. Since the bank is receiving 5 percent interest on its assets, its net interest margin is 2 percent (5 minus 3). This margin is the bank's profit.

Now look at what happens if interest rates rise 1 percent for interest-sensitive assets and liabilities. For each $100 in assets, the bank's revenue goes up from $(0.05 \times \$100) = \$5$ to $[(0.05 \times \$80) + (0.06 \times \$20)] = \$5.20$. But the cost of its liabilities goes up too, from $(0.03 \times \$100) = \$3$ to $[(0.03 \times \$50) + (0.04 \times \$50)] = \$3.50$. So a one-percentage point rise in the interest rate reduces the bank's profit from $(\$5 - \$3) = \$2$ per $100 in assets to $(\$5.20 - \$3.50) = \$1.70$, a decline of $0.30. This example illustrates a general principle: When a bank's liabilities are more interest rate sensitive than its assets are, an increase in interest rates will cut into the bank's profits.

The first step in managing interest rate risk is to determine how sensitive the bank's balance sheet is to a change in interest rates. Managers must compute an estimate of the change in the bank's profit for each one-percentage-point change in the interest rate. This procedure is called *gap analysis*, because it highlights the gap, or difference, between the yield on interest rate–sensitive assets and the yield on interest rate–sensitive liabilities. In our example, the gap is (20 percent − 50 percent) = −30 percent. Multiplying this gap times the projected change in the interest rate yields the change in the bank's profit. A gap of −30 tells us that a one-percentage-point increase in the interest rate will reduce the bank's profit by 30 cents per $100 in assets, which is the same answer we got in the last paragraph. Gap analysis can be refined to take account of differences in the maturity of assets and liabilities, but the analysis quickly becomes complicated.[6] Table 12.3 summarizes all of these calculations.

Bank managers can use a number of tools to manage interest rate risk. The simplest approach is to match the interest-rate sensitivity of assets with the interest-rate sensitivity of liabilities. For instance, if the bank accepts a variable-rate deposit, it then uses the funds to purchase short-term securities. A similar strategy is to make long-term loans at a floating interest rate—such as a mortgage with a a variable interest rate. But while this approach reduces interest-rate risk, it increases credit risk. Rising

---

[6] A more sophisticated examination of interest-rate risk, called *duration analysis*, includes a measure of the interest-rate sensitivity of bond prices. A bond's duration is related to its maturity. The percentage change in the market value = − (duration of the bond) × (percentage-point change in the interest rate). Bankers compute the weighted-average duration of their liabilities and subtract it from the weighted-average duration of their assets to get a duration gap, which can be used to guide the bank's risk management strategy. For a complete treatment, see Chapter 9 in Anthony Saunders and Marcia Miller Cornett, *Financial Institutions Management: A Modern Perspective*, 4th ed. (Boston: McGraw-Hill/Irwin, 2003).

**Table 12.3**   An Example of Interest-Rate Risk

| The impact of an interest-rate increase on bank profits (per $100 of assets) | | |
|---|---|---|
| | **Assets** | **Liabilities** |
| Interest-rate sensitive | $20 | $50 |
| Not interest-rate sensitive | $80 | $50 |
| Initial interest rate | 5% | 3% |
| New interest rate on interest-rate-sensitive assets and liabilities | 6% | 4% |
| | **Revenue from Assets** | **Cost of Liabilities** |
| At initial interest rate | (0.05 × $20) + (0.05 × $80) = $5.00 | (0.03 × $50) + (0.03 × $50) = $3.00 |
| After interest-rate change | (0.06 × $20) + (0.05 × $80) = $5.20 | (0.04 × $50) + (0.03 × $50) = $3.50 |
| Profits at initial interest rate: ($5.00) − ($3.00) = $2.00 per $100 in assets | | |
| Profits after interest-rate change:($5.20) − ($3.50) = $1.70 per $100 in assets | | |
| **Gap Analysis** Gap between interest-rate-sensitive assets and interest-rate-sensitive liabilities: (Interest-rate-sensitive assets: $20) − (Interest-rate-sensitive liabilities: $50) = (Gap: −$30) | | |

interest rates put additional strain on floating-rate borrowers, increasing the likelihood that they will default on their payments.

While restructuring assets to better match those of liabilities can reduce risk, the fact that it also reduces potential profitability has led bankers to look for other ways to control interest rate risk. Alternatives include the use of derivatives, specifically interest rate swaps, to manage interest-rate risk. Recall from Chapter 9 that an interest-rate swap is an agreement in which one party promises to make fixed-interest-rate payments in exchange for floating-interest-rate payments. For a bank that is holding long-term assets and short-term liabilities, an interest-rate swap is exactly the sort of financial instrument that will transfer the risk of rising interest rates to another party.

## Trading Risk

There was a time when banks merely took deposits and made loans, holding them until they were completely paid off. Today, banks not only engage in sophisticated asset and liability management but also hire traders to actively buy and sell securities, loans, and derivatives, using a portion of the bank's capital, in the hope of making additional profits for the bank's shareholders. But trading financial instruments is risky. If the price at which an instrument is purchased differs from the price at which it is sold, the risk is that the instrument may go down in value rather than up. This type of risk is called **trading risk**, or sometimes *market risk*.[7]

---

[7]  Since regulators won't allow banks to hold stock (equity), the traders employed by the bank can't, either. But since the traders buy and sell derivatives that are based on bonds, commodities, and foreign exchange, the rule against stock ownership doesn't restrict their ability to take risks.

## IN THE NEWS

### BMO Trader Pleads Guilty

# U.S. prosecutors probe cozy dealing with broker that cost bank $853M

**Financial Post**

**Eoin Callan**

November 19, 2008

When David Lee walked into the Borgata Spa on this day two years ago, he was greeted by a tranquil oasis of soothing aromas and warm hands trained to knead stresses from the muscles of Wall Street bankers.

Amid chauffeured limousine trips to casinos in Atlantic City, the trader and his boss at Bank of Montreal, Robert Moore, ran up a bill at the spa that was not excessive by the standards of bankers at the peak of a bull-market run, $1,218.46.

It was not the price of the indulgence that piqued the interest of U.S. federal investigators, but the name that appeared on the bill: Kevin Cassidy, an executive at New Jersey–based Optionable, a brokerage that handled billions in transactions for Bank of Montreal's natural-gas derivatives trading operation in New York.

After a lengthy investigation, U.S. prosecutors yesterday unsealed a raft of suits and criminal charges against the two former BMO officers and executives at the brokerage alleging collusion in a scheme to conceal losses on natural gas trades.

Mr. Lee is pleading guilty, and has admitted overvaluing the bank's gas-options portfolio by inflating the worth of trading positions.

The illegal activity first came to light last year after disclosures by the Bay Street bank and enquiries by *The*

*Financial Post*, and prompted BMO to record related losses of $853-million.

The trader has admitted he would regularly sit at his desk in BMO's Times Square office in Manhattan and create flattering values for his "book" of trading positions by using his own mathematical model, when market prices were difficult to ascertain or unavailable.

These generous calculations made the performance of the New York unit look better than it was in reality and allowed Mr. Lee to collect bigger bonuses.

"Lee inflated the value of his book so that it would appear to BMO that his trading was more," investigators said.

To help cover up the distortions and meet his bank's requirement for independent verification of the value of his portfolio, the trader would then e-mail the figures to his personal e-mail address.

After arriving home from the office, the 37-year-old would then forward the over-inflated estimates by e-mail in a spreadsheet to brokers at Optionable, with whom a close relationship had been developed, according to investigators who pieced together a trail of electronic communications that Mr. Lee had attempted to destroy.

The next morning, brokers at Optionable, including Mr. Cassidy, would forward the numbers fabricated by BMO's own trader to BMO's compliance office, prosecutors alleged yesterday.

The "brokers knowingly deceived and defrauded BMO" by passing the falsified figures off as independent estimates, federal officials said in court documents.

The motive of Mr. Lee was to maintain his high-living lifestyle, inflate his performance and conceal losses, according to investigators who accused his supervisor, Mr. Moore, of looking the other way.

The investigators found a lengthy list of "gambling vacations" and visits to men's grooming clubs by Mr. Moore, the BMO executive, sometimes accompanied by Mr. Lee, that

Managing trading risk is a major concern for today's banks. Some of the largest banks in the world have sustained billions of dollars in losses as a result of unsupervised risk taking by employees in their trading operations. The problem is that traders normally share in the profits from good investments, but the bank pays for the losses. Heads, the trader wins; tails, the bank loses. This arrangement creates moral hazard: Traders have an incentive to take more risk than bank managers would like.

were paid for by executives at Optionable and appear to form a pattern of expensive gifts that violated the bank's policy.

A person close to the investigation said there were indications Mr. Lee had sought a seat on the board of the brokerage, though the complaints and indictments unsealed yesterday focused on the cosy relationship that existed between traders at BMO and its broker.

The person pointed out that BMO was Optionable's biggest customer and that this gave the broker an interest in maintaining a good working relationship with the Canadian bank.

In turn, it was trades executed by Mr. Lee that accounted for the bulk of the fees collected by Optionable, which prosecutors allege showered the trader with gifts and helped cover up losses.

The scheme operated successfully for years, but came undone when BMO insisted multiple outside brokers periodically value trading portfolios.

Mr. Cassidy, 49, a founder of Optionable, faces sentences of up to 70 years, on charges of wire fraud, securities fraud and false bank entry.

"We are pleased with the actions taken today by the authorities to bring proceedings against those involved with the commodities trading losses," said a spokesperson for BMO.

## Back Story

May 5, 2007 BMO's explanation for $450-million in losses is questioned widely. BMO had claimed it was left with a bunch of bad trades when the demand for natural gas options dried up and there was a sharp decline in price volatility, claims that turned out to be false.

May 10, 2007 The Financial Post discovers the existence of a Deloitte and Touche report identifying irregularities in the company's New York natural gas trading book. BMO confirms that David Lee, the BMO trader blamed for the losses, is on a leave of absence.

May 11, 2007 *The Financial Post* reports that three senior executives had cashed in US$27-million before the company received the Deloitte and Touche report. David Lee is found to have a close personal relationship with executives at Optionable.

May 17, 2007 BMO reports further losses from natural gas trades, bringing the total to $680-million.

May 25, 2007 *The New York Post* reports that the U.S. Securities and Exchange Commission is investigating Optionable Inc.

Nov. 18, 2008 David Lee pleads guilty to hiding trading losses from BMO

### LESSONS OF THE ARTICLE

Trading operations are notoriously difficult to monitor, and they can go dramatically wrong. The problem is analogous to moral hazard in debt finance (discussed in Chapter 11). Traders are gambling with someone else's money, sharing the gains but not the losses from their risk taking. As a result, they are prone to taking too much risk—and in the cases discussed here, to hiding their losses when their trades turn sour. This moral hazard presents a challenge to the bank's shareholders, who must find ways to rein in traders' tendencies to take too much risk. The tip-off to unbridled risk taking can come when a trader makes too big a profit. Odds are that someone who is making large profits on some days will register big losses on other days. There is no way to make a large profit without taking a big risk.

SOURCE: *By Eoin Callan*, Financial Post, November 19, 2008. *Material reprinted with the express permission of "The National Post Company," a CanWest Partnership.*

The solution to the moral hazard problem in trading is to compute the risk the portfolios traders generate using measures such as standard deviation and value at risk (see Chapter 5). The bank's risk manager then limits the amount of risk any individual trader is allowed to assume and monitors each trader's holdings closely, at least once a day. Moreover, the higher the risk inherent in the bank's portfolio, the more capital the bank will need to hold to make sure the institution remains solvent.

## Other Risks

Beyond liquidity, credit, interest-rate, and trading risk, banks face an assortment of other risks. A bank that operates internationally will face foreign exchange risk and sovereign risk. **Foreign exchange risk** comes from holding assets denominated in one currency and liabilities denominated in another. For example, a bank might purchase bonds issued by Sony Corporation or make a loan to a Japanese business. Both those assets would be denominated in yen. Thus, when the dollar–yen exchange rate moves, the dollar value of the bank's assets will change. Banks manage their foreign exchange risk in two ways. We saw that Canadian banks work to attract deposits that are denominated in the same currency as their loans, thereby matching their assets with their liabilities, and they use foreign exchange futures and swaps to hedge the risk.

Banks also worry a lot about **reputational risk**. We have seen that information is at the core of financial intermediation. The maturity mismatch that characterizes banks makes them particularly vulnerable to reputation risk. As we will discuss in Chapter 14, deposit insurance means that small depositors (those depositing less than $100,000) do not worry about the bank not being able to repay them. But there are other risks. First, large depositors could withdraw their term deposits. A similar problem would occur if the bank had raised funds by selling short-term commercial paper; commercial paper issuers frequently count on being able to roll over (that is, to pay off the old loan with a new loan) their commercial paper. A challenge to the reputation of a bank might mean that they could not roll over their commercial paper, which could present a serious liquidity problem.

While small depositors might not withdraw deposits because they fear for a bank's soundness, they might withdraw deposits if they felt that a bank was acting unethically. As we have seen, a bank's profits come from lending out funds at a higher interest rate than they pay to their depositors. No deposits, no profits. So the banks work to maintain a solid reputation so that they keep deposits.

**Sovereign risk** arises from the fact that some foreign borrowers may not repay their loans, not because they are unwilling to, but because their government prohibits them from doing so. When a foreign country is experiencing a financial crisis, the government may decide to restrict dollar-denominated payments, in which case a Canadian bank would have difficulty collecting payments on its loans in the country. Such circumstances have arisen on numerous occasions. Examples include Asia in 1997, Russia in 1998, and Argentina in 2002. In all these cases governments and corporations alike had difficulty raising enough dollars to repay their dollar-denominated debts. In such crises, a bank has very little recourse in the courts and little hope of recovering the loans.

Managing sovereign risk is difficult. Banks have three options. The first is diversification, which means distributing the bank's loans and securities holdings throughout the world, carefully avoiding too much exposure in any country where a crisis might arise. Second, the bank can simply refuse to do business in a particular country or set of countries. And third, the bank can use derivatives to hedge sovereign risk.

The final risk that banks face is the risk that their computer systems may fail or their buildings burn down (or blow up), what's called **operational risk**. When terrorists destroyed the World Trade Center towers on September 11, 2001, power and communications were disrupted in a large and important part of lower Manhattan. Many financial firms located in or near the World Trade Center quickly switched to backup sites, but others couldn't. The Bank of New York, a large commercial bank, was one of those that fell victim to operational risk. The Bank of New York plays

Figure 12.7     The Bank of New York and September 11, 2001

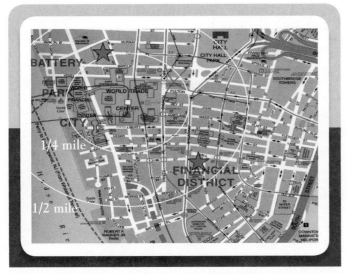

The two red stars show the location of the Bank of New York's primary operations and the backup site. They are both within half a mile of the centre of the World Trade Center complex that was destroyed by terrorists on September 11, 2001. Because these buildings became inaccessible, the Bank of New York ceased operation for several days.

SOURCE: *Copyright American Map Corporation, Lic. No. AMC033007.*

an extremely important role in the U.S. financial system, handling hundreds of billions of dollars worth of transactions each day in the U.S. Treasury securities market. Prior to September 11, the bank maintained both its primary and backup operations within blocks of the World Trade Center (see Figure 12.7). Not only were power and communications to these buildings knocked out by the terrorist attack, but also no one could even get to them. The bank practically shut down for several days and recovered only slowly, losing an estimated $140 million in the process. In placing the backup site so close to the bank's primary operations, managers had made an enormous mistake: They had failed to take account of a significant operational risk.[8]

These risks are serious business. One study estimates that over the 10 years ending in 2002, there were more than 100 events in which financial institutions lost a total of $100 million.[9]

---

[8] For a discussion of the problems that occurred in the U.S. financial system following the destruction of the World Trade Center towers, see the Federal Reserve Bank of New York's *Economic Policy Review,* November 2002, special issue on the economic effects of September 11. Of particular note are Michael J. Fleming and Kenneth D. Garbade, "When the Back Office Moved to the Front Burner: Settlement Fails in the Treasury Market after September 11," and James J. McAndrews and Simon Potter, "Liquidity Effects of the Event of September 11, 2001" retrieved from http://www.newyorkfed.org/research/epr/2002.html.

[9] See Patrick de Fountnouville, Virginia DeJesus-Rueff, John Jordan, and Eric Rosengren, "Capital and Risk: New Evidence on Implications of Large Operational Losses" *Journal of Money Credit and Banking* October 2006, v.38.issue7, pp. 1819–46.

**Table 12.4** Risks Banks Face and How They Manage Them

| Type of Risk | Source of Risk | Recommended Responses |
|---|---|---|
| Liquidity Risk | Sudden withdrawals by depositors | 1. Hold sufficient cash reserves to meet customer demand.<br>2. Manage assets—sell securities or loans (contracts the size of the balance sheet)<br>3. Manage liabilities—attract more deposits (maintains the size of the balance sheet) |
| Credit Risk | Default by borrowers on their loans | 1. Diversify to spread risk.<br>2. Use statistical models to screen for creditworthy borrowers.<br>3. Monitor to reduce moral hazard. |
| Interest-Rate Risk | Mismatch in maturity of assets and liabilities coupled with a change in interest rates | 1. Closely match the maturity of both sides of the balance sheet.<br>2. Use derivatives such as interest-rate swaps. |
| Trading (Market) Risk | Trading losses in the bank's own account | Closely monitor traders using risk management tools, including value at risk. |

In principle, managing operational risk is straightforward, but in practice it can be difficult. The bank must ensure that its computer systems and buildings are sufficiently robust to withstand potential disasters. That means both anticipating what might happen and testing to ensure the system's readiness. Forecasting the possibilities can be daunting. Who could have predicted what happened on September 11?

Table 12.4 summarizes the four major risks banks face and the recommended risk-management strategies.

## Terms

balance sheet, 254
bank capital, 259
credit risk, 268
depository institution, 253
foreign exchange risk, 274
interest rate spread, 263
interest rate risk, 269
liquidity, 254
liquidity risk, 266
loan loss reserves, 260
net interest margin, 263

nondepository institution, 253
off-balance-sheet activities, 263
operational risk, 274
repurchase agreement (repo), 259
reputational risk, 274
return on assets (ROA), 261
return on equity (ROE), 262
sovereign risk, 274
trading risk, 271

## Chapter Summary

1. Bank assets equal bank liabilities plus bank capital.
   a. Bank assets are the uses for bank funds.
      i. They include liquid assets, securities, and loans.
      ii. Over the years, securities have become less important and mortgages more important as a use for bank funds.
   b. Bank liabilities are the sources of bank funds.
      i. They include transaction and nontransaction deposits as well as borrowings from other banks.
      ii. Over the years, transaction repos have become more important and personal savings accounts less important as a source of bank funds.

c. Bank capital is the contribution of the bank's shareholders; it acts as a cushion against a fall in the value of the bank's assets or a withdrawal of its liabilities.

d. Banks make a profit for their shareholders. Measures of a bank's profitability include return on assets (ROA), return on equity (ROE), net interest income, and net interest margin.

e. Banks' off-balance-sheet activities have become increasingly important in recent years. They include:

   i. Loan commitments, which are lines of credit firms can use whenever necessary.

   ii. Letters of credit, which are guarantees that a customer will make a promised payment.

   iii. Liquidity commitments to special investment vehicles.

2. Banks face several types of risk in day-to-day business. They include

a. Liquidity risk—the risk that customers will demand cash immediately.

   i. Liability-side liquidity risk arises from deposit withdrawals.

   ii. Asset-side liquidity risk arises from the use of loan commitments to borrow.

   iii. Banks can manage liquidity risk by adjusting either their assets or their liabilities.

b. Credit risk—the risk that customers will not repay their loans. Banks can manage credit risk by

   i. Diversifying their loan portfolios.

   ii. Using statistical models to analyze borrowers' creditworthiness.

   iii. Monitoring borrowers to ensure that they use borrowed funds properly.

c. Interest rate risk—the risk that a movement in interest rates will change the value of the bank's assets more than the value of its liabilities.

   i. When a bank lends long and borrows short, increases in interest rates will drive down the bank's profits.

   ii. Banks use a variety of tools, such as gap analysis, to assess the sensitivity of their balance sheets to a change in interest rates.

   iii. Banks manage interest rate risk by matching the maturity of their assets and liabilities and using derivatives like interest rate swaps.

d. Trading risk—the risk that traders who work for the bank will create losses on the bank's own account. Banks can manage this risk using complex statistical models.

e. Other risks banks face include foreign exchange risk, reputation risk sovereign risk, and operational risk.

## Conceptual Problems

1. Why do you think that Canadian banks have grown so dramatically in the last 20 years?

2. Banks hold more liquid assets than most businesses do. Explain why.

3. The volume of general loans made by banks has declined over the past few decades. Explain why. What item has counterbalanced the decline in the value of loans on banks' balance sheets?

4.* Why do you think that banks are prohibited from holding equity as part of their own portfolios?

5. In the Bank of Canada's Banking and Financial Statistics, (http://www.bankofcanada.ca/pdf/bfs.pdf) there are tables containing the "Assets and Liabilities of Chartered Banks." Download the most recent data and construct a table that matches Table 12.1.

a. Compare your table to Table 12.1. What are the differences in the data, and how can you explain them?

b. Find the current level of nominal GDP in Canada and use it as a scale for the numbers in your table. What pattern do you see?

6. Explain how a bank uses liability management to respond to a deposit outflow. Why do banks prefer liability management to asset management?

7. Banks carefully consider the maturity structure of both their assets and their liabilities. What is the significance of the maturity structure? What risks are banks trying to manage when they adjust their maturity structure?

8. A bank has issued a one-year GIC for $50 million at an interest rate of 2 percent. With the proceeds, the bank has purchased a two-year Government bond that pays 4 percent interest. What risk does the bank face in entering into these transactions? What would happen if all interest rates rose by 1 percent?

* Indicates more difficult problems.

9. Define operational risk and explain how a bank manages it.

10. In response to changes in banking legislation Canadian banks now all own large investment dealer subsidiaries. How do you think this development affects the level of risk in banking business?

## Analytical Problems

11. Consider the balance sheets of Bank A and Bank B. Which bank do you think faces the greater liquidity risk? Explain your answer.

**Bank A**
**(in millions)**

| Assets | | Liabilities | |
|---|---|---|---|
| Liquid assets | $50 | Demand deposits | $200 |
| Loans | $920 | Term deposits | $600 |
| Securities | $250 | Borrowings | $100 |

**Bank B**
**(in millions)**

| Assets | | Liabilities | |
|---|---|---|---|
| Liquid assets | $30 | Demand deposits | $200 |
| Loans | $920 | Term deposits | $600 |
| Securities | $50 | Borrowings | $100 |

12. Looking again at Bank A and Bank B, based on the information available, which bank do you think is at the greatest risk of insolvency? What other information might you use to assess the risk of insolvency of these banks?

13.* Bank Y and Bank Z both have assets of $1 billion. The return on assets for both banks is the same. Bank Y has liabilities of $800 million while Bank Z's liabilities are $900 million. In which bank would you prefer to hold an equity stake? Explain your choice.

14. You are a bank manager and have been approached by a swap dealer about participating in fixed- for floating-interest-rate swaps. If your bank has the typical maturity structure, which side of the swap might you be interested in paying and which side would you want to receive?

15. If off-balance-sheet activities such as lines of credit do not, by definition, directly affect the balance sheet, how can they influence the level of liquidity risk to which the bank is exposed?

16. Suppose a bank faces a gap of −20 between its interest-sensitive assets and its interest-sensitive liabilities. What would happen to bank profits if interest rates were to fall by 1 percentage point? You should report your answer in terms of the change in profit per $100 in assets.

17. Suppose you were the manager of a bank with the following balance sheet.

**Bank Balance Sheet**
**(in millions)**

| Assets | | Liabilities | |
|---|---|---|---|
| Liquid assets | $30 | Transaction Deposits | $200 |
| Loans | $820 | Nontransaction Deposits | $600 |
| Securities | $150 | Borrowings | $100 |

You want to hold 10 percent of transaction deposits in liquid assets. If you were faced with unexpected withdrawals of $30 million from transaction deposits, what portfolio management options do you have, and which would you choose?

## CHAPTER 13

# Financial Industry Structure

For much of Canadian history, the financial sector was structured around what were termed, "four pillars": banking, trust companies, insurance, and brokerage, and government policy and regulation ensured that each pillar was distinct. Furthermore, foreign institutions were largely prohibited from entering the Canadian market: there were Canadian banks, Canadian life insurance companies, Canadian trust companies. By the beginning of the 21st century the separation between the pillars had largely broken down as had some of the nationalistic isolation. Today, banks own trust companies, insurance companies, and securities dealers; insurance companies own banks. To a large extent, this breakdown was technology driven, but it also reflected a change in regulatory ethos. The rationale for the nationalist and four pillar approaches had been that they increased the stability of the financial system. As we will see in chapters 14 and 15, regulators have continued to focus on stability but believe that the efficiency gains from the broader scope of financial institutions are significant and that the stability concerns can be addressed in other ways.

To understand the structure of the financial industry we need to step back and see how the sector evolved, putting the various components into a broader perspective. We begin by looking at the depository institutions and show how the basic industry structure emerged. Then we turn to the many different nondepository financial institutions. Finally we look at the impact of the trends of globalization, technological innovation and regulation on the structure of the financial sector of the future.

## Depository Institutions

Depository institutions encompass chartered banks, and also trust and loan companies, credit unions, caisses populaires and the Alberta Treasury Branch (ATB), but the banking system is far and away the largest component. In 2006 (the last year for which there are comparable data), the banks had total assets of about $2.4 trillion while the credit unions and caisses populaires had assets of $193 billion and the trust and loan companies (other than the subsidiaries of the banks) had assets of about $18 billion. ATB had assets close to $20 billion.[1] So we begin with the banking system. To understand the structure of the Canadian banking system we show how it evolved and contrast it with a very different system that evolved in almost the same circumstances—the U.S. banking system. Why did two such different systems evolve in such parallel circumstances? Is one system better? Are there forces in today's economy that will lead them to become more similar? We begin with the history.

### A Short History of Canadian Banking

Canada, a nation of 33 million people, has 21 domestic banks. If the United States had the same ratio of banks to population, the country would have approximately 190 banks.

---

[1] Data are from Bank of Canada, Banking and Financial Statistics, August 2009. For Banks: Table C2, p. s21; Trust and mortgage loan companies, Table D1 p. s40; Credit Unions and Caisses populaires, Table D2 p. s42. Data for ATB are from their 2007 Annual Report, p. 78.

In fact, 7,400 commercial banks and roughly 17,000 depository institutions exist within U.S. borders, all vying to serve some 300 million Americans. While the United States and Canada are extremes, most countries' banking systems more closely resemble the Canadian structure. In Japan, for example, 127 million people depend on 196 banks; in the United Kingdom, 60 million people are served by fewer than 250 banks.

The Canadian banking system has always been relatively concentrated: there have never been more than 50 domestic banks (in 1901) and today the Big 6 banks own 90 percent of the assets of the banking system. The United States once had even more banks than it does today: the number peaked at 15,000 in 1984 and has been falling ever since. The basic reason for the difference lies in the early days of banking in the two countries. Canada established a **branch banking** system, with each bank having many offices. In most American states, banks were **unit banks**, or banks without branches. Although there has been consolidation in the industry in both countries, the legacy of that initial design remains.

The Bank of Montreal and the Bank of Nova Scotia were among the first banks established in what is now Canada, in the early 1800s. The banks took deposits of coins and gave the depositors either credit in their deposit account or bank notes. What did the banks do with the coins deposited? Some—about 20 percent—they kept as reserves to pay out to those who wanted to redeem their notes or withdraw their deposits, and the rest they lent out to merchants or the government. (Consumer lending was prohibited until the mid-20th century.[2]) So the banks lent out about 80 percent of the monies entrusted to them and earned interest on their loans. Banking was a profitable business.

A $10 banknote issued by the Bank of Montreal, 1835.

SOURCE: *Currency Museum, Bank of Canada.*

There was no central bank so bank notes were issued by the private banks. What stopped the banks from just printing unlimited quantities of bank notes? First, they had to be willing to exchange the notes for gold or silver coins on demand, so they had to keep a reserve of gold and silver coins. If the note holders got the idea that the bank didn't have enough reserves they might all come to the bank demanding coins. This was called a bank run. Second, the bank owners had "double liability"—if the bank went bankrupt then the owners not only would lose the capital they put in, but also would be billed for as much again. Finally, note-issuing banks needed a special Act of Parliament—a bank "charter"— and there were initially very few banks. A **bank charter** was very valuable as the chartered banks had at least some monopoly power. The bank charter stated the powers of a bank, such as issuing notes and making loans. The charter also limited the powers of a bank: banks had to be willing to redeem their notes in coin on demand, and banks could make loans with only very specific collateral.[3] All the charters allowed the banks to open branches.

After Confederation in 1867 there were a few years of confusion as the monetary systems of the former colonies were harmonized to create a single monetary system with a common set of rules for banks. Prior to Confederation, each bank charter was idiosyncratic and each charter expired at a different time. The *Bank Act* of 1871 renewed all the charters for 10 years. Since 1871, the *Bank Act* has been renewed

---

[2] Households would obtain mortgages from insurance companies, trust companies or specialized mortgage loan companies. Loans for buying cars or household appliances were often made by the selling firms—or family members.

[3] The collateral was essentially limited to accounts receivable, which was called "real bills." Banks could not accept real estate (as in mortgages) or securities (stocks) as collateral.

roughly every 10 years, which gives the government the opportunity to review the conditions under which the banks operate.

Between Confederation and 1900, the number of banks increased, reaching a maximum of 50. In part that reflected the growth of the Canadian population but mostly it was the realization of the profitability of banks and the government's willingness to issue new charters. Not all banks were successful, however; 20 failed. Today it is hard to imagine the impact of a bank failure, because deposits are insured and the bank notes we use are issued by the Bank of Canada. Imagine if the only bank notes we could use were issued by banks without insurance— it was a risky environment. At the *Bank Act* renewal in 1881 the government had introduced mandatory insurance for bank notes and after that date noteholders were reimbursed if a bank failed. But depositors were not, and sometimes experienced losses despite the double liability of shareholders.

*"Of course, you could try another bank, if there were any other banks."*

Although some banks failed, Canada did not experience the banking panics that seemed to occur every decade in the United States. The reason for the stability of the Canadian system is not completely understood, although we know it was not a result of careful government monitoring or assistance: these did not exist. The branch banking system was clearly part of the answer as it enabled the banks to diversify their liabilities and, especially, their assets. The banks made loans across the country and across different types of business. The restrictions on collateral did not preclude lending on a wide range of agricultural and commercial activities.

Another source of stability was the "elastic" note issue of the Canadian banks. In the agricultural economy of the 19th century, the demand for bank notes was highest in the fall when crops were being brought to market. In Canada, the banks would issue more notes in the fall and then redeem them over the winter. In the United States, bank notes were issued by the national banks (described below) and those banks had to send government bonds to Washington to receive notes for circulation. This was a long process and while the banks would stock up for the fall, demands were difficult to predict exactly, and banks often ran short. The U.S. banking system was particularly vulnerable to panics in the fall.

Some historians have argued that the stability of the Canadian system was due to the tight-knit nature of the Canadian industry, and the role of the Canadian Bankers Association. If a bank might become insolvent, the Minister of Finance could discuss the potential consequences for the industry with a few of the larger banks and encourage them to take over the bank for the good of the system. (As discussed in Chapter 14, this is one way the Canada Deposit Insurance Corporation responds to potential insolvency today.) While there were 23 mergers and amalgamations of banks between 1900 and 1920 (and only 8 bank failures) it is hard to know if this consolidation reflected a search for economies of scale or a solution to imminent failure.

Although some Canadians had advocated for government supervision of banks, the Canadian Bankers Association argued that it wasn't necessary and that the industry could be self-regulating. But in 1923 the Home Bank, a large Ontario bank, failed and the government finally required that there be at least monitoring of the banking system; it created the office of the Inspector General of Banks. (Sixty years later the next bank failure would also lead to the first real change in supervision with the creation of the Office of the Superintendent of Financial Institutions.)

The Canadian banking system remained relatively stable through much of the 20th century, including the Great Depression. Gradually though, in the second half of the century, the banking sector changed in response to factors such as technology, globalization, and competition from nonbanks. The decennial review of the *Bank Act* provided a key tool for these adjustments. (With the changing pace of those forces, the *Bank Act* is now reviewed every five years.)

In 1954, the *Bank Act* was amended to permit the banks to lend against government-insured mortgages and the National Housing Act was amended to permit CMHC to insure mortgages (with down payments of 25 percent). The banks moved slowly into the mortgage lending field but today are the largest originators of mortgages.[4] In the late 1960s the banks expanded their exposure to retail debt by sponsoring Visa (initially Chargex) and Mastercard. In 1987 the government amended the *Bank Act* again to permit the banks to hold investment dealer subsidiaries. Very quickly each of the large banks bought one of the larger investment dealers and today each of the largest securities firms is owned by a bank. The *Bank Act* of 1991 permitted banks to hold trust companies and insurance companies as subsidiaries. The banks begin to operate insurance firms, and insurance companies were allowed to own banks, however, to date, Manulife is the only insurance company to take advantage of this possibility, opening Manulife Banking 1993. Other entrants came from outside the financial sector when President's Choice and Canadian Tire both established banks in 1993 and 2003 respectively.

In 1996, the government created a task force on the future of Canadian financial services, signalling more clearly that it saw the industry as a whole and not as four pillars. The task force report (the "MacKay Report" after its Chairman, Harold MacKay) led the way to the 2001 amendments to the *Bank Act*, which created the Financial Consumer Agency of Canada, and allowed the creation of bank holding companies that owned banks and other financial firms. The 2001 amendments also relaxed the ownership structure of banks. Historically, domestic banks were required to be "widely held"; that is, no one person could own more than 10 percent of the shares. MacKay's task force recommended that smaller banks be permitted to have narrower share holding and the 2001 amendments created three types of bank: banks with equity in excess of $5 billion must be widely held; banks with equity between $1 billion and $5 billion can have up to 65 percent of shares held by one person; and small banks with less than $1 billion in equity can be held by a single person.

Until 1999, foreign banks were not allowed to establish branches in Canada although wholly owned subsidiaries of foreign banks were permitted to operate. Then in 1999, an amendment to the *Bank Act* (also prompted by the MacKay Report) permitted operation of branches of foreign banks, although they were restricted from accepting deposits of less than $150,000. This meant that they were not active in the retail deposit market and were primarily in commercial and industrial lending. Table 13.1 summarizes the structure of the Canadian banking system in 2009. While the sector has opened up, the Big 6 domestic Canadian banks remain dominant.

## A Short History of U.S. Banking

In the 19th-century United States, just as in Canada, you needed a charter to open a bank. But unlike in Canada, most charters prohibited branching, creating a unit banking system. Advocates of legal limits on branching argued that such limits prevented concentration and monopoly in banking in the same way that antitrust

---

[4] A 1967 *Bank Act* amendment allowed the banks to lend against conventional mortgages even without insurance. For a longer description, see Charles Freedman (1998) "The Canadian Banking System," *Bank of Canada Technical Report*, 81.

**Table 13.1**   Canadian Banking System

Schedule I: Domestic banks (21)
- Includes the Big 6 Canadian banks plus other domestic banks, such as First Nations Bank of Canada and Manulife Bank of Canada
- Total assets of this group (April 30, 2009): $2,740 billion.

Schedule II: Foreign bank subsidiaries (26)
- Can accept deposits and are typically members of CDIC
- Includes BNP Paribas (Canada) and Citibank Canada
- Total assets of this group (April 30, 2009): $149 billion.

Schedule III: Foreign bank branches (30)
- Two types: full service branches can accept deposits (over $150,000) and make loans, while lending branches cannot accept deposits.
- Full service branches include Deutsche Bank AG and UBS AG Canada Branch; lending branches include Credit Suisse, Toronto Branch.
- Total assets of this group (April 30, 2009): $76 billion.

SOURCE: OSFI, *Data on bank numbers and assets http://www.osfi-bsif.gc.ca. There are three schedules appended to the Bank Act listing each type of bank, so the banks are often identified by their schedule number; e.g., the Big 6 are Schedule I banks.*

laws prevented concentration in manufacturing. They feared that without such limits, a few large banks could drive small ones out of business, reducing the quality of financial services available in small communities.[5]

The unit banking system meant that there were many different banknotes circulating, so that telling the sound money from the unsound became inordinately confusing and inefficient. The whole point of printing money is to reduce information costs and facilitate trade. People hesitated to accept banknotes issued by banks they weren't familiar with, so money was not widely accepted. In the end, the system just didn't work.

Radical change came during the Civil War, when Congress passed the *National Banking Act* of 1863, initiating a gradual shift in power away from the states. While the new law didn't eliminate state-chartered banks, it did impose a 10 percent tax on their issue of banknotes. At the same time, the act created a system of federally chartered banks, or *national banks,* which would be supervised by the Office of the Comptroller of the Currency, inside the U.S. Department of the Treasury. These new national banks could issue banknotes tax-free. Congress's intent was to put the state banks out of business by taking away their source of funds.

While the act did get rid of state-issued banknotes, state banks devised another way to raise funds, by creating demand deposits. Today the United States has a **dual banking system**, in which banks can choose whether to get their charters from the Comptroller of the Currency at the U.S. Treasury or from state officials, leading to what is called "regulatory arbitrage." State banking authorities have been more permissive than federal authorities in the types of operations they allow. Because greater flexibility in a

[5] The United States did have one large branching bank from 1792 to 1812, the Bank of the United States. In 1812, that Bank's 20-year charter was not renewed but a few years later, Congress did charter another nationally branching bank, which became known as the Second Bank of the United States. Again, the charter was not renewed as President Andrew Jackson argued that the Bank represented big-city Eastern moneyed interests and hurt Westerners and farmers.

The first national banknote issued in 1863.

bank's operations means a better chance of making a profit, state charters have been the overwhelming choice. Roughly three-quarters of U.S. banks now have a state charter; the rest have a federal charter.

But national banks were still unit banks, and remained particularly fragile. In 1907, a run on banks across the country provoked the federal government to create a system of Federal Reserve Banks, a central bank that had a monopoly over the note issue. Federal Reserve notes were convertible into gold on demand and each of the 12 Federal Reserve banks, which were spread across the United States, held reserves against those notes.

The next major event in U.S. banking history occurred in 1933 in the midst of the Great Depression. From 1929 to 1933, more than one-third of all U.S. banks failed; individual depositors lost $1.5 billion, or about 3 percent of total bank deposits. At the time, total personal income was less than $50 billion, or about $1 billion a week. So on average, the bank failures of the Great Depression cost depositors one and a half weeks' pay. (Today, total personal income in the United States is over $10 trillion, or roughly $200 billion a week, so the equivalent loss would be about $300 billion. This is far more than the combined losses to depositors and the FDIC in mid-2009, but not outside the possible bounds of costs by the end of 2010.) But since failures were concentrated in small banks, small depositors bore the brunt of the collapse. Millions of small savers lost their life savings.

Congress responded to the crisis with the Glass-Steagall Act of 1933, which created the Federal Deposit Insurance Corporation (FDIC) and severely limited the activities of commercial banks. It also prohibited banks from dealing in securities, providing insurance, or engaging in any of the other activities undertaken by nondepository institutions. But by separating commercial banks from investment banking, the law limited the ability of financial institutions to take advantage of economies of scale and scope that might exist in various lines of business.[6]

In 1980, a gradual process of deregulation of the banking system undid the regulation of the 1930s (though not deposit insurance). Gradually, banks were allowed to pay interest on deposits (1978–86),[7] to branch (the 1994 *Riegle-Neal Act*) and to own securities firms (the 1999 *Gramm-Leach-Bliley Act*).

The effects have been dramatic. In 1935, the vast majority of U.S. banks had no branches; today, nearly three-quarters of them do. In fact, in 1935 there were 14,125 banks in the United States, with a total of 17,237 offices; by 2006 there were 7,480 banks with 80,473 offices. But although there are many banks, the system is very concentrated: roughly 1 percent of the banks hold more than 75 percent of all bank assets. In 2007, Bank of America alone accounted for around 10 percent of both assets and deposits in the U.S. banking system. Deregulation has also spurred the profitability of the banking sector: banks' operating costs and loan losses fell, and the interest rates paid to depositors rose while the interest rates charged to borrowers fell.

But the verdict on deregulation is not yet in. In 2008, the five largest investment banks "disappeared." Bear Sterns was bought by JP Morgan (with the help of a $30 billion federal loan); Merrill Lynch was bought by Bank of America; Lehman Brothers

---

[6] The 1956 Bank Holding Company Act effectively prohibited interstate bank ownership.

[7] For detail on the gradual elimination of interest rate ceilings for deposits, see Anton Gilbert, (n.d.) "Requiem for Regulation Q: What It Did and Why It Passed Away" at http://research.stlouisfed.org/publications/review/86/02/Requiem_Feb1986.pdf.

filed for Chapter 11 bankruptcy protection, and Morgan Stanley and Goldman Sachs applied to become bank holding companies (BHC). As bank holding companies they will be regulated by the Federal Reserve (rather than the SEC) but will also be eligible for financial support from the Fed. In the first half of 2009, 22 banks failed (only 44 had failed in the decade between 1997 and 2007). Many observers blamed deregulation for the financial crisis; however, much of the deregulation happened a decade or more ago, making the link between deregulation and the crisis tenuous. The role of deregulation in the financial crisis is hotly debated and we return to it in subsequent chapters.

Furthermore, banks became more profitable: their operating costs and loan losses fell; the interest rates paid to depositors rose while the interest rates charged to borrowers fell.

## Nondepository Financial Institutions

A survey of the financial industry reveals a broad array of intermediaries. Besides depository institutions, there are five categories of nondepository institution: insurance companies; pension funds; securities firms, including brokers, mutual fund companies, and investment dealers; finance companies; and government-sponsored enterprises. This classification is neither exhaustive nor meant to imply that an institution's activities are restricted to a particular category. Nondepository institutions also include an assortment of alternative intermediaries, such as pawnshops (see Your Financial World: Pawnshops, page 286), payday loan centres (see Your Financial World: The Cost of Payday Loans, page 263), rent-to-own centres, and even loan sharks. Figure 13.1 shows that banks hold the majority of assets in the Canadian financial system, with mutual fund companies and life insurance companies next in terms of asset size. The measurement of the role of the various players in the financial sector is complex because of the interconnections in the industry. For example, the banks and insurance companies own mutual funds (in Figure 13.1 the mutual fund assets have been separated out from the bank and insurance assets).

Our goal in this section is to understand the role of each of these types of nondepository institution in our financial system. We will do so by focusing on the functions

**Figure 13.1**   Financial Services Sector Assets in Canada: 2008

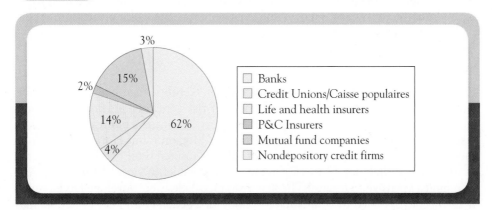

SOURCES: *Chart 1: Financial Services Sector Assets in Canada by Sector, 2000. The Canadian Financial Services Sector, June 2002. Department of Finance Canada. At: http://www.fin.gc.ca/toc/2002/fact-cfss_-eng.asp. Reproduced with permission of the Minister of Public Works and Government Services, 2009.*

## YOUR FINANCIAL WORLD
### Pawnshops

Contrary to their portrayal in the movies and on TV, pawnshops are not disreputable establishments frequented by criminals who are selling stolen goods. They are legitimate businesses that provide a useful service. Think of a pawnshop as a neighbourhood nondepository institution that makes collateralized loans and sells a wide variety of merchandise on the side. The pawnshop's main business is to provide very small loans—smaller than a bank would consider—to people who lack access to the conventional financial system.

Say you have something valuable, like a piece of jewellery, a bicycle, or a camera. You need cash, so you take the valuable item to a pawnshop. The pawnbroker will offer you a loan on the condition that you leave the item there as collateral. When you repay the loan along with interest and fees, the pawnbroker will return your collateral. But if you don't repay the loan on time, the pawnbroker takes the collateral and sells it. The merchandise that's for sale in the pawnshop was collateral for defaulted loans.

Needless to say, the terms of the loan are favourable to the pawnbroker, not to you. The loan amount is usually less than half the value of the collateral, and the interest rate is high: 3 to 5 percent *per month* is standard. There is also a fee that can drive up the interest rate to several hundred percent per year. While such an arrangement may seem outrageous, it is better than the payday loan described in Chapter 12. Because pawnbrokers' loans are collateralized, the interest rates charged are more reasonable than the ones on payday loans. So if you ever find yourself in dire straits, with no other source of credit, by all means go to a pawnshop.

SOURCE: © *Angela Redish.*

of each. Recall from Chapter 11 that the functions of financial institutions can be divided into five categories: (1) pooling the resources of small savers; (2) providing safekeeping and accounting services, as well as access to the payments system; (3) supplying liquidity by converting savers' balances directly into a means of payment whenever needed; (4) providing ways to diversify risk; and (5) collecting and processing information in ways that reduce information costs. We will use the same system to classify nondepository institutions.

## Insurance Companies

Insurance companies began with long sea voyages. Centuries ago, transoceanic trade and exploration were fraught with risk, and that risk generated a demand for insurance. Over time, as long, risky voyages of discovery became the norm and the nature of sea travel changed, insurance changed with it. Modern forms of insurance can be traced back to around 1400, when wool merchants insured their overland shipments from London to Italy for 12 to 15 percent of their value. (Overseas shipments were even more expensive to insure.) The first insurance codes were developed in Florence in 1523. They specified the standard provisions for a general insurance policy, such as the beginning and end of the coverage period and the time frame for receipt of payment following a loss. They also stipulated procedures for handling fraudulent claims in an attempt to reduce the moral hazard problem.

In 1688, Lloyd's of London was established. Today, Lloyd's is famous for insuring singers' voices, dancers' legs, even food critics' taste buds, as well as more traditional assets such as airplanes and ships. The best-known insurance company in the world, Lloyd's began in a small London coffeehouse whose proprietor, Edward Lloyd, catered to retired sea captains who had prospered in the East Indies spice trade. Having sailed many of the trade routes themselves, these captains possessed special knowledge of the hazards of sea voyages. They used their knowledge to assess the risks associated with particular routes and to dabble in marine insurance. The risks were not inconsequential. In the 17th century, a typical voyage to the Spice Islands (part of Indonesia) and back lasted three years. Only one in three ships returned with its cargo, and as few as one in eight sailors lived to tell of the adventure. The rewards of a successful voyage were coveted spices such as nutmeg, a single sack of which could make a sea captain wealthy for the rest of his life.

To obtain insurance, a ship's owner would write the details of the proposed voyage on a piece of paper, together with the amount he was willing to pay for the service, and then circulate the paper among the patrons at Edward Lloyd's coffeehouse. Interested individuals would decide how much of the risk to accept and then sign their names under the description of the voyage. This customary way of doing business became the source of the term "underwriter." Underwriting was open to anyone who wished to assume the risk associated with sea voyages. Because Lloyd's predated by several centuries the concept of limited liability, in which investors' losses were confined to the amount of their investment, underwriting implied unlimited liability. The saying was that an underwriter was liable down to his last cufflink.

Lloyds is better thought of as an insurance market than as an insurance company. To participate in the market, individuals known as *names* join together in groups called syndicates. When a new insurance contract is offered, several syndicates sign up for a portion of the risk in return for a portion of the premiums.

Historically, becoming a name with Lloyd's brought both reputation and risk. The risks were never more apparent than in the early 1990s, when Lloyd's racked up losses in excess of $10 billion as a result of claims on policies that protected firms against the legal damages associated with asbestos. The huge amount exceeded the estimated combined assets of all 34,000 Lloyd's names. Because of their unlimited liability, nearly 2,000 individuals were driven into personal bankruptcy; many of them filed lawsuits claiming that Lloyd's management had misled them. As a result, Lloyd's was reorganized. Today Lloyd's operates in much the same way that it did three centuries ago but through the more conventional structure of a limited liability company. The losses of individual investors in a syndicate are limited to the amount of their initial investment, and no person is exposed to the possibility of financial ruin.

## Two Types of Insurance

At their most basic level, all insurance companies operate like Lloyd's of London. They accept premiums from policyholders in exchange for the promise of compensation if certain events occur. A homeowner pays a premium in return for the promise that if the house burns down, the insurance company will pay to rebuild it. For the individual policyholder, then, insurance is a way to transfer risk. In terms of the financial system as a whole, insurance companies specialize in three of the five functions performed by intermediaries: they pool small premiums and make large investments with them; they diversify risks across a large population; and they screen and monitor policyholders to mitigate the problem of asymmetric information.

Insurance companies offer two types of insurance: life insurance and **property and casualty insurance**. Life insurers—companies such as Sunlife and Canada Life—sell policies that protect the insured against the loss of earnings from disability, retirement, or death. Property and casualty companies sell policies that protect households and businesses from losses arising from accident, fire, and natural disaster. Both types of intermediary allow individuals to transfer their risk to a group. In Canada there are nearly 300 insurance companies of which two-thirds are property and casualty. Half the firms are Canadian and half are foreign. Like the banking sector, the life insurance industry is quite concentrated, with the four largest companies accounting for about 60 percent of industry assets. While a single company may provide both kinds of insurance, the two businesses operate very differently.

Life insurance comes in two basic forms, called term and whole life insurance, as well as a variety of hybrids. Term life insurance provides a payment to the policyholder's beneficiaries in the event of the insured's death at any time during the policy's term. The premium depends on the very predictable proportion of people (of a given age) who will die. Term policies are generally renewable periodically, often every five or ten years, so long as the policyholder is less than 65 years old. Many people obtain term life insurance through their employers, an arrangement called group life insurance. Whole life insurance is a combination of term life insurance and a savings account. The policyholder pays a fixed premium over his or her lifetime in return for a fixed benefit when the policyholder dies. Should the policyholder decide to discontinue the policy, its cash value will be refunded. As time passes and the policyholder ages, the emphasis of the whole life policy shifts from insurance to savings. In fact, most whole life policies can be cashed in at any time. Whole life insurance tends to be an expensive way to save, though, so its use as a savings vehicle has declined markedly as people have discovered cheaper alternatives.

Most adults have experience with property and casualty insurance because driving a car without it is illegal. Auto insurance is a combination of property insurance on the car itself and casualty insurance on the driver, who is protected against liability for harm or injury to other people or their property. Holders of property and casualty insurance pay premiums in exchange for protection during the term of the policy.

On the balance sheets of insurance companies, promises to policyholders show up as liabilities. On the asset side, insurance companies hold a combination of stocks and bonds. Property and casualty companies profit from the fees they charge for administering the policies they write; the claims are covered by the premiums. Because the assets are essentially reserves against sudden claims, they have to be liquid. A look at the balance sheet of a property and casualty insurer will show a preponderance of very short term money-market instruments.

Life insurance companies hold assets of longer maturity than property and casualty insurers. Since most life insurance payments will be made well into the future, this better matches the maturity of the companies' assets and liabilities. Furthermore, while stocks may carry a relatively low degree of risk when held for periods of 25 years or more (recall the discussion in Chapter 8), insurance companies cannot risk the possibility that they may be forced to sell stocks when prices are low in order to pay policyholders' claims. As a result, life insurance companies hold mostly bonds.

**The Role of Insurance Companies** Like life insurers, property and casualty insurers pool risks to generate predictable payouts. That is, they reduce risk by spreading it across many policies. Recall from Chapter 5 that a group of investments with uncorrelated returns is less risky than any individual investment. The same is true of insurance contracts. While there is no way to know exactly which policies will require payment—who will have an automobile accident, lose a house to fire, or die—

# YOUR FINANCIAL WORLD
## How Much Life Insurance Do You Need?

We discussed disability insurance in Chapter 3 and auto-mobile insurance in Chapter 5. What about life insurance? How much should you buy? The first question is whether you should buy any at all. The purpose of life insurance is to take care of the people you are supporting should some-thing unpleasant happen to you. Think of it as replacement income that will be there when you're not. People with young children are the ones who need life insurance the most. If a parent dies, someone will have to raise those children and put them through school, and a life insurance policy will pay the bills. Life insurance is *not* for an unmar-ried postsecondary student with no obligations, so don't let anyone sell it to you if you don't need it.

If you think you need life insurance, the next step is to decide what kind. The best approach is to buy *term life insurance*, which will pay off only if you die. Because other kinds of life insurance include investment compo-nents, they are more costly. And since the people who need life insurance most are young families with limited incomes and big expenses, the more affordable the policy, the better. Making your insurance and investment decisions separately is also easier than trying to achieve all your goals with a single vehicle.*

Finally, how much life insurance should you buy? If you are married with two small children, most advisors recommend that you buy a term policy worth six to eight times your annual income. While that might cover your family's living expenses until the children are grown, con-sider carefully whether it will be enough for their post-secondary education. If you and your spouse each earn $35,000 a year, each of you might need $400,000 worth of life insurance. For someone who is between 30 and 40 years old, a $400,000 policy costs about $500 a year, so out of your joint annual income of $70,000, you and your spouse would be spending $1,000 on term life insurance. That's expensive, so don't buy more than you need.

* Your parents and grandparents may have purchased whole life insurance policies for two reasons. First, in the past, individuals did not have access to all the investment choices that are available today. Second, tax laws were different; for some people, saving through a whole life insurance policy had tax advantages. But with the creation of tax-deferred savings vehicles such as registered retirement savings plans (RRSPs), those benefits disappeared. Today, you would likely pay a life insurance company much more than the value of any tax benefits to you to administer a whole life insurance policy.

the insurance company can estimate precisely the percentage of policyholders who will file claims. Doing so allows managers to accurately compute how much the firm will need to pay out in any given year. From the point of view of company sharehold-ers, property and casualty insurance allows them to spread the risk of accident and damage across a large group of individuals.

In Chapter 11, we discussed the problem of asymmetric information in stock and bond finance. Recall that when a lender or investor cannot tell a good borrower or investment from a bad one, the tendency is for only the worst opportunities to pres-ent themselves. This phenomenon is adverse selection. Furthermore, once borrowers or entrepreneurs have received financing, they have less incentive to avoid risk than the lender or investor. That problem is called moral hazard.

While *adverse selection* and *moral hazard* create significant problems in the stock and bond markets, they create worse problems in the insurance market. A person who has terminal cancer surely has an incentive to buy life insurance for the largest amount possible—that's adverse selection. And without fire insurance, people would have more fire extinguishers in their houses. Fire insurance creates moral hazard, encouraging homeowners to be less careful in protecting their homes than they would be otherwise. Insurance companies work hard to reduce both these problems. By screening applicants, they can reduce adverse selection. A person who wants to buy a life insurance policy must undergo a physical evaluation: weight, blood pressure, blood tests, and health history. Only those who pass the exam are allowed to purchase policies. And people

"*We cannot write a life policy for your husband, Mrs. Blaine, because he is already dead. In insurance terms, that is considered a preëxisting condition.*"

who want automobile insurance must provide their driving records, including traffic citations and accident histories. While bad drivers may be allowed to buy car insurance, they will need to pay more for it. By screening drivers and adjusting their premiums accordingly, then, insurance companies can reduce their losses due to adverse selection.

Insurance companies have ways to reduce moral hazard as well. Policies usually include restrictive covenants that require the insured to engage or not to engage in certain activities. To qualify for fire insurance, a restaurant owner might be required to have the sprinkler system examined periodically; to obtain insurance against physical injury, a baseball or basketball player might be precluded from riding a motorcycle. Beyond such covenants, insurance policies often include *deductibles*, which require the insured to pay the initial cost of repairing accidental damage, up to some maximum amount. Or they may require *coinsurance*, in which the insurance company shoulders a percentage of the claim, perhaps 80 or 90 percent, and the insured assumes the rest of the cost.

It is interesting to speculate about the future of insurance in an age in which firms can collect more and more information at lower and lower cost. Remember that insurance is meant to shift risk from individuals to groups, not to shift the responsibility for events that are certain to happen. For example, no one expects an insurance company to sell life insurance to a person with a terminal disease. Herein lies a problem. With the decoding of the human genome, a battery of tests will soon be available to determine each person's probability of developing a terminal disease. Using this information, each of us will have a fairly good idea of our life expectancy and the relative cost of our health care. If applicants withhold this kind of information from insurance companies, the adverse selection problem will become so severe that the industry could collapse. But if applicants reveal the information, those who are unfortunate enough to carry undesirable genes will not be able to obtain insurance. Someone who has a high probability of getting heart disease at a young age will still be able to get automobile insurance, but getting life or health insurance will be very difficult.

The solution to this problem is not obvious, but it seems likely that any answer will involve government intervention. The government could either require insurance companies to provide coverage to everyone or act as an insurer of last resort.

## Pension Funds

Like an insurance company, a pension fund offers people the ability to make premium payments today in exchange for promised payments under certain future circumstances. Also like an insurance company, pension funds do not accept deposits. They do help people to develop the discipline of saving regularly, getting them started early and helping them to stick with it. As we saw in Chapter 4, the earlier a person begins saving and the more disciplined he or she is, the better off that person will be later in life. Saving from an early age means enjoying a higher income at retirement. Pension plans not only provide an easy way to make sure that a worker saves and has sufficient

### APPLYING THE CONCEPT
#### REINSURANCE AND "CAT BONDS"

To get a mortgage on a home, you'll need insurance. Regardless of where you live, your lender will require you to have fire insurance, and in some places you may also need insurance against natural disasters such as floods, earthquakes, or hurricanes. Without such insurance you won't get a mortgage, and without a mortgage you won't buy a house. Clearly, it's in everyone's interest for insurance companies to provide such insurance and spread the risk. But sometimes this kind of insurance isn't easy to obtain.

Imagine that an insurer is thinking of offering earthquake insurance in British Columbia. Unlike automobile accidents, when an earthquake hits, a large number of policyholders will all file claims at the same time. The result for the insurance company is a large, undiversified risk. To offer earthquake insurance and stay in business, a property and casualty insurance company must find some way to insure itself against catastrophic risks—large natural disasters that generate a significant number of payouts simultaneously.

*Reinsurance companies* offer a solution to this problem by providing insurance to insurance companies. Say the B.C. insurer estimates that an earthquake would generate payments of $15 billion (the approximate loss in the 1994 earthquake in Northridge, Los Angeles). The company may have the resources to cover only the first $1 billion of policyholders' claims. To write the full $15 billion worth of insurance, the company will need to buy $14 billion of reinsurance.

Reinsurance companies are enormous; they operate all over the world. Their geographic spread allows them to diversify their risk, since earthquakes don't happen at the same time in both B.C. and Japan. The fact that reinsurance companies can spread their risk globally gives them the ability to withstand individual losses, even if they are catastrophic.

For this to work, reinsurers have to be big. So big, in fact, that they have become near monopolies, driving up the price of reinsurance in the process.

The rising cost of reinsurance has spurred the creation of a second solution to the problem of insuring catastrophic risk. Financial experts have designed catastrophic bonds, or *cat bonds*, which allow individual investors to share a very small portion of the reinsurance risk. It works like this. Through an investment dealer, an insurance company will sell a substantial quantity of cat bonds, immediately investing proceeds in low-risk financial instruments such as U.S. Treasury bonds. If a catastrophe occurs, the U.S. Treasury bonds are sold and the resulting funds used to pay the claims the insurance company faces. But if no earthquake, fire, or hurricane hits during the policy period, the cat bond owners receive a substantial return.* This high level of compensation, coupled with a very low correlation with the return on most other investments, means that cat bonds can both improve the expected return and lower the risk of a typical investor's portfolio.

The existence of reinsurance and cat bonds has clear benefits. These mechanisms for transferring and spreading the risk of catastrophic disaster improve the risk-return tradeoff for individual investors, enable insurance companies to offer more insurance than they could otherwise, and allow prospective homeowners to get the insurance they need—and the mortgage financing they want—to purchase a home.

---

* One recent example of a cat bond was created by Allianz. The bond raised $150 million, which would be repaid unless there were severe floods in the United Kingdom or an earthquake in North America (excluding California). The bonds paid 3.14 percent over LIBOR. Notice that the risks are uncorrelated and also that the development of this bond reflects the existence of precise ways to measure "severe floods" so that there can be no dispute over whether or not the conditions have been met.

---

resources in old age but also help savers to diversify their risk. By pooling the savings of many small investors, pension funds spread the risk, ensuring that funds will be available to investors in their old age.

People can use a variety of methods to save for retirement, including employer-sponsored plans and individual savings plans, both of which allow workers to defer income tax on their savings until they retire. Nearly everyone who works for a large corporation in Canada has an employer-administered pension plan. There are two basic types: defined-benefit (DB) pension plans and defined-contribution (DC) pension plans. Regardless of the type, many employer-sponsored plans require a person to work for a certain number of years before qualifying for benefits. This qualifying process is called **vesting**. Think of vesting as the point at which the contributions your employer has made to the pension plan on your behalf belong to you. Changing jobs before your pension contributions have been vested can be very costly.

# IN THE NEWS

## Pension Plans Facing a Funding Crisis: Survey

**John Greenwood, Financial Post**

**April 20, 2009**

TORONTO — An overwhelming majority of Canadian senior executives believe defined-benefit pensions have become a crisis for the companies that have them, threatening to sap corporate resources already under stress from the downturn in the economy, according to a survey by the global consultancy [firm] Watson Wyatt.

The firm's sixth annual survey of pension risk, released Monday, found that 88 percent of chief financial officers and vice-presidents of human resources believe that pension plans that promise specified retirement income are in a "widespread funding crisis."

Slightly more than half the 161 respondents said the crisis will be long-lasting while 35 percent called it a cyclical problem.

"Finance people see their company pensions as subsidiaries that they have to put money into and last year (from their perspective) the situation was completely out of control," said Ian Markham, director of pension innovation at Watson Wyatt.

"These plans can be very large, and the amount of money they have to put in can become a drain on the company, limiting the amount they have left for capital investment and expansion. So when they say pensions are in crisis, they're thinking, "I'm supposed to be investing in the business, I need to be investing in the company, but unfortunately my pension is driving me down."

Markham said without some form of government funding relief for pension sponsors, the crisis could have a domino effect on the rest of the Canadian economy, reducing demand for other company's [sic] goods and services and pushing down employment.

In the wake of the financial crisis, many pension plans, both public and private, are facing steep losses. Corporate sponsors of defined-benefit plans are under particular stress because they are on the hook to make up the shortfall and accounting rules give them only a small window—usually about five years—to do that.

Three-quarters of respondents said that without government funding relief, they would make large or moderate reductions in capital spending in order to meet their pension obligations.

---

Let's take a look at how the two types of pension plan work. **Defined-benefit plans** were the norm in the 1970s but have declined from 90 percent of plans in the private sector to only 74 percent today.[8] Participants in defined-benefit plans receive a lifetime retirement income based on the number of years they worked at the company and their final salary. For example, someone who worked for the same company for 30 years and retired at a salary of $100,000 might receive 2 percent of that salary for each year of service, or $60,000 per year. That may seem good, but to reap such benefits, most people would need to work a very long time for the same firm.

**Defined-contribution plans** are replacing defined-benefit plans, and they are very different. In a defined-contribution plan, the employee and employer both make contributions into an investment account that belongs to the employee. Unlike a defined-benefit plan, in a defined-contribution plan the employer takes no responsibility for the size of the employee's retirement income. Instead, at retirement the employee receives the accumulated funds in the account and must decide what to do

---

[8] Public-sector plans have a higher share of defined-benefit but even if they are included, the share has fallen from 93 percent to 81 percent according to B. Baldwin "Determinants of the Evolution of Workplace pensions in Canada," Caledon Institute of Social Policy, March 2007; pp. 1–43.

The stock market turmoil of the past six months has forced sponsors of defined-benefit plans all over the world to rethink their strategy, with many players in the United States and the United Kingdom converting to a defined-contribution structure (in which the amount the company pays out is fixed) as a way to reduce the pressure and help companies to survive. Others are cranking back on the amount of risk pension managers are allowed to take on. But the vast majority of Canadian sponsors have so far declined to take any action.

Only three per cent of survey respondents said they planned to convert to defined-contribution plans in the next few months.

Part of the reason sponsors are taking so long to act may have something to do with the difficulty of persuading employees to accept pension plan changes, Markham said.

Another possibility is that players are hoping that stock markets will rise again if they wait long enough, eliminating the need for tough decisions.

"I think we've got a waiting game now," he said.

### LESSONS OF THE ARTICLE:

Defined-benefit plans are regulated to ensure that companies are able to pay out the pensions they are committed to. But when stock markets plunged by 50 percent in 2008, most pension funds became underfunded. While the government gives them five years to make up their losses, companies need to start making large contributions immediately, at a time when their revenues are also likely at a low point. The companies argue that they don't need to make the pension payments for many years and so should be given a bit of breathing space, in the hope that the market will come back up and reduce the shortfall.

The impact of the stock market decline on pensions depended on whether it was a defined-benefit plan—in which case the burden fell on the company, or a defined-contribution plan—in which case the burden fell on the employee.

SOURCE: "*Pension Plans Facing a Funding Crisis: Survey,*" by John Greenwood, Financial Post, *April 20, 2009. Material reprinted with the express permission of "The National Post Company," a CanWest Partnership.*

with them. The options include accepting a lump sum, removing small amounts at a time, or converting the balance to a fixed monthly payment for life by purchasing an annuity. One big difference between defined-benefit and defined-contribution plans is who bears the market risk. In a defined-contribution plan, the individual bears the risk—doing well when the market goes up and not doing so well when the market falls. In a defined-benefit plan it is the company—which is legally obliged to maintain the value of the assets in the plan—that benefits or loses from market ups and downs (see In the News: Pension Plans Facing a Funding Crisis: Survey).

You can think of a pension plan as the opposite of life insurance. One pays off if you live, the other if you don't. The two vehicles are similar enough that the same institution often offers both. And not surprisingly, the balance sheets of pension funds look a lot like those of life insurance companies; both hold long-term assets such as corporate bonds and stocks. The only difference is that life insurance companies hold only half the equities that pension funds do.[9]

---

[9] The heavier emphasis on equities makes pension funds more risky. This is a risk that is potentially borne by the plans' participants. But as mentioned later in this section, defined-benefit pension plans are partially government insured so some of the risk is borne broadly by taxpayers.

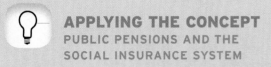

## APPLYING THE CONCEPT
### PUBLIC PENSIONS AND THE SOCIAL INSURANCE SYSTEM

Providing for the elderly is a tremendous challenge for any society. Traditionally, children cared for their parents when they became old. But with the advent of modern industrial societies and an associated increase in geographic mobility, many elderly parents no longer live with their children. Today the expectation is that people will save enough while they are working to pay their own way when they retire. If they don't, the general view is that in a civilized society, government should care for the elderly.

The first public pensions were introduced in Canada in 1927 and were intended to provide retirement support for low-income families. They were initially restricted to those over 70 and were means-tested. In 1952, this old age security (OAS) program was amended to provide a flat-rate pension and over time the minimum age was reduced to 65. In 1989, the government introduced a clawback of the OAS for high-income earners and introduced the Guaranteed Income supplement (GIS) to provide a top-up for low-income seniors. Two major programs have been introduced to supplement the OAS, the deferral of taxes on retirement savings (e.g. through RRSPs) and the Canada Pension Plan. The RRSP program began in 1957, and the CPP in 1966. The Canada Pension Plan (except in Quebec, where the QPP is similar) was a defined benefit plan funded by contributions from employers and employees. Unlike the OAS which is funded from general government revenues, the revenues and expenditures of the CPP—which is administered by the Federal government—are segregated from general government accounts.

The CPP was introduced as a pay-as-you-go system—the monthly payments were funded by contributions, not by earnings. As long as workers' incomes were growing quickly enough and the population itself was growing, the arrangement worked well. However, changing demographics, benefit enhancements and slow earnings growth led to an incipient funding crisis: In 1996 the CPP paid out more in benefits ($17 billion) than it received in contributions ($11 billion). An actuarial report projected that the plan's contingency reserve would be exhausted by 2015. In 1997 the provinces and the federal government agreed on major reforms that included: a reduction in future benefits; an increase in contribution rates; and the creation of the CPP Investment Board (CPPIB) that would operate at arm's length from governments to manage the fund for the benefit of future generations. In 2009 the contribution rate is 9.9% of earnings (split between employer and employee and to a maximum income of $46,300) and the maximum benefit is $10,905 per year. The goal was a fund that would be sustainable over a 75 year horizon, and in July 2009, the Chief Actuary of Canada reaffirmed that indeed the CPP is sustainable through a 75 year timeframe.

The situation in the United States, is very different. There, the Social Security system's finances are in bad shape. It continues to be a "pay-as-you-go" system, and, according to the government's 2005 estimates, by 2040 tax income will be sufficient to finance only 74 percent of promised benefits. It remains to be seen if the U.S. government will have the political will to change the system before that time.

For more information about benefits payable under the Canada Pension Plan see www.servicecanada.gc.ca/eng/sc/cpp/retirement/canadapension.shtml; for more information about how the CPP funds are invested see www.cppib.ca.

**CPP INVESTMENT BOARD**

SOURCE: Logo is used with permission, *www.cppib.ca.*

Finally, it is worth noting that the Ontario government does provide some insurance for private, defined-benefit pension systems. If a company goes bankrupt, the Pension Benefits Guarantee Fund (PBGF) will take over the fund's liabilities. While the PBGF's insurance is capped, so that highly paid employees such as airline pilots are not fully protected, it still increases the incentive for a firm's managers to engage in risky behaviour. To guard against this possibility, regulators monitor pension funds closely. Even so, many experts believe that PBGC could end up owing hundreds of millions of dollars in the not-too-distant future. We'll have to wait and see.

## Securities Firms: Brokers, Mutual Funds, and Investment Dealers

Securities firms provide a range of services including brokerage, underwriting, and sales of mutual funds. In Canada, the large banks all undertake these activities either directly or through whole owned subsidiaries (see Table 13.2). The primary services of brokerage firms are accounting (to keep track of customers' investment balances), custody services (to make sure valuable records such as stock certificates are safe), and access to secondary markets (in which customers can buy and sell financial

| Table 13.2 | Bank Ownership of Integrated Securities Firms |
| --- | --- |

| Firm | Majority owner |
| --- | --- |
| BMO Nesbitt Burns | Bank of Montreal |
| CIBC World Markets | Canadian Imperial Bank of Commerce |
| National Bank Financial | National Bank of Canada |
| RBC Dominion Securities | Royal Bank of Canada |
| Scotia Capital | The Bank of Nova Scotia |
| TD Securities | TD Bank Financial Group |

SOURCE: Canada's Securities Industry, *July 2002. Department of Finance Canada. At: http://www.fin.gc.ca/toc/2002/cansec_-eng.asp. Reproduced with the permission of the Minister of Public Works and Government Services, 2009.*

instruments). Brokers also provide loans to customers who wish to purchase stock on margin. And they provide liquidity, both by offering cheque-writing privileges with their investment accounts and by allowing investors to sell assets quickly.

Mutual fund companies offer liquidity services as well; their money market mutual funds are a key example. But the primary function of mutual funds is to pool the small savings of individuals in diversified portfolios that are composed of a wide variety of financial instruments.

All securities firms are very much in the business of producing information and information is at the heart of the underwriting business. The securities firms are the conduits through which firms raise funds in the capital markets. Through their **underwriting** services, these firms issue new stocks and a variety of other debt instruments. Most commonly, the underwriter guarantees the price of a new issue and then sells it to investors at a higher price, a practice called *placing the issue*. The underwriter profits from the difference between the price guaranteed to the firm that issues the security and the price at which the bond or stock is sold to investors. But since the price at which the investment dealer sells the bonds or stocks in financial markets can turn out to be lower than the price guaranteed to the issuing company, there is some risk to underwriting. For most large issues, a group of firms will band together and spread the risk among themselves rather than one of them taking the risk alone.

Information and reputation are central to the underwriting business. Underwriters collect information to determine the price of the new securities and then put their reputations on the line when they go out to sell the issues. A large, well-established investment dealer will not underwrite issues indiscriminately. To do so would reduce the value of the dealer's brand, along with the fees the bank can charge.

In addition to underwriting, investment dealers provide advice to firms that want to merge with or acquire other firms. Investment dealers do the research to identify potential *mergers and acquisitions* and estimate the value of the new, combined company. The information they collect and the advice they give must be valuable because they are paid handsomely for them. In facilitating these combinations, investment dealers perform a service to the economy. Mergers and acquisitions help to ensure that the people who manage firms do the best job possible. Managers who don't get the most out of the resources entrusted to them risk having their company purchased by executives who can do a better job. This threat of a takeover provides discipline in the management of individual companies and improves the allocation of resources across the economy.

# TOOLS OF THE TRADE
## Hedge Funds

Hedge funds are strictly for millionaires. These investment partnerships (sometimes referred to as *alternative investment management funds*) bring together small groups of people who have over $1 million in investible funds and are willing to make an investment at least $100,000. The larger hedge funds also accept funds from institutional investors such as pension funds, mutual funds, and insurance companies.

Hedge funds are run by a general partner, or manager, who is in charge of day-to-day decisions. Managers are very well paid, receiving an annual fee of at least 2 percent of assets plus 20 percent of profits. In a year in which the fund's return on investment is 10 percent, the manager of an average-size fund of $500 million will receive $20 million in fees.

Because these funds are unregulated, finding out what their portfolios contain can be a challenge even for the fund's investors: the manager simply doesn't tell anyone. This secrecy creates the very real possibility of moral hazard. If a fund starts to incur losses, determining the reason for the fall in value is often impossible. To ensure that the manager's incentives match those of the investors, the manager is required to keep a large fraction of his or her own wealth in the fund. By and large, this requirement solves the problem of moral hazard; but fraudulent behaviour can still occur. In 2005, Boaz Manor, who owned a hedge fund called Porter, was charged with fraud and money laundering in the collapse of a Canadian hedge fund with $800 million in assets.

The name "hedge fund" may suggest that these funds employ the diversification techniques discussed in Chapter 5, but many of them do not. Hedging reduces risk by grouping together individual investments whose returns tend to move in opposite directions, but hedge funds are not low-risk enterprises. Because they are organized as private partnerships, hedge funds are not constrained in their investment strategies; they can trade in derivatives and borrow to create leverage.

A.W. Jones founded the first hedge fund in 1949. His fund combined leverage with short selling (the practice of borrowing a stock or bond whose price you believe will fall, selling it, and then buying it back at a lower price before repaying the lender). Jones divided the fund's equities into two groups: companies whose stock prices he thought would fall and companies whose stock prices he thought would rise. He sold the first group short and used the proceeds to buy shares in the second group. The term *"hedge"* in the name *"hedge fund"* comes from the fact that when the market in general went up or down, moving all stocks in the same direction, the fund would take losses on one group of stock but turn a profit on the second. It was hedged against movements in the market as a whole. Instead, Jones turned a profit when the stocks he sold short went down relative to the stocks he purchased. And those profits were substantial.

Today we would refer to Jones's fund as a "long-short hedge fund," since he was long on some stocks and short on others. *Funds of funds* combine investments in multiple individual funds. Long-short funds, and funds of funds are the most popular Canadian hedge funds. *Macro fund* managers take unhedged positions in the hope of benefiting from shifts in interest rates or national market conditions. *Global fund* managers engage in international stock picking, and the managers of *relative value funds* try to exploit small, transitory differences in the prices of related securities, such as U.S. Treasury bills and bonds. Long-Term Capital Management, the hedge fund that collapsed in September 1998 (see Chapter 9), was following this last strategy, trying to exploit price differences between U.S. Treasury bonds of slightly different maturities. Playing games with interest rates is what led the firm to amass $1.25 trillion in interest rate swaps.

Regardless of the strategies they use, all hedge fund managers strive to create returns that roughly equal those of the stock market (as measured by a comprehensive index such as the S&P 500) but are uncorrelated with it. So while individual hedge funds are very risky—something like 10 percent of them close down every year—a portfolio that invests in a large number of these funds can expect returns equal to the stock market average with very little risk at all. That is why people like hedge funds and why successful hedge fund managers are so well paid.

## Finance Companies

Finance companies are in the lending business. They raise funds directly in the financial markets by issuing commercial paper and securities and then use them to make loans to individuals and corporations. Since these companies specialize in making loans, they are concerned largely with reducing the transactions and information costs that are associated with intermediated finance. And because of their narrow focus, finance companies are particularly good at screening potential borrowers' creditworthiness, monitoring their performance during the term of the loan, and seizing collateral in the event of a default.

Most finance companies specialize in one of three loan types: consumer loans, business loans, and what are called sales loans. Some also provide commercial and home mortgages. *Consumer finance* firms provide small installment loans to individual consumers. If you visit an appliance store to purchase a new refrigerator, you may be offered a deal that includes "no money down and no payments for six months." If you accept this loan offer, you'll be asked to fill out an application and to wait a few minutes while someone checks your credit. The credit is usually supplied not by the store but by a finance company such as Household Finance Corporation. This kind of consumer credit allows people without sufficient savings to purchase appliances such as television sets, washing machines, and microwave ovens.

*Business finance* companies provide loans to businesses. If you want to start your own airline, for example, you will need to acquire some airplanes. That isn't as difficult as it may sound, because you don't need to shell out the entire $100 million price of a new plane. Airplanes, like automobiles, can be leased. That is, a business finance company buys the plane and then leases it back to you, an approach that significantly reduces the cost of starting your new enterprise. While this example is extreme, finance companies will purchase many types of equipment and lease them back to firms.

In addition to equipment leasing, business finance companies provide both inventory loans and accounts receivable loans. Inventory loans enable firms to keep their shelves stocked so that when a customer asks for a product, the firm can fill the order. Accounts receivable loans provide firms with immediate resources in anticipation of receipt of customers' payments. The purpose of both these loan types is to provide short-term liquidity to firms.

*Sales finance* companies specialize in larger loans for major purchases, such as automobiles. Car dealers customarily offer financing to people who are shopping for a new car. When you purchase a car, at a certain point in the negotiations the salesperson will ask how you intend to pay for it. Unless you have sizable savings or are buying a very cheap car, you will need to borrow. The car business is organized so that you don't need to leave the dealership to get your loan; someone there will take care of it for you. The financing is arranged through a finance company that specializes in making car loans. Every major auto manufacturer owns a finance company, as do large retailers such as Sears.

## Government-Sponsored Enterprises

You may be surprised to learn that the Canadian government is directly involved in the financial intermediation system. In some cases the government provides loan guarantees; in others, it charters financial institutions to provide specific types of financing, such as home, farm, and business loans.

The largest government-owned financial intermediary is the Canada Mortgage and Housing Corporation (CMHC), which had assets of $200 billion in 2008. The CMHC began as a mechanism for the government to assist veterans returning from World War II to afford housing. In the early 1950s, Canadian banks were not permitted to make residential mortgages and most of the mortgage funds came from the trust and loan companies. Then in 1954, government (through the *National Housing Act*) allowed CMHC to offer insurance to home buyers who had a 25 percent downpayment, and then permitted the banks to make mortgage loans. Today, both CMHC and private insurers offer mortgage insurance, which is required for mortgages by banks if the down payment is less than 20%. This insurance is a support for the mortgagor (who lends the funds) and the provision of insurance enables households

## APPLYING THE CONCEPT
### THE SHADOWY LINE BETWEEN PUBLIC AND PRIVATE FINANCIAL AGENCIES

In recent years, Fannie Mae and Freddie Mac have been heavily criticized. Because they are private corporations rather than government agencies, their solvency is not explicitly guaranteed by the government. Instead, both benefit from an implicit guarantee and a line of credit from the U.S. Treasury. The general belief was that because of these corporations' size and their importance to the economy, the federal government would not allow them to fail. This perception allowed Fannie Mae and Freddie Mac to borrow at rates lower than those available to private competitors.

Federal Reserve officials were particularly vocal about the problems they saw in the structure of the two corporations, suggesting that those problems could precipitate a financial crisis. During the 1990s, the two companies grew rapidly and by 2006 they either owned or guaranteed more than half of all residential mortgages in the United States. They did so by borrowing more cheaply than institutions without Treasury connections. As a result, they were very

highly leveraged, much more so than any commercial bank is permitted to be. The average U.S. bank has a leverage ratio (assets divided by capital) of about 11 to 1. Fannie Mae and Freddie Mac had debt-to-equity ratios more than twice as high. Their financial statements for the end of 2005 revealed that both had a leverage ratio of about 30 to 1. With such low levels of capital, Fannie Mae and Freddie Mac could not withstand significant numbers of defaults. Government officials worried that a dramatic decline in home prices could create enough mortgage defaults to cause these institutions to fail.

They were right to worry. As we discuss in Chapter 23, the fall in house prices in 2007 did threaten the solvency of Fannie Mae and Freddie Mac in September 2008. And those who believed the government would not let them fail were also right. In September 2008, the U.S. government took them into government conservatorship and agreed to an equity injection financed by the Treasury. The future for Fannie Mae and Freddie Mac is unclear. In a sense, Fannie Mae and Freddie Mac were victims of their own success. Managers took the government's implicit guarantees, borrowed cheaply, and created an enormous mortgage market that encouraged home ownership. In other words, they achieved Congress's goal.

to which perhaps the banks would not otherwise lend, to obtain a mortgage. The CMHC also acts as an intermediary by issuing Canada mortgage bonds and holding securitized mortgages.

The Business Development Bank and Export Development Canada (EDC) are two other large government-owned financial intermediaries that increase the availability of funds for small businesses and export companies, respectively. The government argues that information problems create a market failure and that there is a need for such organizations to help business. Nevertheless, these are small organizations with roughly $10 billion and $30 billion in assets, respectively (compared to assets of the Canadian banking system of over $2 trillion).

Perhaps surprisingly, government-sponsored enterprises play a larger role in the United States than in Canada. When Congress wanted to make sure that low- and moderate-income families could get mortgages, it created the Federal National Mortgage Association (Fannie Mae), a private corporation, and the Government National Mortgage Corporation (*Ginnie Mae*), a corporation that is wholly owned by the federal government. Later, Congress chartered the Federal Home Loan Mortgage Corporation (Freddie Mac). To encourage farm loans, Congress created the Farm Credit System. And to provide student loans, Congress chartered the Student Loan Marketing Association (*Sallie Mae*).

All these government-sponsored enterprises have the same basic structure. They issue short-term bonds and use the proceeds to provide loans of one form or another. Because of their relationship to the government, these associations and corporations can obtain lower than average interest rates on their liabilities, which they then pass on to homeowners, farmers, and students in the form of subsidized mortgages and loans.

Table 13.3 summarizes the characteristics and roles of financial intermediaries.

**Table 13.3**   Summary of Financial Industry Structure

| Financial Intermediary | Primary Sources of Funds (Liabilities) | Primary Uses of Funds (Assets) | Services Provided |
|---|---|---|---|
| Depository Institution | Chequable deposits<br>Savings and time deposits<br>Borrowing from other banks | Cash<br>Loans<br>Securities | • Pooling of small savings to provide large loans<br>• Diversified, liquid deposit accounts<br>• Access to payments system<br>• Screening and monitoring of borrowers |
| Insurance Company | Expected claims | Corporate bonds<br>Government bonds<br>Stocks<br>Mortgages | • Pooling of risk<br>• Screening and monitoring of policyholders |
| Securities Firm | Short-term loans | Commercial paper<br>Bonds | • Management of asset pools<br>• Clearing and settling trades<br>• Immediate sale of assets<br>• Access to spectrum of assets, allowing diversification<br>• Evaluation of firms wishing to issue securities<br>• Research and advice for investors |
| Mutual Fund Company | Shares sold to customers | Commercial paper<br>Bonds<br>Mortgages<br>Stocks<br>Real estate | • Pooling of small savings to provide access to large, diversified portfolios, which can be liquid |
| Finance Company | Bonds<br>Bank loans<br>Commercial paper | Mortgages<br>Consumer loans<br>Business loans | • Screening and monitoring of borrowers |
| Pension Fund | Policy benefits to be paid out to future retirees | Stocks<br>Government bonds<br>Corporate bonds<br>Commercial paper | • Pooling of employees' and employers' contributions<br>• Diversification of long-term investments to ensure future income for retirees |
| Government-Sponsored Enterprise | Commercial paper<br>Bonds | Mortgage insurance<br>Farm loans<br>Exporter loans insurance | • Access to financing for borrowers who cannot obtain it elsewhere |

# The Future of the Financial Sector

The forces that have driven changes in the financial sector to date are not going away. Globalization, innovations in information and computing systems, and changes in regulatory culture will determine the shape and dynamics of the financial sector over the next decade.

Toward the end of the 20th century, banking underwent not only a national but also an international transformation. An explosion in international trade increased the need for international payments services. Very simply, every time a Japanese company purchased software produced in the United States or a Canadian bought a television set manufactured in China, payments had to be made across national boundaries. Today, the international banking system has adjusted to the needs of an interdependent, globalized world.

**MARKETS**

A borrower in France, Brazil, or Singapore can shop for a loan virtually anywhere in the world, and a depositor seeking the highest return can do the same. All the large Canadian banks have offices in New York and—as we saw in Chapter 12—they all have very significant foreign assets and liabilities. Similarly, there are many foreign bank subsidiaries and branches operating in Canada. All this competition has surely made banking a tougher business. Profits are harder for bankers to come by today than they were in 1970, when depositors and borrowers were captive to a small set of Canadian banks. But while bankers' lives may be more difficult, on balance the improved efficiency of the financial system has enhanced growth.

One of the most important aspects of international banking is the eurodollar market. **Eurodollars** are U.S. dollar–denominated deposits held in banks outside the United States. A number of forces conspired to create the euromarket. Originally, it was a response to restrictions on the movement of international capital that were instituted at the end of World War II with the creation of the Bretton Woods system. (We will learn more about the international monetary system and capital controls in Chapter 22.) To ensure that the pound would retain its value, the British government imposed restrictions on the ability of British banks to finance international transactions. In an attempt to evade these restrictions, London banks began to offer dollar deposits and dollar-denominated loans to foreigners. The result was what we know today as the eurodollar market. The Cold War accelerated the market's development when the Soviet government, fearful that the U.S. government might freeze or confiscate them, shifted its dollar deposits from New York to London. In the United States, a combination of factors propelled the eurodollar market. In the 1960s, U.S. authorities tried to prevent dollars from leaving the country and made it costly for foreigners to borrow dollars in the United States for use elsewhere in the world. Then in the early 1970s, a combination of domestic interest rate controls and high inflation rates made domestic deposits much less attractive than eurodollar deposits, which paid comparatively high interest rates. Today, the eurodollar market in London is one of the biggest and most important financial markets in the world, and the interest rate at which banks lend each other eurodollars, called the **London Interbank Offered Rate (LIBOR)**, is the standard against which many private loan rates are measured.

Today's banks are bigger, fewer in number, and more international in reach than the banks of yesteryear; they also have more to offer in the way of services, and the Canadian banking industry, like that elsewhere, is moving closer to the universal bank model. True **universal banks** are firms that engage in nonfinancial as well as financial activities. Depending on the country, such an arrangement provides more or less separation among the banking, insurance, and securities industries. The most extreme example is Germany, where universal banks do everything under one roof, including direct investment in the shares of nonfinancial firms. In Canada, different financial activities must be undertaken in separate subsidiaries, and banks are still prohibited from making equity investments in nonfinancial companies.

The owners and managers of these large financial firms cite three reasons to create them. First, they are well diversified, so their profitability does not rely on one particular line of business. This reduced risk should increase the value of the firm.[10] Second, these firms are large enough to take advantage of economies of scale. A financial holding company needs only one CEO and one board of directors regardless of its size. Only one accounting system is required to run the company. Third, these companies hope to benefit from economies of scope. In the same way that a supermarket offers all sorts of food and nonfood items under one roof, financial holding companies offer customers a wide variety of services, all under the same brand name. This, too, should reduce costs—or maybe the people who run these firms are just trying to build empires.

But while the banks are growing larger the non-bank depository institutions are also growing. For the period 2000–2006 (the last period for which there are comparable data) the credit union sector grew as rapidly as the chartered banks. And it is not just that banks are getting involved in other parts of the financial services sector. Other firms are working to provide customers with the same services they could obtain from more traditional financial intermediaries. Money market mutual fund issuers compete with banks in providing liquidity services to customers (and the banks each own money market mutual funds so that they don't lose this market segment). Mortgage brokers give consumers a choice in how to borrow for the purchase of a home and then sell the mortgages in the financial marketplace. Today, people who need an auto loan or any kind of insurance can get dozens of price quotes in a few hours just by logging onto the Internet. The screening of loan applicants, which was once the job of the neighbourhood banker, has been standardized and now can be done by virtually anyone. Then there are discount brokerage firms such as Qtrade, which provide low-cost access to the financial markets.

In fact, thanks to recent technological advances, almost every service traditionally provided by financial intermediaries can now be produced independently, without the help of a large organization. Loan brokers can give large borrowers access to the pooled funds of many small savers. A variety of financial firms, including brokerage firms and mutual fund companies, provides connections to the payments system, as well as the ability to transform assets into money quickly and at low cost. One of these days, even the electric company may get into the act. And many intermediaries, including mutual fund companies and pension funds, help customers to spread, share, and transfer risk. Finally, the production of information to mitigate the problems of adverse selection and moral hazard has become a business in and of itself.

As we survey the financial industry, then, we see two trends running in opposite directions. On the one hand, large firms are working hard to provide one-stop shopping for financial services. On the other hand, the industry is splintering into a host of small firms, each of which serves a very specific purpose. Will the future be one of generalists, specialists, or both? We will have to wait and see.

---

[10] Financial economists disagree on whether the reduced risk would actually increase the firm's value. Some people argue that firms should not diversify themselves but leave the choice to their stockholders. An investor can always purchase shares in two companies that would otherwise merge, in proportion to whatever risk exposure the investor desires.

## Terms

## Chapter Summary

1. Canada has a highly concentrated banking system:
   a. Six banks hold 93 percent of banking assets and over 50 percent of the assets of the financial system.
   b. Until the 1960s, the Canadian financial sector comprised four distinct pillars: banking, trust companies, insurance, and brokerage; today the large banks own subsidiaries that are trust companies, insurance companies, and brokerage houses.
   c. Banking has been expanding not only across sectors but also across international boundaries.
      i. Many Canadian banks operate abroad, and a large number of foreign banks do business in Canada.
      ii. Eurodollars—dollar deposits in foreign banks—play an important part in the international financial system.
   d. The banking industry is constantly evolving. With changes in regulations, financial services can now be provided in two ways:
      i. Through a large universal bank, which provides all the services anyone could possibly need.
      ii. Through small specialized firms, which supply a limited number of services.

2. The United States has a comparatively large but declining number of banks.
   a. The large number of banks in the United States is explained by historical restrictions on branching.
   b. Since 1997, banks have been permitted to operate in more than one state. This change has increased competition and driven many small, inefficient banks out of business.
   c. Between 1933 and 1999, the *Glass-Steagall Act* prohibited U.S. banks from engaging in the securities and insurance businesses.
   d. In 1999, the *Glass-Steagall Act* was repealed, permitting banks to engage in investment banking and commercial banking.
   e. In 2008, the five big investment banks disappeared: they failed, were bought out, or applied to become bank holding companies.

3. Nondepository institutions are playing an increasingly important role in the financial system. Five types of financial intermediary may be classified as nondepository institutions.
   a. Insurance companies.
      i. Life insurance companies insure policyholders against death through term life insurance and provide a vehicle for saving through whole life insurance.
      ii. Property and casualty companies insure individuals and businesses against losses arising from specific events, such as accidents and fires.
      iii. The two primary functions of insurance companies are to
         • Allow policyholders to transfer risk.
         • Screen and monitor policyholders to reduce adverse selection and moral hazard.
   b. Pension funds perform two basic services.
      i. They allow employees and employers to make payments today so that employees will receive an income after retirement.
      ii. They spread risk by ensuring that those employees who live longer than others will continue to receive an income. For this reason, pension funds may be thought of as the opposite of life insurance.
   c. Securities firms may undertake brokerage activities, underwriting, and creation of mutual funds.

i. Brokers give customers access to the financial markets, allowing them to buy and sell securities.

ii. Mutual fund companies provide savers with small-denomination shares in large, diversified investment pools.

iii. Underwriting involves screening and monitoring firms before issuing their securities.

d. Finance companies specialize in making loans to consumers and businesses for the purchase or lease of specific products, such as cars and business equipment.

e. Government-sponsored enterprises supply direct financing or insurance for housing, exports, and agricultural loans, among other things.

## Conceptual Problems

1. One day you hear that two large Canadian banks are about to merge. From your vantage point as a retail bank customer, what are the costs and benefits of such a merger?

2. What market failures motivate the existence of government-owned financial intermediaries? Do you believe there should be more or fewer government owned financial intermediaries? Why?

3. Banks have been losing their advantage over other financial intermediaries in attracting customers' funds. Why?

4. Describe the economies of scope that large banks hope to realize. Do you believe they will be successful?

5. An industry with a large number of small firms is usually thought to be highly competitive. What are the costs and benefits to consumers of the current market structure of the Canadian banking industry?

6.* What was the main rationale behind the separation of commercial and investment banking activities in the *Glass-Steagall Act* of 1933? Why was the act repealed?

7. Discuss the problems life insurance companies will face as genetic information becomes more widely available.

8. When the values of stocks and bonds fluctuate, they have an impact on the balance sheet of insurance companies. Why is that impact more likely to be a problem for life insurance companies than for property and casualty companies?

9.* As a current member of the workforce, what advantage would there be for you to privatizing part of the Canada Pension Plan to allow for individual private accounts? What do you see as the main potential problem?

10. What are the benefits of collaboration between a large appliance retailer and a finance company?

## Analytical Problems

11. Consider two countries with the following characteristics. Country A has no restrictions on bank branching, and banks are permitted to offer investment and insurance products along with traditional banking services. In Country B, there are strict limits on branch banking and on the geographical spread of a bank's business. In addition, banks in Country B are not permitted to offer investment or insurance services.

a. In which country do you think the banking system is more concentrated?

b. In which country do you think the banking system is more competitive?

c. In which country do you think, everything else being equal, banking products are cheaper?

Explain each of your choices.

12. You examine the balance sheet of an insurance company and note that its assets are made up mainly of Treasury bills and commercial paper. Is this more likely to be the balance sheet of a property and casualty insurance company or a life insurance company? Explain your answer.

13.* Statistically, teenage drivers are more likely to have an automobile accident than adult drivers. As a result, insurance companies charge

* Indicates more difficult problems.

higher insurance premiums for teenage drivers. Suppose one insurance company decided to charge teenagers and adults the same premium based on the average risk of an accident among both groups. Using your knowledge of the problems associated with asymmetric information, explain whether you think this insurance company will be profitable.

14. Use your knowledge of the problems associated with asymmetric information to explain why insurance companies often include deductibles as part of their policies.

15. Suppose you have a defined-contribution pension plan. As you go through your working life, in what order would you choose to have the following portfolio allocations—(a) 100 percent bonds and money-market instruments, (b) 100 percent stocks, (c) 50 percent bonds and 50 percent stocks?

16. As an employee, would you prefer to participate in a defined-benefit pension plan or a defined-contribution pension plan? Explain your answer.

17.* How could the imposition of capital requirements on government-sponsored enterprises such as Fannie Mae and Freddie Mac protect the financial system from dangers associated with a dramatic decline in house prices?

18. Suppose a well-known investment dealer agreed to be the underwriter for a new stock issue. After guaranteeing the price to the issuing company but before selling the stocks, a scandal surrounding the business practices of the bank is revealed. How would you expect this scandal to affect (a) the investment bank and (b) the issuing company?

# CHAPTER 14

## Regulating the Financial System

In the fall of 2008, the financial crisis in the United States threatened to paralyze the global economic system, and although immediate disaster was averted, the crisis is imposing huge costs in terms of unemployment and fiscal burdens around the world. While the scale of this crisis is unusual, financial crises themselves are not; such events are quite common. In the past quarter century, 93 countries have experienced a total of 117 systemwide and 51 smaller disruptions in their financial systems. Virtually no part of the world has been spared; large industrialized countries have suffered along with smaller, less developed ones.

When financial crises occur, governments step in and put financial intermediaries back on track. They often do so by assuming responsibility for the banking system's liabilities so that depositors won't lose their savings. But the cleanup can also require the injection of capital into failed institutions. These crises not only are expensive to clean up, but also have a dramatic impact on growth in the countries where they occurred.

Figure 14.1 on page 306 plots information on the fiscal cost and growth consequence of banking crises between 1980 and 2002. On the horizontal axis of the figure is a measure of the cost of the cleanup and on the vertical axis is the change in economic growth. The data show what one would expect: Bigger crises are worse for growth. Using a slightly different methodology and data from 1970 to 2007, other economists computed that the average cost of banking crises in industrial economies was 15 percent of GDP.[1] Some degree of default is normal at every bank, including well-run ones. But the crisis in the fall of 2008 was not just the result of one bank failing. The IMF estimated the global cost of the financial crisis to be on the order of $4 trillion; and if the U.S. costs were 15 percent of that country's GDP, the U.S. share of that number would be about $2 trillion.

Financial crises are not a recent phenomenon; the history of commercial banking over the last two centuries is replete with periods of turmoil and failure. By their very nature, financial systems are fragile and vulnerable to crisis. Unfortunately, when a country's financial system completely collapses, its economy goes with it, and with economic crisis comes the risk of violence and revolution. Keeping banks open and operating, then, is as essential to maintaining our way of life as a ready military defence. Because a healthy financial system benefits everyone, governments are deeply involved in the way banks and other intermediaries function. Because financial institutions work globally, international organizations have been created to monitor and regulate them. As a result, the financial sector is subject to voluminous rules and regulations, and financial institutions must withstand constant scrutiny by domestic and international monitors. Moreover, the regulations are ever-changing as regulators try to keep up with innovations in the financial sector. The importance of this oversight in ensuring financial stability is hard to exaggerate.

In this chapter, we focus primarily on banking system regulation, and especially on regulations whose goal is to promote financial stability. Historically, financial crises began with banking crises and so regulators were particularly interested in banks. This approach was sufficient when the financial system was primarily a domestic system and financial institutions were organized around the four pillars. However, as we saw

---

[1] Measuring the cost of financial crises is tricky because of the need to separate out what economists call "'transfers" from dead weight loss. If your loss is someone else's gain it is possibly unfair (and may have a long-run cost because you will make sure it doesn't happen again) but it is not necessarily an inefficiency.

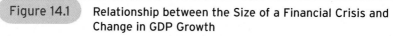

Figure 14.1      Relationship between the Size of a Financial Crisis and Change in GDP Growth

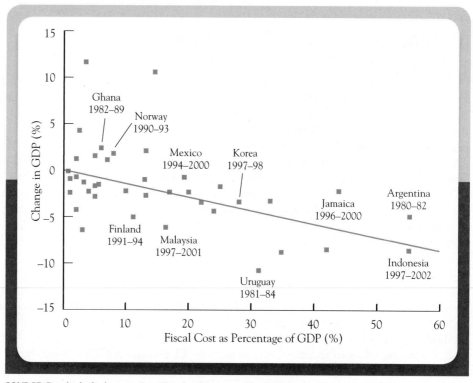

SOURCE: *Data for the fiscal costs are from "Episodes of Systemic and Borderline Financial Crises," by Gerald Caprio Jr. and Daniela Klingebiel. © 2003 The World Bank. Used with permission. Change in GDP is computed as the average annual rate from the three years prior to the crisis to the three years following the crisis; data are from the Inter-American Development Bank's annual report 2004.*

in Chapter 13, today the four pillars have melded together and financial markets are global. At the end of the chapter we discuss how these trends are reshaping the regulatory landscape. But we begin by looking at the sources and consequences of bank fragility. Then, we look at the institutional safeguards—for instance, deposit insurance—the government has built into the system in an attempt to avert financial crises and study the regulatory and supervisory environment of the banking industry. The last section looks briefly at regulation of non-bank financial intermediaries and the challenges facing regulators today.

## The Sources and Consequences of Runs, Panics, and Crises

In a market-based economy, the opportunity to succeed is also an opportunity to fail. New restaurants open and others go out of business. Only one in 10 restaurants survives as long as three years. In principle, banks should be no different from restaurants: new ones should open and unpopular ones close. But few of us would want to live in a world where banks fail at the same rate as restaurants. Banks serve some essential functions in our economy: they provide access to the payments system, and they screen and monitor borrowers to reduce information problems.

Banks' particular fragility arises from the fact that they have a **maturity mismatch**. That is, they allow depositors to withdraw their balances on demand, while using those deposits to make long-term loans. If you want the entire amount in your chequing account converted into cash, all you need to do is go to your bank and ask for it; the teller is obligated to give it to you. If a bank cannot meet this promise of withdrawal on demand because of insufficient liquid assets, it will fail.

Banks not only guarantee their depositors immediate cash on demand but also promise to satisfy depositors' withdrawal requests on a first-come, first-served basis. This commitment has some important implications. Suppose depositors begin to lose confidence in a bank's ability to meet their withdrawal requests. They have heard a rumour that one of the bank's largest loans has defaulted, so that the bank's assets may no longer cover its liabilities. True or not, reports that a bank has become **insolvent** can spread fear that it will run out of cash and close its doors. Mindful of the bank's first-come, first-served policy, frenzied depositors may rush to the bank to convert their balances to cash before other customers arrive. Such a **bank run** can cause a bank to fail.

Crowds trying get into the Northern Rock bank branch, Birmingham, September 2007.

SOURCE: *Lee Jordan, photographer.*

A bank run can be the result of either real or imagined problems. No bank is immune to the loss of depositors' confidence just because it is profitable and sound. A recent example is the Abacus Savings Bank, which serves large numbers of immigrants in New York City's Chinatown. In April 2003, news spread through the Chinese-language media that one of the bank's managers had embezzled more than $1 million. Frightened depositors, unfamiliar with the safeguards in place at U.S. banks, converged on three of the institution's branches to withdraw their balances. Because Abacus Savings was financially sound, it was able to meet all requested withdrawals during the course of the day. In the end, as one government official observed, the real danger was that depositors might be robbed carrying large quantities of cash away from the bank. Leaving their funds in the bank would have been safer, but rumour and a lack of familiarity with government-sponsored deposit insurance caused depositors to panic.[2]

What matters during a bank run is not whether a bank is solvent, but whether it is liquid. Solvency means that the value of the bank's assets exceeds the value of its liabilities—that is, the bank has a positive net worth. Liquidity means that the bank has sufficient reserves and immediately marketable assets to meet depositors' demand for withdrawals. False rumours that a bank is *insolvent* can lead to a run that renders a bank **illiquid**. If people believe that a bank is in trouble, that belief alone can make it so.

When a bank fails, depositors may lose some or all of their deposits, and information about borrowers' creditworthiness may disappear. For these reasons alone, government officials work to ensure that all banks are operated in a way that minimizes their chance of failure. But that is not their main worry. The primary concern is that a single bank's failure might cause a small-scale bank run that could turn into a systemwide **bank panic**. This phenomenon of spreading panic on the part of depositors is called **contagion**.

Information asymmetries are the reason that a run on a single bank can turn into a bank panic that threatens the entire financial system. Recall from Chapter 11 that if there is no way to tell a good used car from a bad one, the only used cars on the

---

[2] See James Barron, "Chinatown Bank Endures Run as Fear Trumps Reassurances," *The New York Times,* April 23, 2003, A1.

market will be lemons. What is true for cars is even truer for banks. Most of us are not in a position to assess the quality of a bank's balance sheet. In fact, since banks often make loans based on sophisticated statistical models, only an expert can estimate the worth of a bank's assets. Depositors, then, are in the same position as uninformed buyers in the used car market: They can't tell the difference between a good bank and a bad bank. And who wants to make a deposit in a bank if there is even a small chance that it could be insolvent? So when rumours spread that a certain bank is in trouble, depositors everywhere begin to worry about their own banks' financial condition.

While banking panics and financial crises can easily result from false rumours, they can also occur for more concrete reasons. Since a bank's assets are a combination of loans and securities, anything that affects borrowers' ability to make their loan payments or drives down the market value of securities has the potential to imperil the bank's finances. Recessions—widespread downturns in business activity—have a clear negative impact on a bank's balance sheet. When business slows, firms have a harder time paying their debts. People lose their jobs and suddenly can't make their loan payments. As default rates rise, bank assets lose value, and bank capital drops. With less capital, banks are forced to contract their balance sheets, making fewer loans. This decline in loans, in turn, means less business investment, which amplifies the downturn. If a recession gets really bad, banks can begin to fail, particularly if the system is inherently fragile.

Canadian experience in the 1980s shows how a downturn can put pressure on banks. The Canadian Commercial Bank and the Northland Bank were Western banks that began operations in 1975. They both invested heavily in oil and gas and in real estate. The recession in the early 1980s hit these sectors particularly hard and both banks failed in 1985—the first Canadian bank failure since 1923. Bank panics start with real economic events, not just rumours.

Financial disruptions can also occur whenever borrowers' net worth falls, as it does during a deflation. Companies borrow a fixed number of dollars to invest in real assets such as buildings and machines, whose values fall with deflation. So a drop in prices reduces companies' net worth (but not their loan payments). This decline in firms' net worth aggravates the adverse selection and moral hazard problems caused by information asymmetries, making loans more difficult to obtain. If these firms cannot get new financing, business investment will fall, reducing overall economic activity and raising the number of defaults on loans. As more and more borrowers default, banks' balance sheets deteriorate, compounding information problems and creating a full-blown crisis.

## The Government Safety Net

Before we discuss the types of regulation and support of financial markets, we need to step back and consider the rationale for regulation. For many products, markets are amazingly effective at what economists call "allocative efficiency": the price system coordinates the interests, wants, and abilities of millions of people so that economic resources are put to their best use. But market failures—such as monopoly power, asymmetric information or externalities—hamper the ability of the price mechanism to allocate resources efficiently, and government regulations are introduced to improve the operation of the system.[3] Because government regulation can bring its own inefficiency, it is not enough to identify a market failure; the principle of regulation is to identify the market failure and to design regulations that improve the operation of the markets. In extreme cases, the government may completely substitute for the market.

---

[3] In addition, governments intervene in the economy to achieve a more equitable allocation of resources, but the majority of financial market regulation is aimed at market efficiency.

The necessary extent of financial market regulation has always been hotly debated and recently it has become even more so. For example, economists who accept the efficient-market hypothesis typically argue for less government intervention than behaviouralists (we discussed these two views in Chapter 8). As we discuss the types of financial regulation, try to be clear in your mind what the market failure is and whether the regulation is improving the market. One way to do this is to consider whether the rationale proposed for financial market regulation would also work to argue for regulating other businesses—say coffee shops or travel agencies; also consider whether the regulation causes more problems than it solves. Getting the right balance of regulation in an environment in which institutions are changing their form and are facing global competition is exceedingly challenging.

The motivation for financial market regulation is twofold: consumer protection and financial system stability. The first is similar to regulation in other fields (for example, food safety). Because it is expensive for consumers to individually monitor institutions and to assess the value of financial products, the government insists on disclosure of the financial conditions of a financial firms. In addition, as in any industry, there is an incentive for small firms to band together (for example, through mergers or takeovers) into large ones to reduce competition, ultimately ending in monopolies. In general, monopolies exploit their customers, raising prices to earn unwarranted profits. Because monopolies are inefficient, the government intervenes to prevent the firms in an industry from becoming too large. In the financial system, that means ensuring that even large banks face competition. In Canada, with its small number of large banks, the government has intervened to deter mergers among the bigger banks on the grounds that it would give those banks undue market power.

The concern with financial system stability derives from the externalities associated with the system. Historically, the emphasis was on payments system stability because the payments system is a network and the collapse of one piece of the network would affect all the others. And, because banks were (1) closer to the payments system than other financial institutions since their liabilities such as demand deposits are a means of payment, and (2) as we have seen they are inherently fragile, regulation and support focused on the banking sector.

The combustible mix of liquidity risk and information asymmetries means that the financial system is inherently unstable. A financial firm can collapse much more quickly than an industrial company. For a steel corporation, an electronics manufacturer, or an automobile maker, failure occurs slowly as customers disappear one by one. But a financial institution can create and destroy the value of its assets in an astonishingly short period, and a single firm's failure can bring down the entire system. The real culprit in creating this high degree of risk is derivatives. When used properly, derivatives are extremely beneficial, allowing the transfer of risk to those who can best bear it. But in the wrong hands, derivatives can bring down even the largest, most respected institutions. The failure of Barings Bank in 1995 is an example. One of the oldest and best-known banks in England, Barings collapsed in just two months after a single trader wiped out the bank's capital with losses of more than $1 billion on futures positions worth over $17 billion. Bets like that can be made only using derivatives. And, because they can be made in ways that are extremely difficult for government regulators to detect, these high-risk actions have the potential to put the entire financial system at risk.[4]

STABILITY

---

[4] The collapse of Lehman brothers—an investment bank, not a commercial bank—and near collapse of AIG—an insurance company—in 2008 show how the difficulties that were thought to be particular to the banking system have spread to other sectors of the financial market.

## YOUR FINANCIAL WORLD
### The Canadian Investor Protection Fund

Investment dealers advertise that they are members of the CIPF—that's the Canadian Investor Protection Fund. The CIPF provides insurance in the event that an investment dealer firm fails, owing its customers cash and securities. It is insurance against insolvency.

If a bank accepts your deposits and uses the funds to make bad loans, your savings are protected by the CDIC against the bank's failure. By contrast, CIPF insurance replaces missing securities or cash that was supposed to be there—up to a limit of $1,000,000 per account. It does not compensate individuals for investments that lost value because market prices fell, nor will it cover individuals who

were sold worthless securities. The CIPF protects against an investment dealer being bankrupt. Mutual fund dealers have a similar insurance scheme—MFDA IPC—to protect eligible customers of members of their association (the MFDA) in case of the members' bankruptcy or insolvency.

For more information on the CIPF, go to http://www.cipf.ca. For information on the MFDA IPC, go to http://www.mfda.ca/ipc/ipc.html. For comprehensive information on what to do if your financial institution fails, check the federal government's Web site, http://www.financeprotection.ca, which provides links to provincial as well as federal programs.

Government officials employ a combination of strategies to protect investors and ensure the stability of the banking system. First, they provide the safety net to insure small depositors. Authorities both operate as the *lender of last resort*, making loans to banks that face sudden deposit outflows, and provide deposit insurance, guaranteeing that depositors receive the full value of their accounts should an institution fail. But this safety net causes bank managers to take on too much risk, leading to the regulation and supervision that we will discuss later in the chapter.

This section will examine the unique role of depository institutions in our financial system. The point is that we need banks. However, although they are essential, they are also fragile. This leads to a discussion of the components of the safety net, the problems it creates, and how the government responds to these problems. The final section looks forward at how financial innovation and the globalization of financial services are blurring the distinctions between depository and nondepository institutions and changing the required scope of government responses.

## The Government as Lender of Last Resort

The best way to stop a bank failure from turning into a bank panic is to make sure solvent institutions can meet their depositors' withdrawal demands. In 1873, British economist Walter Bagehot described the need for a lender of last resort to perform this function. A lender of last resort would make loans to prevent the failure of solvent banks and could provide liquidity in sufficient quantities to prevent or end a financial panic. Specifically, Bagehot proposed that Britain's central bank should "lend freely on good collateral at a high rate of interest to solvent but illiquid banks." By lending freely, he meant providing liquidity on demand to any bank that asked for it. Lending to solvent banks would ensure that the central bank was not bailing out failing institutions. Good collateral would ensure the borrowing bank's solvency and that the central bank profited from the transaction. The high interest rate would penalize the borrowing bank for failing to hold enough reserves or easily salable assets to meet deposit outflows.

Bagehot's advice worked well for liquidity crises in 19th-century England but the changing structure of the financial system requires adaptations in government

## APPLYING THE CONCEPT
### THE DAY THE BANK OF NEW YORK BORROWED $23 BILLION

While the existence of a lender of last resort may encourage bank managers to take too many risks, very few people would argue for abolishing the safeguard outright. There have been days when the system worked exactly as it should. November 20, 1985, was one of them. On that day, the Bank of New York's computer system went haywire. BONY, as it is known, plays a central role in the U.S. Treasury securities market. The bank acts as a clearinghouse, buying bonds from sellers and then reselling them to buyers.

On November 20, a software error prevented BONY from keeping track of its Treasury bond trades.* For 90 minutes transactions poured in, and the bank accumulated and paid for U.S. Treasury bonds, notes, and bills. Importantly, BONY promised to make payments without actually having the funds. But when the time came to deliver the securities and collect from the buyers, BONY employees could not tell who

the buyers and sellers were or what quantities and prices they had agreed to. The information had been erased. By the end of the day, the Bank of New York had bought and failed to deliver so many securities that it was committed to paying out $23 billion that it did not have.

Without a way to come up with $23 billion, BONY wasn't able to make payments to sellers who had delivered their securities. These sellers had made additional transactions in the expectation that they would be paid. Unless BONY found a way to make the promised payments, the problem would spread to other institutions. The Federal Reserve, as lender of last resort, stepped in and made a loan of $23 billion, preventing a computer problem at one very important bank from becoming a full-blown financial crisis.

*BONY's computers could store only 32,000 transactions at a time. When more transactions arrived than the computer could handle, the software's counter restarted at zero. Since the counter number was the key to where the trading information was stored, the information was effectively erased. (Had all the original transactions been processed before the counter restarted, there would have been no problem.)

responses. Bagehot advocated assisting solvent but illiquid banks, but in "normal" times such institutions would rather use their "good" collateral to borrow from a private-sector lender without paying a penalty rate. In abnormal times there are other issues. For the system to work, central bank officials who approve the loan applications must be able to distinguish an illiquid from an insolvent institution. But during a crisis, computing the market value of a bank's assets is almost impossible, since there are no market prices. (If a bank could sell its marketable assets in the financial markets, it wouldn't need a loan from the central bank.) Because a bank will go to the central bank for a direct loan only after having exhausted all opportunities to sell its assets and borrow from other banks without collateral, its illiquidity and its need to seek a loan from the government raise the question of its solvency. Anxious to keep the crisis from deepening, officials are likely to be generous in evaluating the bank's assets and to grant a loan even if they suspect the bank may be insolvent. Knowing this, bank managers will tend to take too many risks.

In other words, the central bank's difficulty in distinguishing a bank's insolvency from its illiquidity creates moral hazard for bank managers. It is important for a lender of last resort to operate in a manner that minimizes the tendency for bankers to take too much risk in their operations.

At the time, Bagehot's prescription for a lender of last resort was meant to address the problem of bank runs that plagued England—that is, to address systemic liquidity crises. By the end of the 20th century, the advice was seen as encompassing responses to both systemic needs for liquidity and emergency needs of individual banks. The Bank of Canada created facilities for each case. The Emergency Liquidity Facilities (ELF) enable the Bank to lend to an institution that is solvent but struggling. The ELF operate along the lines of Bagehot's prescription with the borrowing bank posting good collateral (although perhaps not only government securities) and paying above-market interest rates. Following the failure of the Canadian Commercial Bank and the Northland Bank in the mid-1980s, two other banks, the Bank of British Columbia and the Continental Bank of Canada, faced runs in the market for wholesale deposits. These banks were solvent and the Bank of Canada provided support for them, but they ended up merging with larger banks, and are today part of HSBC Canada.

The Bank of Canada also provides liquidity through what it calls Standing Liquidity Facilities (SLF). These are essentially overnight loans to banks that had a surprise withdrawal of funds. As we describe in Chapter 17, the banks will usually borrow from each other rather than from the Bank of Canada so this source of funds too is only lightly used.

## Government Deposit Insurance

In 1967, the Canadian government created the Canada Deposit Insurance Corporation (CDIC). It required all the chartered banks to pay into a fund (proportionately to their deposits) that would be used to reimburse depositors if the bank failed. The CDIC guarantees that a depositor will receive the full account balance up to $100,000 even if a bank fails. Bank failures, in effect, become the problem of the insurer; bank customers need not concern themselves with their bank's risk taking. So long as a bank has deposit insurance, customers' deposits are safe, even in the event of a run or bank failure.

Here's how the system works. When a bank fails, the CDIC resolves the insolvency either by closing the institution or by finding a buyer. The first approach, closing the bank, is called the *winding-up method*. The CDIC pays off all the bank's depositors, then sells all the bank's assets in an attempt to recover the amount paid out. Under the winding-up method, depositors whose balances exceed the insurance limit, currently $100,000, suffer some losses.

In the second approach, called the **purchase-and-assumption method**, the CDIC finds a firm that is willing to take over the failed bank. Since the failed institution is insolvent—on the balance sheet, its liabilities exceed its assets—no purchaser will do so for free. In fact, the CDIC has to pay banks to purchase failed institutions. That is, the CDIC sells the failed bank at a negative price. For example, when HSBC took over the Bank of British Columbia in 1986, it received some funding from CDIC. Depositors prefer the purchase-and-assumption method to the payoff method because the transition is typically seamless, with the bank closing as usual at the end of the week and reopening on Monday morning under new ownership. In a purchase and assumption, no depositors, even those whose account balances exceed the deposit insurance limit, suffer a loss.

No private insurance fund is big enough to withstand a run on all the banks it insures—that is, no insurance fund except the CDIC. Because the Canadian government backs the CDIC, it can withstand virtually any crisis.

## Problems Created by the Government Safety Net

We know that insurance changes people's behaviour; protected depositors have no incentive to monitor their bankers' behaviour. Knowing this, bankers take on more risk than they would normally, since they get the benefits while the government assumes the costs. In protecting depositors, then, the government creates moral hazard. We can find evidence for this assertion by comparing bank balance sheets before and after the implementation of deposit insurance in the United States in 1934.[5] Commercial banks in the United States have significant leverage; their assets are 12 times the size of their

---

[5] There is no comparable Canadian study.

capital. In the 1920s, before the U.S. deposit insurance system (FDIC) was created, banks' ratio of assets to capital was about 4 to 1. Most economic and financial historians believe that government insurance led directly to the rise in risk. Similar results occurred when the deposit insurance limit was quadrupled to $100,000 in 1980. Over the following ten years, several thousand depository institutions (banks, savings and loans) failed, more than four times the number that failed in the nearly half century since deposit insurance was created in 1935. While a vast majority of the institutions that failed in the 1980s were small, the cost of reimbursing depositors exceeded $180 billion. A summary of research concludes that explicit deposit insurance actually makes financial crises more likely. When countries have either implemented a new scheme or expanded an existing one, the probability of crises has increased.[6]

And that is not the only problem. Because government officials are obsessed with avoiding financial crises, they pay close attention to the largest institutions. While the failure of a small community bank is unfortunate, the prospect of a large financial conglomerate going under is a regulator's worst nightmare. The disruption caused by the collapse of an institution that holds hundreds of billions of dollars in assets is too much for most people even to contemplate. In effect, some banks are just too big to fail. The managers of these banks know that if their institutions begin to founder, the government will find a way to bail them out. The deposit insurer will quickly find a buyer or the government, as lender of last resort, will make a loan. Depositors will be made whole, and the managers of the bank may even keep their jobs.

The government's too-big-to-fail policy limits the extent of the market discipline depositors can impose on banks. Normally, a corporation with millions of dollars to deposit is concerned about the riskiness of its bank's assets, given the limits of government deposit insurance. If the bank fails, the corporation could face significant losses. Thus, the threat of withdrawal of these large balances restrains the bank from taking on too much risk.[7] But for very large banks, the deposit insurance ceiling is meaningless, because everyone knows that authorities will not permit the bank to fail.[8] With virtually no monitoring by depositors and no threat that their balances will be withdrawn, bank managers can take whatever risks they like. The too-big-to-fail policy compounds the problem of moral hazard, encouraging managers of large banks to engage in extremely risky behaviour (and putting small banks at a competitive disadvantage).

## Regulation and Supervision of the Banking System

Government officials employ two strategies to ensure that the risks created by the safety net are contained. Government *regulation* establishes a set of specific principles or rules for bank managers to follow. Government *supervision* provides oversight of financial institutions. As we look at each of these, keep in mind that the goal of government regulation is not to remove all the risk that investors face. Financial intermediaries themselves facilitate the transfer and allocation of risk, improving

---

[6] A. Demirgüç-Kunt and E. Kane, 2002, "Deposit Insurance around the Globe: Where Does It Work?" *Journal of Economic Perspectives* 16(2), pp. 175–95.

[7] Today, large depositors can engage in what is known as a *silent run* on a bank. Rumours that a bank is in trouble can lead to the electronic withdrawal of individual deposits that exceed the $100,000 insurance ceiling. Since the withdrawals are made by wire transfer, no customers can be seen lining up at the bank; these runs are silent and invisible.

[8] The United States temporarily raised the limit of deposit Insurance from $100,000 to $250,000 in October 2008 (until December 2009). At the same time, the United Kingdom raised its limit and in Ireland changed its policy so that a number of institutions have unlimited deposit insurance.

economic efficiency in the process. Regulating risk out of existence would eliminate one of the purposes of financial institutions.

Wary of asking taxpayers to pick up the bill for bank insolvencies, officials created regulatory requirements that are designed to minimize the cost of such failures to the public. The first screen, put in place to make sure the people who own and run banks are not criminals, is for a new bank to obtain a charter. Once a bank has been chartered and has opened for business, a complex web of detailed regulations restricts competition, specifies what assets the bank can and cannot hold, requires the bank to hold a minimum level of capital, and makes public information about the bank's balance sheet. Although all countries have regulations binding their banks, some national regulators (including that of the United States) pursue a rules-based approach while others (including Canada and the United Kingdom) use a principles-based regulatory framework. The principles-based approach allows the individual institutions to determine how they will satisfy the principles, and are more flexible. Consider the difference between the instruction "drive safely" and the rules, "drive at the speed limit" and "without alcohol." On an icy road, the "safe'" speed limit may be less than the speed limit, and while a driver in an accident could say he obeyed the rules, he would find it harder to argue that he obeyed the principle.

As we all know, rules and principles are one thing; enforcement is another. Posting a speed limit on a highway is only the first step in preventing people from driving too fast. Unless the police patrol the highways and penalize speeding drivers, such laws are worthless. The same is true of banking regulations. The best-designed regulatory structure in the world won't be worth the paper it's written on unless someone monitors banks' compliance. Government supervisors are the highway patrol of the banking world. They monitor, inspect, and examine banks to make sure their business practices conform to regulatory requirements.

The **Office of the Superintendent of Financial Institutions (OSFI)** is responsible for the regulation and supervision of banks in Canada. OSFI works with the Ministry of Finance, the Bank of Canada, and the Canada Deposit Insurance Corporation to ensure the safety and soundness of the Canadian banking system. To ensure that the agencies do not work at cross purposes, they meet regularly as members of FISC—Financial Institutions Supervisory Committee (which also includes the Financial Consumer Agency of Canada.)[9]

## Restrictions on Competition

One long-standing goal of financial regulators has been to prevent banks from growing too big and powerful, both because their failure might threaten the financial system and because banks that have no real competition exploit their customers. As we saw in Chapter 13, historically Canadian regulators required that the four pillars of the financial system—banking, insurance, brokerage, and trust companies—remain distinct. In the second half of the 20th century, the barriers between the pillars weakened and the large Canadian banks now all own large securities dealers. However, the government has continued to limit the entry of banks into insurance and, without developing a specific policy, has stood in the way of attempts of the large banks to merge (see In the News: Bizarre World of Bank Mergers on page 316).

---

[9] The mandates of OSFI and CDIC overlap somewhat; since CDIC is on the hook for the costs of a bank failure the organization is very concerned with how well OSFI does its job. That is, the costs and benefits are not completely aligned.

## YOUR FINANCIAL WORLD
### Are Your Deposits Insured?

The sign says "Each depositor insured to $100,000." But what does it really mean? Are your deposits fully insured? The answer to this question can be complicated. Here are a few things to keep in mind.

First, deposit insurance basically covers individuals, not accounts. It insures depositors. That means that if you have a savings account, a chequing account and a GIC all at the same CDIC-covered institution, all in the same name, your total coverage has a maximum of $100,000. This is the case even if the accounts are at different branches. In contrast, accounts at different financial institutions are treated separately.

If you have some accounts in your own name and also some money in a joint account with another person at the same financial institution, the monies in the joint account would be treated separately from the accounts in your own name. Similarly, money in a TFSA, RESP or RRSP, is considered separately.

This information shows some of the complexities. If you want to know the details (and also because, like all government regulations, the rules for government deposit insurance can change, find the latest information on the coverage of your deposits, at www.cdic.ca. (or the provincial ministry of finance for deposits insured by a provincial agency).

But government officials also worry that the greater the competition among banks, the more difficulty banks will have making a profit. Competition reduces the prices customers must pay and forces companies to innovate in order to survive. These effects are as true of the market for deposits and loans as they are of the markets for cars and computers. Competition raises the interest rate bankers pay on deposits and lowers the interest rate they receive on loans; it spurs them to improve the quality of the services they provide. Normally we think of these effects of competition as being positive, but there is a negative side as well. Lower interest margins and reduced fee income cause bankers to look for other ways to turn a profit. Some may be tempted to assume more risk—that is, to make loans and purchase securities that are riskier than advisable.

There are two ways to avoid this type of moral hazard. First, government officials can explicitly restrict competition.[10] That is the solution regulators have chosen in a number of countries; it was also one of the purposes of branching restrictions in the United States. (Branching restrictions may create networks of small, geographically separated independent banks that face very little competition in their regions.) A second way to combat bankers' tendency to take on too much risk is to prohibit them from making certain types of loans and from purchasing particular securities.

## Asset-holding Restrictions and Minimum Capital Requirements

The simplest way to prevent bankers from exploiting their safety net is to restrict banks' balance sheets. Such regulations take two forms: restrictions on the types of asset banks can hold and requirements that they maintain minimum levels of capital. While banks are allowed to build big office buildings and buy corporate jets for top executives, their financial assets are restricted by the Bank Act and OSFI. The basic rule in the Bank Act is that Canadian banks "shall adhere to investment and lending policies, standards and procedures that a reasonable and prudent person would apply in respect of a portfolio of

---

[10] Until the early 1970s, regulation restricted the interest rates U.S. banks could pay on deposits. Regulation Q prohibited interest payments on demand deposits and placed a ceiling on interest payments on time and savings deposits. Its purpose was to restrict competition in order to improve banks' profitability.

# IN THE NEWS
## Bizarre World of Bank Mergers

# Financial Post

### Keith Kalawsky

#### August 10, 2005

In the comic strip Bizarro World, society is ruled by the Bizarro Code, which decrees that doing anything well or making anything too perfect or beautiful is a crime.

Although this fictional planet is inhabited by disfigured and slow-witted versions of Superman and Lois Lane, you can count Ralph Goodale, the Finance Minister, among its inhabitants. On Parliament Hill, an imperfect place if there ever was one, things are truly getting strange.

Just when some bank investors and analysts started to believe Goodale wasn't yanking their chains for the millionth time about allowing mergers, the issue is supposedly dead now until after the next election.

Then yesterday, the NDP interrupted the summer doldrums with a quasi-endorsement of bank mergers—on its terms, mind you. The NDP wants restrictions on branch closures and layoffs, among other conditions.

The weirdness continued when Judy Wasylycia-Leis, the NDP's finance critic, threw a few haymakers at Goodale and the Liberals, and actually made some sense while doing it.

"People have compared Parliament to a soap opera. Well, Ralph Goodale is quickly becoming the Phantom of the Opera with his invisible bank merger policy. It is bizarre, it is not governing," she said yesterday at a press conference in Toronto. "They are so fixated on political benefits and electoral success, that that's their deciding factor on every public policy issue. They have to get over this, because minority government may be around for a long time."

The debate over bank mergers, a term mentioned more than 900 times in National Post stories since 1998, could be forever stuck in a quagmire of confusion, political manoeuvring and incompetence in Ottawa. Wasylycia-Leis is right when she complains that nothing is getting done, though you get the feeling that the NDP is pushing mergers to give the Liberals some rope to hang themselves with.

For all of the money and manpower the banks have blown on the merger file, and all the distraction it has generated, why should anyone believe consolidation is coming now? Why do we even care? The banks' argument that mergers are needed to ensure their international competitiveness has lost what little resonance it had.

Throw all the Canadian banks together into some kind of fantasy mega-merger and they'd still only have a collective market value of about $180-billion, compared to the $225US-billion for Citigroup Inc.

The Canadian banks will only ever be niche players outside our country. At home, they will continue to make scads of money and nice returns for their shareholders. It's an acceptable reality. Live with it. Make the best of it.

All of the government's delays and flip-flopping on the merger issue just provide fodder for conspiracy theories. In a column for this newspaper, John Turley-Ewart recently

investments and loans to avoid undue risk of loss and obtain a reasonable return." The implementation of that rather ambiguous rule is the role of the Superintendent. OSFI does have some specific rules but in general operates by overseeing that each Bank holds a well-diversified portfolio of liquid, high-grade bonds and loans.

Minimum capital requirements complement limitations on bank assets. Recall that bank capital represents the net worth of the bank to its owners. Capital serves as both a cushion against declines in the value of the bank's assets, lowering the likelihood of the bank's failure, and a way to reduce the problem of moral hazard. Capital requirements take two basic forms. The first requires most banks to keep their ratio of capital to assets above some minimum level, regardless of the structure of their balance sheets. The second requires banks to hold capital in proportion to the riskiness of their operations. The computation is extremely complicated and the rules change frequently, but basically a bank must first compute the risk-adjusted level of its assets given the likelihood argued that the federal government will continue to tease Liberal loyalists in the government-relations departments of the major banks. As long as the government keeps whispering that mergers are possible, it can rely on the political and financial support of the banks.

This provocative theory is being taken a small step further on Bay Street, with some arguing that the political popularity of the Liberals, even after all the scandals, largely hinges on their management of the economy.

The chief economists working for the big banks are instrumental in shaping the public's view of whether the government is doing a good job on this crucial file.

If Goodale continues to say that mergers might be allowed, even if he doesn't mean it, the theory is that bank economists will abstain from heavy criticism of his government's economic policy. However, if mergers were actually permitted or explicitly banned, economists would be free to rip the Liberal Party for its mistakes and its already tenuous popularity would decline.

Are the Liberals smart enough for this Machiavellian scheming? It might just be crazy talk. But you can't blame people for trying to decipher the government's behaviour.

What about the NDP then? Bank mergers can't be very high on Jack Layton's agenda. But the NDP has something to gain. With its conditional support for mergers, Goodale can no longer blame the opposition parties for the delay on the merger guidelines, so he is running out of excuses. The NDP comes across as the loyal defender of Main Street interests because it can still object to mergers based on its list of conditions that might deter any of the banks from even pursuing a deal.

At the same time, credit unions in Canada, a source of support for the NDP, would like to see mergers so they can fill the void left by the big banks in smaller communities.

The whole situation is like Charlie Brown getting repeatedly suckered by Lucy into kicking at the same football before she pulls it away. It never seems to end.

### LESSON OF THE ARTICLE:

Bank mergers have been hotly debated in Canada for over a decade but remain a low priority for the government (even in 2009). Politicians don't believe the gain in international competitiveness will be large and believe that the decline in domestic competitiveness will harm Canadian consumers. While the debate lingered on, the relative success of Canadian banks in 2008–09, when large international banks saw their capital significantly impaired, resulted in Canadian banks becoming large on the international scene, with 4 Canadian banks in the top 10 by mid-2009.

SOURCE: Financial Post, Keith Kalawsky, "Risk & Reward," 10 August 2005. *Material reprinted with the express permission of "The National Post Company," a CanWest Partnership.*

of a loan or bond default. Then a capital charge is assessed against that level. Of course, banks face a multitude of other risks, including trading risk, operational risk, and the risk associated with their off-balance-sheet operations. Regulators require banks to hold capital based on assessments of those risks as well. (See Tools of the Trade: The Basel Accords, I and II on page 318 for a description of the capital requirements.)

## Disclosure Requirements

Banks are required to provide information, both to their customers about the cost of their products and to the financial markets about their balance sheets. Regulations regarding disclosures to customers are responsible for the small print on loan applications and deposit account agreements; their purpose is to protect consumers. A bank must tell you the interest rate charged on a loan and must do so in a standardized way

# TOOLS OF THE TRADE

## The Basel Accords, I and II

Global financing took off in the 1980s as bankers realized they could expand their operations across national boundaries and turn a profit internationally. While this was a welcome development for most bank customers, not everyone appreciated the competition from abroad. In some countries, bankers complained that the foreign banks invading their turf held an unfair competitive advantage.

Because no one likes competition, we should always be suspicious of this sort of complaint. But in this case, the bankers did have a point. Since foreign banks operate under different regulatory rules, competing with a bank whose home country allows it to hold a lower level of capital is impossible. Holding extra capital is costly. Banks that hold less capital than others, and therefore take on more leverage, have lower costs and can offer borrowers lower interest rates.

This legitimate complaint led to a movement to create international regulations that would promote financial stability within countries and ensure a competitive balance with banks that operate globally. The Bank for International Settlements (BIS), a forum for international cooperation among central bankers and monetary and financial institutions, developed the 1988 Basel Accord, named after the Swiss town where the world's bank regulators meet. The accord established a requirement that internationally active banks must hold capital equal to or greater than 8 percent of their risk-adjusted assets. Assets would be placed in one of four different categories based on their risk of default. The associated risk weights would range from zero to 100 per-

cent. For example, bonds issued by industrialized countries carried a zero risk weight, but residential mortgages carried a 50 percent weight.

The first Basel Accord (Basel I) had several positive effects. First, by linking minimum capital requirements to the risk a bank takes on, it forced regulators to change the way they thought about bank capital. Second, it created a uniform international system. Finally, the accord provided a framework that less developed countries could use to improve the regulation of their banks.

While the Basel Accord was constructive, it did have some severe limitations. In adjusting for asset risk, the accord failed to differentiate between bonds issued by the U.S. government and those issued by emerging-market countries such as Turkey: both received a weight of zero. And a corporate bond received a weight of 100 percent regardless of whether it was AAA-rated or junk. Not only that, but a bank got no credit for reducing risk through diversification. Making one loan of $100 million received the same risk weight as making 1,000 loans of $100,000 each. These shortcomings encouraged banks to shift their holdings toward riskier assets in ways that did not increase their required bank capital.

By the mid-1990s, bank regulators and supervisors had concluded that the Basel Accord needed revision. Starting in 1998, the Basel Committee on Banking Supervision, which wrote the original accord, negotiated a revised framework for determining whether banks have sufficient capital. The new Basel Accord (Basel II) is based on three pillars: a revised set

that allows you to compare interest rates at competing banks. (This regulation is similar to the one that requires grocery stores to show the price of cheese, peanut butter, or popcorn per 100 grams, allowing customers to tell which brand or size is cheapest.) The bank must also tell you the fees it charges to maintain a chequing account—the cost of cheque clearing, the monthly service charge, the fee for overdrafts, and the interest rate paid on the balance, if any.

Disclosure of accounting information to the financial markets protects depositors in a different way. It allows both regulators and the financial markets to assess the quality of a bank's balance sheet. Since the information is published in a standardized format according to clearly specified accounting rules, government officials can easily tell whether a bank is obeying the regulatory rules, and financial analysts can compare one bank to another. With this information, both regulators and the financial markets can penalize banks that are taking too much risk.[11]

---

[11] Writing disclosure rules turns out to be extremely difficult, especially for off-balance-sheet activities. For example, regulators need to know whether a bank that buys or sells interest rate swaps is hedging risk on its balance sheet or taking on more risk. Since positions can change very quickly, sometimes minute by minute, regulators are challenged to figure out exactly what should be reported and when.

## Table 14.1

| Borrower | Risk Weight |
| --- | --- |
| Bonds issued by sovereigns (rated AAA to AA⁻) | Zero |
| Claims on banks rated (AAA to AA⁻) | 20 percent |
| Standard residential mortgages | 35 percent |
| Corporate loans (rated AAA to AA⁻) | 20 percent |
| Consumer and corporate loans (unrated) | 100 percent |

of minimum capital requirements; supervisory review of bank balance sheets; and increased reliance on market discipline to encourage sound risk management practices. The first measure refines the estimation of risk-adjusted assets to reflect more accurately the risk banks actually take. For example, bonds issued by highly rated corporations receive a 20 percent weight; junk bonds, a 150 percent weight (see Table 14.1 for some examples). The second measure requires supervisors to attest to the soundness of bank managers' risk estimation and control methods. Supervisors now review the way banks assess their risk and decide how much capital they should hold. The third measure requires banks to make public their risk exposure and the level of capital they hold. Banks that can show they are behaving responsibly will be rewarded in the market with better credit ratings and higher stock prices.

The Basel Accord is not a law but a set of recommendations for banking regulation and supervision. The Committee that writes and amends the accord has no direct authority over the banks in any country. Instead, its members work to develop a code of best practice that will help government officials around the world ensure the safety and soundness of their banking systems. In Canada, OSFI monitors compliance with the Basel II recommendations.

Following the crisis that began in 2007, the BIS began a review of its processes and planned to expand its coverage to better incorporate liquidity risks and risks due to banks' exposures to complex financial instruments such as derivatives.* As we will discuss further in Chapter 23, governments (including through the Basel Committee) are developing new approaches to financial stability going beyond Basel II to include macroprudential regulation.

---

\* For information about the Basel Committee on Banking Supervision's activities and the Basel Accords in general, see its Web site at http://www.bis.org/bcbs/aboutbcbs.htm.

## Supervision

The government enforces banking rules and regulations through an elaborate oversight process called supervision, which relies on a combination of monitoring and inspection. OSFI examiners measure the risk of a bank using the structure underlying the Risk Matrix in Figure 14.2 on page 320. Each activity of the bank is separately identified, and assessed for its risk in each of seven dimensions: Credit risk, market risk, liquidity risk, insurance risk, operational risk, legal risk, and strategic risk. The "materiality" column reflects the scale of the risk, which can be low, moderate, or high. If an activity is highly material, a given amount of risk is much more significant.

The objective of supervisors is not to eliminate risk but to ensure that it is understood and managed appropriately. The right-hand side of the risk matrix has space for the amount of risk mitigation that the bank has undertaken. When the inherent risks are adjusted for risk mitigation, the examiner can derive the net risk of each activity, which again could be low, moderate, or high. The output of the risk matrix is a measure of "overall net risk." The net risk is then contextualized by the direction (is the institution overall becoming riskier or less risky) and by earnings performance and adequacy of capital.

Figure 14.2 OSFI Risk Matrix

**Institution Name**
**Risk Matrix as at DATE**

| Signifigant Activities | Materiality | Inherent Risks | | | | | | | Quality of Risk Management | | | | | | | Net Risk | Direction of Risk |
|---|---|---|---|---|---|---|---|---|---|---|---|---|---|---|---|---|---|
| | | Credit | Market | Liquidity | Insurance | Operational | Legal & Regulatory | Strategic | Operational Mgmt | Financial Analysis | Compliance | Internal Audit | Risk Mgmt | Senior Mgmt | Board Oversight | | |
| Activity 1 | | | | | | | | | | | | | | | | | |
| Activity 2 | | | | | | | | | | | | | | | | | |
| Activity 3 | | | | | | | | | | | | | | | | | |
| etc. | | | | | | | | | | | | | | | | | |
| Overall Rating | | | | | | | | | | | | | | | | | |

| Capital | | Earnings | | | |
|---|---|---|---|---|---|
| Composite Rating | | Direction of Risk | | Time Frame | |

SOURCE: *Office of the Superintendent of Financial Institutions (OFSI), Supervisory Framework, 1999 and Beyond. Reproduced with the permission of the Minister of Public Works and Government Services, 2009.*

Having done the assessment, what happens next? OSFI has a four-step intervention program. If a bank's risk is low, then it is in Stage 0, which is simply ongoing monitoring. Stages 1 through 4 go from increased monitoring at Stage 1 to provision for winding down at Stage 4. OSFI also translates the information in the Risk Matrix into a CAMELS rating, which is the rating system that CDIC uses (and many other supervisors internationally use) to evaluate the health of the banks they monitor. This acronym stands for Capital adequacy, Asset quality, Management, Earnings, Liquidity, and Sensitivity to risk. Banks are given a rating from one to five in each of these categories, one being the best, and then combine the scores to determine the overall rating. The CAMELS ratings are *not* made public. Instead, they are used to make decisions about whether to take formal action against a bank or even to close it. Current practice is for supervisors to act as consultants, advising banks how to get the highest return possible while keeping risk at an acceptable level that ensures they will stay in business.

## Financial System Regulation

Banks receive a disproportionate amount of attention from government regulators, both because they play a central role in the economy and because they face a unique set of problems. But non-bank depository institutions and other financial intermediaries have the same properties, if on a smaller scale, and are also subject to regulation and supervision. Government regulations require insurance companies to provide proper information to policyholders and restrict the ways the companies manage their assets. The same is true for securities firms and pension funds, whose assets must be structured to ensure that they will be able to meet their obligations many years into the future.

Each sector of the industry has a regulatory and supervisory framework, and in Canada this complexity is added to by the range of federal and provincial regulations. Broadly speaking, federally chartered institutions are regulated federally, and provincially chartered institutions are regulated by either federal or provincial authorities. Most insurance companies are regulated by OSFI; credit unions are mostly regulated provincially, and trust companies are mixed. For example, the British Columbia Financial Institutions Commission (part of the Ministry of Finance) supervises 50 credit unions and as many trust companies, and also administers the Credit Union Deposit Insurance Corporation, which insures credit union deposits and non-equity shares. In addition, an independent agency of the Ministry of Finance, the BC Securities Commission (BSCS), regulates securities trading in BC, for example, monitoring securities issuers and dealers and enforcing legislation against illegal securities sales and insider trading. Currently, Canada is the only G-7 country without a national securities commission; therefore, each province oversees securities legislation. The federal government is currently proposing to introduce such a national securities regulator.

## The Challenge to Regulators and Supervisors

Regulatory focus on depository institutions was motivated in part by the unique interconnectedness of balance sheets between institutions. But recent changes in the law, together with technological innovation, have challenged the traditional structure of regulation and supervision. Today, we bank in a bazaar where a wide range of intermediaries offers a broad array of financial services. We no longer know or care whether the product or service we buy is supplied by someone in town or on the other side of the country. In fact, when you call the bank, the person who answers the phone may live in India, for all you know. Telecommunications has made the location of financial service providers irrelevant.

"Yes, we do have the authority to regulate you."

Besides the globalization of financial services, other changes have challenged regulators and supervisors. First, today's marketplace offers financial instruments that allow individuals and institutions to price and trade almost any risk imaginable. Moreover, because derivatives allow the transfer of risk without a shift in the ownership of assets, a financial institution's balance sheet need not say much about its health. To understand the meaning of this change, consider the traditional rules for computing the minimum required level of bank capital. Historically, the minimum capital level was based on measures such as the default risk of a bank's assets. But in a world where banks can buy and sell derivatives that promise payment in the event of default such measures become almost meaningless. Regulators and supervisors need to adapt. (See the discussion in Tools of the Trade: The Basel Accords, I and II on page 318.)

As regulators responded to the financial crisis of 2007–09, many other gaps in regulation were identified. The Basel II capital requirements were argued to be insufficient in a number of ways. Firstly they were procyclical in that in the "good times" risks were lower so the risk-weighted capital requirements were lower. This meant that the banks were not well capitalized when markets turned down, and also that the banks needed to recapitalize just when it was harder to raise capital. Basel II also had allowed the banks to use their own models of risk (typically the VaR models we discussed in Chapter 5) although supervisors had to approve the modelling. Many financial institutions' models were found to be based on data that did not include the kind of financial meltdown that occurred in 2008–09.

Many other concerns with financial market regulation were raised. One concern was that the regulation focused on narrow activities—banking or securities trading for example, but financial institutions span activities. Relatedly, as institutions became larger, more became "too big to fail"; as well, regulation was national but financial institutions span national borders. Finally, a concern that regulators focus on individual institutions' behaviour may not provide safeguards against systemic risk. At meetings of the G20 finance ministers in November 2008 and April 2009, there was agreement that new, broad, and coordinated approaches to financial regulation were needed. It remains to be seen if such approaches will be found.

Finally, it is important that regulators recognize that the goal of financial stability does not mean guaranteeing the stability of individual financial institutions. Too often supervisors have viewed their role as ensuring that no firm fails. but to do so would defeat the purpose of competition, rendering the entire system less efficient than it could be. Rather, the regulator's goal should be to prevent large-scale catastrophes.

## Terms

## Chapter Summary

1. The collapse of banks and the banking system disrupts both the payments system and the screening and monitoring of borrowers.
   a. Banks fail when their liabilities exceed their assets.
   b. Because banks guarantee their depositors cash on demand on a first-come, first-served basis, they are subject to runs.
   c. A bank run can occur simply because depositors have become worried about a bank's soundness.
   d. The inability of unsophisticated depositors to tell a sound from an unsound bank can turn a single bank's failure into a bank panic, causing even sound banks to fail through a process called contagion.
   e. A financial crisis in which the entire banking system ceases to function can be caused by
      i. False rumours.
      ii. The actual deterioration of bank balance sheets for economic reasons.

2. The government is involved in every part of the financial system.
   a. Banks are heavily regulated because they are central to the payments system and a bank failure or liquidity crisis could threaten the stability of the financial system.
   b. Nondepository institutions are also heavily regulated, but because they were not considered to be prone to runs, government oversight of these institutions is less intrusive than in the banking industry.
   c. The government has established a two-part safety net to protect the nation's banking system.
      i. The Bank of Canada acts as the lender of last resort, providing liquidity to solvent institutions in order to prevent the failure

of a single bank from becoming a system-wide panic.

ii. The Canada Deposit Insurance Corporation (CDIC) insures individual depositors, preventing them from withdrawing their deposits at the first whiff of trouble, thus eliminating bank runs.

d. The government's safety net encourages bank managers to take more risk than they would otherwise, increasing the problem of moral hazard.

3. Through regulation and supervision, government officials reduce the amount of risk banks can take, lowering their chances of failure. Regulators and supervisors
   a. Restrict competition.
   b. Restrict the types of assets banks can hold.
   c. Require banks to hold minimum levels of capital.
   d. Require banks to disclose their fees to customers and their financial indicators to investors.
   e. Monitor banks' compliance with government regulations.

4. Financial system regulation is dynamic and must respond to changes in the structure of the financial system. Today's regulatory system will evolve to address the challenges posed by:
   a. The use of credit derivatives.
   b. The emergence of financial institutions that span functions (banking, insurance, securities dealers).
   c. Financial institutions that span national regulatory authorities.
   d. Institutions that are "too big to fail."

## Conceptual Problems

1. Explain how a bank run can turn into a bank panic.

2. Current technology allows large bank depositors to withdraw their funds electronically at a moment's notice. They can do so all at the same time, without anyone's knowledge, in what is called a silent run. When might a silent run happen, and why?

3. In analyzing data from around the world, a researcher observes that countries whose governments offer deposit insurance are more likely to have financial crises than other countries. Why?

4. Discuss the regulations that are designed to reduce the moral hazard created by deposit insurance.

5. How does the lender of last resort create moral hazard?

6. Distinguish between illiquidity and insolvency. Why is it difficult for a lender of last resort to tell insolvency from illiquidity? Does the distinction matter?

7. Why do regulators insist that banks hold a minimum level of capital?

8.* Why is the banking system much more heavily regulated than other areas of the economy?

9. Using the example of the Great Depression, explain why the existence of a lender of last resort is no guarantee of financial stability.

10.* Explain why, in seeking to avoid financial crises, the government's role as regulator of the financial system does not imply it should protect individual institutions from failure.

## Analytical Problems

11. For each of the following events, state whether you think the immediate problem a typical bank is most likely to encounter is one of illiquidity or of insolvency. Explain your choice in each case.
    a. The government announces it is abolishing its deposit insurance program.
    b. The economy falls into recession and job losses are rampant.
    c. The central bank imposes reserve requirements, effective immediately.

12. Suppose you have two deposits totalling $130,000 with a bank that has just been declared insolvent. Would you prefer that the CDIC resolve the insolvency under the "payoff method" or the "purchase and assumption" method? Explain your choice.

13.* How might the existence of the government safety net lead to increased concentration in the banking industry?

* Indicates more difficult problems.

14. If banks' fragility arises from the fact that they provide liquidity to depositors, as a bank manager, how might you reduce the fragility of your institution?

15.* Why do you think bank managers are not always willing to pursue strategies to reduce the fragility of their institutions?

16. Regulators have traditionally required banks to maintain capital-asset ratios of a certain level to ensure adequate net worth based on the size and composition of the bank's assets, based on the size and composition of the assets on the bank's balance sheet. Why might the effectiveness of such capital adequacy requirements have fallen in more recent times?

17. You are the lender of last resort and an institution approaches you for a loan. You assess that the institution has $800 million in assets, mostly in long-term loans, and $600 million in liabilities. The institution is experiencing unusually high withdrawal rates on its demand deposits and is requesting a loan to tide it over. Would you grant the loan?

18. You are a bank examiner and have concerns that the bank you are examining may have a solvency problem. On examining the bank's assets, you notice that the loan sizes of a significant portion of the bank's loans are increasing in relatively small increments each month. What do you think might be going on, and what should you do about it?

# CHAPTER 15

## Central Banks in the World Today

On September 15, 2008, Lehman Brothers, one of the largest investment banks in the world, filed for bankruptcy protection in the United States. On September 16, the largest insurance company in the United States, AIG, would have done the same if it had not been "bailed out" by an $85 billion loan from the Federal Reserve Bank. Over the next few days there was essentially a run on the entire U.S. financial system.[1] Over the next few months the financial crisis spread globally and, as credit markets dried up, businesses couldn't borrow and began laying off workers.

The financial crisis came after two decades of stable economic growth, a period economists called "the Great Moderation." In response to the crisis, central banks around the globe introduced a series of measures to attempt to get credit markets functioning and to stimulate the economy. The crisis raised many questions about the role of central banks: Were central banks responsible for the crisis itself through too-easy monetary policy or too lax regulation? How should a central bank respond to the crisis? Would easy monetary policy, put in place to stimulate the economy, end up generating inflation? What limits are there—legally and economically—to

[1] Phillip Swagel, "The Financial Crisis: An Inside View," Brookings Paper (March 30, 2009), retrieved August 23, 2009, from http://www.brookings.edu/economics/bpea/~/media/Files/Programs/ES/BPEA/2009_spring_bpea_papers/2009_spring_bpea_swagel.pdf.

the powers of a central bank? While the crisis began in the United States, its impact was felt globally and the Bank of Canada faced the same questions, although with slightly less urgency.

But we need to begin at the beginning. What do central banks do? Why do we have central banks? How do central bank policies influence the economy? Despite the constant presence of central banks in the news and their unprecedented power, most people have only a vague idea of what they are and what they do. This chapter explains the evolution of modern central banks and describes the structure and functions of central banks. In the following chapter, we describe how particular central banks such as the Bank of Canada, the Federal Reserve and the European Central Bank have chosen among competing priorities and structures.

## How Central Banks Originated

Central banks began at different times in different countries and for different reasons. Indeed, central banking is largely a 20th-century phenomenon: In 1900, only 18 countries had central banks; today there are more than 170.[2] While they all perform a core set of functions, there is considerable heterogeneity in the range of functions and in the way that central banks are organized. That said, as financial markets become more integrated globally, central banks will become more similar. We begin by looking at the origins of some central banks and then look at the structure of a modern central bank.

The earliest central banks, such as the Bank of Sweden and the Bank of England, were created in the 1600s. The king gave the central bank the right to issue bank notes and in return the Bank had to lend money to the king to help finance wars. For example, the Bank of England was chartered in 1694 for the express purpose of raising taxes and borrowing to finance a war between Austria, England, and the Netherlands on one side and Louis XIV's France on the other.

By the 1800s the role of the Bank of England had gradually changed from being primarily a "government bank" to becoming a "bankers' bank."[3] This meant that the other banks in England began to keep deposits at the Bank of England that they used as reserves in case of a sudden demand for cash and as a way of making payments between banks. If one bank owed another one money, the first bank would write a cheque on its account at the Bank of England to transfer the funds. By the mid-1800s Bank of England notes had become "as good as gold" and, by the late 19th century the Bank of England acted as a lender of last resort when needed by lending to other banks facing a liquidity crisis. After 1873, there were no widespread financial panics in England. By the 20th century, acting as a lender of last resort was a core function of central banks, indeed almost a defining function.

Unlike the Bank of England, the United States created a central bank, the Federal Reserve System, not as a source of government revenue, but to stabilize the financial system.[4] Between 1870 and 1907, the United States experienced 21 financial panics of

---

[2] The Bank for International Settlements (BIS) Web site has a link to all central bank Web sites: http://www.bis.org/cbanks.htm

[3] For a more detailed discussion, see Glyn Davies' *The History of Money from Ancient Times to the Present Day* (Cardiff: University of Wales Press), 1994.

[4] For two short periods in the 19th century, the United States did have a national bank that served many of the functions of a central bank. Early American dislike for the centralization of power doomed these institutions, the First Bank of the United States (1791–1811) and the Second Bank of the United States (1816–1836). See Michael F. Bryan and Bruce Champ's "Fear and Loathing of Central Banks in America," *Economic Commentary* of the Federal Reserve Bank of Cleveland, June 2002, for a brief description of this history.

varying severity. In the mostly agrarian economy of the time, a typical crisis began with either a crop failure that left farmers with nothing to sell or a bumper crop that drove prices below costs. Either way, farmers defaulted on their loans. The losses damaged the balance sheets of rural banks, leading them to withdraw funds from larger banks in New York or Chicago, where they held deposits. If the rural banks' withdrawals were large enough, the urban banks would be forced to call in their own loans or to refuse renewal of loans that were coming due. As word of the financial difficulties spread, other banks would become concerned and begin to call in their loans as well. Finally, when average people (small depositors) heard of the problem, they would flock to their local banks, demanding to receive their balances in the form of currency or gold.

Unless confidence in the system was restored quickly, such runs left bankers with no choice but to close their doors. During the Panic of 1907, an astonishing two-thirds of banks found themselves temporarily unable to redeem deposits in cash. The situation led one prominent German banker to observe that the U.S. banking system was at the same point in the early 1900s that Europe's had been in the 1400s. In the intervening centuries, Europeans had developed a system of central banks; Americans hadn't. The prevailing philosophy of many 19th-century Americans was that centralized government of any form should be kept to a minimum. But the punishing effects of frequent financial panics led people to reconsider the merits of a powerful central bank and in 1913, Congress passed the *Federal Reserve Act*, which created the U.S. Federal Reserve System.

The Bank of Canada opened for business in 1934. There had been earlier proposals to create a central bank but it was not until the Great Depression that the advocates of central banking had sufficient political strength to get legislation passed to create a central bank. The severity of the Great Depression led many to call for a central bank for a variety of different reasons. Some people held the view that a central bank would print money, which would stimulate the economy. (In practice, the Bank was not very expansionary.) Others argued that the Bank of Canada would operate as the government's bank, managing the public debt and the foreign exchange reserves. At the time, the Department of Finance performed those activities and it was argued that it would be better to have an arm's-length institution to do these functions. Still others argued that the instability in global financial markets created a role for a lender of last resort. The Canadian bankers argued that in the United States there was a central bank but thousands of banks were failing and there were frequent bank runs. In Canada, despite the absence of a central bank, there had been no bank failures or runs.

Prime Minister R.B. Bennett said that he saw the need for a central bank when he realized that in order to buy pounds sterling, a Canadian had to buy U.S. dollars and go to New York to buy sterling.

> *I learned to my surprise that there was no direct means of settling international balances between Canada and London, that the only medium was New York, and the value of the Canadian dollar would have to be determined in Wall Street. I made up my mind then and there that this country was going to have a central bank because there must be some financial institution that can with authority do business for the whole of the Dominion with the other nations of the World.*[5]

Bennett created a Royal Commission to study the need for a central bank and the Commission quickly reported back in favour. The *Bank of Canada Act* was passed in 1933 and the Bank began operating in March 1934. Initially the Bank was partly privately owned, but in 1939 the government bought out the private shareholders,

---

[5] Cited in Milton L. Stokes, "Bank of Canada" (Toronto: 1939) p. 65.

arguing that the Bank should operate in the public interest and it was therefore necessary that it be wholly government owned.

The European Central Bank (ECB) is the most recent central bank to be created. While central banking had stabilized European financial systems before 1900, the 20th century was another story. In that century, Europe experienced high inflation rates, low growth, high and volatile interest rates, and unstable exchange rates. After two world wars, governments' free spending led to unrelenting fiscal deficits. When European economies stagnated in the 1970s and 1980s, a consensus built that inflation was a fundamental problem and poor monetary policy was to blame. Leaders came to believe that the only way to ensure both political and economic stability was to forge closer ties among the continent's countries. They decided the best solution was a common currency and a single central bank.

The agreement to form a European monetary union was formalized in the Treaty of Maastricht, named for the Dutch city in which it was signed in 1992. The treaty initiated a lengthy process that led ultimately to the creation of the European System of Central Banks (ESCB), which is composed of the European Central Bank (ECB) in Frankfurt, Germany, and the National Central Banks (NCBs) in all 27 countries in the European Union. Only 16 of the EU countries have adopted the euro (in 2009). The ECB and the NCBs of those 16 countries that adopted the euro make up what is known as the Eurosystem, which shares a common currency and common monetary policy. On January 1, 1999, the European Central Bank (ECB) began operations. At this writing, Denmark, Sweden, and the United Kingdom, as well as 9 of the 12 countries that joined the European Union since May 1, 2004, remain outside the Eurosystem and retain control over their monetary policy.

## The Functions of a Modern Central Bank

As the government's bank, the central bank occupies a privileged position: It has a monopoly on the issuance of currency and the provision of settlement balances.[6] *The central bank creates money.* The ability to print currency means that the central bank can control the availability of money and credit in a country's economy. As we'll see in later chapters, most central banks go about this by adjusting short-term interest rates. This activity is what we refer to as monetary policy. In today's world, central banks use monetary policy to stabilize economic growth and inflation. An expansionary or accommodative policy, through lower interest rates, raises both growth and inflation over the short run, while tighter or restrictive policy reduces them. We will discuss the mechanics of monetary policy in more detail in later chapters.

Understanding why a country would want to have its own monetary policy is important. At its most basic level, printing paper money is a very profitable business. A $100 bill costs only a few cents to print, but it can be exchanged for $100 worth of goods and services. It is logical that governments would want to maintain a monopoly on printing paper money and to use the revenue it generates to benefit the general public. (Although, when we list the objectives of the central bank later in this chapter, profit maximization will not be one of them.)

Government officials also know that losing control of the printing presses means losing control of inflation. A high rate of money growth creates a high inflation rate, which is why the republics of the former Soviet Union needed to establish their own

---

[6] The monopoly over settlement balances means that banks settle their accounts by transferring balances between accounts at the central bank.

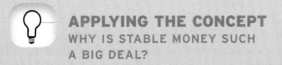

## APPLYING THE CONCEPT
### WHY IS STABLE MONEY SUCH A BIG DEAL?

**by David E. Altig***

On Wednesday, July 10, 1940, Adolf Hitler's Luftwaffe attacked British air bases along the coasts of Scotland and eastern and southeastern England. Four months later, the Battle of Britain was over, bringing an end to German hopes of direct military conquest of the British Isles.

But the end of the air raids would not end the attack on the United Kingdom. Shortly after their defeat in the Battle of Britain, the Germans began to produce a new weapon that, while less obviously violent than Luftwaffe bombs, was recognized as no less virulent. That weapon was counterfeit British pounds.

Operation Bernhard, as the counterfeiting enterprise would be known, was named for Bernhard Kruger, the SS officer who oversaw the production of the bogus notes by slave labor in the Sachsenhausen concentration camp near Berlin. By contemporary accounts, the plan resulted in the manufacture of about £150,000,000 in counterfeit notes of various denominations—in the neighborhood of $7 billion by today's standards. Kruger's operation enlisted the support of known counterfeiters as well as professionals and skilled tradesmen among the camp's population. It incorporated production techniques that ran the gamut from detailed material analyses to the manual labour of prisoners who "seasoned" the bogus bills by passing them from one another, folding and soiling them to give them a realistic worn appearance.

The objective was simple, devious, and pernicious: To undermine public confidence in the pound and, by so doing, irreparably damage the British economy. In the end, the plot did not succeed in destroying confidence in Britain's currency, and eventually, the counterfeiting program shifted toward financing various clandestine Nazi activities outside the United Kingdom. Ironically, this shift in the operation's focus was made possible precisely because the initial goal of undermining the pound's value was not realized.

Operation Bernhard is a particularly interesting example of the use of counterfeiting as warfare, but it is by no means unique or unprecedented. One of the earliest known instances of counterfeiting as a weapon occurred during the city-state conflicts of Renaissance Italy (the historical period that would inspire Machiavelli's *The Prince*). The instigator in this case was one Galeazzo Sforza, a Milanese duke, who in 1470 (when Machiavelli was an infant) attempted to undermine the economic well-being of his enemies in the rival city-state of Venice by adding counterfeiting Venetian currency to the corpus of general treachery that he regularly practiced. (History records the duke as a particularly odious character, whose cruelty led to a successful assassination plot by Milanese elites in 1476.)

There are many, many more examples, including American counterfeiting of North Vietnamese dong during the Vietnam War and modern terrorist aggressions. The ubiquitous impulse to undermine the value of, and confidence in, the currency of one's enemies is testament to the indispensable role of a stable and reliable monetary standard in modern economies. In fact, so broad and deep is the potential damage of a successful counterfeiting campaign, some reports indicate that professional German military officers initially opposed Operation Bernhard partly on the grounds that it constituted an unacceptable attack on civilian populations. What do attempts to counterfeit an enemy's currency during wartime have in common with decisions to adopt another country's currency during peacetime? Both are inspired by the power of a stable monetary standard and, conversely, the consequences of losing it. Both illustrate why preserving the value of the nation's currency is one of a central bank's most important responsibility.

*Excerpt from *Why Is Stable Money Such a Big Deal?* Economic Commentary of the Federal Reserve Bank of Cleveland, May 1, 2002.

central banks. After the collapse of the Soviet Union, the Russian ruble circulated throughout the area, and the central bank of the Russian Republic controlled how quickly the quantity of rubles increased. This arrangement did not work well; by 1992, the inflation rate throughout the *ruble zone* exceeded 1,000 percent per year. Not surprisingly, the monetary system soon collapsed as people lost confidence that the ruble would retain its value. By late 1993, countries were issuing their own currencies in an attempt to control inflation locally. Moldova, one of the more successful, was able to reduce its rate of inflation to 30 percent by 1995.

The primary reason for a country to create its own central bank, then, is to ensure control over its currency. Giving the currency-printing monopoly to someone else can be disastrous, resulting in high inflation and damage to the economy's ability to function smoothly. (In fact, attempts to destabilize the value of a country's currency through counterfeiting have been used as a weapon in wars. (See Applying the Concept: Why Is Stable Money Such a Big Deal? on page 329.) Nevertheless, some countries have done it; the European Monetary Union comes to mind immediately. Many European countries have ceded their right to conduct independent monetary policy to the European Central Bank, as part of a broader move toward economic integration. But they did it after instituting strict controls that ensured inflation would remain low to minimize the risk that European monetary policy will be misused.

The central bank's ability to create money means that it can make loans even when no one else can, including during a crisis. We discussed financial panics in Chapter 14, where we learned that a bank will collapse if all its depositors try to withdraw their account balances at the same time. No bank, no matter how well managed, can withstand a run. To stave off such a crisis, the central bank can lend reserves or currency to sound banks. By ensuring that sound banks and financial institutions can continue to operate, the central bank makes the whole financial system more stable. Many people believe this is the most important function of any modern central bank.

But other functions are also important. Every country needs a secure and efficient payments system. People require ways to pay each other, and financial institutions need a cheap and reliable way to transfer funds to one another. The fact that all banks have accounts at the central bank makes it the natural place for these *interbank* payments to be settled.

Finally, as we saw in our discussion of banking regulation, someone has to watch over commercial banks and nonbank financial institutions so that savers and investors can be confident they are sound. Those who monitor the financial system must have sensitive information. For example, they need to know the exact methods institutions use to make lending and credit decisions. Needless to say, such knowledge would be very useful to the institutions' competitors. Government examiners and supervisors are the only ones who can handle such information without conflict of interest. In some countries they are housed in the central bank, while in others they work in separate agencies. Central banks are the biggest, most powerful players in a country's financial and economic system. Central bankers are supposed to use this power to stabilize the economy, making us all better off. And for the most part, that is what they do. But any institution with the power to ensure that the economic and financial systems run smoothly also has the power to create problems. Central bankers who are under extreme political pressure, or are simply incompetent, can wreak havoc on the economic and financial systems. By lending to weak financial institutions that should have been closed, the Bank of Thailand helped to create the Asian financial crisis of 1997. And the failure of the Bank of Russia to exert any control over the expansion of money and credit led to a very high inflation rate, contributing to the fact that the Russian economy shrank by nearly 50 percent during the 1990s.

Before we go on to examine the goals and objectives of central bankers in detail, it is essential that we understand what a modern central bank is *not*. First, a central bank does not control securities markets, though it may monitor and participate in bond and stock markets. Second, the central bank does not control the government's budget. It provides a place for money paid to the government to be deposited, making good on the government's cheques, and helping to borrow funds when they are needed. In other words, the central bank serves the government in the same way that a commercial bank serves a business or an individual.

Table 15.1 lists the functions of a modern central bank.

**Table 15.1**   The Functions of a Modern Central Bank

1. Manages the currency and manages or oversees the payments system.
2. Sets the overnight interest rate and controls the quantity of money.
3. Guarantees that sound banks can do business by *lending* to them, even during crises.
4. Works with government agencies to oversee financial institutions.
5. Manages the government's debt.

# Stability: The Primary Objective of All Central Banks

The central bank is essentially part of the governance of an economy.[7] Whenever we see an agency of the government involving itself in the economy, we need to ask why. What makes individuals incapable of doing what we have entrusted to the government? In the case of national defence and pollution regulation, the reasons are obvious. Most people will not voluntarily contribute their resources to the army. Nor will they spontaneously clean up their own air. To put it slightly differently, government involvement is justified by the presence of externalities or public goods; that is, when individuals do not pay the full costs or capture the complete benefits from their actions.

The rationale for the existence of a central bank is equally clear. The economy functions more smoothly when there is a single issuer of notes and, while the value of money may vary over time because of inflation, citizens can be confident that the issuer of the money will not go bankrupt. In addition, while economic and financial systems may be fairly stable most of the time, when left on their own they are prone to episodes of extreme volatility.

Central bankers work to reduce the volatility of the economic and financial systems by pursuing five specific objectives:

STABILITY

1. Low and stable inflation.
2. High and stable real growth, together with high employment.
3. Stable financial markets and institutions.
4. Stable interest rates.
5. A stable exchange rate.

It is important to realize that instability in any of these—inflation, growth, the financial system, interest rates, or exchange rates—poses an economy-wide risk that individuals can't diversify away. Recall from Chapter 5 that systematic risk, where everyone is affected, differs from idiosyncratic risk, which affects only a particular organization or individual. The job of the central bank is to improve general economic welfare by managing and reducing systematic risk. Keep in mind that it is probably impossible to achieve all five of the central bank's objectives simultaneously. Tradeoffs must be made, and in Chapter 16 we will see which tradeoffs particular central banks made.

---

[7] There is an important nuance here. Central banks are usually an independent agency of a central government. We discuss later in this chapter how a central bank can be independent yet accountable. Technically, the legal organization of central banks can be quite complex. Some are inside their country's government, some are private banks, and others are a combination. The Bank of Canada began as a combination but in 1939 the government bought out the private shareholders. The Federal Reserve remains in the "combination" category, part government and part private bank. As a practical matter, since they all have a set of tasks that only they are allowed to perform, we will treat central banks as if they are a part of the government.

## Low, Stable Inflation

In 2002, the director of research of the International Monetary Fund (the closest institution there is to a world central bank) summarized virtually every economist's view when he said, "Uncontrolled inflation strangles growth, hurting the entire populace, especially the indigent."[8] That is why many central banks take as their primary job the maintenance of price stability. That is, they strive to eliminate inflation. The consensus is that when inflation rises, the central bank is at fault.

The rationale for keeping the economy inflation-free is straightforward. Standards, everyone agrees, should be standard. A pound should always weigh a pound, a cup should always hold a cup, and a yard should always measure a yard. Similarly, a dollar should always be worth a dollar. What is true for physical weights and measures should be true for the unit of account as well. The purchasing power of one dollar, one yen, or one euro should remain stable over long periods. Maintaining price stability enhances money's usefulness both as a unit of account and as a store of value.

Prices are central to everything that happens in a market-based economy. They provide the information individuals and firms need to ensure that resources are allocated to their most productive uses. When a seller can raise the price of a product, for example, that is supposed to signal that demand has increased, so producing more is worthwhile. But inflation degrades the information content of prices. When all prices are rising together, understanding the reasons becomes difficult. Did consumers decide they liked an item, shifting demand? Did the cost of producing the item rise, shifting supply? Or was inflation responsible for the jump in price? If the economy is to run efficiently, we need to be able to tell the difference.

If the inflation rate were predictable—say, 10 percent year in and year out—we might be able to adjust, eventually. But unfortunately, as inflation rises, it becomes less stable. If our best guess is that the rate of inflation will be 2 percent over the coming year, we can be fairly certain that the result will be a price level increase of between 1 and 3 percent. But experience tells us that when we expect the inflation rate to be around 10 percent, we shouldn't be surprised if it ends up anywhere between 8 and 12 percent. The higher inflation is, the less predictable it is, and the more systematic risk it creates.[9]

Moreover, high inflation is bad for growth. This fact is obvious in extreme cases, such as in 1985, when the inflation rate reached 11,000 percent in Bolivia, or in 1983, when it reached nearly 5,000 percent in Ukraine. In such cases of hyperinflation—when prices double every 2 to 3 months—prices contain virtually no information, and people use all their energy just coping with the crisis, so growth plummets. In Bolivia, growth went from more than plus 6 percent in the late 1970s to minus 5 percent during the hyperinflation. The Ukrainian economy shrank by more than 20 percent the year inflation peaked. Only when inflation was brought under control did these economies begin to grow again.

Because low inflation is the basis for general economic prosperity, most people agree that it should be the primary objective of monetary policy. But how low should inflation be? Zero is probably too low. There are a couple of reasons for this. First, if the central bank tries to keep the inflation rate at zero, there is a risk of deflation—a drop in prices. Deflation makes debts more difficult to repay, which increases the default rate on loans, affecting the health of banks. Deflation reduces the value of a firm's collateral and net worth, exacerbating the problems of moral hazard and adverse

[8] Kenneth S. Rogoff, "An Open Letter to Joseph Stiglitz," International Monetary Fund, July 2, 2002.

[9] Inflation is costly for other reasons as well. They include the cost of going to the bank more often, the cost of changing prices more often, and distortions created by the way the tax system is written.

## YOUR FINANCIAL WORLD
### Why Inflation Is Bad for You

If you ask most people why inflation is bad, they will say it is responsible for a decline in what they can purchase with their incomes. For them, inflation causes a drop in their standard of living: Prices have gone up, but their incomes, including their wages, haven't. Economists view inflation differently. To them, inflation is when everything that is denominated in dollars goes up proportionally—prices, incomes, savings account balances, everything. It is as if everything is suddenly measured in cents instead of dollars. How could this possibly make anyone worse off?

The problem is that high inflation tends to be more volatile than low inflation, so the higher inflation is, the greater the risk. When inflation is averaging 2 percent per year, chances are slim that it will more than double to 5 percent (an increase of 3 percentage points). Such an increase would mean that the central bank had lost control, at least temporarily. But if the rate of inflation is closer to 15 percent, an increase of 3 percentage points to 18 percent, a change of only one-fifth, could easily happen.

To see how this affects virtually everyone, recall from Chapter 6 that unpredictable inflation makes bonds risky.

Higher-than-expected inflation reduces the real return a bondholder receives. Since the real return is the nominal return minus expected inflation, if the nominal interest rate is 5 percent and inflation turns out to be 2 percent, then the real return drops to 3 percent. If the inflation rate ends up at 5 percent, the real return is zero. That's a risk. Since risk requires compensation, inflation risk drives up the interest rate required to entice investors to hold bonds.

Now think about two common financial transactions: getting a home mortgage and saving for retirement. When you buy a house, your goal is to get the lowest mortgage interest rate you can find. Inflation risk drives up mortgage interest rates, increasing your monthly payments and forcing you to purchase a less expensive house. Turning to your retirement savings, inflation risk makes it more difficult to know how much to save, because you are unsure what the purchasing power of your savings will be 40 or 50 years from now. Long-term planning is hard enough without the added burden of inflation risk.

selection we discussed in Chapter 11, which may prevent some borrowers from obtaining loans. Second, if the inflation rate were zero, an employer wishing to cut labour costs would need to cut nominal wages, which is difficult to do. With a small amount of inflation, the employer can simply leave wages as they are, and workers' real wages will fall. So a small amount of inflation makes labour markets work better, at least from the employer's point of view.

## High, Stable Real Growth

Booms are popular, but recessions are not. In recessions, people get laid off and businesses fail. Without a steady income, individuals struggle to make their auto, credit card, and mortgage payments. Consumers pull back, hurting businesses that rely on them to buy products. Reduced sales lead to more layoffs, and so on. The longer the downturn goes on, the worse it gets.

By adjusting interest rates, central bankers work to moderate these cycles and stabilize growth and employment. The idea is that there is some long-run *sustainable* level of production called **potential output** that depends on things like technology, the size of the capital stock, and the number of people who can work. Growth in these *inputs* leads to growth in *potential output—***sustainable growth**. In Canada, growth usually runs around 3 percent per year. Over the short run, output may deviate from this potential level, and growth may deviate from its long-run sustainable rate. In recessions, the economy stalls, incomes stagnate, and unemployment rises. By lowering interest rates, monetary policymakers can moderate such declines.

Similarly, there are times when growth rises above sustainable rates, and the economy overheats. These periods may seem to bring increased prosperity, but since they don't last forever, they are followed by reduced spending, lower business invest-ment, and layoffs. A period of above-average growth has to be followed by a period of below-average growth. The job of the central bank during such periods is to raise interest rates and keep the economy from operating at unsustainable levels.

Importantly, in the long run, stability leads to higher growth. The reason is that unstable growth creates risk for which investors need to be compensated in the form of higher interest rates. With higher interest rates, businesses borrow less, which means that they have fewer resources to invest and grow. To understand how this works, think about getting a loan to buy a car. The more certain you are that you will have a good, steady job over the next few years, the larger the loan you will feel comfortable taking on. If you are nervous that you might lose your job, you will be cautious. What is true for you and your car loan is true for every person and every company. The greater the uncertainty about future business conditions, the more cautious people will be in mak-ing investments of all kinds. Stability leads to higher growth.[10]

The importance of keeping sustainable growth as high as possible is hard to over-state. The difference between an economy that grows at 4 percent per year and one that grows at 2 percent per year is the difference between an economy that doubles in size over 18 years and one that grows by less than 50 percent in the same period. (This calculation uses the rule of 72 described in Your Financial World: How Long Does Your Investment Take to Double? on page 64.) Keeping employment high is equally important. In the same way that you can never get back the study time you lost when you went to the movies before an exam, it is impossible for the economy to recover what unemployed people would have produced had they been working during a downturn. You can't get the lost time back. Policymakers are expected to manage the country's affairs so that we will stay on a high and sustainable growth path.

The levels of growth and employment aren't the only things of importance, though. Stability matters too. Fluctuations in general business conditions are the primary source of systematic risk, a kind of risk that can't be diversified away. As we have said a number of times, uncertainty about the future makes planning more dif-ficult, so getting rid of uncertainty makes everyone better off.

## Financial System Stability

Financial system stability is an integral part of every modern central banker's job. It is essential for policymakers to ensure that the markets for stocks, bonds, and the like continue to operate smoothly and efficiently. The financial system is like plumb-ing: When it works, we take it for granted, but when it doesn't work, watch out. If people lose faith in banks and financial markets, they will rush to low-risk alterna-tives, and intermediation will stop. Savers will not lend and borrowers will not be able to borrow. Getting a car loan or a home mortgage becomes impossible, as does selling a bond to maintain or expand a business. When the financial system collapses, economic activity does, too.

The possibility of a severe disruption in the financial markets is a type of system-atic risk. Nothing that a single individual does can eliminate it. Central banks must control this systematic risk, making sure that the financial system remains in good working order. The *value at risk*, not the standard deviation, is the important measure here. Recall from Chapter 5 that value at risk measures the risk of the maximum

---

[10] For a discussion on the relationship between the level and volatility of growth, both the evidence and the theory, see Garey Ramey and Valerie A. Ramey's "Cross-Country Evidence on the Link between Volatility and Growth," *American Economic Review* 85 (December 1995) p. 1138–1151.

potential loss. When thinking about financial stability, central bankers want to minimize the risk of a disaster and keep the chance of this maximum loss as small as possible.

## Interest Rate Stability

It is easy to see why interest rate volatility is a problem. First, most people respond to low interest rates by borrowing and spending more. Individuals take out loans to purchase cars, new appliances and the like, while corporations issue more bonds and use the proceeds to enlarge their operations. Conversely, when interest rates rise, people borrow and spend less. So, by raising expenditure when interest rates are low and reducing expenditure when interest rates are high, interest rate volatility makes output unstable.

"Personally, I liked this roller coaster a lot better before the Federal Reserve Board got hold of it."

SOURCE: © The New Yorker Collection 1997. Robert Mankoff from cartoonbank.com. All Rights Reserved.

Second, interest rate volatility means higher risk—and a higher risk premium—on long-term bonds. (Remember from Chapter 7 that the long-term interest rate is the average of expected future short-term interest rates plus a risk premium that compensates for the volatility of short-term interest rates.) Risk makes financial decisions more difficult, lowering productivity and making the economy less efficient. Since central bankers control short-term interest rates, they are in a position to control this risk and stabilize the economy.

### Exchange-Rate Stability

Stabilizing exchange rates is the last item on the list of central bank objectives. The value of a country's currency affects the cost of imports to domestic consumers and the cost of exports to foreign buyers. When the exchange rate is stable, the dollar price of a car produced in Germany is predictable, making life easier for the foreign automobile manufacturer, the domestic retailer, and the Canadian car buyer. Planning ahead is easier for everyone.

Different countries have different priorities. While the Bank of Canada and the European Central Bank may not care much about exchange-rate stability, the heads of central banks in small, less developed, trade-oriented countries do. In *emerging-markets countries* where exports and imports are central to the structure of the economy, officials might reasonably argue that good overall macroeconomic performance follows from a stable exchange rate.

Table 15.2 on page 336 summarizes the five objectives of a modern central bank.

# Meeting the Challenge: Creating a Successful Central Bank

The period from 1980 to 2007 saw many remarkable changes. The Internet and cell phones came into widespread use. In Canada, the inflation rate fell from 6 percent to 2 percent. Meanwhile, real growth rose from less than 3 percent to more than 4 percent.

Outside Canada, improvements were even more dramatic. In 1980, nearly two-thirds of the countries in the world were experiencing an inflation rate in excess of 10 percent per year and nearly one in three was experiencing negative growth.

STABILITY

**Table 15.2**     The Objectives of a Modern Central Bank

| | |
|---|---|
| 1. Low, stable inflation | Inflation creates confusion and makes planning difficult. When inflation is high, growth is low. |
| 2. High, stable growth | Stable, predictable growth is higher than unstable, unpredictable growth. |
| 3. Financial system stability | Stable financial markets and institutions are a necessity for an economy to operate efficiently. |
| 4. Stable interest rates | Interest rate volatility creates risk for both lenders and borrowers. |
| 5. Stable exchange rates | Variable exchange rates make the revenues from foreign sales and the cost of purchasing imported goods hard to predict. |

Twenty-five years later, only one country in six had a two-digit inflation rate, while approximately 150 countries were growing at rates in excess of 2 percent per year. And not only was inflation lower and growth higher, both were more stable.

What explains this phenomenon? A prime candidate is that technology sparked a boom just as central banks became better at their jobs. First, monetary policymakers realized that sustainable growth had gone up, so they could keep interest rates low without worrying about inflation. Second, central banks were redesigned. It wasn't just that new central banks were established, like the ones set up in the 15 republics of the former Soviet Union. The structure of existing central banks changed significantly. The Bank of England is over three centuries old (its building in London has stood for nearly 200 years) but its operating charter was completely rewritten in 1998. The same year brought major changes in the organizational structure of the Bank of Japan. Federal Reserve operations have changed, too. In the United States, the first public announcement of a move in the federal funds rate was made on February 4, 1994, and on January 19, 2002, the regular issuance of a statement explaining interest rate decisions became an official part of Federal Reserve procedures. The Bank of Canada made operational changes too. In 1996, the Bank of Canada began issuing press releases to explain changes in the bank rate and in 2000 the Bank switched from making changes to the policy interest rate at any time it chose, to having eight "FADs"—fixed announcement dates—annually. It changes the interest rate outside those dates only in very unusual circumstances such as following the 9/11 attacks on New York City or in the worst of the financial crisis in October 2008.

Many people believe that improvements in economic performance during the 1990s were related at least in part to the policy followed by these restructured central banks. Improving monetary policy is not just a matter of finding the right person for the job. There is an ample supply of highly qualified people. In fact, in many countries there is a long history of central bankers who have tried but failed because they weren't free to pursue effective policies. Successful policymaking is as much a consequence of the institutional environment as of the people who work in the institutions. Nowhere is that more true than in central banking.

Today there is a clear consensus about the best way to design a central bank and what to tell monetary policymakers to do. To be successful, a central bank must (1) be independent of political pressure, (2) make decisions by committee, (3) be

## YOUR FINANCIAL WORLD
### Does News about the Bank of Canada Affect Your Daily Life?

On an average day, *The Wall Street Journal* mentions the Federal Reserve in about five stories. Similarly the Canadian newspapers routinely report on the Bank of Canada. Reporters and editors obviously think people should care what the central bank is doing. Do we really need to follow news about the central bank every day?

The preoccupation with the central bank comes from the fact that it adjusts interest rates. News reports invariably predict the timing and direction of the next move in interest rates. While we all care about interest rates—they measure the cost of a car loan or mortgage, and the return we get on investments—on a normal day, the interest rate on a loan doesn't change.

But over periods of weeks or months, changes in interest rates can be noteworthy. During the summer and fall of 2005, the inflation rate rose significantly. These increasingly ominous readings led to not only immediate interest rate increases, but also the expectation that the

Bank of Canada would continue to raise short-term interest rates into the summer. All of this caused long-term interest rates to go up too. (Recall from Chapter 7 that the long-term interest rate is the average of expected short-term interest rates, plus a risk premium.) The result was an increase in the costs to borrow. To take one example, during the second half of 2005, the interest rate on a 25-year, fixed-rate home mortgage rose from around 5.7 percent to 6.3 percent. This increase alone drove up the monthly payment on a $200,000 mortgage by $70 per month.

Events like this one don't happen often. Understanding when and how they might occur requires knowing how the Bank of Canada operates and what sort of news is likely to precipitate changes in interest rates. That means following long-term economic trends to gain some sense of what the Bank is likely to do, and when.

accountable to the public and transparent in communicating its policy actions, and (4) operate within an explicit framework that clearly states its goals and makes clear the tradeoffs among them.

## The Need for Independence

The idea of central bank independence—that central banks should be independent of political pressure—is a new one. After all, the central bank originated as the government's bank. It did the bidding first of the king or emperor and then of the democratically elected congress or parliament. Politicians rarely give up control over anything, much less something as important as monetary policy. However, in the 1990s, nearly every government that hadn't already done so made the central bank independent of the finance ministry. The Banque de France became independent in 1993. Political control of the Bank of England and the Bank of Japan ended in 1998. And the new European Central Bank was independent from the day it opened on July 1, 1998.

Independence has two operational components. First, monetary policymakers must be free to control their own budgets. If politicians can starve the central bank of funding, then they can control the bank's decisions. Second, the bank's policies must not be reversible by people outside the central bank. Prior to 1998, policymakers at the Bank of England merely recommended interest rate changes to the Chancellor of the Exchequer, a political official. That is, interest rate policy was ultimately decided by the British equivalent of the Canadian Minister of Finance. Since 1998, the Bank of England's Monetary Policy Committee has made those decisions autonomously. The same is true in the United States, where the Federal Open Market Committee's decisions on when to raise or lower interest rates cannot be overridden by the President, Congress, or the Supreme Court.

Successful monetary policy requires a long time horizon. The impact of today's decisions won't be felt for a while—several years, in many instances. Democratically elected politicians are not a particularly patient bunch; their time horizon extends only to the next election. The political system encourages members of Parliament and members of Congress to do everything they can for their constituents before the next election—including manipulating interest rates to bring short-term prosperity at the expense of long-term stability. The temptation to forsake long-term goals for short-term gains is simply impossible for most politicians to resist. Given the ability to choose, politicians will select monetary policies that are overly accommodative. They will keep interest rates too low, raising output and employment quickly (before the election), but causing inflation to go up later (after the election). Low interest rates are very popular because there are more borrowers than lenders.

Knowing these tendencies, governments have moved responsibility for monetary policy into a separate, largely apolitical, institution. To insulate policymakers from the daily pressures faced by politicians, governments must give central bankers control of their budgets and authority to make irreversible decisions and must appoint them to long terms.

## Decision Making by Committee

Should important decisions be made by an individual or by a committee? Military planners know they can't have groups making decisions in the heat of a battle; someone has to be in charge. But monetary policy isn't war. Monetary policy decisions are made deliberately, after significant amounts of information are collected and examined. Occasionally a crisis does occur, and in those times someone does need to be in charge. But in the course of normal operations, it is better to rely on a committee than an individual. Though extraordinary individuals can be trusted to make policy as well as a committee, building an institution on the assumption that someone of exemplary ability will always be available to run it is unwise. And given the difficulty of removing a central bank governor—a feature that is built into the central bank system—the cost of putting the wrong person in charge can be very high.

The solution, then, is to make policy by committee. Pooling the knowledge, experience, and opinions of a group of people reduces the risk that policy will be dictated by an individual's quirks. Besides, in a democracy, vesting so much power in one individual poses a legitimacy problem. For these reasons, monetary policy decisions are made by committee in all major central banks in the world. As we will discuss in Chapter 16, Canadian monetary policy decisions are made by the Governing Council of the Bank of Canada, which includes the governor of the Bank, the senior deputy governor, and the four deputy governors. The Federal Reserve has its Federal Open Market Committee, the European Central Bank its Governing Council, and the Bank of Japan its Monetary Policy Committee. The number of members varies from 6 in Canada to (currently) 22 at the ECB—but, crucially, it is always bigger than one.

## The Need for Accountability and Transparency

There is a big problem with central bank independence: It is inconsistent with representative democracy. The idea of putting appointed technocrats in charge of one of the most important government functions is inherently undemocratic. Politicians answer to the voters; by design, independent central bankers don't. How can we have faith in our financial system if there are no checks on what the central bankers are doing? The economy will not operate efficiently unless we trust our policymakers.

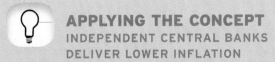

## APPLYING THE CONCEPT
### INDEPENDENT CENTRAL BANKS
### DELIVER LOWER INFLATION

What finally drove politicians to give up control over monetary policy? It was the realization that independent central bankers would deliver lower inflation than the politicians themselves could. Researchers noticed that the degree of control politicians can exert over central banks varies greatly across countries, and is related to inflation outcomes. Figure 15.1 shows an index of central bank independence[*] on the horizontal axis and average inflation rates from 1973 to 1988 on the vertical axis. Note that Germany and Switzerland, the two countries with the most independent central banks, had the lowest inflation, averaging around 3 percent per year over the 15-year period. Conversely, New Zealand and Spain, the two countries with the least independent central banks, had the highest inflation—between 7 and 9 percent. Even the politicians were convinced. They knew that the more control they had over the central bank, the more money they were likely to create. While printing more money relieves short-term fiscal problems, it eventually drives inflation higher. Politicians voluntarily tied their own hands, handing over control of monetary policy to an independent central bank.

The design of the European Central Bank (ECB) is a clear example of the logic that independence leads to lower inflation. Politicians in Spain, Italy, and France, where inflation had been running over 6 percent per year for several decades, wanted their economies to be more like Germany's. In hopes that the new institution would deliver low inflation, they chose the German central bank, the Deutsche Bundesbank, as a model. By most accounts, the ECB is the most independent central bank in the world. And, as one would expect, inflation has been consistently low in Europe.

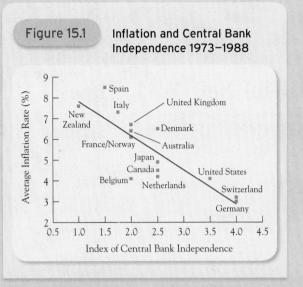

**Figure 15.1**   Inflation and Central Bank Independence 1973–1988

SOURCE: *"Central Bank Independence and Macroeconomic Performance: Some Comparative Evidence," Journal of Money, Credit, and Banking* 25 (May 1993), pp. 151–162. Used with permission.

[*] The index of central bank independence measures the ability of the central bank to select its policy objectives without political interference. It is constructed using information on things like the length of the central bank governor's term, whether the governor can be fired, whether government representatives participate directly in monetary policy decisions, and whether the central bank is required to finance government deficits. The less the central bank is constrained by the government, the more independent it is.

---

Proponents of central bank independence realized they would need to solve this problem if their proposals were to be adopted. Their solution was twofold. First, politicians would establish a set of goals; second, the policymakers would publicly report their progress in pursuing those goals. Explicit goals foster accountability and disclosure requirements create transparency. While central bankers are powerful, our elected representatives tell them what to do and then monitor their progress. That means requiring plausible explanations for their decisions, along with supporting data.

The institutional means for assuring accountability and transparency differ from one country to the next. In some cases, the government establishes an explicit numerical target for inflation, while in others the central bank defines the target. In Canada, the government and the Bank of Canada agree on an inflation target for a five-year period (the current target runs until 2011). In the United Kingdom, the government sets a specific target each year; in the European Union, the central bank is asked only to pursue "price stability" as its primary objective; in the United States, the Federal Reserve is asked to deliver price stability as one of a number of objectives,

# The New York Times

**Edmund L. Andrews**

**January 30, 2007**

When Ben S. Bernanke took over as chairman of the Federal Reserve Board one year ago, he brought with him a long-held conviction that the central bank should be more explicit about its goals and less personalized than it had been under his predecessor Alan Greenspan.

Yet as Mr. Bernanke celebrates his first anniversary on the job, the Fed is still far away from acting on his major proposal of setting an explicit target for inflation.

Mr. Bernanke has long argued that publicly committing the central bank to an inflation target—probably 1 to 2 percent a year—would make its policy more transparent and open to the public. Its decisions would be easier for investors to anticipate, he argued, and the public might have greater confidence that inflation would indeed remain low.

It is an idea that Mr. Greenspan staunchly opposed, arguing that it would bind the Fed to rigid rules and deprive it of crucial flexibility in reacting to economic surprises.

But even though a majority of those on the Fed board agree with Mr. Bernanke in principle, officials have, if anything, become more cautious over the last year about making a change.

Outside experts say the caution stems from deeper concerns: a reluctance to change a practice that appears to be working well already; a fear among some that the Fed may become trapped by its own promises; and perhaps a worry about opposition from Democratic lawmakers, who now control Congress and who have publicly fretted that the Fed will focus on inflation while ignoring unemployment.

As a practical matter, Mr. Bernanke will reach his first anniversary with the economy heading toward the Fed's goal of a "soft landing"—a modest slowdown in economic growth and a slight ebb in inflation, yet with strong wage increases and continued low unemployment.

The outlook for Mr. Bernanke's goal of setting inflation targets remains uncertain. A majority of Fed governors and presidents of the Federal Reserve's district banks support the idea as an important move toward greater openness.

Mr. Bernanke has taken pains to build a consensus before making any changes, and has gone so far as to put Donald L. Kohn, the Fed's highly respected vice chairman and the leading opponent of inflation targeting, in charge of a special committee to review "communication issues," including the prospects for inflation targets.

But even many longtime supporters of the idea predict that the Fed is unlikely to change gears this year.

Adam S. Posen, who was a co-author with Mr. Bernanke on a 1999 book about inflation targeting, said Mr. Bernanke would need at least a year to build consensus.

"Bernanke has to build three consensuses at once," said Mr. Posen, a senior fellow at the Peterson Institute for

and many have speculated that Ben Bernanke will introduce inflation targets in the future (see In the News: Fed Has Yet to Set Target on Inflation).

Similar differences exist in the timing and content of information made public by central banks. Today every central bank announces its policy actions almost immediately after the committee meeting has concluded, but the extent of the statements that accompany the announcement and the willingness to answer questions vary.

The Bank of Canada publishes a detailed analysis of its view of the economy and rationale for policy in the quarterly *Monetary Policy Report* and at that time also holds a press conference. The governor and deputy governor also appear before Standing Committees of the Senate and House of Commons at least once a year. The Federal Reserve's statements tend to be only a few sentences long, and no one answers questions. In contrast, the president and vice president of the European Central Bank hold a press conference to answer questions on a statement several pages in length.

International Economics. In addition to persuading the Fed's other governors, Mr. Posen said, Mr. Bernanke must also build support from the central bank's influential staff and with Congress.

It remains unclear whether the Fed needs legislation from Congress to adopt explicit inflation targets. But many Democrats have been quick to criticize the central bank for not focusing enough attention on wages and job creation.

Indeed, the new chairman of the House Financial Services Committee is Representative Barney Frank of Massachusetts, who often challenged Mr. Greenspan about rising income inequality and stubbornly high unemployment.

Mr. Bernanke is set to testify about the economic outlook before Mr. Frank's committee on Feb. 15. In an indication that Mr. Bernanke will face a more combative political environment than he did last year, aides to Mr. Frank said he was planning a second hearing to get contrasting views from economists and people with "other real world experience."

But perhaps the biggest reason for the slow movement is that Mr. Bernanke's approach may not end up being much different from Mr. Greenspan's.

In recent years, Fed officials under Mr. Greenspan made it clear they had an informal target or "comfort zone" on inflation. For many, that zone was a "core" inflation rate—excluding volatile prices for food and energy—of 1 to 2 percent a year.

Even if the Fed were to set a public target for inflation, Mr. Bernanke and other supporters have not said how quickly the Fed would need to meet the target.

Mr. Bernanke and others now stress that the Fed will not react mechanically if inflation climbs above the target, as it has over the last year. Mr. Bernanke has argued for defining an "optimal long-run inflation rate" and originally suggested the Fed should aim to hit that target within three years.

But some of Mr. Bernanke's allies now contend that there should be no specific time frame at all.

## LESSON OF ARTICLE

As an economics professor at Princeton University, Ben Bernanke wrote about the virtues of central banks adopting explicit inflation targets. So, when he became Chairman of the Board of Governors of the Federal Reserve System in 2006, everyone knew what he thought the Fed should do. But the adoption of a new policy framework depends on building political support both among the members of the FOMC and in the U.S. Congress that oversees the Fed. Has the FOMC, under Chairman Bernanke's leadership, adopted an explicit inflation target?

It is difficult to know how important these differences in communications strategy are. Central bank statements are very different today than they were in the early 1990s. Until 1996, for example, the Bank of Canada didn't even announce its policy decisions publicly. Secrecy, once the hallmark of central banking, is now understood to damage both the policymakers and the economies they are trying to manage. For monetary policy to be a stabilizing force, central bankers need to explain their actions in periodic public statements, such as the press releases issued on each fixed announcement date. In essence, the economy and financial markets should respond to information that everyone receives, not to speculation about what policymakers are doing. Thus, policymakers need to be as clear as possible about what they are trying to achieve and how they intend to achieve it. There really shouldn't be any surprises.

## The Policy Framework, Policy Tradeoffs, and Credibility

We've seen that a modern central bank has a long list of objectives—low, stable inflation; high, stable growth; a stable financial system; and stable interest and exchange rates. To meet these objectives, central bankers must be independent, accountable, and good communicators. Together these qualities make up what we will call the monetary policy framework. The framework exists to resolve ambiguities that arise in the course of the central bank's work. Looking at the bank's objectives, we can see the problem. Setting a goal of low inflation is easy, but there are many ways to measure inflation. The central bank needs to decide which measure to use and then stick with it. The Bank of Canada is explicit about the measure of inflation it uses in evaluating the success or failure of its policy. It targets the Consumer Price Index. The European Central Bank targets the so-called the harmonized index of consumer prices, or HICP. More important than the details, though, is the fact that officials have told us what they are trying to do. Their statement helps people to plan at the same time that it holds officials accountable to the public.

The monetary policy framework also clarifies the likely responses when goals conflict with one another. There is simply no way that policymakers can meet all their objectives at the same time. They have only one instrument—the interest rate—with which to work, and it is impossible to use a single instrument to achieve a long list of objectives. To take a recent example, by mid-2004, the economy had recovered completely from the recession of 2001. Businesses were increasing production and hiring new workers. But, as the economy boomed, the inflation rate started to rise. And when this happens, the appropriate response is to tighten policy, raising interest rates. So, starting in September 2004, the Bank of Canada's Governing Council did just that. Over the next 20 months they raised the Bank rate by 200 bps (recall from Chapter 4 that a basis point is 1/100 of a percent, so 200 bps means they raised the rate by 2 percent). As a result, inflation remained low. Obviously, if interest rates are changing every few months, they are not stable. More importantly, raising the interest rate means reducing the availability of money and credit at the risk of slowing growth. The goal of keeping inflation low and stable, then, can be inconsistent with the goal of avoiding a recession. By the end of 2006, inflation remained low while growth had slowed slightly, but most people thought the Bank had done a good job balancing these two objectives.

Central bankers face the tradeoff between inflation and growth on a daily basis and policymakers must choose among competing objectives. That means that central bankers must make their priorities clear. For example, the public needs to know whether they are focusing primarily on price stability, as is the case in many countries, or whether they are willing to allow a modest rise in inflation to avoid an appreciation of the exchange rate. This important part of the policy framework limits the discretionary authority of the central bankers, ensuring that they will do the job they have been entrusted with. Thus, it is an essential part of the bank's communication responsibilities.

Finally, a well-designed policy framework helps policymakers establish credibility. For central bankers to achieve their objectives, everyone must believe that they will do what they say they will do. This is particularly important when it comes to keeping inflation low. The reason is that most economic decisions are based on expectations about future inflation. We saw this relationship when we studied the determination of interest rates: The nominal interest rate equals the real interest rate plus expected inflation. The same is true for wage and price decisions. Firms set prices based partly on what they believe inflation will be in the future. They make wage agreements with workers based on expected future inflation. The higher their expectations for future inflation, the

| Table 15.3 | The Principles of Central Bank Design |
| --- | --- |
| Independence | To keep inflation low, monetary decisions must be made free of political influence. |
| Decision making by committee | Pooling the knowledge of a number of people yields better decisions than decision making by an individual. |
| Accountability and transparency | Policymakers must be held accountable to the public they serve and clearly communicate their objectives, decisions, and methods. |
| Policy framework | Policymakers must clearly state their policy goals and the tradeoffs among them. |

higher prices, wages, and interest rates will be. Expected inflation creates inflation. Successful monetary policy, then, requires that inflation expectations be kept under control. The most straightforward way for the central bank to do so is to announce its objectives, show resolve in meeting them, and explain its actions clearly along the way.

Table 15.3 summarizes the principles of central bank design and can serve as a checklist for evaluating the operation of any central bank we come across.

## Fitting Everything Together: Central Banks and Fiscal Policy

Before a European country can join the common currency area and adopt the euro, it must meet a number of conditions. Two of the most important are that the country's annual budget deficit—the excess of government spending over revenues each year—cannot exceed 3 percent of GDP and the government's total debt—its accumulated level of outstanding bonds and other borrowings—cannot exceed 60 percent of GDP.[11] Once a country gains membership in the monetary union, failure to maintain these standards triggers substantial penalties.[12]

Remember that the central bank does not control the government's budget. Fiscal policy, the decisions about taxes and spending, is the responsibility of elected officials. But by specifying a range of "acceptable" levels of borrowing, Europeans are trying to restrict the fiscal policies that member countries enact. For the European Central Bank to do its job effectively, all the member countries' governments must behave responsibly.[13]

[11] In practice, these limits were open to political interpretation, so countries that failed to meet them were allowed to join anyway. For example, in fall of 1998, Belgium's debt was 122 percent of its GDP—more than double the stated limit. But because the debt was forecasted to decline in the future, the requirement was waived.

[12] The "Stability and Growth Pact of 1997" dictates that "medium-term budgets" must be "close to balance or in surplus." The exact mechanism came under significant strain in 2003. The previously agreed upon penalties that would be triggered by budget deficits in excess of 3 percent of GDP were not levied on the offending countries. The strength of the pact will be tested by the high fiscal deficits in 2009/10.

[13] While at this writing the United States has no explicit government budget restrictions, it has in the past. Following the large deficits of the 1980s, the U.S. Congress put restrictions on the size of the federal deficit. These expired in the late 1990 and, during the first few years of the 21st century, deficits began to rise again. One has to suspect that Congress will eventually be forced to address these problems and the likely outcome will be budget restrictions of the type that are in place in Europe.

While fiscal and monetary policymakers share the same ultimate goal—to improve the well-being of the population—conflicts can arise between them. Fiscal policymakers are responsible for providing national defence, educating children, building and maintaining transportation systems, and aiding the sick and poor. They need resources to pay for these services. Thus, funding needs create a natural conflict between monetary and fiscal policymakers. In their effort to stabilize prices and provide the foundation for high sustainable growth, central bankers take a long-term view, imposing limits on how fast the quantity of money and credit can grow. In contrast, fiscal policymakers tend to ignore the long-term inflationary effects of their actions and look for ways to spend resources today at the expense of prosperity tomorrow. For better or worse, their time horizon extends only until the next election. Some fiscal policymakers resort to actions intended to get around restrictions imposed by the central bank, eroding what is otherwise an effective and responsible monetary policy.

In the earliest days of central banks, a government that needed money would simply order the bank to print some. Of course, the result was inflation and occasionally hyperinflation. That is what led to the evolution of the independent central banks. Today the central bank's autonomy leaves fiscal policymakers with two options for financing government spending. They can take a share of income and wealth from the country's citizens through taxes, or they can borrow by issuing bonds in the financial markets.

Because no one likes taxes, and officials fear angering the electorate, politicians often turn to borrowing in order to finance some portion of their spending. But a country can issue only so much debt. Beyond some limit, future tax revenues will not cover the payments that are due to lenders. At that point, the only solution is to turn to the central bank for the means to finance spending. As a technical matter, the government will "sell" new bonds directly to the central bank—bonds that no one else wants to buy. But doing so creates a monetary expansion, which leads to inflation. In fact, if officials can't raise taxes and are having trouble borrowing, inflation is the only way out.

While central bankers hate it, inflation is a real temptation to shortsighted fiscal policymakers. It is a way to get resources in their hands. The mechanism is straightforward. The government forces the central bank to buy its bonds and then uses the proceeds to finance spending. But doing so increases the quantity of money in circulation, sparking inflation. While the rise in inflation may ultimately do great damage to the country's well-being, it also benefits fiscal policymakers: It reduces the value of the bonds the government has already sold, making them easier to repay. Inflation is a way for governments to default on a portion of the debt they owe.

While many politicians do act in their countries' long-term interests, there are plenty of examples of poor fiscal policymaking. Following the collapse of the Soviet Union, Russia had very few sources of revenue. Taxes were hard to collect and lenders were skeptical of the new government's ability to repay its loans, so interest rates were extremely high. Then there was the fact that almost everyone worked for the government. In short, expenses were high and revenue was low. Russian politicians turned to the Central Bank of Russia. The result was an inflation rate of more than 14 percent per *month* for five consecutive years.

In early 2002, Argentina's economy collapsed when banks refused to honour their depositors' withdrawal requests. Unemployment skyrocketed, output plummeted, and the president was forced to resign. The full story is complicated, but we can understand one aspect of it without much trouble. During 2001, Argentina's provincial governments began to experience significant budget problems. Their response was to start paying their employees with government bonds. But unlike the bonds we normally see, these were in small denominations—1, 2, 5, 10, 20 pesos, and so on.

Not surprisingly, these small-denomination bonds were immediately used as means of payment, becoming money in effect. By mid-2002, this new form of money accounted for roughly 40 percent of the currency circulating in Argentina, and the Central Bank of Argentina lost control over the amount of money circulating in the economy.

So we see that the actions of fiscal policymakers can subvert the best efforts of central bankers. The Central Bank of Argentina was independent and its policymakers were well regarded. But if the government can shut down the banking system and issue its own money, then the central bank's independence is irrelevant. The Bank of Canada, the Federal Reserve, the Bank of Japan, and 170 other central banks around the world are independent only as long as their governments let them be. When faced with a fiscal crisis, politicians often look for the easiest way out. If that way is inflating the value of the currency today, they will worry about the consequences tomorrow.

This brings us back to the criteria for inclusion in the European Monetary Union. The founders of the system wanted to ensure that participating governments kept their fiscal houses in order so that none of them would be tempted to pressure the European Central Bank to create inflation and bail them out. Monetary policy can meet its objective of price stability only if the government lives within its budget and never forces the central bank to finance a fiscal deficit.

In summary, responsible fiscal policy is essential to the success of monetary policy. Our discussions earlier in the chapter allowed us to conclude that there is no way for a poorly designed central bank to stabilize prices, output, the financial system, and interest and exchange rates, regardless of the government's behaviour. To be successful, a central bank must operate in a particular way. It must be independent, accountable, and clear about its goals. It must have a well-articulated communications strategy and a sound decision-making mechanism. We turn in Chapter 16 to a detailed discussion of the structure of major central banks to see what makes them successful.

## Terms

accountability, 339
central bank, 326
central bank independence, 337
credibility, 342
European Central Bank (ECB), 328
European System of Central Banks (ESCB), 328
Eurosystem, 328

financial system stability, 334
fiscal policy, 343
hyperinflation, 332
monetary policy, 328
monetary policy framework, 342
potential output, 333
price stability, 332
sustainable growth, 333
transparency, 339

## Chapter Summary

1. Central banks evolved for different reasons in different countries but today virtually all countries have a central bank and all central banks perform similar functions.

2. The functions of a modern central bank are to:
   a. Manage the currency and manage or oversee the payments system.
   b. Set the overnight interest rate and control the quantity of money.
   c. Guarantee that sound banks can do business by lending to them, even during crises.
   d. Work with government agencies to oversee financial institutions.
   e. Manage the government's debt.

www.mcgrawhill.ca/olc/cecchetti

3. Central banks have multiple objectives and because these objectives often conflict, policymakers must have clear priorities:
   a. Low and stable inflation.
   b. High and stable growth and employment.
   c. Stable financial markets and institutions.
   d. Stable interest rates.
   e. Stable exchange rates.

4. The best central banks:
   a. Are independent of political pressure.
   b. Make decisions by committee rather than by an individual.
   c. Are accountable to elected representatives and the public.
   d. Communicate their objectives, actions, and policy deliberations clearly to the public.
   e. Articulate clearly how they will act when their goals conflict.
   f. Are credible in their efforts to meet their objectives.

5. Fiscal policy can make the central bank's job impossible because
   a. Politicians take a short-term view, ignoring the inflationary impact of their actions over the long term.
   b. Politicians are predisposed toward financing techniques that will create inflation.
   c. Inflation provides immediate revenue and reduces the value of the government's outstanding debt.
   d. Responsible fiscal policy is a precondition for successful monetary policy.
   e. Central banks remain independent at the pleasure of politicians.

## Conceptual Problems

1. In 1900, there were 18 central banks in the world; 100 years later, there were 174. Why does nearly every country in the world now have a central bank?

2. The power of a central bank is based on its monopoly over the issuance of currency. Economics teaches us that monopolies are bad and competition is good. Would competition among several central banks be better? Provide arguments both for and against.

3. Explain the costs of each of the following conditions and explain who bears them.
   a. Interest rate instability.
   b. Exchange-rate instability.
   c. Inflation.
   d. Unstable growth.

4. Provide arguments for and against the proposition that a central bank should be allowed to set its own objectives.

5. The Maastricht Treaty, which established the European Central Bank, states that the governments of the countries in the European Monetary Union must not seek to influence the members of the central bank's decision-making bodies. Why is freedom from political influence crucial to the ECB's ability to maintain price stability?

6.* Explain why even the most independent central banks are still dependent on the support of the government to meet their policy objectives effectively.

7. In the 1970s and 1980s, Argentina experienced a series of hyperinflationary episodes, during which inflation averaged about 300 percent per year. Finally, after two decades, authorities decided to create a system in which the Argentinean peso could be converted to U.S. dollars on a one-to-one basis. If the central bank wanted to print more pesos, it would need to obtain dollars to back them. Discuss the possible sources of Argentina's high inflation, and explain why the change in policy was expected to eliminate it. (For 10 years, the system worked with virtually no inflation. But in January 2002, the monetary system collapsed, along with the Argentinean economy.)

8. Explain how transparency helps eliminate the problems that are created by central bank independence.

9.* While central bank transparency is widely accepted as desirable, too much openness may have disadvantages. Discuss some of these drawbacks.

10.* Since 1993, the Bank of England has published a quarterly *Inflation Report*. Similarly, the Bank of Canada publishes a *Monetary Policy*

*Indicates more difficult problems.

Report four times a year. Compare a recent issue or one from each Web site (http://www.bankofengland.co.uk, http://www.bankofcanada.ca). Would you propose any changes to the Bank of Canada's *Monetary Policy Report*?

## Analytical Problems

11. Which do you think would be more harmful to the economy—an inflation rate that averages 5 percent a year and has a high standard deviation or an inflation rate of 7 percent that has a standard deviation close to zero?

12. Consider the structure of the Bank of Canada. If you were asked by the minister of finance whether monetary policy decisions should be made by a well-qualified individual with an extremely strong dislike of inflation or by a committee of equally well-qualified people with a wide range of views, which choice would you recommend?

13. Suppose a newly independent economy has asked you for advice in designing its central bank. For each of the following design features, choose which one you would recommend and briefly explain your choice:
    a. Central bank policy decisions are irreversible or central bank policy decisions can be overturned by the democratically elected government.
    b. The central bank has to submit a proposal for funding to the government each year or the central bank finances itself from the earnings on its assets and turns the balance over to the government.
    c. The central bank policymakers are appointed for periods of four years to coincide with the electoral cycle for the government or the central bank policymakers are appointed for 14-year terms.

14. "A central bank should remain vague about the relative importance it places on its various objectives. That way, it has the freedom to choose which objective to follow at any point in time." Assess this statement in light of what you know about good central bank design.

15.* The long list of central bank goals includes the stability of interest rates and exchange rates. You look on the central bank Web site and note that it has increased interest rates at every one of its meetings over the last year. You read the financial press and see references to how the exchange rate has moved in response to these interest rate changes. How could you reconcile this behaviour with the central bank's pursuit of its objectives?

16. Suppose, in an election year, the economy started to slow down. At the same time, clear signs of inflationary pressures were apparent. How might the central bank with a primary goal of price stability react? How might members of the incumbent political party who are up for reelection react?

17. Assuming that they could, which of the following governments do you think would be more likely to pursue policies that would seriously hinder the pursuit of low and stable inflation by the central bank? Explain your choice.
    a. A government that is considered highly creditworthy both at home and abroad in a politically stable country with a well-developed tax system, or
    b. A government of a politically unstable country that is heavily indebted and considered an undesirable borrower in international markets.

18.* Suppose the government is heavily indebted. Why might it be tempting for the fiscal policymakers to sell additional bonds to the central bank in a move that it knows would be inflationary?

# CHAPTER 16

## The Structure of Central Banks: The Bank of Canada, the Federal Reserve, and the European Central Bank

In Chapter 15, we saw that while all central banks share common functions and objectives, not all central banks play exactly the same role in the economy, and within their objectives central banks can focus on different priorities. This should not be a surprise since we saw that central banks began for different reasons and at different times. In this chapter we look at how the Bank of Canada is structured and which objectives it has chosen to focus on. Then we compare the Bank of Canada with two other major central banks, the Federal Reserve System (the Fed) and the European Central Bank (ECB).

## The Bank of Canada

Prior to the creation of the Bank of Canada, most of its functions of the Bank were carried out, but by a different organization. Bank notes were issued by each of the chartered banks, as well as by the Department of Finance. Instead of having the Bank of Canada manage government bank accounts, the Department of Finance did that too. Since Canada was on the gold standard most of the time, there was no scope for an independent monetary policy (as we shall see in Chapter 22). But the absence of a central bank meant that there was no lender of last resort. After World War I, the Department of Finance played that role as well (or at least had the capacity to do so) but before the war there was no lender of last resort. Academic research has suggested several different interpretations of the consequences of the lack of such a facility. One line of research emphasizes the lack of banking panics in Canada and argues that when a Canadian bank ran into difficulties, another Canadian bank would take it over. Others have emphasized the role of double liability in reducing risk taking in Canadian banks, while others have argued that the Canadian banks kept reserves in the much larger New York market to provide a buffer in case of need. Intriguingly, Canadian banks continue to have a deserved reputation for stability in the 21st century.

### The Organizational Structure of the Bank of Canada

The Bank of Canada was created by the *Bank of Canada Act* in 1934, and, although the act has been amended a few times, most of the legislation is unchanged. The CEO of the bank is the governor who is appointed by the Bank's board of directors with the approval of the minister of finance and federal cabinet. In 2008, Mark Carney was named the eighth governor of the Bank for a seven-year term. The appointment of the senior deputy governor (Paul Jenkins in 2009) also requires ministerial approval, while there are four other deputy governors who are appointed by the governor with the board's approval. Together these officers form the Governing Council, which is the key policymaking body of the Bank.

There are 12 directors, appointed by the minister of finance for three-year terms, who are chosen to represent the views of Canadians from all across the country. The governor chairs the board, the senior deputy is a member of the board, and the deputy minister of finance sits on the board but has no vote. While the governance of the Bank of Canada seems like rather dry stuff, remember that independence from the government is a key feature of effective central banks and the balance between accountability to a democratically elected government and independence is critical.

The Bank's head office and most of its staff are in Ottawa but there are major regional offices in Montreal and Toronto as well as branches in Vancouver, Calgary, and Halifax. Regional representatives liaise with the business community, and each quarter regional representatives interview leaders in about 100 firms. The interview results are summarized and published on the Bank's Web site http://www.bankofcanada.ca/en/bos/index.html. The interviews give the Bank a qualitative view of the state of the economy and supplement the statistical information that the Bank collects.

"I don't know a damn thing about monetary policy, but I know what I like."

## The Objectives of the Bank of Canada

We have seen that a central bank has multiple objectives, which it must define in such a way that it can be held accountable for its performance. The first step in setting priorities is established in the preamble to the *Bank of Canada Act*:

> WHEREAS *it is desirable to establish a central bank in Canada to regulate credit and currency in the best interests of the economic life of the nation, to control and protect the external value of the national monetary unit and to mitigate by its influence fluctuations in the general level of production, trade, prices and employment, so far as may be possible within the scope of monetary action, and generally to promote the economic and financial welfare of Canada.*

SOURCE: *Bank of Canada.*

This mandate gives the Bank of Canada responsibility for currency, monetary policy, and financial system stability. The currency issue function is critical as the smooth functioning of the economy depends on Canadians being able to trust the banknotes that they are handed every day. The Bank of Canada spends considerable resources ensuring that this remains the case. See Your Financial World: The Production of Money, on page 350.

**Monetary Policy**   Monetary policy can be broken into two components: choice of a monetary policy framework and implementation of that framework. The Bank of Canada and the minister of finance have jointly agreed on an inflation targeting framework with a flexible exchange rate. The Bank's job is to achieve that target.

In November 2006, the Bank and the government renewed their agreement to set the inflation target at 2 percent until the end of 2011. The Bank of Canada will use monetary policy to achieve a rate of inflation of 2 percent, and to avoid as far as reasonably possible letting the rate of inflation exceed 3 percent or fall below 1 percent. The target is in terms of the Consumer Price Index and the Bank operates

# YOUR FINANCIAL WORLD
## The Production of Money

The Bank of Canada manages the bank note system (but not the coinage, which is the responsibility of the Royal Canadian Mint). The main parts of this responsibility include producing notes that will be hard to counterfeit, ensuring that the notes are distributed across the country according to the needs of each region, and withdrawing worn notes from circulation. Because a bank note costs little to produce and is worth anywhere from $5 to $100, successful counterfeiting is very profitable. The Bank of Canada notes have many security features designed to make it easy to detect a counterfeit note, including a holographic stripe. The most common note to counterfeit is the $20 as counterfeiters hope that businesses won't check a $20 bill as often as a high-denomination note. In 2007, there were about $1.5 billion notes in circulation and only 150 000 were counterfeit. If you are holding a counterfeit note you won't get compensated by the Bank of Canada and it is illegal to pass it on, so you should support businesses that are vigilant about checking for counterfeiting. The Web site of the Bank of Canada has many aids to help in detecting counterfeit notes and provides educational material for schools and the retail sector (http://www.bankofcanada.ca/en/banknotes/index.html)

The Bank also withdraws worn notes from circulation. The worn notes are shredded and sent to a landfill, although you can buy a small amount of shredded notes (see photo) at the Boutique in the Bank Museum in Ottawa.

SOURCE: *Currency Museum, Bank of Canada, Gord Carter.*

to keep the inflation rate close to 2 percent over a two-year horizon.[1] Suppose inflation rose (say because of increasing prices of imports). If the Bank had a very short horizon, it would have to raise interest rates sharply to get inflation back to the target. This might stabilize inflation but at the expense of sharp fluctuations in economic growth. On the other hand, if the horizon is too long then price stability is reduced. The Bank's experience with inflation targeting since 1991 has indicated that a two-year horizon is an appropriate balance between these two forces.

The choice of inflation target is the result of considerable research by the Bank of Canada and the Ministry of Finance. In setting the target in 2006 the Bank stated that it would begin a research program to determine whether the target should be lowered in the future, or whether the target should be changed to a target for the price level rather than a target for the inflation rate.

Having set the inflation target, how does the Bank of Canada achieve it? The operational tool of monetary policy is the overnight interest rate. Eight times a year the Governing Council of the Bank deliberates and determines the target for the overnight rate (the rate at which large financial institutions lend to each other). Sometimes the council leaves the rate unchanged, often it changes the rate by 25 bps up or down, and when the economy is changing rapidly it moves the rate by more than 25 bps. The Tools of the Trade: The Bank of Canada Announcement Statement on page 352 presents a sample press release announcing a change in the target overnight rate.

We will discuss the details of how the Bank can set the interest rate for the economy in subsequent chapters. For now, keep in mind that the rate the Bank of

---

[1] Alternative measures of inflation include the GDP deflator and the "core" CPI, which excludes the most volatile components of the CPI basket. To distinguish total CPI from core, total CPI is sometimes referred to as "headline" CPI.

Canada controls is a nominal interest rate. Since inflation doesn't change quickly, however, this is almost the same as controlling the short-term *real* interest rate. (Recall that the real interest rate equals the nominal interest rate minus expected inflation.) The real interest rate plays a central role in economic decisions. The higher the real interest rate, the more expensive borrowing is, and the less likely a company is to build a new factory or an individual is to purchase a new car. Furthermore, the lower the level of purchases by firms and households, the lower the level of growth will be. So by controlling the overnight interest rate the Bank of Canada influences real growth. (The macroeconomic model that explains this mechanism is presented in Part IV.)

The second part of the monetary policy framework is a flexible exchange rate. Canadians export 40 percent of the goods and services they produce, so for Canadians exchange rates are crucial prices—the price of foreign currency. Unfortunately, there is a tradeoff between exchange rate stability and the other objectives of monetary policy: high and stable economic growth and stable consumer prices. Canada could reduce exchange rate instability by fixing the exchange rate against the U.S. dollar or in the extreme case by adopting the U.S. dollar as our currency. Note that neither of these would completely eliminate exchange rate instability as the U.S. dollar fluctuates against many Asian and European currencies.

But if Canada tied the price of a Canadian dollar to the U.S. dollar, then the exchange rate couldn't help the economy adjust to major changes in commodity prices. In 1998, following the Asian crisis, commodity prices on world markets fell dramatically. In Canada, the value of the Canadian dollar fell relative to the U.S. dollar and the fall in Canadian commodity prices was less than the fall in the (US$) world price, which helped Canadian exporters adjust to the fall in demand. The Bank of Canada no longer intervenes in foreign exchange markets to ensure an orderly market, but rather "reserves such actions for times of major international crisis or a clear loss of confidence in the currency or in Canadian dollar–denominated securities."[2]

**Financial System Stability**   The Bank of Canada works to enhance the stability and efficiency of the financial system of Canada through a variety of channels. The Bank provides liquidity to the financial system both through routine provision of liquidity to major financial institutions needing overnight funds and by providing emergency liquidity to financial institutions in a time of crisis. While in many countries the central bank supervises the financial system, the Bank of Canada does not regulate or oversee financial institutions. The Office of the Superintendent of Financial Institutions (OSFI) oversees the soundness of federally chartered financial institutions and the Financial Consumer Agency of Canada monitors their treatment of consumers.

Unlike in many countries, the Bank of Canada does not own or operate the payments system. The payments system organizes the clearing (e.g., the movement of cheques from the bank they were deposited in to the bank they were drawn on) and settlement (offsetting transfer of funds between the financial institutions).[3] The Canadian Payments Association (CPA) is a nonprofit organization in which most of the large financial institutions are members. The CPA manages the clearing and

---

[2] "The Bank in Brief: The Exchange Rate" April 2006. http://www.bankofcanada.ca/en/backgrounders/bg-e1. html; accessed August 24, 2009.

[3] The rationale for the private ownership of the payments system is historical. For decades the (private) Canadian Bankers' Association ran the payments system. This meant that non-bank financial intermediaries did not have access to the payments system on equal terms to banks. The government proposed that a new clearing and settlement system be established that levelled the playing field across financial institutions, and the CPA was created.

# TOOLS OF THE TRADE

## The Bank of Canada Announcement Statement

On each Fixed Announcement Date (FAD), the Bank of Canada issues a press release stating the change in the target overnight rate if there is one. The details of the Bank statement change periodically, but the basic structure stays the same:

- It begins with a clear statement of the current target for the overnight rate and the corresponding Bank rate.
- Next is a summary of the Bank's view of current economic conditions; how they have changed since the last announcement and how they are expected to change in the near future.

- The summary is followed by a description of the "balance of risks." This is a summary of the major sources of uncertainty about the future path of the economy and how they affect the prospects of achieving the inflation target.
- Finally, the Bank notes the next Fixed Announcement Date and also the release date of any upcoming Monetary Policy Report or Update.

To see this structure, let's have a look at the July 15, 2008 statement:

---

FOR IMMEDIATE RELEASE   15 July 2008

### Bank of Canada Keeps Overnight Rate Target at 3 percent

OTTAWA – The Bank of Canada today announced that it is maintaining its target for the overnight rate at 3 percent. The operating band for the overnight rate is unchanged, and the Bank Rate remains at 3¼ percent.

Three major developments are affecting the Canadian economy: the protracted weakness in the U.S. economy; ongoing turbulence in global financial markets; and sharp increases in many commodity prices. The first two developments are evolving roughly in line with expectations in the April Monetary Policy Report. However, commodity

prices are continuing to outstrip earlier expectations. This has led to further increases in Canada's terms of trade and real national income, and has altered the outlook for global and domestic inflation.

Although Canadian economic growth in the first quarter was weaker than expected, final domestic demand continues to expand at a solid pace. The economy is judged to have moved into slight excess supply in the second quarter of this year; excess supply is expected to increase over the balance of the year. High terms of trade, accommodative monetary pol-

---

settlement system but settlement is done on the books of the Bank of Canada. The Bank of Canada is responsible for overseeing the CPA.

The financial crisis of 2008–09 raised questions about how central banks should promote financial stability see In the News: BoC Needs More Power of Oversight, Crow Says; Former Governor, on page 356. The lender of last resort function had traditionally involved lending only to banks, but in 2008 some nonbanks were critical to the financial system—such as the large insurance company AIG mentioned in the introduction. The crisis also led to a blurring of the line between monetary policy and financial stability policy. The Bank of Canada expanded the range of its liquidity facilities, lending to more financial institutions, for longer periods and against a wider range of securities. In Chapter 23, we examine the response of the Bank of Canada and the Fed in 2008–09 in detail.

## Assessing the Bank of Canada's Structure

In the last chapter, we developed a checklist for assessing a central bank's structure. We said that an effective central bank is one in which policymakers are independent of icy, and a gradual recovery in the U.S. economy are expected to generate above-potential growth starting early next year, bringing the economy back to full capacity around mid-2010. Canadian GDP is projected to grow by 1.0 percent in 2008, 2.3 percent in 2009, and 3.3 percent in 2010.

Total CPI inflation over the next year is expected to be much higher than projected at the time of the April Report. Assuming energy prices follow current futures prices over the projection period, total CPI inflation is projected to rise temporarily above 4 percent, peaking in the first quarter of 2009. As energy prices stabilize and with medium-term inflation expectations remaining well anchored, total inflation is then projected to converge to the core rate of inflation at the 2 percent target in the second half of 2009. Core inflation is projected to remain well contained and broadly in line with earlier expectations, averaging close to 1.5 percent through the third quarter of this year and then rising to 2 percent in the second half of 2009.

The three major developments affecting the Canadian economy pose significant upside and downside risks to the Bank's base-case projection. Weighing the implications of these, the Bank views the risks to its base-case projection for inflation as balanced.

Against this backdrop, the Bank judges that the current level of the target for the overnight rate remains appropriate. The Bank will continue to monitor carefully the evolution of risks, together with economic and financial developments in the Canadian and global economies, and set monetary policy consistent with achieving the inflation target over the medium term.

The Bank's detailed projection for the economy and inflation, and its assessment of risks to the projection, will be published in the Monetary Policy Report Update on 17 July 2008.

**Information note:**
The Bank of Canada's next scheduled date for announcing the overnight rate target is 3 September 2008.

The statement is read carefully by financial analysts who want to be able to predict what the Bank's next move might be. They particularly read the "balance of risks" so that they know what new data might influence the Bank's next rate setting. On September 3, 2008, the Bank again kept the rate unchanged and then lowered the rate quickly with the onset of the financial crisis in October 2008.

SOURCE: *Bank of Canada. The Bank of Canada Announcement Statement, July 15, 2008. At http://www.bankofcanada.ca/en/fixed-dates/2008/rate_150708.html.*

political influence, make decisions by committee, are accountable and transparent, and state their objectives clearly. Let's evaluate the Bank of Canada using these criteria.

**Independence from Political Influence**   We set out three criteria for judging a central bank's independence: budgetary independence, irreversible decisions, and long terms. The Bank of Canada made roughly $2 billion in net income in 2008. Much of that income is seignorage revenue, the profit from the right to print money. There were $53 billion outstanding Bank of Canada notes, and those notes represent an interest-free loan to the Bank of Canada. The Bank sends all its net revenue to the Receiver General of Canada. The Bank controls its own budget, which is overseen by the board of directors. The decisions of the Governing Council cannot be overturned by the government. The governor and senior deputy governor are appointed for seven-year terms.

As we noted in Chapter 15, a central bank should be independent but accountable to a democratically elected government. Initially the line between the Bank's authority and that of the government was unclear, and in 1961 conflict between the governor and the minister of finance went so far as the government introducing a bill in the House of Commons declaring the position of governor of the Bank of Canada vacant, since he did not resign when asked![4] The governor, James Coyne, eventually resigned but the new governor insisted on a clarification of roles. The *Bank of Canada Act* was amended to state that if the minister disagrees with a governor's policy he or she may issue a **directive** telling the governor what policy to follow. But such a directive must be published in the *Canada Gazette*, and it is widely understood that the governor would resign in that situation. Since it would be very likely to lead to concern among international financial institutions, and possibly a run on the dollar, a directive would be used only in extreme circumstances. It has not been used to date.

**Decision Making by Committee**   The Governing Council, comprising the governor, the senior deputy governor, and the four deputy governors, makes the monetary policy decisions.

**Accountability and Transparency**   The Bank of Canada has become considerably more transparent over the last decade. The Bank issues a press release on each of the Fixed Announcement Dates saying what decision has been made and why. Surveys of senior loans officers at major financial institutions and information from interviews of businesses across the country are available on the Bank's web site. The Bank issues quarterly *Monetary Policy Reports* that give a detailed analysis of the state of the economy and rationale for policy decisions. At that time the governor and deputy governor hold a press conference and answer questions from the media. They also appear annually before the House of Commons and Senate Finance Committees to answer questions. All members of the Governing Council frequently make speeches across the country to explain the stance of monetary policy.

**Clear Statement of Intentions**   While transparency has increased, the Bank of Canada is rather more opaque than the Federal Reserve, or even the Bank of England. Both those central banks publish the minutes of the discussions of the decision-making committee (without attributing views to individuals) after a two- or three-week delay. The Fed also publishes entire transcripts of the meetings of the Federal Open Market Committee (FOMC) after a five-year delay.

# The Federal Reserve System
## The Organizational Structure of the Federal Reserve

The Federal Reserve is a much more complicated institution than the Bank of Canada. There are three components with overlapping responsibilities (see Figure 16.1 and Table 16.1). There are 12 regional *Federal Reserve Banks*, distributed throughout the country; a central governmental agency, called the Board of Governors of the Federal Reserve System, located in Washington D.C.; and the *Federal Open Market Committee*. This complex organization reflects the history of central banking in the United States and at least in theory diffuses power, creating a system of checks and balances that reduces the tendency for power to concentrate at the centre.

---

[4] The stated reason for the resignation request was an increase in the governor's pension (previously approved by the board) but the governor believed that it was due to a policy disagreement—the governor had increased interest rates—and refused to resign as a matter of principal. The House approved the legislation declaring the governorship vacant but the Senate defeated the bill, whereupon the governor resigned.

Figure 16.1    The Structure and Policy Organization of the Federal Reserve System

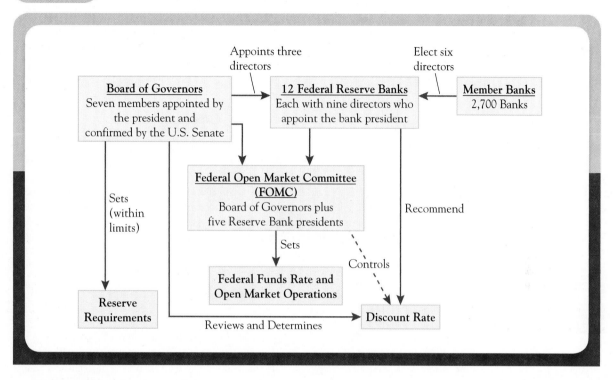

Table 16.1    A User's Guide to the Fed

The Federal Reserve System is complicated, so here is a list of the key players:

| | |
|---|---|
| *Chair of the Board of Governors* | Most powerful person in the federal reserve system. Also chair of the FOMC. Effectively controls FOMC meetings and interest-rate policy. Appointed by the president to a four-year term; must be one of the governors. |
| *Governors of the Board* | Supervise and regulate much of the financial industry. All are voting members of the FOMC. Appointed by the president to 14-year terms. |
| *President of the Federal Reserve Bank of New York* | Runs the biggest and most important of the Reserve Banks, where monetary policy operations are carried out and much of the Fed's work for the Treasury is done. Appointed by the Bank's board of directors with the approval of the Board of Governors, for a five-year term. Also vice chair of the FOMC. |
| *Presidents of the other federal Reserve Banks* | Provide services to commercial banks in their districts. Also attend FOMC meetings and vote every two or three years. |

The board and all the Reserve Banks maintain Web sites that publish data, economic research, speeches, and information about customer services. In addition, the FOMC maintains a Web site that lists meeting times and links to the transcripts, minutes, and statements of the committee: http://www.federalreserve.gov.

## IN THE NEWS

### BoC Needs More Power of Oversight, Crow Says; Former Governor

# Financial Post

**Paul Vieira**

**June 23, 2009**

Regardless of how well Canada's banking system fared during the economic crisis, the financial regulatory scheme is inadequate and in need of change, including handing the Bank of Canada more responsibility for overseeing system-wide risks, says a former governor of the central bank.

"The bank [should] be given a clearly acknowledged oversight and investigative mandate regarding financial stability—linked with the responsibility to report on the same," said John Crow, who was Bank of Canada governor for a seven-year term beginning in February, 1987. "The bank would have the clear authority and responsibility to decide what needs to be tackled and to form and publish its own considered views on broad matters."

Mr. Crow, in a paper for the C.D. Howe Institute, said the collapse of Canada's non-bank commercial paper market—and how the Office of the Superintendent of Financial Institutions argued it bore no responsibility for the fall—should have

opened policy-makers' eyes to the need for change. The ABCP debacle showed, he said, how OSFI is ill equipped or ill suited to oversee systemic, or macroprudential, risks.

Moreover, the former governor indicated it is unclear whether Canada's relatively solid financial system coming out of the financial crisis could be attributed to either superior regulatory work, conservative lending practices among banks or just "plain luck."

Mr. Crow has waded into the regulatory debate just as the White House announced plans last week to give the U.S. Federal Reserve new powers and position it as a key play in a council of regulators with broader co-ordinating responsibility.

Further, Mr. Crow's recommendations would support changes championed last week by the current Bank of Canada governor, Mark Carney. Mr. Carney used a speaking appearance in Regina to criticize the current global banking regulatory scheme as too rigid and not flexible enough to deal with sudden changes in financial markets. He called for changes to the regulatory regime that would make the system more dynamic and better positioned to identify systemic risks, and vowed to lobby world financial leaders and his domestic partners for such reforms.

The Group of 20 nations, of which Canada is a member, has already endorsed this move to so-called system-wide oversight.

SOURCE: © Courtesy of the Federal Reserve Bank of New York

**The Federal Reserve Banks** In the heart of Wall Street, two blocks from the site where the World Trade Center towers once stood, sits a large, fortress-like building that is the home of the Federal Reserve Bank of New York. Deep in the fourth subbasement is the largest gold vault in the world, stocked with many more bars than Fort Knox. All of this gold belongs to foreign countries and international organizations such the International Monetary Fund. The Federal Reserve Bank of New York is the largest of the 12 Federal Reserve Banks, which, together with their branches, form the heart of the Federal Reserve System.

Reserve banks are strange creations, part public and part private. They are federally chartered banks and private, nonprofit organizations, owned by the commercial banks in their districts. As such, they are overseen by both their own boards of directors and the Board of Governors, an arm of the federal government. The method for choosing the nine members of the boards of directors ensures the inclusion of not only bankers but also other business leaders and people who represent the public interest. Six

In his paper for the Toronto think-tank, Mr. Crow said he does not envisage the central bank obtaining new regulatory authority over the financial system. Instead, it should be given access to data compiled by supervisory agencies and, if needed, use its expertise and moral suasion to get authorities to tackle what it views as the big risks to the stability of the marketplace.

Moreover, the bank should work with other regulatory agencies, and be asked to lead a committee of key players such as the Office of the Superintendent of Financial Institutions, [and] the Department of Finance.

"There is a great deal to be said for having the Bank of Canada play the central role in identifying and providing answers for potential risks to the financial system," Mr. Crow said, noting the bank "ought to have the sense of direction, intellectual capability and the ability to staff appropriately."

Mr. Crow also cited how the Bank of Canada has been "hauled into financial stability issues" that are outside its jurisdiction, most notably with ABCP.

"It is ... worth noting that in the ABCP episode the Bank of Canada, while not having any formal responsibility, played a vital leadership role in pulling the situation back from chaos and finding a defensible solution," the former governor wrote.

**LESSONS OF THE ARTICLE:**

The roles of central banks are fluid. We have described the functions of the Bank of Canada today—a lender of last resort without responsibility for supervising financial institutions—but over time functions and priorities can change. Central banks, perhaps because of their budgetary independence, tend to have greater research and analytical capacity than government agencies. As all financial and monetary authorities re-examine their regulatory and supervisory structures in the wake of the financial crisis, it is likely that the roles of central banks will expand.

SOURCE: *BoC Needs More Power of Oversight, Crow Says; Former Governor,"* by Paul Vieira, Financial Post & FP Investing (Canada), June 23, 2009. *Material reprinted with the express permission of "The National Post Company,"* a CanWest Partnership.

directors are elected by the commercial bank members, and the remaining three are appointed by the Board of Governors. Though the range of views represented is wide, everyone has an interest in ensuring economic and financial stability.

Each Reserve Bank has a president who is appointed for a five-year term by the bank's board of directors with the approval of the Board of Governors. (All 12 presidents' terms run concurrently, starting and ending at exactly the same time.) The Reserve Banks conduct the day-to-day business of the central bank, serving as both the government's bank and the bankers' bank. The Reserve Banks perform the same functions as the Bank of Canada. That is, they

- Issue new currency (Federal Reserve notes) and destroy old, worn currency
- Operate as the banker for the U.S. Treasury and manage government debt
- Hold deposits for the banks in their districts
- Make funds available to commercial banks within the district through *discount loans* on which they charge interest at the *discount rate*

The Reserve Banks also perform some functions that are managed by other agencies in Canada, such as OSFI, the FCA and the CPA. They

- Operate and ensure the integrity of a payments network for clearing paper cheques and transferring funds electronically.
- Supervise and regulate financial institutions in the district to ensure their safety and soundness, as well as evaluate proposed bank mergers and new operations.

In addition to these duties, the Federal Reserve Bank of New York provides services to foreign central banks and to certain international organizations that hold accounts there. The Federal Reserve Bank of New York is also the system's point of contact with financial markets. It is where Treasury securities are auctioned, foreign currency is bought and sold, and the Federal Reserve's own portfolio is managed through what are called *open market operations*.

Finally, the Reserve Banks play an important part in formulating monetary policy. They do it both through their representation on the FOMC, which makes interest-rate decisions, and through their participation in setting the discount rate, the interest rate charged on loans to commercial banks. The Federal Reserve Act specifies that the discount rate is to be set by each of the Reserve Banks' board of directors, with the approval of the Board of Governors and, strictly speaking, it is. But the directors have virtually no say over the discount rate, because it is set automatically at a premium above the overnight interest rate that the FOMC controls. Once the FOMC makes its decision, there is nothing left for anyone else to do. That's why in Figure 16.1, detailing the complex structure of the Federal Reserve System a dashed line labelled "controls" runs from the FOMC to the discount rate.

## The Board of Governors

While the New York Federal Reserve Bank is often the public face of the Fed, the Board of Governors in Washington is its official headquarters. The board comprises the seven governors who are appointed by the president and confirmed by the U.S. Senate for 14-year terms, plus a staff of several thousand. The long terms of governors are intended to protect the board from political pressure. The fact that the terms are staggered—one beginning every two years—limits any individual president's influence over the membership.[5] The board has a chairman and a vice chairman, appointed by the president from among the seven governors for four-year renewable terms. The board's membership usually includes academic economists, economic forecasters, and bankers. To ensure adequate regional representation on the board, no two governors can come from the same Federal Reserve district. The Federal Reserve Act explicitly requires "a fair representation of the financial, agricultural, industrial, and commercial interests."

The Board of Governors of the Federal Reserve System performs the following duties:

- Sets the reserve requirement, which determines the level of reserves banks are required to hold
- Approves or disapproves discount rate recommendations made by the Federal Reserve Banks

---

[5] In recent years, four out of every five governors have resigned prior to the end of their terms. Someone has been appointed to fill the remaining portion of the term. A person who has been appointed under those circumstances can be reappointed for a full term. (That is how Alan Greenspan, Ben Bernanke's famous predecessor, was able to remain chair for nearly 20 years.) A board member who serves a full term may not be reappointed, however.

- Administers consumer credit protection laws
- Approves bank merger applications
- Supervises and regulates the Reserve Banks, including their budgets and their presidents' salaries
- Along with the Reserve Banks, regulates and supervises the banking system, examining individual banks for safety and soundness and for compliance with the law
- Analyzes financial and economic conditions, both domestic and international

**The Federal Open Market Committee**   When most people think about the Federal Reserve, what comes to mind is not the payments system or bank supervision but interest-rate setting. And when the business press discusses the Fed, its attention is really on the Federal Open Market Committee (FOMC). This is the group that sets interest rates to control the availability of money and credit to the economy. The FOMC has been around since 1936 and has 12 voting members. These are the seven governors, the president of the Federal Reserve Bank of New York, and four Reserve Bank presidents. The chair of the Board of Governors chairs the FOMC as well, and the committee's vice chair is the president of the Federal Reserve Bank of New York. While only five of the 12 Reserve Bank presidents vote at any one time, all of them participate in the meeting. The FOMC could control any interest rate, but the rate it chooses to control is the federal funds rate, the rate banks charge each other for overnight loans of their excess deposits at the Fed. The federal funds rate is similar to the overnight interest rate in Canada. Table 16.2 compares the structure of the FOMC to that of the Bank of Canada's Governing Council.

The FOMC currently meets eight times a year, or roughly once every six weeks, in the Board Room at the Federal Reserve Building in Washington, D.C. During times of crisis, the committee can confer and change policy over the telephone. Because these "inter-meeting" policy shifts signal the financial markets that the FOMC believes conditions are dire, they are reserved for extraordinary times, such as the aftermath of the terrorist attacks on the World Trade Center of September 2001 or the financial crisis in October 2008. The policy directive simply instructs the New York Fed's staff to buy and sell U.S. Treasury securities so as to maintain the market federal funds rate at the target.

The chair of the Fed is the FOMC's most important member. So, if you want to know whether interest rates are likely to go up, down, or stay the same, that is the person you should listen to most closely. To have an impact on policy, governors or Reserve Bank presidents must build support for their positions through their statements at the meeting and in public speeches until finally the chair has no choice but to acquiesce. While the chair is very powerful, the committee structure provides an important check on his or her power.

## Objectives of the Federal Reserve

The U.S. Congress has set the Federal Reserve's objectives: "The Board of Governors of the Federal Reserve System and the Federal Open Market Committee shall maintain long run growth of the monetary and credit aggregates commensurate with the economy's long run potential to increase production, so as to promote effectively the goals of maximum employment, stable prices, and moderate long-term interest rates."

What should we make of this vague statement? Some people see ambiguity as advantageous. Because laws are difficult to change, they argue, we wouldn't want the Fed's

**Table 16.2** Comparing the FOMC to the Bank of Canada's Governing Council

|  | FOMC | Governing Council |
|---|---|---|
| **Independence** | | |
| Budgetary control | Controlled by the Board of Governors | Controlled by the board of directors. |
| Decisions irreversible | Yes | Yes, subject to the Directive power |
| Terms of appointment | Governors, 14 years; Reserve Bank presidents, 5 years | Governor and senior deputy governor 7 years |
| Threat of legislative change | Requires an act of Congress | Requires an Act of Parliament |
| **Decision making** | Committee of 19 members, 12 voting at one time | Committee of 6 decide by consensus |
| **Accountability and Transparency** | | |
| Policy deliberations | Immediate release of target interest rate with a brief statement and the votes of the committee members | Immediate release of target interest rate with an explanatory statement; the governor and senior deputy governor answer questions |
|  | Minutes of the meeting released after 3 weeks | No minutes released |
|  | Transcripts released after 5 years | No transcripts |
| Other information | Twice-yearly reports to Congress | Annual report to the Parliament |
|  | Public speeches of members | Public speeches of members |
|  | Data collection and dissemination | Data collection and dissemination |
|  | Publication of research reports, along with forecasts of inflation and growth | Publication of research reports, along with forecasts of inflation and growth |
| **Policy framework** | Dual mandate of price stability and sustainable economic growth. No clear definition or statement of tradeoffs between the two goals | Price stability is paramount and defined in terms of an inflation target. All else are secondary goals |
| **Cooperation with Fiscal Policymakers** | No explicit mechanism | Regular meetings between the governor and the minister of finance |

objectives to be extremely specific; the imprecision of the language means the Fed can essentially set its own goals. In the past, the FOMC has been unwilling to tell us exactly how it interprets this broad mandate and at this writing still has not. But prior to becoming chairman, when he was a professor at Princeton University, Ben Bernanke argued that the best way to make monetary policy is to announce a specific numerical objective for inflation over some horizon. Before the 2008 financial crisis, there was every reason to believe that he would move the FOMC in this direction, but instead his term has been dominated by immediate and longer-term responses to the crisis.

## Assessing the Structure of the Fed

**Independence from Political Influence**   The Fed meets the three criteria for judging a central bank's independence: budgetary independence, irreversible decisions, and long terms. The Fed controls its own budget. The Fed's substantial revenue is a combination of interest on the government securities it holds and fees charged to banks for payments system services, including cheque clearing, electronic funds transfers, and the like. In fact, the Fed's income is so large that, in a typical year, 95 percent of it is returned to the U.S. Treasury.[6] Interest-rate changes are implemented immediately and can be changed only by the FOMC—no one else can reverse or change them. The terms of the governors are 14 years; the chair's term runs for four years; and the Reserve Bank presidents serve for five years (and they aren't even appointed by politicians).

Even though the structural elements required to maintain an independent monetary policy are in place, the Fed does occasionally come under political attack. As we have said, raising interest rates is never popular. But so long as policymakers are successful in stabilizing inflation, growth, and the financial system, political problems can be minimized.

**Decision Making by Committee**   The Fed clearly makes decisions by committee, because the FOMC *is* a committee. While the chair of the Board of Governors may dominate policy decisions, the fact that there are 12 voting members provides an important safeguard against arbitrary action by a single individual. In the Federal Reserve, no one person can become a dictator.

**Accountability and Transparency**   The FOMC releases huge amounts of information to the public. Prior to each meeting, the committee publishes, and makes publically available, a report on "Current Economic Conditions," which summarizes anecdotal information on conditions in each of the Federal Reserve districts. (The information used to be compiled in a booklet with a beige cover, and so is now known as the "beige book.") Immediately after the meeting comes the announcement of the policy decision, together with the explanatory statement. Then, three weeks later, a detailed anonymous summary—the minutes—is published. After a five-year waiting period, the FOMC publishes the word-for-word transcript of a meeting. Added to these documents is the twice-yearly Monetary Policy Report to Congress, which includes the members' forecasts for inflation and growth over the next two years. This report is accompanied by the chair's appearance before Congress to discuss the state of the nation's economy. Members of the FOMC also give frequent public speeches, and occasionally testify before Congress. In an average year, the chair gives 15 to 20 speeches, and other governors and Reserve Bank presidents speak 5 to 10 times each. All of these communications—the beige book, the statement, the minutes, the transcripts, the biannual report, the testimony, and the speeches—can be found on various Fed Web sites.

This avalanche of information certainly seems enough to give everyone a sense of what the FOMC is doing and why. But lots of information isn't always the right information. A few things are missing from the Fed's communications. First and foremost, there is no regular press conference, nor any real questioning of the chair on the FOMC's current policy stance. And there is the short period before and after the FOMC's meeting when no member will comment publicly on monetary policy. Second, the inputs into

---

[6] You can approximate the Fed's interest income in a typical year by multiplying the value of its securities holdings—about $800 billion in 2007—by the U.S. Treasury's one-year interest rate, roughly 5 percent in 2007. You'll get a number around $40 billion.

## YOUR FINANCIAL WORLD
### The Fed Can't Save You from a Stock Market Crash

Will the Federal Reserve keep the stock market from crashing, helping us all to sleep better at night? We have already said that the central bank's job is to reduce systematic risk by stabilizing prices, output growth, and the financial system. But there is only so much that a central bank can, should, or will do. In the end, no one can save us from all the risks we face.

The history of the stock market in the late 1990s and early 2000s provides a stark illustration of the pressures central bankers face and the limits of their actions. As equity prices rose in 1998 and 1999, many investors came to believe that then Federal Reserve Board chairman Alan Greenspan would not let the stock market decline significantly. He and his colleagues on the FOMC would bail everyone out. Their reasoning went like this: Changes in wealth change consumption patterns. That is, the richer we all become, the more we spend; conversely, the poorer we are, the less we spend. A stock market crash would reduce spending, sending the economy into a severe recession—something the "Greenspan Fed" would

not allow. For investors, this assumption meant that they could buy stocks without worrying about the downside; they need not fear a crash. While owning stock used to be risky, it wasn't anymore. Or so many people believed in 1999. And the lower the perceived risk, the smaller the risk premium became. This drove prices up even further. (Remember that the lower the risk, the more you will pay for a financial instrument.)

What happened? The answer is that the Fed doesn't control the stock market; it merely sets interest rates and ensures that banks have funds to honour their commitments. As the stock market declined through 2001 and 2002, the FOMC lowered its interest-rate target from 6 percent to 1 percent to avert a recession. Growth was sluggish for a few years, and inflation rose only slightly. Then, in 2008/9 many blamed the low interest rate policies of the Fed for the housing price bubble and its subsequent collapse. No one can eliminate the risk that is inherent in an investment—not even the most powerful central bank in the world.

the decision-making process—documents such as the staff forecast which is distributed in a green book, (known as "the green book") and the policy options in the "blue book"—and the meeting transcript are not made public until five years after the fact.

"I've called the family together to announce that, because of inflation, I'm going to have to let two of you go."

## The European Central Bank

In 1995, Romans shopped with lire, Berliners with deutsche marks, and Parisians with francs. The Banca d'Italia, Italy's central bank, controlled the number of lire that circulated, while the Bundesbank managed the quantity of deutsche marks and the Banque de France, the volume of francs. But on January 1, 1999, the majority of Western European countries adopted a common currency. Today, residents of Rome, Berlin, and Paris all make their purchases in euros, and monetary policy is the job of the European Central Bank (ECB). In the same way that a dollar bill is worth a dollar everywhere in the United States, a euro note is worth a euro everywhere in the euro area. By 2009, the euro had become the currency of 16 countries (see the map in Figure 16.2).

Figure 16.2    The European System of Central Banks

Countries using the euro in 2009

European Union Member countries not using the euro in 2009

Countries that are not members of the European Union in 2009

A myriad of names and abbreviations are associated with central banking in Europe. To avoid confusion, we will refer to the institution that is responsible for monetary policy in the euro area as the European Central Bank (ECB). Our goal is to understand its basic organizational structure.[7]

---

[7] Two publications are helpful in understanding European monetary policy. *The Monetary Policy of the ECB* published by the ECB in 2004, provides a technical description of how things work. For a more academic discussion of monetary policy strategy, written by the top economists at the ECB, see Otmar Issing, Vitor Gaspar, Ignazio Angeloni, and Oreste Tristani, *Monetary Policy in the Euro Area* (Cambridge, UK: Cambridge University Press, 2001).

## Organizational Structure of the ECB

The Eurosystem, like the Federal Reserve system, comprises a set of interrelated institutinons (see Table 16.3). There is the six-member Executive Board of the ECB, which is similar to the Board of Governors; the national central banks, which play many of the same roles as the federal Reserve Banks; and the Governing Council, which formulates monetary policy, just as the FOMC does.[8] The executive board has a president (currently Jean Claude Trichet of France) and a vice president (Lucas Papademos of Greece), who play the same role as the Fed's chair and vice chair. Executive board members are appointed by a committee composed of the heads of state of the countries that participate in the monetary union.

The ECB and the NCBs together perform the traditional operational functions of a central bank, which we learned about in the last chapter. In addition to using interest rates to control the availability of money and credit in the economy, they are responsible for the smooth operation of the payments system and the issuance of currency. While the details differ from country to country, the National Central Banks continue to serve as bankers to the banks and governments in their countries.

There are several important differences between the Fed and the ECB, however. First, the ECB does not supervise and regulate financial institutions. Second, the implementation of monetary policy—the ECB's day-to-day interaction with the financial markets—is accomplished at all the national central banks, rather than being centralized as it is in the United States. Third, the ECB's budget is controlled by the national central banks, not the other way around. This arrangement means that the NCBs control the finances of the executive board and its headquarters in Frankfurt.

**Table 16.3** Key Players in the European Central Bank

| | |
|---|---|
| European Central Bank (ECB) | The central authority in Frankfurt, Germany, that oversees monetary policy in the common currency area (established July 1, 1998) |
| National Central Banks (NCBs) | The central banks of the countries that belong to the European Union |
| European System of Central Banks (ESCB) | The ECB plus the NCBs of all the countries in the European Union, including those that do not participate in the monetary union |
| Eurosystem | The ECB plus the NCBs of participating countries; together, they carry out the tasks of central banking in the euro area |
| ECB Executive Board | The six-member body in Frankfurt that oversees the operation of the ECB and the Eurosystem |
| Governing Council | The (currently) 22-member committee that makes monetary policy in the common currency area |
| Euro | The currency used in the countries of the European Monetary Union |
| Euro area | The countries that use the euro as their currency |

[8] The structure of the ECB is based on that of the Deutsche Bundesbank, the German central bank. While Europeans uniformly viewed the Bundesbank as being successful in stabilizing the post–World War II German economy, the real reason for the new structure was politics. The designers of the ECB had to find a way to create a common central bank that incorporated all of the existing national central banks. This meant adding a new central administration while retaining what was already there.

Before we move on, it is worth noting that a number of additional European Union countries, particularly those in eastern Europe, are likely to enter the monetary union in the coming years. As they do, some difficult decisions must be made. When it began in 1999, people already wondered how the ECB's 22-member Governing Council managed to make decisions. Imagine what could happen if membership were enlarged to 33; 6 executive board members plus one representative from each of the 27 member countries! In anticipation of this problem, the Governing Council of the ECB has adopted a complex system of rotation that bears a passing resemblance to the system used by the FOMC. The executive board members have permanent places on the Governing Council, just as the board of governors of the Federal Reserve System does, while the remaining central bank governors rotate.

## The Objectives of the ECB

The Treaty of Maastricht states that "the primary objective of the European System of Central Banks (ESCB) shall be to maintain price stability. Without prejudice to the objective of price stability, the ESCB shall support the general economic policies in the [European] Community," including the objective of sustainable and noninflationary growth. Like the Fed's legislatively dictated objectives, this statement is quite vague. The Governing Council's response has been to explain its interpretation of the statement and describe the factors that guide its policy decisions. Before assuming operational responsibility on January 1, 1999, the council prepared a press release entitled "A Stability-Oriented Monetary Policy Strategy." The strategy has two parts. First, there is a numerical definition of price stability. Second, it intends to focus on a broad-based assessment of the outlook for future prices, with money playing a prominent role.[9]

The ECB's governing council defines price stability as an inflation rate of close to 2 percent, based on a euro-area-wide measure of consumer prices. The index, called the harmonized index of consumer prices (HICP), is similar to the Canadian consumer price index (CPI). The HICP is an average of retail price inflation in all the countries of the monetary union, weighted by the size of their gross domestic products. So inflation in Germany, where roughly one-third of the total economic activity in the euro area occurs, is much more important to policy decisions than inflation in Ireland, whose economy is about one-30th the size of Germany's. This arrangement has important implications for monetary policy operations, because there will surely be times when the proper policy for Ireland is to raise interest rates but the proper policy for Germany is to lower them. Given Ireland's relative size, a change in inflation or growth there has little impact on the euro area as a whole. The same is true for a number of other small countries in the union.

The fact that the economically large countries matter much more than the small ones can affect the dynamics of the governing council's policymaking. Remember that a group including the heads of all the euro-area national central banks, as well as the members of the executive board, makes interest-rate decisions. While the governing council's job is to stabilize prices in the euro area as a whole, one wonders whether activities in the smaller countries will have undue influence on its policy decisions. To understand this concern, imagine what would happen if all the governing council's members pressed for actions appropriate to their own countries. The result would be a policy appropriate to the median country. And since there are only three large countries in the ECB—Germany, France, and Italy—the median country is likely to be fairly

---

[9] The ECB refers to this statement as its "two-pillar" strategy. Observers have been critical of the way money is included in the policy framework. If the goal is to stabilize prices, why isn't money growth just one of a wide range of indicators that are factored into policy decisions?

small. The custom of drawing half the executive board members from the large countries and half from the small ones is not a foolproof counterweight to this tendency.

These potential shortcomings notwithstanding, evidence strongly suggests that the ECB is doing the job it is supposed to do. That is, the governing council's policy has been appropriate to the euro area; it has not been skewed toward smaller countries' concerns. The specificity of the price stability objective set forth in the Treaty of Maastricht holds policymakers accountable, giving them very little discretion in their decision making.

## Assessing the Structure of the ECB

**Independence from Political Influence**   A number of important safeguards were included in the Treaty of Maastricht to ensure the central bank's independence. First, there are the terms of office: executive board members serve eight-year terms (without the possibility of reappointment), and member nations must appoint their central bank governors for a minimum of five years. Second, the ECB's financial interests must remain separate from any political organization. Third, the treaty states explicitly that the governing council cannot take instructions from any government, so its policy decisions are irreversible. The fact that the ECB is the product of a treaty agreed to by all of the countries of the European Union makes it extraordinarily difficult to change any of the terms under which it operates. People who study central banks generally agree that these provisions make the ECB the most independent central bank in the world.

**Decision Making by Committee**   The focus of the ECB's activity is on the control of money and credit in the Eurosystem—that is, on monetary policy. The governing council, the equivalent of the Fed's FOMC, is composed of the six executive board members and the governors of the 13 (as of 2007) central banks in the Euro area. Meetings to consider monetary policy actions are held monthly in Frankfurt, at the ECB's headquarters. Decisions are made by consensus; no formal votes are taken. The issue of voting has been a contentious one, but the ECB is adamant in its refusal to take votes (or to publicly admit to it). The rationale for this position seems very reasonable. The governing council members are charged with setting policy for the euro area as a whole, regardless of economic conditions in the individual countries they come from. If votes were taken, they would ultimately become public. For the governor of the Banque de France to vote to raise interest rates at a time when the French economy is on its way into a recession would be difficult, even if it is the right thing to do for Europe as a whole. Formal voting, as it is done at the FOMC, would get in the way of good policy.[10]

**Accountability and Transparency**   Like the Federal Reserve, the ECB distributes large volumes of information both on paper and on its Web site, in all of the ECB's official languages. Included are a weekly balance sheet, a monthly statistical bulletin, an analysis of current economic conditions, biannual forecasts of inflation and growth, research reports relevant to current policy, and an annual report. In addition, the president of the ECB appears before the European Parliament every quarter to report on monetary policy and answer questions, and governing council members speak regularly in public. But the most important aspect of the ECB's communication strategy concerns statements about the governing council's policy deliberations. (Like the Bank of Canada, the governing council of the ECB targets a short-term interest rate on interbank loans.)

[10] An important difference between the ECB's governing council and the FOMC is that the governors of the Federal Reserve board always hold the majority of the seats on the FOMC (7 out of 12) while the executive board members are always a minority on the governing council (6 out of a current 19). In the Eurosystem, power is less centralized than it is at the Fed.

Following each of the governing council's monthly meetings on monetary policy, the president and vice president of the ECB hold a news conference in Frankfurt. The proceedings begin with the president reading a several-page statement announcing the council's interest-rate decision, together with a brief report on current economic and financial conditions in the euro area. The president and vice president then answer questions. A transcript of all their remarks is posted on the ECB's Web site (http://www.ecb.int) soon afterward. This procedure contrasts starkly with the FOMC's practice of issuing a terse statement and refusing to answer questions immediately after its meetings. On the other hand, the FOMC issues minutes of its meetings within six weeks, while the ECB does not make its minutes public for 20 years. Minutes of the ECB's very first governing council meeting, which do not identify who said what, are not scheduled to be released until 2019. Furthermore, the governing council does not keep verbatim transcripts of meetings. While observers generally sympathize with the view that transcripts eliminate spontaneity from a meeting, the same cannot be said of minutes. It is hard to justify such a long lag in making public an anonymous summary of the governing council's deliberations.

In assessing whether the ECB's communications strategy is sufficient, we need to ask two questions. First, does the information that is released minimize the extent to which people will be surprised by future policy actions? Second, does it hold policymakers accountable for their decisions? On the first issue, the primary problem turns out to be that often a number of conflicting opinions are expressed. While confusion in communication was a problem when the ECB first got started, the governing council now knows the importance of providing a unified public front, and its members' public statements are more consistent. On the second issue, indications are that the system is working and that there is accountability. The ECB is forced to justify its actions to the European public, explaining its policies and responding to criticisms.

## APPLYING THE CONCEPT
### THE NEW BANK OF JAPAN

The 1990s were difficult for Japan. After two decades of real growth averaging 4.5 percent per year, the growth rate fell to about 1.5 percent a year. At the same time, the Japanese stock market fell by two-thirds, and the banking system practically stopped functioning.

The Japanese Ministry of Finance (commonly known as the MoF) was largely blamed for the mess. Until 1998, the MoF controlled virtually every aspect of the financial system, including monetary policy. It could tell the Bank of Japan (BoJ) where to set its interest-rate target, whom to hire and fire, and what its budget should be. When times were good, the fact that the BoJ worked for the politicians didn't really matter. With high growth rates, resources were abundant, and there was little to fight over. But a decade of stagnation coupled with the meltdown of the country's banking system created strains that the system simply couldn't withstand.

Since 1998, Japanese interest-rate decisions have been made by a nine-member board at the Bank of Japan that is independent of the MoF. The board includes the governor, two deputy governors, and six "outside" experts appointed by the prime minister and approved by the Japanese Parliament (called the Diet). The Bank of Japan Law, which established this structure, states that the policy board's primary goal is the "pursuit of price stability, contributing to the sound development of the national economy." The wording and implications of this statement of BoJ's objective closely resemble the ECB's, with its primary goal of price stability.

The Bank of Japan's policy board meets twice a month, announces its decisions at a press conference following each meeting, and publishes detailed minutes about a month later. These actions, together with frequent public speeches by the nine board members and numerous publications posted on the BoJ Web site, ensure that the financial markets and the public are well informed about the way monetary policy is made in Japan. Furthermore, important BoJ documents are translated into English.

All in all, the BoJ's system of independence, accountability, transparent communication, and monetary policy framework meets most of the requirements we have listed for success. Even so, the Japanese economy continued to struggle for a number of years after the structure was put into place. The most likely explanation is that the Japanese financial system remained in terrible shape, so banks were not playing their essential role as intermediaries. That is, resources were not being transferred from savers to investors, regardless of what the central bank did. There was really little that the Bank of Japan could do. But by 2006, things were looking up; the Japanese economy looked to be poised to return to normal levels of growth, and the BoJ should be able to do the job it is designed to do.

## Terms

Board of Governors of the Federal Reserve System, 358
directive, 354
discount rate, 358
euro area, 362
European Central Bank (ECB), 362
European System of Central Banks (ESCB), 365
Eurosystem, 364
Executive Board of the ECB, 364
federal funds rate, 359

Federal Open Market Committee (FOMC), 359
Federal Reserve Banks, 356
Federal Reserve System, 356
Governing Council of the ECB, 364
Governing Council of the Bank of Canada 350
national central banks (NCBs), 364
seignorage revenue, 353

## Chapter Summary

1. The Bank of Canada is the central bank of Canada.
   a. The monetary policy framework includes an inflation target, currently set as a 2 percent increase in the CPI, and a flexible exchange rate.
   b. The Bank is independent. The governor's decisions can be overridden only by the government if the minister of finance issues a public directive.
   c. The Bank of Canada issues Canadian currency, manages monetary policy, promotes the soundness of the financial system, and is the government's banker.
   d. The Bank of Canada does not operate the payments system or regulate the banking system.

2. The Federal Reserve System is the central bank of the United States. Its decentralized structure comprises three primary elements:
   a. Twelve Federal Reserve Banks, each with its own board of directors, issue currency and act as the Treasury's bank. They also hold deposits of commercial banks, operate a payments system, make loans to commercial banks, and evaluate the safety and soundness of financial institutions in their districts.

   b. The seven-member Board of Governors in Washington, D.C., including the chair, regulates and supervises the financial system.
   c. The Federal Open Market Committee (FOMC) makes monetary policy by setting interest rates. It has 12 voting members, including the 7 governors and 5 of the 12 Reserve Bank presidents and meets eight times a year. It is controlled largely by the chair.

3. The FOMC's success in meeting its objectives is enhanced by
   a. Its independence, which comes from its members' long terms, budgetary autonomy, and the irreversibility of its policy decisions.
   b. Clear communication of its policy decisions through an explanatory statement that is distributed immediately and minutes that are published following the next meeting.
   c. Regular public appearances of the committee's members.
   It is impaired by
   a. Its unwillingness to define exactly what it means by the stated goals of price stability and sustainable economic growth.
   b. Its unwillingness to respond to questions about its policy stance in a timely manner.

4. The European Central Bank (ECB) is the central bank for the countries that participate in the European monetary union.
   a. The ECB is composed of three distinct parts:
      i. The national central banks (NCBs) provide services to the banks and governments in their countries.
      ii. The European Central Bank in Frankfurt, with its six-member executive board, oversees the monetary system.
      iii. The governing council makes monetary policy decisions.
   b. The ECB's primary objective is to stabilize prices in the common currency area.
   c. The ECB's success in meeting its policy objectives is aided by the timely announcement of policy decisions, press conferences in which top ECB officials respond to questions, and the release of twice-yearly forecasts.
   d. The ECB's success is impaired by the fact that the minutes of its policy meetings are not published for 20 years.

## Conceptual Problems

1. What is the target of the Bank of Canada's monetary policy? Is the Bank of Canada as transparent as the Federal Reserve and the ECB?

2. What are the Federal Reserve's goals? How are Fed officials held accountable for meeting them?

3. Go to the Bank of Canada's Web site (http://www.bankofcanada.ca) and locate the Bank's press release for the most recent Fixed Announcement Date. What does the statement say about the state of the economy? Does the statement say anything about the risks to meeting its goals? Now read the committee's last two statements to see if the balance of risks has changed. If it has, can you figure out why?

4. Some people have argued that the high inflation of the late 1970s was a consequence of the fact that Federal Reserve Board Chairman Arthur Burns did what President Richard Nixon wanted him to do. Explain the connection.

5 What factors increase and what factors decrease the independence of the Bank of Canada?

6. What are the goals of the ECB? How are its officials held accountable for meeting them?

7. Go to the ECB's Web site (http://www.ecb.int) and locate the most recent statement of the president of the ECB about monetary policy. What was the governing council's policy decision? How was it justified?

8. Do you think the Bank of Canada has an easier or a harder time agreeing on monetary policy than the governing council of the ECB? Why?

9.* What are the two most important factors in ensuring that power is decentralized in the Eurosystem?

10. The Monetary Policy Committee (MPC) of the Bank of England is responsible for setting interest rates in the United Kingdom. Go to the Bank's Web site at http://www.bankofengland.co.uk, and get as much information about the MPC as you can. How big is it? Who are its members? How often does it meet? What sorts of announcements and publications does it offer? Is it independent of Parliament?

## Analytical Problems

11. Do you think it would be a good idea for the Bank of Canada to release minutes or a transcript of the meetings of the governing council at which interest rates are set? Explain your answer.

12.* Currently, all the national central banks in the Eurosystem are involved with the implementation of monetary policy. What do you think would be the advantage of centralizing the conduct of these day-to-day interactions with financial markets at the ECB in Frankfurt? Can you think of any disadvantages?

13. Do you think it would be a good idea to have regional central banks in Canada? Why or why not?

14. Do you think members of the Bank of Canada's governing council should take formal votes? Why or why not?

15. If members of the Bank of Canada's governing council do decide to take formal votes on monetary policy decisions, do you think these votes should be published? Why or why not?

16. Why do you think the statement released by the Bank of Canada on each Fixed Announcement Date retains the same basic structure?

17. Consider the objectives of a central bank (summarized in Table 15.2 on page 336). To which objectives has the Bank of Canada assigned the highest priorities, and how does the Bank measure achievement?

18.* If you were asked to design a new central bank, what two institutional design features of (a) the Federal Reserve System and (b) the Bank of Canada would you adopt? Explain your choices.

* Indicates more difficult problems.

# CHAPTER 17

## The Central Bank Balance Sheet and the Tools of Monetary Policy

Being the governor of a central bank is a bit like being an airline pilot: when things go smoothly there is not a huge amount to do; when things go wrong, making the right decision is critical. For much of the first decade of this century, for example, central bank announcements were rather mundane as central banks announced that inflation was slightly above or below the target and responded by raising or lowering the interest rate a little to steer the inflation rate back on course. From October 2004 to September 2005 the Bank did not change its interest rate setting at all, leaving the target for the overnight rate at 2.5 percent the whole time. Then, in late 2008, the standard tools suddenly looked insufficient and central bank governors everywhere went into crisis mode, turning to new or at least rusty tools to mitigate the effects of the financial crisis. Between October 2008 and April 2009 the target overnight rate fell from 3 percent to just 0.25 percent, in six large steps. Once the interest rate couldn't go any lower, other tools were developed. (Of course, very quickly questions were raised about whether or not the "pilot'" had been asleep at the wheel during the calmer times, and had either led the economy into the crisis, or not taken evasive action.)

In this chapter, we study the calmer times. How is monetary policy conducted when the economy is relatively stable? Central bankers have a long list of goals and a short list of tools they can use to achieve them. They are supposed to promote the stabilization of prices, output, the financial system, exchange rates, and interest rates yet the only real power they have comes from their control over their own balance sheet and their monopoly on the supply of currency and reserves. We need to understand how the central bank interacts with the financial system. What is it that central banks buy and sell? What are the assets and liabilities on their balance sheets? How do they control those assets and liabilities, and why might they want to hide them from the public? More to the point, how is the central bank's balance sheet connected to the money and credit that flow through the economy? Where *do* the trillions of dollars in our bank accounts actually come from? In answering these questions, we will combine our knowledge of how central banks work with our understanding of commercial bank operations.

We will begin by looking at the balance sheet of a generic central bank and describe the forces that can change the balance sheet. The central bank has unique powers to determine its balance sheet and we show how this enables it to implement monetary policy. In Chapter 15, we noted that the Bank of Canada gives first priority to stabilizing the rate of inflation at 2 percent. It does this by setting the overnight interest rate. In the second half of the chapter we show how the central bank uses its balance sheet to control the very short term interest rate. We look at both at the Bank of Canada and more briefly at the operation of the Federal Reserve and the European Central Bank. In the following two chapters we will analyze how the overnight interest rate affects the aggregate economy, which will allow us to determine the level the central bank should set for the interest rate to achieve a particular target rate of inflation. Finally, in Section V we turn to the question of how the central bank can use its tools in crisis situations.

# The Central Bank's Balance Sheet

The central bank is both the government's banker and the bankers' banker, and as such engages in numerous financial transactions. It can supply currency, provide deposit accounts to the government and commercial banks, make loans, and buy and sell securities and foreign currency. All these activities cause changes in the central bank's balance sheet. Because the balance sheet is the foundation of any financial institution, understanding the day-to-day operation of a central bank must start with an understanding of its assets and liabilities and how they change. The structure of the balance sheet gives us a window through which we can study how the institution operates. Here we will examine a generic central bank balance sheet and in later sections of the chapter we will see how the operating procedures of particular central banks affect the composition of their balance sheet.

Central banks publish their balance sheets regularly. The Bank of Canada and the Federal Reserve both do so weekly; you can find the information on their Web sites. (To get a sense of the relative size of the balance sheets of the Fed, the ECB, and the People's Bank of China, see Applying the Concept: Central Bank Balance Sheets on page 372.) Publication is a critical part of the transparency that makes monetary policy effective. The published data are complicated and in fall 2008 when central banks began using their balance sheet to address the financial crisis, they became even more so. Figure 17.1 shows a stripped-down version of the balance sheet listing the major assets and liabilities that appear in every central bank's balance sheet in one form or another. Note that the entries are divided into not only columns, with assets on the left and liabilities on the right, but also categories. The top row shows the assets and liabilities the central bank holds in its role as the government's bank, and the bottom row shows the assets and liabilities it holds as the bankers' bank. Let's examine each entry, starting with the assets.

## Assets

The central bank's balance sheet shows three basic assets: securities, foreign exchange reserves, and loans. The first two are needed so that the central bank can perform its role as the government's bank; the loans are a service to commercial banks. Let's look at each one in detail.

1. *Securities* are the primary assets of most central banks. Though some central banks hold a wide variety of public and private debt, the Bank usually holds only Government of Canada securities. The quantity of securities it holds is controlled through purchases and sales known as *open market operations*. It is important to emphasize that independent central banks, not fiscal authorities, determine the quantity of securities they purchase.

**Figure 17.1**    The Central Bank's Balance Sheet

|  | **Assets** | **Liabilities** |
|---|---|---|
| Government's Bank | Securities<br>Foreign exchange reserves | Currency<br>Government's deposits |
| Bankers' Bank | Loans | Financial institutions'<br>deposits (reserves) |

## APPLYING THE CONCEPT
### CENTRAL BANK
### BALANCE SHEETS

To get some idea of the size and composition of central bank balance sheets, we can look at Table 17.1, which summarizes the balance sheet data for the Bank of Canada, the Federal Reserve System, and the People's Bank of China (the Chinese central bank).

Let's start by comparing the Fed and the Bank of Canada. On the asset side, both hold the vast majority of their assets in the form of securities, which includes securities they may be holding under repos. The liability sides are also similar with the vast majority of liabilities being notes outstanding. The U.S. banks were required to hold reserves against demand deposits but since vault cash counts toward the reserve requirements, the amount that they need to keep on deposit at the Fed is minimal.

Turning to the People's Bank of China, the PBOC, this balance sheet has a completely different structure. Foreign exchange reserves and loans are enormous, close to US$2 trillion. A full explanation for this will have to be deferred to Chapter 22. The short version is that the Chinese have been keeping their exchange rate fixed, and to do it, the central bank has been forced to purchase massive quantities of foreign reserves. (To neutralize the potential inflationary impact of these massive purchases, the PBOC has been issuing bonds of its own in order to control the rate of growth of the monetary base. As of the date of the data in Table 17.1, it had issued 4,392 billion yuan worth of these "sterilization" bonds—about US$640 billion

Taking the PBOC's published balance sheet and putting it into the format for Table 17.1 is made difficult by the presence of something called simply "claims on financial institutions." These are recorded in Table 17.1 as loans, but they could just as easily have been put under securities since they are surely long term. To understand these "loans," you should realize that a significant part of the Chinese economy remains state owned, a leftover from the communist era. In order to continue to operate, state-owned enterprises often require subsidies. These are subsidies that have come in the form of bank loans that are ultimately financed by the central bank. In other words, these central bank loans do not play the same role as those from the Fed or the Bank of Canada. They are the channel through which the government keeps state-owned companies afloat.

Finally, the line showing nominal GDP enables you to get a rough measure of the size of the central bank relative to the size of the economy. The People's Bank is much larger proportionately, reflecting the greater use of cash in the economy (a central bank liability) and the greater role of the state in the economy. The Bank of Canada is smaller relative to the economy than the Fed, both because Canadians tend to use less cash and because the banks do not hold any significant quantity of reserves (remember that the U.S. data are in billions).

2. **Foreign exchange reserves** are the central bank's and government's balances of foreign currency. These are held in the form of bonds issued by foreign governments. For example, the Fed holds euro-denominated bonds issued by the German government as well as yen-denominated bonds issued by the Japanese government. These reserves are used in **foreign exchange interventions**, when officials attempt to change the market values of various currencies.

3. Loans are extended to commercial banks. There are several kinds, and their importance varies depending on how the central bank operates.

Government bonds are the biggest, most important asset on the Bank of Canada's balance sheet. Through these holdings the Bank controls the overnight interest rate and the availability of money and credit. While central banks such as the Fed and the ECB hold foreign exchange reserves, Canada's foreign exchange reserves are owned by the government and show up on the government's balance sheet.[1] In contrast, in some countries the central bank's primary focus is the level of foreign exchange reserves.

---

[1] The foreign exchange reserves are held in the Exchange Fund equalization account. This fund is managed by the Bank of Canada for the government.

| Table 17.1 | Balance Sheets of the Bank of Canada, the Federal Reserve, and the People's Bank of China, July 2008 |

|  | People's Bank of China 100 mn yuan Dec-08 | Federal Reserve US$bn Jul-08 | Bank of Canada C$mn Jun-08 |
| --- | --- | --- | --- |
| Securities | 16,279 | 770 | 51,376 |
| Foreign exchange | 149,580 | 88 |  |
| Loans | 20,287 | 17 | 2 |
| Gold |  | 11 |  |
| Other assets | 7,958 | 32 | 1,239 |
| Total | 194,104 | 918 | 52,770 |
| Currency | 33,075 | 795 | 50,040 |
| Government accounts | 27,414 | 4 | 1,443 |
| Commercial FI deposits | 82,277 | 29 | 180 |
| Other liabilities | 51,338 | 130 | 1,255 |
| Capital | 0 | 40 | 148 |
| Total | 194,104 | 918 | 52,770 |
| GDP | 297,471 | 14,204 | 1,618,380 |

For the People's Bank of China, "Securities" refers to claims on the central government, "Loans" to claims on all financial institutions and nonfinancial institutions, and "Other liabilities" include $336 billion of bonds issued by the central bank.

For the Federal Reserve, "Securities" include all forms of repurchase agreements; "Foreign exchange reserves" does not include U.S. Treasury Exchange Stabilization Fund, which is of exactly equal size; and "Currency" excludes cash in bank vaults, which is included in commercial bank reserves.

For the Bank of Canada, Commercial FI deposits are deposits of CPA members.

SOURCES: *Bank of Canada Banking and Financial Statistics, (September 2009): Tables B1 (p. s10–11) and H1 (p. s96–97); Federal Reserve release H.4.1; U.S. Treasury and Federal Reserve Foreign Exchange Operations, Quarterly Report, Table 1; Chinese data are from www.pbc.gov.cn.*

## Liabilities

Turning to the liabilities side of the central bank's balance sheet, we see three major entries: currency, the government's deposit account, and the deposit accounts of financial institutions. Again, these can be divided into two groups based on their purpose. The first two items allow the central bank to perform its role as the government's bank, while the third allows it to fulfill its role as the bankers' bank. Let's look at each in turn, again using the example of Canada to illustrate some important details.

1.  Nearly all central banks have a monopoly on the issuance of the *currency* used in everyday transactions. Take a look at the top of any dollar bill and you will see the words "Bank of Canada." Currency is a central bank's principal liability.

2.  Governments need a bank account just like the rest of us. They have to have a place to deposit their income and a way to pay for the things they buy. The central bank provides the government with an account into which the government deposits funds (primarily tax revenues) and from which the

government writes cheques and makes electronic payments. We will see that as the manager of the *government account*, the Bank of Canada can use its ability to shift funds between the government accounts at private financial institutions and at the Bank to affect the size of its balance sheet.

3. *Deposits of financial institutions* (**reserves**) are held by financial institutions at the Bank. (Note that these are assets for the private institutions and a liability for the central bank.) Traditionally, such accounts were restricted to commercial banks, and their primary function was to hold the bank's **required reserves**. They also were used for interbank settlements. Today in many countries commercial banks are not required to hold reserves, but they still hold accounts at the central bank to use for interbank settlements. In the same way that you can take cash out of a commercial bank, the bank can withdraw its deposits at the central bank. And just as you can write a cheque instructing your bank to transfer some part of your account balance to someone else, a commercial bank can transfer a portion of its deposit account balance to another bank. The Bank of Canada records deposits of financial institutions as *Deposits of CPA members*, which includes but is not restricted to banks.[2]

The Canadian financial institutions are not required to hold deposits at the Bank of Canada and they typically do not (despite the interest that the Bank of Canada pays on reserves.)

## The Importance of Disclosure

Buried in the mountain of paper that every central bank publishes is a statement of the bank's own financial condition. This balance sheet contains what is probably the most important information that any central bank makes public. Every responsible central bank in the world discloses its financial position regularly, most of them every week. In the same way that shareholders require a periodic accounting of the activities of the companies they own, we are all entitled to the information on our central bank's balance sheet. Without public disclosure of the level and change in the size of foreign exchange reserves and currency holdings, it is impossible for us to tell whether the policymakers are doing their job properly. Publication of the balance sheet is an essential aspect of central bank transparency. Delays, such as those during the Mexican debt crisis of 1994–1995, are a clear sign of impending disaster.

Another sign of trouble is misrepresentation of the central bank's financial position. A particularly egregious case of lying by a central bank occurred in the Philippines in 1986, when then-President Ferdinand Marcos was desperate to remain in power. We know now that Marcos ordered the central bank to print enormous amounts of money so that he could try to buy enough individual votes to win the election. In the four months leading up to the election, the quantity of money circulating in the Philippine economy rose 40 percent. While a government can usually print money whenever it wants, that was not the case in the Philippines. As part of a loan agreement with the International Monetary Fund (IMF), the Central Bank of the Philippines had promised to limit the rate of money growth. Since Filipinos used currency for the vast majority of transactions, the easiest way for the IMF to enforce the agreement was to monitor the serial numbers on new bills. Because each bill has a unique serial number, figuring out how many of them are being printed shouldn't be difficult. But instead of printing one

---

[2] In 2008, in addition to some banks , the Caisse centrale Desjardins du Québec, Credit Union Central of Canada, and Alberta Treasury Branches held settlement accounts at the Bank of Canada.

bill per serial number, the Philippine government printed bills in triplicate—three bills per serial number. And the central bank kept quiet about the scheme.[3]

The central bank of Thailand was similarly evasive in the summer of 1997. The Bank of Thailand was committed to stabilizing the value of its currency, the Thai *baht*, at an exchange rate of about 26 to one U.S. dollar. To do so, officials had to convince foreign exchange traders that they had enough dollars to buy baht if market participants started to sell. To be convinced, currency traders had to see the numbers. But in summer 1997, officials at the Bank of Thailand refused to tell anyone, even their own Minister of Finance, how many dollars the bank held. When the truth got out, and everyone learned that the cupboard was bare, the baht collapsed, ending 1997 at 50 to one dollar.[4]

## The Monetary Base

Together, currency in the hands of the public and deposits of financial institutions (FIs)—the privately held liabilities of the central bank—make up the monetary base, also called high-powered money. As we will see in the next section, the central bank can control the size of the monetary base, the base on which all other forms of money stand. (The term "high-powered" comes from the fact that the quantity of money and credit in the economy is a multiple of currency plus banking system reserves.) As we will see in Chapter 20, when the monetary base increases by a dollar, the quantity of money rises by several dollars.

To get some sense of the relationship between the monetary base and the quantity of money, we can look at a few numbers. In June 2008, the Canadian monetary base was $50 billion. At the same time, M1+ was $443 billion and M2++ was $1.69 trillion. So M1 was nearly 10 times the size of the monetary base, and M2 was more than 30 times the monetary base. The fact is that when the financial institutions hold no reserves in the central bank, the monetary base is just the amount of notes in circulation.

# Changing the Size and Composition of the Balance Sheet

Unlike you and me, the central bank controls the size of its balance sheet. That is, policymakers can enlarge or reduce their assets and liabilities at will, without asking anyone. We can't do that. To see the point, think about a simple transaction you engage in regularly, such as buying $50 worth of groceries. When you arrive at the checkout counter, you have to pay for your purchases. Let's say you do it with a cheque. When the supermarket deposits your cheque in the bank, your $50 moves through the payments system. It is credited to the supermarket's account and, eventually, debited from yours. As long as you started with at least $50 in your chequing account, the process works smoothly. The grocery store's bank account is $50 larger and yours is $50 smaller.

---

[3] Newspaper stories at the time documented what happened in the Philippines. See, for example, Chris Sherwell, "Banknotes in Triplicate Add to Filipino's Confusion," *Financial Times*, February 22, 1986.

[4] The Bank of Thailand hadn't actually sold its dollar reserves on the open market. Officials had engaged in forward transactions that committed them to sell the dollars in the future. Thus, they could claim to have dollars that in reality were committed to others. For a detailed description of this episode, see Paul Blustein, *The Chastening: Inside the Crisis That Rocked the Global Financial System and Humbled the IMF* (New York: Public Affairs, 2001).

Now think about a standard transaction in which the central bank buys a $1 million government security. What's the difference between this purchase and yours at the grocery store? First, there is its size. The central bank's transaction is 20,000 times as big as yours. But that's not all. To see another important difference, let's look at the mechanics of the security purchase. To pay for the bond, the central bank writes a $1 million cheque payable to the bond dealer that sells the bond. (In real life, the transaction is done electronically.) After the cheque is deposited, the dealer's bank account is credited $1 million. The commercial bank then sends the cheque back to the central bank. When it gets there, something unusual happens. Remember, at the end of your cheque's journey, your bank debited your chequing account $50. But when the central bank's $1 million cheque is returned, the central bank credits the reserve account of the bank presenting it $1 million. And that's it. The central bank can simply buy things (the $1 million bond, for instance) and then create liabilities to pay for them (the $1 million increase in reserves in the banking system). It can increase the size of its balance sheet as much as it wants.

We can use the balance sheet of the central bank to write the monetary base as

$$\text{Monetary Base} = \text{Central Bank Assets (Securities + Loans + Foreign Exchange holdings)} - \text{Deposits in the Government Account} \tag{17.1}$$

Clearly, the size of the monetary base is determined by the balance sheet items on the right-hand side of the equation.

Turning to the specifics of this process, we'll look at four types of transaction: (1) an *open market operation,* in which the central bank buys or sells a security; (2) the extension of a *loan* to a commercial bank by the central bank; (3) a transfer of funds out of the government account and (4) the decision by an individual to *withdraw cash* from her private bank. Each of these has an impact on both the central bank's balance sheet and the banking system's balance sheet. Equation (17.1) tells you that items 1 to 3 will affect the monetary base and item 4—although it changes the composition of the central bank's balance sheet—does not change the monetary base.

To figure out the impact of each of these transactions on the central bank's balance sheet, we need to remember one simple rule: When the value of an asset on the balance sheet increases, either the value of another asset decreases so that the net change is zero or the value of a liability rises by the same amount. What's true for assets is also true for liabilities. An increase in a liability is balanced either by a decrease in another liability or by an increase in an asset. The principle is the same regardless of whose balance sheet we are looking at.

## Open Market Operations

When the Bank of Canada buys or sells securities in financial markets, it engages in **open market operations**. These open market purchases and sales have a straightforward impact on the Bank's balance sheet. To see how the process works, take the common case in which the Bank of Canada purchases $1 billion in government bonds from a commercial bank. To pay for the bonds, the Bank of Canada transfers $1 billion into the deposit account of the seller. The exchange is done electronically. Panel A of Figure 17.2 shows the change in the Bank of Canada's balance sheet. This is called a **T-account**. The left side shows the change in assets and the right side gives the change in liabilities. Panel A of Figure 17.2 shows the impact of this **open market purchase** on the Bank of Canada's balance sheet: Its assets and liabilities both go up $1 billion, increasing the monetary base by the same amount.

# YOUR FINANCIAL WORLD
Why We Still Have Cash

For years experts have been predicting the demise of paper currency—cash. First, credit cards were going to take over; now it is electronic forms of money. But still we have cash. In fact, we have more cash than ever. During the 1990s, as more and more people got credit cards and clever people tried to introduce e-money, the volume of dollar bills outstanding rose 8 percent per year. To put it in concrete terms, the amount of Canadian currency in the hands of the public doubled in 10 years. By 2008, cash holdings amounted to something like $1,600 per Canadian resident. (See the Applying the Concept: Where Are All Those $100 Bills? on page 29.) Similarly large amounts are held in the United States and Europe. Nothing seems to dissuade people from holding paper notes issued by the central bank.

There are a number of explanations for this phenomenon. First, there is convenience: the easiest way to repay $20

you borrowed from a friend is to use cash. Second, many people prefer to receive cash to avoid paying taxes. Servers in restaurants, for instance, don't want to pay income tax on their tips. Finally, there is the fact that cash provides anonymity. When you pay with cash, no one cares who you are and the transaction can't be traced back to you. This arrangement has obvious advantages for people engaged in drug dealing, smuggling, and other black-market activities. But if the demand for cash came solely from people engaged in illegal activities, the proper response would be to outlaw it. The fact is that law-abiding people use cash for legal transactions in which they would prefer to remain nameless. Surely we don't want to lose the ability to hide some of our purchases from public view.

Until there are electronic currencies that maintain anonymity, there is little chance that electronic products will replace paper currency.

What is the impact of the Bank of Canada's open market purchase on the banking system's balance sheet? The Bank of Canada exchanged $1 billion in securities for $1 billion in Deposits of FIs, both of which are assets for the banking system. (We will use the more generic term "deposits of FIs" rather than "deposits of CPA members" as these operations could describe actions by central bank, and they each have slightly different names for these accounts.) Panel B of Figure 17.2 shows the balance-sheet effect of the exchange. Note that there are no changes on the liabilities side of the banking system's balance sheet, and the changes on the asset side sum to zero.

Looking at Figure 17.2, you'll notice that deposits of FIs at the Bank of Canada are an asset to the banking system but a liability to the Bank of Canada. This may seem confusing, but it shouldn't be. It's like your own bank account. The balance in that account is your asset, but it is your bank's liability.

Before we move on, we should note that if the Bank of Canada *sells* a government bond through what is known as an open market sale, the impact on everyone's balance

**Figure 17.2**   Balance Sheet Changes after the Bank of Canada Purchases a Government Bond

| A. Bank of Canada's Balance Sheet | | B. Banking System's Balance Sheet | |
|---|---|---|---|
| Assets | Liabilities | Assets | Liabilities |
| Securities (Government bond) +$1 billion | Deposits of FIs +$1 billion | Deposits at Bank of Canada +$1 billion<br>Securities (Government bond) −$1 billion | |

sheet is reversed. All the credits in the two figures become debits and vice versa. The Bank of Canada's balance sheet shrinks, as does the monetary base; the banking system's reserves decline, while its securities holdings increase.

## Loans to a Financial Institution

In Canada these take the form of advances to members of the CPA and are provided under the Bank of Canada's Standing Liquidity Facilities (SLF). The Bank of Canada does not force financial institutions to borrow money; they ask for loans. To get one, a borrowing FI must provide collateral, usually in the form of government bonds.[5] Not surprisingly, when the Bank of Canada makes such a loan, it changes the balance sheet of both institutions. For the borrowing FI, the loan is a liability that is matched by an offsetting increase in the level of its "advances" account. For the Bank of Canada, the loan is an asset that is created in exchange for a credit to the borrower's account. The impact on the Bank of Canada's balance sheet is shown in Panel A of Figure 17.3.

Note that the increase in loans is an asset to the Bank of Canada, while the change in the Advances increases its liabilities. The impact on the Bank of Canada's balance sheet is the same as that of an open market purchase. The extension of credit to the financial system raises the level of reserves and expands the monetary base.

The impact on the financial system's balance sheet mirrors the impact on the Bank of Canada, with deposits at the Bank of Canada and advances both increasing. In this case, however, FIs have increased the size of their balance sheet by borrowing from the Bank of Canada (see Panel B of Figure 17.3).

## Shifting Government Deposits

The Bank of Canada can also affect its balance sheet by moving government of Canada balances from the government account at the Bank to the government's accounts in the financial system. When it does this, it will transfer the funds to the deposit accounts of the FIs at the Bank of Canada. Figure 17.4 shows the effect of this change. The Bank of Canada now holds deposits of the financial institutions and not of the government of Canada. The financial system has an added asset, the funds on deposit at the Bank of Canada, and an added liability, the deposit of the government of Canada.

---

**Figure 17.3**   Balance Sheet Changes after the Bank of Canada Makes an Advance

| A. Bank of Canada's Balance Sheet | | B. Banking System's Balance Sheet | |
|---|---|---|---|
| **Assets** | **Liabilities** | **Assets** | **Liabilities** |
| Advances +$100 billion | Deposits of FIs +$100 billion | Deposits at Bank of Canada +$100billion | Advances +$100million |

---

[5] Remember, "collateral" is the term used to describe specific assets pledged by a borrower that a lender can seize in the event of nonpayment. To obtain a discount loan, a bank must identify specific assets (usually bonds) that the Bank of Canada can take if the bank doesn't repay the loan. Details of policies for Standing Liquidity Facilities and Emergency Lending Assistance are described in the Bank of Canada's *Financial Stability Review*, 2004, pp. 49–55.

Figure 17.4   Balance Sheet Changes after the Bank of Canada Transfers Deposits to the Banking System

| A. Bank of Canada's Balance Sheet | | | B. Banking System's Balance Sheet | | |
|---|---|---|---|---|---|
| Assets | Liabilities | | Assets | Liabilities | |
| | Deposits of FIs | +$1 million | Deposits in Bank of Canada   +$1 million | Gov't deposits | +$1million |
| | Government Deposits | -$1million | | | |

## Cash Withdrawal

The Bank of Canada has almost no control over its biggest liability: notes in circulation. If you decide to use less cash and so deposit $100 into your bank, the bank will then have $100 in vault cash. This increase is not noted on this balance sheet of the Bank of Canada. A more detailed balance sheet of the Bank of Canada would make it clear that there has been a reduction in the notes in the hands of the public and an increase in the notes held by the banking system. Figure 17.5 shows how this transaction affects the balance sheets of you, the Bank of Canada, and your bank. The composition of your assets has changed from cash to a bank deposit; the composition of the Bank of Canada's liabilities has changed from a liability to you to a liability to your bank; the balance sheet of your bank has expanded, adding a liability to you and an asset—cash in the bank.

Table 17.2 summarizes the impact of each of the four transactions we have just studied on the size and composition of the Bank of Canada's balance sheet. Open market operations and government deposit transfers are both done at the discretion of the central bank, while the level of discount borrowing is decided by the financial institutions. The nonbank public decides how much currency to hold.

It is worth noting that there are countries in which the process works differently. As we will see in Chapter 22, when a central bank wishes to control its country's exchange rate rather than the domestic interest rate, one way to do so is to stand ready to buy and sell foreign currency. In such cases, foreign exchange intervention is not truly under the central bank's control. Instead, the private sector decides when the purchases and sales are made and how large they are. That is essentially what the Bank of Thailand was doing in 1997, and when it started to run out of foreign currency reserves, the system collapsed.

Figure 17.5   Balance Sheet Changes after a Private Person Deposits Cash into Her Bank Account

| A. Nonbank Public's Balance Sheet | | | |
|---|---|---|---|
| Assets | | Liabilities | |
| Currency | -$100 | | |
| Chequable deposits | +$100 | | |

| B. Bank of Canada's Balance Sheet | | | C. Banking System's Balance Sheet | | |
|---|---|---|---|---|---|
| Assets | Liabilities | | Assets | Liabilities | |
| | Currency (public) | -$100 | Vault Cash   +$100 | Chequable deposits | +$100 |
| | Currency (banks) | +$100 | | | |

**Table 17.2** Changes in the Size and Composition of the Bank of Canada's Balance Sheet

| Transaction | Initiated by | Typical Action | Impact |
|---|---|---|---|
| Open market operation | Central bank | Purchase of government security | Increases deposits of FIs |
| CPA Advance | Private bank | Loan to a financial institution | Increases deposits of FIs |
| Transfer government deposit | Central bank | Move deposits from central bank to FI | Increase deposits of FIs |
| Cash deposit | Nonbank public | Deposit cash at ATM | Increases deposits of FIs |

Note: All these transactions could be done in reverse to decrease deposits of FIs.

## APPLYING THE CONCEPT
### THE FED'S RESPONSE ON SEPTEMBER 11, 2001

On a normal day, U.S. banks have $40 billion worth of cash in their vaults and $10 billion in reserve deposits at Federal Reserve Banks. Their discount loan balance is virtually zero. And on a normal day, the Federal Reserve Bank of New York's trading desk buys $3 billion to $5 billion worth of bonds in temporary open market operations but does not intervene in the foreign exchange markets.

The days following September 11, 2001, were not normal. On the morning of September 11, 2001, four hijacked planes crashed: two into the World Trade Center Towers in New York City; one into the Pentagon in Washington, D.C.; and one into a field in western Pennsylvania. Thousands of people died, and the world changed. The disruptions were enormous. All nonmilitary aircraft in the United States were immediately grounded and U.S. airspace was closed. In the Wall Street area, power and communications networks were shut down, closing the financial markets. Airplanes were grounded, and the Wall Street area in lower Manhattan became inaccessible. The fact that civilian planes couldn't fly had important implications for the way in which paper cheques were handled. As the first step in clearing a paper cheque, the Fed credits the reserve account of the bank that presents it by the amount written on the cheque. If the bank on which the cheque is drawn (the one whose account is to be debited) is located in a different Federal Reserve District from the bank that presented the cheque (whose account has been credited), then the cheque must be physically transported to the paying bank's district before that bank's reserve account is debited. Since the credit occurs first, the process creates something called *float*. By Thursday, September 13, float had exploded, rising from its usual level of about $500 million to a whopping $50 billion.

Meanwhile, people's inability to reach their offices in downtown New York had closed some very large banks. Though those banks could still receive payments from other banks, they couldn't make any payments to anyone. Funds were flowing into a few huge reserve accounts, but nothing was coming out. These banks were sucking up the lifeblood of the financial system, its liquidity.

Fed officials saw the looming crisis and reacted immediately, providing reserves to anyone who needed them. Most of us never realized how close we came to catastrophe. A group of about 20 Fed employees slept in the Fed's building the night of September 11 so they could carry out open market operations the next morning. Then they moved to a contingency site across the Hudson River to continue their work. On Thursday, September 13, and Friday, September 14, the Fed increased its securities holdings by between $70 and $80 billion, made $8 billion in discount loans, and bought almost $20 billion worth of euros. Adding these transactions to the nearly $50 billion in float, we see that over a two-day period the Fed increased banking system reserves by almost $150 billion.[*] This massive injection of reserves was quickly drained over the next week as the system got back to normal. The banking system withstood the enormous shock, meeting its commitments and leaving people's finances more or less unaffected. This was one of the great successes of modern central banking. In extraordinary circumstances, quick action by the Fed kept the financial markets afloat. While some institutions and individuals will never recover from the terrorist attacks, the financial system—one of the terrorists' primary targets—returned to near normal within weeks.

This is all described in detail in the Federal Reserve Bank of New York's annual report of Open Market Operations for 2001, available on the Bank's Web site at http://www.newyorkfed.org/markets/omo/omo2001.pdf.

# The Operation of Monetary Policy

Now that we have learnt about the structure of central banks we can return to the core question: How does the central bank implement monetary policy? (In the next chapter we turn to the question of how it determines what monetary policy to implement.) Each central bank has its own operating framework and we will discuss the Canadian system in detail while presenting that of the ECB and the Fed in less detail as a point of comparison. As before, we will focus on the Bank of Canada's operating framework during "normal'" times and leave to Chapter 23 a discussion of the Bank's operating framework during crisis times.

## The Bank of Canada's Operational Framework

The Bank of Canada implements monetary policy by setting a target overnight rate and then making sure that the overnight rate is at or close to its target. Eight times a year the Governing Council of the Bank of Canada meets and decides on the target for the overnight rate. The overnight rate is the rate at which financial institutions borrow and lend to each other overnight, i.e., very short term, well-collateralized loans.[6] The Bank of Canada has a variety of tools that can ensure that the overnight rate is at its target. First, the Bank sets what it calls "the operating band." The band is 50 basis points (50 bps) wide. The top of the band is the **Bank rate**—the rate at which the central bank will lend to an eligible CPA member; the bottom of the band is the rate at which the Bank will pay interest on deposits. The mid-point of the band is the "target for the overnight rate." This structure ensures that the overnight rate will never exceed the Bank rate (as the Bank is willing to lend at that rate, why pay more?) and that the overnight rate will never fall below the bottom of the operating band—if the Bank of Canada pays interest at that rate, no institution would lend money for less (see Figure 17.6).

**Figure 17.6**   **Bank of Canada Operating Framework**

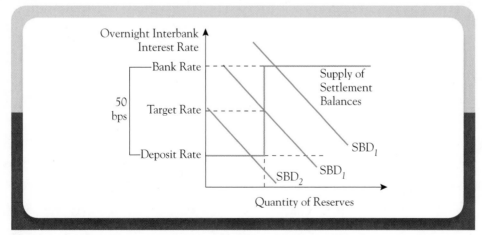

The Bank of Canada targets an overnight rate. The Bank rate (at which CPA members can borrow) is 25 bps higher than the target overnight rate and the Deposit rate is 25 bps lower.

SOURCE: *Bank of Canada*.

[6] For further details see, Walter Engert, Toni Gravelle, and Donna Howard, "The Implementation of Monetary Policy in Canada," Bank of Canada Discussion Paper 2008–9.

# TOOLS OF THE TRADE
## Clearing and Settling

The clearing and settlement system refers to the process where cheques (or electronic transfers) deposited in one bank generate a payment of funds into that account from the account on which the cheque is drawn. "Clearing" refers to the transfer of the actual cheque while "settlement" refers to the transfer of the funds. While somewhat arcane, the clearing and settlement system is the lynchpin of the payments system. In many countries the clearing house is owned and operated by the central bank, but in Canada the Canadian Payments Association (CPA) owns and operates the payments system, although settlement occurs on the books of the Bank of Canada. Consider how this system would work in a simple example with three banks, the Royal Bank, Scotiabank, and TD Canada Trust.

Table 17.3 shows the balances owing at the end of a trading day. The Royal Bank owes the other two banks $18 million. This means (for example) that the other two banks brought in cheques totalling $18 million that their clients had deposited drawn on the Royal Bank. But the Royal Bank brought in cheques drawn on the other two banks that totaled $20 million. So the net difference is that the Royal Bank will on balance receive $2 million. By the same logic, TD Canada Trust owes $35 million and is owed $22 million, for a negative net balance of $13 million.

Scotiabank also owes less than it is owed, by $11 million. Notice that by construction the net balances have to add up to zero. We can see that more clearly in Table 17.3 Panel B.

At the end of the day (literally!) TD has to find $13 million to pay to the other two banks, and there are three ways that it could do so:

1. If TD has funds in its deposit account at the Bank of Canada, it could transfer those balances.

2. It could borrow the funds from the Bank of Canada, which would put the balances into TD's account and then TD could make its payments.

3. It could borrow funds—possibly from Scotiabank and Royal Bank.

Before we analyze which of these options TD will use, notice that under options 1 and 2 the other banks will carry positive balances overnight in their accounts at the Bank of Canada. The choice between the three options will mostly depend on prices. How much would a loan from the Bank of Canada cost? How much would the other banks charge for a loan? How much would the Bank of Canada pay in interest on deposits accounts?

## Table 17.3 Example of Clearing and Settlement

### PANEL A: Gross Balances

|  | Royal Bank is owed | TD Canada Trust is owed | Scotiabank is owed | Total |
|---|---|---|---|---|
| Royal owes | N/A | $12 | $6 | $18 |
| TD Canada Trust owes | $15 | N/A | $20 | $35 |
| Scotiabank owes | $5 | $10 | N/A | $15 |
|  | $20 | $22 | $26 | $68 |

### PANEL B: net balances

|  | Royal Bank | TD Canada Trust | Scotiabank | Total |
|---|---|---|---|---|
| Royal receives | N/A | $3 | −1 | 2 |
| TD Canada Trust receives | −3 | N/A | −$10 | −$13 |
| Scotiabank receives | +$1 | +$10 | N/A | $11 |

\* A negative amount means that the bank pays.

| Figure 17.7 | The Target Overnight Rate and Daily Market Rate, January 1995–July 2008. |

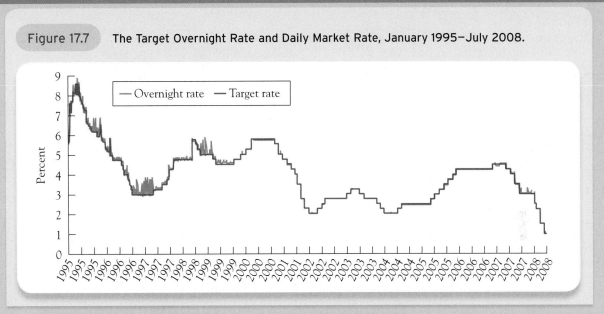

SOURCE: *Bank of Canada. Overnight rate v39050; Target for overnight rate v39079; both from Table 176-0048.*

And this is where monetary policy comes in. As described in the text, the Bank of Canada sets the "Bank rate"—the rate at which the central bank will lend to a financial institution—and the deposit rate—the rate at which the Bank will pay interest on reserves. The banks have half an hour to trade between each other at the end of the day and most likely they will come to an agreement that Scotiabank and Royal Bank will lend balances to TD, at a rate between the top and bottom of the range.

But the Bank doesn't just want the overnight rate to be within the operating band, it wants the overnight rate to be at the mid-point. Financial institutions use the overnight market extensively for very short term loans and the Bank of Canada can see on any morning if the rate is moving above or below the target. Suppose that the overnight rate was higher than the target. The Bank of Canada would offer to lend funds at the target rate, which would lower the overnight rate. In practice the Bank uses repos or "SPRAs" to do this (see Chapter 12 for a description of repos). This move has two effects: it brings down the overnight rate and it injects funds into the system. If the payments system was balanced initially (as in Table 17.3), then the Bank has to withdraw these funds if it wants the net supply of settlement balances to be zero. This is called neutralizing the repo, and it is done by removing some of the government of Canada's funds from an account at a commercial bank and depositing them into the government's account at the Bank of Canada.[7]

The Bank defines its facility for lending to financial institutions at the Bank rate as Standing Liquidity Facilities (SLF), in distinction to Emergency Lending Assistance (ELA). The SLF are meant to be used routinely by direct clearers that are not in financial difficulties and need an overnight loan because of a surprise at the clearings, for example. The ELA facility is for institutions that are not as robust financially and is often for longer than an overnight term. This is the facility that we discussed under "lender of last resort" in Chapter 14.

[7] If the overnight rate was too low, then the opposite operations would be conducted with a Sale and Prepurchase Agreement (SRA) more commonly known as a "reverse" used to raise the overnight rate. Again, the Bank would likely neutralize the operation by shifting funds from the Government of Canada account at the Bank of Canada and putting them into commercial banks.

## YOUR FINANCIAL WORLD
What the Target Overnight Rate Means to You

On learning that the Bank of Canada controls the overnight rate, most people's reaction is, "I'm not a bank and I don't borrow overnight, so why should I care?" What they do care about is the interest rate they pay on student loans, or auto loans, or home mortgages. But since all interest rates move together, people who care about long-term interest rates must care about short-term interest rates.

Remember from our discussion of the term structure of interest rates in Chapter 7 that the long-term interest rate is the average of expected future short-term interest rates. Thus, the rate charged on a five-year, fixed-rate home mortgage is the average of the expected one-year rates for the next five years. Those one-year interest rates, in turn, are averages of the expected one-day interest rates for the next 365 days. Unless everyone expects the Bank of Canada to keep interest rates at the same level for a very long time, the interest rates you care about will move—by less than the target federal funds rate, but they will move.

To see how important this is, we can look at the example of a five-year fixed rate mortgage. In September 2005, with the Bank's target for the overnight rate at 2.75 percent, the interest rate on a five-year, fixed-rate mortgage was 5.8 percent, and the monthly payment on a $200,000 loan was roughly $1,250. By July 2006, the Bank of Canada had raised the overnight rate target to 4.25 percent, and the mortgage interest rate had risen to 6.95 percent. At the higher interest rate, the monthly payment on a $200,000 mortgage was something like $1400—more than $150 a month higher!

The Bank of Canada's operational framework has been remarkably successful. Figure 17-7 on page 383 shows that the overnight rate remained very close to the target. Furthermore, this happened with very limited use of repos; between January 1999 and January 2008 the Bank performed SPRA/SRA operations on average fewer than 30 days per year.[8]

[8] For further details see, Walter Engert, Toni Gravelle, and Donna Howard, "The Implementation of Monetary Policy in Canada," Bank of Canada Discussion Paper 2008–9.

## The Federal Reserve's Operational Framework

The primary monetary policy tool of the Federal Reserve is the target federal funds rate, the interest rate at which banks make overnight loans to each other. Federal funds are funds that a commercial bank has in its deposit account at the Fed. These loans are very similar to the overnight loans among the Canadian financial institutions except that these are uncollateralized. If the bank were to fail, the lender would not have recourse.

Financial market participants are constantly speculating about movements in the target federal funds rate. FOMC meetings always end with a decision on the target level, and the statement released after the meeting begins with an announcement of that decision. To a large extent, this is U.S. monetary policy. But because the federal funds rate is the rate at which banks lend reserves to each other overnight, it is determined in the market, not controlled by the Fed. With this qualification in mind, we will distinguish between the target federal funds rate set by the FOMC and the market federal funds rate, at which transactions between banks take place.

The term "federal funds" comes from the fact that the funds that banks lend are their deposit balances at Federal Reserve Banks. On any given day, banks target the level of reserves they would like to hold at the close of business. But as the day goes by, the normal flow of business may leave them with more or fewer reserves than they want to hold. This discrepancy between actual and desired reserves gives rise to a market for reserves, with some banks lending out their excess funds and others borrowing to cover a shortfall. Without this market, banks would need to hold substantial quantities of excess reserves as insurance against shortfalls. While transactions are often made through brokers (third parties who bring buyers and sellers together), they

Figure 17.8    Target Federal Funds Rate and the Daily Market Rate, January 1992–July 2006.

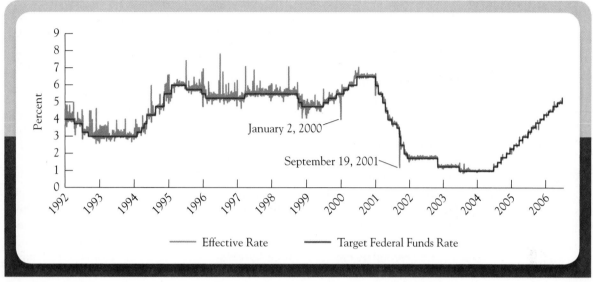

SOURCE: *Board of Governors of the Federal Reserve.*

are all bilateral agreements between two banks. Since the loans are unsecured—there is no collateral to fall back on in the event of nonpayment—the borrowing bank must be creditworthy in the eyes of the lending bank, or the loan cannot be made.

If the Fed wanted to, it could force the market federal funds rate to equal the target rate all the time by participating directly in the market for overnight reserves. Instead, the Fed chooses to control the federal funds rate by manipulating the quantity of reserves. Using *open market operations,* the Fed adjusts the supply of reserves, with the goal of keeping the market federal funds rate close to the target rate. That is, the Fed buys or sells securities to add or drain reserves as required to meet the expected demand for reserves at the target rate.

Let's take a moment to compare the FOMC's target rate with the market rate over the last few years, to see how well the Fed's staff has met its objective. Figure 17.8 plots both the target federal funds rate (the dark line that moves stepwise) and the market federal funds rate (the lighter line that jumps around) beginning in 1992. As you can see, the market interest rate was close to the target on most days. Every so often, though, the system seemed to go haywire, creating occasional spikes in the market interest rate. Changes in the reserve accounting rules in 1998 combined with improvements in information systems, both within banks and at the Fed, mean that there are now fewer surprises. Changes that were made to the discount-lending program in 2002 appear to have stabilized the market rate even further. As a result, the daily deviations from the target rate are now very small.

Just as the Bank of Canada distinguishes between Standing Liquidity Facilities and Emergency Lending Assistance, the Federal Reserve distinguishes between primary and secondary credit.

**Primary credit** is extended on a very short-term basis, usually overnight, to institutions that the Fed's bank supervisors deem to be sound. Banks seeking to borrow must post acceptable collateral to back the loan. The interest rate on primary credit is 100 basis points *above* the federal funds target rate. This is called the primary discount rate.

The term "discount rate" usually refers to this primary discount rate. As long as a bank qualifies and is willing to pay the penalty interest rate, it can get the loan. Primary credit is designed to provide additional reserves at times when the open market staff's forecasts are off and so the day's reserve supply falls short of the banking system's demand. In that case, the market federal funds rate will rise above the FOMC's target. Providing a facility through which banks can borrow at a penalty rate 100 bps above the target puts a cap on the market federal funds rate. Banks will go to the discount window and borrow reserves from the Fed rather than go into the federal fund market and pay a rate above the primary discount rate. So the system is designed both to provide liquidity in times of crisis, ensuring financial stability, and to keep reserve shortages from causing spikes in the market federal funds rate. By restricting the range over which the market federal funds rate can move, this system helps to maintain interest-rate stability.

Secondary credit is for banks that are experiencing longer-term problems that they need some time to work out. There are times when banks have serious financial difficulty that they can resolve without failing. A bank that takes a large loss from poor lending decisions will become undercapitalized, but it may be able to raise funds to continue operating if it is given enough time. Such a bank has nothing to lose by requesting secondary credit. Without it, it will fail anyway. But before the Fed makes the loan, it has to believe there is a good chance the bank will be able to survive. You can see why secondary credit is rare.

The Federal Reserve requires that member banks keep balances at the Fed. Historically, such required reserves were thought to ensure that banks were sound but the introduction of deposit insurance reduced that use. Later it was thought that the ability to change the reserve requirement would give central banks a necessary tool of monetary policy but the experience of Canada (and many other central banks) has shown that other tools give greater precision. In practice, the reserve requirements in the United States are sufficiently low that they have little impact and the Fed does not use them for monetary control. Table 17.4 summarizes the monetary policy tools of the Fed.

**Table 17.4**  The Tools of U.S. Monetary Policy

|  | What Is It? | How Is It Controlled? | What Is Its Impact? |
|---|---|---|---|
| Target Federal Funds Rate | Interest rate charged on overnight loans between banks | Supply of reserves adjusted through open market operations to meet expected demand at the target rate | Changes interest rates throughout the economy |
| Discount Rate | Interest rate charged by the Federal Reserve on loans to commercial banks | Set as a premium over the target federal funds rate | Provides short-term liquidity to banks in times of crisis and aids in controlling the federal funds rate |
| Reserve Requirement | Fraction of deposits that banks must keep either on deposit at the Federal Reserve or as cash in their vaults | Set by the Federal Reserve Board within a legally imposed range | Stabilizes the demand for reserves |

The target federal funds rate is the Federal Open Market Committee's primary policy instrument. Financial market participants are constantly speculating about movements in this rate. FOMC meetings always end with a decision on the target level, and the statement released after the meeting begins with an announcement of that decision. To a large extent, this *is* U.S. monetary policy. But because the federal funds rate is the rate at which banks lend reserves to each other overnight, it is determined in the market, not controlled by the Fed. With this qualification in mind, we will distinguish between the *target* federal funds rate set by the FOMC and the market federal funds rate, at which transactions between banks take place.

The name "federal funds" comes from the fact that the funds banks trade are their deposit balances at Federal Reserve Banks. On any given day, banks target the level of reserves they would like to hold at the close of business. But as the day goes by, the normal flow of business may leave them with more or less reserves than they want to hold. This discrepancy between actual and desired reserves gives rise to a market for reserves, with some banks lending out their excess funds and others borrowing to cover a shortfall. Without this market, banks would need to hold substantial quantities of excess reserves as insurance against shortfalls. While transactions are often made through brokers (third parties who bring buyers and sellers together), they are all bilateral agreements between two banks. Since the loans are unsecured—there is no collateral to fall back on in the event of nonpayment—the borrowing bank must be creditworthy in the eyes of the lending bank, or the loan cannot be made.

## The European Central Bank's Operational Framework

Like the Federal Reserve's, the ECB's monetary policy toolbox contains an overnight interbank rate, the rate at which the central bank lends to commercial banks, and a reserve requirement. Since the ECB pays interest on reserve deposits, there is also a reserve deposit rate.

While the ECB occasionally engages in outright purchases of securities, it provides reserves to the European banking system primarily through what are called refinancing operations. The main refinancing operation is a weekly auction of two-week repurchase agreements in which the ECB, through the national central banks, provides reserves to banks in exchange for securities and then reverses the transaction two weeks later. The policy instrument of the ECB's governing council is the minimum interest rate allowed at these refinancing auctions, which is called the main refinancing operations' minimum bid rate. This is the European equivalent of the Bank of Canada's target overnight rate, so we will refer to it as the target refinancing rate. The main refinancing operations provide banks with virtually all their reserves and account for 40 percent of the ECB's balance sheet.

The ECB's Marginal Lending Facility is the analogue to the Bank of Canada's Standing Liquidity Facilities. Through this facility, the ECB provides overnight loans to banks at a rate that is normally well *above* the target-refinancing rate. The spread between the marginal lending rate and the target refinancing rate is set by the governing council and is currently 100 bps. Commercial banks initiate these borrowing transactions when they face a reserve deficiency that they cannot satisfy more cheaply in the marketplace. Banks do borrow regularly, and on occasion the amounts they borrow are large.

Banks with excess reserves at the end of the day can deposit them overnight in the ECB's Deposit Facility at an interest rate substantially below the target-refinancing rate. Again, the spread is determined by the governing council and is currently 100 bps. While they are usually small, these deposits can be substantial, since they include all the excess reserves in the Eurosystem's banks. But, as in Canada, the existence of

| Figure 17.9 | Euro-Area Overnight Cash Rate and ECB Interest Rates, January 1999–July 2006 |

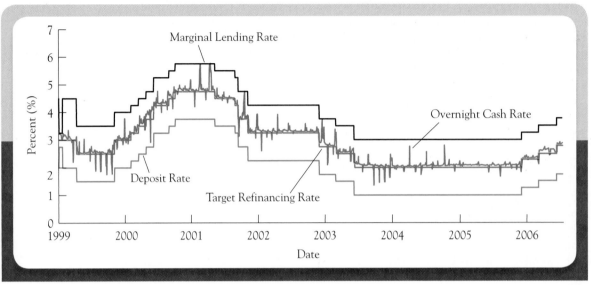

SOURCE: *European Central Bank.*

the deposit facility places a floor on the interest rate that can be charged on reserves. Because a bank can always deposit its excess reserves in the deposit facility at a rate 100 bps below the target refinancing rate, it will never make a loan at a lower rate.

The ECB requires that banks hold minimum reserve levels based on the level of liabilities they hold. The reserve requirement of 2 percent is applied to chequing accounts and some other short-term deposits. Deposit levels are averaged over a month, and reserve levels must be held over the following month. Because the ECB pays interest on reserves, the cost of meeting the reserve requirement is relatively low, and banks do not go out of their way to escape it.

The European system is designed to give the ECB tight control over the short-term money market in the euro area. And it works. Figure 17.9 shows the target refinancing rate, which is the minimum bid rate in the weekly auctions, as the heavy line running through the centre of the graph, with the marginal lending rate 100 bps above and the deposit rate 100 bps below. The **overnight cash rate** is the European analogue to the market federal funds rate, the rate banks charge each other for overnight loans. As you can see, this rate fluctuates quite a bit, but it always remains inside the 200-bps band—the target refinancing rate plus or minus 100 bps.

## Linking Tools to Objectives: Making Choices

Monetary policymakers use the various tools they have to meet the objectives society gives them. Their goals—low and stable inflation, high and stable growth, a stable financial system, stable interest, and exchange rates—are (or should be) given to them by their elected officials. But day-to-day policy is left to the technicians, who must then decide which tools are the best for the job.

Over the years, a consensus has developed among monetary policy experts, both inside and outside central banks, that (1) the reserve requirement is not useful as an operational instrument; (2) central bank lending is necessary to ensure financial stability; and (3) short-term interest rates are the tool to stabilize short-term fluctuations in prices and output. The logic of this conclusion is straightforward. To follow it, let's start by listing the features that distinguish good policy instruments from bad ones.

## Desirable Features of a Policy Instrument

A good monetary policy instrument has three features:

1. It is easily *observable* by everyone.
2. It is *controllable* and quickly changed.
3. It is tightly *linked* to the policymakers' objectives.

These features seem obvious. After all, a policy tool wouldn't be very useful if you couldn't observe it, control it, or predict its impact on your objectives. But beyond the obvious, it is important that a policy instrument be easily observable to ensure transparency in policymaking, which enhances accountability. Controllability is important in both the short term and the long term. An instrument that can be adjusted quickly in the face of a sudden change in economic conditions is clearly more useful than one that takes time to adjust. And the more predictable the impact of an instrument, the easier it will be for policymakers to meet their objectives.

Requiring that a monetary policy instrument be observable and controllable leaves us with only a few options from which to choose. The reserve requirement won't work. Since banks cannot adjust their balance sheets quickly, changes need to be announced some time in advance. Then there are the components of the central bank's balance sheet: commercial bank reserves, the monetary base, loans, and foreign exchange reserves—as well as their prices, various interest rates, and the exchange rate. (Exchange rate policy is discussed in Chapter 22.) But how do we choose between controlling quantities and controlling prices? Over the years, central banks have switched from one to the other. From 1975 to 1982 the Bank of Canada targeted the growth rate of M1. Similarly, from 1979 to 1982, the Fed did try targeting bank reserves. In both cases the goal was to reduce the inflation rate from double-digit levels. Inflation fell quickly, so in a sense the policies were a success. But one side effect of choosing to control reserves was that interest rates became highly variable, rising from 14 percent to over 20 percent and then falling to less than 9 percent, all in a period of less than six months.

The consensus today is that the Fed's strategy of targeting reserves rather than interest rates in the period from 1979 to 1982 was a way of driving interest rates to levels that would not have been politically acceptable had they been announced as targets. Even in an environment of double-digit inflation rates, the FOMC could not explicitly raise the target federal funds rate to 20 percent. By saying they were targeting the quantity of reserves, the committee members escaped responsibility for the high interest rates. When inflation had fallen and interest rates came back down, the FOMC reverted to targeting the federal funds rate. And that is what it has done ever since.

Appearances and politics aside, there is a very good reason the vast majority of central banks in the world today choose to target an interest rate rather than some quantity on their balance sheet. For example, consider a system with reserve requirements and reserve targets. With reserve supply fixed, a shift in reserve demand changes the short-term interest rate. When reserve demand increases, the overnight rate will go up and when reserve demand falls, the overnight rate will go down. If the central bank chooses to target the quantity of reserves, it gives up control of the overnight rate. Figure 17.10 on page 390 shows what happens: As reserve demand increases and falls, the market interest rate fluctuates over a range that is determined by the intersection of supply and demand.

Figure 17.10 **The Market for Bank Reserves When the Central Bank Targets the Quantity of Reserves**

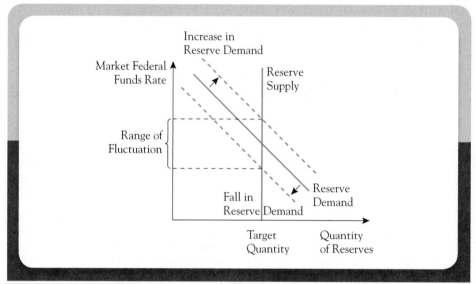

When the central bank targets the quantity of reserves, a shift in reserve demand causes the overnight rate to move. An increase in reserve demand forces the interest rate up, while a fall in reserve demand forces the interest rate down.

From the discussion in Chapter 15, we can infer that in order to meet their objectives, central bankers will tend to adopt operating procedures that keep interest rates from becoming volatile. Interest rates are the primary linkage between the financial system and the real economy, so stabilizing growth means keeping interest rates from being overly volatile. In the context of choosing an operating target, that means keeping unpredictable changes in reserve demand from influencing interest rates and feeding into the real economy. The best way to do this is to target interest rates.

## Operating Instruments and Intermediate Targets

Before continuing, we should pause to consider some terms and concepts that often crop up in discussions of central banking. Central bankers sometimes use the terms "operating instrument" and "intermediate target." Operating instruments refer to actual tools of policy. These are instruments that the central bank controls directly. Every central bank can control the size of its balance sheet, for instance. It can choose to use this power to control the monetary base if it wishes, or to control the interest rate in the market for reserves, as the FOMC does. These are the operating instruments.

Central bankers use the term intermediate targets to refer to instruments that are not directly under their control but lie instead somewhere between their policymaking tools and their objectives (see Figure 17.11). The monetary aggregates are a prime example of intermediate targets. The idea behind targeting M1, for example, is that changes in the monetary base, or reserves, affect the monetary aggregates before they influence inflation or output. So in targeting M1, central bankers can more effectively meet their objectives. They don't actually care about money growth itself, in other words; it is just a useful indicator. And announcing targets for money growth that can be monitored by the public increases policymakers' accountability.

## APPLYING THE CONCEPT
### INFLATION TARGETING

If you can focus central bankers' attention clearly on a well-articulated objective, you will get better policy. The problem is how to do it. During the 1990s, a number of countries including Canada adopted a policy framework called inflation targeting in an effort to improve monetary policy performance. And it seems to have worked. Countries that embraced inflation targeting achieved both lower inflation and higher real growth.

Inflation targeting bypasses intermediate targets and focuses directly on the objective of low inflation. It is a monetary policy strategy that involves the public announcement of a numerical inflation target, together with a commitment to make price stability the central bank's primary objective to which all other objectives are subordinated. This approach creates an environment in which everyone believes policymakers will keep the inflation rate low, so long-term expectations of inflation remain low, anchoring long-term interest rates and promoting growth. As we saw in Chapter 15, one of the keys to any successful central bank policy is for policymakers to convince the public that they will keep inflation low. Their commitment must be credible. Inflation targeting is designed to convince people that monetary policy will deliver low inflation.

Central banks that employ inflation targeting operate under what has been described as a *hierarchical mandate,* in which inflation comes first and everything else comes second. Canada, the United Kingdom, Australia, Chile, and South Africa are among the roughly two dozen countries that target inflation. Most observers put the ECB in the group as well. This approach contrasts with the Federal Reserve's *dual mandate,* in which inflation and growth are on an equal footing. Because of this dual mandate, the Fed has shied away from adopting inflation targeting.

By focusing on a clearly defined and easily observable numerical inflation statistic and requiring frequent communication with the public, inflation targeting increases policymakers' accountability and helps to establish their credibility. Not only do central bankers know what they are supposed to do, but everyone else does, too. The result is not just lower and more stable inflation but higher and more stable growth as well.

Over the last two decades of the 20th century, central bankers largely abandoned intermediate targets, having realized that they didn't make much sense. There may be something special about monetary aggregates, and it may be particularly helpful in forecasting future economic developments and in guiding policy. But then again, it may not be helpful. More importantly, circumstances may change in ways that make an intermediate target unworkable. Link #1, between the operating instruments and the intermediate target, may shift or link #2, between money growth and the final inflation and growth objectives, may change (we will discuss these problems in Chapter 21). If either of these happened, the central bank would need to explain why it was changing its target and it would look as if policymakers don't know what they are doing. So instead, policymakers focus on how their actions directly affect their target objectives—link #3, for example, by practising *inflation targeting,* which is discussed in Applying the Concept: Inflation Targeting.

### Figure 17.11    Instruments, Targets, and Objectives

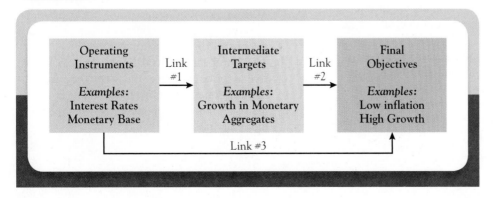

## Terms

Advances to members of the Canadian Payments Association, 378
bank rate, 381
central bank's balance sheet, 371
discount loans, 378
discount rate, 386
ECB's Marginal Lending Facility, 387
Emergency Lending Assistance (ELA), 383
foreign exchange intervention, 372
foreign exchange reserves, 372
high-powered money, 375
inflation targeting, 391
intermediate targets, 390

lender of last resort, 383
market federal funds rate, 387
minimum bid rate, 387
monetary base, 375
open market operations, 376
open market purchase, 376
open market sale, 377
overnight cash rate, 388
overnight rate, 370
primary credit, 385
primary discount rate, 385
required reserves, 374
reserves, 374
Standing Liquidity Facilities (SLF), 378
T-account, 376
target federal funds rate, 384
target overnight rate, 370
vault cash, 386

## Chapter Summary

1. The central bank uses its balance sheet to control the quantity of money and credit in the economy.
   a. The central bank holds assets and liabilities to meet its responsibilities as the government's bank and the bankers' bank.
   b. Central bank assets can include securities, foreign exchange reserves, and loans.
   c. Central bank liabilities include currency, the government's account, and deposits of financial institutions.
   d. Reserves equal commercial bank account balances at the central bank plus vault cash.
   e. The monetary base, also called high-powered money, is the sum of currency and reserves, the two primary liabilities of a central bank.

2. The central bank controls the size of its balance sheet.
   a. The central bank can increase the size of its balance sheet, raising reserve liabilities and expanding the monetary base, through
      i. Open market purchases of domestic securities.
      ii. The purchase of foreign exchange reserves (in the form of bonds issued by a foreign government).
      iii. The extension of a loan to a commercial bank.
   b. The central bank can decrease the size of its balance sheet, lowering reserve liabilities and reducing the monetary base, through the sale of domestic or foreign securities.
   c. The public's cash withdrawals from banks shift the central bank's liabilities from reserves to currency and shrink the size of the banking system balance sheet.

3. The Bank of Canada sets the operating range, which includes
   a. The target for the overnight rate.
   b. The Bank rate, 25 bps above the overnight rate.
   c. The interest rate on deposits of financial institutions at the Bank of Canada, 25 bps below the target for the overnight rate.

4. The Bank of Canada ensures that the overnight rate stays close to its target
   a. Because the direct clearers in the Canadian Payments Association settle their balances on the books of the Bank of Canada.
   b. By using open market operations (SPRAs) and movements of government deposits between the Bank of Canada and the financial institutions.

5. Other central banks operate in a similar but not identical fashion:
   a. The target federal funds rate is the primary instrument of monetary policy for the Federal Reserve, which uses open market operations to control the federal funds rate.
   b. The European Central Bank's primary objective is price stability and it targets the refinancing rate (the minimum bid rate on the main refinancing operations) to implement monetary policy.

c. Unlike the Bank of Canada, both the Fed and the ECB have required reserves but these are not used very often for monetary policy implementation.

6. Central banks have routine lending facilities (Standing Liquidity Facilities in Canada) and emergency lending facilities (Emergency Lending Assistance in Canada).

7. Monetary policymakers use several tools to meet their objectives.
   a. The best tools are observable, controllable, and tightly linked to objectives.
   b. Short-term interest rates are the best tools for monetary policymaking.
   c. Modern central banks do not use intermediate targets such as money growth.

## Conceptual Problems

1. Follow the impact of a $100 cash withdrawal through the entire banking system, showing the impact on both a chartered bank and the Bank of Canada.

2. Suppose your friend with a bank account at CIBC paid a debt to you with a cheque for $250. Explain the cash flows and settlement that would result if you deposited this cheque at your branch of TD Canada Trust.

3.* Using material on the Web site of the Bank of Canada, explain how your answer to question 2 would be different if you banked at a credit union that was an indirect clearer in the CPA.

4.* Why is currency circulating in the hands of the nonbank public considered a liability of the central bank?

5. Economists believe that central banks should be as transparent as possible, allowing the public to accurately forecast changes in interest policy. Explain the justification for this belief. What would happen if policymakers constantly surprised the public?

6. The federal government maintains accounts at commercial banks. What would be the consequences if the government shifted funds from one of those banks to the Bank of Canada?

7. In an effort to diversify, the Central Bank of China has decided to exchange some of its dollar reserves for euros. Follow the impact of this move on the U.S. banking system's balance sheet, the Federal Reserve's balance sheet, and the European Central Bank's balance sheet. What is the impact on the U.S. and Chinese monetary bases?

8. Suppose the Bank of Canada buys $1 billion in government bonds. What is the impact on the monetary base? What could the Bank of Canada do to keep the monetary base from changing following the purchase?

9. The Bank of Canada pays a market-based interest rate on required reserves and a lower rate on excess reserves. Explain why the system is structured this way.

10.* Explain why central banks use an overnight interest rate rather than a longer-term interest rate as their policy tool.

## Analytical Problems

11. Suppose that the economists on the Bank of Canada's trading desk noticed that the overnight rate was below the target the Bank had set. How would they respond?

12. Continuing question 11, if the traders were then asked to neutralize the impact of their work on the monetary base, how could they do so?

13.* Explain the factors that could cause the overnight rate to deviate from the target overnight rate. Why has this gap changed over time? What factors might make this gap larger in the United States or Eurosystem?

14.* In carrying out open market operations, the Bank of Canada buys and sells federal government securities. Suppose the Canadian government paid off all its debt. Could the Bank of Canada continue to carry out open market operations?

* Indicates more difficult problems.

15. Suppose you observe a rise of $100 million in reserves on the liability side of the central bank's balance sheet with all other liabilities remaining unchanged. On the asset side, the entries under "securities" and "loans" remained unchanged. What might have accounted for the change in reserves and how would this action be reflected on the central bank's balance sheet?

16. In which of the following cases will the size of the central bank's balance sheet change?
    a. The Bank of Canada conducts an open market purchase of $100 million government securities.
    b. A commercial bank borrows $100 million from the Bank of Canada.
    c. The amount of cash in the vaults of commercial banks falls by $100 million due to withdrawals by the public.

17. You are an economic adviser to a country whose central bank has recently been granted the power to conduct monetary policy. The central bank is considering increasing reserve requirements in an effort to ensure the stability of the banking system and seeks your advice. What factors would you recommend the central bank take into account when trying to predict the impact of such a policy?

18.* You pick up the morning newspaper and note a headline reporting a major scandal about the Canada Deposit Insurance Corporation that is likely to undermine the public's confidence in the banking system. What impact, if any, do you think this scandal might have on the relationship between the monetary base and the money supply?

# CHAPTER 18

## Output, Inflation, and Monetary Policy

Governments publish economic data constantly. Almost every day we receive new information on some aspect of the economy, with news stories quoting experts on what it all means. Is inflation on the way up? Is the economy on the verge of recession? An important part of such analyses is speculation about the impact of the new data on monetary policy. In our discussion of central banking, we noted that conjectures about policymakers' likely reaction fills the financial news. And no wonder, since members of the committees that set interest rates—the governing council at the Bank of Canada and the FOMC in the United States—always tie their policy actions to current and expected future economic conditions.

Needless to say, everyone is preoccupied with monetary policy. While traders in the financial markets are trying to outguess each other, to make a profit by betting on the next move in interest rates, the rest of us are just hoping the central bank will succeed in keeping inflation low and real growth high. How do policymakers do it? What is the mechanism through which changes in the interest rate influence inflation and output? And what are the limits of policymakers' power to control the economy?

As we will see in Chapter 20, in the long run, inflation is tied to money growth. Over periods of several decades, high money growth leads to high inflation. Furthermore, long-run growth depends on technology, the size of the capital stock, and the number of people who can work. But over shorter periods of months or years, changes in the rate of money growth tell us little about future movements in the inflation rate. That is especially true when inflation is low, as it has been throughout much of the industrialized world over the past decade or two.

The objective of this chapter is to understand fluctuations in inflation and real output, and how central banks use interest-rate policy to stabilize them during the "normal" times when the economy is suffering neither a financial crisis nor a hyperinflation. To do it, we will develop a macroeconomic model of fluctuations in the business cycle in which monetary policy plays a central role. From this, we will see that short-run movements in inflation and output can arise from two sources: shifts in the quantity of aggregate output demanded (that is, changes in consumption, investment, government spending, or net exports) and shifts in the quantity of aggregate output supplied (that is, changes in the costs of production). Modern monetary policymakers work to eliminate the volatility that each of these creates by adjusting the target interest rate.

We will develop our macroeconomic model in three steps, beginning with a description of long-run equilibrium. We then move on to derive the *dynamic aggregate demand curve*, which shows the quantity of real output demanded by those people who use it at each level of inflation; that is, how real output is related to changes in the prices, not just their level. Here we will see the critical role of monetary policy. Finally, we introduce aggregate supply, which is the level of real output supplied by firms at each level of inflation. There is both a short-run and a long-run version of the aggregate supply curve. In the short run, equating dynamic aggregate demand with short-run aggregate supply gives us the equilibrium levels of output and inflation. Business cycles are movements in this short-run equilibrium. And because we have built monetary policy into the model, we will see how modern central banks can use their policy tools to stabilize short-run fluctuations in output and inflation.

As we proceed through the chapter, keep in mind that our ultimate objective is to understand how modern central bankers set interest rates. When policymakers change the target interest rate, what are they reacting to, and what is the impact on the economy?

# Output and Inflation in the Long Run

The best way to understand fluctuations in the business cycle is as deviations from some benchmark or long-run equilibrium level. The booms and recessions that make up business cycles are temporary movements away from this long-run equilibrium level. So we begin with the following question: What would the levels of inflation and output be if nothing unexpected happened for a long time? The answer to this question is that in the long run, current output equals potential output—full-employment output—and the inflation rate equals the level implied by the rate of money growth.

## Potential Output

Potential output is what the economy is capable of producing when its resources are used at normal rates. Imagine you are running a company that produces hockey sticks for the Montreal market. You have estimated the demand for sticks based on the information available to you, purchased machines, and hired workers to operate them. If everything goes according to plan, you'll make a nice profit. But suddenly the Canadiens win the Stanley Cup and the number of kids who play hockey increases dramatically. Your hockey stick sales skyrocket. To meet the increased demand, you begin running your factory around the clock.

What happened? The fact that the Canadiens have won the Stanley Cup has driven your output above the normal level—that is, above your potential output. Now, what if the local professional football team, the Montreal Alouettes, were suddenly successful? This could create a boom in the sale of footballs at the expense of hockey equipment, forcing you to cut back on production below normal levels. The reduction in the rate at which you use your resources would drive your output level below the potential level at which you could produce.

Over time, conditions at your hockey stick factory are likely to change. First, if you come to believe that an increase or decrease in the demand for your product is permanent, you will change the scale of your factory, redesigning it to enlarge or reduce its size. And second, technological improvements allow you to increase the factory's production at given levels of capital and labour. In other words, your factory's normal level of output evolves over time—usually going up, but occasionally going down. So, in the short run production can deviate from normal, while in the long run the normal level itself changes.

What is true for the Montreal hockey stick manufacturer is true for the economy as a whole. There is a normal level of production that defines potential output. But potential output is not a fixed level. Because the amount of labour and capital in an economy can grow, and improved technology can increase the efficiency of the production process, potential output tends to rise over time. Furthermore, unexpected events can push current output away from potential output, creating what is called an **output gap**. When current output climbs above potential it creates an **expansionary output gap**; when current output falls below potential, it creates a **recessionary output gap**. These output gaps eventually cancel each other out, so that *in the long run, current output equals potential output.*

## YOUR FINANCIAL WORLD
### Using the Word *Inflation*

Everyone talks about *"inflation"*, but what do they mean? In normal conversation, when people use the word "inflation," they are referring to price increases. If the price of gasoline or the cost of a basket of groceries rises, that's inflation. When *The Globe and Mail* reports that the inflation rate was one- or two-tenths of 1 percent over the past month, it means that the average price level went up. But, as it is commonly used, the term "inflation" does not distinguish a one-time change in the price level from a situation in which prices are rising continuously.

Economists use the term more precisely. To them, inflation means a *continually rising price level*. That is, inflation refers to a *sustained rise* that continues for a substantial period. In discussing changes in inflation, economists emphasize the distinction between *temporary* and *permanent* changes. A temporary increase is a one-time adjustment in the price level, while a permanent change is a rise or fall in the long-run course of inflation.

To see the difference, consider an example in which the inflation rate is zero. Then, suddenly, gasoline prices rise, driving that month's Consumer Price Index (CPI) up by 1 percent. The next month, however, since energy prices don't change again, the CPI is unchanged as well. At the end of this episode, the inflation rate is where it started, at zero, but the price level as measured by the CPI is 1 percent higher. Temporary changes in inflation lead to adjustments in the price level. Only changes in monetary policy can cause permanent increases or decreases in inflation.

## Long-Run Inflation

The other key to long-run equilibrium is inflation. In the long run, economists expect that the demand for money is proportional to the level of output in the economy. If we write the level of nominal output as the product of real output and the price level, then we can summarize this relationship as $M = kPY$, where M is the quantity of money, $k$ is a factor of proportionality, $P$ is the price level, and Y is real output.[1] Assuming that $k$ is fixed (remember we are looking at the long-run here), this implies that money growth equals inflation plus real growth:

$$\%\Delta M = \%\Delta P + \%\Delta Y,$$

where "%Δ" stands for percentage change. We can restate this equation in terms of potential output, which we will call $Y^P$. In the long run, since current output equals potential output, real growth must equal growth in potential output ($\%\Delta Y = \%\Delta Y^P$). From this we can conclude that, *in the long run, inflation equals money growth minus growth in potential output* ($\%\Delta P = \%\Delta M - \%\Delta Y^P$).

Policymakers know that money growth is an important benchmark for tracking long-run inflation trends, so they pay close attention to it. In fact, when faced with very high inflation, central bankers focus almost exclusively on controlling money growth. Reducing the growth of the money supply is the only way to bring down inflation of 50 or 100 percent per year. But with 1 or 2 or even 5 percent inflation, restraining money growth is not a central short-run policy objective. Over periods even as long as a few years, the link between the quantity of money and prices (summarized by the parameter $k$ above) can fluctuate significantly, so central banks focus on the direct link between interest rates and the inflation rate.

[1] In Chapter 20, we explore this relationship in more detail, and in particular note that the factor of proportionality $k$ is a function of the interest rate. To make the argument clearer, we abstract from that relationship here but you can think about how the analysis would be affected if we assumed that $k$ depended (negatively) on the interest rate.

We turn now to a discussion of the role of monetary policy in the determination of fluctuations in current output and inflation. To understand that role, we need to develop a simple macroeconomic model—a shorthand description of the economy that helps us to organize our thinking. We begin with the dynamic aggregate demand curve, then develop an aggregate supply relationship and finally see how the two together determine output and inflation.

## Monetary Policy and the Dynamic Aggregate Demand Curve

Since our task is somewhat complex, it is useful to have an overview of where we are going. The goal is to understand the relationship between inflation and the quantity of aggregate output demanded by those people who use it. To get there, we will proceed in three steps. First, we examine the relationship between aggregate expenditure and the real interest rate. Next, we study how monetary policymakers adjust their interest-rate instrument in response to changes in inflation. And finally, we put these two together to construct the dynamic aggregate demand curve that relates output and inflation. A short summary is as follows:

1. **Aggregate expenditure and the real interest rate:** We begin with a description of how *aggregate expenditure*—especially investment, consumption, and exports—depends on the real interest rate. As the real interest rate rises, investment and consumption fall, reducing the level of aggregate expenditure. As the real interest rate rises, the exchange rate appreciates and net exports also decline. There is a *downward sloping* relationship between the quantity of aggregate expenditure and the real interest rate.

2. **Inflation, the real interest rate, and the monetary policy reaction curve:** Next, we will see that monetary policymakers respond to increases in inflation by raising their policy-controlled interest rate. And, importantly, they raise their nominal policy rate by more than the change in inflation. So, because of the way policymakers react, when inflation rises, the real interest rate goes up. There is an *upward sloping* relationship between inflation and the real interest rate that we will call the *monetary policy reaction curve*.

3. **The dynamic aggregate demand curve:** Putting 1 and 2 together—the fact that monetary policymakers react to higher inflation by raising the real interest rate and that a higher real interest rate reduces the level of aggregate expenditure—

**Figure 18.1**    Inflation, Monetary Policy, and Aggregate Demand

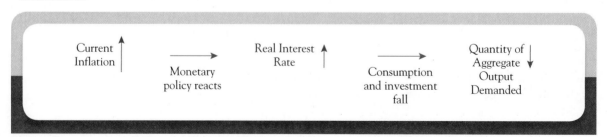

When inflation rises, policymakers react by raising the real interest rate. Higher real interest rates reduce consumption and investment, lowering the quantity of aggregate output demanded.

**Figure 18.2**    Short Term Interest Rates

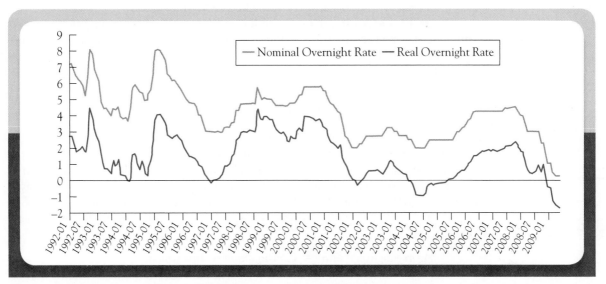

The real interest rate is computed as nominal overnight rate minus the difference between the real and nominal long term bond yield.

SOURCE: *Bank of Canada. Nominal interest rate v122514; Real interest rate v122514 minus measure of expected inflation (difference between v122553 and v122544). CANSIM Table 176-0043.*

gives us a relationship between inflation and the quantity of aggregate output demanded that we will call the *dynamic aggregate demand curve*. And, like conventional demand curves, this one slopes down, so that's how we will draw it. The dynamic aggregate demand curve is a downward-sloping relationship between inflation and aggregate output. This approach is summarized in Figure 18.1

Before continuing, it is important to keep in mind that economic decisions of households to save and of firms to invest depend on the *real* interest rate, not the nominal interest rate. So, to alter the course of the economy, central banks must influence the real interest rate. As it turns out, in the short run, when monetary policymakers change the nominal interest rate, they change the real interest rate. To see why, remember that the nominal interest rate ($i$) equals the real interest rate ($r$) plus expected inflation ($\pi^e$): $i = r + \pi^e$. Solving this for $r$, tells us that $r = i - \pi^e$, or the real interest rate equals the nominal interest rate minus expected inflation. Importantly, inflation expectations adjust slowly in response to changes in economic conditions. This means that when policymakers change $i$, $\pi^e$ doesn't change, so changes in the nominal interest rate change the real interest rate.

Data for the past several decades make it clear that movements in the short-term nominal interest rate are also movements in the short-term real interest rate. To see this, look at Figure 18.2, which plots the nominal overnight rate—the one the Bank of Canada controls—against a measure of the real overnight rate constructed using data on expected inflation.[2] The figure shows that the nominal and real overnight rise

[2] Data on inflation expectations are not readily available in Canada. We used the differential between the yield on a nominal long-term government of Canada bond and that on a real long-term government of Canada bond to proxy for the expected inflation rate. But the liquidity of the market for real return bonds is much less than that of the nominal bond market so that changes in the relative yields also capture changes in the liquidity premium, making it a far-from-perfect proxy.

and fall together. So when the Bank of Canada raises the nominal overnight rate, it raises the real overnight rate as well. Conversely, when the Bank lowers the nominal overnight rate, it lowers the real overnight rate with it.

The real interest rate, then, is the lever through which monetary policymakers influence the real economy. In changing real interest rates, they influence consumption, investment, and other components of aggregate expenditure. Let's see how this all works.

## Aggregate Expenditure and the Real Interest Rate

**The Components of Aggregate Expenditure and the Real Interest Rate**    To understand the impact of monetary policy on the economy, we need to link the real interest rate to the level of output. This task requires a detailed description of aggregate expenditure and its relationship to the real interest rate. The best way is to start with the national income accounting identity from principles of economics that analyzes the uses of the economy's output. Doing so allows us to divide aggregate expenditure into four parts:

$$\text{Aggregate expenditure} = \text{Consumption} + \text{Investment}$$
$$+ \text{Government purchases} + (\text{Exports} - \text{Imports})$$

$$Y = C + I + G + (X - M)$$

The terms in this expression are defined as follows:

1. **Consumption** (C) is spending by individuals for items such as food, clothing, housing, transportation, entertainment, and education—accounting for more than half of GDP.

2. **Investment** ($I$) is spending by firms for additions to the physical capital they use to produce goods and services.[3] Examples include new buildings and equipment. The cost of newly constructed residential homes, as well as the change in the level of business inventories, is also included. All together, these expenditures usually total about 20 percent of GDP.

3. **Government purchases** (G) is spending on goods and services by federal, provincial, and local governments. New military equipment and schools fall into this category, as well as the salaries of public school teachers, police officers, and firefighters; however, transfers such as employment insurance payments and social assistance are not included. Total federal, provincial, and municipal government purchases in Canada fluctuate around 25 percent of GDP.

4. **Net exports** equals *exports* minus *imports* ($X - M$). Remember that exports are goods and services produced in one country and sold to residents of another country; imports are purchases of foreign-made goods and services. The difference between the two represents the net expenditure for domestically produced goods. Over the past two decades, while Canadian exports have averaged close to 35 percent of GDP, net exports have been averaging only 3 percent of GDP.

---

[3] Remember that economists use the term investment differently from the way it is used in the business press. In the business press, an investment is a financial instrument such as a stock or bond that people use as a means of holding their wealth. Importantly, though, people who make such a "financial investment" aren't creating anything new; they are buying something that already exists. To an economist, investment is the creation of new physical capital.

For our purposes, it is helpful to think of aggregate expenditure as having two parts, one that is sensitive to changes in the real interest rate and one that is not. Three of the four components of aggregate expenditure—consumption, investment, and net exports—are sensitive to changes in the real interest rate. Among these, investment is the most important. Deciding whether to replace an existing machine or purchase a new one is a complicated matter, dependent on a comparison of the revenue generated by the investment with the cost of financing it. This decision boils down to a comparison of the return on the investment and the cost of borrowing to finance it.[4] An investment can be profitable only if its internal rate of return exceeds the cost of borrowing. From this, we can conclude that the higher the cost of borrowing, the less likely that an investment will be profitable. Since borrowers and lenders both care about the real return, we see immediately that the higher the real interest rate, the lower the level of investment.

While investment may be the most important component of aggregate expenditure that is sensitive to real interest rates, it isn't the only one. Consumption and net exports respond to the real interest rate as well. What is true for a business considering an investment, for example, is true for a family thinking of buying a new car. Higher real interest rates mean higher inflation-adjusted car-loan payments, which make new cars more costly. Furthermore, as the real interest rate rises, the reward to saving goes up. More saving means lower consumption.

The case of net exports is more complicated. Briefly, when the real interest rate in Canada rises, Canadian financial assets become more attractive to foreigners.[5] This rise in the desirability of Canadian assets to foreigners increases the foreign demand for Canadian dollars, causing the Canadian dollar to appreciate. The higher the value of the Canadian dollar, the more expensive Canadian exports will be, and the cheaper Canadian imports will be. Together, lower exports and higher imports mean lower net exports. Again, the higher real interest rate has reduced a component of aggregate expenditure.

Finally, there is government expenditure. While changes in the real interest rate may have an impact on the government's budget by raising the cost of borrowing, the effect is likely to be small, so we will ignore it.

For three of the four components of aggregate expenditure, then, our conclusion is the same: When the real interest rate rises

- Consumption (C) *falls* because the reward to saving is now higher.
- Investment (I) *falls* because the cost of financing has gone up.
- Net exports (X − M) *fall* because the domestic currency has appreciated, making imports cheaper and exports more expensive.

Thus, as shown in Figure 18.3 on page 402, *a rise in the real interest rate reduces the level of aggregate expenditure*.[6]

Bear in mind, though, that the components of aggregate expenditure can change for reasons unrelated to the real interest rate. Consumption or investment can rise when individuals or businesses become more confident about their future income or sales. Government purchases can increase because of a change in fiscal policy, and net exports can climb because of an exogenous movement in the exchange rate.[7] Any

---

[4] See the discussion of internal rate of return in Chapter 4.

[5] There is a more detailed discussion in Chapter 10.

[6] If you have studied intermediate macroeconomics, you may recognize this relationship as the "IS" curve.

[7] The treatment of the exchange rate is very subtle here. If the exchange rate changes because the interest rate rose, it is captured by a movement along the curve, but if it shifts for unrelated reasons—for reasons exogenous to the model—then it causes a shift of the curve.

Figure 18.3 **Aggregate Expenditure and the Real Interest Rate**

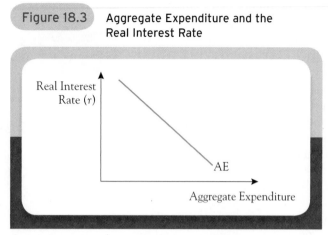

A fall in the real interest rate leads to an increase in aggregate expenditure.

of these would shift the aggregate expenditure curve in Figure 18.3 to the right, increasing the level of aggregate expenditure at every level of the real interest rate.

Table 18.1 provides a summary of the relationship between aggregate expenditure and the real interest rate.

We can see immediately how the relationship between the real interest rate and the level of aggregate expenditure helps central bankers to achieve one of their objectives: stabilizing current output at a level close to potential output. When economic activity speeds up or slows down and current output moves above or below potential output, policymakers can adjust the real interest rate in an effort to close the expansionary or recessionary gap. But, as we have emphasized repeatedly throughout our study of monetary policy, central bankers spend much of their time worrying instead about keeping inflation low.

**The Long-Run Real Interest Rate**   Before diving into a description of the relationship between monetary policy and inflation, there is one more thing we must do. We need to figure out what happens to the real interest rate over the long run. Earlier we discussed the concept of potential output and noted the economy's tendency to move toward that normal level over time. In this section we have examined how various components of aggregate expenditure respond to the real interest rate. We have seen that higher real interest rates, holding constant things like business and consumer confidence as well as government expenditure, are associated with lower levels of aggregate expenditure. Putting these two discussions together, we can conclude that there must be some level of the real interest rate at which aggregate expenditure equals potential output. That is, there is some level of aggregate expenditure that is consistent with the normal level of output toward which the economy moves over the long run. This concept is important enough that we will give it a name, the long-run real interest rate. *The long-run real interest rate equates the level of aggregate expenditure to the quantity of potential output.*

**Table 18.1**   **The Relationship between Aggregate Expenditure and the Real Interest Rate**

| | |
|---|---|
| **What is it?** | The downward-sloping relationship between the quantity of aggregate expenditure ($C + I + G + NX$) and the real interest rate ($r$). |
| **Why does it slope down?** | When the real interest rate rises, the exchange rate appreciates and the components of aggregate expenditure fall. |
| **When does it shift?** | When aggregate expenditure goes up for reasons unrelated to changes in the real interest rate, the relationship shifts to the right. Examples include: 1. Increases in individual optimism that drive up consumption. 2. Rising business confidence that increases investment. 3. Changes in fiscal policy that raise government expenditure or reduce taxes. 4. Increases in net exports that are unrelated to changes in the real interest rate. |

To figure out the level of the long-run real interest rate, take the aggregate expenditure curve drawn in Figure 18.3 and find the interest rate that is consistent with the quantity of potential output $(Y^P)$.[8] You can see how to do it in Figure 18.4. This figure helps us to understand the two possible reasons that the long-run real interest rate can change: (1) shifts in the aggregate expenditure curve, and (2) changes in the level of potential output.

First, take the case in which the level of potential output remains fixed, but there is a rise in some of the components of aggregate expenditure that do not respond to the real interest rate. One example of this is a rise in government purchases (all other things held equal). When G goes up, it increases the level of aggregate expenditure at every real interest rate, shifting the aggregate expenditure curve to the right. The result is shown in Panel A of Figure 18.5. For the level of aggregate expenditure to remain equal to the (unchanged) quantity of potential output, the interest-sensitive components of aggregate expenditure must fall. For that to happen, the long-run real interest rate must rise.[9] Besides government purchases, there are portions of consumption, investment, and net exports that are not sensitive to the real interest rate. If any of those components rises, driving aggregate expenditure up at every level of the real interest rate, the long-run real interest rate must go up.

**Figure 18.4**   The Long Run Real Interest Rate

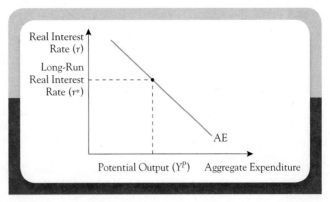

The long-run real interest rate ($r*$) equates aggregate expenditure with potential output.

**Figure 18.5**   Change in the Long-Run Real Interest Rate

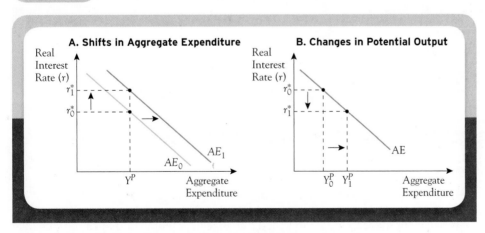

[8] Unfortunately, computing a numerical estimate for the long-run real interest rate is complicated because it is related to the return on capital investment (adjusted for risk) in the economy as a whole, a quantity that is very difficult to calculate. In the United States, most estimates are around 2.5 percent. See John C. Williams, "The Natural Rate of Interest," Federal Reserve Bank of San Francisco Economic Letter, 2003–32, October 31, 2003.

[9] This effect is related to what is sometimes called "crowding out." The idea is that government spending can take the place of investment. Crowding out occurs when the government borrows funds to increase spending, thereby increasing the supply of bonds. An increase in the supply of bonds drives the price of bonds down, increasing the interest rate, and reducing investment. When the government borrows, firms can't, so investment is crowded out.

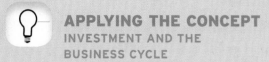

## APPLYING THE CONCEPT
### INVESTMENT AND THE
### BUSINESS CYCLE

Fluctuations in investment are one of the most important sources of changes in aggregate expenditure. Over short periods of a quarter or a year, consumption and government purchases tend to be fairly stable; and net exports are just too small to account for much of the variation in aggregate output. So understanding fluctuations in the business cycle means understanding changes in investment.

To grasp this point, look at Figure 18.6, which plots the ratio of investment to gross domestic product over the past 45 years. The shaded bars designate recessions. Note that from 1960 to 2008, investment fluctuated from 14 percent of GDP to more than 22 percent of GDP. More to the point,

during every recession, investment itself falls by between 2 and 10 percent of GDP. When we talk about a recession, what we are really talking about is a drop in investment.

What causes the level of investment to change? The tools we have developed suggest two possibilities: changes in the real interest rate and changes in expectations about future business conditions. Remember, an investment will be profitable when its real internal rate of return exceeds its real cost of financing. Once again, the real interest rate is what matters in economic decisions. The higher the real cost of financing, the less likely that an investment will be profitable. And the lower the expected future revenue from an investment is, the lower the real internal rate of return will be. So the higher the real interest rate and the less optimistic business people are about the future, the fewer investments firms will undertake and the more likely the economy will fall into recession.

**Figure 18.6**    Investment and the Business Cycle: The Ratio of Investment to GDP

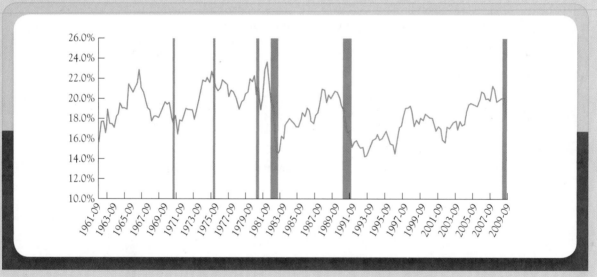

SOURCE: *Statistics Canada CANSIM database, http://cansim2.statcan.ca, Ratio of Investment, sum of personal (v498504) and Corp + GBE (v498505) both from Table 380-0031, to GDP (v498074) from Table 380-0002. Accessed 28 July 2009.*

What about the second case in which a change in potential output causes a change in the long-run real interest rate? This has an inverse effect on the real interest rate. When the quantity of potential output rises, the level of aggregate expenditure must rise with it. As we have seen, an increase in the level of aggregate expenditure requires a decline in the real interest rate. (Take a look at Panel B of Figure 18.5 on page 403.) When potential output goes up, the long-run real interest rate falls.

In summary, the long-run real interest rate ($r^*$) is that level at which aggregate expenditure ($C + I + G + NX$) equals potential output ($Y^p$). When components of aggregate expenditure that are not sensitive to the real interest rate rise, the long-run real interest rate rises with them. But when potential output rises, the long-run real interest rate falls. Importantly, the level of the long-run real interest rate is a consequence of the structure of the economy; it is not something policymakers can choose.

## Inflation, the Real Interest Rate, and the Monetary Policy Reaction Curve

We now move to the *second of the three steps* in our derivation of the relationship between inflation and the level of aggregate output demanded: In response to changes in inflation, policymakers adjust their policy-controlled interest rate.

In April 2006, CPI inflation was 2.4 percent, and although the core rate of inflation was less than 2 percent, the Bank of Canada's economic models implied that this low level of core inflation reflected the temporary impact of an exchange rate depreciation. The Bank expected that the strength of the underlying economy would keep inflationary pressures high unless it took action. The Bank responded by raising the target for the overnight interest rate from 3.75 percent to 4 percent. The Bank's press release included the statement "In line with the Bank's outlook for the Canadian economy, some modest further increase in the policy interest rate may be required to keep aggregate supply and demand in balance and inflation on target over the medium term." That is, the governing council of the Bank of Canada had concluded that economic conditions justified raising nominal interest rates so that they could raise the real interest rate in an effort to lower aggregate expenditure and close the expansionary output gap. The statement also made clear that in practice the Bank of Canada moves gradually and often chooses a path for interest rates that may be rising or falling.

Statements made by the Federal Reserve at that time reveal similar thinking. In May 2006, the FOMC raised its target for the federal funds rate from 4.75 percent to 5 percent and the statement read in part: "The Committee judges that some further policy firming may yet be needed to address inflation risks but emphasizes that the extent and timing of any such firming will depend importantly on the evolution of the economic outlook as implied by incoming information." While the specifics of the FOMC's and the governing council's statements may differ, both clearly indicate that policymakers set their short-run nominal interest rate targets in response to economic conditions in general, and inflation in particular.[10] High inflation leads to high nominal and real interest rates.

These two examples are representative of the sorts of things central bankers commonly say. Looking at the details, we can conclude that when current inflation is high or current output is running above potential output, central bankers will raise nominal interest rates; when current inflation is low or current output is well below potential, they will lower interest rates. Importantly, while central bankers state their policies in terms of nominal interest rates, they do so knowing that changes in the nominal interest rate will translate into changes in the real interest rate. As we have discussed, these changes in

"*How many times have I asked you not to discuss stubbornly high interest rates in front of the children?*"

---

[10] The fact that policy does not have an immediate impact on either inflation or output complicates matters substantially. In fact, interest-rate changes must anticipate changes in inflation and output, so they must be based on forecasts as much as on current levels. That is why, in their public comments, central bankers nearly always refer to likely future developments.

Figure 18.7  The Monetary Policy Reaction Curve

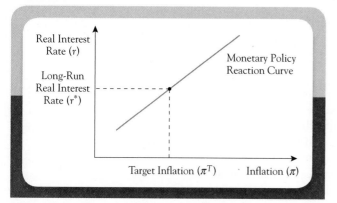

Monetary policymakers react to increases in current inflation by raising the real interest rate, while decreases lead them to lower it. The monetary policy reaction curve is located so that the central bank's target inflation is consistent with the long-run real interest rate, which equates aggregate expenditure with potential output.

the real interest rate influence the economic decisions of firms and households. We can summarize all of this in the form of a **monetary policy reaction curve** that approximates the behaviour of central bankers.

### Deriving the Monetary Policy Reaction Curve

We can summarize the reactions of the central banks in the following response function: in order to ensure that deviations of inflation from the target rate are only temporary, policymakers respond to changes in inflation by changing the real interest rate in the same direction. That is, *higher current inflation requires a policy response that raises the real interest rate*, and *lower current inflation requires a policy response that lowers the real interest rate*. This means that the monetary policy reaction curve slopes upward as shown in Figure 18.7.

Where do we draw the reaction curve? What determines its location? The location depends on where policymakers would like the economy to end up in the long run, which is the equilibrium toward which the economy tends over time. For the real interest rate, the economy moves toward the long-run real interest rate that equates aggregate expenditure with potential output. That interest rate is shown as $r^*$ in Figure 18.7. For inflation, the answer is the central bank's target level ($\pi^T$). *The monetary policy reaction curve is set so that when current inflation equals target inflation, the real interest rate equals the long-run real interest rate.* That is, $r = r^*$ when $\pi = \pi^T$.

While the long-run real interest rate and the inflation target tell us the location of the monetary policy reaction curve, what governs its slope? Is the curve steep or flat? The answer is that the slope depends on policymakers' objectives. When central bankers decide how aggressively to pursue their inflation target, and how willing they are to tolerate temporary changes in inflation, they are determining the slope of the monetary policy reaction curve. They are deciding whether to respond to deviations of current inflation from target inflation with small or large changes in the real interest rate. Policymakers who are aggressive in keeping current inflation near target will have a steep monetary policy reaction curve, while those who are less concerned will have a reaction curve that is relatively flat. We look at the implications of this difference at the end of the next chapter.

### Shifting the Monetary Policy Reaction Curve

When policymakers adjust the real interest rate, they are either moving along a fixed monetary policy reaction curve or shifting the curve. A movement along the curve is a reaction to a change in current inflation. A shift in the curve represents a change in the level of the real interest rate at every level of inflation. To see what can shift the monetary policy reaction curve, we need to examine the variables we held constant when we drew the curve in Figure 18.7. In that analysis, we held both target inflation $\pi^T$ and the long-run real interest rate $r^*$ fixed. If either of these variables changes, the entire curve shifts. Looking at Figure 18.8, we can see that an *increase* in $r^*$ shifts the curve to the left, as does a *decrease* in the $\pi^T$. Analogously, a decline in the long-run real interest rate $r^*$, or an increase in the inflation target $\pi^T$, shifts the monetary policy reaction curve to the right.

**Figure 18.8**   Shifting the Monetary Policy Reaction Curve

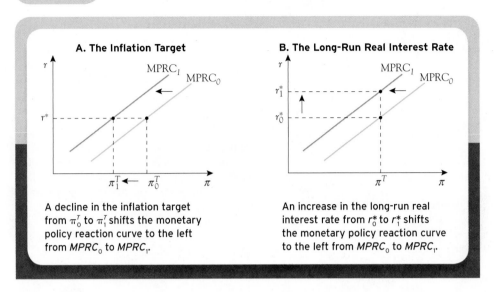

A decline in the inflation target from $\pi_0^T$ to $\pi_1^T$ shifts the monetary policy reaction curve to the left from $MPRC_0$ to $MPRC_1$.

An increase in the long-run real interest rate from $r_0^*$ to $r_1^*$ shifts the monetary policy reaction curve to the left from $MPRC_0$ to $MPRC_1$.

From our earlier discussion, we know that the long-run real interest rate $(r^*)$ is determined by the structure of the economy. Policymakers cannot choose it. What if $r^*$ were to rise as a consequence of an increase in government purchases, or some other component of aggregate expenditure that is not sensitive to the real interest rate? The result of such an increase is a shift to the left in the monetary policy reaction curve as shown in Panel B of Figure 18.8. Remember that the curve is drawn so that the real interest rate equals its long-run level at the point where inflation meets the central bank's target. An increase in the long-run real interest rate means that policymakers have set a higher real interest rate at every level of current inflation. Assuming that policymakers have not changed their inflation target, this shift means that the long-run nominal interest rate rises as well.

Table 18.2 provides a summary of the properties of the monetary policy reaction curve.

**Table 18.2**   The Monetary Policy Reaction Curve

| | |
|---|---|
| **What is it?** | The upward-sloping relationship between inflation $(\pi)$ and the real interest rate $(r)$ set by monetary policymakers. |
| **Why does it slope upward?** | When inflation rises, monetary policymakers raise the real interest rate. |
| **What determines its location?** | Drawn so that, when current inflation equals target inflation $(\pi = \pi^T)$ policymakers set the real interest rate equal to the long-run real interest rate $(r = r^*)$. |
| **When does it shift?** | 1. When the central bank's inflation target $(\pi^T)$ changes. A decline shifts the inflation curve to the left.<br><br>2. When the long-run real interest rate $(r^*)$ changes. An increase shifts the curve to the left. |

## IN THE NEWS

### FOCUS SHIFTS TO INFLATION; Bank of Canada holds rates steady to join sea-change in policy

# Financial Post; p. FP1

### By Jacqueline Thorpe

June 11, 2008

The global war on inflation has begun and it will not be pretty.

Throwing Bay Street its widest curve ball in years, the Bank of Canada bucked market expectations for an interest-rate cut yesterday and held interest rates at 3% joining the U.S. Federal Reserve, the European Central Bank and even emerging markets in an all-out offensive to keep global prices from spiralling even higher.

It will undoubtedly mean a prolonged period of lacklustre global growth and continuing anxiety for stock markets.

Whether Mark Carney actually got on the phone with Ben Bernanke and Jean-Claude Trichet to discuss their three-pronged attack we will probably never know, but it is clear we are in the middle of a sea-change in global monetary policy.

Only in April, the Bank of Canada was slashing interest rates by 50 basis points and saying "further monetary stimulus will likely be required." Yesterday, the bank said inflation could hit 3%, up from 1.7% now, if energy prices persist. Inflation risks had tilted to the upside, global growth had been stronger than expected, and commodity prices "sharply higher."

Just in March, the Fed was rescuing investment banks and inventing new liquidity instruments to manage the biggest credit market blow-up since the Chinese invented the abacus.

But in a speech late Monday, Mr. Bernanke virtually dismissed a half-point jump in the U. S. unemployment rate, focusing instead on surging oil prices that have added to inflation risks and inflation expectations.

As for the ECB's Mr. Trichet, he's always hawkish, but when he suggested last week that European rates could go up as early as July, the markets' inflation hackles were raised.

Two things have happened to change the view—growth and $10US-a-day gains in the price of oil.

The Bank of Canada perhaps believes the 0.3% contraction in first-quarter GDP was an aberration, likely caused by harsh weather and a plunge in auto production that could be made up this quarter.

Meanwhile, Mr. Bernanke down-played the rise in the U.S. unemployment rate to 5.5% from 5.0%—the biggest jump in more than 22 years—noting the risk the United States had entered a substantial downturn "appears to have diminished over the past month or so."

Inflation-focused central banks simply cannot ignore the surge in oil prices and rising inflation rates from China to the United States.

## The Dynamic Aggregate Demand Curve

### Deriving the Dynamic Aggregate Demand Curve

We are now ready to move to the *third* and *final step* outlined at the beginning of this section: The construction of the dynamic aggregate demand curve that relates inflation and the level of output, accounting for the fact that monetary policymakers respond to changes in current inflation by changing the interest rate. Doing it means answering the following question: What happens to quantity of aggregate output demanded when current inflation changes? From our earlier discussion, we know that central bankers respond to an increase in current inflation by raising the real interest rate. That is, they move along their monetary policy reaction curve (shown in Figure 18.7 on page 406). We also know that a higher real interest rate lowers the level of aggregate expenditure by reducing investment, consumption, and net exports. (That's in Figure 18.3 on page 402.) Putting these two together, we see that when inflation rises, the quantity of aggregate output demanded falls.

"I think it's quite possible every central bank has been spooked by oil prices and the upward march we've seen in headline inflation just about everywhere," said Douglas Porter, deputy chief economist at BMO Capital Markets.

Even emerging markets have stepped up the tightening with China ordering banks to set aside record reserves, Vietnam raising rates yesterday and other countries peeling back fuel subsidies.

Markets, however, do not take kindly to central banks hinting at interest rate hikes when growth is still struggling.

There has been mayhem in the bond markets in recent days, with yields surging and the recovery stock markets have been nurturing since the credit market stabilized now clearly under threat. With the central bank failing to provide expected stimulus and oil prices listing, the S&P/TSX composite dumped 224.56 points to 14,736.20 yesterday.

"Stocks had been dependent on the Fed getting the stimulus in place and not adjusting until 2009," said Andrew Pyle, investment advisor at ScotiaMcleod. "If you're looking at Canada now, it's a double whammy. What you're going to get is the drag on U.S. sentiment from what the Fed's doing and if the U.S. dollar goes up and commodity prices go down you are going to get a hit on that, too."

Still, many economists believe the central banks will be all talk and no action, that plunging home values, wonky stock markets and soaring gasoline prices will do more to wring inflation out of the system than rising rhetoric ever could.

It will certainly take some nerve to actually pull the trigger on rates.

**LESSONS OF THE ARTICLE:**

Our characterization of monetary policy as the response of the target interest rate to inflation captures the essence of monetary policy, but in practice it is a lot more complex. The Bank of Canada focuses on long-run drivers of inflation and so the analysts who try to predict the Bank's next move do so similarly. Notice that this article is from June 2008. The Bank did not change the interest rate but three months later, as the financial crisis took hold, the Bank joined other central banks and lowered the rate by 50 bps.

SOURCE: *Focus Shifts to Inflation; Bank of Canada holds rates steady to join sea-change in policy*, by Jacqueline Thorpe, Financial Post, *National Edition*, *June 11, 2008. Material reprinted with the express permission of "The National Post Company," a CanWest Partnership.*

Inflation and the quantity of aggregate output demanded move in opposite directions, so the *dynamic aggregate demand curve* shown in Figure 18.9 on page 410 slopes downward.[11]

To understand the dynamic aggregate demand curve, think about what happens when current inflation rises. In response, monetary policymakers raise the real interest rate, moving the economy upward along the monetary policy reaction curve. The higher real interest rate reduces the interest-sensitive components of aggregate expenditure (consumption, investment, and net exports), causing a fall in the quantity of aggregate output demanded by the people in the economy who use it.

[11] Figuring out the location of the dynamic aggregate demand curve is somewhat complicated. To do it, recall that along the monetary policy reaction curve the real interest rate equals the long-run real interest rate at the point where inflation equals the central bank's target level. And the long-run real interest rate is the level at which aggregate expenditure equals potential output. This all means that the dynamic aggregate demand curve must go through the point where output equals potential output at the same time that inflation equals target inflation. We will come back to this in the next chapter.

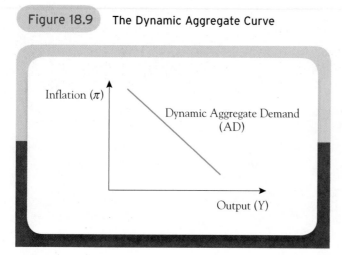

Figure 18.9 The Dynamic Aggregate Curve

As inflation rises, monetary policymakers increase the real interest rate, lowering interest-rate-sensitive components of aggregate expenditure.

Higher current inflation means less aggregate output demanded. In contrast, in response to lower current inflation, policymakers reduce the real interest rate, moving downward along the monetary policy reaction curve. Their action raises consumption, investment, and net exports, causing the quantity of aggregate output demanded to rise. Thus, *changes in current inflation move the economy along a downward-sloping dynamic aggregate demand curve*. (Take a look back at Figure 18.1 on page 398 and the summary that goes along with it.)

### Why the Dynamic Aggregate Demand Curve Slopes Down

To recap, the dynamic aggregate demand curve slopes down because higher current inflation induces policymakers to raise the real interest rate, depressing various components of aggregate expenditure. But this is only one reason that increases in inflation are associated with falling levels of aggregate output demanded by the people who use it. Economists have suggested a number of others.

First, higher inflation reduces wealth, which lowers consumption. It does this in two ways: inflation means that the money everyone holds is gradually declining in value; also, inflation is bad for the stock market, since as it rises, uncertainty about inflation rises with it, rendering equities a relatively more risky and hence less attractive investment. A drop in the value of stocks reduces wealth.

Yet another reason for the downward slope of the dynamic aggregate demand curve is that inflation can have a greater impact on the poor than it does on the wealthy, redistributing income to those who are better off. For example, minimum wages often don't rise with inflation even when other wages do, so inflation erodes the purchasing power of minimum-wage workers. And since the rich consume a smaller portion of their income than others, saving a greater portion than the poor (who can't afford to save at all), this redistribution lowers consumption in the economy as a whole, reducing quantity of aggregate output demanded.

Then there is the fact that inflation creates risk; the higher the inflation rate, the greater the risk. Most people want to insure themselves against risk, and that means increased saving, just in case. More saving means a lower level of consumption and lower quantity of aggregate output demanded. Finally, there is the fact that rising inflation makes foreign goods cheaper in relation to domestic goods, driving imports up and net exports down. All these possibilities imply that even if the monetary policymakers do not change the real interest rate when inflation goes up—the monetary policy reaction curve is flat—the effect of inflation on real money balances causes the dynamic aggregate demand curve to slope down.

### Shifting the Dynamic Aggregate Demand Curve

In deriving the dynamic aggregate demand curve, we saw that increases in inflation bring a monetary policy response that raises the real interest rate. Those movements in the real interest rate, in turn, cause changes in the quantity of aggregate output demanded by those who use it, moving the economy along the dynamic aggregate demand curve. In our derivation we held constant the location of both the aggregate expenditure curve and

# YOUR FINANCIAL WORLD
It's the Real Interest Rate that Matters

Suppose you want to buy a car and have to borrow $20,000 and will repay the loan over four years. Consider two cases. In the first, Case A, the interest rate is 8 percent so your monthly payment is $488.26; in the second, Case B, the interest rate is 10 percent and your monthly payment is $507.25. But the real cost of the loan depends on the inflation rate, and in particular how much your salary rises. Suppose that in Case A your wages are going up at 1 percent per year and in Case B your wages are rising at 5 percent per year.

The table below compares the two cases. Case A has a lower nominal interest but a higher real rate of interest. Notice that even though the nominal interest rate is higher in case B, after three years the loan payment takes a smaller share of your monthly paycheque than in Case A. Second, notice that in Case A the first payment is a smaller share of your monthly paycheque than in Case B. This reflects the front-end loading of payments when inflation is high: essentially you are paying down the principal faster.

| | Interest rates on a $20,000 loan paid off over 4 years. | | | | Base salary $2500/month | | |
| | Nominal Interest Rate | Monthly Payment | Inflation Rate | Real Rate of Interest | Real Salary after 3 years | Fraction of Salary Used for car Payment | |
| | | | | | | Initially | After 3 years |
| A | 8% | $488.26 | 1% | 7% | $2575 | 19.5% | 18.9% |
| B | 10% | $507.25 | 5% | 5% | $2894 | 20.3% | 17.5% |

the monetary policy reaction curve. In the first case, we assumed that components of aggregate expenditure not dependent on the real interest rate were fixed; and in the second that the inflation target and the long-run real interest rate were fixed. Shifts in any of these will shift the dynamic aggregate demand curve.

Let's start by looking at shifts in the aggregate expenditure curve. In the absence of any change in monetary policy, changes in components of aggregate expenditure not caused by movements in the real interest rate shift the dynamic aggregate demand curve. That is, changes in consumption, investment, government purchases, or net exports that are unrelated to changes in the real interest rate shift the dynamic aggregate demand curve, with declines leading to contractions and increases leading to expansions.

To understand these sources of shifts in the dynamic aggregate demand curve, take the case of an increase in consumer confidence. When people become more optimistic about the future, believing that the risk of being laid off has eased, they are more likely to purchase a new car or go on an expensive vacation. Increases in consumer confidence tend to raise consumption at every level of the real interest rate, increasing the level of aggregate expenditure. Assuming unchanged monetary policy, this shifts the dynamic aggregate demand curve to the right (as shown in the top panel of Figure 18.10 on page 412).

What is true for consumer confidence is true for all of the components of aggregate expenditure. Increased optimism about future business prospects raises investment at every level of the real interest rate, shifting the dynamic aggregate demand curve to the right. Increases in government spending (or decreases in taxes) increase aggregate expenditure and have the same effect. And increases in net exports that are unrelated

**Figure 18.10**   Shifting the Dynamic Aggregate Demand Curve

**Changes in Components of Aggregate Expenditure**

$C \uparrow, I \uparrow, G \uparrow, NX \uparrow$

*Increases* in consumption, investment, government expenditure, or net exports (all unrelated to the real interest rate) shift the dynamic aggregate demand curve to the *right*.

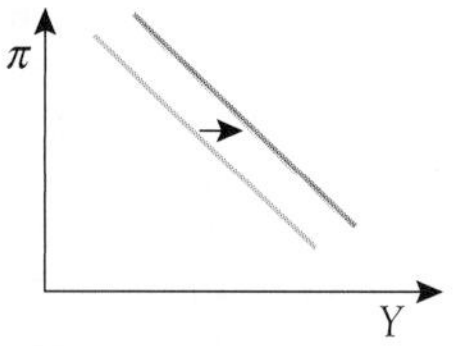

**Shifts in the Monetary Policy Reaction Curve**

$\pi^T \uparrow$

*Increases* in the central bank's inflation target shift the dynamic aggregate demand curve to the *right*.

$r^* \downarrow$

*Decreases* in the long-run real interest rate shift the dynamic aggregate demand curve to the *right*.

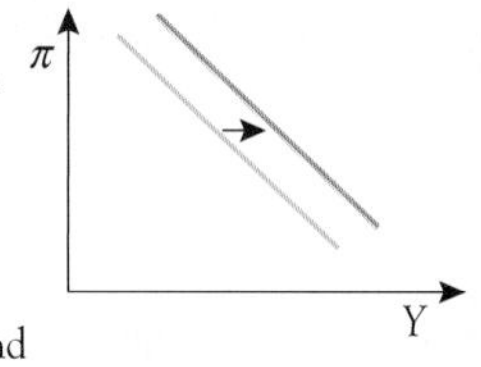

to the real interest rate do the same thing—they are expansionary, shifting the dynamic aggregate demand curve to the right.

Turning to the monetary policy reaction curve, whenever it shifts, the dynamic aggregate demand curve shifts, too. To see why, consider an increase in the central bank's inflation target, what some people might characterize as a permanent easing of monetary policy. The result is the opposite of the decline shown in Panel A of Figure 18.8 on page 407. The rise in the inflation target shifts the monetary policy reaction curve to the right, lowering the real interest rate that policymakers set at every level of inflation. At the new, higher inflation target, the lower real interest rate increases the quantity of aggregate output demanded at every level of inflation, shifting the dynamic aggregate demand curve to the right.

Changes in the long-run real interest rate shift the dynamic aggregate demand curve as well. To see why, consider a case in which the long-run real interest rate changes because the level of potential output increases. Because the long-run real interest rate equates aggregate expenditure with potential output, when potential output rises, the long-run real interest rate must fall, driving up the interest-rate-sensitive components of aggregate expenditure. This has the same effect on the monetary policy reaction curve as an increase in policymakers' inflation target. A fall in the long-run real interest rate shifts the curve to the right, reducing the real interest rate policymakers set at every level of inflation and shifting the dynamic aggregate demand curve to the right.

Looking at these two changes, we see that any shift in the monetary policy reaction curve shifts the dynamic aggregate demand curve in the same direction. Expansionary monetary policy that lowers the interest rate associated with each level of inflation increases the quantity of aggregate output demanded at each level of inflation and

**Table 18.3**   The Dynamic Aggregate Demand Curve

| | |
|---|---|
| **What is it?** | The downward-sloping relationship between inflation and the quantity of aggregate output demanded by the people who use it. |
| **Why does it slope down?** | 1. A rise in inflation leads monetary policymakers to raise the real interest rate (along the monetary policy reaction curve). |
| | 2. A higher real interest rate drives down the interest-sensitive components of aggregate expenditure (especially consumption and investment). |
| **When does it shift?** | When aggregate expenditure goes up for reasons unrelated to changes in the real interest rate, the relationship shifts to the right. Examples include: |
| | 1. Changes in components of aggregate expenditure not sensitive to the real interest rate (monetary policy unchanged). |
| | 2. Shifts in the monetary policy reaction curve. |

shifts the dynamic aggregate demand curve to the right (as shown in the bottom panel of Figure 18.10). And contractionary monetary policy that raises the interest rate associated with each level of inflation decreases the quantity of aggregate output demanded at each level of inflation and shifts the dynamic aggregate demand curve to the left.

## Aggregate Supply

The dynamic aggregate demand curve is downward sloping. It tells us that higher current inflation is associated with a lower quantity of aggregate output demanded. But this alone doesn't explain how inflation and the quantity of output are determined. To do that, we need to introduce an aggregate supply curve. The aggregate supply curve tells us where

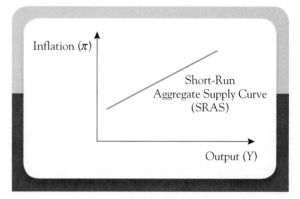

**Figure 18.11**   Short-Run Aggregate Supply Curve

Inflation persistence means the short-run aggregate supply curve slopes up.

along the dynamic aggregate demand curve the economy ends up. So, to complete the analysis, we now move to an examination of aggregate supply and the behaviour of the firms that produce the economy's output. Critically, there are short-run and long-run versions of the aggregate supply curve. When combined with the dynamic aggregate demand curve, the short-run aggregate supply curve tells us where the economy settles at any particular time; while the long-run curve, together with dynamic aggregate demand, tells us the levels of inflation and the quantity of output that the economy is moving toward in the long term.

### Short-Run Aggregate Supply

The **short-run aggregate supply curve** tells us that as inflation rises, producers increase the quantity of output supplied. It *is the upward-sloping relationship between current inflation and the quantity of output*. The reason is that prices of factors used as inputs in production, especially wages paid to workers, are costly to adjust, so they change infrequently. In the short run, they are sticky. For producers, this means that costs of production—wages paid to workers, rents paid for buildings, prices paid for raw material inputs—are fixed in the short run, so increases in prices of the things that firms sell mean higher profits and more supply. Put another way, in the short-term production costs don't change much, so when product (or retail) prices rise firms increase supply in order to take advantage. From this, we can conclude that in the short run higher inflation elicits more aggregate output supplied by the firms that produce it (see Figure 18.11).[12]

### Shifts in the Short-Run Aggregate Supply Curve

Changes in product-price inflation create movements *along* a short-run aggregate supply curve. In coming to this conclusion, we assumed that production costs didn't change. But what if they do? When production costs change, the short-run aggregate supply curve *shifts*. This can happen for any of three reasons:

---

[12] The short-run aggregate supply curve is a close relative of the Phillips Curve that you may have already seen. The Phillips Curve is the downward-sloping relationship between inflation and unemployment. Since unemployment is related to the level of output—higher output means lower unemployment—there is a clear correspondence.

| Figure 18.12 | Shifting the Short-Run Aggregate Supply Curve |

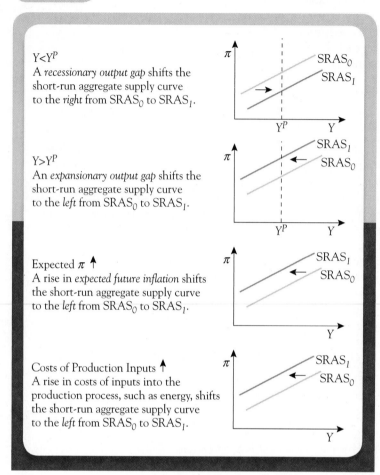

$Y < Y^P$

A *recessionary output gap* shifts the short-run aggregate supply curve to the *right* from $SRAS_0$ to $SRAS_1$.

$Y > Y^P$

An *expansionary output gap* shifts the short-run aggregate supply curve to the *left* from $SRAS_0$ to $SRAS_1$.

Expected $\pi$ ↑

A rise in *expected future inflation* shifts the short-run aggregate supply curve to the *left* from $SRAS_0$ to $SRAS_1$.

Costs of Production Inputs ↑

A rise in costs of inputs into the production process, such as energy, shifts the short-run aggregate supply curve to the *left* from $SRAS_0$ to $SRAS_1$.

1. Deviations of current output from potential output.
2. Changes in expectations of future inflation.
3. Factors that drive production costs up or down.

Let's look at each one of these in some detail.

When current output equals potential output, so that there is no output gap, the short-run aggregate supply curve remains stable. But when current output rises above potential output, inflation rises, and when current output falls below potential output, inflation falls. To understand the relationship between output gaps and inflation, recall that potential output is the level at which firms are using labour and capital at normal rates. But when current output falls below potential output, creating a *recessionary output gap*, part of the economy's capacity is idle. Firms have little trouble hiring new workers under these conditions, and their plants and equipment are underutilized. As a result, firms tend to raise the prices of the products that they sell and wages they pay their workers by less than they did when current output equalled potential output. That is, production costs rise more slowly, so inflation falls.

When current output exceeds potential output, creating an *expansionary output gap*, the opposite happens. Firms have difficulty hiring new workers and retaining those already on the payroll. They pay overtime to their employees and use their plants and equipment at levels they can maintain only temporarily. Under these circumstances, firms will increase their product prices and the wages that they pay their workers by more than they would if they were operating at normal levels. So, when there is an expansionary gap, production costs rise more quickly and inflation goes up.

We can conclude that when current output deviates from potential output, inflation adjusts. A recessionary output gap, in which current output falls below potential output, forces inflation down; an expansionary output gap, in which current output rises above potential output, drives inflation up (see the top two panels of Figure 18.12).

Output gaps are only one of the sources of production cost changes that shift the short-run aggregate supply. A change in expectations about future inflation is another. Workers and firms care about real wages and real product prices—the level of compensation and profits measured in goods and services that they can purchase. As we noted earlier, it is costly to adjust wages and prices, so they change infrequently. More importantly, during months or even years for which they are fixed, inflation erodes the real wages paid to workers and real prices charged by firms. This makes everyone concerned about future inflation, and the higher expected inflation is, the more nominal wages and nominal prices will rise. As a result, changes in inflation expectations are analogous to changes in production costs. An increase in expected inflation increases production costs, lowering production at every level of current inflation and shifting the short-run aggregate supply curve to the left as shown in the third panel of Figure 18.12.

Finally, changes in the prices of raw material inputs, as well as other external factors that change production costs, shift the short-run aggregate supply curve. The most common example of an input price change is a movement in the price of energy. When oil prices rise, increasing the cost of production, firms are forced to raise the prices of their products. The sharp increases in oil prices in the 1970s, from $3.50 a barrel in 1973 to $10 a barrel in 1976 and $39 a barrel in 1980, were a major cause of inflation during that decade. Conversely, when oil prices fall, as they did in 1986 and again in 1999, inflation tends to fall. The same thing happens when labour costs rise, as they do when payroll taxes increase or the cost of employer-provided extended health care insurance rises. *An increase in production costs causes the short-run aggregate supply curve to shift to the left*, as shown in the last panel of Figure 18.12.

## The Long-Run Aggregate Supply Curve

The final step in completing our discussion of output and inflation fluctuations is to examine the long run. What happens after everyone has had time to make the adjustments that in the long run bring output and inflation back to normal? The answer (from the first part of this chapter) is that the economy moves to the point where current output equals potential output, while inflation is determined by money growth. The implications of this answer are that, in the long run, current output must equal potential output, and inflation must be determined by monetary policy. That is, in the long run, output and inflation are unrelated, and *the* long-run aggregate supply curve *is vertical at the point where current output equals potential output*.

This conclusion makes sense. From our earlier discussion, we know that the short-run aggregate supply curve shifts whenever current output rises above or falls below potential output, creating an expansionary or recessionary output gap. When current output equals potential output, the short-run aggregate supply curve does not shift. The fact that the short-run aggregate supply curve is stable when there is no output gap means that the long-run aggregate supply curve is vertical at that point.

In deriving the short-run aggregate supply curve, we noted that inflation depends on inflation expectations. That is, when workers and firms make the wage and price decisions that determine today's inflation, they do it with an eye toward future inflation. And an increase in expected inflation is just like an increase in production costs, shifting the short-run aggregate supply curve to the left (as in the bottom panel of Figure 18.12).

To summarize, the short-run aggregate supply curve shifts *both* when current output deviates from potential output *and* when expected inflation deviates from current inflation. For the economy to remain in long-run equilibrium, then, in addition to current output equalling potential output, current inflation must equal expected inflation. So *at any point along the long-run aggregate supply curve, current output equals potential output ($Y = Y^p$) and current inflation equals expected inflation ($\pi = \pi^e$)*. This is drawn in Figure 18.14 on page 417, where the upward-sloping short-run aggregate supply curve (SRAS) intersects the vertical long-run aggregate supply curve (LRAS) at the point where inflation equals expected inflation.

**APPLYING THE CONCEPT**

INFLATION AND THE OUTPUT GAP

The idea that inflation responds to the output gap is confirmed by a close examination of the data. To see, take a look at Figure 18.13, which plots the output gap (the red line) against the core inflation rate six quarters later (the green line) over the period 1993 to 2009. Inflation tends to fall when there is a recessionary output gap and rise when current output exceeds potential output. Importantly, an output gap has little immediate impact on inflation; its effect takes roughly a year and a half to be felt. While central banks are importantly guided by the output gap, there are frequent and large revisions to the measured output gap, which is a challenge to policymaking.

**Figure 18.13** Inflation and the Output Gap

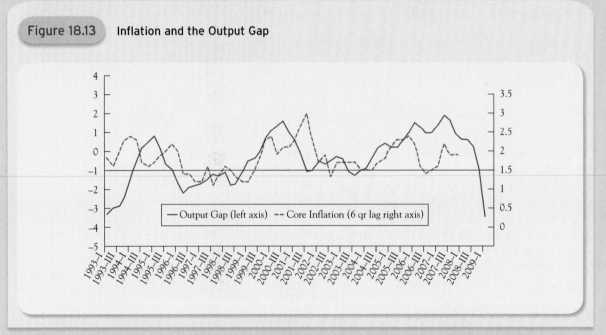

In this figure the output gap is measured as the percentage deviation of current real gross domestic product from potential real gross domestic product. The core inflation rate is the Bank of Canada's measure of core inflation, a variant of the CPI that excludes the eight most volatile components (mostly food, fuel, and tobacco) and the effects of indirect taxes.

SOURCE: *Output gap and Inflation rate (Core CPI is used), www.bankofcanada.ca/en/rates/indinf/product_data_en.html," accessed 23 July 2009.*

Table 18.4 provides a summary of the properties of the short- and long-run aggregate supply curves.

# Equilibrium and the Determination of Output and Inflation

## Short-Run Equilibrium

We now have the tools we need to understand both the movements in output and inflation in the short run and their determination in the long run. Short-run equilibrium is determined by the intersection of the dynamic aggregate demand curve (AD) with the short-run aggregate supply curve (SRAS). Combining the AD curve from Figure 18.9 on page 410 and the SRAS curve from 18.11, we get Figure 18.15 on page 418. Current output and inflation are determined by the intersection at point E in the figure. And, like all supply and demand diagrams, changes in inflation and output arise from shifts in either supply, demand or both. We'll have a detailed look at the sources and consequences of these shifts in Chapter 19.

## Adjustment to Long-Run Equilibrium

What happens when current output deviates from potential output so that there is an output gap? Earlier we saw that output gaps lead to *shifts* in the short-run aggregate supply curve. This means that if there is either an expansionary or a recessionary output gap, the economy cannot be in long-run equilibrium. To see how adjustment to long-run equilibrium works, let's look at two cases: One in which current output is above potential ($Y > Y^p$), and one in which it is below potential ($Y < Y^p$). When current output exceeds potential, the resulting expansionary output gap

**Figure 18.14**   Short- and Long-Run Aggregate Supply Curves

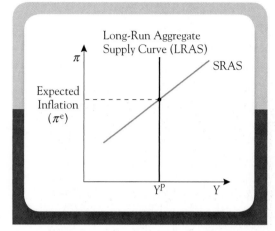

The long-run aggregate supply curve (LRAS) is vertical at the point where current output equals potential output.

**Table 18.4**   Aggregate Supply

|  | Short-Run Aggregate Supply Curve (SRAS) | Long-Run Aggregate Supply Curve (LRAS) |
|---|---|---|
| **What is it?** | The upward-sloping relationship between inflation ($\pi$) and the quantity of aggregate output ($Y$) supplied by the firms that produce it. | The vertical relationship between inflation ($\pi$) and the quantity of aggregate output supplied. |
| **What is its slope?** | Since production costs adjust slowly, increases in product prices make it profitable to increase quantity supplied, so the SRAS is upward sloping. | In the long run, the economy moves to the point where current output equals potential output so the LRAS is vertical at $Y = Y^p$. |
| **What determines its location?** | It intersects the long-run aggregate supply curve (LRAS) where inflation equals expected inflation ($\pi = \pi^e$). | The LRAS is vertical at potential output. |
| **When does it shift?** | 1. When there is a recessionary output gap ($Y < Y^p$), the SRAS shifts to the right.<br>2. When there is an expansionary output gap ($Y > Y^p$), the SRAS shifts to the left.<br>3. When expected inflation increases, the SRAS shifts to the left.<br>4. When production costs rise, the SRAS shifts to the left. | When potential output ($Y^p$) changes, the LRAS shifts. An increase in $Y^p$ shifts the LRAS to the right; a decrease shifts it to the left. |

## Figure 18.15  Short-Run Determination of Output and Inflation

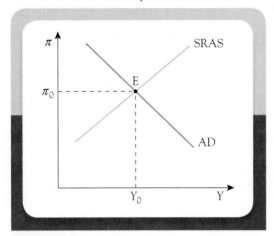

In the short run, inflation and output are determined by the intersection of the short-run aggregate supply curve (SRAS) and the dynamic aggregate demand curve (AD), point E above.

exerts upward pressure on production costs, shifting the short-run aggregate supply curve to the left. This process continues until output returns to potential, as shown in Panel A of Figure 18.16. At first, quantity of aggregate output demanded equals the quantity supplied in the short run at point 1, where current output $Y_0$ exceeds potential output $Y^p$. The resulting expansionary output gap puts upward pressure on production costs, shifting the short-run aggregate supply curve to the left until it reaches point 2, where current output equals potential output and there is no output gap. Only at this point do inflation and output stop changing. Notice that the inflation rate at point 2 is not the same as at point 1. Here we will simply assume that point 2 represents the target level of inflation. Whether or not it does depends on the factor that caused the economy to be out of equilibrium. In Chapter 19 we will examine cases in which the economy is pushed off its inflation target and show how the central bank returns inflation to target.

Now consider the second case, in which current output, $Y_0$, is lower than potential output, $Y^p$. This recessionary output gap places downward pressure on production costs, shifting the short-run aggregate supply curve to the right. Again, the process continues until current output returns to potential, as shown in Panel B of Figure 18.16. At first, the quantity of aggregate output demanded equals the quantity supplied in the short run at point 1, where current output falls short of potential output. The resulting recessionary output gap causes the short-run aggregate supply curve to shift to the right as shown. As it does, current output increases until it equals potential output and inflation falls, until the economy reaches point 2. At this point, output and inflation are steady.

This example has several important implications. First, it shows that the economy has a self-correcting mechanism. When output moves away from its long-run equilibrium level, inflation moves away from the central bank's target and policymakers respond by changing the real interest rate. This moves the economy along the dynamic aggregate

## Figure 18.16  Adjustment to Long-Run Equilibrium

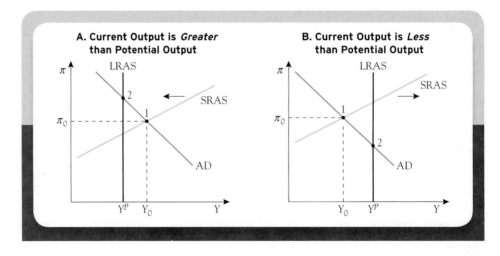

# TOOLS OF THE TRADE
## Output Growth and Output Gaps

In a press release on July 14, 2008, the Bank of Canada noted that "Although Canadian economic growth in the first quarter was weaker than expected, final domestic demand continues to expand at a solid pace. The economy is judged to have moved into slight excess supply in the second quarter of this year; excess supply is expected to increase over the balance of the year."

Central bankers say this sort of thing all the time. They talk about the risks that economic growth will move above or below its maximum sustainable level. But if you open an economics textbook, or even look at current research on how to best conduct monetary policy, you will see everything written in terms of the *level* of current output, *potential output,* and the *output gap;* not real growth. What's going on? When central bankers mention growth, are they speaking the same language as the macroeconomists who study output gaps?

To reconcile monetary policymakers' words with the models in economics textbooks, we can start with the fortunate fact that the economy is usually growing. Investment increases the size of the capital stock used for production, and new hires raise the number of people working. And then there are

technological improvements: inventions and innovations are continually raising individual productivity. Increases in the available amounts of capital and labour, together with improvements in productivity, are the sources of economic growth. And because economic growth implies an increase in the normal level of production, potential output is usually rising. These increases in the economy's productive capacity shift the long-run aggregate supply curve (LRAS) to the right.

When monetary policymakers use the term "growth," they are talking about increases in both actual and potential output. Unless these are equal, an output gap opens up. That is, when $Y$ grows faster than $Y^p$, it creates an expansionary output gap and when $Y$ grows more slowly than $Y^p$, it creates a recessionary output gap. Only when $Y$ and $Y^p$ grow at the same rate—that's the maximum sustainable growth rate—will the economy be at its long-run equilibrium with output equal to potential output.

So, while it may appear that policymakers' words about growth don't match their deeds in addressing output gaps, they do. Just remember that the economy is always growing, and so long as actual and potential output both grow at the same pace, no output gap will develop.

demand curve until it returns to its long-run equilibrium. Second, the fact that inflation changes whenever there is an output gap reinforces our conclusion that in the long run output returns to potential output. This is why we drew the long-run aggregate supply curves as a vertical line in the figures.

Long-run equilibrium is the point at which the economy comes to rest. Since we will be using it as a benchmark for understanding fluctuations, it is important to list its properties. As we noted earlier, in the long run, current inflation must equal expected inflation. Furthermore, when current output equals potential output, the real interest rate equals the long-run real interest rate. And going back to the monetary policy reaction curve, we know that policymakers set the real interest rate equal to this long-run level when current inflation equals their inflation target. So there are four conditions for long-run equilibrium:

1. Current output equals potential output $(Y = Y^p)$,
2. Current inflation is steady and equal to target inflation $(\pi = \pi^T)$,
3. Current inflation equals expected inflation $(\pi = \pi^e)$, and
4. The real interest rate equals the long-run real interest rate $(r = r^*)$.

## Terms

## Chapter Summary

1. In the long run
   a. Current output equals potential output, which is the level of output the economy produces when its resources are used at normal rates.
   b. Inflation equals money growth minus growth in potential output.

2. The dynamic aggregate demand curve is a downward-sloping relationship between inflation and the quantity of output demanded by those who use it:
   a. Aggregate expenditure = consumption + investment + government purchases + net exports.
      i. Aggregate expenditure falls when the real interest rate rises.
      ii. The long-run real interest rate equates aggregate expenditure with potential output.
   b. Monetary policy is described by an upward-sloping monetary policy reaction curve.
      i. When policymakers change the nominal interest rate, they change the real interest rate as well, because inflation doesn't change quickly.
      ii. Policymakers react to increases in inflation by increasing the nominal and therefore real interest rate.
      iii. The monetary policy reaction curve is set so that the real interest rate equals the long-run real interest rate when inflation equals the central bank's target.

   iv. The monetary policy reaction curve shifts when either the inflation target changes or the long-run real interest rate changes.
   c. Movements along the dynamic aggregate demand curve occur when monetary policymakers react to changes in inflation by adjusting the real interest rate.
   d. The dynamic aggregate demand curve shifts when
      i. Changes in consumer confidence, business optimism, government purchases, or net exports shifts the dynamic aggregate demand curve.
      ii. The monetary policy reaction curve shifts.

3. The aggregate supply curve tells us the amount of output producers are willing to supply at given levels of inflation.
   a. The short-run aggregate supply curve slopes up because, in the short run, costs of production adjust more slowly than the output prices.
   b. Production cost changes shift the short-run aggregate supply curve. These occur when
      i. There is a recessionary or expansionary output gap.
      ii. Expectations about future inflation change.
      iii. Raw material prices, such as the cost of energy, change.
   c. The long-run aggregate supply curve is vertical at potential output.
      i. Along the long-run aggregate supply curve, expected inflation equals current inflation.
      ii. The long-run aggregate supply curve shifts when either the amounts of capital and labour used in the economy change or productivity changes.
      iii. The short-run aggregate supply curve intersects the long-run aggregate supply curve at the point where inflation equals expected inflation.

4. Equilibrium output and inflation are determined by the intersection of the dynamic aggregate demand curve and either the short-run or long-run aggregate supply curve.
   a. The short-run equilibrium point is located where the dynamic aggregate demand curve intersects the short-run aggregate supply curve.
   b. The long-run equilibrium point is located where the dynamic aggregate demand curve intersects the long-run aggregate supply curve.

At that point, current output equals potential output and inflation equals the inflation target, which equals expected inflation.

c. Fluctuations in output and inflation come from either
   i. Demand shifts, which cause them to rise and fall together.
   ii. Supply shifts, which cause one to rise as the other falls.

## Conceptual Problems

1. Explain the determinants of potential growth.

2.* Explain how a recessionary output gap would emerge in an economy in which the long-run aggregate supply curve is persistently shifting to the right.

3. Describe the determinants of the long-run real interest rate and speculate on the sort of events that would make it fluctuate. Given your answer, do you think the real interest rate is more likely to have gone up or down over the past five years?

4. Explain how and why the components of aggregate expenditure depend on the exchange rate.

5. Explain how and why the components of aggregate expenditure depend on the real interest rate. Be sure to distinguish between the real and nominal interest rates, and explain why the distinction matters.

6. The Bank of Canada's primary objective is keeping inflation close to 2 percent. In contrast, the FOMC has a dual objective of price stability and high economic growth. How would you expect the monetary policy reaction curves of the two central banks to differ? Why?

7. In the United Kingdom, the Chancellor of the Exchequer (equivalent to the Minister of Finance in Canada) sets the Bank of England's inflation target. For years, the Chancellor set the target rate at 2.5 percent, but after a new government was elected, the new Chancellor set the rate at 3.5 percent. Describe the impact of this change in the inflation target on
   a. The monetary policy reaction curve.
   b. The aggregate demand curve.

\* Indicates more difficult problems.

8. Use data for the quarter or month before each of the last two recessions (1981-III–1982-IV; 1990-II–1991-I) and at their end to construct a table showing the change in the one-month Treasury bill rate and the percentage change in real GDP between the beginning and end of the recession. Both series can be found from CANSIM (interest rate: v122529; real GDP v1992067). Comment on any interesting patterns you find.

9. Using the same data sources as in question 8, collect data on the 1- and 3-month treasury bill rate for 1970 to the present. Note the behaviour of the interest rates just before the recessions of 1981 and 1990. Did interest rates rise or fall before peaks in the business cycle? Do your findings suggest that monetary policy causes recessions? (The one-month T-bill rate data start in 1980; there was no target for the overnight rate in 1970).

10.* Explain why the short-run aggregate supply curve is upward sloping. Under what circumstances might it be vertical?

## Analytical Problems

11. Suppose the real interest rate falls. What would you expect to happen to (a) consumption, (b) investment, and (c) net exports in the economy?

12.* Economy A and Economy B are similar in every way except that in Economy A, 70 percent of aggregate expenditure is sensitive to changes in the real interest rate and in Economy B, only 50 percent of aggregate expenditure is sensitive to changes in the real interest rate.
   a. Which economy will have a steeper aggregate expenditure curve?
   b. How would the dynamic aggregate demand curves differ given that the monetary policy reaction curve is the same in both countries?

Explain your answers.

13. State whether each of the following will result in a movement along or a shift in the monetary policy reaction curve and in which direction the effect will be.

www.mcgrawhill.ca/olc/cecchetti

a. Policymakers increase the real interest rate in response to a rise in current inflation.

b. Policymakers increase their inflation target.

c. The long-run real interest rate falls.

14. Suppose a natural disaster wipes out a significant portion of the economy's capital stock, reducing the potential level of output. What would you expect to happen to the long-run real interest rate? What impact would this have on the monetary policy reaction curve and the dynamic aggregate demand curve?

15. Suppose there were a wave of investor pessimism in the economy. What would be the impact on the dynamic aggregate demand curve?

16. Explain how each of the following affects the short-run aggregate supply curve:

a. Firms and workers reduce their expectations of future inflation.

b. There is a rise in current inflation.

c. There is a fall in oil prices.

17. Suppose the economy is in short-run equilibrium at a level of output that exceeds potential output. How would the economy self-adjust to return to long-run equilibrium?

18.* You read a story in the newspaper blaming the central bank for pushing the economy into recession. The article goes on to mention that not only has output fallen below its potential level but also that inflation has risen. If you were to write to the newspaper defending the central bank, what argument would you make?

# APPENDIX 18

The model that we have presented in this chapter can be summarized algebraically. Begin with the aggregate expenditure curve

$$E = e_0 + e_1 r \tag{A1}$$

where $e_1 < 0$, reflecting the negative relationship between the real interest rate and aggregate expenditure, and $e_0$ captures all the factors (such as business confidence, government expenditure etc.,) that also affect aggregate expenditure. We defined the long-run real rate of interest as the rate at which aggregate expenditure equals potential output, which we can write implicitly as

$$e_0 + e_1 r^* = Y_P \tag{A2}$$

Notice that the long-run real interest rate ($r^*$) depends on $e_0$ and $Y^p$.

Next we derived the monetary policy reaction curve, which showed how the central bank varied the real interest rate as a function of inflation.

$$r = m_0 + m_1 \pi \tag{A3}$$

where $m_1 > 0$, as the central bank raises the rate when inflation rises. The slope of this curve ($m_1$) captures how aggressively the central bank reacts to inflation. The intercept ($m_0$) is determined by the condition that when the inflation rate is at its target, the real interest rate equals its long-run level.

$$r^* = m_0 + m_1 \pi^T \tag{A4}$$

Combining equations (A3) and (A4), we can write the monetary policy reaction function in terms of the long-term real interest rate and the target inflation rate:

$$r = r^* + m_1 (\pi - \pi^T) \tag{A5}$$

To derive the dynamic aggregate demand curve, substitute the monetary policy reaction in equation (A5) function into the expenditure curve in equation (A1):

$$E = e_0 + e_1 (r^* + m_1 [\pi - \pi^T])$$
$$E = (e_0 + e_1 r^* - e_1 m_1 \pi^T) + e_1 m_1 \pi \tag{A6}$$

The substitution tells you that the aggregate demand curve is the relationship between inflation and expenditure incorporating the dependence of aggregate demand on the real interest rate and the reaction of the central bank to inflation. It is very important to notice that, unlike demand curves in microeconomics, not all variables are constant along the dynamic aggregate demand curve. Specifically, the real interest rate is varying as you move along the curve. Given our assumption that $e_1 < 0$ and $m_1 > 0$, the curve capturing the relationship between aggregate expenditure and inflation is negatively sloped.

The equation for long-run aggregate supply is simple

$$Y = Y^P \tag{A7}$$

and the equation for short run aggregate supply is

$$Y = s_0 + s_1\pi \tag{A8}$$

where $s_1 > 0$. The slope of the short-run aggregate supply curve (SRAS) depends on how much output can respond in the short run to unexpectedly or temporary high prices. The intercept of the SRAS is determined by the condition that the SRAS intercepts potential output where actual inflation equals expected inflation. That is, the intercept ($s_0$) is a function of expected inflation. If there is a recessionary gap, then actual inflation will be less than expected and we assume that expected inflation falls; that is, that $s_0$ rises. Notice that when we draw the SRAS, we have inflation on the vertical axis and output and expenditure on the horizontal axis. That means that an upward shift in the SRAS reflects a decline in $s_0$, or to put it another way, an upward shift in SRAS means a lower level of output for each level of inflation.

Now we can put it all together! In equilibrium, expenditure will equal output,

$$E = Y \tag{A9}$$

In long-run equilibrium we know that $Y = Y^P$ and $\pi = \pi^T$. Using (A2), we see that this implies $r^* = \dfrac{Y^P - e_0}{e_1}$; and using (A8) we see that $s_0 = Y^P - s_1\pi^T$.

To find the short-run equilibrium, we equate short-run aggregate supply in equation (A8) and dynamic aggregate demand in equation (A6) to find the rate of inflation (let the overbar indicate it is the short-run equilibrium):

$$s_0 + s_1\overline{\pi} = (e_0 + e_1 r^* - e_1 m_1 \pi^T) + e_1 m_1 \pi$$

$$\overline{\pi} = \frac{e_0 + e_1 r^* - e_1 m_1 \pi^T - s_0}{s_1 - e_1 m_1}\pi = \frac{e_0 + e_1 r^* - e_1 m_1 \pi^T - s_0}{s_1 - e_1 m_1} \tag{A10}$$

Then we can substitute this back into either equation (A8) or (A6) to find the level of output:

$$\overline{Y} = s_0 + s_1 \left\{ \frac{e_0 + e_1 r^* - e_1 m_1 \pi^T - s_0}{s_1 - e_1 m_1} \right\} \tag{A11}$$

The point $(\overline{Y}, \overline{\pi})$ corresponds to the intersection point in Figure 18-15. To fully characterize the equilibrium, you would also have to find the level of the real interest rate by substituting the expression for $\overline{Y}$ for E in equation (A1) or insert the expression for $\overline{\pi}$ into equation (A5).

One of the reasons to do the algebraic analysis is that it makes clear how the endogenous variables ($Y$, $r$, and $\pi$) depend on all the parameters and variables of the model. If you know how a variable (say government expenditures) affects a parameter (in this case $e_0$), then you can determine how it affects the equilibrium levels of output and inflation. Consider an exogenous increase in government expenditures, which would increase $e_0$. We begin with the short-run analysis and assume that $s_0$ is constant and that the monetary authority does not shift the MPRC. This latter means that we can substitute (A3) rather than (A5) into the expenditure function (A1) to derive the aggregate demand curve to get:

$$E = e_0 + e_1(m_0 + m_1\pi) \tag{A12}$$

Letting $E = Y$, we can solve (A12) and (A8) to find expressions for Y and $\pi$:

$$\overline{Y} = s_0 + s_1 \left\{ \frac{e_0 + e_1\pi - s_0}{s_1 - e_1 m_1} \right\} \text{ and } \overline{\pi} = \frac{e_0 + e_1\pi - s_0}{s_1 - e_1 m_1} \tag{A13}$$

An increase in $e_0$ will increase output and inflation in the short run. This could correspond to a point like 1 in Panel A of Figure 18.16 on page 418. To derive the long-run consequences, we begin by maintaining the assumption that the monetary authority moves only along the MPRC, but we allow the SRAS curve to shift up ($s_0$ falls) in response to the expansionary output gap. From (A11), clearly inflation will rise with a fall in $s_0$, and by rearranging the equation for $\overline{Y}$ to isolate the $s_0$ terms we see that output also falls. $s_0$ will continue to fall until the output gap is closed, or $Y = Y^p$. This corresponds with point 2 in Panel A of Figure 18.16. But at that point inflation is above the inflation target. To return to long-run equilibrium, the monetary authority raises the real interest rate so that the interest-rate sensitive components of aggregate demand fall. (If this were literally done sequentially, then we would see the SRAS curve fall ($s_0$ rise) as the inflation rate declined. In practice the two long-run adjustments occur concurrently.)  In the long-run equilibrium, the initial increase in $e_0$ is exactly offset by a decrease in the interest-sensitive components of aggregate demand; that is, $-e_1\Delta r^* = \Delta e_0$. This corresponds to the equilibrium in Figure 18.14 on page 417.

# CHAPTER 19

## Understanding Business Cycle Fluctuations

In the last chapter we constructed a framework for understanding fluctuations in output and inflation. We discussed the fact that central bankers respond to rising inflation by increasing the real interest rate, causing interest-sensitive components of aggregate expenditure—especially investment—to fall, driving down the quantity of aggregate output demanded by the people who use it. So, higher inflation means a lower level of demand in the economy as a whole. The *dynamic aggregate demand curve slopes down*.

On the supply side, we saw that the sluggish response of production costs means that higher inflation elicits more production from firms, and is associated with a greater level of output supplied in the short run. The *short-run aggregate supply curve slopes upward*. Finally, we learned that in the long run, the economy moves to the point where output equals potential output, so the *long-run aggregate supply curve is vertical*. While the economy can and does move away from this long-run equilibrium, it has a natural self-correcting mechanism that returns it to the point where resources are being used at their normal rates and gaps between current and potential output disappear.

We will now use this framework to improve our understanding of business cycles— the fluctuations in aggregate economic output from quarter to quarter and year to year. What drives these fluctuations and what determines their extent? Figure 19.1 illustrates the long-run trends in the Canadian inflation rate together with indicators of business cycle recessions over the past 50 years. From the mid-1950s to the 1970s Canadian inflation averaged 2.5 percent. In the mid-1970s inflation rose rapidly to nearly 13 percent, and after a brief respite returned to that level in the early 1980s. Then the inflation rate fell sharply to 4 percent and remained there for a few years before rising again at the end of the 1980s, peaking at nearly 7 percent. In the early 1990s the Bank of Canada introduced inflation targets, initially to reduce the inflation rate and then to stabilize it. By the end of 1991, prices were increasing at a rate of less than 4 percent per year and inflation until 2009 has remained close to 2 percent.

In addition to data on the rate of inflation, Figure 19.1 displays a series of shaded bars representing recessions—periods when the Canadian real GDP was falling. While there is no apparent relationship between the *level* of inflation and these recessions, it does appear that the inflation rate falls during or after a recession.

One final point about Figure 19.1 is worth noting. In recent years, the frequency of recessions has fallen markedly. In the 30 years from 1955 to 1984, there were six recessions; in the 20 years from 1984 to 2004 there was only one. In the early years of the 21st century economists spoke of this reduction in the volatility of real growth as "the great moderation." More recently, of course, such language has been scarce.

To help understand the patterns in Figure 19.1, we will start by cataloguing the various reasons that the dynamic aggregate demand curve and the aggregate supply curve shift. These are the potential sources of fluctuations in both output and inflation described at the end of the last chapter. We trace the initial impact of shifts in aggregate demand such as an increase in government spending or shifts in short-run aggregate supply such as a movement in oil prices. Next, we examine what happens during the transition as the economy moves to long-run equilibrium. Our goal is to take the macroeconomic model and use it to understand practical real-world examples.

Figure 19.1    Inflation and the Business Cycle, 1955–2006

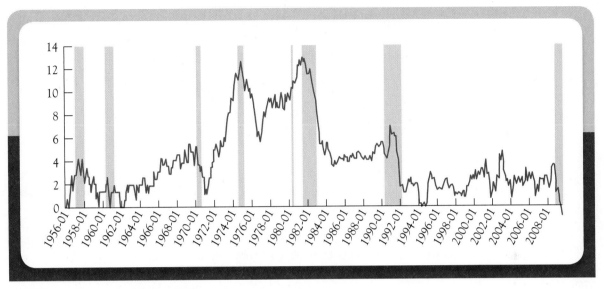

This figure shows the 12-month change in consumer prices.

SOURCE: *Statistics Canada CANSIM database, http://cansim2.statcan.ca, Table 326-0020 (v41690973), accessed 18 September 2009.*

In the second part of the chapter, we will use the model to understand how central bankers work to achieve their stabilization objectives, together with a series of examples that highlight the pitfalls and limitations that monetary policymakers face. The section is organized around a series of questions of increasing complexity. We will examine how, in practice, policymakers work to achieve their stabilization goals; the appropriate actions to take when potential output changes; and the difficulty central bankers have figuring out why output has fallen, among other things.

In the final section of the chapter we introduce the "Taylor rule," first proposed by economist John Taylor, which determines the interest rate that should be set in an economy based on the desired inflation rate and the level of the output gap. By the end of this chapter you should have a good understanding of the complexity of the problem of choosing the target for the overnight interest rate, and a knowledge of some of the tools that central banks use to select the rate.

## Sources of Fluctuations in Output and Inflation

In the earlier discussion we learned that the economy naturally moves toward its long-run equilibrium where output equals potential output ($Y = Y^P$) and inflation equals the central bank's target ($\pi = \pi^T$), which equals the level of inflation firms and individuals expect ($\pi = \pi^e$). This tells us that the long-run aggregate supply curve is vertical at potential output. But because costs of production adjust slowly, higher inflation means higher profits and more supply; that is, the short-run aggregate supply curve slopes upward. Short-run equilibrium is where the dynamic aggregate demand curve intersects this short-run aggregate supply curve. So, immediately after either the short-run aggregate supply curve or the dynamic aggregate demand curve shift, the economy will move away from its long-run equilibrium. This means that understanding short-run fluctuations in output and inflation requires that we study shifts in dynamic aggregate demand and short-run aggregate supply.

Before moving to an analysis of various demand and supply curve shifts, let's take a brief detour to define one of the few new terms in this chapter: *shock*. Economists use the word "shock" to mean something unexpected. For example, when oil prices rise or when consumers become less confident about the future, these are almost always unpredictable *shocks*. In our framework, a shock shifts the dynamic aggregate demand or short-run aggregate supply curve. Since it affects costs of production, the oil price increase is a **supply shock**, while the shift in consumer confidence, which affects consumption expenditure, is a **demand shock**. So, a shock is something that creates a shift in the demand or supply curve.

## Shifts in the Dynamic Aggregate Demand Curve

Recall that a shift in the dynamic aggregate demand curve can be caused by either a shift in the monetary policy reaction curve or a change in components that are not sensitive to the interest rate such as government purchases that shift aggregate expenditure. Let's look at the impact of each of these. We will first look at a decline in the central bank's inflation target that shifts the monetary policy reaction curve, and then at a fiscal policy contraction that decreases government purchases and shifts the aggregate expenditure curve.

### A Decline in the Central Bank's Inflation Target
Over the past several decades, numerous countries have succeeded in reducing their inflation rates from fairly high levels to the modest ones we see today. For example, Chile was able to reduce its inflation rate from over 20 percent in the early 1990s to roughly 2 percent today. In the mid-1980s, Israel's inflation rate peaked at nearly 400 percent before it was brought down in a series of steps, first to 20 percent and eventually to 1 percent. And Sweden entered the 1990s with an inflation rate that was over 10 percent. The Riksbank, the Swedish central bank, spent a number of years driving the country's inflation rate down below 2 percent, where it has stayed. All of these cases involved permanent declines in inflation that reflect a decrease in the central bank's inflation target.

To analyze the impact of a reduction in the policymaker's inflation target, let's begin with the monetary policy reaction curve. A fall in $\pi^T$ shifts the monetary policy reaction curve to the left, as shown in Figure 19.2 (which reproduces Figure 18.8A on page 407). The decrease in the inflation target raises the real interest rate policymakers set at each level of inflation.

This reduces aggregate expenditure at every level of inflation, shifting the dynamic aggregate demand curve to the left as well, as shown in Panel A of Figure 19.3. You can see that as the dynamic aggregate demand curve shifts to the left, from $AD_0$ to $AD_1$, the economy moves from original short-run equilibrium point, 1, to new short-run equilibrium point, 2. At point 2, inflation and current output are both lower than they were prior to the monetary policy tightening. The immediate consequence of the reduction in the central bank's inflation target is to shift the dynamic aggregate demand curve to the left, moving the economy along the short-run aggregate supply curve (SRAS), driving both current output and inflation down.

Following the policy change, potential output has not changed. This means that the fall in current output creates a

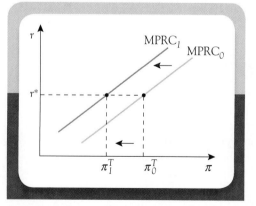

**Figure 19.2**  **A Decline in the Central Bank's Inflation Target**

A decline in the inflation target from $\pi^T_0$ to $\pi^T_1$ shifts the monetary policy reaction curve to the left from $MPRC_0$ to $MPRC_1$.

Figure 19.3     A Decline in the Central Bank's Inflation Target

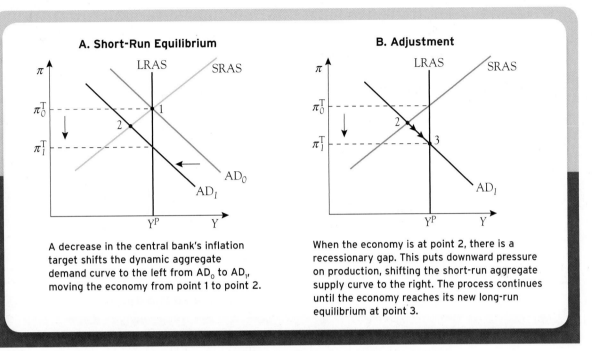

**A. Short-Run Equilibrium**

A decrease in the central bank's inflation target shifts the dynamic aggregate demand curve to the left from $AD_0$ to $AD_1$, moving the economy from point 1 to point 2.

**B. Adjustment**

When the economy is at point 2, there is a recessionary gap. This puts downward pressure on production, shifting the short-run aggregate supply curve to the right. The process continues until the economy reaches its new long-run equilibrium at point 3.

recessionary gap: $Y < Y^P$. And a recessionary gap puts downward pressure on production costs, shifting the short-run aggregate supply curve to the right. Eventually, the economy moves along the new dynamic aggregate demand curve $AD_1$ from point 2 to the new long-run equilibrium at point 3. There, inflation equals the central bank's (new) target and output equals potential output.[1]

**A Decrease in Government Purchases**   From 1990 to 1995, the Canadian federal government ran budget deficits of over $30 billion each year, which caused the ratio of government debt to GDP to rise to over 60 percent. In 1995, Finance Minister Paul Martin argued that Canadians might have trouble borrowing in international capital markets if the deficits continued, and also that the interest costs of such a high debt level were too much of a burden on tax payers. He decided to eliminate the deficit and from 1996 to 2008 the federal government ran a budget surplus. What are the macroeconomic implications of such a large expansionary move in fiscal policy?

In the last chapter we learned that decreases in government purchases (G) and cuts in taxes both represent a decrease in components of aggregate expenditure that are not sensitive to the interest rate. For example, a decrease in G shifts the dynamic aggregate demand curve to the left. Panel A in Figure 19.4 on page 430 shows how such a change in fiscal policy shifts the dynamic aggregate demand curve from its original position $AD_0$ to its new position $AD_1$. As a result, the economy moves from the original short-run equilibrium point 1 to the new short-run equilibrium point 2. Not surprisingly, the immediate impact of this decrease in government purchases is to decrease both current output and inflation. But, because potential output has not

---

[1] With a lower inflation target ($\pi^T$), we also know that at the new long-run equilibrium, expected inflation ($\pi^e$) must be lower as well.

Figure 19.4    A Decrease in Government Expenditure

A. Short-Run Equilibrium

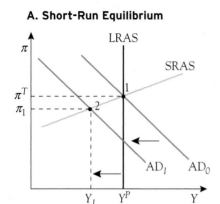

B. Adjustment

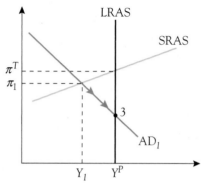

A decrease in government expenditure shifts the AD curve to the left from $AD_0$ to $AD_1$. This moves the economy from point 1 to point 2. In the short run, output falls to $Y_1$ while inflation decreases to $\pi_1$.

When the economy is at point 2, there is a recessionary gap, which puts downward pressure on inflation. This causes the short-run aggregate supply curve to shift to the right, moving the economy along $AD_1$ toward point 3.

changed, this can't be the long-run effect. Instead, the higher level of current output means that $Y < Y^P$, so that there is now a recessionary gap. Since current output does not equal potential output, the economy cannot stay at point 2. Instead, it must move back to its long-run equilibrium on the long-run aggregate supply curve.

Here's how the adjustment works. At point 2 there is a recessionary output gap, $Y < Y^P$. With current output below potential output, firms decrease both their product prices and the wages that they pay their workers by more than they would if they were operating at normal levels. So, when there is a recessionary gap, production costs fall more quickly and inflation goes down. This shifts the short-run aggregate supply curve to the right, driving inflation even lower. As inflation falls, monetary policymakers lower the real interest rate, moving the economy *along* the dynamic aggregate demand curve $AD_1$ (as shown in Panel B of Figure 19.4). Eventually, as the economy travels along $AD_1$, output begins to rise back toward its long-run equilibrium level, potential output.

Unless something else happens, the economy settles at point 3 in Panel B of Figure 19.4, where $AD_1$ crosses the long-run aggregate supply curve (LRAS) and current output once again equals potential output. It is extremely important to realize that at point 3 inflation is below where it started at point 1, and that this is below the policymakers' original inflation target $\pi^T$. Unless monetary policy adjusts, when the dynamic aggregate demand curve shifts to the left, inflation will fall.

While central bankers could allow a decrease in government purchases to drive down their inflation target, permanently lowering inflation and the monetary growth rate, it seems unlikely. So long as monetary policymakers remain committed to their original inflation target, they need to do something to get the economy back to the point where it began—point 1 in Panel A of Figure 19.4, at the intersection of the original dynamic aggregate demand curve with the long-run aggregate supply curve. This is the point where current output equals potential output, and current inflation equals the policymaker's original inflation target.

In Chapter 18, we noted that an increase in government purchases raises the long-term real interest rate. The higher the level of government purchases, the higher the level of the real interest rate needed to equate aggregate expenditure with potential output. Conversely, of course, lowering government expenditures lowers the real interest rate. Realizing this, monetary policymakers react by shifting their monetary policy reaction curve to the right, lowering the real interest rate at every level of inflation. Remember, the central bank controls the real interest rate in the short run. When the monetary policy reaction curve shifts, the dynamic aggregate demand curve shifts with it. In this case, looser monetary policy shifts the dynamic aggregate demand curve to the right (back to $AD_0$), bringing the economy back to long-run equilibrium where output equals potential output and inflation equals the central bank's target at point 1 in Figure 19.4.[2]

We can summarize the path the economy takes after a decrease in government purchases as follows: Output initially falls below potential output until monetary policymakers push it back up to its long-run equilibrium level. Meanwhile, inflation falls initially and then rises back to the central bank's target level. From this we can conclude that, without a change in target inflation, *a decrease in government purchases causes a temporary decrease in both output and inflation*. The same is true for any factor that shifts the dynamic aggregate demand curve to the left. Immediately following such a shift and, in the absence of any monetary policy response, output and inflation both fall. With time, and in the absence of any monetary policy response, the recessionary output gap drives down production costs, shifting the short-run aggregate supply curve to the right, moving the economy along the new dynamic aggregate demand curve. This movement drives inflation down further as current output rises, returning to the level of potential output. If policymakers do react, inflation and output will return to their original long-run levels.

A rise in aggregate expenditure, perhaps caused by a rise in consumer or business confidence, has the opposite impact from a decrease in government expenditure. The dynamic aggregate demand curve shifts to the right, driving output up. Thus, *a rise in aggregate expenditure causes a temporary increase in both output and inflation*. With time, and in the absence of any monetary policy response, the expansionary output gap causes the short-run aggregate supply curve to shift to the left, moving the economy along the new dynamic aggregate demand curve (see Table 19.1 on page 432). This movement drives inflation up further, and current output begins to fall toward potential output. If policymakers do react, inflation and output will return to their original long-run levels.

Over the years, policymakers have reacted to shifts in aggregate expenditure in different ways, with differing results. In the second half of the 1970s, government deficits expanded and the rate of inflation rose. What could have been a temporary increase in inflation became a permanent one, in effect increasing the Bank of Canada's implicit inflation target to the point where the new dynamic aggregate demand curve intersected the long-run aggregate supply curve. In contrast, the elimination of deficits in the 1990s didn't cause a significant reduction in inflation. Between the 1970s and the 1990s, the Bank of Canada successfully adopted inflation targeting, which meant that it was committed to not allowing fiscal policy to change the inflation rate.

This discussion implies that whenever we see a *permanent* increase in inflation, it must be the result of monetary policy. That is, if inflation goes up or down and remains at its new level, the only explanation is that central bankers must be allowing it to happen. They have changed their inflation target, whether implicitly or explicitly.

---

[2] The model implicitly assumes that monetary policymakers respond immediately and automatically to deviations of inflation from their target but, since the long-run real interest rate is unobservable, only gradually to changes in the long-run real interest rate. Although for clarity we have discussed the adjustments sequentially, in practice they occur concurrently. The Appendix to Chapter 18 helps clarify the timing.

| Table 19.1 | Impact of an Increase in Dynamic Aggregate Demand on Output and Inflation |
|---|---|
| Source | Monetary policy reaction curve shifts right<br>• Increase in inflation target<br>• Decrease in long-run real interest rate<br><br>Increase in aggregate expenditure:<br>• Consumer confidence up<br>• Business optimism up<br>• Government purchases up<br>• Net exports up |
| Result | Dynamic aggregate demand shifts right |
| Short-Run Impact | $Y$ increases<br>$\pi$ increases |

**Figure 19.5**    A Negative Supply Shock

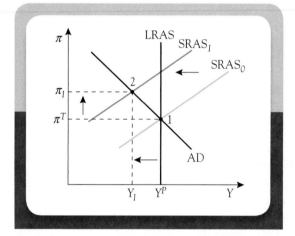

A negative supply shock shifts the short-run aggregate supply curve to the left, moving short-run equilibrium from point 1 to point 2. Inflation rises and output falls.

## Shifts in the Short-Run Aggregate Supply Curve

Changes in production costs *shift the short-run aggregate supply curve*. Using the aggregate demand/aggregate supply diagram, we can trace the effects of such an increase in the costs of production—a *negative supply shock*. The immediate effect of something that increases production costs is to move the short-run aggregate supply curve to the left, reducing the amount supplied at every level of inflation. (These bad consequences—higher inflation and lower growth—are why we label such a shock as "negative.") Figure 19.5 shows the result. Short-run equilibrium—the point where the short-run aggregate supply and dynamic aggregate demand curves intersect—moves to point 2 in the figure, where output is lower and inflation is higher. This creates a condition that is sometimes referred to as *stagflation*—economic stagnation coupled with increased inflation (see Table 19.2).

| Table 19.2 | Impact of a Decline in Short-Run Aggregate Supply on Output and Inflation |
|---|---|
| Source | Negative supply shock<br>• Increase in production costs<br>• Increase in expected inflation |
| Result | Short-run aggregate supply curve shifts left |
| Short-Run Impact | $Y$ falls<br>$\pi$ increases |

What happens next? The recessionary gap $(Y < Y^p)$ exerts downward pressure on production costs and inflation. As a result, the short-run aggregate supply curve begins to shift to the right, moving the economy along the dynamic aggregate demand curve, driving inflation down and output up. Inflation continues to fall and output continues to rise until the economy returns to the point where current output equals potential output (which we are assuming is unchanged) and inflation equals the central bank's (unchanged) target level, point 1 in Figure 19.5.

As was the case with the decrease in government purchases (when combined with an appropriate monetary policy response), a supply shock has no effect on the economy's long-run equilibrium point. Only a change in either potential output or the central bank's inflation target can accomplish that.

## Using the Aggregate Demand–Aggregate Supply Framework

We are now ready to use the macroeconomic framework to address a series of interesting questions. We examine the following (in increasing order of complexity):

1. What causes recessions?
2. How do policymakers achieve their stabilization objectives?

# TOOLS OF THE TRADE
### Defining a Recession

Statistics Canada is the official arbiter of when Canada is in recession, and makes the determination based primarily on the behaviour of output and employment. While the rule of thumb that a recession is any episode in which real gross domestic product (GDP) declines for two consecutive quarters provides a rough guide, it is not infallible. For example, if output fell for two quarters because a one quarter decline was followed by particularly bad weather leading to a second quarter of decline, it would not necessarily be defined as a recession.

In the United States, the arbiter for declaring "official" recessions is the National Bureau of Economic Research (NBER, a research organization founded in 1920, is devoted to studying how the economy works). The NBER's definition of a recession is as follows:

*A recession is a significant decline in economic activity spread across the economy, lasting more than a few months, normally visible in production, employment, real income, and other indicators. A recession begins when the economy reaches a peak of activity and ends when the economy reaches its trough. Between trough and peak, the economy is in an expansion.\**

This definition has three important implications. First, a recession is a decline in activity, not just a dip in the growth rate. Second, the exact length of the economic contraction is ambiguous. A severe decline in economic activity that lasted less than two quarters could still be considered a recession according to this definition. And third, since key economic indicators often change direction at different times, there is an element of judgment in dating the peaks and troughs of business cycles. As a result, the NBER's Business-Cycle Dating Committee takes its time in declaring the beginning and end of a recession. Delays of six months to a year are common.

The term "business cycle" is somewhat misleading when used to refer to fluctuations in economic activity. The word "cycle" calls up images of recurring waves that rise and fall in a periodic pattern. Economic fluctuations aren't like that. Both the length of recessions and the time between them are irregular.

Panel A of Figure 19.6 on page 434 plots real GDP in Canada with shaded periods representing recessions as defined by two quarters of declines in GDP. Panel B plots the NBER's business-cycle reference dates against the growth in U.S. real GDP over the period. The figures show that whichever definition you use, the two economies experienced very similar business cycles.

SOURCE: "Determination of the December 2007 peak in Economic Activity" December 2008, retrieved August 25, 2009 from http://www.nber.org/cycles/dec2008.html. For more information on the procedures used to date U.S. business cycles, go to the NBER's Web site at www.nber.org. For more information on the dating of Canadian business cycles see "The Impact of recessions in the United States on Canada" by Philip Cross, Canadian Economic Observer, Section 3, March 2009.

(continued)

## Figure 19.6 Growth in Real GDP over the Business Cycle

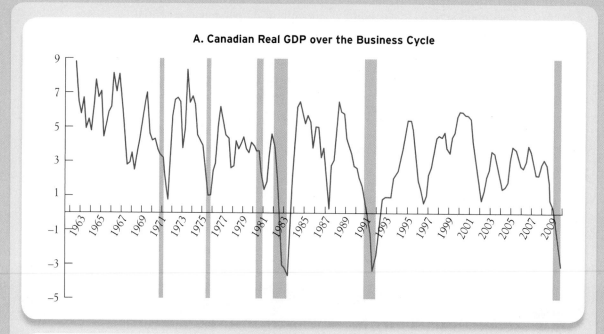

### A. Canadian Real GDP over the Business Cycle

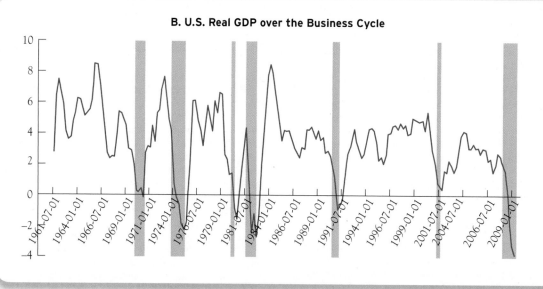

### B. U.S. Real GDP over the Business Cycle

The figure shows the four-quarter percentage change in real GDP. The shaded areas represent recessions as defined by Statistics Canada and the NBER (United States). The data on US recessions are from NBER at: http://www.nber.org/cycles/cyclesmain.html.

SOURCES: *Figure 19.6A (Canadian data): Statistics Canada CANSIM database, http://cansim2.statcan.ca, Table 380-0002, v1992067, accessed 18 September 2009 || Figure 19.6B: The data on U.S. recessions are from: a) NBER at: http://www.nber.org/cycles/cyclesmain.html; b) Federal Reserve Bank of St. Louis. FRED, Series GDPPC1_PC1 at: http://research.stlouisfed.org/fred2, accessed 28 September 2009. [This is the GDPc1 series. The percentage change is from one year ago.]*

3. What happens when potential output changes?
4. What are the implications of globalization for monetary policy?
5. Can policymakers distinguish a recessionary gap from a fall in potential output?
6. Can policymakers stabilize output and inflation simultaneously?

## What Causes Recessions?

Looking at the macroeconomic model, we can see that output and inflation movements can arise from either demand or supply shifts. To figure how we might tell them apart, notice that while shifts in either the dynamic aggregate demand curve or the short-run aggregate supply curve can have the same effect on inflation, they have opposite effects on output. So, if the dynamic aggregate demand curve shifts to the right, increasing inflation, it will result in higher output as well. By contrast, when the short-run aggregate supply curve shifts to the left, inflation rises and output falls. That is, the possible sources of fluctuations are (1) shifts in the dynamic aggregate demand curve that cause output and inflation to rise and fall together, moving in the *same* direction; and (2) shifts in the short-run aggregate supply curve that move output and inflation in *opposite* directions, one rising when the other one is falling.

So, what are the likely sources of economic fluctuations? Let's start with inflation. Recall that in long-run equilibrium, inflation equals the central bank's target, which is equal to inflation expectations. So, if we see inflation rise or fall permanently, it must be that policymakers changed their inflation target, consciously or not. By contrast, short-run inflation fluctuations have more than one possible source. Inflation goes up in the short run when either the dynamic aggregate demand curve shifts to the right, or when the short-run aggregate supply curve shifts to the left. The first of these comes from either increases in the components of aggregate expenditure that are not sensitive to the real interest rate (higher government expenditure, business optimism, or consumer confidence) or a permanent easing of monetary policy (when the monetary policy reaction curve shifts to lower the real interest rate at every level of inflation). Each of these shifts dynamic aggregate demand to the right, increasing inflation. The second comes from increases in the costs of production, like a rise in oil prices or higher inflation expectations—each of which shifts the short-run aggregate supply curve to the left, driving inflation up.

Turning to output, there are again two possible sources of fluctuations. Output drops when either the dynamic aggregate demand curve or the short-run aggregate supply curve shift to the left. For demand, either a decline in aggregate expenditure or a shift to the left in the monetary policy reaction curve drives current output below potential output. This brings up the interesting possibility that policymakers could be the sources of recessions. On the supply side, increases in either production costs or inflation expectations drive output down (at the same time that they drive inflation up). Which is it? Let's see if we can figure it out.

If demand shifts were the cause of recessions, we should see inflation fall when output falls. And if production cost increases were the source, then we should see inflation rise as the economy slows down. Look back at Figure 19.1 on page 427. Note that inflation fell after six of the last seven recessions. It appears that many of the recessions in the past half century can be traced to shifts in the dynamic aggregate demand curve. Let's go further and figure out what caused these AD shifts. Was it falling aggregate expenditure brought about by changes in people's attitudes, or was it the actions of monetary policymakers? To see, we can look at one more piece of evidence: the behaviour of interest rates. Figure 19.7 on page 436 shows that shortly

Figure 19.7    Interest Rates and the Business Cycle

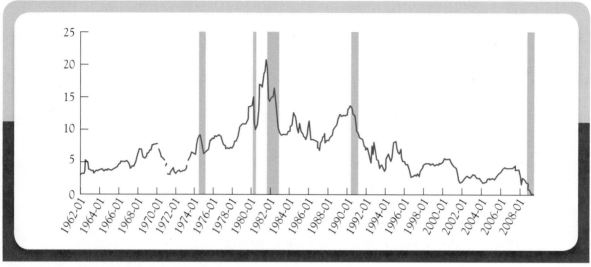

SOURCE: *Bank of Canada, v122531, Table 176-0043.*

before most recessions start, just to the left of each of the shaded bars, the interest rate tends to rise. This suggests that Bank of Canada policy may be at least partly to blame for the business cycle downturns over the past half century. But why would policy-makers have chosen to cause these recessions? The answer is to bring down inflation. Especially in the late 1970s, when the inflation rate was over 10 percent per year, something had to be done. The only thing the Bank of Canada could do under such circumstances was to raise interest rates, reducing the interest-sensitive components of aggregate expenditure in the process and triggering a recession. The low inflation we enjoy today is the result of the Bank of Canada's tough policy decisions.

Notice that, unlike in most recessions, before the onset of the 2009 recession interest rates were falling. This is a sign that it is an unusual event—and not just in its severity. The simultaneous decline in output and inflation signals an aggregate demand shift but interest rates show it's not a (direct) result of monetary policy. In Chapter 23, we discuss the triggers of the financial crisis that led to the recession but here note that the collapse of financial markets led to a sharp contraction of aggregate demand.

## How Do Policymakers Achieve Their Stabilization Objectives?

The aggregate demand–aggregate supply framework is useful in understanding how monetary and fiscal policymakers seek to stabilize output and inflation using what is called stabilization policy. In thinking about the way monetary policy can be used to reduce the economic fluctuations, recall that movements in output and inflation can be caused both by shifts in the dynamic aggregate demand curve and in the short-run aggregate supply curve. But when shifting their reaction curve, central bankers shift the dynamic aggregate demand curve. They cannot shift the short-run aggregate supply curve. What this means is that monetary policymakers can neutralize demand shocks, but they cannot offset supply shocks. That is to say, they can counter aggregate expenditure changes that shift the dynamic aggregate demand curve, but they cannot eliminate the effects of changes in production costs that shift the short-run aggregate supply curve.

As for fiscal policy, our macroeconomic framework allows us to study the impact of changes in government taxes and expenditures as well. As we have seen in the previous section, these shift the dynamic aggregate demand curve. This means that fiscal policy can work to stabilize the economy. While both monetary and fiscal policy can in principle stabilize the economy, as we will discuss, the lags and uncertainties in policy making limit the potential for stabilization.

**Monetary Policy**   To see how monetary policy can stabilize the economy following a shift in the dynamic aggregate demand curve, consider what happens when consumers and businesses suddenly become more pessimistic about the future. Such a change reduces consumption and investment, shifting the dynamic aggregate demand curve to the left. In the absence of any change in monetary policy, this drop in consumer and business confidence would cause current output to fall below potential output ($Y < Y^P$), creating a recessionary output gap. Panel A of Figure 19.8 shows the dynamic aggregate demand curve shifting to the left (from $AD_0$ to $AD_1$) and the economy moving to a new short-run equilibrium point where current output falls short of potential output (at the point where $AD_1$ crosses SRAS).

Realizing that consumer and business confidence have fallen, driving down the consumption and investment components of aggregate expenditure, policymakers will conclude that the long-run real interest rate has gone down. Assuming that their inflation target remains the same, the drop in aggregate expenditure prompts them to shift their monetary policy reaction curve to the right, reducing the level of the real interest rate at every level of inflation. This is the shift from $MPRC_0$ to $MPRC_1$ shown in Panel B of Figure 19.8. Recall that when the monetary policy reaction curve shifts, the dynamic aggregate demand curve shifts in the same direction. This means that the policymakers' action shifts the dynamic aggregate demand curve back to its initial position as shown in Panel A of Figure 19.8. So, in the absence of a policy response, following the decline in aggregate expenditure, output would fall. But instead, the policy response means that the dynamic aggregate demand curve remains at its initial position, so output remains equal to potential output and inflation remains steady at the central bank's target.[3]

While central bankers can offset aggregate demand shocks in theory, in practice it is extremely difficult to keep inflation and output from fluctuating when aggregate expenditure changes. There are two reasons for this. First, it takes time to recognize what has happened. Fluctuations in the quantity of aggregate output demanded arising from things such as changes in consumer or business confidence can be very difficult to recognize as they are occurring. Second, changes in interest rates—the tool monetary policymakers use to offset aggregate demand shocks—do not have an immediate impact on the economy. Instead, when interest rates rise or fall, it takes time for output and inflation to respond. A good rule of thumb is that interest rate changes start to influence output in 6 to 9 months and inflation after 18 months, but our knowledge is not all that precise. In short, while in theory we can neutralize aggregate demand shocks; in reality they create short-run fluctuations in output and inflation.

**Discretionary Fiscal Policy**   There are two very different types of fiscal policy. One is automatic, operating without any further actions on the part of government officials, and the other is discretionary, relying on fiscal policymakers' decisions. Automatic stabilizers, including employment insurance and the proportional nature of the tax

---

[3] Stabilizing aggregate demand shocks in this way also ensures that expected inflation remains equal to the central bank's inflation target.

| Figure 19.8 | Stabilizing a Shift in Dynamic Aggregate Demand |

**A. Aggregate Expenditure Decline**

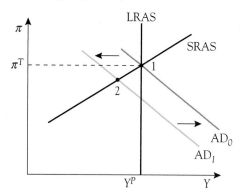

**B. Monetary Policy Response**

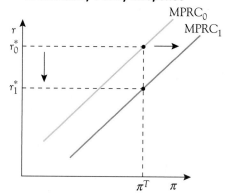

Following a drop in consumer or business confidence, the dynamic aggregate demand shifts to the left from $AD_0$ to $AD_1$, moving the economy from point 1 to point 2. Realizing this, monetary policymakers shift their MPRC to the right, shifting the dynamic aggregate demand curve back to where it started and returning the economy to point 1.

Following a drop in consumer confidence, the long-run real interest rate falls from $r_0^*$ to $r_1^*$. Policymakers respond by shifting their reaction curve from $MPRC_0$ to $MPRC_1$, shifting the AD curve back to its original position, $AD_0$.

system, are in the first group. These adjust mechanically to stimulate an economy that is slowing down and put the brakes on an economy that is speeding up. They operate countercyclically to eliminate fluctuations in aggregate expenditure and keep the economy stable. But there are times when automatic stabilizers are not enough; and that's when politicians face the temptation to enact temporary expenditure increases and tax reductions—what is called *discretionary* fiscal policy. Discretionary fiscal policy changes aggregate expenditure, shifting the dynamic aggregate demand curve.

As noted earlier in the chapter, a rise in government purchases or a decrease in taxes drives up aggregate expenditure, shifting the dynamic aggregate demand curve to the right. Thus, fiscal policy can act just like monetary policy to offset shifts in the dynamic aggregate demand curve and stabilize inflation and output. In fact, it has been used exactly this way on a number of occasions.

At least in principle, then, discretionary fiscal policy offers a clear alternative to monetary policy. On closer examination, however, it has at least two shortcomings. First, discretionary fiscal policy works slowly, and second, it is almost impossible to implement expeditiously. Most recessions are short, lasting a year or less. Furthermore, since economic data become available only several months after they are collected, the economy is often halfway through a recession before there is a consensus that a downturn has actually started. Only in exceptional circumstances can the government pass new legislation in less than several months. And fiscal policies do not have an immediate impact on the economy. Even after a tax cut has been passed, individual consumption and corporate investment tend to remain sluggish. Odds are that, by the time the spending does start, the recession will be over. This means that discretionary fiscal policy is likely to have its biggest impact when it is no longer needed.

# YOUR FINANCIAL WORLD

Stabilizing Your Consumption

Stability improves welfare. That's the fifth core principle of money and banking, and it is what guides the work of central bankers. In recent years monetary policymakers have succeeded in delivering low, stable inflation and high, stable growth. And a less volatile overall economy makes it easier for each of us to stabilize our own financial lives. As individuals, we care about paying our bills and stabilizing our standard of living. While the economy as a whole may be less volatile today than it was in the 1970s, individual incomes still rise and fall in ways that can make it difficult for a person to stabilize his or her consumption.

In earlier chapters we learned how to use the financial system to help reduce the risks we face in our everyday lives. We discussed life insurance, automobile insurance, and disability insurance, as well as the need for an emergency reserve in case of disaster. But even so, there are still times things don't quite work out, and for these times there is credit.

Individuals use credit in two ways. First, they borrow to purchase expensive things such as cars and houses without having to save the full amount and pay cash. Without a mortgage, very few young people could afford to purchase a home. Second, the ability to borrow means that an unemployed person who has run through his or her savings will still have something to eat and a place to sleep until a new job comes along. Borrowing allows individuals to keep their purchases of consumer goods and services—their consumption—smooth, despite fluctuations in income.

While credit can help us to smooth our consumption, it is only a stop-gap measure that we should use for as short a time as possible. Loans do need to be repaid, and borrowing for current consumption is something you should repay as quickly as possible.

The problems with discretionary fiscal policy don't end there since economists don't write economic stimulus packages; politicians do. And economics clearly collides with politics where fiscal stimulus is concerned. From an economic point of view, the best policies are the ones that influence a few key people to change their behaviour, avoiding rewarding people to do what they would have done anyway. Examples of economically efficient fiscal policies include temporary investment incentives and income tax reductions targeted toward those who are less well off. Politicians have a different set of incentives. They want to be reelected, so they look for programs that reward the largest number of people possible, to ensure their reelection. This means that discretionary fiscal policy is likely to be based more on political calculation than on economic logic. Though we can't hold public officials' opportunism against them, we need to recognize its existence. Because politicians want to remain popular with their constituencies, economic slowdowns—when some voters are suffering and the rest are worried—play to their worst instincts. In short, discretionary fiscal policy is a poor stabilization tool. While an economically sensible stimulus package can be designed, such legislation does not often become law.

Both monetary and fiscal stabilization policies have drawbacks. Central bankers can operate quickly and independently, but changes in the interest rate take a long time to affect the economy. Fiscal policy takes a long time to enact and may reflect political biases, but it may have an immediate impact. Under most circumstances, stabilization policy is left to the central bankers. Fiscal policy's automatic stabilizers are clearly important parts of the economic landscape, but discretionary government expenditure and tax changes have a role only after monetary policy has run its course—that is, when conditions are so bad that using every available tool makes sense.

"I had no idea our marriage was so interest-rate sensitive."

## What Happens When Potential Output Changes?

In order to concentrate on the impact of shifts in dynamic aggregate demand and short-run supply, we have neglected movements in potential output. But potential output does change, and the consequences are important both for short-run movements in output and inflation and for long-run equilibrium.

To understand what happens when potential output changes, let's trace out the consequences of a rise in $Y^P$ brought on by an increase in productivity. First, recall that the long-run aggregate supply curve (LRAS) is vertical at the point where current output equals potential output, so when potential output rises this curve shifts to the right. But that's not all. An increase in productivity reduces costs of production, so it is a positive supply shock as well. This shifts the short-run aggregate supply curve (SRAS) to the right. But how far does SRAS shift? To see, recall from Chapter 18 that the short-run aggregate supply curve intersects the long-run aggregate supply curve at the point where current inflation equals expected inflation ($\pi^e$)—that's where production costs are not changing. Immediately following the increase in potential output, expected inflation does not change, so the SRAS shifts the same distance as the LRAS does. From this we can conclude that an *increase in potential output shifts both the long- and short-run aggregate supply curves to the right* as shown in Panel A of Figure 19.9.

The short-run impact of an increase in potential output is straightforward. In the short run, output and inflation are determined by the intersection of the short-run aggregate supply (SRAS) and the dynamic aggregate demand (AD). The increase in potential output doesn't affect the quantity of output demanded, so AD is unchanged. Panel B of Figure 19.9 shows what happens. The economy starts at point 1 where the original short-run aggregate supply curve (SRAS$_0$) intersects the dynamic aggregate demand curve (AD). At this original equilibrium point, output equals the initial level of potential ($Y_0^P$) and inflation equals the central bank's target ($\pi^T$), which equals expected inflation ($\pi^e$). When potential output increases to $Y_1^P$, the short-run and

**Figure 19.9**    **An Increase in Potential Output**

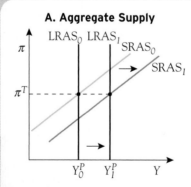

**A. Aggregate Supply**

An increase in potential output shifts both the short- and long-run aggregate supply curves to the right. Before and after the shift, the short-run aggregate supply curve crosses the long-run aggregate supply curve at the point where $\pi = \pi^e$

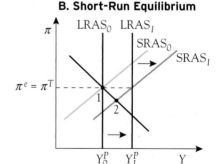

**B. Short-Run Equilibrium**

In the short run, the economy moves from point 1 to point 2.

long-run aggregate supply curves shift to SRAS$_1$ and LRAS$_1$. In the short run, the new equilibrium is at point 2 where SRAS$_1$ intersects AD. We can see from the figure, initially output is higher and inflation is lower.

What happens next? In the long run, output must go to the new level of potential output, $Y_1^P$. The path it takes to get there depends on what monetary policymakers do. If policymakers are happy with their inflation target—it could already be low enough—then they will work to move the economy to the point on the new long-run aggregate supply curve (LRAS$_1$) consistent with that initial target. But since the higher level of potential output comes along with a lower long-run real interest rate (look back at Figure 18.5 on page 403), returning inflation to its initial (higher) level means shifting the monetary policy reaction curve to the right. This change in monetary policy shifts the dynamic aggregate demand curve to the right. The policy adjustment will quickly drive output and inflation up until they reach their new long-run equilibrium levels where output equals $Y_1^P$ and inflation equals its original target $\pi^T$ (which equals expected inflation). This case is shown in Panel A of Figure 19.10.

Without a conscious shift in monetary policy, at point 2 in Panel B of Figure 19.10 there is a recessionary gap—current output is less than potential output—so there is downward pressure on production costs that will start to shift the short-run aggregate supply curve to the right, driving inflation down even further. We know that the SRAS continues to shift until output equals potential output. Looking at Panel B of Figure 19.10, we see that this process naturally brings us to point 4, where output equals the new higher level of potential output $Y_1^P$ and inflation is below the original target level $\pi_0^T$. When the policymakers see the change in the real interest rate, they will adjust the interest rate, shifting the monetary policy reaction function and returning inflation to its target level.[4]

---

**Figure 19.10**   Policy Options Following an Increase in Potential Output

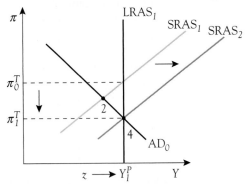

**A. Inflation Target Unchanged**

If, following an increase in potential output, policymakers' inflation target is unchanged, they must shift the dynamic aggregate demand curve to the right, bringing output and inflation to point 3.

**B. Inflation Target Reduced**

If, following an increase in potential output, policymakers wish to lower their inflation target, they will allow the economy to move to point 4.

---

[4] Alternatively, if the monetary policymaker wants to lower inflation it could take the opportunity to lower inflation without generating a fall in output. A central bank with an explicit inflation target would not do this as it would jeopardize the credibility of future targets.

Throughout our discussion of business cycle fluctuations, we have assigned a major role to shifts in the quantity of aggregate output demanded. This has led us to focus on how shifts in the dynamic aggregate demand curve change its point of intersection with an upward-sloping short-run aggregate supply curve and lead to movements in output and inflation.

An alternative explanation for business cycle fluctuations focuses on shifts in potential output. This view, known as **real-business-cycle theory**, starts with the assumption that prices and wages are flexible, so that inflation adjusts rapidly. That is to say, the short-run aggregate supply curve shifts rapidly in response to deviations of current output from potential output. This assumption renders the short-run aggregate supply curve irrelevant. Equilibrium output and inflation are determined by the point of intersection of the dynamic aggregate demand curve and the long-run aggregate supply curve, where current output equals potential output. Thus, any shift in the dynamic aggregate demand curve, regardless of its source, influences inflation but not output. Neither changes in aggregate expenditure nor changes in monetary policy have any impact on the level of output. Since inflation ultimately depends on the level of money growth, it is determined by monetary policy.

To explain recessions and booms, real-business-cycle theorists look to fluctuations in potential output. They focus on changes in productivity and their impact on GDP. Productivity is a measure of output at a fixed level of inputs. An increase in productivity means an increase in GDP for a given quantity of capital and number of workers. Shifts in productivity can be either temporary or permanent. Examples of such shifts include changes in the availability of raw materials, changes in government regulation of labour and product markets, and inventions that improve the economy's productive capacity. Any of these events will shift potential output. According to real-business-cycle theory, they are the primary sources of fluctuations in output.[5]

## What Are the Implications of Globalization for Monetary Policy?

If you look at the label of the shirt or blouse you are wearing, chances are it was imported from the Philippines, Cambodia, Vietnam, or somewhere else in Asia. The reason is that it is less costly to manufacture clothing in places where labour is inexpensive. The result is that clothes are cheaper in Canada: Trade lowers prices. But does it also lower inflation?

The simplest way to understand the macroeconomic impact of international trade is to think about it as a source of productivity-enhancing technological progress. Shifting production of clothes from domestic factories to foreign ones is the same as Canadian producers finding a new, cheaper technology for producing the same things at home. And improvements in technology increase potential output. That is something we understand.

Recall from the previous section that an increase in potential output shifts both the long-run and short-run aggregate supply curves to the right. This has the immediate impact of shifting the economy along its dynamic aggregate demand curve to a point where output is higher and inflation is lower. All of this is shown in Figure 19.9 on page 440. In the long run, we know that output goes to the new, higher level of potential output. But, as we discussed in the previous section, the long-run level of inflation depends on how monetary policymakers respond. Our conclusion is that globalization and trade do reduce inflation in the short run and just like any positive supply shock, they provide an opportunity to reduce inflation permanently.

[5] For a more detailed discussion of real business cycle theory see Chapter 19 of N. Gregory Mankiw's *Macroeconomics*, 6th edition (New York: Worth Publishing, 2007).

Is globalization likely to have a sizeable impact on inflation even in the short run? To see, we can look at a few numbers. Between January 2003 and January 2004 the Canadian dollar appreciated from US$0.64 to US$0.78—a 22 percent appreciation. The appreciation would mean that the cost of goods priced in U.S. dollars or Chinese yuan (which was tied to the dollar) would fall. How much impact did this have on the Canadian inflation rate? The inflation rate fell from 3.7 percent to 1.2 percent— a decline of 2.5 percentage points. A study by Statistics Canada found that most of this decline came from products that had a high import content ("high" means over 30 percent; there is a very large component of domestic content in imported goods reflecting retailing charges and transportation).[6] But the decline in the cost of imported goods reflected not only the exchange rate but also a significant reduction in world crude oil prices. The study concludes that about half of the decline in inflation may have been a result of the exchange rate appreciation—1.25 percent. So even very large exchange rate changes have only a small impact on the inflation rate.

We just can't get away from the fact that domestic inflation is tied to domestic monetary policy. In the long run, the inflation rate equals the money growth rate less the growth rate of potential output ($\pi = \%\Delta M - \%\Delta Y^P$).

## Can Policymakers Distinguish a Recessionary Gap from a Fall in Potential Output?

Throughout the 1960s, GDP growth averaged more than 5 percent per year. But in the early 1970s GDP growth began to fall, averaging less than 2 percent in 1975. While this was happening, inflation rose dramatically, from 5 percent in 1972 to nearly 12 percent in late 1975. (Take a look at Figures 19.1 on page 427 and 19.6 on page 434 to see the pattern.) When inflation rises at the same time that output falls, the appropriate policy response depends on whether potential output has fallen. If $Y^P$ is lower, then the long-run real interest rate $r^*$ is higher, and policymakers need to shift their monetary policy reaction curve to the left, setting higher policy-controlled interest rates at every level of inflation. This ensures that inflation and expected inflation remain at the central bank's target. By contrast, if the simultaneous fall in output and increase in inflation is the result of a supply shock that simply shifted the short-run aggregate supply curve to the left, then policymakers should focus on moving the economy back to the same point where they started. Distinguishing a recessionary gap from a fall in potential output is critical.

The proximate cause of the 1970s episode was a tripling of the price of oil, from $3.56 to $11.16 a barrel. That increase in production costs translates into a negative supply shock. It's no wonder that inflation rose and output fell. But the right reaction depends crucially on what happened to potential output at the time. In retrospect we know that as oil prices rose, the productive capacity of the economy fell, and potential output went down with it. At the time, policymakers didn't realize that. Instead, they thought lower output reflected a recessionary gap. This led to an inappropriate response that drove inflation up, where it stayed for longer than it should have.

We can use the dynamic aggregate demand and aggregate supply apparatus to understand the importance of recognizing changes in potential output and see the consequences of the mistake made by policymakers in the 1970s. To do this, let's look at two cases. In the first, a supply shock drives inflation up and output down, but potential output is unchanged, so there is a recessionary gap. This is the case we studied in Figure 19.5 on page 432. Here's what happens. Following any supply shock, policymakers

---

[6] Chiru, Rady, "The Soaring Loonie and Prices: Lower Inflation for Consumers?" Statscan: 11-621-MIE2004014, retrieved September 3, 2009, from http://www.statcan.gc.ca/pub/11-621-m/11-621-m2004014-eng.pdf.

have a choice. They can either leave their inflation target as it is, and simply react by adjusting interest rates along an unchanged monetary policy reaction curve, or they can change their inflation target. As we saw earlier in this chapter, a positive supply shock presents a pleasant choice—allow output to rise and then fall, or lower inflation permanently. By contrast, a negative supply shock presents two less appealing alternatives. Policymakers can either allow output to remain below potential output longer so that inflation falls, or raise the inflation target. Central bankers rarely believe their inflation target is too low, so they almost always respond to a negative supply shock by allowing a recessionary gap to develop in order to return inflation to its original target. Operationally, this means raising interest rates along an unchanged monetary policy reaction curve at the same time that output is already falling.

If, however, the negative supply shock is associated with a decline in potential output, matters are quite different. This is the case shown in Panel A of Figure 19.11 on page 444. Initially, the economy moves to point 1, where inflation is higher and output is lower. So far, things are identical to the case where potential output is unchanged. But what happens next is not. At point 1, there is now an *expansionary gap*. Even though output has fallen, potential output has fallen by more and output remains above the new, lower, $Y_1^P$. Without any change in the monetary policy reaction curve, the economy starts moving to point 2. That is, inflation continues to rise and output continues to fall.

The challenge for policymakers is to figure out that potential output has fallen and that this has increased the long-run real interest rate. Under these circumstances, keeping inflation at its target requires a leftward shift in the monetary policy reaction curve, as shown in Panel B of Figure 19.11. Policymakers need to raise the real interest rate by even more than they would in the case of a recessionary gap.

## Figure 19.11    A Drop in Potential Output

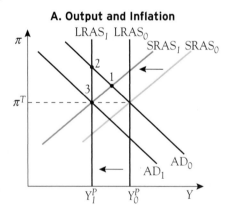

**A. Output and Inflation**

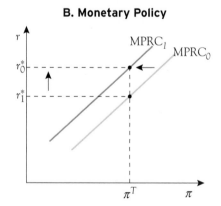

**B. Monetary Policy**

A drop in potential output shifts the long- and short-run aggregate supply curves to the left. Initially, the economy moves to point 1 where there is an expansionary gap. At point 1, there is upward pressure on production costs, so in the absence of a change in monetary policy, the SRAS will start to shift to the left, driving inflation up further.

Since lower potential output means a higher long-run real interest rate, monetary policymakers must respond to the fall in $Y^P$ by shifting their reaction curve from $MPRC_0$ to $MPRC_1$. This shifts the dynamic aggregate demand curve from $AD_0$ to $AD_1$ and ensures that the economy moves to point 3 rather than 2.

By the end of the 1970s, inflation had been over 6 percent for five straight years. The Bank of Canada realized its estimate of potential output was too high and that it would need to raise interest rates to keep inflation from rising. Over the next few years, tighter monetary policy eventually had the desired impact so that inflation was back down below 5 percent by 1983.

## Can Policymakers Stabilize Output and Inflation Simultaneously?

Our analysis of business cycles has been based on the idea that short-run fluctuations in output and inflation are caused by either demand shifts or supply shifts. And, as we have seen repeatedly, dynamic aggregate demand curve shifts move inflation and output in the same direction; while short-run aggregate supply shifts move inflation and output in opposite directions. Earlier in this chapter, we discussed how, by shifting their monetary policy reaction curve, policymakers offset demand shocks. (This is shown in Figure 19.8 on page 437.)

Unfortunately, supply shocks are a different story. There is no way to neutralize them. For instance, take the case of a negative supply shock such as an oil price increase that raises production costs. This has the immediate effect of driving output down and inflation up (see Figure 19.5 on page 432). Now consider the tools that are available to policymakers. By shifting the monetary policy reaction curve, central bankers can shift the dynamic aggregate demand curve. Is there any way to use this tool to bring the economy back to its original long-run equilibrium point quickly and painlessly? The answer is no. Monetary policymakers can shift the dynamic aggregate demand curve, but they are powerless to move the short-run aggregate supply curve. And there is no shift in the dynamic aggregate demand curve that can quickly move

## TOOLS OF THE TRADE
GDP vs. GDI

Economists love acronyms and these two are so similar you might think the difference is unimportant; but for policymakers it could be crucial. First, the definitions. GDP— gross domestic product—measures the goods produced in the economy, and real GDP measures that in volume terms to control for inflation. GDI—gross domestic income— measures the purchasing power or income of Canadians, and, again, real GDI measures that purchasing power in terms of goods. The difference between the two matters when the terms of trade change significantly. Suppose that Canada exports oil, and the world price of oil rises. If Canada didn't increase oil production at all, then real GDP wouldn't change. But since Canadians could buy many more imported goods with the export revenues, Canadians' real purchasing power would have risen.

The difference between GDP and GDI can be quite large. Between 2002 and 2005, Canadian real GDP grew by 8.3 percent, while real GDI grew 13.4 percent. Similarly over short periods, when there is a rapid change in the terms

of trade, the impact can be dramatic. In early 2009 Prime Minister Harper suggested that the Canadian economy did better than the United States in the second half of 2008. But the Parliamentary Budget Officer pointed out that the Department of Finance had argued before that real GDI growth "provides the best measure of income growth in the overall economy—and is a more relevant indicator of change in well-being of Canadians than real GDP."* He went on to note that falling commodity prices caused Canada's real GDI to decline in the second half of the year, "plunging by 15.3 percent in the fourth quarter—ten times larger than the (1.5 percent) decline observed in the U.S."

The central bank needs to monitor GDI in addition to real GDP as increases in GDI also can represent inflationary increases in aggregate expenditure.

*Office of the Parliamentary Budget Officer, "Canada's Recent Economic Performance," March 11, 2009, http://www2.parl.gc.ca/Sites/PBO-DPB/documents/ Recent_Economic_Performance.pdf, retrieved September 8, 2009.

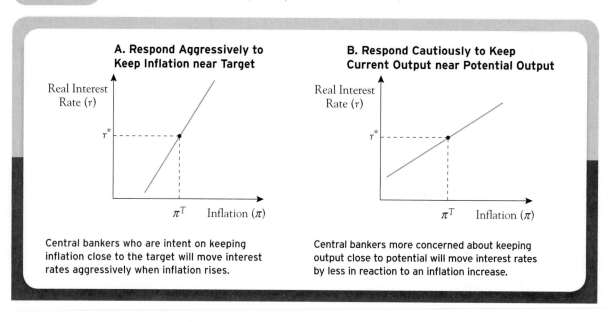

Figure 19.12    The Slope of the Monetary Policy Reaction Curve

A. Respond Aggressively to Keep Inflation near Target

Central bankers who are intent on keeping inflation close to the target will move interest rates aggressively when inflation rises.

B. Respond Cautiously to Keep Current Output near Potential Output

Central bankers more concerned about keeping output close to potential will move interest rates by less in reaction to an inflation increase.

the economy back to its long-run equilibrium point, where current output equals potential output and current inflation equals the central bank's target.

But that's not the end of the story. Central bankers can choose how aggressively they react to deviations of inflation from their target caused by supply shocks. They can do this by picking the slope of their monetary policy reaction curve, which then determines the slope of the dynamic aggregate demand curve. The more aggressive policymakers are in keeping current inflation close to target, the steeper their monetary policy reaction curve and the flatter the dynamic aggregate demand curve. By controlling the slope of the dynamic aggregate demand curve, policymakers choose the extent to which supply shocks translate into changes in output or changes in inflation. This means that the slope of the monetary policy reaction curve—how aggressively to react to deviations of inflation from their target—is really a choice about the relative volatility of inflation and output. The more central bankers stabilize inflation, the more volatile output will be, and vice versa. There is a tradeoff.

To see why policymakers face a tradeoff between inflation and output volatility, we can compare two policymakers, one with a relatively steep monetary policy reaction curve (as in Panel A of Figure 19.12), and one with a relatively flat monetary policy reaction curve (as in Panel B of Figure 19.12). The first policymaker cares more about keeping inflation close to its target level than the second one does.

Turning to the dynamic aggregate demand curve, Panel A of Figure 19.13 on page 447 shows the relatively flat AD curve implied by the steep monetary policy reaction curve in which small deviations in inflation from the target level elicit large changes in the real interest rate. A flat dynamic aggregate demand curve, corresponding to the steep monetary policy reaction curve in Panel A of Figure 19.13, means that a supply shock creates large changes in current output. So an increase in production costs—a negative supply shock—drives output down sharply, opening

Figure 19.13    The Policymaker's Choice

### A. Respond Aggressively to Keep Inflation near Target

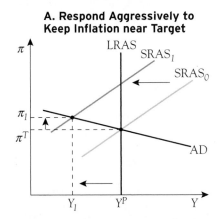

### B. Respond Cautiously to Keep Current Output near Potential Output

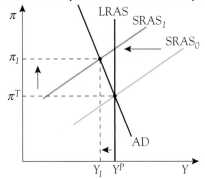

Central bankers intent on keeping inflation close to the target will move interest rates aggressively when inflation rises and create bigger fluctuations in output.

Policymakers more concerned about keeping output close to potential will move interest rates by less in reaction to an inflation change, resulting in bigger fluctuations in inflation.

up a large recessionary output gap. We can assume that the larger the output gap, the greater the pressure on inflation. A large recessionary gap should force inflation down faster than a small recessionary gap. In fact, policymakers are counting on that mechanism when they choose to follow this path. By reacting aggressively to supply shocks, policymakers force current inflation back to target quickly. The cost of following this path, however, is that it causes output to fall substantially. Stable inflation means volatile output.

Panel B of Figure 19.13 shows what happens when policymakers are less concerned about keeping inflation close to target in the short run, and more concerned about keeping current output near potential output. When policymakers worry more about short-run fluctuations in output than about temporary movements in inflation, they will choose a relatively flat monetary policy reaction curve in which movements in the real interest rate are small, even when inflation strays far from its target level. The result is a steep dynamic aggregate demand curve such as the one in Panel B. Notice what happens in this case following a supply shock. Once more, inflation rises, creating a recessionary output gap. But the output gap is small, so the downward pressure on inflation is relatively weak. As a result, inflation adjusts slowly, remaining high for a longer period than it would have if policymakers had reacted more aggressively. Stable output means volatile inflation.

When choosing how aggressively to respond to supply shocks, central bankers are deciding how to conduct stabilization policy. Do they want to ensure that inflation remains near target, or that output remains close to potential? When faced with a supply shock, policymakers cannot stabilize both output and inflation. And by stabilizing one, the other becomes more volatile. Monetary policymakers face an inflation-output volatility tradeoff.

## IN THE NEWS

### Issues Dogging Dodge Pile up; Bay Street Divided on What Rates Will Do

### Financial Post's Financial Post & FP Investing (Canada)

**By Jacqueline Thorpe**

December 3, 2007, p. FP1

The mental monetary policy gymnastics David Dodge in all likelihood was subjected to in the past few days must have been intense. As he met with his deputies at Bank of Canada ahead of tomorrow's interest rates announcement, the economic uncertainties were piling up by the minute.

Here are some of the issues they likely tossed around:

– Man who set this schedule? The November labour market report comes out three days after we issue our announcement. Surely that great big public hiring spree has started to cool off by now.
– If we hold interest rates steady at 4.50% and that fellow Bernanke at the Fed cuts U.S. rates to 4.25% or heaven forbid 4.0% next week, what the heck is the loonie going to do?
– This credit crunch is bad, but how much is it really going to squeeze borrowing in this country? And didn't we want things to cool off anyway?

– Looks like exporters are really starting to take it in the neck but business investment is really zooming, Christmas has got to be big this year and there's a whack of tax cuts coming.
– What's with that loonie anyway, now it's below par?
– Hey look, core consumer prices are at 1.8%, below our 2% target!

Bay Street is quite divided over whether the bank will actually pull the trigger on a rate cut tomorrow. They appear convinced, however, Mr. Dodge will leave his job at the end of January by kicking off a rate-cutting cycle.

According to a Reuters survey last week, eight of 13 firms that deal securities with the bank forecast it would hold rates steady tomorrow while five called for a cut of 25 basis points to 4.25%. Eleven expected the bank to chop a quarter point in January and two forecast it to stand pat.

As has been the case through much of Mr. Dodge's term, the bank is faced with a trade sector that is dragging in the face of a strong loonie but a domestic economy that rolls along unperturbed.

As Friday's third-quarter GDP report showed, consumer spending eased off somewhat, but robust business, government and construction activity pushed overall growth to a higher-than-expected 2.9%. Employment continues to be relentlessly

## A Guide to Central Bank Interest Rates: The Taylor Rule

The previous section mentioned some of the many factors that can go into interest rate–setting decisions. American economist John Taylor wanted to cut through the complexity to provide the Federal Reserve with a simple formula or rule of thumb that central bankers could use to set the interest rate. The Taylor rule is

$$\text{Target fed funds rate} = 2\tfrac{1}{2} + \text{Current inflation} + \tfrac{1}{2}(\text{Inflation gap})$$
$$+ \tfrac{1}{2}(\text{Output gap}) \tag{1}$$

This expression assumes a long-term real interest rate of 2½ percent, which is added to current inflation, the inflation gap, and the output gap. The inflation gap is current inflation minus an inflation target, both measured as percentages; the output gap is current GDP minus its potential level—that is, the percentage deviation of current output from potential output. When inflation exceeds the target level, the inflation strong, generating an unemployment rate of 5.8% and average hourly wage gains of 4.1% on a year-over-year basis in October.

The hit to the trade sector looks like it's intensifying, however. TD Securities said it subtracted 4.7 percentage points from growth in the third quarter, the biggest drag since 1995.

The bank also faces three major new wrinkles: a slowing U.S. economy; a global credit crunch; and a loonie that is beginning to put noticeable downward pressure on inflation.

The credit crunch has already resulted in $2-billion in writedowns at the big six Canadian banks, amounting to 10% of profits. More importantly, borrowing is becoming more difficult for both companies and consumers.

Borrowing in the commercial paper market has dropped 20% from its peak in July while the five-year mortgage rate averaged 7.4% in October, the highest in five years.

Meanwhile, the great Canadian supersale has begun as retailers begin to pass on the savings from a strong loonie, spurred on by waves of cross-border shoppers.

Inflation, the bank's primary concern, slipped below the bank's target for the first time in 16 months in October. The question is, is the inflation rate now set to fall so far below the bank's 2 target it needs the bank to ease up on monetary policy?

## LESSONS OF THE ARTICLE

Interest rate setting can be a very challenging task. In December 2007, core CPI, which the Bank often uses as a gauge of underlying inflation was below 2 percent, but the economy was growing, unemployment was falling, and wage increases were rising. Should Governor Dodge raise the interest rate to slow down an overheating economy or lower the rate to bring inflation back up to the target? This article highlights the challenges facing the governor. The Bank ended up lowering the interest rate by 25 basis points, although it highlighted both the upside and downside risks for inflation in its statement.

SOURCE: *"Issues Dogging Dodge Pile up; Bay Street Divided on What Rates Will Do,"* *Jacqueline Thorpe.* Financial Post, *National Edition, Dec. 3, 2007. Material reprinted with the express permission of "The National Post Company," a CanWest Partnership.*

gap is positive; when current output is above potential output, the output gap is positive. For example, if inflation is currently 3 percent, the target rate is 2 percent, and GDP equals its potential level so there is no output gap, then the target federal funds rate should be set at 2½ + 3 + ½ = 6 percent.

This rule makes intuitive sense: When inflation rises above its target level, the response is to raise interest rates; when output falls below the target level, the response is to lower interest rates. If inflation is currently on target and there is no output gap (current GDP equals potential GDP), then the target federal funds rate should be set at its neutral rate of target inflation plus 2½.

The Taylor rule has some interesting properties. Consider what happens if inflation rises by 1 percentage point, from 2 percent to 3 percent, and the inflation target is 2 percent (assume that everything else remains the same). What happens to the target federal funds rate? The increase in inflation affects two terms in the Taylor rule, current inflation and the inflation gap. Since the inflation target doesn't change, both these terms rise 1 percentage point. The increase in current inflation feeds one for one into the target federal funds rate, but the increase in the inflation gap is halved.

When the inflation rate increases by *1 percentage point, the Federal Reserve should raise the target federal funds rate by 1½ percentage points.*

Significantly, the Taylor rule tells us that for each percentage point that the inflation rate exceeds its target, the real interest rate, which is equal to the nominal interest rate minus expected inflation, should be raised by half a percentage point. Since economic decisions depend on the real interest rate, this means that higher inflation leads policymakers to raise the inflation-adjusted cost of borrowing, thereby slowing the economy and ultimately reducing inflation. If central banks fail to do this, if they allow the real interest rate to fall following an increase in inflation, the result is further increases in production and further increases in inflation.

The Taylor rule also states that for each percentage point that output is above potential—that is, for each percentage point in the output gap—interest rates should be raised half a percentage point. The fractions that precede the terms for the inflation and output gaps—the halves in equation (1)—depend both on how sensitive the economy is to interest rate changes and on the preferences of central bankers. The more central bankers care about inflation, the bigger the multiplier for the inflation gap and the lower the multiplier for the output gap. It is not unusual for central banks to raise the target interest rate by twice the increase in inflation while virtually ignoring the output gap.

The Taylor rule was designed for the U.S. economy and economists have suggested versions of the Taylor rule more appropriate for a small open economy like Canada. However, for the moment we will stay with the U.S. version and compare its predictions with the behaviour of the Fed. We see that implementing the Taylor rule requires four inputs: (1) the constant term, set at 2½ in equation (1); (2) a measure of inflation; (3) a measure of the inflation gap; and (4) a measure of the output gap. The constant is a measure of the long-term risk-free real interest rate, which is about 1 percentage point below the economy's growth rate. Since the U.S. economy has been growing at a rate of about 3½ percent per year, we set this term at 2½. But the number can and does change.

Next we need to add measures of current inflation and the inflation gap. As for the inflation target to use in measuring the inflation gap, we will follow Taylor and use 2 percent, so the neutral target federal funds rate is 4½ percent (2½ plus 2). For the output gap, the natural choice is the percentage by which GDP deviates from a measure of its trend, or potential.

Figure 19.14 plots the FOMC's actual target federal funds rate, together with the rate predicted by the Taylor rule. The result is striking: From 1992 (when Professor Taylor created his rule) to 2002, the two lines are very close to each other. The FOMC changed the target federal funds rate when the Taylor rule predicted it should. While the rule didn't match policy exactly, it did predict what policymakers would do in a general way. From 2003 on, the Taylor rule proposed tighter monetary policy than the Fed actually followed, a fact that gives support to those who argue that loose monetary policy created the bubble conditions that led, or at least promoted, the financial crisis in 2008.

Figure 19.14    The Taylor Rule, 1990–2006

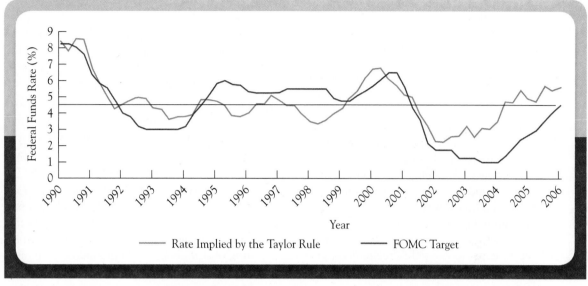

SOURCE: *Board of Governors of the Federal Reserve and author's calculations.*

## Terms

business cycles, 426
demand shock, 428
gross domestic income
   (GDI), 445
real-business-cycle

theory, 441
recession, 433
stabilization policy, 436
supply shock, 428
Taylor rule, 447

## Chapter Summary

1. Short-run fluctuations in output and inflation arise from shifts in either the dynamic aggregate demand curve or the short-run aggregate supply curve.
   a. A decrease in the central bank's inflation target shifts the dynamic aggregate demand curve to the left.
      i.  In the short run, this decreases both output and inflation.
      ii. It creates a recessionary output gap, exerting additional downward pressure on inflation.
      iii. In the long run, inflation falls to the new target as output returns to potential output.
   b. A government expenditure decrease shifts the dynamic aggregate demand curve to the left.
      i.  In the short run, this decreases both output and inflation.
      ii. It creates a recessionary output gap, exerting additional downward pressure on inflation.
      iii. To keep inflation from falling, monetary policymakers shift their reaction curve to the right, lowering the real interest rate at every level of inflation.
      iv. Unless the central bank's target inflation changes, the economy eventually returns to its original long-run equilibrium point.
   c. A negative supply shock shifts the short-run aggregate supply curve to the left.
      i.  In the short run, this decreases output and increases inflation.
      ii. It creates a recessionary output gap that places downward pressure on inflation.
      iii. Unless the central bank's target inflation changes, the economy returns to its original long-run equilibrium point.

2. Applying the dynamic aggregate demand–aggregate supply framework we see that

   a. Most postwar recessions have originated in tight monetary policy.

   b. Stabilization policy is the use of monetary and fiscal policy tools to stabilize output and inflation.

      i. Monetary policy can be used to shift the dynamic aggregate demand curve to offset changes in the quantity of aggregate output demanded. In practice, lack of information and lags in the impact of policy changes makes this very difficult.

      ii. Fiscal policy can shift the dynamic aggregate demand curve as well, but it is difficult to do in a timely way.

      iii. A positive supply shock that lowers production costs and shifts the short-run aggregate supply curve to the right creates an opportunity for policymakers to permanently lower inflation.

   c. An increase in potential output shifts both the short- and long-run aggregate supply curves to the right, driving output up and inflation down, as well as creating an expansionary output gap.

   d. Globalization has the same impact as an increase in potential output. In the long run it raises output, but inflation changes only if the central bank adjusts its target.

   e. It is difficult (but crucial) for monetary policymakers to distinguish a decline in the quantity of aggregate output demanded from a fall in potential output.

   f. When confronted with a shift in the short-run aggregate supply curve, central bankers face a tradeoff between output and inflation volatility.

3. The Taylor rule offers a rule of thumb for setting the U.S. interest rate and captures how the Fed has set monetary policy from 1992 to 2002.

## Conceptual Problems

1. Define the term "stabilization policy" and describe how it can be used to reduce the volatility of economic growth and inflation. Do stabilization policies improve everyone's welfare?

2. Should government authorities pursue economic stabilization through monetary or fiscal policies? Why or why not?

3. Explain why monetary policymakers cannot restore the original long-run equilibrium of the economy if, in the short run, the economy has moved to a point where inflation is above target inflation and output is below potential output.

4. Will changes in technology affect the rate at which the short-run aggregate supply curve shifts in response to an output gap? Why or why not? Provide some specific examples of how technology will change the rate of adjustment.

5. Go to Statistics Canada and collect data on output per hour since 1980. Compute the percentage change in productivity. Compare this plot to the plot of inflation data at the beginning of this chapter. Do productivity changes explain inflation performance?

6. The 2001 recession was extremely mild. Can you explain why? Be sure to use information on the path of interest rates in your answer.

7. Suppose the economy has been sluggish so, in an effort to increase growth, government officials have decided to cut taxes. They are considering two possible tax cuts of equal size. The first would reduce the taxes everyone pays by 10 percent. The second would eliminate taxes on people in the lowest income bracket, leaving everyone else's taxes the same. Does it matter which one of these plans the government implements? Why or why not?

8.* Using Canadian GDP data from Statistics Canada, calculate the annual percentage changes in GDP for each quarter starting with the first quarter of 1961. Plot these percentage changes and comment on the pattern you see. Using the same data, calculate the standard deviation of GDP growth rates for the periods 1961–1991 and 1992 to the present, and comment on what you find.

9. Suppose that the price of potash rises and potash represents 10 percent of the exports of Saskatchewan. How would this affect the real GDP and the real GDI of Saskatchewan?

* Indicates more difficult problem.

10.* According to real-business-cycle theory, can monetary policy affect equilibrium output in either the short run or the long run?

# Analytical Problems

11. Starting with the economy in long-run equilibrium, use the aggregate demand–aggregate supply framework to illustrate what would happen to inflation and output in the short run if there were a rise in consumer confidence in the economy. Assuming the central bank takes no action, what would happen to inflation and output in the long run?

12. Consider again the rise in consumer confidence described in question 11. What would happen to inflation and output in the long run if the central bank remained committed to its original inflation target and responded with policy tightening? Compare the outcome to the one in question 11 using the aggregate demand–aggregate supply framework.

13. How would a shock that reduces production costs in the economy (a positive supply shock) affect equilibrium output and inflation in both the short run and the long run? Illustrate your answer using the aggregate demand–aggregate supply framework. You should assume that the shock does not affect the potential output of the economy.

14. Suppose, instead of waiting for the economy described in question 13 to return to long-run equilibrium, the central bank opted to use the positive supply shock as an opportunity to move to a lower inflation target. Illustrate the impact of this change in the inflation target using an aggregate demand–aggregate supply diagram. Compare this with a graph of a situation in which the central bank lowers its inflation target in the absence of a positive supply shock.

15.* Suppose a natural disaster reduces the productive capacity of the economy. How would the equilibrium long-run real interest rate be affected? Assuming the central bank maintains its existing inflation target, illustrate the impact on the monetary policy reaction curve and on equilibrium inflation and output both in the short run and in the long run.

16.* Monetary policymakers observe an increase in output in the economy and believe it is a result of an increase in potential output. If they were correct, what would the appropriate policy response be to maintain the existing inflation target? If they were incorrect and the increase in output resulted simply from a positive supply shock, what would the long-run impact be of their policy response?

17.* Consider a previously closed economy that opens up to international trade. Use the aggregate demand-aggregate supply framework to illustrate a situation in which this would lead to lower inflation in this economy in the long run.

18.* In the face of global oil price shocks, what could monetary policymakers do to minimize the resulting recessionary gaps? What would be the tradeoff of such a policy? Illustrate your answer using the aggregate demand–aggregate supply framework.

# PART V

## Modern Monetary Economics

# CHAPTER 20

## Money Supply and Money Demand

Given our discussions up to this point you might get the idea that monetary policy has little to do with money. Indeed, anyone who listens carefully to what central bankers say, or reads what they write, will form the impression that 21st-century monetary policy has very little to do with money, despite its focus on inflation. That impression is reinforced by the technical papers that monetary economists write. Everyone talks about interest rates and exchange rates; no one talks about money.

But, digging deeper, you will find that central bankers and monetary economists *do* care about money. After decades of studying the economy, Nobel Prize–winning economist Milton Friedman wrote, "Inflation is always and everywhere a monetary phenomenon." Most economists would agree. We see concern for money, too, in statements made by officials of the European Central Bank (ECB). In Chapter 16, we discussed the stability-oriented strategy that the ECB's governing council adopted in the fall of 1998 to achieve the objective of price stability. The council's strategy assigned money a prominent role that was, in its members' words, "signaled by the announcement of a quantitative reference value for the growth rate of a broad monetary aggregate."[1] The idea was that deviations of money growth from the reference value signalled a risk to European price stability. Since then, the ECB's monthly announcements of its target interest rate have regularly mentioned money growth.

Obviously, money plays a central role in the formulation of European monetary policy. The contrast with Canada could not be more striking: a typical Bank of Canada press release

[1] Press Release of European Central Bank, December 1, 1998.

on a fixed announcement date uses the word "monetary" in the context of "monetary policy" and "monetary conditions," even "monetary stimulus," but almost never in the context "monetary aggregate" or "quantity of money." Similarly at the Fed, the quantity of money is rarely discussed in decisions (or even the minutes) of the FOMC meetings. In 2001, Federal Reserve Board Governor Laurence H. Meyer even went so far as to say that money "plays virtually no role in the conduct of monetary policy."[2]

What accounts for the distinctly different treatment of money growth in the two different central banks? If money growth is tied to inflation, why don't central bankers in Canada pay more attention to it? The goal of this chapter is twofold. First, it examines the link between money growth and inflation in order to clarify the role of money in monetary policy. Second, it explains the logic underlying central bankers' focus on interest rates.

## Why We Care about Monetary Aggregates

We start with the single most important fact in monetary economics: the relationship between money growth and inflation rates. Panel A of Figure 20.1 on page 455 shows the average annual inflation and money growth in 150 countries over the 25 years from 1981 to 2005. This graph is striking for two reasons. The first is its scale: some countries suffered inflation of more than 500 percent *a year* for two decades. Second, every country with high inflation had high money growth. History provides no examples of countries with high inflation and low money growth or with low inflation and high money growth.

Figure 20.1   Inflation Rates and Money Growth

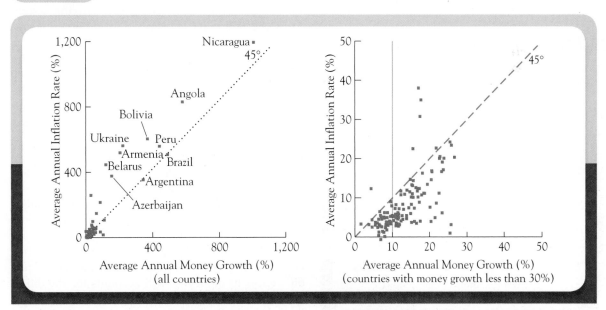

Inflation was computed from each country's analog to the consumer price index; money is the rough equivalent of M2. Data are from 1981 to 2005. Changing the definition of either inflation or money does not alter the graph.

SOURCE: *These figures are based on data from the International Monetary Fund's International Financial Statistics.*

[2] Laurence H. Meyer, "Does Money Matter?" The 2001 Homer Jones Memorial Lecture, Washington University, St. Louis, Missouri, March 28, 2001.

STABILITY

One thing the figure does not show because of its scale is the huge number of points that fall very close to the origin, representing countries with both low inflation and low money growth. Panel B of Figure 20.1 displays the data for the 118 countries that experienced moderate money growth (averaging less than 30 percent per annum) over the two decades from 1981 to 2003. While the relationship between money growth and inflation is less striking, it is still clearly there. The higher the rate of money growth is, the higher the inflation rate is likely to be. The two variables move together. This evidence alone tells us that *to avoid sustained episodes of high inflation, a central bank must be concerned with money growth. Avoiding high inflation means avoiding rapid money growth.*

Both panels of Figures 20.1 include a 45-degree line. Note that the points representing countries with very high inflation tend to lie above the line, while the points representing countries with moderate to low inflation tend to fall below it. As the simplified graph in Figure 20.2 shows, points lying above the 45-degree line represent countries in which average inflation exceeds average money growth; points lying below the 45-degree line represent countries in which money growth exceeds inflation. To understand this relationship, think about what would happen if the inflation rate rose to 1,200 percent a year, as was the case in Nicaragua (see Panel A of Figure 20.1). That means prices would be rising about 5 percent a week. When the currency that people are holding loses value that rapidly, they will work to spend what they have as quickly as possible.[3] As we will see shortly, spending money more quickly has the same effect on inflation as an increase in money growth.

Connecting this relationship to central bank policy is straightforward. Recall from Chapter 17 that the central bank controls the size of its own balance sheet. Policymakers can purchase as many assets as they want, issuing currency and commercial bank reserve liabilities to do so. Those liabilities, in turn, form the monetary base. Through the process of deposit expansion, the banking system turns the monetary base into the monetary aggregates. Thus, the monetary aggregates cannot grow rapidly without at least the tacit consent of the central bank. By limiting the rate at which they purchase securities, policymakers can control the rate at which aggregates such as M2 grow. In other words, *it is impossible to have high, sustained inflation without monetary accommodation.*

Not surprisingly, evidence of the link between inflation and money growth is the foundation on which modern monetary policy is built. That is why the ECB pays close attention to growth in the monetary aggregates. But to use the link as a policy guide, central bankers must understand how it works. Looking back at Figure 20.1, we can see that all money growth is not created equal. Something beyond just differences in money growth accounts for the differences in inflation across countries. To see the point, look at Panel B of Figure 20.1 and note the vertical

**Figure 20.2**    **Money Growth and Inflation**

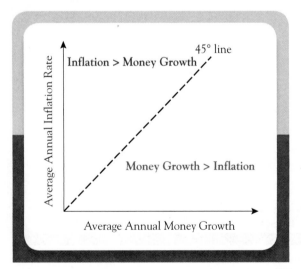

---

[3] In some countries suffering from hyperinflation, workers may be paid more than once a day because cash loses value so quickly. Stories have been told about children travelling to their parents' workplace at midday to collect the morning's pay and spend it on food before its value declined.

## APPLYING THE CONCEPT
### INFLATION AND THE COLLAPSE OF THE SOVIET UNION

In 1990, the Soviet Union collapsed, leaving in its place 15 independent countries known as the "former Soviet Republics." These new countries had several characteristics in common. One of them was their horrible inflation experience. In Latvia from 1991 to 1994, the inflation rate averaged just below 300 percent per year—the lowest rate of the 15 countries. In Georgia in 1994, prices rose 15,600 percent, or roughly 10 percent per week.

The source of these extraordinary levels of inflation was not hard to find: It was rapid money growth. Because the governments of these countries were the successors to the Soviet Union, a command economy, at first they were responsible for controlling every aspect of their citizens' economic lives. Virtually everyone worked for and was paid by the government. But while these states were committed to extremely high levels of expenditure, they had virtually no sources of revenue. There was no way to collect taxes and no way to borrow. The only available source of revenue was to print money, so that is what government officials did. They printed lots of it, raising money growth rates to well over 100 percent a year. From 1992 to 1993, for example, the Ukrainian equivalent of M2 increased by a factor of 20. Not surprisingly, such high money growth was matched by high inflation. Ukraine's 2,000 percent rate of money growth was accompanied by 4,000 percent inflation.

*Former Soviet Republics*

Officials in these countries realized that inflation had to be brought under control, or people would revolt (again). So they made a number of changes. The most important was to take the authority to print money out of the hands of politicians and turn it over to an independent central bank. Together with vast economic reforms that shrank the size of most of the governments dramatically, this depoliticizing of monetary policy produced an amazing transformation. By 2001, the rate of inflation had dropped to less than 10 percent in nine of the 15 countries; only Belarus had an inflation rate of over 50 percent. As money growth fell, inflation dropped with it.

line drawn at the point where annual money growth averages 10 percent. Points lying on or near the line represent countries that experienced average annual inflation rates of between 2 percent and 9 percent. What accounted for the differences in inflation among those countries, which had almost the same rate of monetary growth?

Still other questions arise. For instance, Figure 20.1 on page 455 shows average inflation and money growth over a 25-year period. The results suggest that money growth is a useful guide to understanding long-term movements in inflation. But what happens over shorter periods of a few months or years? Answering such questions requires moving beyond the simple statistical relationship shown in Figure 20.1. We do this in two steps. First we look at how the monetary base is connected to the quantity of money and then we show how economic decisions influence the link between money growth and inflation.

In June 2008, Z$1,000,000,000 were worth just US$1. A loaf of bread cost Z$600 million. By the end of 2008, the inflation rate in Zimbabwe was over 200 million percent. The central bank printed notes in larger and larger denominations—up to Z$100 trillion. But in January 2009, it stopped. People refused to accept Zimbabwe dollars and insisted on payments in real goods or U.S. dollars. At the end of the month the Reserve Bank accepted reality and legalized the dollarization. The hyperinflation had been the second highest ever experienced (second to Hungary) and had played a significant part in the destruction of the economy.

# Deposit Expansion and the Money Multiplier

Central bank liabilities form the base on which the supplies of money and credit are built; that is why they are called the *monetary base*. The central bank controls the monetary base, causing it to expand and contract. But most of us don't focus much attention on the monetary base. Our primary interest is in the broader measures of money, M1 and M2, which are multiples of the monetary base. Recall from Chapter 2 that M1 is currency plus demand deposits and M2 adds time deposits to M1.[4] This is the *money* we think of as available for transactions. What is the relationship between the central bank's liabilities and these broader measures of money? How do reserves become bank deposits? The answer is that the banking system makes them, in a process called **multiple deposit creation**.

The linkage between the monetary base and the monetary aggregates depends in part on whether the monetary policy environment includes a system of required reserves: that is, a rule that banks have to hold deposits at the central bank proportional to their outstanding deposits. The United States and the ECB require banks to hold reserves but others such as Canada and the United Kingdom do not. In Canada, required reserves were standard until the early 1990s, with banks required to hold a central bank deposit balance (in the 1980s) of 5 percent of demand deposits and 2 percent of notice or savings deposits. Now they are not required to hold reserves but do have accounts at the Bank of Canada for settlement balances. Deposits in these accounts are the reserves of the banking system.[5]

## Deposit Creation in a Single Bank

To see how deposits are created, let's start with an open market purchase in which the Bank of Canada buys $100,000 worth of securities from RBC. While RBC may have its own reasons for selling the securities, we are assuming that the Bank of Canada initiated the transaction. So if RBC doesn't sell the securities, some other bank will.

The Bank of Canada's purchase leaves RBC's total assets unchanged, but it shifts $100,000 out of securities and into reserves, increasing reserves by the amount of the open market purchase. The impact on RBC's balance sheet is shown in Panel A of Figure 20.3. (It is similar to Panel B of Figure 17.2 on page 377.)

What does RBC do in response to this change in the composition of its assets? The bank's management must do something. After all, it just sold an interest-bearing government bond to the Bank of Canada and received low-interest bearing reserves in exchange. If it does nothing, the bank's revenue will fall, and so will its profits. With liabilities unchanged, the increase in RBC's reserves doesn't affect the quantity of reserves the bank wants to hold, so it counts as an increase in *excess reserves*. When reserves rise in response to the sale of a security, something profitable has to be done with the proceeds.

The most natural thing for a bank to do is to lend out the excess—and no more. To keep the example simple, assume that RBC has just received a loan application from Ontario Builders Incorporated (OBI). OBI is seeking $100,000 to finance the continued construction of an office building. RBC approves the loan and credits OBI's chequing account with an additional $100,000. Panel B in Figure 20.3 shows RBC's balance sheet immediately after the loan is made.

---

[4] Here we will use the terms "M1" and "M2" but you should recall from Chapter 2 that the Bank of Canada most often speaks of adjusted aggregates M1+ and M2++.

[5] We use the term "banks" throughout this section rather than the more long-winded terms "deposit-taking institutions" or "direct clearer members of the Canadian Payments Association."

Figure 20.3   Changes in RBC's Balance Sheet after the Bank of Canada's Purchase of Securities

**A. Immediate Impact**

| Assets | | Liabilities |
|---|---|---|
| Reserves | +$100,000 | |
| Securities | −$100,000 | |

**B. After the Extension of a Loan**

| Assets | | Liabilities | |
|---|---|---|---|
| Reserves | +$100,000 | Chequable deposits | +$100,000 |
| Securities | −$100,000 | | |
| Loans | +$100,000 | | |

**C. After Withdrawal by the Borrower**

| Assets | | Liabilities | |
|---|---|---|---|
| Reserves | $0 | Chequable deposits | $0 |
| Securities | −$100,000 | | |
| Loans | +$100,000 | | |

OBI did not take out its $100,000 loan to leave it in its Royal Bank chequing account. The company borrowed to pay suppliers and employees. So OBI's financial officer proceeds to write cheques totalling $100,000. As RBC makes good on OBI's cheques, OBI's chequing account balance falls, but so does RBC's reserve account balance. When the entire $100,000 loan has been spent, RBC's balance sheet looks like Panel C of Figure 20.3.

In summary, following a $100,000 open market purchase of securities by the Bank of Canada, RBC makes a loan equal to the amount of newly created excess reserves. That loan replaces the securities as an asset on RBC's balance sheet.

## Deposit Expansion in a System of Banks

RBC's loan and OBI's expenditures can't be the end of the story because the suppliers and employees paid by OBI took their cheques to the bank and deposited them. As the cheques made their way through the payments system, RBC's reserves were transferred to the reserve accounts of the suppliers' and employees' banks. *Only the Bank of Canada (the central bank) can create and destroy the monetary base.* The nonbank public determines how much of it ends up as reserves in the banking system and how much is in currency; all the banks can do is move the reserves they have around among themselves. So, assuming cash holdings don't change following an open market purchase, the reserves created by the Bank of Canada must end up somewhere. Let's follow them to see where they go.

We'll start by making three assumptions that allow us to focus on the essential parts of the story: (1) banks want to hold reserves equal to 10 percent of chequing account deposits;[6] (2) when the level of chequing account deposits and loans changes, the quantity of currency held by the nonbank public does not; and (3) when a borrower writes a cheque, none of the recipients of the funds deposit them back in the bank that initially made the loan. Now, let's say that OBI uses the $100,000 loan to pay for steel girders from Canadian Steel Co. Canadian Steel deposits the $100,000 in its bank, TD Canada Trust, which credits Canadian's

---

[6] In practice the banks usually hold far less than 10 percent but these larger numbers help to make the example clear.

Figure 20.4      Changes in Balance Sheets

**A. TD Canada Trust after Canadian Steel's Deposit**

| Assets | | Liabilities | |
|---|---|---|---|
| Reserves | +$100,000 | Canadian Steel's Chequing account | +$100,000 |

**B. TD Canada Trust after Extension of a Loan**

| Assets | | Liabilities | |
|---|---|---|---|
| Reserves | +$10,000 | Canadian Steel's Chequing account | +$100,000 |
| Loan | +$90,000 | | |

**C. BMO after Deposit and Extension of a Loan**

| Assets | | Liabilities | |
|---|---|---|---|
| Reserves | +$9,000 | Chequing account | +$90,000 |
| Loan | +$81,000 | | |

Assuming desired reserves are 10% of deposits, and there are no changes in currency holdings.

chequing account. When OBI's cheque clears, TD's reserve account at the Bank of Canada is credited with $100,000. That's the transfer of reserves from the Royal. The result is shown in Panel A of Figure 20.4.

The additional $100,000 in Canadian Steel's chequing account is costly for TD Canada Trust to service. Canadian Steel will want to receive interest on its idle balance as well as access to it for payments. And the reserves TD Canada Trust just received don't pay much interest. In the same way that RBC lent out its new reserves following the Bank of Canada's open market purchase, TD Canada Trust will make a loan after Canadian Steel has made its deposit. How large will the loan be? Since the bank wants to hold reserves equal to 10 percent of deposits, TD Canada Trust must hold an additional $10,000 in reserves against the new $100,000 deposit so the largest loan TD Canada Trust can make is $90,000—and that's what it does. (Remember, we're assuming banks hold no excess reserves.) If the borrower immediately uses the $90,000 loan, TD Canada Trust's balance sheet will look like Panel B in Figure 20.4.

This new loan, and the reserves that go with it, must go somewhere, too. Let's say that it is deposited in yet another bank, BMO, which makes a loan equal to 90 percent of the new deposit. The change in BMO's balance sheet is shown in Panel C of Figure 20.4. (Recall, we're assuming that the owner of the chequing account at BMO doesn't withdraw any cash.)

At this point, a $100,000 open market purchase has created $100,000 + $90,000 = $190,000 in new chequing account deposits at TD Canada Trust and BMO and $100,000 + $90,000 + $81,000 = $271,000 in new combined loans at RBC, TD Canada Trust, and BMO. But the process doesn't stop there. The $81,000 loan from BMO is deposited into Scotiabank, where it creates an additional $81,000 in chequing account deposits. Scotiabank then makes a loan that is 90 percent of $81,000, or $72,900, and the $72,900 is deposited. And so on, as shown in Figure 20.5.

Table 20.1 on page 462 shows the consequences of a $100,000 open market purchase for the banking system as a whole. As the $100,000 in new reserves spreads through the banking system, it generates $1,000,000 in deposits and $1,000,000 in loans. With a 10 percent reserve requirement, each added dollar in reserves expands to $10 in deposits, increasing the quantity of money by a factor of 10.

With a bit of algebra, we can derive a formula for the **deposit expansion multiplier**—the increase in commercial bank deposits following a one-dollar open market purchase (assuming there are no changes in the amount of currency held by the nonbank public).

There's an easy way and a hard way to figure out the size of the deposit expansion multiplier. Let's start with the easy way. Imagine that the entire banking system is composed of a single bank—call it the Monopoly Bank. When the country's banking system is made up of just one bank, everyone has to use it. That means that any payment made from one person to another is just a transfer between two accounts in the Monopoly Bank. Because the managers of the Monopoly Bank know this, they don't need to worry about losing reserves when they make a loan.

So here's the question. For each dollar change in reserves arising from a transaction with the Bank of Canada, how much can the Monopoly Bank change its deposits? Monopoly Bank's reserves are just the desired reserve ratio $r_D$ times its deposits. If desired reserves are $RR$ and deposits are $D$, the level of reserves can be expressed

$$RR = r_D D \qquad (1)$$

Any change in deposits creates a corresponding change in desired reserves, expressed as

$$\Delta RR = r_D \Delta D \qquad (2)$$

Now let's go back to the question we started with: What is the change in the level of deposits following a one-dollar change in reserves? From equation (2), we can see that the answer is

$$\Delta D = \frac{1}{r_D} \Delta RR \qquad (3)$$

So for every dollar increase in reserves, deposits increase by $(1/r_D)$. This is the simple deposit expansion multiplier. If the desired reserve requirement is 10 percent, as it was in our example, then the simple deposit expansion multiplier equals $(1/0.1) = 10$, and a \$100,000 open market purchase generates a \$1,000,000 = 10 times \$100,000 increase in the quantity of money. To see why this makes sense, note that if deposits rose by more than \$1,000,000 following the addition of \$100,000 in reserves, the banking system would be holding less than its desired level of reserves. And if deposits rose by less than 10 times the change in reserves, some banks would be holding excess reserves, which violates one of the assumptions we made at the outset.

The hard way to compute the simple deposit expansion multiplier is to look at Table 20.1 and add up the entries. Notice that starting with BMO Bank, each entry in the column "Increase in Deposits" equals $(1 - r_D)$ times the entry above it, where $r_D$

---

**Figure 20.5**   **Multiple Deposit Creation**

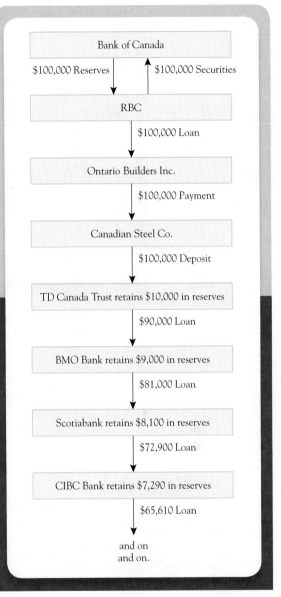

Assuming desired reserves are 10 percent of deposits, and there are no changes in currency holdings.

| Table 20.1 | | Multiple Deposit Expansion following a $100,000 Open Market Purchase Assuming a 10% Desired Reserve Ratio | |

| Bank | Increase in Deposits | Increase in Loans | Increase in Reserves |
|---|---|---|---|
| RBC | $0 | $100,000 | $0 |
| TD Canada Trust | $100,000 | $90,000 | $10,000 |
| BMO | $90,000 | $81,000 | $9,000 |
| Scotiabank | $81,000 | $72,900 | $8,100 |
| CIBC | $72,900 | $65,610 | $7,290 |
| National | $65,610 | $59,049 | $6,561 |
| . | . | . | . |
| . | . | . | . |
| . | . | . | . |
| The Banking System | $1,000,000 | $1,000,000 | $100,000 |

is the reserve requirement (measured as a decimal). With a desired reserve ratio of 10 percent, $r_D = 0.10$, $(1 - r_D) = 0.90$, so each entry is 0.90 times the one above it. For example, $90,000 equals 0.90 times $100,000; $81,000 equals 0.90 times $90,000. Thus, a one-dollar increase in reserves creates an increase in deposits equal to the sum of this series: $[1 + (1 - r_D) + (1 - r_D)2 + (1 - r_D)3 + \ldots]$. Using a formula from Appendix 4, we can determine that this expression equals $(1/r_D)$.

Before we continue, it is important to emphasize that there is nothing magical about *increases* in reserves and deposit *expansion*. A *decrease* in reserves will generate a deposit *contraction* in exactly the same way. That is, a $100,000 open market sale, in which the Bank of Canada sells a security in exchange for reserves, will reduce the level of deposits. From equation (3), we see that with a 10 percent desired reserve ratio, the contraction in deposits is $10 \times \$100,000 = \$1,000,000$.

## Deposit Expansion with Cash Withdrawals

We have made considerable headway in understanding the link between the central bank's balance sheet and the quantity of money in the economy. A change in reserves precipitates a significant change in the level of loans and chequable deposits in the banking system. But the simple deposit expansion multiplier is too simple. In deriving it, we ignored the fact that the nonbank public holds cash. As people's account balances rise, they have a tendency to hold more cash. From our discussion of the central bank's balance sheet, we know that when individuals change their cash holdings, they change the level of reserves in the banking system. Let's go back through the deposit expansion story, this time taking cash withdrawals into account. Assume that the holder of a chequing account withdraws 5 percent of a deposit in cash. Recall that the desired reserve ratio is 10 percent.

*"God bless you, sir."*

SOURCE: © *The New Yorker Collection 2001. Lee Lorenz from cartoonbank.com. All Rights Reserved.*

To understand the implication of these changes, let's use the example in the last section, in which the Bank of Canada purchased $100,000 worth of securities from RBC (Panel A of Figure 20.3 on page 459), which proceeded to make a $100,000 loan to Ontario Builders Incorporated (Panel B of Figure 20.3). OBI then used the $100,000 to purchase steel from Canadian Steel, which withdrew the funds from RBC and deposited them in a chequing account in TD Bank. This brings us to the T-account in Panel A of Figure 20.4 on page 460. If Canadian Steel takes some of the $100,000 in cash then the next loan cannot be $90,000.

| Figure 20.6 | Change in *TD Bank* Balance Sheet following a Deposit and Extension of a Loan |
|---|---|

| Assets | | Liabilities | |
|---|---|---|---|
| Reserves | +$9,500 | Canadian Steel's | |
| Loan | +$85,500 | Chequing account | +$95,000 |

Assuming desired reserves are 10% of deposits and cash holdings are 5%. Note: Canadian Steel also has $5,000 in cash.

Assuming that Canadian Steel removes 5 percent of its new funds in cash, that leaves $95,000 in the chequing account and $95,000 in TD Bank's reserve account. Since TD Bank wishes to hold reserves equal to 10 percent of deposits, it will want to keep reserves of 10 percent of $95,000, or $9,500. That means making a loan of only $85,500. Instead of Panel B of Figure 20.4, TD Bank's balance sheet looks like Figure 20.6 above.

We can continue as before, following the proceeds of TD Bank's loan as it is deposited in BMO. Assuming that the depositor of the loan's proceeds wishes to hold 5 percent of the deposit in cash, the increase in deposits will be $85,500 minus $4,275 equals $81,225 and BMO will make a loan of $73,102.50, keeping reserves of $8,122.50. Compare these numbers with the ones in Table 20.1 and you will see how much smaller the deposit expansion becomes if we take into account cash withdrawals.

In the last section, we derived the result that a one-dollar change in reserves created a change in deposits equal to one over the reserve requirement, or $(1/r_D)$. So, for an $r_D$ of 10 percent, a $1 change in reserves generated a $10 change in deposits. But now the analysis is more complicated and the deposit expansion is smaller. The desire of account holders to withdraw cash reduces the impact of a given change in reserves on the total deposits in the system. The more cash the public withdraws, the smaller the impact.

## The Arithmetic of the Money Multiplier

To better understand the relationship between deposits and reserves, we can derive the **money multiplier**, which shows how the quantity of money (chequing account deposits plus currency) is related to the monetary base (reserves in the banking system plus currency held by the nonbank public). Keep in mind that the monetary base is the quantity that the central bank can control.

If we label the quantity of money $M$ and the monetary base $MB$, the money multiplier $m$ is defined by the relationship

$$M = m \times MB \qquad (4)$$

To derive the money multiplier, we start with a few simple relationships: money equals currency $(C)$ plus chequable deposits $(D)$; the monetary base $(MB)$ equals currency plus reserves in the banking system. Writing these relationships as simple equations, we have

$$M = C + D$$
$$Money = Currency + Chequable\ deposits \qquad (5)$$

$$MB = C + R$$
$$Monetary\ base = Currency + Reserves \qquad (6)$$

These are just accounting definitions; the next step is to incorporate the behaviour of banks and individuals. Starting with banks, we know that their desired holdings of reserves is given by $r_D$, *but what determines this ratio?* In the absence of reserve requirements *the amount of reserves a bank holds depends on the costs and benefits of holding them*. The cost of excess reserves is the interest on the loans that could be made with them, while the benefits have to do with safety should deposits be withdrawn suddenly. The higher the interest rate, the lower banks' excess reserves will be; the greater banks' concern over the possibility of deposit withdrawals, the higher their reserves will be.

Turning to the nonbank public, we need to take account of their currency holdings. Again, as in the preceding example, we assume that people hold currency as a fraction of their deposits. That is,

$$C = \{c_D\}D \qquad (7)$$

where $\{c_D\}$ is the **currency-to-deposit ratio**. The *decision of how much currency to hold depends on costs and benefits* in the same way as the decision to hold excess reserves. The cost of currency is the interest it would earn on deposit, while the benefit is its lower risk and greater liquidity. As interest rates rise, cash becomes less desirable. But if the riskiness of alternative holdings rises or liquidity falls, then cash becomes more desirable, and $\{c_D\}$ will rise.

Bringing these elements together, we can rewrite the expression for the monetary base using the reserve and currency expressions. That gives us

$$MB = C + R$$
$$\text{Monetary base} = \text{Currency} + \text{Reserves}$$
$$MB = (c_D)D + (r_D)D \qquad (8)$$
$$= (c_D + r_D)D.$$

But our interest is in the relationship between the quantity of money and the monetary base. To find the relationship between the quantity of money and the monetary base, we can solve equation (8) for the level of deposits.

$$D = MB/(c_D + r_D) \qquad (9)$$

This expression tells us how much deposits change with a change in the monetary base. Notice that if we ignore cash withdrawals, we get the same result as in equation (3), that a change in deposits equals $(1/r_D)$ times the change in the monetary base. For a reserve requirement of 10 percent, that meant that a \$1 change in the monetary base increased deposits by \$10. Assuming a 5 percent currency-to-deposit ratio, equation (9) tells us that a \$1 increase in the monetary base will increase deposits by $[1/(0.10 + 0.05)] = 6.67$.

Returning to the derivation of the money multiplier, we can take the expression for money as the sum of currency and deposits and rewrite it as

$$M = \{c_D\}D + D \qquad (10)$$
$$= (c_D + 1)D$$

Substituting $D$ from the equation (9) gives us the final answer:

$$M = \left\{\frac{c_D + 1}{c_D + r_D}\right\} \times MB \qquad (11)$$

$$\text{Money} = \text{Money multiplier} \times \text{Monetary base}$$

This result is somewhat complicated, but it is worth studying. Equation (11) tells us that the quantity of money in the economy depends on three variables:

# YOUR FINANCIAL WORLD
## Your Excess Reserves

Banks hold excess reserves to ensure that they have sufficient resources to meet unexpected withdrawals. Your bank guarantees that it will provide you with immediate access to the funds in your chequing account, either by giving you cash or by honouring your cheque when it arrives. Sound business practice means having a little extra on hand, just in case people withdraw more money than usual. That is a cost of operating the bank.

In the same way that a bank holds excess reserves to insure itself against unexpectedly large withdrawals, individuals need to have an emergency fund to pay for unexpected expenses that can't be postponed. The appropriate size of the emergency fund varies from person to person; the exact amount depends on considerations such as your tolerance for risk, the number of income earners in your household, the amount of your income, the deductible on your insurance policies, and the stability of your employment. Most financial planners recommend that individuals hold emergency funds equal to a minimum of three, and preferably six to nine, months' income in cash accounts. The accumulation of an emergency fund is the first step in any investment program. Unless you really like risk, make sure you have such a fund before you make any other investments. Like a bank, we all need excess reserves.

1. The monetary base, which is controlled by the central bank.
2. The desire on the part of banks to hold reserves.
3. The demand for currency by the nonbank public.

To see how the quantity of money in the economy changes, we can look at the impact of each of these three elements. The first is the easiest. We know that if the monetary base increases, holding bank and public behaviour constant, the quantity of money increases. Looking at the second element, we see that an increase in banks' desired reserve holdings decreases the money multiplier. So for a fixed level of the monetary base, an increase in $r_D$ reduces M.

Finally, there is the currency-to-deposit ratio. What happens when individuals increase their currency holdings at a fixed level of the monetary base? Since $\{C_D\}$ appears in both the numerator and the denominator of the money multiplier in equation (13), we can't immediately tell whether the change creates an expansion or a contraction. Fortunately, logic gives us the answer. When an individual withdraws cash from the bank, he or she increases currency in the hands of the public and decreases reserves, so the monetary base is unaffected. But the decline in reserves creates a multiple deposit contraction. (Remember, every dollar in reserves creates more than a dollar's worth of deposits, raising the quantity of money more than a dollar.) Because each extra dollar held in currency raises M by only a dollar, when reserves are converted to currency, the money supply contracts. Table 20.2 on page 466 summarizes the effect of changes in the three components of the money supply.

A short numerical example illustrates the computation of the money multiplier. In January 2008, Canadian banks held reserves of $5.1 billion. Currency in the hands of the public was $48.5 billion, while deposit accounts (demand deposits plus other chequable deposits) amounted to $379 billion. These amounts imply that the reserve to deposit ratio $r_D$ was (5.1/379) = 0.0135; and the currency-to-deposit ratio $c_D$ was (48.5/379) = 0.128. Substituting these amounts into equation (13), we get the M1+ money multiplier:

$$m = \frac{1 + 0.128}{0.0135 + 0.128} = \frac{1.128}{0.1415} = 7.97$$

**Table 20.2** Factors Affecting the Quantity of Money

| Factor | Who Controls It | Change | Impact on *M* |
|---|---|---|---|
| Monetary base | Central bank | Increase | Increase |
| Desired reserve-to-deposit ratio | Commercial banks | Increase | Decrease |
| Currency-to-deposit ratio | Nonbank public | Increase | Decrease |

We can see the impact of eliminating required reserves by looking at how the money multiplier has changed. Thirty years ago, the currency-to-deposit ratio was much higher, as was the reserve ratio with the net effect that the money multiplier was much lower. In 1980, for example, currency was $9.1 billion, while deposits were $34.8 billion, so the ratio was 0.26. Banks held reserves of $6.1 billion, so $r_D$ was 0.175. Substituting these values into equation (11) shows the M1+ money multiplier was only 2.88.

Finally, notice that there is a specific money multiplier for each definition of money. Since from equation (4) the money multiplier is defined as the money stock divided by the monetary base, it is larger for the broader monetary aggregates (such as M2++) than for narrow monetary aggregates (such as M1+). Equation (5) makes clear that the "deposits" in the reserve ratio and the currency ratio include all the components of a particular monetary aggregate other than currency.

# The Velocity of Money

We know how the central bank can change the monetary base, and we know how that translates into changes in the monetary aggregates, but what explains the relationship between the money stock and prices? What accounts for the fact that high money growth is accompanied by high inflation? Recall that during times of inflation, the value of money is falling. If we think about the value or purchasing power of money in terms of the goods needed to get money, the impact of inflation becomes clear. Normally, we think of how many dollars we need to buy a cup of coffee or a sandwich; that's the money price of the sandwich. But we can turn the question around and ask how many cups of coffee or sandwiches a person needs to buy one dollar. A fall in the number of cups of coffee it takes to buy one dollar represents a decline in the price, or value, of money.

If someone asked you how the price of a cup of coffee is determined, having learned your microeconomics, you would answer that it depends on the supply of and demand for coffee. When the supply of coffee rises but demand does not, the price falls. Not surprisingly, the same is true of the price of money: it is determined by supply and demand. Given steady demand, an increase in the supply of money drives the price of money down. That's inflation. If the central bank continuously floods the economy with large amounts of money, inflation will reach very high levels.

## Velocity and the Equation of Exchange

To understand the relationship between inflation and money growth, we need to focus on money as a means of payment. Imagine a simple economy that is composed of four university students: One has $100 in currency; the second has two tickets to the weekend football game, worth $50 each; the third has a $100 calculator; and the fourth has a set of 25 high-quality drawing pencils that sell for $4 apiece. Each of these students wants something else. The one with the $100 in currency needs a calculator, so she buys it. The student who sold the calculator to her wants to see the football game, so he uses the cash she paid him to buy the two tickets. Finally, the student who sold the football tickets needs some pencils for a drawing class, so the cash changes hands again.

Let's analyze the effect of these transactions. Their total value is $100 × (1 calculator) + $50 × (2 football tickets) + $4 × (25 drawing pencils) = $300. In this four-person economy, the $100 was used three times, resulting in $300 worth of transactions. In general terms, we can write this calculation as

$$\text{(Number of dollars)} \times \text{(Number of times each dollar is used)}$$
$$= \text{Dollar value of transactions} \qquad (12)$$

To interpret this expression, note that the number of dollars is the quantity of money in the economy. The number of times each dollar is used (per unit of time) is called the **velocity of money**. The more frequently each dollar is used, the higher the velocity of money.

Applying this same logic to the economy as a whole is straightforward, since virtually every transaction uses money at some stage. For our purposes here, we will restrict the analysis to sales and purchases of final goods and services produced in a country during a given period and measured at market prices. That is, we will focus on **nominal gross domestic product**. Every one of the purchases counted in nominal GDP requires the use of money. So,

$$\text{(Quantity of money)} \times \text{(Velocity of money)} = \text{Nominal GDP} \qquad (13)$$

Since we have data on both the quantity of money and nominal GDP, we can use equation (13) to compute the velocity of money. Each definition of money—each monetary aggregate—has its own velocity. In 2008, GDP equalled $1.581 trillion and M1+ equalled $445 billion, so M1+ had a velocity of 3.5. In the same year, M2++ equalled $1.68 trillion, so the velocity of M2++ was less than one.[7] We will come back to this topic shortly.

To manipulate the expression for velocity in equation (13), we can rewrite it using algebraic symbols. We'll use the letter M to represent money and V to represent velocity. Nominal GDP can be divided into two parts, the price level and the quantity of real output (or real GDP). Calling these two factors $P$ and $Y$, we can state that nominal GDP = $P$ times $Y$. Using this notation, we can rewrite equation (13) as

$$MV = PY \qquad (14)$$

This expression, called the **equation of exchange**, tells us that *the quantity of money multiplied by its velocity equals the level of nominal GDP*, written as the price level times the quantity of real output.

With money on the left-hand side and prices on the right, the equation of exchange provides the link between money and prices that we are looking for. But our real concern is with inflation, not the price level, and money growth, not the quantity of money. We need to manipulate equation (14) to allow for the percentage change in each factor. Noting that the percentage change of a product such as MV or PY is the sum of the percentage changes in each factor, we can write

$$\%\Delta M + \%\Delta V = \%\Delta P + \%\Delta Y$$
$$\text{Money growth} + \text{Velocity growth} = \text{Inflation} + \text{Real growth} \qquad (15)$$

[7] Bank of Canada, Banking and Financial Statistics, August 2009; p. 52 for M1+ and M2++, and p. 97 for GDP.

where the symbol "%Δ" stands for percentage change. We know that the percentage change in the quantity of money is money growth; the percentage change in the price level is inflation; and the percentage change in real GDP is real growth. So equation (15) tells us that *money growth plus velocity growth equals inflation plus real growth.*

The equation of exchange accounts for some important characteristics of the patterns shown in Figure 20.1 on page 455. First, it tells us why high inflation and high money growth go together. Second, it explains the tendency for moderate- and low-inflation countries to fall below the 45-degree line in Panel B of Figure 20.1. That is, money growth tends to be higher than inflation in those countries because they are experiencing real growth. Looking at equation (15), we can see that if velocity is constant, then money growth equals the sum of inflation and real growth. At a given level of money growth, the higher the level of real growth is, the lower the level of inflation will be. So in countries that are growing, inflation will be lower than money growth, causing their economies to fall below the 45-degree line in Panel B of Figure 20.1.

## The Facts about Velocity

Looking at equation (15), we see that the behaviour of the velocity of money has important implications for monetary policy. Since the trend in real growth is determined by the structure of the economy and the rate of technological progress, if velocity is constant, countries could control inflation directly by limiting money growth. This logic led Milton Friedman to conclude that central banks should simply set money growth at a constant rate.[8] That is, policymakers should strive to ensure that the monetary aggregates such as M1 and M2 grow at a rate equal to the rate of real growth plus the desired level of inflation. One challenge to this policy is that central bankers control the monetary base rather than the monetary aggregates, but if we leave this to one side for the moment (we take it up in Chapter 21) we see that a constant growth rate of the money stock would stabilize inflation only if velocity were constant. In countries with inflation rates above 10 or 20 percent per year, changes in velocity can probably be safely ignored. In those economies, lowering inflation really does require lowering money growth. But in countries in which the inflation rate is below 10 percent per year, changes in the velocity of money could have a significant impact on the relationship between money growth and inflation.

How much does the velocity of money fluctuate? To find out, we can look at some data. Panel A of Figure 20.8 on page 420 shows the velocity of M1+ and M2++ from 1968 to 2009. There is a very noticeable downward trend in both series. In the long run, the velocity of M2++ looks very stable, decreasing gradually from 2 to 1. These historical data confirm Fisher's conclusion that *in the long run, the velocity of money is stable, so that controlling inflation means controlling the growth of the monetary aggregates.* The velocity of M1+ is less stable than that of M2++ but since 1990 it has declined relatively steadily.

But central bankers are concerned with inflation rates over quarters or years, not half a century. The monetary aggregates, even broad ones, can be useful guides to short-term policy only to the extent that they signal changes in inflation during the periods monetary policymakers care about. And the long-run view in the Panel A of Figure 20.8 masks some important short-run movements. Even the velocity of M2++, which seems stable, moves dramatically from quarter to quarter. To see this, we can look at the four-quarter (short-run) percentage change in M2++ velocity, shown in Panel B of Figure 20.8. The shaded bars in the figure represent recessions. Looking at

---

[8] The original statement of what has come to be known as Friedman's *k-percent rule* is in Milton Friedman, *A Program for Monetary Stability* (New York: Fordham University Press, 1960).

# YOUR FINANCIAL WORLD

## Understanding Inflation Statistics

When people think about inflation, they usually have the consumer price index (CPI) in mind. The CPI is the most commonly used and closely watched measure of inflation in Canada.* Given its prominence, we should understand its limitations.

The CPI, published monthly by Statistics Canada, is used widely to make adjustments for inflation and to measure changes in the cost of living from month to month and year to year. The index is designed to answer the following question: How much more would it cost today to purchase the same basket of goods and services that was bought on a fixed date in the past? To calculate the CPI, every two years government statisticians ask a representative sample of people what they actually buy. Then they construct a representative "market basket" of goods and services and track how much it costs from month to month. Inflation, as measured by the CPI, is the percentage change in the price of this basket of goods.

The CPI systematically overstates inflation. That is, its estimates of the change in the cost of living are biased upward. There are several sources of bias. The first comes from the fact that consumers' *buying patterns* change all the time, while Statistics Canada's surveys are infrequent. (Figure 20.7 shows the relative weights used to divide the market basket among different types of expenditures in 2005.) Consumers tend to shift their purchases away from goods that have become relatively more expensive and toward those that have become less expensive. Their willingness to make such substitutions lessens the impact of price changes on their standard of living. To the extent that statisticians fail to take such substitutions into account, the measure of consumer price inflation that they compile will overstate changes in the cost of living.

A second source of bias arises from the fact that statisticians have tremendous difficulty taking into account improvements in the *quality* of goods and services included in the consumer price index. Suppose, for example, that all cinemas introduce an elaborate new sound system that enhances the movie-going experience, raising ticket prices at the same time. If consumers are willing to pay the higher ticket prices because they value the improved sound quality, statisticians may simply record the increase

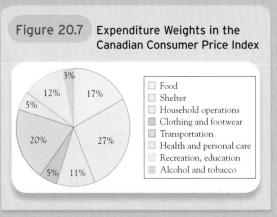

**Figure 20.7** Expenditure Weights in the Canadian Consumer Price Index

- Food
- Shelter
- Household operations
- Clothing and footwear
- Transportation
- Health and personal care
- Recreation, education
- Alcohol and tobacco

SOURCE: *Statistics Canada. Weighting Diagram of the Consumer Price Index—2005 basket at April 2007 Prices, Canada, Provinces, Whitehorse and Yellowknife. Catalogue number 62-001X. Accessed May 13, 2009. At: http://www.statcan.gc.ca/imdb-bmdi/document/2301_D34_T9_V1_B.pdf.*

in ticket prices without accounting for the increase in quality. The result is that inflation is overstated.

Statisticians are aware of all of these problems and are constantly working to minimize the bias they create. Nevertheless, the CPI still overstates inflation by about 0.5 percentage point per year. So when the CPI rises by 2 percent, the real cost of living, correctly measured, rises only about 1.5 percent. While a bias of that size doesn't amount to much if prices are rising at 10 or 15 percent a year, it becomes significant to both policymakers and consumers at the low levels of inflation common in recent years. For central bankers who wish to maintain price stability—zero inflation, correctly measured—the CPI's bias means that they need to systematically adjust their inflation objective, raising it about half a percentage point. That is, rather than setting their objective at zero measured inflation, they must choose some positive rate above that. For the rest of us, the CPI's bias means that if the index goes up 2 percent a year, we need only a 1.5 percent raise to maintain our standard of living.

* *Tools of the Trade in Chapter 2 on page 26 gives a brief introduction to the CPI.*

the figure, we can see that in the short run, velocity fluctuates quite a bit, sometimes by very large amounts. The scale of the figure runs from –14 to +6 percent!

The first step in understanding short-run movements in velocity is to examine what happened in the past. Returning to Panel A of Figure 20.8 on page 470, notice the increase in M1+ velocity in the late 1970s and early 1980s. This was a period of both high nominal interest rates, which peaked at over 20 percent, and significant financial innovations, including the introduction of stock and bond mutual funds

Figure 20.8 The Velocity of Money

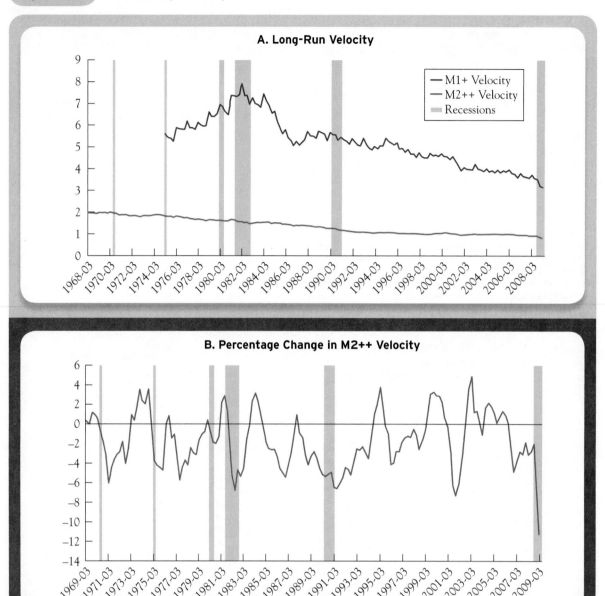

SOURCE: *Bank of Canada M1+ v37258; M2++ v41552790, both Table 176-0020; Statistics Canada, nominal GDP, v498074, from Table 380-0001, accessed 17 June 2009.*

that allow investors chequing privileges. The first of these innovations made holding money very costly; the second allowed individuals to economize on the amount of money they held. Together these reduced the amount of money individuals held for a given level of transactions, raising the velocity of money.

This discussion of velocity suggests that there is a close connection between fluctuations in velocity and changes in the demand for money. To understand and predict changes in the velocity of money, then, policymakers must understand the demand for money. We turn to that topic next.

# Velocity and the Demand for Money

We emphasized earlier that the equation setting nominal GDP equal to the money stock multiplied by the velocity of money (equation (14)) is an identity. Now we show that it is a small step to go from this identity to a behavioural model. Suppose that we assume temporarily that individuals decide to hold an amount of money proportional to their nominal income. In the economy as a whole we have

$$M^d = k\,P\,Y \tag{16}$$

where k represents that constant proportion. And suppose that the central bank creates a monetary base that, combined with the money multiplier, gives a money supply, $M^S = \overline{M}$. Then in equilibrium, with money supply equal to money demand,

$$\overline{M} = k\,P\,Y \tag{17}$$

Equation (17) tells us that the level of nominal income (PY) is determined by the quantity of money—a view (unsurprisingly) called the quantity theory of money. Notice that if you decided to calculate the velocity in this economy, you would find that

$$V = \frac{1}{k}$$

In other words, if we want to understand the determinants of velocity, we can use the framework of supply and demand, which enables us to develop a richer model of money demand than the simple assumption that individuals hold money in fixed proportion to their income.

The best way to understand money demand, and therefore the determinants of the velocity of money and the relationship between money and inflation, is to ask why individuals hold money. What do they do with the money that is supplied to them? Recall from Chapter 2 that money can be a means of payment, a unit of account, and a store of value. While the unit-of-account function is crucial to the economy, it provides no justification for holding money, so we will ignore it here and focus on the first and third functions. People hold money in order to pay for the goods and services they consume (the means-of-payment function) and as a way of holding their wealth (the store-of-value function). These two forms of demand are referred to as the transactions demand for money and the portfolio demand for money, respectively.[9] As we look at each of them, keep in mind that our objective is to understand fluctuations in the velocity of money. The more money individuals want to hold (all other things equal), the lower the velocity of money will be.

## The Transactions Demand for Money

The quantity of money people hold for transactions purposes depends on their nominal income, the cost of holding money, and the availability of substitutes. Let's look at each of these briefly, taking income first. The higher people's nominal income, the more they will spend on goods and services. The more they purchase, the more money they will need. This observation is the basis for the conclusion that nominal money demand rises with nominal income, part of the quantity theory of money (look back at equation (5)). Thus, *the higher nominal income is, the higher nominal money demand will be.*

[9] This framework for discussing the demand for money was originally developed by John Maynard Keynes and is known as Keynes' liquidity preference theory.

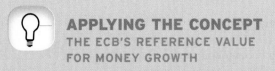

### APPLYING THE CONCEPT
### THE ECB'S REFERENCE VALUE
### FOR MONEY GROWTH

The monetary policy strategy of the European Central Bank assigns a prominent role to money. Many of the ECB's practices are modelled on those of its predecessor, the German Bundesbank, widely viewed as one of the most successful central banks in the world. In the 1970s, as inflation rose into the double digits in the United States and throughout most of Europe, the Bundesbank kept inflation in Germany at levels that would be acceptable even today. Policymakers there did so by setting annual targets for the monetary aggregates. Several decades later, in the hope that the Bundesbank's reputation for controlling inflation would rub off on them, ECB policymakers decided to set a "quantitative reference value for the growth rate of a broad monetary aggregate."

For the first four years of its existence, the ECB announced what amounted to a target growth rate of 4½ percent for euro-area M3 (the European equivalent of M2). Officials computed the rate using the percentage-change version of the equation of exchange (equation (4)). That meant they had to make assumptions about real growth, velocity growth, and the desired level of inflation. They assumed the euro-area economy was growing at a rate of 2 to 2½ percent per year, velocity was declining by ½ to 1 percent per year, and inflation should be 1 to 2 percent annually. Substituting the midpoints of those ranges into equation (4), we get

Money growth $- \frac{3}{4} = 1\frac{1}{2} + 2\frac{1}{4}$

so money growth = 4½ percent.

The ECB was heavily criticized for its use of money growth targets. Observers claimed that the relationship between money growth and inflation was too unpredictable to be useful in the short run. They argued that the velocity of money in the newly created euro area would be difficult to forecast. For a new central bank with no proven record of controlling inflation, they charged, this was a potentially dangerous move that could damage policymakers' credibility. Possibly in response to their critics, in May 2003 ECB policymakers decided to downgrade the role of money growth in their strategy. From then on, money growth would be used as "a crosscheck," not a major part of their strategy. And the governing council would no longer review the reference value every year, emphasizing its usefulness only as a long-run benchmark.

Deciding how much money to hold depends on the costs and benefits. The benefits are easy to appreciate: holding money allows people to make payments. The costs are equally easy to understand. Because money can always be used to purchase an interest-bearing bond, the interest that people lose in not buying the bond is the opportunity cost of holding money. The nominal interest rate is the one that matters here. Compare money, which pays zero interest, to a bond that pays interest. The difference between the two is the rate that matters, and that's the nominal interest rate. Of course, the bond is not a means of payment; it must be converted into money before it can be used to pay for transactions. So the decision to hold money or bonds depends on how high the bond yield is and how costly it is to switch back and forth between the two. For a given cost of switching between bonds and money, as the nominal interest rate rises, then, people reduce their chequing account balances, shifting funds into and out of higher-yield investments more frequently. Thus, the fact that the transactions demand for money falls as the interest rate rises has immediate implications for velocity. *The higher the nominal interest rate—that is, the higher the opportunity cost of holding money—the less money individuals will hold for a given level of transactions, and the higher the velocity of money.*[10]

---

[10] The fact that higher interest rates raise velocity means that they put upward pressure on inflation. And yet, as we will see in the following chapters, monetary policymakers combat high inflation by raising interest rates. The apparent contradiction is resolved by the fact that, while interest rate increases might drive velocity higher, they reduce real growth by even more—enough to make the overall effect the one that we have come to expect.

This relationship explains why inflation tends to exceed money growth in the high-inflation countries shown in Panel A of Figure 20.1 on page 455; that is why the points representing high-inflation countries tend to lie above the 45-degree line. At high levels of inflation, when prices are rising at a rate of 1,000 or 1,500 percent a year, money is losing value very quickly. At those levels, the opportunity cost of holding money is equivalent to the cost of inflation, a real return of –1,000 or –1,500 percent a year. People respond to the high cost of holding money by keeping as little of it as possible, getting rid of it as quickly as they can. They purchase durable goods that have a zero real return, which is quite a bit better than the real return of –1,000 percent they would get from holding money. Their frantic spending drives up the velocity of money. The quantity theory of money tells us that with national income held constant, inflation equals money growth plus growth in velocity. Since high inflation brings an increase in velocity, inflation must be higher than money growth in these countries, placing them above the 45-degree line in Panel A of Figure 20.1.

Besides interest rates, *the transactions demand for money is affected by technology*. Financial innovation allows people to limit the amount of money they hold. The best way to think about this is to imagine that innovation reduces the cost of shifting funds from an interest-bearing bond to a chequing account. The lower the transactions cost, the more people will shift money from their bond funds to their chequing accounts, and the less money people will choose to hold.

This has direct implications for the impact of financial innovation on the transactions demand for money. To see what they are, think about a case in which your bank offers a new kind of product that features free automatic transfers between an account with interest at the level of a bond and your traditional chequing account. You sign up for the account, but continue using your old cheques and debit card. This new account has the feature that each time you make a purchase, your bank automatically shifts the amount of the purchase from the bonds you are holding to your chequing account, where it remains for one day before being paid to your creditor. As a result, your chequing account will never have more than one day's worth of purchases in it, so you will hold much less money. Financial innovations that lower the cost of shifting money between bonds (or other investments) and a chequing account will lower money holdings at a given level of income. The immediate implication is that financial innovations that economize on the money holding increase the velocity of your money.

Thus, an increase in the liquidity of stocks, bonds, or any other asset reduces the transactions demand for money. The advent of automatic teller machines and financial products that allow customers to make payments directly from their stock or bond mutual funds, often at no extra cost, means that today people don't need to hold as much cash in their wallets and their chequing accounts as their parents and grandparents once did.

Finally, *we all hold money to insure ourselves against unexpected expenses*. We will include this form of demand, sometimes called the **precautionary demand for money**, as a part of transactions demand. The idea is that emergencies may arise that require immediate payments, for which we hold some amount of money in reserve. As we saw in Your Financial World: Your Excess Reserves on page 465, an individual's rainy-day fund is analogous to a bank's excess reserves. The level of precautionary balances we hold in such funds is usually related to our income and our level of expenditures. The higher our normal expenses, the larger our rainy-day funds will be. The precautionary demand for money also rises with risk. While this effect is probably small, the higher the level of uncertainty about the future, the higher the demand for money and the lower the velocity of money will be.

## YOUR FINANCIAL WORLD

### Free Chequing Accounts Are Rarely Free

Banks are always trying to attract new customers. To do so, some banks advertise free chequing accounts. But are these accounts really free? The answer is almost surely no. In fact, bankers joke that *"free* chequing" really means *"fee* chequing" because of all the fees customers end up paying. While banks don't normally impose a monthly service charge on such accounts, that doesn't make them free.

Depending on the bank, customers with "free chequing" may pay a fee to use the ATM or to visit a teller in person. They pay additional fees for notary public services, certified bank cheques, and bounced cheques. The insufficient funds charge is especially high for customers with "free chequing," who are more likely than other customers to overdraw their accounts.

Overdrafts, in fact, are very profitable for banks. Here's why. If you write a cheque for $100 more than your account balance, the bank will cover it but will charge you a fee, usually $25 to $30. You will have only a week or so to pay back the overdraft. In other words, the bank is offering you a $100 loan at a weekly interest rate of 25 percent or more. While banks are normally required to disclose the interest rates they charge on loans, regulators have decided that overdrafts are not loans. As a result, banks don't have to tell people who overdraw their accounts that they are paying a compound annual interest rate of over 10,000,000 percent!

There are two lessons here. First, don't be fooled by offers of free chequing. Before you open a chequing account, figure out what services you are going to need and find the bank that meets your needs most cheaply. Second, don't overdraw your account. There is almost always a cheaper way to borrow money.

## The Portfolio Demand for Money

Money is just one of many financial instruments that we can hold in our investment portfolios. As a store of value, money provides diversification when held along with a wide variety of other assets, including stocks and bonds. To understand the portfolio demand for money, note that a chequing account balance or a money market account is really just a "bond" with zero time to maturity. That means we can use the framework presented in Chapter 6, where we discussed the demand for bonds, to understand the portfolio demand for money.

Recall that the demand for bonds depends on several factors, including wealth, the return relative to alternative investments, expected future interest rates on bonds, risk relative to alternative investments, and liquidity relative to alternative investments. Each of these affects the portfolio demand for money. As wealth increases, individuals increase their holdings of all assets. A prudent person holds a diversified portfolio that includes stocks, bonds, real estate, and money. As wealth rises, the quantity of all these investments, including money, rises with it. So money demand varies directly with wealth. Note that this rule applies even at a fixed level of expenditures: a rich person who has the same expenses as a poor person will still hold more money.

In studying the demand for bonds, we noted that an investor's desire to hold any specific financial instrument depends on how well it compares with alternative investments. The higher the expected return relative to the alternatives, the higher the demand for an asset will be. The same is true for money: the higher its return relative to the alternatives, the higher the demand. Put slightly differently, a decline in bond yields will increase the portfolio demand for money.

Because expectations that interest rates will change in the future are related to the expected return on a bond, they will affect the demand for money as well. To understand why, remember that the price of a bond varies inversely with the interest rate. When interest rates rise, bond prices drop and bondholders suffer a capital loss. So if you think interest rates are likely to rise, bonds will become less attractive than money to you. (Recall that the prices of short-term bonds fluctuate less than the prices of long-term bonds. Money is the ultimate short-term bond because it has zero time to maturity.) As a result, you will sell the bonds in your portfolio and increase your money holdings—at least until interest rates stop rising. When interest rates are expected to rise, then, money demand goes up.

Next there is risk. In our discussion of bonds, we noted that a decline in risk relative to that of alternative investments increases the demand for bonds. While the riskiness of money can decrease, what usually happens is that the riskiness of other assets increases, driving up the demand for money.[11] Looking back at Panel B of Figure 20.8 on page 470, we can see that during the financial crisis of 2008/9, the velocity of M2 declined. The cause was an increase in uncertainty (risk), which drove investors to shift their funds into money.

Finally there is liquidity, a measure of the ease with which an asset can be turned into a means of payment. While some forms of money are more liquid than others, they are all closer to becoming a means of payment than other alternatives. If a sudden decrease in the liquidity of stocks, bonds, or other assets occurred, we would expect to see an increase in the demand for money.

Table 20.3 summarizes all of the factors that increase the demand for money.

**Table 20.3**   Determinants of Money Demand: Factors That Cause Individuals to Hold More Money

| **Transactions Demand for Money** | |
| --- | --- |
| Nominal income | The higher nominal income, the higher the demand for money. |
| Interest rates | The lower interest rates, the higher the demand for money. |
| Availability of alternative means of payment | The less available alternatives means of payment, the higher the demand for money. |
| **Portfolio Demand for Money** | |
| Wealth | As wealth rises, the demand for money goes up. |
| Return relative to alternatives | As the return on alternatives falls, the demand for money goes up. |
| Expected future interest rates | As expected future interest rates rise, the demand for money goes up. |
| Risk relative to alternatives | As the riskiness of alternatives rises, the demand for money goes up. |
| Liquidity relative to alternatives | As the liquidity of alternatives falls, the demand for money goes up. |

[11] To grasp why money can be risky, think of an example in which the nominal interest rate on money is zero (that is literally true for cash and nearly true for many bank deposits). When money pays no interest, its return is minus inflation. That is, money loses value at the rate of inflation. The less certain inflation is, the more uncertain the return on money, and the more risky it is. So inflation uncertainty increases the riskiness of holding money.

# Money Supply and Money Demand[12]

Our model of money demand suggests that the demand for money (and therefore the velocity of money) depends on a large number of variables. When we looked at velocity we focused on the relationship between money, prices, and real income, and saw that since real income grows relatively slowly, high inflation and high money growth are necessarily correlated. Here, we want to turn the focus toward the relationship between money and short-term interest rates, an analysis that is more relevant for economies with low levels of monetary growth. To focus on that relationship, we will assume that other variables are unchanging although in practice the world is not that simple.

Figure 20.9 depicts a money demand function showing that at higher interest rates there is less demand for money. It also depicts a money stock that is a constant. The money stock represents the monetary base supplied by the central bank multiplied by the money multiplier. Notice that panels A and B of Figure 20.9 are subtly different. In Panel A the money stock is fixed and equilibrium between the supply and demand for money determines the short-term interest rate. In Panel B the interest rate is fixed and equilibrium between the supply and demand for money determines the stock of money.

Central banks have a choice: they can set the interest rate or they can set the monetary base. If the money demand function and the money multiplier were stable and known, these policies would be the same. In practice, fluctuations in the money multiplier and in the level of all those other variables in Table 20.3 mean that if the central bank sets the interest rate, the money supply may not be what it anticipates. Similarly, if the central bank sets the monetary base, the interest rate may be higher or lower than anticipated. The choice of the central bank depends on which variable it really want to sets and whether the money demand or money supply function is more stable. Currently, the Bank of Canada determines an interest rate and the money stock is demand determined (as in Panel B of Figure 20.9. In the next chapter we look at the rationale for that choice in more detail.

Figure 20.9    Supply and Demand for Money

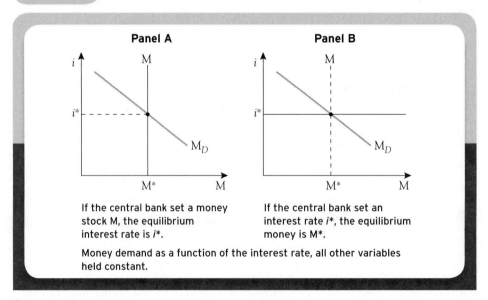

**Panel A**

If the central bank set a money stock M, the equilibrium interest rate is $i^*$.

**Panel B**

If the central bank set an interest rate $i^*$, the equilibrium money is M*.

Money demand as a function of the interest rate, all other variables held constant.

[12] We have avoided the term "money market" here to avoid confusion between the market for short-term bonds (the "money market" in popular usage) and the demand and supply for aggregates such as M1+ and M2++, which is the subject of this section.

## Terms

| | |
|---|---|
| currency-to-deposit ratio, 464 | portfolio demand for money, 471 |
| deposit expansion multiplier, 461 | precautionary demand for money, 473 |
| equation of exchange, 467 | quantity theory of money, 471 |
| money multiplier 463 | reserve ratio, 461 |
| mulitple deposit creation, 458 | transactions demand for money, 471 |
| nominal gross domestic product, 467 | velocity of money, 467 |

## Chapter Summary

1. There is a strong positive correlation between money growth and inflation.
   a. Every country that has had high rates of sustained money growth has experienced high rates of inflation.
   b. At very high levels of inflation, inflation exceeds money growth.
   c. At moderate to low inflation, money growth exceeds inflation.
   d. Ultimately, the central bank controls the rate of money growth.

2. Bank reserves are transformed into chequable deposits through multiple deposit creation. In the simplest case, this process is limited by the desire to hold reserves in proportion to deposits.
   a. When a bank's reserves increase, the bank makes a loan that becomes a deposit at a second bank.
   b. The second bank then makes another loan, but the amount of the loan is limited by the desired reserve ratio.
   c. This process continues until deposits have increased by a multiple that is equal to one over the reserve ratio.

3. The money multiplier links the monetary base to the quantity of money in the economy.
   a. The size of the money multiplier depends on
      i. Banks' desire to hold reserves.
      ii. The public's desire to hold currency.
   b. While the central bank controls the level of the monetary base, it cannot control the money multiplier.

4. The equation of exchange defines velocity as nominal GDP divided by the quantity of money, implying that money growth plus velocity growth equals inflation plus real growth.

5. If velocity and real growth were constant, the central bank could control inflation by keeping money growth constant.
   a. In the long run, velocity is stable, so controlling inflation means controlling money growth.
   b. In the short run, the velocity of money is volatile.

6. Shifts in velocity are caused by changes in the demand for money.
   a. The transactions demand for money depends on income, interest rates, and the availability of alternative means of payment.
   b. The portfolio demand for money depends on the same factors that determine the demand for bonds: wealth, expected future interest rates, and the return, risk, and liquidity associated with money relative to alternative investments.

7. Combining the models of money demand and money supply shows that the central bank can choose the short-term interest rate or the quantity of money—not both.

## Conceptual Problems

1. Why is inflation higher than money growth in high-inflation countries and lower than money growth in low-inflation countries?

2.* Explain why giving an independent central bank control over the quantity of money in the economy should reduce the occurrences of periods of extremely high inflation, especially in developing economies.

3. If velocity were constant at 2 while M2 rose from $5 trillion to $6 trillion in a single year, what would happen to nominal GDP? If real GDP rose 3 percent, what would be the level of inflation?

4. If velocity were predictable but not constant, would a monetary policy that fixed the growth rate of money work?

* Indicates more difficult problems.

www.mcgrawhill.ca/olc/cecchetti

5. Describe the impact of financial innovations on the demand for money and velocity.

6. If the interest rate on bonds dropped to zero, what would happen to the transactions demand for money?

7. Suppose that expected inflation rises by 3 percent at the same time that the yields on nonmoney assets such as bonds rise by 3 percent. What will happen to the demand for money? What if the yield on nonmoney assets rose by 4 percent?

8.* Explain how money growth reduces the purchasing power of money.

9. Provide arguments both for and against the adoption of a target growth rate for M2. What assumptions would be necessary to compute such a target rate?

10. Comment on the ECB's use of the reference value for money growth.

## Analytical Problems

11. Countries A and B both have the same money growth rate and in both countries, real output is constant. In country A, velocity is constant, while in country B, velocity has fallen. In which country will inflation be higher? Explain why.

12. Consider a country in which the level of desired reserves fluctuates widely and unpredictably. Would such a country be a good candidate for a money growth rule to guide monetary policy? Explain your answer.

13.* Assuming velocity were constant, could an open economy with a fixed-exchange rate follow a money growth rule successfully if capital moved freely across its borders? Explain your answer.

14. Draw a graph of money demand and money supply with the nominal interest rate on the vertical axis and money balances on the horizontal axis. Assume the central bank is following a money growth rule where its sets the growth rate of money supply to zero. Use the graph to illustrate how fluctuations in velocity imply that targeting money growth results in greater volatility of interest rates.

15. Using the same graph as that described in question 14, show how the central bank could use its control over the stock of money to target a particular level of interest rate in the face of changes in velocity.

16. Which of the following factors would increase the transactions demand for money? Explain your choices.
   a. Lower nominal interest rates.
   b. Rumors that a computer virus had invaded the ATM network.
   c. A fall in nominal income.

17. Which of the following factors would increase the portfolio demand for money? Explain your choices.
   a. A new Web site allows you to liquidate your stock holdings quickly and cheaply.
   b. You expect future interest rates to rise.
   c. A financial crisis is looming.

18.* Suppose a central bank is trying to decide whether to target money growth. Proponents of the move are confident that the new policy would be successful as, under the existing policy regime, they observed a stable statistical relationship between money growth and inflation. What warning might you issue to the central bank when they ask your advice?

# CHAPTER 21

## Modern Monetary Policy and the Challenges Facing Central Bankers

In November 2006, the Bank of Canada and the Minister of Finance announced that they were jointly renewing the commitment that the Bank would operate monetary policy to target a 2 percent CPI inflation rate. This led some to conclude that the 2 percent inflation target was an ideal target for monetary policy, but the Bank of Canada simultaneously began a research agenda to test that conclusion. Is 2 percent CPI inflation the right target? Should it be zero? Should it be a different measure of inflation? Does Canada need an explicit target or, like the United States, should the goal be vaguer?

Textbooks naturally emphasize what is known about a subject, and this one is no exception. But the fields of monetary economics and finance are alive with debate; there are many areas in which current events and research results are changing our understanding of monetary policy. In this chapter we introduce some of these research areas and discuss some of the challenges facing central banks.

We begin by taking up the question in the opening paragraph. What should be the target of the central bank? Monetary economists sometimes use the phrase "**nominal anchor**" to capture the notion of a target for the central bank as the target is seen as the object that ties down the value of the nominal variables in the economy, such as the nominal interest rate, the nominal exchange rate, and the price level. We discuss the need for a nominal anchor and the relative merits of alternative nominal anchors such as an inflation target, a money supply target, or a price level target. (A fixed exchange rate is an alternative target but given its broad ramifications it has a whole chapter following this one.)

A second area of ongoing research at central banks and in academic economics departments is the transmission mechanism of monetary policy. How does monetary policy affect the real economy? How can the interest rate on assets that are held in small amounts by a few institutions really affect the entire economy? In chapters 18 and 19 we argued that changing the overnight rate affected aggregate demand through its effect on the exchange rate and the whole structure of interest rates. Some economists have proposed alternative transmission mechanisms that we review later in the chapter. Finally, we look at one important operational area of monetary policy: the measurement of potential output. In chapters 18 and 19, we blithely used the term "potential output" in discussing central bank decision making, but the level of potential output is unobservable! How do central bankers measure the unobservable?

## Choosing a Nominal Anchor

The Bank of Canada uses inflation targets as a way of "anchoring" inflation expectations. Why is this necessary? Economists Finn Kydland and Ed Prescott received the Nobel Prize in Economics in 2004 in part for their neat way of describing the challenge faced by central bankers. Figure 21.1 on page 480 illustrates the problem. The analysis is based on three critical assumptions: (1) that, other things being equal, central banks would want to set inflation above expected inflation, (2) that central banks don't like high inflation, and (3) that you can't intentionally surprise people. Let's look at these one at a time.

Assumption (1) could reflect the possibility that if inflation is higher than expected the output gap will shrink, so if the central bank wants to raise employment it will try to have a "surprise" inflation. Another reason that the central bank might want surprise inflation is that then the government could borrow cheaply and repay in less valuable dollars. This is sometimes called inflating the debt away. Both these factors will be more important if the central bank is not independent of the government, and independence of central banks is advocated precisely to reduce these incentives.

Assumption (2) reflects the understanding that, again other things being equal, less inflation is better than more inflation. In part, this is because even if inflation is fully anticipated, a world of 10 percent inflation imposes costs on individuals whether from marking up their goods every month or from trying to figure out how much of a price increase is a change in relative prices and how much is inflation. But, more importantly, inflation is never exactly factored into contracts. In Canada, inflation expectations were well anchored at 2 percent in the early 21st century, but the tax code was not fully indexed to take account of the inflation.

Together assumptions (1) and (2) give us the line $\pi(\pi^e)$, a line with a slope less than one and a positive intercept. This line shows the rate of inflation that the central bank would like to set as a function of the expected rate of inflation. The intercept is the rate of inflation the central bank would like to set if the public expected no inflation. That will depend on the tradeoff between how much the central bank dislikes high inflation and how much it would want to reduce the output gap. Notice that if the public expects very high inflation, the central bank would actually prefer to disappoint the public and set inflation less than expected. That is because the costs of high inflation outweigh the benefits of reducing the output gap. At low inflation, the tradeoff goes the other way: low inflation isn't very costly so the benefits of a surprise inflation outweigh the costs.

Now we come to assumption (3). That assumption is that the central bank can't surprise the public. Basically this is saying that the public understands the incentives of the central bank. They know that the central bank would like to have a surprise inflation, other things being equal. The only point that can satisfy all three assumptions is the point where the $\pi(\pi^e)$ intersects the 45° line. At that point the central bank is setting the inflation rate at its preferred rate given inflation expectations, and the public is not being surprised since actual inflation equals expected inflation.

Why is point A the only equilibrium? Suppose it happened that the expected inflation rate was zero. The central bank would want to have a "surprise" inflation of 2 percent. But the public knows the central bank would do so, so everyone would have set their inflation expectations at 2 percent; however, then the central bank would try to cheat anyway by setting the inflation rate even higher—again an incentive widely known and understood. The only equilibrium is for the central bank to set the inflation rate so high that the public knows that the central bank wouldn't want a higher inflation rate because the gains (say from reducing the output gap) would be less than the cost of the high inflation.

**Figure 21.1** Expectations and Monetary Policy Credibility

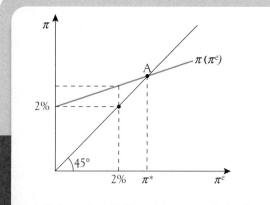

$\pi(\pi^e)$ shows the inflation rate an unconstrained central bank would choose as a function of inflation expectations. If individuals expect an inflation rate of 2% the central bank would have an incentive to set inflation above 2%.

Point A is the equilibrium. Is that the best the economy can do? No. Suppose that the ideal inflation rate is 2 percent (for example, due to biases in the CPI measure or because of the problems of the zero interest bound, discussed in Chapter 23). If the central bank could be constrained to set an inflation rate of 2 percent then expected inflation and actual inflation would both be 2 percent. To see that this is better than at Point A, notice that in both cases actual inflation equals expected inflation so there is no gain on the output and employment front in either case, but point A has lower inflation so is unambiguously better.

How could the central bank be constrained to set an inflation rate of 2 percent? Economists have proposed a number of mechanisms, many of which have been implemented, and none of which is foolproof! In the late 19th and early 20th century the gold standard tied the quantity of money to the amount of gold in an economy and so limited the discretion of the central bank. In the 1990s the government of New Zealand imposed legislation, including a clause declaring that the governor of the central bank would be fired if the inflation rate exceeded a certain level. Alternatively, it has been proposed that central bankers with a visceral hatred of inflation be appointed so that the tradeoff underlying the $\pi(\pi^e)$ curve disappears. In practice, reputation seems to have been the key. Countries announce that they will have a 2 percent inflation rate and then stick to that rule, so that over time the expected inflation rate is 2 percent. Now, if a country took advantage of the low expectations, it would get a short-term gain but a long-term loss, as it would be stuck at the bad equilibrium (A) for a long time or until undergoing a painful disinflation.

## Targeting Money Growth

In the long run, inflation is tied to money growth. In a high-inflation environment, where money growth and inflation are both running higher than 100 percent, moderate variations in the growth of velocity are a mere annoyance. What is important is the resolve of central bank officials (and politicians) to bring inflation down. There is no magic to it; the only solution is to reduce money growth.

In a low-inflation environment, controlling inflation is not so simple. The quantity theory of money tells us that our ability to use money growth as a policy guide depends on the stability of the velocity of money. The velocity of the broad monetary aggregate M2 appears sufficiently stable for M2 to serve as a benchmark for controlling inflation over the long run—over periods of several decades. But in the short run, the velocity of money varies substantially. Yet the mere fact that velocity fluctuates is not reason enough to dismiss money growth as a policy target.

As we saw in Chapter 17, an intermediate target can be useful when it is predictably linked to the policymakers' operating instrument, on the one hand, and their policy objective on the other. This statement implies two criteria for the use of money growth as a direct monetary policy target: (1) a stable link between the monetary base and the quantity of money and (2) a predictable relationship between the quantity of money and inflation. The first of these allows policymakers to predict the impact of changes in the central bank's balance sheet on the quantity of money. The second allows them to translate changes in money growth into changes in inflation. These criteria cannot be solely qualitative in nature; central bankers need numerical estimates of these relationships. Policymakers must be able to say that a 1 percent change in the monetary base will generate an $x$ percent change in a monetary aggregate such M2, which will then translate into a $y$ percent change in inflation, and over what time period. The relationship between money demand and its determinants listed in Table 20.3 must be stable and predictable—a problem for policymakers. We look at these two requirements in turn.

"Forgive the mess. Warren just put everything into cash."

**The Relationship between the Monetary Base and the Money Supply**   For changes in the monetary base to lead to predictable changes in the quantity of money the components of the money multiplier need to be predictable. That is, they don't actually have to be constant, but they have to move in predictable or consistent ways. For example, market interest rates affect the cost of holding both excess reserves and currency. So as interest rates increase, we would expect to see both $\{R/D\}$ and $\{C/D\}$ fall, increasing the money multiplier and the quantity of money. If these changes in the money multiplier were predictable, a tight link would exist between the monetary base and the quantity of money—a link the central bank might choose to exploit in its policymaking. While such a link made sense in a discussion of the economy in the 1930s, and might still be important in emerging countries such as China and India, for countries with sophisticated financial systems it no longer is. In countries such as Canada and the United States, the link between the central bank's balance sheet and the quantity of money circulating in the economy has become too weak and unpredictable to be exploited for policy purposes.

The problem is that the money multiplier is just too variable; you can see it in the data. Figure 21.2 plots the ratio of the M1 and M2 to the monetary base from 1980 to 2009. Notice the difference in the scales. The M1 money multiplier uses the left scale and rose from about 3 to 8, while the M2 multiplier is drawn against the right-hand

**Figure 21.2**   M1+ and M2++ Multipliers, 1980–2009

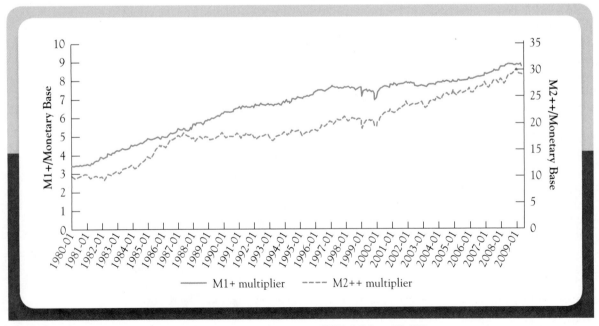

scale and grew from 12 to 30. Both money multipliers rose throughout the period but the growth rate was far from constant, showing both long swings and short-run fluctuations. (The two dramatic dips in 1999 reflect high amounts of reserves put into the system for the introduction of LVTS in February of that year, and in preparation for Y2K in December.)

The relationship between the monetary base and the quantity of money is too volatile for a central bank to exploit for short-run policy purposes.

**The Instability of Money Demand**   To study the demand for money quantitatively, we will focus on the impact of the two factors that affect the transactions' demand for money, nominal income and interest rates. Recalling the logic of the equation of exchange, we can conclude that the first factor, nominal income, is roughly proportional to money demand. Doubling people's nominal income means doubling the dollar value of the transactions they engage in, which requires double the original amount of money. That means we can focus on nominal income divided by the quantity of money, which equals velocity. This brings us to the second factor, interest rates (or more precisely, the opportunity cost of holding money). Is there a stable relationship between the velocity of money and the opportunity cost of holding it?

The data displayed in Figure 21.3 bear directly on this question. The figure shows the velocity of M1 on the vertical axis and a proxy for the opportunity cost of holding M1 on the horizontal axis The red dots show data from before 1975 and the blue show data from 1975 to 1981. The difficulty in part is that in targeting money growth rates the monetary authorities need a very precise answer to the question: if interest rates rise by 25 bps how much will velocity respond by? Figure 21.3 shows that the answer changed over time and it did not change in a predictable way.

**Figure 21.3**   Velocity

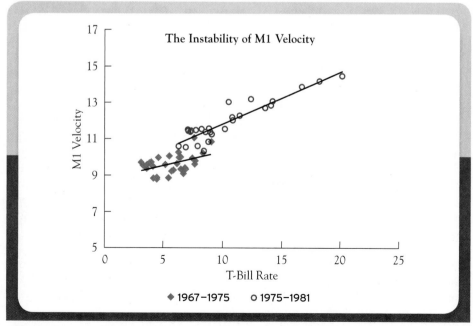

SOURCE: *Bank of Canada. M1 (net) v37198 from 176-0020; Tbill rates v122531 from Table 176-0043; Statistics Canada, nominal GDP, v498074, from Table 380-0001, accessed 17 June 2009.*

## TOOLS OF THE TRADE
Using Statistical Models in Policy Evaluation

To do their jobs, policymakers need to know how changes in policy will affect their objectives. An essential question in any monetary policy decision is how much to adjust interest rates in order to keep prices stable and economic growth high. Unlike theory, policymaking is about numbers; it requires quantitative estimates of the relative impact of alternative policies. These estimates are based on statistical models that summarize the correlations among economic variables. To obtain the necessary information, economists at the central bank collect historical information and analyze it in an attempt to determine how past changes in policy have affected the economy. Their estimates allow policymakers to answer questions such as "If we raise the federal funds rate from 4 to 5 percent, how much lower will the rate of inflation be two years from now?"

Such an exercise may seem straightforward, but it has pitfalls. For an economic prediction to be valid, it must be based on data drawn from a historical period in which the same set of policies was in place. If it isn't, the results can be seriously misleading. A sports analogy will help to make the point. In the United States, a football team has four downs to make 10 yards, but in Canada, a football team gets only three downs before being forced to give up the ball. As a result, Canadian football teams regularly kick the ball away on the third down. Needless to say, no one would think of using data from Canadian football games to predict third-down behaviour in a U.S. game.

In the mid-1970s, Nobel Prize–winning economist Robert Lucas observed that what is true in sports is true in economics.[*] In the same way that altering the rules of a game will change the players' strategies, altering economic policy will change people's economic decisions. For example, no one would use data from a fixed-exchange-rate period to model the impact of interest rate policy in a floating-exchange-rate system. Nor would anyone use information from a period when central bankers targeted money growth, allowing interest rates to vary, to predict the impact of a shift to targeting interest rates. Economic and financial decisions, Lucas noted, are based on expectations about the future, including what policymakers will do. Any change in policymakers' behaviour will change people's expectations, altering their behaviour and the observed relationships among economic variables.

This observation, known as the Lucas critique, has had a profound influence on the way policymakers formulate their recommendations. It implies that in predicting the effects of a change in policy, policymakers must take into account how people's economic behaviour will change with it. To understand the impact of policies never before implemented, Lucas emphasized, policymakers must rely heavily on economic theory, modelling people's reactions to changes in their environment.

[*] The original Lucas critique is described in Robert E. Lucas, Jr., "Econometric Policy Evaluation: A Critique," Carnegie-Rochester Conference on Public Policy 1, 1976, pp. 19–46.

There are several possible explanations for the instability of money demand over the last quarter of the 20th century. The primary one has to do with the introduction of financial instruments that paid higher returns than money but could still be used as means of payment. While officials have tried to account for the new instruments by changing the composition of the monetary aggregates (see Applying the Concept: Financial Innovation and the Shifting Definition of Money), money demand continues to appear unstable.

The breakdown in the relationship between money demand and interest rates that occurred in the Canada during the early 1990s drove researchers back to their computers to build better, more robust statistical models. Nevertheless, the debate over the stability of money demand serves as a cautionary note for policymakers.

### Experience with Money Growth Targets
Though today virtually no central bank conducts monetary policy solely by targeting money growth, the practice was common in the 1970s. In 1975, when Canadian inflation was over 10 percent, the Bank of Canada introduced monetary aggregate targeting.

The Bank set a target range for the growth rate for M1 of 10 to 15 percent and expected to reduce that growth rate over time to gradually reduce the inflation rate

**APPLYING THE CONCEPT**
FINANCIAL INNOVATION
AND THE SHIFTING
DEFINITION OF MONEY

Financial innovation means that the assets that families and individuals hold for transacting and saving change over time. The Bank of Canada tries to respond to this by expanding the definition of the monetary aggregates to reflect the changing behaviour. Figure 21.4 shows the behaviour of velocity based on three different definitions of M2. The original definition was intended to capture the store of value and included savings accounts at banks in addition to the demand deposits included in M1. As individuals began to use money market mutual funds for saving, and the accounts at trust companies and credit unions were less distinct from bank accounts, the preferred definition shifted to M2+, which incorporates those accounts.

As you can see from Figure 21.4, the velocity of M2 and M2+ began to rise in the early 1990s. Did that mean that households were not saving? The behaviour of M2 ++ velocity has the answer. M2++ includes non−money market mutual funds and Canada savings bonds as well as the account included in M2+. M2++ velocity did not rise. The increase in M2+ velocity combined with the decrease in M2++ velocity indicates that households were switching their savings out of the accounts in M2+ and into non−money market mutual funds and CSBs. If the same amount of saving was happening, it would have the same effect on prices and spending so the Bank argued that M2++ reflected the underlying behaviour in the economy better than M2+.

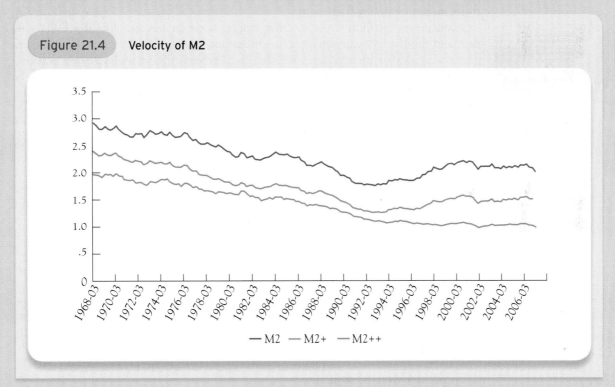

**Figure 21.4**    Velocity of M2

— M2    — M2+    — M2++

SOURCE: *Bank of Canada. M2 (net) v37198; M2+(net) v37216; M2++(gross) v41552790, all from 176-0020; Statistics Canada, nominal GDP, v498074, from Table 380-0001, accessed 17 June 2009.*

in Canada. The result was that the growth rate of M1 fell from 13.8 percent in 1975 to 8.4 percent in 1977. But the growth rate of M2 barely changed (falling from 15 percent to 14 percent) and the rate of inflation remained high. By 1981 the growth rate of M1 was 3.3 percent but the growth rate of M2 was still 14 percent and the inflation rate was 12 percent. When Governor of the Bank of Canada Gerald Bouey explained to a House of Commons committee why the Bank was abandoning monetary growth targets, he commented that "We did not abandon M1, M1 abandoned us."[1] This result is an example of Goodhart's Law, which states that when a variable (for example, money growth) is used as a policy instrument, a relationship between the instrument and the target (for example, inflation) that previously existed will break down.[2] While the Bank considered adopting an M2 target, finally, like the Federal Reserve, it abandoned targets. By the summer of 2003, even Milton Friedman had given up. "The use of the quantity of money as a target has not been a success," he conceded. "I'm not sure I would as of today push it as hard as I once did."[3]

European monetary policymakers view matters differently. The ECB's governing council periodically announces a money growth rate that is intended to serve as a long-run reference value. Large deviations from this reference value require an explanation. The difference of opinion between the Europeans and the North Americans on this matter can be traced to their divergent views on the stability of money demand. Researchers who study the demand for money in the euro area have concluded that the demand is stable, which implies that changes in velocity are predictable. This assumption is the justification for the ECB's emphasis on money in its monetary policy framework.

Even given this difference in their emphasis on money growth, the ECB, the Fed, and the Bank of Canada have all chosen interest rates as their operating target. The reason is that interest rates are the link between the financial system and the real economy. Changes in interest rates are one of the primary tools central bankers have for influencing the economy. By keeping interest rates stable, policymakers can insulate the real economy from disturbances that arise in the financial system. For example, the payments system can change quickly. The introduction of more liquid financial instruments or newly configured electronic systems can have a direct impact on the way money is used and therefore on velocity. If policymakers wanted to, they could keep money growth constant in the face of such innovations. But doing so would create volatility in interest rates, which could destabilize the real economy. This point was made in Chapter 17, which discussed the rationale for choosing the interest rate rather than the quantity of reserves as an operating instrument. There we noted that the best way to keep changes in reserves from influencing interest rates and affecting the real economy is to target interest rates. While inflation is tied to money growth in the long run, interest rates are the tool policymakers use to stabilize inflation in the short run.

The idea that targeting money growth destabilizes interest rates is not just a theoretical possibility. Figure 21.5 shows the path of the overnight interest rate. The shaded area represents the period when the Bank of Canada was targeting M1 growth rates. Notice how volatile the interest rate was during that period. This sort of volatility, caused by policymakers' inability to forecast shifts in the velocity of money, would surely damage the real economy.

## Inflation Targets

After the abandonment of money growth targets, Canadian monetary policy had no clear nominal anchor. The Bank of Canada operated to stabilize output and prices but without a specific target for either. In 1988 the Governor of the Bank of Canada,

---

[1] Cited in James Powell, "A History of the Canadian Dollar" Bank of Canada, p. 77.

[2] This is a variant of the Lucas critique described on page 484, which notes that reduced-form relationships, such as that between money growth and inflation, are sensitive to changes in the policy environment.

[3] Simon London, "Lunch with the FT: Milton Friedman," *Financial Times*, June 7, 2003, p. 12.

Figure 21.5   The Overnight Rate and Money Growth Targeting

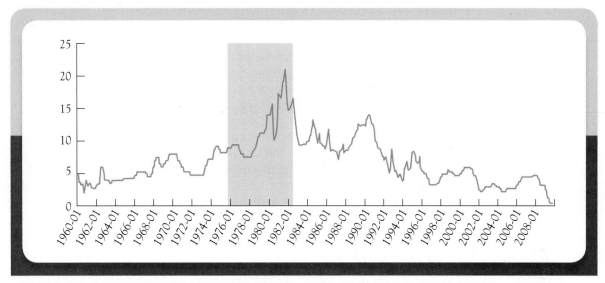

The shaded bar represents the period from 1975 to 1981, when the Bank of Canada targeted the quantity of money.

SOURCE: *Bank of Canada. Overnight rate v39050 from Table 176-0048.*

John Crow, issued what was effectively a call to arms. He declared that the goal of the central bank should be "stable prices," albeit without defining "stable prices" more explicitly. The Bank began to operate policy with the goal of lowering inflation, and in February 1991 inflation targeting was adopted formally in a joint statement by the Minister of Finance and Governor Crow. Initially the goal was an inflation rate for the consumer price index within the range of 2 percent to 4 percent, a range that would be reduced to 1 percent to 3 percent by 1995. The target was set for a five-year term and in 1996 the target range of 1 to 3 percent was confirmed, as it was in 2001 and again in 2006. The only major change in the target was that the Bank shifted toward a clearer commitment to keep inflation at the mid-point of the range (that is, a 2 percent inflation rate) rather than simply within the band.

New Zealand was the first country to adopt inflation targeting—in 1989—but since then many other industrialized countries, including the United Kingdom and Sweden, as well as some emerging market countries, such as Chile and Korea, and transition economies, such as the Czech Republic and Poland, have adopted inflation targets.

Inflation targets make it very clear what the central bank is trying to do, and so make monetary policy more predictable. The adoption of inflation targets has been accompanied by a radical change in how the central bank operates. In the 1980s, it seemed as though central banks were trying to "fool" the markets, but now central bankers aim for transparency, not opacity.

Advocates of inflation targeting point out how much inflation declined in inflation-targeting countries. On the other hand, skeptics point out that the countries that adopted inflation targeting were those with an inflation problem, so improvement wasn't hard. It is not completely clear that countries that are not inflation targeters, like the United States, have done significantly worse than Canada or New Zealand in achieving low inflation. Other critics of inflation targeting note that 2 percent is not price stability but rather inflation stability. Even if we acknowledge that there are biases in inflation measurement, those biases are estimated to be about 0.5 percent in Canada so price stability would require a target of 0.5 percent inflation, not 2 percent.

A more challenging criticism argues for a higher rather than lower target inflation rate on the grounds that the nominal interest rate can never be less than zero—termed the **zero nominal-interest-rate bound**.[4] Suppose that there is a serious recessionary gap so that economic conditions require the central bank to set a real interest rate of –2 percent. Now, if the rate of inflation is at the bottom of a 1 to 3 percent range, that is at 1 percent, the central bank would want to set a nominal interest rate of –1 percent but can't do that. If the target inflation range had been (for example) at the bottom of a 3 to 5 percent range, then the central bank could have set the nominal interest rate at 1 percent and achieved the desired real rate. As we will see in Chapter 23, the zero nominal interest bound is a serious challenge in low-inflation environments.

A final criticism of inflation targeting argues that by targeting inflation rather than the price level, the central bank increases the uncertainty regarding inflation over the long run. These critics advocate price-level targets rather than inflation targets and we examine these next.

## Price-Level Targets

Advocates of price level targets do not necessarily advocate a stable price level—some argue for a rising price level—but that is subtly different from advocating an inflation target. Consider the example in Figure 21.6.

Panel A represents an inflation-targeting central bank. Suppose today the price level is at 100 and that the inflation target is 2 percent over the next year, or a price level of 102. Now suppose what actually happens is that the price level rises to 110. The inflation-targeting central bank will set the following year's target to 112 (110 plus 2 percent). Contrast this behaviour with the central bank (shown in Panel B) that targets a price level increase of 2 percent. Again, the price level begins at 100 and unexpectedly rises to 110. The price level–targeting central bank will now target a price level of 104. That is, the inflation-targeting central bank always targets 2 percent from wherever the price level happens to be, while the price level–targeting central bank sticks to the original path. A simpler way to say this is that the inflation-targeting central bank lets bygones be bygones, while the price level–targeting central bank does not.

Some consequences are obvious. If there was a burst of high inflation, the price level–targeting central bank would have to create a disinflation to bring the price level back down to the path, which might cause unemployment and slow growth. On the other hand, if prices had stagnated at 100, the price level–targeting central bank would pursue a more expansionary monetary policy with 4 percent inflation to bring the price level up to 104 in the second year. The inflation-targeting central bank would again target 2 percent inflation to bring the price level up to 102.

An advantage of price-level targeting over inflation targeting is that it reduces the uncertainty about the price level (and the rate of inflation) over a long horizon. For example, suppose you are in a union that is making a long-term wage contract (as many BC government employees did in 2006). You need to know what the inflation rate will be over the entire period, and with inflation targeting you will be much less certain than with price-level targeting. Or, suppose you are considering financing a project that will take 10 years to pay off. The real rate of interest that you will pay

---

[4] The Bank of Canada argues that the target for the overnight rate should not be set below 25 bps "to preserve the effective functioning of markets in a low inflation environment" and thus defines 25 bps as 'the effective lower bound" for the overnight rate. Bank of Canada, "Monetary Policy Report," April 2009, p. 25.

Figure 21.6    Inflation Targeting and Price-Level Targeting

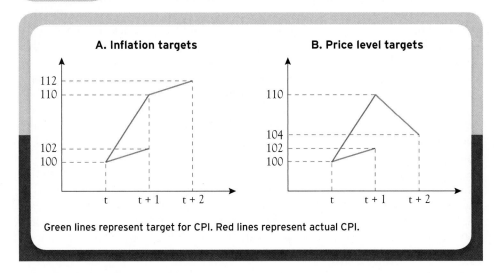

Green lines represent target for CPI. Red lines represent actual CPI.

depends on the rate of inflation over 10 years, so you too will benefit from the lower variability of the price level under price-level targeting. Similarly for someone planning for retirement, inflation uncertainty is an important source of risk.

Both inflation targeting and price-level targeting policies require a definition of the price level. Many definitions have been proposed. Canada states its inflation target in terms of the Consumer Price Index, a readily available, easily understood magnitude. The Federal Reserve keeps its eye more closely on the Personal Consumption Expenditure (PCE) deflator. This measure suffers from less substitution and new good bias (and so shows lower inflation) than the CPI, but is somewhat more arcane. Statistics Canada does not compute a monthly PCE deflator. A more contentious issue is that neither index directly includes asset prices—such as stock market prices or real estate.[5] Until the financial crisis, the consensus of central bankers was that targeting asset prices (for example, trying to burst asset price bubbles) is too difficult. Since the financial crisis, there is greater awareness of the cost (even in the very narrow terms of the consequences for achieving the 2 percent inflation target) of not bursting a bubble.

## The Monetary Policy Transmission Mechanism

We know from Chapter 17 that a central bank's ability to influence the economy comes from its ability to determine the size of its balance sheet and that they use this power to control the interest rate that banks charge each other for overnight loans. Because inflation changes only slowly, policymakers can use this tool to influence the short-run *real* interest rate. In Chapter 18, we saw that the components of aggregate expenditure are sensitive to the real interest rate, so by changing the real interest rate,

[5] The case for intervening in a bubble is summarized in Stephen G. Cecchetti, Hans Genberg, and Sushil Wadhwani, "Asset Prices in a Flexible Inflation Targeting Framework," in William C. Hunter, George G. Kaufman, and Michael Pomerleano, eds., *Asset Price Bubbles: Implications for Monetary, Regulatory, and International Policies* (Cambridge, MA: MIT Press, 2002), pp. 427–444. For the case against, see Ben Bernanke and Mark Gertler, "Should Central Banks Respond to Movements in Asset Prices?" *American Economic Review*, May 2001, pp. 253–257.

policymakers can influence real economic activity. Yet the Japanese experience in the 1990s (described in Applying the Concept: What Happened in Japan on page 540) suggests that this standard policy tool doesn't always work. To see why, we need to look at all the ways monetary policy actions can affect economic activity. That means recalling the role of financial intermediaries in solving the information problems that keep lenders and savers apart.

Any time the central bank alters the size of its balance sheet, the effects ripple through the economy, changing nearly everyone's behaviour. Households adjust their spending on houses and cars. Companies rethink their decisions about how much and how fast to grow. Exchange rates change, bond and stock prices move, and banks adjust their balance sheets. In fact, we would be challenged to find a financial or economic decision that is unaffected. To fully appreciate how monetary policy works, then, we need to examine the various ways in which changes in the policy-controlled interest rate influence the quantity of aggregate output demanded in the economy as a whole. These are referred to collectively as the channels of the monetary policy transmission mechanism. We will begin with the traditional interest rate and exchange-rate channels. Next we will study the role of banks and finally the importance of stock price movements.

## The Traditional Channels: Interest Rates and Exchange Rates

Central banks, such as the Bank of Canada, Federal Reserve, and the Bank of Japan, target a very short-term (usually overnight) interest rate. In the Bank of Canada's case, for example, a policy change is a change in the target for the overnight rate. And as we saw in Chapter 18, a change in the monetary policymakers' target interest rate leads to a change in the real interest rate, which has a direct effect on total spending. The lower the real interest rate, the higher investment, consumption, and net exports will be.

Let's review this process. As the real interest rate falls, financing becomes less expensive, so firms become more likely to undertake investment projects and families more likely to purchase new cars. Changes in the real interest rate also affect the exchange rate. When the real interest rate falls, investor demand for Canadian assets falls with it, lowering the demand for and increasing the supply of dollars, reducing their value. That is, an easing of monetary policy—by which we mean a decrease in the overnight nominal interest rate, which lowers the real interest rate—leads to a depreciation of the dollar. A less valuable dollar, in turn, drives up the cost of imported goods and services, reducing imports from abroad. At the same time, however, the lower value of the dollar makes Canadian goods and services cheaper to foreigners, so they will buy more of them. Together, lower imports and higher exports mean higher net exports, or an increase in total spending.

While these traditional channels of monetary policy transmission make sense theoretically, they present a practical problem. Though changes in monetary policy do influence firms' decisions to purchase new equipment and build new buildings, empirically the interest rate channel appears to be a weak one. That is, data suggest that the investment component of total spending isn't very sensitive to interest rates, which should not be a surprise to us. At the end of our discussion of financial intermediation in Chapter 11, we saw that information problems often make external financing too difficult and costly for firms to undertake, either directly in the financial markets or indirectly through institutions. As a result, the vast majority of investments are financed by businesses themselves, through their own funds. While a

## TOOLS OF THE TRADE
Correlation Does Not Imply Causality

Suppose we notice that the higher the crime rate in a neighbourhood, the more often police are present. Should we infer that the police are causing crime? Surely not. Nor should we conclude from the fact that hospitals are filled with doctors that doctors make people ill. A fundamental principal of sound logical reasoning is that correlation does not imply causality. The fact that two events happened together does not indicate a causal link.

In the physical sciences, where researchers can conduct controlled experiments, establishing a causal link is not a serious challenge. We know from scientific trials that antibiotic drugs really do eliminate infections. It's not just chance that the people who take them feel better. But in economics, establishing a causal relationship is much more difficult. How can we be sure that monetary policy affects real economic activity? Our theories tell us that when policymakers raise the nominal interest rate, the real interest rate goes up, depressing aggregate expenditure and lowering real economic activity. But do we have any hard evidence of this relationship?

The answer is that we do have some evidence that higher interest rates are associated with lower levels of real growth. Look back at Figure 19.7 on page 436, and you'll see the pattern: when interest rates rise, growth falls. But does that mean that increases in the interest rate cause recessions? What if, simultaneously, an increase in oil prices depresses real growth, causing policymakers to raise the interest rate in order to head off rising inflation? That is, what if some third factor drives up the interest rate, forcing growth down at the same time? In that case, the interest rate becomes another implication of the fundamental cause of recession, an increase in oil prices.

How can we eliminate this problem and determine the extent to which monetary policy actually causes economic fluctuations? The answer is that we need to look for clear evidence that particular monetary policy actions are unrelated to this sort of third factor. Some years ago, Christina Romer and David Romer of the University of California at Berkeley read through the records of the Federal Reserve's interest rate decisions since 1946. They identified a series of dates on which FOMC members stated unambiguously that they were raising interest rates to combat inflation. Each of these episodes was followed by a recession. Romer and Romer argued that, because the intention in each of these instances was to fight inflation, the FOMC's actions were not the result of the level of GDP at the time. Instead, it was monetary policy actions that were the fundamental cause.* With hard work and ingenuity, economists are ultimately able to distinguish causality from correlation.

---

* See Christina D. Romer and David H. Romer, "Does Monetary Policy Matter? A New Test in the Spirit of Friedman and Schwartz," in O.J. Blanchard and S. Fischer, eds., *NBER Macroeconomic Annual* (Cambridge, MA: MIT Press, 1989), pp. 121–170.

---

change in the interest rate does change the cost of external financing, it doesn't have much of an effect on investment decisions.

The impact of short-term interest rates on household decisions is also rather modest. The problem is that people's decisions to purchase cars or houses depend on longer-term interest rates rather than the policymakers' short-run target rate. So household consumption decisions will change only to the extent that changing the target interest rate affects long-term interest rates. And the overall effect isn't that large.

As for the effect of monetary policy on the exchange rate, once again, theory and practice differ. In the real world, the policy-controlled interest rate is just one of many factors that shift the demand and supply for the dollar on foreign exchange markets. The rather long list, described in Chapter 10, includes a change in the riskiness of domestic investment relative to foreign investment; a change in the preference of Canadian consumers for foreign-produced goods and services; and a change in foreigners' income and wealth. The influence of these other factors renders the impact of monetary policy on the exchange rate and net exports unpredictable.

Thus, after careful analysis, we must conclude that the traditional channels of monetary policy transmission aren't very powerful. Yet evidence shows that monetary policy *is* effective. When policy-controlled interest rates go up, the quantity of aggregate output demanded does go down. The dynamic aggregate demand curve slopes down. Something else must be amplifying the impact of monetary policy changes on real economic activity. Otherwise, no one would care about the central bank's periodic policy statements. To figure out what that link might be, we turn now to a discussion of two alternative transmission channels: the stock and real estate markets, and the behaviour of banks.

## Bank-Lending and Balance-Sheet Channels

Four times a year the Bank of Canada conducts an opinion survey on bank-lending practices. Addressed to the senior loan officers who oversee lending policies at the largest banks in the country, the survey contains questions about both the demand for and the supply of loans. On the demand side, the questions have to do with the quantity and quality of loan applications. On the supply side, they have to do with the relative difficulty of getting a loan, as well as the rates borrowers must pay. This survey provides important information to monetary policymakers. Without it, they would not be able to tell whether a change in the quantity of new loans granted resulted from a shift in supply or a shift in demand. Was a drop in the quantity of new loans the result of fewer applications or a tightening of credit standards? Did interest rate spreads climb because the quality of borrowers declined or because banks became more stingy? Policymakers at the Bank of Canada collect this data because if banks stop making loans, businesses can't borrow to finance their investment projects, and economic growth slows.

The fact is that banks are essential to the operation of a modern industrial economy. They direct resources from savers to investors and solve problems caused by information asymmetries. Financial intermediaries specialize in screening borrowers to ensure they are creditworthy and in monitoring loan recipients to guarantee that they use borrowed funds as they said they would. But banks are not only the hub of the financial system; they are also the conduit through which monetary policy is transmitted to the economy. When policymakers change the size of the central bank's balance sheet, their action has an immediate impact on commercial bank balance sheets because it affects the level of reserves they hold. To understand monetary policy changes completely, then, we need to look carefully at how they affect the banking system. That means we need to examine the impact of policy changes on banks and bank lending.

**Banks and Bank Lending** For the vast majority of individuals and firms, the cost of issuing either stocks or bonds is prohibitive. These borrowers do not have access to direct capital market financing; instead, they must go to banks, which step in to reduce the information costs small borrowers face. A small business that is denied a bank loan has nowhere else to turn, so the project it wishes to undertake goes unfunded. When banks stop lending, a large class of borrowers simply can't obtain financing. Thus, bank lending is an important channel through which monetary policy affects the economy.[6] By altering the supply of funds to the banking system, policymakers can affect banks' ability and willingness to lend. This policy mechanism is referred to as the **bank-lending channel** of monetary policy transmission.

---

[6] Studies of how and why monetary policy is transmitted through bank lending and balance sheets include Ben Bernanke and Mark Gertler, "Inside the Black Box: The Credit Channel of Monetary Policy Transmission," *Journal of Economic Perspectives* 9 (Fall 1995), pp. 27–45.

## YOUR FINANCIAL WORLD
### Don't Count on Inflation to Bail You Out

When policymakers lower interest rates, their aim is to encourage people to borrow. Central bankers know that low-interest mortgages make it possible for people to buy homes they otherwise couldn't afford. And low-interest car loans allow them to buy a new car earlier than they would otherwise. In lowering interest rates, the Bank of Canada is counting on a surge in borrowing to drive output higher. But while the increase in debt may help the economy as a whole, it can be dangerous for some individuals. They may borrow too much and end up with more debt than they can manage.

The problem with debt is that it must be repaid. Making sure you can repay your debts means carefully calculating what you can afford—not only now but also over the entire term of the loan. To avoid overextending yourself, don't borrow on the assumption that your income is going to rise rapidly. While you will almost surely receive annual increases in your real wage (adjusted for inflation), they are likely to be fairly modest. In fact, for the economy as a whole, pay raises tend to match the rate of productivity growth, which is usually between 2 and 3 percent. So don't be tempted into thinking that, though your budget may be tight when you take out a loan, future salary raises will remedy the problem.

The strategy of counting on salary increases to help eliminate debt amounts to counting on inflation to bail you out. It's true that inflation can be helpful to people who are in debt because it reduces the burden of repayment. But if policymakers at the Bank are doing their job, which is to keep inflation low, hoping inflation will help you pay off your loans is a strategy that is likely to backfire.

To see how the banking-lending channel works, think about the immediate consequences of an open market purchase (see Figure 17.2 on page 377). Recall that an open market operation involves an exchange of securities for reserves between the banking system and the central bank. When the central bank purchases securities from commercial banks, it pays for them with reserves. So after an open market purchase, banks have fewer interest-bearing securities and more noninterest-bearing reserves. The banks then make new loans and these new loans work their way through the banking system through the process of multiple deposit creation, increasing the supply of loans throughout the economy. (Take a look back at the section on the deposit expansion multiplier in Chapter 20, page 461.) In short, an open market purchase has a direct impact on the supply of loans, increasing their availability to those who depend on banks for financing.

Monetary policymakers are not the only people who can influence bank-lending practices; financial regulators can, too. Changes in financial regulations, such as an increase or decrease in the amount of capital banks are required to hold when they make certain types of loans, will have an impact on the amount of bank lending as well. In the early 1990s, the U.S. economy failed to make a strong recovery from the recession after the first Gulf War. Careful examination of U.S. banking practice suggests that the disappointing economic performance was a direct consequence of a slowdown in bank lending. At the time, bank balance sheets were very weak, having been eroded by large loan losses during the banking crises of the 1980s. When an increase in capital requirements was added to the banks' already heavy burden, the result was a reduction in lending.

### Firms' Balance Sheets and Household Net Worth
Besides its influence on the willingness of banks to lend, monetary policy has an important effect on the creditworthiness of borrowers—or at least on their perceived creditworthiness. This balance-sheet channel of monetary policy transmission works because monetary

policy has a direct influence on the net worth of potential borrowers. Specifically, an easing of monetary policy improves firms' and households' balance sheets, increasing their net worth. In turn, these increases in net worth reduce the problems of moral hazard and adverse selection, lowering the information costs of lending and allowing borrowers to obtain financing more easily. Recall that the higher the net worth of a borrower, the more likely that the lender will be repaid.

There are two ways in which expansionary monetary policy can improve borrowers' net worth. First, as we have already discussed, an expansionary policy drives up asset prices, increasing the value of firms and the wealth of households. Higher equity and property prices mean higher net worth, which implies lower information costs and greater ease in obtaining financing. The increase in home equity loans that follows a real estate boom is an example of this process. With an increase in household wealth, banks are willing to step up their lending.

The second way that a monetary policy expansion can improve borrowers' net worth has to do with the drop in interest rates. Most borrowers already have loans that they are in the process of repaying; lower interest rates reduce the burden of repayment. For a firm, the drop in the cost of financing increases the difference between revenues and expenses, raising profits and increasing the firm's value. Something similar happens for individuals. When interest rates fall, people who hold variable-rate loans enjoy lower interest payments. This drop in the cost of their financing reduces the information problems that plague the lending relationship. Why? To evaluate a borrower's creditworthiness, banks look at the percentage of a person's income that is devoted to loan payments. At lower interest rates, that percentage will be lower, so individuals will qualify for larger loans. The conclusion is that *as interest rates fall, the supply of loans increases*.

It is worth pausing to emphasize that information is the driving force in the bank-lending and balance-sheet channels of monetary policy transmission. Information services are central to banks' role in the financial system because they help to address the problems of adverse selection and moral hazard. The primacy of information in banking has some important implications for our understanding of the link between the financial system and the real economy. It means that financial instability, which is characterized by large and unpredictable moves in asset prices, accompanied by widespread bankruptcy, will reduce lenders' willingness to supply financing. It also means that accounting scandals, such as the ones that plagued companies in 2001 and 2002, will have an effect on the economy as a whole. When bankers are worried about the accuracy of accounting information, they will be less willing to make loans to anyone. Inferior information leads to an increase in adverse selection, reducing bank lending, lowering investment, and ultimately depressing the quantity of aggregate output demanded.

The channels of monetary policy transmission depend on the structure of the financial system. The importance of the bank lending channel depends on the banks being important financial intermediaries. In the early years of the 21st century, the banks' share of lending fell as nonbank lenders and asset-backed securities took market share. This process paused in 2008–9, but the innovations in communications systems that drove those changes will continue and may reduce the importance of the bank-lending channel over time. That said, information problems and the balance-sheet effects they create seem likely to persist for some time. While technology has made the processing of increasing amounts of information easier and cheaper, it seems unlikely to solve the problems of adverse selection and moral hazard, which make net worth such an important determinant of a borrower's creditworthiness.

## Asset-Price Channels: Wealth and Investment

When the interest rate moves, so do stock prices. Specifically, a fall in the interest rate tends to push stock prices up. This relationship between the interest rate and the stock market is referred to as the **asset-price channel** of monetary policy transmission. To understand it, we must first figure out why a change in the interest rate might cause a movement in stock prices. Then we must explain how a change in stock prices can influence quality of aggregate output demanded.

To see how the interest rate influences stock prices, recall that the fundamental value of a stock is the present value of the stream of its future dividends. The lower the interest rate, the higher the present value and, therefore, the higher the stock price will be. Added to this relationship is the fact that an easing of monetary policy might well improve consumer and business confidence in the prospects for future growth. More growth means more revenue and higher profits, and that, too, will drive up stock prices. In fact, because current stock prices are based largely on expectations of future growth and future interest rates, they tend to move in anticipation of a cut in interest rates.

Monetary policy affects real estate markets in the same way that it influences stock markets. The mechanism is straightforward. When policymakers reduce their interest rate target, it drives the mortgage rate down. Lower mortgage rates mean higher demand for residential housing, driving up the prices of existing homes.

In short, when the central bank reduces its target interest rate, the stock and real estate markets are likely to boom. Then what? Stock and property prices affect both individual consumption and business investment. For individuals, a rise in stock and real estate prices means an increase in wealth. The richer people become, the more they will consume. If stock values go high enough, shareholders can actually buy the luxury cars they have been wanting, or take the fancy vacations they've been dreaming of, or maybe both. The conclusion is that higher asset prices mean increased wealth and raised consumption.

Just as consumption is affected by stock price movements, so is investment. As stock prices rise, firms find it easier to raise funds by issuing new shares. That is, they gain access to financing in the primary capital market. To see why, think of a simple example in which the price of a company's stock suddenly increases. In the meantime, nothing has happened to the cost of a new investment and hence to its internal rate of return. But at the higher stock price, financing is now cheaper. This story should sound familiar. Recall the way in which the traditional *interest rate channel* influences investment: a lower real interest rate means a lower cost of financing, which raises the profitability of investment projects. As a result, borderline investment projects suddenly become profitable when real interest rates fall. The same thing happens when stock prices rise. As financing becomes less expensive, more investments become profitable. In short, when asset markets boom, so does business investment in new equipment and buildings.[7]

Overall, changes in monetary policy influence aggregate expenditure in the economy through a variety of channels that are summarized in Table 21.1. Each of the

---

[7] This line of reasoning, known as Tobin's q-theory, was originally developed by the Nobel Prize–winning economist James Tobin. Tobin pointed out that the question of whether or not a firm invests should depend on the ratio of the market value of its shares to the replacement cost of its plant and equipment, which he called $q$. When $q$ is greater than one—that is, when a firm's stock market value exceeds its cost of rebuilding—investment in new plant and equipment is cheap relative to the value placed on it in the financial markets. When $q$ is less than one, embarking on new investments isn't worthwhile.

**Table 21.1**    The Monetary Policy Transmission Mechanism

| Channel | Mechanism |
| --- | --- |
| Interest rates (traditional channel) | Lower interest rates reduce the cost of investment, making more projects profitable. |
| Exchange rates (traditional channel) | Lower interest rates reduce the attractiveness of domestic investment, depressing the value of the currency and increasing net exports. |
| Bank lending | An easing of monetary policy raises the level of bank reserves and bank deposits, increasing the supply of funds. |
| Firms' balance sheets | Lower interest rates raise firms' profits, increasing their net worth and reducing the problems of adverse selection and moral hazard. |
| Household net worth | Lower interest rates raise individuals' net worth, improving their credit worthiness and allowing them to increase their borrowing. |
| Asset prices | Higher stock prices and real estate values fuel an increase in both business investment and household consumption. |

transmission mechanisms works slightly differently, but they all lead us to the same conclusion: When interest rates rise, the quantity of aggregate output demanded falls so the dynamic aggregate demand curve slopes down.

## Estimating Potential GDP

Having looked at the myriad of ways in which a central bank can influence economic activity, we could easily come away from this discussion with the impression that monetary policy can be distilled to a hard and fast science—that a few equations, coupled with some statistical analysis, will do. Unfortunately, that isn't true. To do their job well, central bankers need a detailed understanding of how both the financial system and the real economy will react to their policy changes. That would be tough enough in a world that is standing still, but the constant change that is a feature of today's economy makes the job all the more difficult. In fact, policymakers face a series of daunting challenges. In this section, we look at just one of those challenges—estimating potential GDP.

Modern monetary policymakers can't do their job without estimates of both the level and growth rate of potential output. The reason is that interest rate adjustments depend on the difference between current and potential output, referred to in earlier chapters as the output gap. Recall from Chapter 19 that inflation goes up or down depending on whether the output gap is positive (real output greater than potential) or negative (real output less than potential). Thus, stabilizing inflation means adjusting monetary policy to the output gap by raising interest rates when the gap is positive and lowering them when the gap is negative. When we say that central bankers strive to stabilize growth at a high level, what we mean is that they try to keep the economy growing at the same rate as potential output. The growth rate of potential output is the economy's sustainable growth rate. This logic provides the foundation for the Taylor rule and the monetary policy reaction curve (described in Chapter 19).

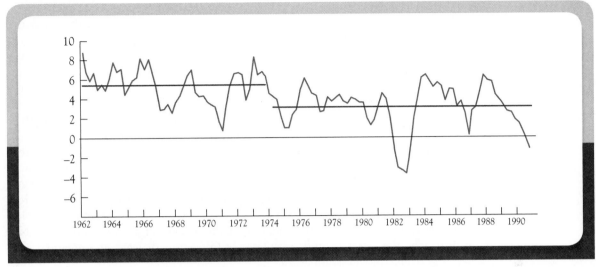

Figure 21.7    GDP Growth

SOURCE: *Table 380-0002, v1992067, GDP Growth v19920637, access date, June 2009.*

The policymaker's challenge is to distinguish movements in measured GDP that represent a change in the output gap from movements that represent a change in potential output. To understand why this is such an important task, consider an unexpected increase in GDP. If potential output has not changed, the correct response to the rise in real output is to tighten policy, raising interest rates in order to reduce the quantity of aggregate output demanded and keep inflation from rising. But if the rise in GDP is permanent and sustainable, so that it represents an increase in potential output, the appropriate response is to allow current output to climb to a new long-run level while stabilizing inflation.

The problem is, telling the difference between temporary and permanent changes in real growth is extremely difficult. Consider the experience of the 1970s. Figure 21.7 shows the average growth rate of Canadian GDP in the 1970s and 1980s. With hindsight we can see that the growth rate of potential output declined—perhaps by as much as 1 percent—but at the time it seemed that the economy was underperforming and that there was a recessionary output gap.

In the terminology of the previous chapters, policymakers may not be able to tell the difference between a leftward shift in the dynamic aggregate demand curve and a leftward shift in the short- and long-run aggregate supply curves. These two shifts require very different policy responses. A decrease in aggregate expenditure that shifts the dynamic aggregate demand curve, but is not accompanied by a change in potential output, creates a recessionary output gap and pushes down the long-run real interest rate. The proper response is a shift in the monetary policy reaction function to the right, decreasing the real interest rate at all levels of inflation. A shift in the short- and long-run aggregate supply curves, on the other hand, represents a decrease in potential output, which creates an expansionary (positive) output gap at the same time that it raises the long-run real interest rate. In this case, the correct response is to raise the real interest rate at all levels of inflation, shifting the monetary policy reaction curve to the left. The question is, when output falls unexpectedly, should policymakers raise or lower the target interest rate? One explanation for the inflation of the late 1970s is that policymakers responded to the apparent recessionary gap with unnecessarily expansionary monetary policy.

Data from U.S. private-sector GDP forecasts in the 1990s give further evidence of how hard it is to differentiate (1) changes in aggregate expenditure that shift the dynamic aggregate demand curve on the one hand, from (2) changes in potential output that shift the short- and long-run aggregate supply curves. Figure 21.8 plots the level of GDP (on a logarithmic scale) against a series of *consensus forecasts*—the median forecasts of a broad survey of professional economists who specialize in predicting GDP growth.[8] For each quarter, the chart shows the forecasted path of GDP over the next two years. In the first quarter of 1996, for example, the figure shows the actual data point plus the forecast for the next eight quarters. Note that actual GDP followed a steeper path than forecasted GDP throughout the period, meaning that forecasters consistently underestimated GDP growth. This systematic underestimation of the growth rate is a clear sign that forecasters were slow to recognize that part of the acceleration in productivity was permanent and so a portion of the unexpected increase in actual output was a result of a shift in potential. Not surprisingly, the series of underestimates of GDP growth were accompanied by a series of overestimates of inflation.

The message is clear. During periods when the growth rate of potential GDP is changing, central bankers face challenges that are even more daunting than usual. (see Applying the Concept: The Challenge of Estimating Potential Output Growth on page 500). Failing to react to a decline in potential output growth, as policymakers did in the 1970s, can result in an extended episode of undesirably high inflation, which can be costly to eliminate. But tightening policy in the face of an increase in potential growth can prevent growth from occurring. The challenge is to figure out, as quickly and accurately as possible, the true growth rate of potential GDP.

Figure 21.8    Forecasted versus Actual GDP, 1995–2001

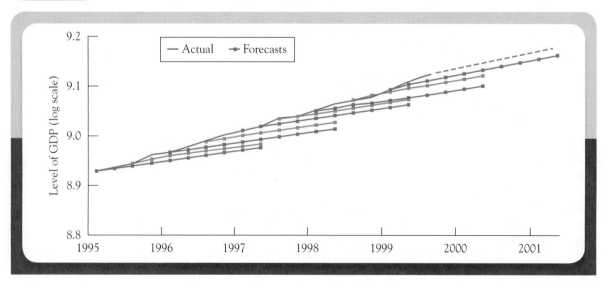

SOURCE: *Statistics Canada CANSIM database, http://cansim2.statcan.ca, Table 380-0002, v1992067, GDP Growth v1992063, accessed June 2009.*

[8] Such data aren't available for Canada, but the Bank of Canada faced a similar problem.

# YOUR FINANCIAL WORLD
## Predicting Inflation

When you sign a car loan or a mortgage, and when you agree to a long-term salary or wage contract you are implicitly betting on the rate of inflation. If the rate of inflation is higher than you expect then you will be paying a lower real rate of interest than you expected; but it would also mean that you are getting a lower real wage than you expected. So, the predictability of the inflation rate matters, but is there a good way to predict the inflation rate?

In Canada, the answer to that question is also an answer to How credible is the Bank of Canada's inflation target? If the Bank is very credible then the best forecast of the inflation rate at the two-year horizon is 2 percent. Nearer term, of course, the inflation rate is likely to deviate from 2 percent. Two ways to begin to answer the question are to look at the forecasts of professionals and to look at the market "bet" on inflation by looking at the forecast implied by the difference between the real return bond and a nominal bond.

Both the Conference Board of Canada (an economic think tank and consulting agency) and Consensus Economics (an organization that produces forecasts based on surveying professional economists) produce forecasts of inflation. The Bank of Canada also surveys firms as to their expectations of CPI inflation. While all these measures are based on surveys, the rate implied by the spread between the real return bond and the nominal bond is market based. The Bank of Canada defines the rate of inflation that would make someone indifferent between holding a real return bond and the equivalent maturity nominal bond the "Break Even Inflation Rate" (BEIR). Since both bonds are traded in the marketplace, someone is actually placing bets on the rate of inflation with these instruments. But research by the Bank of Canada (2004) showed that the BEIR is not a better predictor on average of future inflation, and is more volatile than survey expectations.*

\* *Data from the surveys and the BEIR are available on the Bank of Canada Web site: http://www.bankofcanada.ca/en/rates/indinf.html*

SOURCE: *"Real Return Bonds: Monetary Policy Credibility and Short-Term Inflation Forecasting"* Christopher Reid, Frederic Dion, and Ian Christensen, *Bank of Canada Review, Autumn 2004.*

**APPLYING THE CONCEPT**
THE CHALLENGE OF ESTIMATING
POTENTIAL OUTPUT GROWTH

The growth rate of potential output is a key ingredient in calculating the output gap, which as we have seen, is a key ingredient in interest rate settings. The Bank of Canada reports its projected growth rate for potential output every six months in the *Monetary Policy Report*, and the projected values for the last few years are shown in Table 21.2. Reading across a row tells you the growth rate projected on a given date. Reading down a column shows how the growth predicted for a given year changed over time. You can see that during "normal" times the projected growth rate varied slightly. In April 2006, the Bank was projecting a growth rate of 3 percent in 2007 and 2008, but six months later it revised that downward slightly. The big changes came in the projected growth rates for 2009 and later. In late 2006 the estimate for 2009 was 2.8 percent, and that estimate

moved slightly over the next 18 months. But in October 2008 the growth rate was reduced and then in early 2009 it was reduced even further.

In understanding these revisions to the potential growth rate it is critical to remember that these are not projections or forecasts of the GDP growth rate. They are projections of the growth rate of the amount the economy could produce if there were sufficient demand. (The difference between potential output and demand is the output gap).

Why did the growth rate of potential output decline in 2009? Remember that potential output level is determined by variables such as the capital stock and labour force productivity. When the economy undergoes significant structural change it takes time for factors of production to change sectors, reducing labour productivity. The capital stock is also affected as parts of the existing stock become obsolete, and if investment declines then the capital stock is less than would have been anticipated. The Bank of Canada argued that all these factors were responsible for the revisions to potential output in April 2009.

**Table 21.2**

|        | 2006 | 2007 | 2008 | 2009 | 2010 | 2011 |
|--------|------|------|------|------|------|------|
| Apr-06 | 2.9  | 3    | 3    |      |      |      |
| Oct-06 |      | 2.8  | 2.8  | 2.8  |      |      |
| Apr-07 |      | 2.8  | 2.8  | 2.7  |      |      |
| Oct-07 |      | 2.8  | 2.8  | 2.6  |      |      |
| Apr-08 |      |      | 2.8  | 2.7  | 2.6  |      |
| Oct-08 |      |      |      | 2.4  | 2.5  | 2.5  |
| Apr-09 |      |      |      | 1.2  | 1.5  | 1.9  |
| Oct-09 |      |      |      | 1.2  | 1.5  | 1.9  |

SOURCE: *Monetary Policy Report*, Bank of Canada, various issues. At: *http://www.bankofcanada.ca/en/mpr/mpr_previous.html*.

# Terms

# Chapter Summary

1. Monetary authorities need to credibly commit to a nominal anchor.
   a. Possible nominal anchors include a money supply growth rule, an inflation target, a fixed exchange rate or a price-level target.
   b. The Bank of Canada and the Federal Reserve adopted money growth targets in the 1970s but velocity became unstable and they abandoned the money growth targets.
   c. The Bank of Canada adopted inflation targets in 1991 and has been reasonably successful in keeping inflation within the target range since then.
   d. Central banks are analyzing the properties of alternative targets such as price-level targets.
2. Monetary policy influences the economy through several channels.
   a. The traditional channels of monetary policy transmission are interest rates and exchange rates.
      i. Interest rates influence consumption and investment.
      ii. Exchange rates affect net exports.
   b. Monetary policy affects the supply of bank loans, changing the availability of bank financing to firms and individuals.
   c. Monetary policy can change firms' and households' net worth, affecting their creditworthiness as borrowers.
   d. The asset-price channel of monetary policy transmission works through stock and real estate prices.
      i. Stock and property prices influence household wealth and consumption.
      ii. Stock prices also affect businesses' ability to raise funds and make investments.
3. Monetary policymakers face significant operational challenges. For example, they need to have accurate estimates of potential GDP, even when its growth trend is shifting.

# Conceptual Problems

1. Explain in detail the traditional view of how monetary policy influences the economy.
2. From the senior loan officers' survey, the Bank of Canada governing council members learn that banks are tightening their lending standards. Why should policymakers care about this change? What action are they likely to take, and why?
3. Explain why the traditional interest rate channel of monetary policy transmission from monetary policy actions to changes in investment and consumption decisions may be relatively weak.
4. The Governor of the Bank of Canada gives a speech and says that interest rates are unlikely to rise for the next few years. Will this statement have any impact on the economy? Which channels of monetary policy transmission will be affected by the announcement? Will the speech pose any difficulties when the Bank finally raises the interest rate?
5. The government decides to place limits on the interest rates banks can pay their depositors. Seeing that alternative investments pay higher interest rates, depositors withdraw their funds from banks and place them in bonds. Will their action have an impact on the economy? If so, how?
6. New developments in information technology have simplified the assessment of individual borrowers' creditworthiness. What are the likely consequences for the structure of the financial system? For monetary policy?

www.mcgrawhill.ca/olc/cecchetti

7.* Describe the theory of the exchange-rate channel of the monetary transmission mechanism. How, through the exchange rate, does an interest rate increase influence output? Why is this link difficult to find in practice?

8. Suppose the federal government had a significant debt, and some Canadians were advocating that the Bank of Canada raise the inflation rate to reduce the burden of that debt. Under what circumstances would the debt burden be reduced? How would you advise the Bank of Canada to respond to this request?

9. Discuss the pros and cons of lowering the inflation target from 2 percent to 1 percent.

10. Discuss the credibility problem that would be faced by a central banker with a price level target if the economy had just experienced an unexpected inflation, pushing the price level above the target.

## Analytical Problems

11. For each of the following, explain whether the response is theoretically consistent with a tightening of monetary policy and identify which of the traditional channels of monetary policy is at work:
   a. Firms become more likely to undertake investment projects.
   b. Households become less likely to purchase refrigerators and washing machines.
   c. Net exports fall.

12. Suppose in Country A, changes in short-term interest rates translate quickly into changes in long-term interest rates, while in Country B long-term interest rates do not respond much to changes in short-term rates. In which country would you expect the interest rate channel of monetary policy to be stronger? Explain your answer.

13. Consider a situation in which central bank officials repeatedly express concern that output exceeds potential output so that the economy is overheating. Although they haven't implemented any policy moves as yet, the data show that consumption of luxury goods has begun to slow. Explain how this behaviour could reflect the asset-price channel of monetary policy at work.

14. Do you think the balance-sheet channel of monetary policy would be stronger or weaker if
   a. Firms' balance sheets in general are very healthy.
   b. Firms have a lot of existing variable-rate debt.

15. Suppose there is an unexpected slowdown in the rate of productivity growth in the economy so that forecasters consistently overestimate the growth rate of GDP. If the central bank bases its policy decisions on the consensus forecast, what would be the likely consequences for inflation assuming it maintains its existing inflation target?

16. Compare the impact of a given change in monetary policy in two economies that are similar in every way except that, in Economy A, the financial system is very evolved with many alternatives to bank financing available, while in Economy B, bank loans account for almost all of the financing in the economy.

* Indicates more difficult problems.

## CHAPTER 22

# Exchange Rate Policy and the Central Bank

On September 22, 2000, the Bank of Canada began buying euros for the first time since that currency came into existence 21 months earlier. Meanwhile, central bank officials in Frankfurt, London, Tokyo, and New York did the same. Between them, they bought between €4 and €6 billion. The Fed alone bought €1.5 billion for $1.34 billion. The whole operation took about two hours; when it was over, the central banks announced what they had done. As the ECB wrote in its press release, they did it because of "shared concern about the potential implications of recent movements in the euro exchange rate for the world economy." Since its inception on January 1, 1999, the euro had fallen steadily from US$1.18 to US$0.85, a decline of more than 25 percent. Though its low value had made exports cheap, bolstering the foreign sales of European-made products, it had also forced up the prices of imports. ECB officials, charged with maintaining price stability, found the high price of imports particularly troubling since they really did not want to raise interest rates just to bolster the value of their currency (which is what they would have had to do). Experts debated whether the euro should be worth US$1.10 or US$1, but all agreed that US$0.85 was too low.

The coordinated intervention in the foreign exchange market made headlines around the world. The euro did appreciate briefly, rising to US$0.89 on the day of the intervention, but by mid-October, it had returned to US$0.85. The action may have been dramatic, but it wasn't effective. To understand why the intervention didn't work, and why the Bank of Canada almost never engages in foreign currency transactions, we need to examine the mechanics of how a central bank manages its country's exchange rate.

Argentina provides another example of how external and domestic factors interact in the making of monetary policy. Over the years, Argentina has suffered from severe inflation. During the 1970s, inflation averaged about 100 percent, meaning that prices doubled every year, while the economy grew about 3 percent a year. By 1989, inflation had climbed to more than 2,000 percent per year and the price level was 60 *billion* times what it had been 20 years before. Needless to say, growth fell. In 1990, real GDP was below its 1973 level and Argentina's economy was at a standstill.

The cause of such high inflation is often a combination of failed fiscal policy and failed monetary policy. Politicians want to spend too much, so they lean on central bankers to print more money. To discipline policymakers, in 1991 Argentineans implemented a mechanism called a *currency board*, which had two important attributes. First, Argentina's central bank, the Banco Central de la Republica Argentina, guaranteed that it would exchange Argentinean pesos for U.S. dollars on a one-for-one basis; it fixed its exchange rate. Second, the central bank was required to hold dollar assets equal to its domestic currency liabilities, again at a one-to-one exchange rate. For every peso note that was issued and every peso in commercial bank reserves that it created, the Central Bank of Argentina had to hold one U.S. dollar.

The results were almost miraculous. Inflation fell immediately; after a few years, it had completely disappeared. But as we will see later, the victory didn't last. By early January 2002, the currency board had collapsed, GDP had fallen by a quarter, and inflation had risen to over 30 percent.

The examples of the ECB and Argentina suggest a connection between domestic monetary policy and exchange rate policy. To avoid raising domestic interest rates, the ECB organized a coordinated intervention to shore up the value of the euro. To control the inflationary impulses of fiscal and monetary authorities, Argentina fixed its exchange rate to the dollar.

If exchange rate policy is inseparable from interest rate policy, we have left something essential out of our analysis by ignoring cross-border transactions. To rectify the omission, we turn now to a discussion of exchange rate regimes. Why is a country's exchange rate linked to its domestic monetary policy? Are there circumstances when exchange rate stabilization becomes the overriding objective of central bankers? If so, should they try to fix the rate at which their currency can be exchanged for some other currency? Should a country consider giving up its currency entirely? We look at some examples of countries that have done so and conclude by examining the lessons of these examples for Canada.

## Linking Exchange Rate Policy with Domestic Monetary Policy

Exchange rate policy is integral to any monetary policy regime. The city of Vancouver, for instance, has a fixed exchange rate with the rest of Canada—both use the Canadian dollar—so it has no independent monetary policy. Because Vancouver's monetary policy is made by the Bank of Canada, interest rates in Vancouver are the same as interest rates everywhere else in Canada. Any discrepancy between the price of a bond in Vancouver and the price of the same bond in Toronto is wiped out instantly by arbitrage, as investors buy the bond where it is cheap and sell it where it is expensive (all this is done electronically). What is true for Vancouver is true for any country: *When capital flows freely across a country's borders, a fixed exchange rate means giving up domestic monetary policy.*

There are two ways to see the connection between exchange rates and monetary policy. The first comes from thinking about the market for goods and *purchasing power parity;* the second builds on the Vancouver/Toronto bond market arbitrage example. Purchasing power parity tells us about the long-run tendencies of exchange rates, while capital market arbitrage shows us how short-run movements in exchange rates are tied to the supply and demand in the currency markets. Let's look at each of these approaches in more detail.

### Inflation and the Long-Run Implications of Purchasing Power Parity

In Chapter 10, we studied the long-run determinants of exchange rates starting with the *law of one price*. Ignoring transportation costs, the law of one price says that identical goods should sell for the same price regardless of where they are sold. That is, the same television set should sell for the same price in Toronto and Halifax. The concept of purchasing power parity extends the logic of the law of one price to a basket of goods and services. As long as goods can move freely across international boundaries, one unit of domestic currency should buy the same basket of goods anywhere in the world.

This apparently simple idea has important implications. It means that when prices change in one country but not in another, the exchange rate will adjust to reflect the change. If U.S. inflation is higher than Canadian inflation, for instance, the U.S. dollar should depreciate relative to the Canadian dollar. If everything in the United States costs more U.S. dollars, Canadian dollars should cost more U.S. dollars, too. Figure 10.2 on page 211 confirmed that this principle works well over long periods. *In the long run, changes in the exchange rate are tied to differences in inflation.*

To understand how this works, recall that purchasing power parity means that

$$\text{US\$ per C\$} = \frac{\text{US\$ price of basket of goods in the United States}}{\text{C\$ price of basket of goods in Canada}} \quad (1)$$

Taking the percentage change of both sides of this expression, we get[1]

| Percentage change in number of US\$ per C\$ | = | Percentage change in US\$ price of basket of goods in the United States | − | Percentage change in C\$ price of basket of goods in Canada | (2) |

Since the percentage change in the basket of goods is the same as inflation, we can rewrite this expression as

Percentage change in US\$ per C\$ = U.S. inflation rate − Cdn inflation rate   (3)

Thus, when the U.S. inflation rate is higher than the Canadian inflation rate, the number of U.S. dollars needed to buy a Canadian dollar rises. When the Canadian inflation rate is higher than the U.S. inflation rate, the reverse is true. An example can help us to see how this works. Say we need US\$0.60 to purchase a Canadian dollar (so a US\$ is worth C\$1.67) at the beginning of the year. During the year, the U.S. inflation rate is 5 percent, and the Canadian inflation rate is 2 percent. At the end of the year, we would expect the exchange rate to change so we need 3 percent more U.S. dollars to purchase a dollar, or US\$0.618 per Canadian dollar.

Purchasing power parity has immediate implications for monetary policy, which we can see clearly if we think about the debate over fixing the Canadian dollar to the U.S. dollar. If Canada, wanted to fix its exchange rate to the U.S. dollar, then Canadian monetary policy must be conducted so that Canadian inflation matches U.S. inflation. Alternatively, if Canada wants its inflation rate to diverge from the U.S. inflation rate, the C\$–US\$ exchange rate must be allowed to vary. *The central bank must choose between a fixed exchange rate and an independent inflation policy; it cannot have both.*

We could stop here, except for the fact that purchasing power parity works only over long periods, such as decades. That is, even though the exchange rate *eventually* adjusts to differences between prices at home and abroad, deviations from purchasing power parity can last for years. While this time lag in exchange rate movements might appear to ease restrictions on monetary policy, in fact it does not. To understand why, we need to examine what happens in the capital markets when investors can move their funds freely across international boundaries.

## Interest Rates and the Short-Run Implications of Capital Market Arbitrage

In the short run, a country's exchange rate is determined by supply and demand. The exchange value of the dollar depends on factors such as the preferences of Canadians for foreign assets and the preferences of foreign investors for Canadian assets. In the short run, investors play a crucial role, since they are the ones who can move large

---

[1] In going from equation (1) to equation (2), we are using the approximation that the percentage change in $(X/Y)$ equals the percentage change in $X$ *minus* the percentage change in Y. This approximation works best for small changes.in interest rate

quantities of dollars, euros, pounds, or pesos across international borders. Assuming that governments allow funds to flow into and out of their countries, these movements can occur very quickly.

To understand the implications of international capital mobility, recall the connection between interest rates and exchange rates we described in Chapter 10. Suppose the exchange rate between the Canadian dollar and the pound was fixed. Investors would be indifferent between investing in a dollar-denominated bond in Toronto or a pound-denominated bond in London with the same maturity and risk characteristics only when the interest rates in the two cities are the same. If interest rates differed in Toronto and London, investors would move funds back and forth, wiping out the difference. This example is analogous to a comparison between bonds sold in Toronto and in Vancouver. Since the dollar exchange rate between the two cities is fixed and capital is free to move between them, their interest rates must be the same.

More generally, if capital can flow freely between two countries and investors can invest in identical assets in the each country, then arbitrage ensures that the two assets have the same expected return. We called this the uncovered interest parity condition. This condition (which ignores the exchange rate risk premium) states that the domestic interest rate will equal the foreign interest rate (on an asset with the same risk and maturity characteristics) plus expected exchange rate depreciation:

$$i = i^f + \frac{\Delta E^e}{E} \tag{4}$$

Notice that this implies that under a fixed exchange rate interest rates must be equal across the two countries. Like purchasing power parity, capital market arbitrage has direct implications for monetary policy.

At first glance, it may seem as if policymakers can choose between stabilizing the domestic interest rate and stabilizing the exchange rate. But our discussion of interest rates and arbitrage depended critically on the ability of investors to move capital across international boundaries. If capital cannot flow freely between London and Toronto, there is no mechanism to equate interest rates in the two countries, and our logic falls apart. Thus, we need to revise our conclusion: So long as capital can flow freely between countries, monetary policymakers must choose between fixing their exchange rate and fixing their interest rate. A country *cannot*

- Be open to international capital flows,
- Control its domestic interest rate, and
- Fix its exchange rate.

Policymakers must choose two of these three options.

Looking around the world, we see that different countries have made different choices. Canada, for example, has an open capital market, a controlled domestic interest rate, and a freely floating dollar. During the 1990s, Argentina maintained an open capital market but fixed its exchange rate with the dollar, giving up control of domestic interest rates. But these are not the only alternatives; there is another possibility that is worth exploring. If a country is willing to forgo participation in international capital markets, it can impose capital controls, fix its exchange rate, and still use monetary policy to pursue its domestic objectives.

Capital controls go very much against the grain of modern economic thinking. The consensus among economists is that open capital markets benefit everyone. In the same way that international trade allows countries to exploit their comparative advantage, internationally integrated capital markets ensure that capital goes to its most efficient uses.

## YOUR FINANCIAL WORLD

### Emerging-Markets Crises and You

One morning you awaken to news of a severe financial crisis in an emerging-market country. As in Asia in 1997 and Latin America in 2002, some part of the developing world appears to be near collapse. The guardians of the financial system—officials from the central bank, the finance ministry, and international organizations such as the IMF—are convening to decide what to do. In the meantime, the market value of investments in the emerging world is plummeting as traders flee to safety, moving their money into the United States and Europe. What should you do?

If you followed the advice in Chapter 10, some of your investments are in foreign stocks and bonds, so this crisis looks as if it may have an impact on you. Will it? The answer is it will have virtually no effect at all. Here's why. First, your portfolio should be well diversified, so you will be prepared for the possibility that some of your investments will do poorly. Second, these countries are small in an economic sense—the fact that they are "emerging" means they are at an early stage of development—so your investments there

will be small. To give some idea of just how small these countries are economically and financially, note that Malaysia's GDP is less than one one-hundredth the size of U.S. GDP, and the Malaysian financial market is one five-hundredth the size of the U.S. financial market. In fact, if you diversified your investments internationally, purchasing stocks based on the size of each country's capital market, for each $100 you invested, you would put $46 in the United States, $29 in western Europe, $10 in Japan, and 20 cents in Malaysia! So, even if the Malaysian stock market were to fall by 50 percent, you would only lose 10 cents per $100 you had invested.

Finally, most of your investments are likely to be in a retirement account, which you probably won't need for decades. Over the years that you hold these investments, their value will go up and down; occasional losses are just bumps in the road. As long as you take a long-term perspective and diversify your holdings, these crises will have only a negligible impact on you.

---

The free flow of capital across borders enhances competition, improves opportunities for diversification, and equalizes rates of return (adjusted for risk). As this view took hold in the late 20th century, countries removed the restrictions on the flow of capital that had been initiated earlier in the century.[2]

When we look at large industrialized countries, the benefits of open capital markets are easy to see. Canadian workers benefit from the jobs at Honda's assembly plant in Alliston, Ontario, and Canadian investors benefit from their access to French and German stocks. But for emerging-markets countries, this greater openness has come with certain risks. The problem is that capital that flows into a country can also flow out, and it can do so quickly. That means that countries with open capital markets are vulnerable to sudden changes in investor sentiment. Investors may decide to sell a country's bonds, driving their prices down and their interest rates up. Investors convert the proceeds of the sale into foreign currency, driving the value of the domestic currency down. If everyone loses confidence in a country at the same time, the result is similar to a bank run: All foreign investors leave at once, precipitating a financial collapse. (We will examine the mechanics of these crises later in this chapter.)

It is tempting for government officials to try to avert such crises by restricting people's ability to move capital into and out of a country—by imposing controls on the flow of

---

[2] Like central banks, controls on international capital flows are a 20th-century innovation. One of the hallmarks of the period between the world wars (the 1920s and 1930s) was the strong movement toward national autonomy. As the world economy collapsed during the Great Depression, countries tried to isolate themselves by instituting restrictions on both the trade in goods and services and the transfer of capital. Restrictions on the ability of foreigners to own domestic assets, and on everyone's ability to transfer currency or gold out of a country, became common. Many of these became part of the international financial system after World War II and were maintained by industrialized countries into the 1970s and beyond. Until 1979, the British government maintained controls on investments made abroad by U.K. residents. Until 1974, the United States taxed interest received by Americans on foreign bonds.

## APPLYING THE CONCEPT
### MALAYSIA IMPOSES
### CAPITAL CONTROLS

Following the financial crises that enveloped Thailand and Indonesia in 1997, then Korea and Russia in 1998, most emerging-markets countries suffered extreme stress. To reduce risk, foreign investors simply pulled out. They sold those countries' bonds, driving their prices down and their interest rates up, and then converted the proceeds into foreign currencies, driving the value of the domestic currencies down. As in a bank run, no one wanted to be last in line to sell; everyone rushed to leave at once. Plummeting exchange rates and skyrocketing interest rates brought these economies to their knees. Banks and industrial firms that had once been able to borrow easily became desperately short of funds.

The typical response of countries experiencing such a financial crisis is for the government to borrow from other countries and the International Monetary Fund (IMF) and use the borrowed funds to meet its obligations. Eventually, interest rates come down, the exchange rate recovers, foreign investors return, and the government repays the loans. But Malaysia adopted a different course. Believing there was nothing inher-

ently wrong with the nation's economy and that the crisis resembled a bank run more than anything else, officials took the extreme step of implementing strict capital controls. By placing severe limits on investors' ability to remove money from the country, they ensured that foreign investments would remain there. More important, they could fix the value of their currency, the ringgit, and lower domestic interest rates.

At the time, Western economists condemned the policy, claiming that it would destroy the country's economy for years to come. While experts continue to argue about the wisdom of Malaysia's capital controls, their initial response was clearly mistaken. Malaysia's recovery took only two years, compared to five years for Thailand and Indonesia. Would the recovery have been even faster without the capital controls? We will never know for sure. But if countries start instituting capital controls every time there is a whiff of crisis, they will dramatically increase the risk of investing in emerging-market countries. Investors will become wary of putting money into foreign countries if they aren't sure they will be able to take it out whenever they want.*

*For a detailed description of the Malaysian experience in 1998, see Ethan Kaplan and Dani Rodrik, "Did the Malaysian Capital Controls Work?" *National Bureau of Economic Research Working Paper* No. 8142, February 2001.

capital. There are two basic types of capital control. *Inflow controls* restrict the ability of foreigners to invest in a country; *outflow controls* place obstacles in the way of selling investments and taking funds out. During much of the 1990s, foreigners wishing to invest in Chile were required to make a one-year, zero-interest deposit of 20 percent of the investment at the central bank. This inflow control penalized short-term investments, encouraging investors to invest for a longer period.

Outflow controls include restrictions on the ability of domestic residents to purchase foreign assets, and often include prohibitions on removing currency from the country. In the fall of 1998, Malaysian citizens were prohibited from taking more than 1,000 ringgit in cash (worth a bit more than US$250 at the time) out of the country, while the most foreigners could take out of the country was the amount they had brought with them when they entered the country. Any nonresident who sold a Malaysian security was required to hold the proceeds in the country for at least 12 months before taking it out. These controls effectively cut Malaysia off from the world capital market.

## Mechanics of Exchange Rate Management

Since both the Bank of Canada and the European Central Bank buy and sell securities to maintain their overnight interbank interest rates at target levels, they must have given up control of their exchange rates. No wonder their intervention on September 22, 2000, had almost no effect on the value of the euro. Even so, Bank of Canada and ECB policies *do* have an impact on the value of the dollar and the euro. And if either central bank chose to, it could give up controlling interest rates and target the exchange rate instead.

How would they do it? What are the mechanics of exchange rate management and exchange rate intervention? We have seen that everything the central bank does has something to do with its balance sheet. Foreign exchange intervention is no exception. So to look at the mechanics of exchange rate management, we'll start with the central bank's balance sheet. Once we understand the balance-sheet effects of foreign currency intervention, we can look more closely at what central banks like the Bank of Canada and the ECB actually do.

## Foreign Exchange Intervention

If all policymakers want to do is to fix the exchange rate, there is a simple way to do it: They can offer to buy and sell their country's currency at a fixed rate. For example, if the Canadian government decided to fix the U.S. dollar–Canadian dollar exchange rate at one to one, it would simply tell the Bank of Canada to stand ready to exchange Canadian dollars for U.S. dollars whenever anyone asked. Buying U.S. dollars wouldn't be much of a problem, since the Bank of Canada can print all the dollars it needs. But selling U.S. dollars in exchange for Canadian dollars might pose some difficulty unless the Bank of Canada had a substantial U.S. dollar reserve. We will ignore this complication for now and return to it later in the chapter, when we discuss the problem of speculative attacks.

Canada's foreign exchange reserves are held in the Exchange Fund Account (EFA), which belongs to the Ministry of Finance, not the Bank of Canada. The Ministry of Finance sets the broad objectives of the Fund, but the Bank of Canada manages the fund. Here we will simplify our analysis of the impact of exchange market intervention by consolidating the balance sheets of the EFA and the Bank of Canada. To support the Canadian dollar, the Bank of Canada would sell U.S. dollars and buy Canadian dollars. In buying Canadian dollars it reduces outstanding Canadian dollar liabilities. These interventions have an impact on interest rates and, through the deposit expansion multiplier, on the quantity of money in the economy as well. Similarly, buying U.S. dollars and selling Canadian dollars increases the supply of reserves to the banking system, putting downward pressure on interest rates and expanding the quantity of money. Remember that in taking these actions, the Bank of Canada responds to the market. Under a fixed exchange rate the decision to buy and sell U.S. dollars is made by financial market participants, not the central bank: *controlling the exchange rate means giving up control of the size of reserves so that the market determines the interest rate.*

To see how this process works in practice, let's go back to September 2000, when the largest central banks in the world intervened to bolster the value of the euro. Canada spent C$140 million buying euros that day. (By itself that probably wouldn't have had much impact on the European interest rates but the Fed spent over $1 billion so the scale of the concerted action was significant.) When Bank of Canada employees bought euros, they paid for them by creating reserves for the banking system. Then as soon as they received the €120 million from foreign exchange dealers they spent it on bonds issued by euro-area governments, often the German government.

The balance-sheet implications of this exchange are straightforward. Figure 22.1 on page 510 shows the results of the intervention. Looking at the asset side, and following the standard convention of reporting the value of the central bank's foreign exchange reserves in domestic currency units, we see that the Bank of Canada has increased its euro-denominated foreign exchange reserve assets by $140 million. On the liabilities side of the balance sheet, we see that chartered bank reserves have increased by the same amount.

**Figure 22.1** Change in the Bank of Canada's Balance Sheet Immediately following a Purchase of Euros

| Assets | Liabilities |
|---|---|
| Euro reserves +$140 million (German government bonds) | Chartered Bank reserves +$140 million |

This T-account should look familiar. If we focus on the liabilities side of the balance sheet, we see that the purchase of euro bonds is identical to a purchase of Canadian government bonds. That is, the purchase of a security has added reserves to the banking system. The only difference is the issuer of the bond. Like any other change in reserves, this one has a direct impact on the quantity of money in the economy. In other words, it is expansionary, so it reduces domestic interest rates. *A foreign exchange intervention has the same impact on reserves as a domestic open market operation.*

Will this intervention change the exchange rate? Figure 22.2 shows what happens. Recall from Chapter 10 that the dollar exchange rate is determined by the supply of and demand for dollars. The Bank of Canada did supply dollars to the market through its intervention, but more importantly, the interest rate has fallen. Remember that whenever investing in Canada becomes less attractive relative to investing somewhere else, the result is a decrease in the demand for dollars that will be used by foreigners to purchase Canadian assets and an increase in the supply of dollars that will be used by Canadians to purchase foreign assets. In this example, assuming that the Bank of Canada does nothing but purchase German government bonds, the Canadian interest rate will fall while European interest rates remain the same. Foreign investors will want to buy fewer Canadian bonds, and they will need fewer dollars to do it. As a result, the demand for dollars in the foreign exchange market falls. Meanwhile, Canadian investors will want to buy more foreign bonds, and they

**Figure 22.2** Effect of a Decrease in Canadian Interest Rates Relative to Interest Rates in the Euro Area

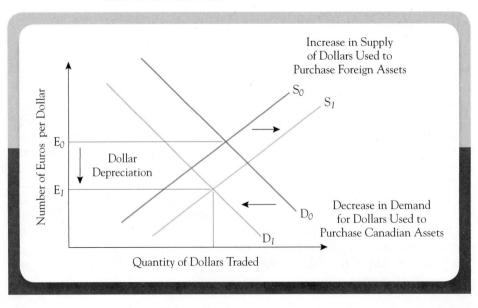

supply more dollars to do that. The demand and supply shifts shown in Figure 22.2 together drive the value of the dollar down and the value of the euro up. The dollar depreciates and the euro appreciates, reducing the number of euros offered per dollar in the foreign exchange market.

You may think there is something strange about this discussion. We started with a foreign exchange intervention in which the Bank of Canada purchased euros and noted its impact on the dollar–euro exchange rate. But the reason the exchange rate moved was that the domestic interest rate changed, shifting the demand for dollars in the foreign exchange market. By making domestic Canadian investment less attractive, the intervention prompted people to purchase fewer dollars, driving the price of dollars down. Our conclusion is that *a foreign exchange intervention affects the value of a country's currency by changing domestic interest rates*.

This conclusion has an important implication. It means that *any central bank policy that influences the domestic interest rate will affect the exchange rate*. The fact that we started with an exchange rate intervention is irrelevant. An open market purchase or sale works exactly the same way. If the Bank of Canada bought Canadian government bonds instead of euro-denominated bonds, the action would drive down Canadian interest rates, decreasing the demand for dollars in the foreign exchange market and causing a decline in the value of the dollar. There is nothing special about a foreign exchange intervention.

## Sterilized Intervention

In September 2000, when the ECB, the Federal Reserve, the Bank of Japan, the Bank of England, and the Bank of Canada all intervened to buy euros, none of them changed their domestic interest rate targets. No wonder the value of the euro didn't change! But that means their transactions must have been different from the one we just studied. We assumed that when the Bank of Canada bought euros, it increased commercial bank reserves, which would reduce interest rates in the absence of any other action. Such a move is an example of an **unsterilized foreign exchange intervention**, one that changes central bank liabilities. But in large countries, central banks don't operate that way. Instead, they engage in **sterilized foreign exchange interventions**, in which a change in foreign exchange reserves alters the asset side of the central bank's balance sheet but the domestic monetary base remains unaffected.

A sterilized intervention is actually a combination of two transactions. First there is the purchase or sale of foreign currency reserves, which by itself changes the central bank's liabilities. But this is immediately followed by an open market operation of exactly the same size, designed to offset the impact of the first transaction on the monetary base. For example, the Bank of Canada's purchase of a German government bond, which would increase reserves, is offset by the sale of a Canadian government bond. Together, these two actions leave the level of reserves unchanged. Such an intervention is sterilized with respect to its affect on the monetary base, or the size of the central bank's balance sheet. *An intervention is unsterilized if it changes the monetary base and sterilized if it does not change the monetary base.*

"If this doesn't help you don't worry, it's a placebo."

| Figure 22.3 | Change in the Bank of Canada's Balance Sheet following a Sterilized Purchase of Euro-Denominated Bonds |
|---|---|

| Assets | | Liabilities |
|---|---|---|
| Euro reserves (German government bonds) | +$140 million | Chartered Bank Reserves unchanged |
| Securities (Canadian T Bills) | −$140 million | |

Figure 22.3 shows the result on the Bank of Canada's balance sheet. Notice two things. First, commercial bank reserves remain unchanged following a sterilized intervention, so domestic monetary policy does not change. Second, the intervention changes the *composition* of the asset side of the central bank's balance sheet. The Bank of Canada has swapped Canadian government bonds for bonds issued by the German government—an action that has no impact on the exchange rate. Prior to 1998 the Bank of Canada had intervened systematically to support the Canadian dollar. Since then, the Bank has acknowledged that such intervention is ineffective and now intervention is reserved for "exceptional" circumstances.[3]

# The Costs, Benefits, and Risks of Fixed Exchange Rates

STABILITY

Many countries allow their exchange rates to float freely, so that the value of their currencies is determined in the financial markets. But others—especially small, emerging-market countries—fix their exchange rates. That is, officials of the central bank and the finance ministry agree that the best policy is to maintain a predictable value for their currency, so they target the exchange rate. Why do some countries make that decision? Surely fixing the exchange rate has costs as well as benefits. We now turn to a brief discussion of the tradeoffs.

## Assessing the Costs and Benefits

The owners of the Blue Jays baseball team, probably wouldn't mind if the Bank of Canada decided to fix the exchange rate with the U.S. dollar. They face a common problem for companies engaged in international trade: they pay most of their expenses in one currency and receive the bulk of their revenues in another. Specifically, the Blue Jays receive about 80 percent of their revenue in Canadian dollars but pay 80 percent of their expenses—including a $75 million annual payroll (in 2006) and the bills for chartered planes and fancy hotel rooms—in U.S. dollars. So if the Canadian dollar depreciates, as it did during the late 1990s, the Blue Jays incur a financial loss. Unless they hedge this exchange rate risk, for each 10 percent drop in the value of the Canadian dollar they will lose something like $11 million. The more volatile exchange rates become, the worse the problem gets. If the exchange rates were fixed, the Blue Jays' risk would disappear.[4]

[3] See the Bank in Brief, "Intervention in the Foreign Exchange Market," accessed August 21, 2009. http://www.bankofcanada.ca/en/backgrounders/bg-e2.html. The policy of intervening to support the Canadian dollar only in exceptional circumstances does not preclude joining international actions to support other currencies—as in the action of September 2000.

[4] The Toronto Blue Jays do hedge their foreign exchange risk in the derivatives market. In effect, they pay someone for insurance against moves in the exchange rate. Doing so makes their expenses and profits more predictable, but it isn't free.

Goods and services aren't the only things that cross international borders; capital does, too. Fixed exchange rates not only simplify operations for businesses that trade internationally, but also, by eliminating exchange rate risk, reduce the risk that investors face when they hold foreign stocks and bonds.

So fixed exchange rates seem to be a good idea for both businesses and investors. They also have another potential benefit. As we discussed in Chapter 21, a fixed exchange rate can serve as a nominal anchor for the monetary system. A fixed exchange rate ties policymakers' hands. Remember that in the long run, the exchange rate is determined by inflation differentials. In countries that are prone to bouts of high inflation, a fixed exchange rate may be the only way to establish a credible low-inflation policy. It enforces low-inflation discipline on both central bankers and politicians, and an exchange rate target enhances transparency and accountability.

There is one serious drawback to a fixed exchange rate, however. It *imports* monetary policy. Fixing your currency's value to that of another country means adopting the other country's interest rate policy. When Argentina fixed the exchange rate of the peso to the U.S. dollar, policymakers gave up control of Argentinean interest rates and effectively handed it over to the FOMC. Needless to say, when the FOMC sets the target federal funds rate, committee members don't worry much about what is going on in Argentina. What this means is that a fixed exchange rate makes the most sense when the two countries involved have similar macroeconomic fluctuations. Otherwise, the country with the flexible exchange rate that is in control of monetary policy (e.g., the United States) might be raising interest rates to combat domestic inflation at the same time that the other country (e.g., Argentina) is going into recession.

In deciding whether to fix their country's exchange rate, policymakers should consider several additional matters. First, when a country fixes its exchange rate, the central bank is offering to buy and sell its own currency at a fixed rate. To honour this commitment to purchase currency, monetary policymakers will need ample currency reserves. For instance, a country that fixes its exchange rate to the dollar needs to hold dollars in reserve. Living up to this promise in a world of free-flowing capital requires a high level of foreign exchange reserves. For many countries, the billions of dollars required are both difficult to obtain and expensive to keep.[5]

Second, since floating exchange rates act as automatic macroeconomic stabilizers, fixing the exchange rate means reducing the domestic economy's natural ability to respond to macroeconomic shocks. Imagine a country on the verge of recession. If monetary policymakers can, they will react by lowering interest rates in an attempt to keep the economy from slowing. Beyond the direct effect on investment and consumption, lower interest rates make domestic bonds less attractive to foreigners, reducing the demand for the domestic currency and driving down its value. The resulting currency depreciation drives down the price foreigners must pay for domestic exports, increasing the demand for them and amplifying the impact of the initial interest rate reduction. With a fixed exchange rate, this stabilization mechanism is completely shut down.

The appreciation of the Canadian dollar in the early 21st century illustrates this shock absorber function of the flexible exchange rate. The rise in demand for Canadian natural resources stimulated aggregate demand in Canada and, other things being equal, would have been inflationary. With a flexible exchange rate, the increased demand for Canadian dollars led to an appreciation of the dollar that dampened aggregate demand (demand for exports in particular), offsetting the initial demand shock.

---

[5] Reserves are often held in very liquid short term foreign securities so the "carry cost" (that is, the cost of holding reserves) is the difference between the interest rate the government borrows at and the rate it earns on its reserves.

## The Danger of Speculative Attacks

While fixed exchange rates may have benefits for a country's economy, they are fragile and prone to a type of crisis called a speculative attack. To understand the nature of a speculative attack, imagine that a country is trying to maintain a fixed exchange rate. Now suppose that for some reason, financial market participants come to believe that the government will need to devalue its currency in the near future. They won't wait; instead, investors will attack the currency and force an immediate devaluation.

The mechanics of the attack are straightforward. Take the example of the attack on the Thai baht in 1997. Through the mid-1990s, the Bank of Thailand was committed to maintaining a fixed exchange rate of approximately 26 baht to the U.S. dollar. To do so, officials had to make sure foreign currency traders believed that the Bank of Thailand had enough dollars on hand to buy however many baht the traders wanted to sell. In summer 1997, financial market participants began to question whether the reserves at the central bank really were big enough, and they swung into action. Speculators borrowed baht at domestic Thai interest rates, took them to the central bank to convert them to dollars at the rate of 26 to one, and then invested the dollars in short-term, interest-bearing securities in the United States. The immediate impact of these transactions was to drain the Bank of Thailand's dollar reserves. The lower the dollar reserves, the less likely that the Thais would be able to meet further requests to convert baht into dollars. And the more baht speculators borrowed to convert into dollars, the further the reserves fell.

The details are instructive. Imagine that, anticipating a severe depreciation, you borrow 2.6 million baht. You take them to the Bank of Thailand and convert them into US$100,000 at the fixed rate of 26 to one. With the proceeds, you buy U.S. Treasury bills. One week later, your expectations are realized and the baht depreciates by 10 percent. Now you need only US$90,909 to obtain the 2.6 million baht with which to repay the loan. You've made an almost instant profit of over US$9,000.[6] Since international currency speculators have very deep pockets, they can quickly drain billions of dollars from a central bank this way—and make a huge profit in the process.[7]

What causes a speculative attack? There are two possibilities. The first brings us back to fiscal policy: Remember that politicians can make the central banker's job impossible. Ensuring that a currency retains its value means keeping domestic inflation at the same level as that of the country to which your exchange rate is pegged. If investors begin to think that at current levels, government spending must ultimately increase inflation, they will stop believing that officials can maintain the exchange rate at its fixed level. This seems to have been an important part of what happened during the Asian crisis of 1997.

[6] This simple example ignores both the interest you would need to pay to borrow the baht and the interest you would receive on the Treasury bills. An exact calculation would take the difference between the two interest rates into account and would likely reduce the profit. But since such transactions are usually done over days or weeks at most, this adjustment would have only a modest impact on the return. It also ignores your need to buy and sell U.S. dollars. However, the Canadian dollar/U.S. dollar exchange rate was unlikely to change by anything like 10 percent over a few days. A speculator would hedge the Canadian dollar/U.S. dollar risk in the forward market. The point is that betting against a fixed exchange rate can be a very profitable transaction, with little downside risk.

[7] In September 1992, the Bank of England belonged to the European Exchange Rate Mechanism, which linked the exchange rates of many countries. It effectively pegged the pound to the then-independent German currency, the deutsche mark. In an attempt to contain domestic inflation, the Germans raised interest rates dramatically, a policy the British did not want to follow. When speculators realized that the situation was untenable—that the Bank of England could not fix its exchange rate and have a lower interest rate than the Germans—they attacked. George Soros is reputed to have made over $1 billion betting that the pound would be devalued.

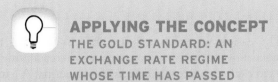

## APPLYING THE CONCEPT
### THE GOLD STANDARD: AN EXCHANGE RATE REGIME WHOSE TIME HAS PASSED

If you take a dollar bill to the Bank of Canada, officials will give you a new one. Should they offer to give you gold instead? That would be returning to the time when the dollar was "as good as gold." Today, advocates of a return to the gold standard claim that it would eliminate inflation. As evidence, they point to the time before World War I, when Canada was on the gold standard and inflation averaged less than 1 percent per year. What these advocates don't advertise is that, while inflation was low on *average*, it was highly variable, fluctuating between $+3\frac{1}{4}$ percent and $-3\frac{1}{4}$ percent. In fact, for much of the late 19th century, prices fell steadily. Only early in the 20th century did they rise back to a level not far above where they started in 1880.

The focus on past inflation obscures the long list of reasons that few economists today advocate a return to the gold standard. To begin with, the gold standard obligates the central bank to fix the price of something we don't really care about. Instead of stabilizing the prices of the goods and services we buy and consume, the central bank fixes the dollar price of gold. In place of fluctuations in the market price of gold, there are fluctuations in the dollar price of goods.

Then there is the fact that, under the gold standard, the amount of money in the economy would depend on the amount of gold available. More gold equals more money. Since, in the long run, inflation is tied to money growth, this means that inflation depends on the rate at which gold is mined. Why should monetary policy be determined by the rate at which South Africa and Russia dig gold from the ground? Moreover, any political disruption in those parts of the world could have dramatic monetary policy effects.

The case for gold grows even less persuasive when we realize that the gold standard is an exchange rate policy, too. The promise to convert dollars into gold means that international transactions must be settled in gold. So when the value of imports does not exactly match the value of exports, gold is transferred from one country to another. Thus, a country with a current account deficit—whose imports exceed its exports—has to pay the difference by transferring gold to countries with current account surpluses. (See Applying the Concept: The Balance of Payments and "Global Imbalances" on page 518 for a description of balance-of-payments accounting.) With less gold, the country's central bank must contract its balance sheet, raising interest rates, reducing the quantity of money and credit in the economy, and driving domestic prices down. Under a gold standard, countries running current account deficits will be forced into deflation. Meanwhile, countries with current account surpluses can allow their gold inflows to generate inflation, but they need not. Under the gold standard, a central bank can have too little gold, but it can never have too much.

Economic historians believe that gold flows played a central role in spreading the Great Depression of the 1930s throughout the world. After World War I, all the major countries in the world worked to reconstruct the gold standard. By the late 1920s, they had succeeded. At the time, both the United States and France were running current account surpluses, absorbing the world's gold into their vaults. But instead of allowing the gold inflows to expand the quantity of money in their financial systems, authorities in both countries tightened monetary policy in an attempt to cool off their overheated, inflation-prone economies. The result was catastrophic, since it forced countries with current account deficits and gold outflows to tighten their monetary policies even more. The resulting deflation increased the likelihood that people would default on loans, destroying the economic and financial system in the United States and elsewhere. Economic historians place the blame squarely on the gold standard. What makes their argument truly convincing is the fact that the sooner a country left the gold standard and regained control of its monetary policy, the faster its economy recovered.

From our vantage point in the 21st century, the gold standard is an historical artifact that caused nothing but trouble. It is hard to understand why anyone would want to bring it back.

But speculative attacks can occur even when a country's fiscal and monetary policy-makers are behaving responsibly. They can arise spontaneously out of nowhere. If by chance enough currency speculators simply decide that a central bank cannot maintain its exchange rate, they will attack it, mobilizing tens of billions of dollars virtually overnight. To make matters even worse, spontaneous speculative attacks are a bit like bank runs; they can be contagious.

Many observers suspect that in today's world, no central bank has the resources to withstand such an attack. It would take substantial foreign exchange reserves to even think about trying.

*"Part of me wants to help you with your crisis, Hargraves, but part of me wants to go to lunch."*

## Summarizing the Case for a Fixed Exchange Rate

The easiest way to summarize this discussion is to make a list of the conditions under which adopting a fixed exchange rate makes sense for a country. A fixed exchange rate makes most sense for a country if it has all three of the following:

- A poor reputation for controlling inflation on its own.
- An economy that is well integrated with the one to whose currency the rate is fixed, trading significantly with it and sharing similar macroeconomic characteristics.
- A high level of foreign exchange reserves.

Regardless of how closely a country meets these criteria, fixed exchange rates are still risky to adopt and difficult to maintain.

## Fixed Exchange Rate Regimes

The gold standard system of the late 19th and early 20th centuries was a form of fixed exchange rate regimes. Each country agreed to convert its currency into a certain weight of gold that determined, and fixed, the relative value of each currency. The gold standard was abandoned during the Great Depression but many forms of fixed exchange rates persist. We will look at managed exchange rate pegs, in which policymakers try to restrict the exchange rate to a certain range; at currency boards, in which the central bank holds foreign currency assets as backing for the domestic monetary base; and at dollarization, in which a country eliminates its own currency and begins using one issued by another country. In the next section we will look at how Canada's exchange rate regime changed over time.

### Exchange Rate Pegs and the Bretton Woods System

Despite the calamity of the 1930s, the world remained enamored of fixed exchange rates and the gold standard. So in 1944, a group of 44 countries agreed to form the **Bretton Woods system**. Named for the New Hampshire resort where the agreement was signed, it was a system of fixed exchange rates that offered more flexibility over the short term than had been possible under the gold standard.

The Bretton Woods system lasted from 1945 to 1971. Though the details of the system were complex, the basic idea is not. Each country maintained an agreed-upon exchange rate with the U.S. dollar—that is, it *pegged* its exchange rate to the dollar. To make the system work, every country had to hold dollar reserves and stand ready to exchange its own currency for dollars at the fixed rate. The dollar was what is known as a *reserve currency*, and it was convertible into gold at a rate of $35 per ounce. The choice of the dollar as the reserve currency was based on several factors. First, the United States was the biggest of the Allies (the victors in World War II), both economically and militarily. Second, dollars were relatively abundant.

Since other countries did not want to adopt U.S. monetary policy, their fixed exchange rates required complex capital controls. Even so, countries had to intervene regularly,

## YOUR FINANCIAL WORLD
### Should You Buy Gold?

Since the gold standard isn't a workable system, central banks don't need to buy gold. But what about you? Gold doesn't pay interest like a bond or dividends like a stock, and its price is highly volatile. From 1974 to 1980, gold more than quadrupled in value, rising in price from $200 per ounce to $850 per ounce; by the year 2000 it had fallen to $250 to $400 per ounce, but by 2009 the price had risen to over $900! Clearly gold is a high-risk investment.

But that isn't all. Governments and central banks own about 30 percent of all the gold that has ever been taken out of the ground, over 900 million ounces. Because they have no use for it, governments are slowly selling it. Europeans are doing most of the selling, at a rate of about 50 million ounces per year. The fact that some of the largest holders of gold are now the biggest sellers just reinforces the metal's poor investment potential.

Some investment advisors might try to convince you to buy gold to reduce risk. What they will tell you is that gold rises in value when inflation goes up and falls when inflation goes down, so it can be used as a hedge against increases in nominal interest rates. Remember that higher inflation means higher interest rates, and higher interest rates mean lower bond prices. Gold appears to provide a hedge against inflation. While there may be some truth to this idea, it isn't very good investment advice. Not only is gold expensive to buy, sell, and store, but also there are better ways to deal with inflation risk. After all, inflation risk is highest for long-term bonds. If inflation risk is what you are worried about, then buy short-term bonds; it's both cheaper and easier than buying gold.

While gold may be a reasonable investment for someone who is fleeing a homicidal dictator, the rest of us should stick to wearing it as jewellery. The best advice is to invest your savings in bonds and stocks.

buying or selling dollars to maintain their exchange rates at the peg. Adjustments were made to the *exchange rate pegs*, but only in response to perceived long-term imbalances. What gave the system some flexibility was the *International Monetary Fund* (IMF). The IMF was created to manage the Bretton Woods System by making loans to countries in need of short-term financing to pay for an excess of imports over exports. For a number of years, the system worked reasonably well, but as capital markets started to open up, it came under increasing strain.

With a fixed exchange rate and the free movements of capital across international borders, countries could not have independent monetary policies. Recall the example of fixing the Canadian dollar to the U.S. dollar cited earlier in this chapter. The long-run implications of purchasing power parity meant that, if U.S. inflation deviated from Canadian inflation, the U.S. dollar–Canadian dollar exchange rate had to change. In the late 1960s, the countries in the Bretton Woods system were in the same position. Since their exchange rate was fixed to the dollar, participating countries were forced to adopt policies that resulted in the same amount of inflation as in the United States. When U.S. inflation began to rise in the late 1960s (yet another disastrous side effect of the Vietnam War), many countries balked; they didn't want to match the rise in inflation.

Canada abandoned the fixed exchange rate in 1970 and by 1973 the Bretton Woods system had completely fallen apart. The response of American officials has been to allow the dollar to float freely ever since. Europeans took a different tack; for much of the time from the collapse of the Bretton Woods system to the adoption of the euro in 1999, they maintained various fixed exchange rate mechanisms. Since capital flowed freely among these countries, that meant giving up their ability to set interest rates.

## APPLYING THE CONCEPT
### THE BALANCE OF PAYMENTS AND "GLOBAL IMBALANCES"

Even before the financial crisis that began in 2008, policymakers in Canada and elsewhere raised concerns about "global imbalances." To understand what they meant, we need to understand how international payments are recorded in the international balance of payments and, in particular, the three components to the balance of payments: the current account balance, the capital account balance, and the official settlements balance.

The *current account* tracks the flow of payments for currently produced goods and services across national boundaries. The *trade balance* is the difference between a country's exports and imports of goods and services. A full accounting of annual flows must also include unilateral transfers, such as the money foreign workers send home to relatives, as well as investment income, such as the interest payments Canadians receive on their holdings of European (and other foreign) bonds. When we include the balance on these items with the trade balance we have the current account balance. When a country's exports and net foreign income exceed its imports, its current account balance will be positive—that is, it will have a *current account surplus*.

To grasp the importance of the current account, you need to realize that countries have budgets, just like individuals. If you spend more than your income, you have two options: sell something you own or get a loan. What is true for an individual is also true for a country. Think of the revenue earned from selling exports to foreigners as the country's income, and the cost of imports bought from overseas as its spending. When spending exceeds income, the result is current account deficit. To pay for its overspending, the country must either sell something it owns or borrow.

The *capital account* tracks the purchase and sale of assets—stocks, bonds, real estate, and the like—between countries. When a German buys shares in RIM, or a Canadian purchases a Brazilian government bond, the transaction appears in the capital account. The *capital account balance* is the difference between a country's capital inflows and capital outflows. When a country's capital account is in surplus, it has a net capital inflow. Its residents are either selling assets to foreigners or borrowing money from abroad.

Finally, the *official settlements balance* is the change in a country's official reserve holdings. During the time of the gold standard, these reserves took the form of gold bars. The official settlements balance shows the change in the central bank's foreign exchange reserves.

The international balance of payments is an accounting framework that relates these three pieces. Their relationship is simple: They must sum to zero.

Current account balance + Capital account balance + Official settlements balance = 0

This accounting identity has important implications. If, as is normally the case in developed economies today, official reserve positions are unchanged so the official settlements balance is zero, then the current account balance plus the capital account balance sum to zero. So, a current account deficit must be matched by a capital account surplus, for example. If a country is importing more than it is exporting, it must either borrow from abroad or sell assets to foreigners to finance excess purchases.

Now we can return to the issue of global imbalances. At the beginning of the 21st century the U.S. current account deficit was about 7 percent of GDP annually. That means that every year the United States borrowed that amount from foreigners, building up its international indebtedness. The current account deficit reflected (1) foreign desire to invest in the United States (which included the desire of foreign central banks to build up reserves of U.S. assets to support their exchange rate pegs) and (2) low U.S. savings rates. Under flexible exchange rates the current account deficit would lead to a U.S. exchange rate depreciation that would stimulate U.S. exports and slow U.S. imports, reducing the deficit. However, a considerable part of the deficit was a result of trade with China, which fixed its exchange rate with the United States, precluding that channel of adjustment. The problem was temporarily eased by the financial crisis in 2008/9, which increased U.S. savings rates and reduced U.S. imports, halving the current account deficit. But of course the debt is still outstanding. If the Chinese decide to reduce their holdings of U.S. securities, then there could be an abrupt decline in the value of U.S. dollars and/or increase in U.S. interest rates. Both would have significant repercussions for the Canadian economy.

## Hard Pegs: Currency Boards and Dollarization

The international monetary system took a big hit in 1971 when the Bretton Woods system collapsed. Gradually, a consensus developed that countries whose economies are open to international capital flows must choose between completely flexible, market-determined exchange rates and what have come to be known as hard pegs. In a hard-peg system, the central bank implements an institutional mechanism that ensures its ability to convert a domestic currency into the foreign currency to which it is pegged. The danger of a speculative attack means anything less is unworkable. In the words of the first deputy managing director of the International Monetary Fund, "pegs are not sustainable unless they are very hard indeed."[8]

Only two exchange rate regimes can be considered hard pegs: currency boards and dollarization.[9] With a **currency board**, the central bank commits to holding enough foreign currency assets to back domestic currency liabilities at a fixed rate. With **dollarization**, one country formally adopts the currency of another country for use in all its financial transactions. Let's look at examples of both systems.

### Currency Boards and the Argentinean Experience

Somewhere between 10 and 20 currency boards operate in the world today. The best known is the one in Hong Kong. The Hong Kong Monetary Authority (HKMA) operates a system whose sole objective is to maintain a fixed exchange rate of 7.8 Hong Kong dollars to one U.S. dollar. Since the HKMA holds roughly $200 billion in foreign currency (dollar) assets, it can issue about 1.5 trillion billion Hong Kong dollars in liabilities. The rules of the currency board provide that the HKMA can increase the size of Hong Kong's monetary base only if it can accumulate additional dollar reserves.

As this example suggests, with a currency board, the central bank's only job is to maintain the exchange rate. While that means that policymakers cannot adjust monetary policy in response to domestic economic shocks, the system does have its advantages. Prime among them is the control of inflation. As we noted in the introduction to this chapter, Argentina decided to adopt a currency board in April 1991 to end triple-digit inflation, and the approach worked. After three years, the inflation rate had dropped to 4 percent; by 1998, it was nearly zero. Forgoing the ability to stabilize domestic growth seems like a small price to pay for this sort of inflation performance, especially in an inflation-prone economy.

But currency boards do have their problems. First, by giving up the ability to control the size of its balance sheet, the central bank loses its role as the lender of last resort to the domestic banking system. The Banco Central de la Republica Argentina solved this problem by establishing standby letters of credit (described in Chapter 12) from large U.S. banks. When the time came to make emergency loans to local banks, officials borrowed dollars from U.S. banks and then made loans in pesos. But their lending was limited to the amount of dollar credit that foreign banks were willing to extend.

In 2001, the Argentinean currency board collapsed and authorities were forced to allow the peso to float. Within a few months, dollars that had once cost one peso apiece cost three. What caused the collapse? Entire books have been written to answer this question, but several points will take us a long way toward understanding what happened. First, the peso was pegged to the U.S. dollar, despite the fact that Argentina's economy doesn't have much to do with the U.S. economy. When the dollar appreciated in the 1990s, it made the peso more valuable as well. The overvalued peso priced Argentinean exporters out of their markets, which were not in the United States. Over a period of years, the fact that exports were too expensive ended up severely damaging Argentina's economy.

---

[8] See Stanley Fischer, "Exchange Rate Regimes: Is the Bipolar View Correct?" *Journal of Economic Perspectives* 15, no. 2 (Spring 2001), pp. 3–24.

[9] Chinese policy suggests a third approach—build up unbreakable stock of foreign reserves. In 2009 China's foreign exchange reserves exceeded $2 trillion, sufficient to convince even the most aggressive speculators of their power to defend the exchange rate. This policy is expensive (the carry cost referred to earlier) and an option for only the very largest economies.

A 5-peso note issued by the government of the Province of Buenos Aires in 2001.

But the overvalued exchange rate was only part of the story; fiscal policy was the other part. While the Argentinean economy grew at a healthy rate of nearly 4½ percent per year through much of the 1990s, government spending rose even faster—so fast that the government needed to borrow an average of nearly 4 percent of GDP per year just to pay its bills. The more the government borrowed, the more wary lenders became of continuing to lend. Undeterred, politicians spent until they simply ran out of money.

The problem was worst at the provincial government level where borrowing became impossible even to meet the payroll. So provincial government officials began printing a sort of bond and using it to pay their employees. The bonds issued by the provincial government of Buenos Aires, called *patacones*, paid 7 percent annual interest and matured in one to five years (see the photo). What made them special was that they were the same physical size as currency and were issued in small denominations of one to 100 pesos in order to pay employees and retirees. Observers estimated that Argentina's provincial governments eventually issued 40 percent of the currency in circulation. When politicians began printing their own money, the claim that Argentinean inflation would roughly mirror U.S. inflation—a requirement for the long-run viability of the fixed exchange rate—was no longer credible and the currency board collapsed. Always remember, irresponsible politicians can undermine any monetary policy regime.

**Dollarization in Ecuador** Some countries just give up and adopt the currency of another country for all their transactions, completely eliminating their own monetary policy. While this approach is commonly known as dollarization, it need not be based on the dollar. Monaco, the small country for the rich and famous on the southern coast of France, adopted the French franc in 1865 and uses the euro today.

Monaco is very small, covering less than 50 square miles (about twice the size of Manhattan), with a population of only 30,000. Ecuador, with a population of 13 million spread over 100,000 square miles, is another story. In 1999, Ecuador experienced a severe financial crisis. Real GDP fell more than 7 percent, the inflation rate rose to 50 percent, the banking system nearly collapsed, and the currency, the *sucre*, went into freefall, losing two-thirds of its value relative to the dollar in a year. In January 2000, Ecuador officially gave up its currency. Within six months, the central bank had bought back all the sucres in circulation. Almost immediately, interest rates dropped, the banking system re-established itself, inflation fell dramatically, and growth resumed. Ecuador's move to dollarization was successful enough that a year later El Salvador followed suit. Panama has been dollarized since 1904.

Why would a country choose to give up its currency? In the case of a small emerging-market country, there are a host of reasons. First, with no exchange rate, there is no risk of an exchange rate crisis—no possibility of either a large depreciation or a sudden capital outflow motivated by the fear of depreciation. Second, using dollars or euros or yen can help a country to become integrated into world markets, increasing its trade and investment. Finally, by rejecting the possibility of inflationary finance, a country can reduce the risk premium it must pay on loans and generally strengthen its financial institutions. But it does need to find some way to get the dollars it will need to keep the monetary base growing, which can prove to be a challenge.

The benefits of dollarization are balanced against the loss of revenue that comes from issuing currency—what is called *seignorage*. Remember, printing a $100 bill costs only a few cents. Before dollarization, issuing currency generated seignorage revenue for Ecuador; since dollarizing, because Ecuador now uses U.S. currency, it forgoes that revenue, which goes to the United States. Second, dollarization effectively eliminates the central bank as the lender of last resort because, again, the Federal Reserve, not the Central Bank of Ecuador, prints dollars. If a banking emergency arises in Ecuador, the government will need to find some way to get dollars to provide the needed liquidity. (This is the problem Argentina solved by paying large U.S. banks for standby letters of credit.) Third, there is the loss of autonomous monetary or exchange rate policy. But since foreign investors' lack of confidence in domestic policymakers was what created Ecuador's crisis, it is hard to see that loss as a serious one. Finally, any country that adopts the dollar as its currency gets U.S. monetary policy, like it or not. Obviously, this drawback is least worrisome for countries whose economies are closely tied to that of the United States. While it might make sense for countries like Mexico or Canada, for Ecuador the decision isn't so clear.[10]

Note that dollarization is not the same as a monetary union. The decision by European countries to create a common currency, the euro, was fundamentally different from a country's decision to adopt the dollar. When the FOMC makes its decisions, the affairs of Ecuador and El Salvador carry no weight. And as we have already noted, dollarized countries forgo the revenue from issuing currency and are forced to make special arrangements to provide emergency loans to domestic banks. In contrast, all European countries participating in the monetary union take part in monetary policy decisions, and all share in the revenue that comes from printing euros. Europe's national banks still operate as lenders of last resort in making euro loans. In sum, a monetary union is shared governance; dollarization is not.

## Canada's Choice of Exchange Rate Regime

Canada abandoned the gold standard during the Great Depression and was a party to the Bretton Woods agreement in 1944, but unlike most industrial countries Canada experimented with a floating exchange rate during the Bretton Woods period. Immediately after the War, the Canadian dollar was fixed to the U.S. dollar at par, but three years later speculative capital outflows forced the government to devalue the dollar to US$.90. Just a year later the military buildup caused by the Korean war led to increases in commodity prices and a capital inflow to Canada. If the inflows weren't sterilized, then the Canadian money stock and prices would rise. As people realized that the Canadian government would not allow inflation to rise, they anticipated a revaluation of the dollar and began speculating on such a rise. This exacerbated the problem as it meant more capital inflows and the government felt that it was in a quandary. It didn't want to raise the value of the Canadian dollar that it had just lowered, and did not want to accept the inflation, so it adopted a floating exchange rate.

In the context of Bretton Woods this made Canada somewhat of a maverick. The IMF was strongly advocating fixed exchange rates, so the Canadian government was careful to say that the floating exchange rate was a temporary policy to be kept in place until the appropriate value of the dollar was clearer. In fact, the temporary policy lasted from 1950 to 1962, and later Canada's success with a floating rate became

---

[10] While Ecuador formally dollarized, other countries dollarize informally as more and more people use the U.S. dollar or other foreign currency. As the hyperinflation in Zimbabwe worsened, people started refusing payment in Zimbabwe dollars and expecting payment in U.S. dollars. The government accepted this and began licensing some industries to transact in U.S. dollars. Time will tell if Zimbabwe moves to official dollarization or introduces another monetary policy reform.

# IN THE NEWS

## Making Sense of Currency Union with the United States: Herein Lies a Bluffer's Guide to a Fixed Dollar

# Financial Post: Canada

By Jacqueline Thorpe

Date: September 28, 2001

Whenever the Canadian dollar brushes its historic low, it raises the question of whether some form of currency association with the U.S. dollar makes economic sense.

Fixed-currency regimes have been tried through much of the last century and much of the world, and various countries —Hong Kong and Argentina, for example—have tied their currencies to the U.S. dollar. The Canadian dollar has itself been a fixed currency at various times, either to gold or the U.S. dollar. Most recently, between 1962 and 1970 it was fixed at U.S.92.50 cents with a fluctuation band of plus or minus 1 percent.

Many observers like the status quo. They argue a floating exchange rate is better because it offers flexibility in dealing with internal and external shocks. It also gives Canada much more flexibility in adjusting monetary policy when needed.

But many economists and public-policy experts have argued persuasively in recent years for currency union, saying it reduces the cost and risk of doing business with the United States and would make Canadian companies more competitive. Here's how.

## The Case for a Fixed Currency

• Canada would benefit from the superior monetary policy of the U.S. Federal Reserve. Many economists say that argument has diminished as the Bank of Canada has improved its inflation-fighting credentials. Canadian interest rates have moved largely in tandem with U.S. rates over the past few years.

• A fixed currency would save the cost of converting currency back and forth between Canadian and U.S. dollars. According to some estimates, it costs Canadian businesses and travellers $3-billion a year in foreign-exchange transaction costs (0.3 percent of Canada's GDP), and those costs are increasing as our trade with the United States increases.

• If—against current odds—the Canadian dollar rises, then the profits a Canadian company makes selling its products in the United States decreases. Of course, when the dollar falls further, the company gets a foreign exchange gain. (Companies use a range of foreign-exchange derivatives to mitigate against the negative effects of currency fluctuation.)

• The low Canadian dollar insulates companies from making the technology improvements that have radically improved U.S. productivity. At the same time, the productivity enhancing computers and equipment that so benefited U.S. companies are too expensive to import. (Others doubt that a fixed currency would induce a com-

part of the argument for the widespread abandonment of fixed exchange rates in the early 1970s. The floating period ended in 1962 following the Coyne Affair (see Chapter 16) and from 1962 to 1970 the Canadian dollar was pegged at US$0.925.

Then again in 1970, wartime expenditures (this time for the Vietnam War) drove up commodity prices and led to capital inflows into Canada. The government had to choose between allowing these inflationary pressures or letting the value of the Canadian dollar rise. The government again chose a "temporary" floating exchange rate, and the dollar appreciated from US$0.925 to US$0.97. But unlike the 1950s Canada's action was soon followed by the major industrial countries and after 1973 the Bretton Woods system was essentially dismantled.

At the beginning of the 21st century, Canada has been on a flexible exchange rate for 30 years, but the choice of exchange rate system continues to be debated. The costs of exchange rate volatility encouraged some economists to advocate a monetary union pany to make productivity improvements.) It's nice to have a Canadian dollar cushion your profit margin, but why would you be satisfied with a 10 percent profit margin if you could bump it up to 15 percent?

- Some say excessive currency appreciation is a disadvantage to Canadian companies. The run-up in the dollar from just over U.S.70 cents in 1986 to near U.S.90 cents in 1992 increased Canadian labour costs by nearly 40 percent, swamping any productivity improvements.

- Canadian businesses suffer when the currency is misaligned in either direction. Currency union would highlight Canadian business's weak points [and] spur improvements.

- When Canadian currency is overvalued, as in the late 1980s, many companies fled to the United States. When it is undervalued, there is risk of a brain drain to the United States, forcing Canadian companies to either raise wages or follow the brains over the border.

## The Options

If Canada were to form some sort of currency union with the United States, there are many ways it could be approached

- Exchange rate targets, pegs and fixed-exchange rates ...

- Currency board ...

- Dollarization ...

- Currency union: The NAMU (North American Monetary Union), or the Amero, would see Canada and the United States forming a currency similar to the EMU. Canada would have a vote on a supranational central bank. Its clout, however, would likely be minor because of its relative size. This rankles many.

**LESSONS OF THE ARTICLE**

There is no simple answer to the question of what exchange rate regime Canada should choose. In the text we describe the options presented here. The political unlikelihood of a currency union and the consensus that only "hard" pegs are likely to be effective implies that the choice is between a flexible exchange rate and de facto dollarization. The debate about currency union flourished in the early years of the 21st century when the Canadian dollar depreciated to nearly US$0.60 (look back to Figure 10.1 on page 203), but then died away as the dollar appreciated. The recent increase in the volatility of the Canadian dollar may regenerate the debate.

SOURCE: "*Making Sense of Currency Union with the United States: Herein Lies a Bluffer's Guide to a Fixed Dollar,*" Jacqueline Thorpe, Financial Post, Sept. 28, 2001. *Material reprinted with the express permission of "The National Post Company,*" *a CanWest Partnership.*

with the United States (see In the News: Making Sense of Currency Union with the United States, above). Others have argued that the flexibility of the exchange rate gives Canada the ability to absorb terms of trade shocks with lower real costs. The form of monetary union is also not clear—would Canada dollarize like Ecuador, or would the United States agree to a North American currency along the lines of the euro (extremely unlikely). With its own currency, Canada can choose a rate of inflation, can credibly act as a lender of last resort for Canadian financial institutions, and can let the exchange rate help the economy adjust to terms of trade shocks. We will let the former Governor of the Bank of Canada David Dodge, have the final word:

*Our empirical analysis shows that these adjustment benefits are quite large during periods of significant shocks. But there is no free lunch. There are costs involved in choosing a floating currency, and these could be avoided under dollarization. These include the costs of currency transactions and the need to mitigate currency risk—costs that can be considerable. At the present time, however, the adjustment benefits clearly outweigh the costs. This is an empirical statement, not a philosophical one. It is possible that, at some future time, the structures of our two economies could converge to the point that the reverse would be true. But for now, and as far into the future as I can see, the floating exchange rate is the best choice for Canada given the degree of integration of the Canadian and U.S. markets for goods and services and labour.*[11]

[11] "Dollarization and North American Integration," Remarks by David Dodge to the Chambre de commerce du Québec, Sherbrooke, Quebec. October 2002.

## Terms

Bretton Woods, 516
capital controls, 506
currency board, 519
dollarization, 519
foreign exchange
   intervention, 510
gold standard, 515
hard pegs, 518

speculative attack, 514
sterilized foreign
   exchange
   intervention, 511
unsterilized foreign
   exchange
   intervention, 511

## Chapter Summary

1. When capital flows freely across a country's borders, fixing the exchange rate means giving up domestic monetary policy.
   a. Purchasing power parity implies that in the long run, exchange rates are tied to inflation differentials across countries.
   b. Capital market arbitrage means that in the short run, the exchange rate is tied to differences in interest rates.
   c. Monetary policymakers can have only two of the following three options: open capital markets, control of domestic interest rates, and a fixed exchange rate.

2. Central banks can intervene in foreign exchange markets.
   a. When they do, it affects their balance sheet in the same way as an open market operation.
   b. Foreign exchange intervention affects the exchange rate by changing domestic interest rates. This is called unsterilized intervention.
   c. A sterilized intervention is a purchase or sale of foreign exchange reserves that leaves the central bank's liabilities unchanged. It has no impact on the exchange rate.

3. The decision to fix the exchange rate has costs, benefits, and risks.
   a. Both corporations and investors benefit from predictable exchange rates.
   b. Fixed exchange rates can reduce domestic inflation by importing the monetary policy of a country with low inflation.
   c. Flexible exchange rates allow countries to have an independent monetary policy and offset some of the impact of terms of trade shocks on aggregate demand.
   c. Fixed exchange rate regimes are fragile and leave countries open to speculative attacks.
   d. The right conditions for choosing to fix the exchange rate include
      i. A poor reputation for inflation control.
      ii. An economy that is well integrated with the one to whose currency the rate is fixed.
      iii. A high level of foreign exchange reserves.

4. After the collapse of Bretton Woods, many economists argued that the only viable fixed exchange rate regimes were hard pegs such as dollarization or a currency board.
   a. With a currency board, the central bank holds enough foreign currency reserves to exchange the entire monetary base at the promised exchange rate. Argentina had a currency board in the 1990s but it collapsed when the regional governments began printing their own money.
   b. Dollarization is the total conversion of an economy from its own currency to the currency of another country.

5. Canada has a flexible exchange rate and a policy of intervening to support the Canadian dollar only in exceptional circumstances.

# Conceptual Problems

1. Explain the mechanics of a speculative attack.

2. Assume that the interest rate on one-year Japanese government bonds is 2 percent, one-year Canadian government bonds pay 3 percent, and the exchange rate is 100 yen per dollar.
   a. Assuming the yen–dollar exchange rate is fixed, explain how you could make a riskless profit.
   b. Assuming the yen–dollar exchange rate is a floating rate, what would you expect it to be in one year?

3. In 1997, the Bank of Thailand was maintaining a fixed exchange rate at 26 baht to the dollar. At the same time, Thai interest rates were substantially higher than those in Japan. Thai bankers were borrowing money in Japan and lending it in Thailand.
   a. Why was this transaction profitable?
   b. What risks were associated with this method of financing?
   c. Describe the impact of a depreciation of the baht on the balance sheets of Thai banks involved in these transactions.

4. During the time of the currency board, Argentinean banks offered accounts in both dollars and pesos, but loans were made largely in pesos. Describe the impact on banks of the collapse of the currency board.

5. Investors became nervous just before the 2002 Brazilian presidential election. As a result, the risk premium on Brazilian government debt increased dramatically and Brazil's currency depreciated significantly.
   a. How could concern over an election drive up the risk premium?
   b. How was the risk premium connected to the value of the currency?

6. During the Asian financial crisis in the summer and fall of 1997, investors became concerned that the Hong Kong Monetary Authority would not be able to maintain its currency board. As a result, the overnight interest rate in Hong Kong rose to about 200 percent. Explain this phenomenon.

7.* Explain why a central bank is usually more effective at holding the value of its domestic currency at an artificially low level for a sustained period than at an artificially high level.

8. When asked about the value of the dollar, the Governor of the Bank of Canada answers, "The foreign exchange policy of Canada is the responsibility of the Minister of Finance; I have no comment." Discuss this answer.

9.* Explain why a consensus has developed that countries should either allow their exchange rates to float freely or adopt a hard peg as an exchange rate regime.

10. Explain the costs and benefits of dollarization. Could a dollarized regime collapse?

# Analytical Problems

11. You observe that two countries with a fixed exchange rate have current inflation rates that differ from each other. You check the recent historical data and find that inflation differentials have been present for several months and that they have not remained constant. How would you explain these observations in light of the theory of purchasing power parity?

12.* The model in Chapters 18 and 19 assumed a flexible exchange rate. How would you modify it to capture the case of a fixed exchange rate?

13. Assuming the country is open to international capital flows, which of the following combinations of monetary and exchange rate policies are viable? Explain your reasoning.
    a. A domestic interest rate as a policy instrument and a floating exchange rate.
    b. A domestic interest rate as a policy instrument and a fixed exchange rate.
    c. The monetary base as a policy instrument and a floating exchange rate.

14. Show the impact on the Bank of Canada's balance sheet of a foreign-exchange market intervention where the Bank sells $1,000 worth of foreign exchange reserves. Explain what impact, if any, the intervention will have on the domestic money supply.

15. If the Bank of Canada decides to sterilize the foreign-exchange market intervention described in question 14, show the impact on the Bank's

---

* Indicates more difficult problems.

balance sheet. What would the overall impact be on the monetary base? What would be the impact, if any, on the exchange rate?

16. Use a supply-and-demand diagram for dollars to show the impact of an increase in Canadian interest rates relative to interest rates in the United States in the wake of a foreign-exchange market intervention by the Bank of Canada.

17.* Consider a small open economy with a wide array of trading partners all operating in different currencies. The economy's business cycles are not well synchronized with any of the world's largest economies and the policymakers in this country have a well-earned reputation for being fiscally prudent and honest. In your view, should this small open economy adopt a fixed exchange rate regime?

18. A small eastern European economy asks your opinion about whether it should pursue the path to joining the European Economic and Monetary Union (EMU) or simply "euroize" (i.e., dollarize by using the euro for all domestic transactions). What advice would you give?

## CHAPTER 23

# Monetary Policy and Financial Crisis

During the 18 years from 1991 to 2008, the Canadian economy grew by nearly 50 percent while inflation was low and stable. The government had eliminated the fiscal deficit and the unemployment rate had fallen to levels that most economists considered full employment. Economists spoke of the "Great Moderation" and monetary policymakers were given much of the credit for that stability. But beneath the calm, pressure was building along the fault lines of the global economy and in 2007 the pressure began to be visible. By September 2008 the global economy was in crisis and Canada, although faring better than many countries, was not immune. Canadian real GDP fell in the last quarter of 2008 and in the first half of 2009, and by the end of June 2009 was 3.2 percent lower than a year earlier.

The crisis had its epicentre in the United States and came to a head in September 2008 when, in a single week, a major investment bank (Lehman Brothers) failed, the other investment banks quickly became commercial banks to ensure that they were eligible for Federal Reserve support, and the Federal Reserve provided emergency support to an insolvent insurance company (AIG). As banks everywhere wondered if their counterparts would still exist the next day, the interbank market and consequently other short-term markets, froze—and not just in the United States. Banks operate globally and the liquidity crisis spread globally too. Central banks provided emergency liquidity and sometimes capital; governments increased deposit insurance limits (sometimes providing insurance for wholesale as well as retail deposits) and lowered interest rates. These actions did restore liquidity to credit markets but most OECD countries fell into a recession and the economic impact of the financial crisis continued for many months.

The financial crisis shocked economists and policymakers, but a little perspective shows that crises are a persistent feature of financial markets. A popular history of financial panics lists the Dutch Tulip Bubble of 1636 as the first large bubble, followed by the South Sea Bubble (UK) and the Mississippi Bubble (France) in 1720.[1] Even if we stick to the late 20th century, we could list the 1987 stock market crash (United States), the Japanese stock market bubble and crash (the Nikkei fell by roughly 50 percent in 1990), the Asian financial crisis in 1997, and the dot.com crash in 2001. Many crises share common features, such as expansionary monetary policy and rapid financial innovation (and unheeded warnings of trouble!) but at other times the same features are innocuous.

Through this book, we have built up a stock of knowledge of the financial system and of the powers of the central bank. Now we use this knowledge to look at the origins of the crisis and the responses of the policymakers. In Chapters 18 and 19, we described the conduct of monetary policy assuming that the economy was functioning "normally." However, 2008 and 2009 were anything but normal economic times, and central banks around the globe (both individually and collectively) turned to new, or at least long-disused, instruments of monetary policy.

We set the scene by describing the stability of the macroeconomy in the years leading up to the crisis and then survey the sources of financial market pressures that led to the crisis. We have discussed many of these as we described the financial system throughout

---

[1] Charles Kindleberger and Robert Z. Aliber (2005) *Manias, Panics and Crashes, A History of Financial Crises*, Wiley Investment Classics, p. 9.

the book. Indeed, many economists had commented on these sources of fragility, but it is a long way from commentary to corrective action. And few appreciated how the combined weaknesses would create such devastation. After providing a brief timeline of the worst months of the crisis, we look at how the Federal Reserve and the Bank of Canada responded. We conclude the chapter looking forward to how financial market regulation may change over the next few years.

## Prelude to the Crisis—the Great Moderation

Monetary policy seemed rather mundane in the early years of this century. Economists spoke of "the Great Moderation" in the volatility of real growth and it seemed as though the policymakers had figured out how to keep the economy on a stable growth path—the economist's version of the "end of history."[2] The last two decades were remarkable. Information technology came of age, bringing the benefits of computerization into our lives through everything from cars to dishwashers. Thanks to the Internet, incredible libraries are now available to us in our homes and offices.

From 1991 to 2007 the Canadian economy did not suffer a single year of decline in output. During these years of phenomenal growth, inflation fell steadily, from more than 5 percent in 1991 to less than 2 percent by the end of the decade. If you look back at Figures 19.1 on page 427 and 19.6 on page 434 you can see that both inflation and growth became substantially less variable than they were 20+ years ago.[3]

This prosperity and stability was shared across the industrialized world. Data from the 63 countries for which we have reliable information show that inflation dropped dramatically between the 1980s and the 1990s. Median inflation fell from an average annual rate of 7 percent in the period 1985–1994 to 3 percent in the period 1995–1999. The decline in average inflation was even sharper, from 83 percent to just 8½ percent. Inflation rose in only 10 of the 63 countries.[4]

This moderation happened despite turbulence in global financial markets. Major economic crises occurred in Latin America and Asia, and Long-Term Capital Management, a U.S. hedge fund nearly collapsed, paralyzing the bond markets. Raw materials prices fluctuated wildly. The price of oil spiked at more than $35 a barrel late in 1990, then plunged below $12 a barrel at the end of 1998 before beginning a steady rise to over $100 a barrel in 2008.

If the size and frequency of external disturbances did not diminish, something must have cushioned

SOURCE: © The New Yorker Collection 1990. Kenneth Mahood from cartoonbank.com. All Rights Reserved.

[2] In 1989 Francis Fukuyama wrote an influential essay called "The End of History" (Summer, 1989, *The National Interest*) suggesting that the history of humankind had been a search for the best form of government and ,following the Fall of the Berlin Wall, liberal democracy was revealed to be the final and best form. The thesis has been contested on both empirical and theoretical grounds.

[3] A similar decline in the United States is documented in detail by Margaret M. McConnell and Gabriel Perez Quiros in "Output Fluctuations in the United States: What Has Changed since the Early 1980s?" *American Economic Review* 90 (December 2000), pp. 1464–1476.

[4] Remember that the median is the middle value; if the inflation rates of the 63 countries were ranked from highest to lowest then the median would be the 32nd value in the list. The median is much less influenced by extreme outliers than the mean, which explains why the mean in the 1985–1994 period is so much higher than the median.

the blows. Economists have suggested that part of the stability reflected advances in information technology, which increased manufacturers' flexibility in responding to changes in demand. The result has been a dramatic decline in inventories at every stage of the production process. In durable manufacturing, the new supply method called "just-in-time" cut the ratio of inventories to sales in half in the period from the early 1990s to the beginning of 2002. Today, an automobile assembly plant keeps only a few hours worth of parts on hand; the rest are in transit to the factory, timed to arrive at just the right moment. Similarly, a supermarket or superstore such as the Bay or Loblaws holds only one to two days' supply of most products. The result is a great deal of flexibility in responding to changes in demand and sales.

In addition, the monetary authorities in Canada and other countries took credit for the stability of the economy, arguing that monetary policy delivered a low and stable inflation rate that helped to keep real growth high and stable. With hindsight, some argue that monetary policy might have been too powerful and created the conditions for short-term growth at the expense of longer-term stability.

## The Negative Undercurrents

Financial crises are almost definitionally characterized by an absence of liquidity in key markets and an excess of leverage in significant financial institutions, but the source of these features can differ. In the years leading up to the crisis in September 2008, low interest rates encouraged investors to seek ways to increase returns. We know from Chapter 5 that increasing leverage is one way to increase returns but that it also increases risk. The search for higher returns also led to new financial instruments that (intentionally or otherwise) obscured the extent of leverage and risk taking from both investors and regulators, and increased the vulnerability of the economy. As the crisis evolved, the opacity of these new instruments reduced the liquidity in many financial markets, amplifying the initial events.

We will begin by looking at the sources of low interest rates and then focus on the financial system and how it is regulated. As we go through the discussion, we will emphasize the role of information, and you should keep in mind Principle 3: "Information is the basis of decisions," and its implication: that the quality of decision making depends completely on the quality of the information.

### Search for Yield

From 2002 to 2005, real (and nominal) interest rates were at long-term lows. For borrowers this was a great thing; for savers, "not so much." Although not equally beneficial for everyone, there is nothing inherently problematic about low interest rates. But if the low interest rates reflected global imbalances, unsustainably accommodative monetary policy, or a mispricing of risk, then low interest rates could be followed by financial difficulties. We look at each possibility in turn and find that, indeed, each played a role.

**Global Imbalances**   One key factor was high rates of saving—exceeding 50 percent—in China, the world's second-largest (2009) and fastest-growing economy. In a global environment with open capital markets, high savings in a large economy will reduce interest rates globally. The investment opportunities in China could not absorb all these savings, which meant that they were available for consumption or investment elsewhere. As we discussed in Chapter 22 (see Applying the Concept: The Balance of Payments and "Global Imbalances": on page 518) China had a surplus in the current account (exports exceeded imports) and a deficit in the capital account (net purchases of foreign assets). In contrast, the United States had a balance of trade deficit (imports exceeded exports) and a capital account surplus (net sales of financial assets).

This situation was inherently unstable. Recall what this scenario implies. Each month the United States was buying goods from the rest of the world, and paying for them with IOUs. At some point, either sellers of goods will stop taking IOUs (the gradual case) or the holders of those IOUs will ask to cash them in (the hard-landing case). Either way, the U.S. economy would have to start consuming less instead of more than it produced. In China, a couple of factors stalled the market's adjustment mechanisms: the exchange rate channel did not operate because the Chinese had a fixed (or almost fixed) exchange rate with the United States, and the monetary channel (whereby the purchase of foreign exchange acts like an expansionary open market operation driving up prices in China) did not operate as the Chinese sterilized the foreign exchange purchases.

The buildup of reserves in China, and the constant current account deficit in the United States did not go unnoticed. Many economists worried about the "global imbalances" and hoped that the adjustment would be gradual rather than sudden. Look at the remarks of David Dodge, then Governor of the Bank of Canada speaking in Chicago in May 2007 to the Chicago Council on Global Affairs:

> The word "global" is the key to seeing both the nature of the problem and the path to its solution. There is no single cause of these imbalances. In China and many other Asian countries, we have seen very high levels of net savings ... The U.S. economy is in the reverse situation. Over the past few years, the United States has become a large net borrower, as government deficits rose and household savings fell. As a result, we have seen lower desired savings relative to desired investment in the United States. In the future, these global imbalances will have to be corrected through an increase of net savings in the United States and a reduction of net savings in Asia and in the oil-exporting countries.
>
> But, given the recent behaviour of international financial markets, and based on recent commentary, one might start to think that global imbalances are no longer something to be concerned about ... However, I worry that it is far too early to start discounting the threat posed by the persistence of global imbalances.[5]

**Accommodative Monetary Policy**  While the high level of savings tended to depress interest rates generally, at the short end of the maturity spectrum monetary policy was an additional force keeping interest rates low. In studies of past financial crises, accommodative monetary policy is almost invariably found to be part of the causal mechanism, and U.S. monetary policy in the early years of the decade was indeed accommodative. Following the attacks of 9/11 and the collapse of the Tech bubble, Alan Greenspan, then chairman of the board of governors of the Federal Reserve lowered interest rates from 3.5 percent to 1 percent. While the NBER did declare that the U.S. economy was in recession in 2001, it was one of the shortest recessions in history and many credited the recovery to Greenspan's policy.

But the Federal Reserve kept the interest low until 2006. Look back at Figure 19.14 on page 450, which shows the FOMC target rate and the rate of interest implied by the Taylor rule. While from 1991 to 2002 the FOMC target rate stayed close to that proposed by the Taylor Rule, from 2002 to 2006 the FOMC target rate was lower than that given by the Taylor rule, sometimes by more than 2 percent. There is no magic to the Taylor rule, and indeed the FOMC believed that the Taylor Rule's prescrip-

---

[5] Remarks by David Dodge, Governor of the Bank of Canada, to the Chicago Council on Global Affairs, Chicago, Illinois 21 May 2007 http://www.bank-banque-canada.ca/en/speeches/2007/sp07-11.html

tion was too tight, but the difference does provide support for those who believe that monetary policy was too easy in the years before 2007.

Critics of the Federal Reserve's policies argue that by keeping interest rates low the Fed supported a housing price bubble that was a key source of the financial crisis. They argue that the Fed should have responded to the rising stock market and house prices in 2005 and 2006. Indeed, some commentators speak of the Greenspan "put." They argue that his policy of lowering rates aggressively when asset prices collapsed, as in 2001, but not raising rates aggressively when asset prices rose meant that households took on too much risk by assuming that the Fed would always support asset prices.

**Mispricing of Risk**    While global savings would lower interest rates across the maturity spectrum, and accommodative monetary policy would lower short-term interest rates, the pre-crisis years were also characterized by a decrease in credit spreads; a fall in the difference between the interest rates on government securities and corporate bonds. As we saw in Chapter 5, this difference could decline for a number of reasons. If people underestimated the risk of an asset then its risk premium would be low; if the riskiness of a particular asset declined then its risk premium would fall; finally, if people didn't know or understand how risky an asset was then its risk premium might fall.

It is hard to know which of these three factors drove down credit spreads in the early years of the century. At the time it was argued that the amount of risk was decreasing as financial innovations were permitting asset holdings to be more diversified and therefore the risk held by an individual could be reduced. With hindsight, it seems that much of the decrease reflected a lack of information and misunderstanding of the riskiness of complex financial instruments. We return to this below as we look at the role of financial innovation in the crisis.

## Financial Innovation

As with accommodative monetary policy, most financial crises reflect the impact of financial innovation. Often, the issue is that the regulatory authorities have not kept up with the pace of financial innovation and this was the case in the early 21st century.

Financial innovation did not begin in the 21st century, and most of the institutions and assets that are held blameworthy for the crisis were employed before the turn of the century. For example, mortgage-backed securities (MBS) have been traded for nearly 20 years. But in the early years of this century there was a dramatic expansion of their use in the United States. Rather than being restricted to "prime borrowers," financial institutions created subprime MBS, which had the distinction that they could not be purchased by one of the housing finance agencies, Fannie Mae or Freddie Mac. So the MBS were bought by other financial institutions. When financial institutions sold MBS, they pooled the mortgages, but didn't simply sell a share of the pool. They divided the pool up into what were called "tranches." Take an example where there are three equal-sized tranches: the arrangement would be that if there were any mortgage defaults, the first losses would go to those holding the bottom tranche, the so-called "equity tranche." That means that those holding the middle tranche would lose only if more than one-third of the mortgages defaulted; and the top tranche would lose only if two-thirds or more of the mortgages were defaulted on. The top tranche was called the "AAA" tranche as these mortgages were considered virtually risk free.

Activity in the MBS market was influenced by the interaction of the credit rating agencies and the regulatory authorities. In Chapter 14 we described the Basel agreements, which required that banks hold capital in proportion to the riskiness of their portfolios. They did not need to hold capital against AAA assets but needed to

Figure 23.1    A Visual Sense of the Complexity: From Mortgages to Securities

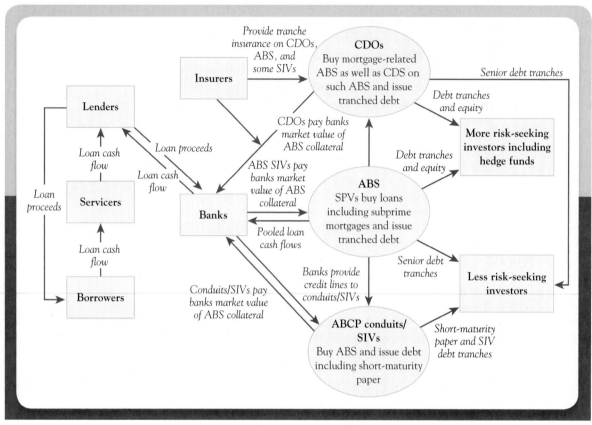

SOURCE: *Adapted from Figure 1.10: Mortgage Market Flows and Risk Exposures, Chapter 1, p. 11. From Global Financial Stability Report, October 2007, International Monetary Fund.*

hold considerable capital against risky loan portfolios. So the banks created subsidiaries that owned these risky loans, getting them off their own balance sheets in the "shadow banking system." If these assets really were off balance sheet then perhaps all would have been well, but when the mortgages started to default, the banks took them back onto their own balance sheet to maintain the reputation of their product line. The result was that they took loan losses, which reduced their capital. The banks then had to either raise capital or reduce their loans—a process called deleveraging.

As with credit default swaps, the securitization of mortgages has the potential to improve the functioning of the financial markets, but only if all parties are informed about the risks that they are taking and have the capacity to take those risks. Figure 23.1 is a sketch of the MBS market. We will not go through each element of the chart but it illustrates the complexity of the arrangements in the market. Again, with hindsight, it is clear that many of those holding MBS were not aware of precisely what risks they were taking.

We can give a couple of examples of how risk was mispriced. Recall from Chapter 5 that institutions measured risk using Value at Risk (VaR) models that were designed to answer how much the institution or an asset class would lose in the worst (say) 5 percent of scenarios. To answer that question you need to compute how likely certain individual events are and how correlated those events are: what are the odds that housing prices fall *and* the exchange rate declines, for example? To measure the correlations, institutions used the experience of the last 10 or 20 years, which is not long enough to measure the probability of events that occur only once every 20 years on average. In the crisis, when returns on one class of assets fell, banks needing liquidity sold other assets, lowering their prices and resulting in much more correlation than the models had anticipated.

Another example is the insurance provided by "monoline insurers." A monoline insurer is a company that sells insurance against credit default. So if you were holding a municipal bond but were worried that the municipality might default (or wanted to raise the credit rating of your portfolio) then you could buy a credit default swap from an insurance company. This intermediation separated two functions of loans—to share risk and to store value. Traditional insurance companies hold a portfolio of risks and so are not vulnerable if one risk defaults, but the monoline companies insured only an array of financial assets; when some assets were defaulted on, the insurance on all the rest evaporated.

While it is of course easy with hindsight to see how innovations were creating vulnerabilities in the financial sector, there were certainly warning signs in advance. Consider the commentary in the Annual Report of the Bank of International Settlements, (the central bankers' central bank) in June 2007, which raised concerns about both the shadow banking system and the broadly accommodative monetary policy:

> *A closely related concern is the possibility that banks have, either intentionally or inadvertently, retained a significant degree of credit risk on their books. Assuming that the big banks have managed to distribute more widely the risks inherent in the loans they have made, who now holds these risks, and can they manage them adequately? The honest answer is that we do not know. Much of the risk is embodied in various forms of asset-backed securities of growing complexity and opacity. They have been purchased by a wide range of smaller banks, pension funds, insurance companies, hedge funds, other funds and even individuals, who have been encouraged to invest by the generally high ratings given to these instruments. Unfortunately, the ratings reflect only expected credit losses, and not the unusually high probability of tail events that could have large effects on market values. Hedge funds might be most exposed, since many have tended to specialise in purchases of the riskiest sorts of these instruments, and their inherent leverage can in consequence be very high. It is not, by definition, possible to put all these uncertainties together and arrive at a prediction. Rather, if one believes that a range of possible developments could all interact in various ways, such interactions could form the basis of a thousand stories. Yet it must be noted that behind each set of concerns lurks the common factor of the highly accommodating financial conditions noted in the Introduction.*[6]

Many others raised concerns but very few suspected how badly the economy would fare in 2008—and raising concerns is very different from prompt corrective action.

## Regulatory Environment

In Chapter 14 we saw that the government's role in the financial system is to safeguard the stability of the financial system, and that it does this in part by providing deposit insurance and acting as a lender of last resort. We went on to argue that by providing those facilities the monetary authority creates moral hazard (i.e., reduces the incentive that financial institutions have to be careful in taking risks and that therefore the authorities regulate and supervise the financial system).

[6] *The BIS 2007 Annual Report*; June 2007, p. 145.

But, almost by definition, regulation means restricting businesses from doing what they want to do, and many will find a way around that regulation. The use of the shadow banking system to reduce the apparent risks that the banks were taking is one example of that process.

**Systemically Important Financial Institutions**   Lender-of-last-resort policies were traditionally viewed as advocating the provision of liquidity to solvent banks, with an emphasis on "'solvent" and on "banks." This made sense when banks were uniquely central to the financial system and when no bank was large enough to imperil the financial system By the 21st century there were critically important nonbank institutions; in the United States these included investment banks and the monoline insurers. Furthermore, some of those institutions had become large enough that, at least in the eyes of Fed officials, their failure could have devastating consequences for the financial system; they were "too big to fail." The emergence of large systemically important nonbank financial institutions mattered because these institutions were not regulated by the Federal Reserve, and had leverage ratios far in excess of those permitted the banks. Remember that an institution with a high leverage ratio loses a much greater proportion of its capital than a institution with a low leverage ratio for a given loss. When losses on, for example, MBS began to occur, the highly leveraged U.S. investment banks were particularly hard hit.

# The Financial Crisis Unfolds

Symptoms of the financial crisis began to show in early 2007, but it was not until 18 months later that the crisis reached its nadir in September 2008. The economic consequences took longer to emerge and show signs of persisting further beyond 2009. We present a brief timeline of the financial crisis beginning with the events in the United States and then discussing the Canadian and international experience.

## The Crisis in the United States

With hindsight we can see the first signs of the crisis in the United States when house prices fell, reducing the asset value of some sub-prime mortgages and leading to tightening in the mortgage market. Table 23.1 traces some of the key events as the crisis unfolded (see http://timeline.stlouisfed.org for many more details, with a U.S. focus). The decision in August 2007 by a French bank to halt redemptions in subprime-related mortgage funds, and the subsequent widening of credit spreads, made investors aware of the potential breadth of the financial market's problems including the extent of opacity in the markets, the potential interconnectedness of financial institution balance sheets, and the international reach of subprime problems.

In March 2008 the Federal Reserve announced that it was providing support to facilitate the purchase of Bear Stearns by JP Morgan Chase.[7] Bear Sterns was an investment bank that managed many funds that had considerable exposure to subprime mortgages. As an investment bank, Bear was not traditionally eligible for support from the Federal Reserve, but the situation was one that called for a lender of last resort: Bear faced a liquidity crisis and it was hugely interconnected with other

---

[7] The Federal Reserve Bank of New York provided a $29 billion guarantee on $30 billion of assets, but JP Morgan would take the first $1billion in losses on the portfolio. The U.S. Treasury agreed to backstop the New York Fed. For details see Stephen D. Cecchetti ,"Crisis and Responses: The Federal Reserve in the Early Stages of the Financial Crisis," *Journal of Economic Perspectives*, Vol. 23, 1, Winter 2009, pp 51–75.

**Table 23.1**   Some Key Events in the Financial Crisis of 2007–9

| February 2007 | Freddie Mac tightened criteria for buying subprime mortgages |
|---|---|
| June 2007 | Moody's and S&P place securities backed by subprime mortgages on credit watch |
| July 2007 | Bear Stearns liquidates two hedge funds invested in MBS |
| August 2007 | BNP Paribas—France's largest bank—halts redemptions in 3 large investment funds exposed to U.S. subprime mortgages |
| August 2007 | Non-bank ABCP market in Canada freezes; $32 billion commercial paper stops trading |
| September 2007 | Northern Rock (U.K. Bank) receives support from Bank of England |
| February 2008 | Northern Rock taken over by U.K. government |
| March 2008 | Bear Stearns "purchased" by JP Morgan Chase with support from Fed |
| June 2008 | S&P downgrades debt of two monoline insurers |
| July 2008 | Fed Board approval for New York Fed to lend to Fannie Mae and Freddie Mac if necessary |
| September 7, 2008 | Fannie Mae and Freddie Mac placed in government conservatorship |
| September 15, 2008 | Lehman Bros files for bankruptcy protection |
| September 15, 2008 | Bank of America announces it will buy Merrill Lynch |
| September 16, 2008 | AIG receives loan from New York Federal Reserve |
| September 16, 2008 | Primary Reserve Money market mutual fund "breaks the buck" |
| September 21, 2008 | Fed approves Goldman Sachs and Morgan Stanley applications to become bank holding companies |
| September 2008 | Washington Mutual and Wachovia (two large banks) are sold with assistance from the FDIC |
| October 2008 | FDIC raised deposit insurance limit to $250,000 |
| October 2008 | Icelandic Banks taken over by government; German banks receive government support |

SOURCE: *Federal Reserve Bank of St. Louis.*

elements of the financial system. (The liquidity crisis arose partly because of the significant amount of leverage the company held, roughly 1:35. Remember that the capital asset ratios mandated by Basel II were imposed on commercial banks, not investment banks.) The Federal Reserve argued that the interdependency between Bear Sterns and the rest of the financial system made it a systemically important financial institution and that this justified the Fed's support for the transaction.

Economists had a mixed reaction to the support for Bear Stearns, with some arguing that the Fed was right to keep the system going and others arguing that the action set a dangerous precedent. One of the goals of lender-of-last-resort policies is to stem future runs on banks. Remember that deposits in investment banks are not insured although investment banks, just like commercial banks, have liquidity risk. Their deposits can be pulled out a lot more quickly than their assets can be liquidated. If Bear Stearns had failed, there would have been knock-on effects as those who were owed money by the company were not repaid. On the other hand many of those people had been paid handsomely for taking risks and some economists argued that they should not be supported by taxpayer money. The tradeoff between the viability of the financial system (a good) and support for those who, at least ex post, made poor decisions (an outcome that generates moral hazard and is often viewed as unfair) would be replayed throughout the crisis.

The week of September 15, 2008, changed the U.S. financial system forever. In early September 2008 Lehman Bros., another large investment bank, with assets of $600 billion, needed to roll over about $100 billion per month. On September 15, the company filed for bankruptcy protection, the largest bankruptcy in U.S. history. Simultaneously, Merrill Lynch was purchased by Bank of America. Lehman's bankruptcy wiped out the value of its commercial paper. The next day, a large money market mutual fund holding that commercial paper—whose shares investors had believed would never fall below $1—fell to $0.97: "broke the buck" in the language of the markets. On the same day, AIG, an insurance company with huge exposures to credit default swaps, turned to the Federal Reserve, which again acted as a lender of last resort to a financial institution outside its normal lending purview. The following week the two remaining large investment banks—Goldman Sachs and Morgan Stanley—applied to become bank holding companies. While this would make them subject to Fed regulation, it gave them the right to Federal Reserve liquidity support. Later in the month two of the largest commercial banks failed and were sold with the assistance of the FDIC. The Federal Reserve introduced a range of new support programs, which we will discuss below, and the Treasury introduced the troubled asset relief program (TARP), which enabled the Treasury to inject capital into financial institutions. Within three months $170 billion had been invested in the banking system. Economists who had had reservations about the Fed's support for the Bear Stearns takeover had even more questions about the government's sudden ownership stake in the financial sector.

## The Financial Crisis in the Rest of the World

The potential severity of the financial crisis became evident in Canada in August 2007 when issuers of non-bank-supported ABCP were unable to roll over their paper. Although initially it was thought that that $32 billion problem could be resolved without government funding, as the restructuring debate went on, the financial markets deteriorated and eventually resolution required a guarantee of $8 billion from provincial and federal governments. (See Applying the Concept: The ABCP Debacle on page 137). On the whole, though, the Canadian financial market continued to function well, and throughout the crisis the Canadian banking system has outperformed many others internationally. This is far from saying that Canadian financial institutions were unscathed. Many had exposures to the U.S. housing market, and all took significant loan provisions and saw their capital eroded.

There are many potential sources of the relative success of the Canadian financial system and here we list a few:[8]

- Stable macro foundations—Canada had low inflation, a current account surplus, and no fiscal deficit going into the crisis.
- Strong regulatory environment—for example, OSFI regulates and oversees all systemically important financial institutions in Canada, avoiding the issues of

[8] This section draws on material from Carol Ann Northcott, Graydon Paulin, and Mark White, "Lessons for Banking Reform: A Canadian Perspective," *Central Banking* Volume 19 (4) pp. 43–53.

regulatory arbitrage in the United States; OSFI also imposed higher capital requirements on banks than the Basel minima.

- Strong banks—unlike in the United States, Canadian banks did not use the originate-to-distribute model for mortgages and held few subprime mortgages; all mortgages with loan-to-value ratios less than 80 percent had to be insured—mostly by CMHC, which had government backing; large banks benefited from geographic diversification.

The question of why Canada had such strong fundamentals remains open. In part, (as we discussed in Chapter 13) the different histories of U.S. and Canadian banking explain why the systems evolved differently. In part, the political pressure for affordable housing, leading to the role of Fannie Mae and Freddie Mac, and regulatory acceptance of subprime mortgages and their securitization, explain the vulnerability of the U.S. housing finance sector. Finally, U.S. leadership in financial innovation left the holders of new instruments exposed.

We have focused our discussion of the crisis on the United States, as the global financial centre where many of the problems began, and Canada. But the crisis was a global phenomenon and indeed that explains part of its severity. It also means that part of the response, both immediate and longer term, is necessarily international.

Many of the financial institutions in industrial economies had lent into the United States and had exposures both directly to the U.S. housing market and indirectly to U.S. financial institutions. In emerging-market economies the problem was less that they were directly exposed to asset losses in the industrial world, but that the deleveraging of banks in the United States and other industrial economies led to a sudden withdrawal both of funds and of lines of credit, generating a credit and an exchange rate crisis.

The IMF attempted to ameliorate both conditions with expanded lending facilities. In Iceland, where the banking system had been deregulated in the 1990s and which had become particularly highly leveraged, the three largest banks were put into receivership, and in late 2008 Iceland became the first industrial economy to access IMF loans since the 1970s. The G-20 leaders in April 2009 agreed to triple resources available to the IMF to $750 billion, as well as support a new SDR allocation and provide at least $100 billion of additional lending by the MDBs, and ensure $250 billion of support for trade finance.

## Monetary Policy Responses

The financial crisis led to a collapse of asset prices (such as share prices and real estate prices) around the globe. In the short run, the crisis severely restricted the availability of credit, leading to sharp production cutbacks. In the longer run, consumer confidence declined along with consumer wealth, and consumer spending, particularly on durables, declined in lockstep. Unemployment rates rose sharply and governments went into deficits as a result of stimulus plans and automatic stabilizers. In Canada the high share of income (for households, firms, and governments) from natural resource exports meant that the decline in prices of natural resource prices had a significant negative impact.

The macro model that we built in Chapters 18 and 19 captures the consequences of a decline in investment due to a fall in business prospects and a decline in individuals' confidence in the future. These depress both aggregate expenditure, driving spending down at every level of inflation and the real interest rate, shifting the

### Figure 23.2    The Impact of the Financial Crisis

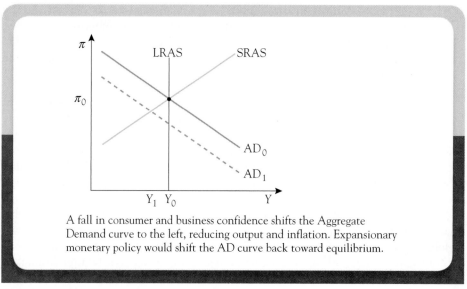

A fall in consumer and business confidence shifts the Aggregate Demand curve to the left, reducing output and inflation. Expansionary monetary policy would shift the AD curve back toward equilibrium.

SOURCE: *Federal Reserve Bank of St. Louis.*

dynamic aggregate demand curve to the left (see Figure 23.2 on page 538). The immediate consequence of this drop in the quantity of aggregate output demanded is that real output falls below potential output, creating a recessionary output gap that puts downward pressure on inflation. Under normal circumstances, monetary policymakers would react to the decline in inflation by cutting the nominal interest rate enough to lower the real interest rate. Their action would increase spending, raise real output, and eliminate the output gap.

But in 2008 inflation was low and to lower the real rate of interest sufficiently would require a negative nominal interest rate. Since anyone can earn a zero nominal interest rate by holding on to a dollar bill, the nominal interest rate can't go below zero—the zero nominal interest bound. In Canada and the United States, the monetary authorities responded with what are known as "unconventional" policies: They expanded their balance sheets, and targeted longer-term interest rates. These policies were effective, but they are not without risk. Central banks lacked any experience with them. Monetary policymaking rests on quantitative estimates of the impact of a change in the target interest rate on the central bank's objectives. While policymakers have some idea of how a 25- or 50-basis-point reduction in their target rate would affect output and inflation over the next year or two, they don't know what the quantitative impact of an unconventional policy option would be. While policymakers can be sure which direction the economy will move, they can't tell how far or how fast.[9] Today policymakers are in uncharted territory.

[9] For an early discussion of Bernanke's views on unconventional monetary policy options, see "Deflation: Making Sure 'It' Doesn't Happen Here," his remarks before the National Economists Club, Washington, D.C., November 21, 2001. The speech is available on the Federal Reserve Board's Web site at http://www.federalreserve.gov.

Figure 23.3   Lowering the Target Fed Funds Rate

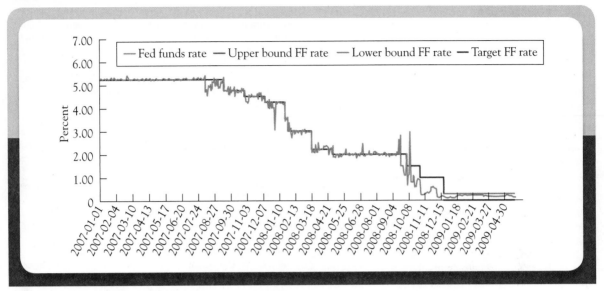

SOURCE: *Federal Reserve Bank of St. Louis*.

## Monetary Policy in the United States

Recall that in normal times the Fed's monetary policy instrument is the target federal funds rate, and it is changed at meetings of the FOMC held about every six weeks. The Federal Reserve initially responded to the crisis using the conventional interest rate instrument, but then moved to a series of unconventional measures as the interest rate approached zero and the crisis became more severe.

**Interest Rate Reductions**   Throughout the early months of the crisis the Fed lowered the target federal funds rate (see Figure 23.3). The first downward move—from 5.25 percent to 4.75 percent occurred in September 2007. In October and December 2007 the target was lowered by 25 bps at each FOMC meeting. You can almost see the crisis tightening in January 2008 when the FOMC lowered the target by 75 bps at one of the rare intermeeting conference calls, and then on January 30, 2008, lowered the rate by a further 50 bps to 3 percent. In March there was a further 75 bp reduction, and in April 25 25 bps more to bring the rate to 2 percent. In June and in early August 2008 the rate was held at 2 percent and it seemed that perhaps a corner had been turned. With hindsight we know it was the calm before the storm. In mid-August the FOMC again had an intermeeting conference call and issued a press release noting "the downside risks to growth have increased appreciably." Two weeks later Fannie Mae and Freddie Mac were placed in government conservatorship, and two weeks after that Lehman brothers failed.

In two separate 50 bps steps, the Fed lowered the target for the federal funds rate from 2 percent to 1 percent in October 2008. Then in December 2008 the FOMC voted to set a target range for the federal funds rate from 0 to 25 basis points. Interest rates were essentially zero. But that was the interest rate on the safest of loans— interest rates on risky loans were high and in some markets funds were simply not available. The Federal Reserve argued that lowering the interest rate was not sufficient but rather liquidity had to be provided directly to the markets.

## APPLYING THE CONCEPT
### WHAT HAPPENED IN JAPAN?

The 1990s were not a pleasant time in Japan. After decades of rapid growth, the Japanese economy ground to a halt. Panel A of Figure 23.4 shows how poor Japan's economic performance was from 1985 to 2006. Over the decade of the 1990s, Japanese growth averaged less than 1 percent per year—far below its average of nearly 4 percent in the 1980s.

Japanese policymakers took action, lowering interest rates throughout the decade. Panel B of Figure 23.4 shows the downward path of the overnight cash rate, the Bank of Japan's policy instrument. Finally, in the winter of 1999, the Bank's policy board lowered the target interest rate to zero. Still, growth didn't pick up. With the interest rate at zero, there didn't appear to be much more the Bank of Japan could do. Nominal interest rates can't fall below zero.

Why did the Japanese economy fail to respond to the Bank of Japan's long sequence of interest-rate reductions? Solving the mystery requires that we look at various channels of monetary policy transmission—in this case, asset prices and bank lending. The collapse of the Japanese stock market provides the first piece of the puzzle. From a peak of nearly 40,000 at the end of 1989, the Nikkei 225 index (the Japanese equivalent to the S&P 500) fell by more than half, to 16,000 in 1992. Property prices fell with it. The impact of this decline in asset prices was severe. Beyond its direct effects on consumption and investment, both of which collapsed, the crash did considerable damage to both the creditworthiness of borrowers and banks' balance sheets. Borrowers' net worth fell with the collapse of equity and property values, worsening information problems and depressing aggregate expenditure even further.

When real growth slowed to a standstill, firms were no longer able to repay their loans. The quantity of nonperforming loans skyrocketed, eroding bank capital and causing loan officers to become extremely wary of extending new loans. By 2000, bad loans accounted for 14 percent of outstanding loans, up from 3 percent in 1993. Bank capital fell from a relatively low $5\frac{1}{4}$ percent of assets early in the 1990s to less than $2\frac{1}{2}$ percent in 2000.*

The dramatic rise in the number of nonperforming loans was compounded by the fact that many were backed by assets whose value had collapsed. As a result, many banks had virtually no capital left. They should have been shut down but, for political reasons, closing them was impossible.** So they were allowed to continue operating. Given the large numbers of both bankrupt firms and impaired banks, it was no wonder that the Bank of Japan's monetary policy had virtually no impact. The fact that the interest rate was zero simply didn't matter, because the channels through which interest-rate reductions would normally have influenced real economic activity were almost completely blocked. There was no way for borrowers to obtain financing. Thus, policymakers had little ability to shift the dynamic aggregate demand curve or even to influence its slope. To clean up the mess, the banking system would need to be put back on a solid footing.

U.S. policymakers kept in mind the lessons of Japan's experience in the 1990s as they responded to the financial crisis. Though Americans suffered many of the same consequences as the Japanese—their wealth declined, reducing consumption and investment and damaging borrowers' balance sheets—if the banking system can continue to function, the economy will recover more quickly. A healthy banking system can make all the difference.

* For a thorough discussion of the problems in the Japanese financial system during the 1990s, see Anil K. Kashyap, "Sorting Out Japan's Financial Crisis," *Economic Perspectives*, The Federal Reserve Bank of Chicago, 2000, 4th Quarter, pp. 42–55.

** A striking feature of the Japanese experience in the 1990s is that regulators and supervisors failed to enforce prudential regulations that would have forced many banks to close for lack of adequate capital. The reasons for their "regulatory forbearance" are complex, but two are particularly noteworthy. First, without a fully developed deposit insurance system, it was unclear to regulators how depositors would be compensated when banks were liquidated. Second, and possibly more important, shutting the doors on banks would have meant foreclosing on defaulted borrowers. Not only were many depositors supporters of the political party that held power at the time, but it was commonly believed that some were members of organized crime who were prone to violence. See Mitsuhiro Fukao, "Japan's Lost Decade and Its Financial System," *The World Economy* 26, no. 5 (March 2003), pp. 365–384.

**Changes in the Fed Balance Sheet** As we saw in Chapter 17, the balance sheet of the central bank reveals its actions, and we can see how the Fed responded to the financial crisis by comparing the Fed's balance sheet at the end of 2007, before the financial markets really tightened, with that of April 2009, in Table 23.2 on page 544. Look first at the balance sheet in December 2007 to remind yourself of the "normal" balance sheet. The Fed had assets of close to $1 trillion, and 85 percent of that was in U.S. government bonds that the Fed owned. On the Liabilities side, Federal Reserve Notes in circulation represented 90 percent of the liabilities, with deposits of the government being close to zero and reserves of banks being just under 5 percent.

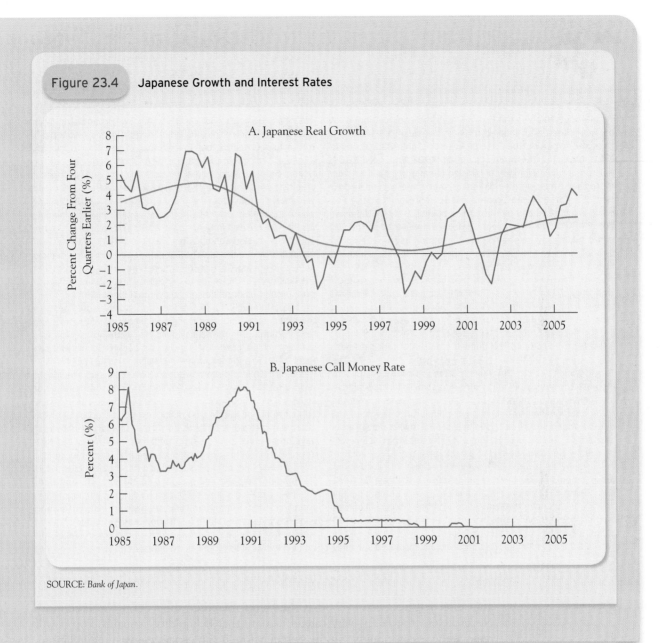

**Figure 23.4**    Japanese Growth and Interest Rates

A. Japanese Real Growth

B. Japanese Call Money Rate

SOURCE: *Bank of Japan.*

Now look at the balance sheet on April 29, 2009. First, the size of the Fed balance sheet has doubled, which means the Fed owns twice as many assets as it did before the crisis. If we look at the liability side (it is simpler to understand) we see that the Fed paid for those assets not by issuing notes, but by (1) increasing the amount of reserves available to the banks, and (2) increasing the amount of deposits in the Treasury account. Recall from Chapter 21 that an expansion in the monetary base will expand the money stock by the same proportion if the money multiplier is constant, but increases in reserves are not inflationary if the banks increase their desired reserve ratios. This is what happened: between December 2007 and April 2009 the money

# TOOLS OF THE TRADE
The Remarkable Expanding Balance Sheet

Throughout 2007–8 the Fed changed the composition of its balance sheet, and doubled its size. Consider the securities that are owned by the Federal Reserve. Table 23.2 on page 544 shows that between December 2007 and April 2009, holdings of U.S. Treasury securities fell slightly but that was more than offset by the holdings of mortgage-backed securities. But the only mortgage-backed securities that the Fed owns are guaranteed by one of the agencies of the U.S. government (Freddie Mac, Fannie Mae, or Ginnie Mae), so the Fed is not taking any risk by holding these mortgages. The banks did not want to hold mortgages and so by buying them the Federal Reserve was increasing the liquidity of the banking system. Ben Bernanke argued that because the banks know that they will be able to sell the MBS to the Federal Reserve they are more willing to originate mortgages and he noted that even by April 2009 mortgage interest rates had fallen.

The second group of assets reflect the Fed's provision of short-term liquidity to the domestic and international financial system—essentially lender-of-last-resort operations. The Term Auction Facility (TAF) was created in December 2007 to increase the supply of liquid funds in response to tightening in interbank funding markets. Discount window lending was the traditional mechanism for supplying liquidity to the markets, but the stigma attached to such visible borrowing made banks hesitant to use that avenue. If markets thought that a bank was in trouble then it might lead to a bank run. The TAF, by encouraging many borrowers (and possibly because the settlement arrangements meant that the funds weren't available for three days and were therefore not an avenue for very urgent liquidity needs), did not have the same stigma. Initially, $100 billion was auctioned, but the amounts increased and in April, 2009 $400 billion was outstanding in loans to depository institutions (see Table 23.2). In December 2007, the Fed also provided currency

swap arrangements with the ECB and Switzerland. The swap arrangements were for $20 billion and $4 billion respectively for up to six months, but the number of countries (including Canada), the amounts, and the term soon increased, and in September they had increased to $620 billion. Like lines of credit, these lines were there in case they were needed and were not all drawn down, and in April 2009 about $250 billion was outstanding. The ABCP Money Market investor lending facility was created in September 2008 in response to the run on money market funds (when Reserve Primary Money Fundamental "broke the buck" after Lehman's failed). The Fed did not (could not legally) directly support the mutual funds; rather the facility extended loans to depository institutions to finance their purchases of money market mutual funds.

Two other facilities to support markets were outside even the broadest definition of traditional lender of last resort, and reflected what Ben Bernanke called the "extraordinary circumstances'" of the crisis: the Term Asset-backed Securities Loan Facility (TALF) and the Commercial Paper Funding Facility. TALF was a $200 billion fund created in November and provided a facility for the New York Fed to lend funds on a wide range of collateral including AAA asset-backed securities. The Treasury agreed to provide up to $20 billion for a credit guarantee. The latter was created in October 2008 to a special company that buys commercial paper using funds borrowed from the New York Fed to provide liquidity in short-term credit markets.

The final line of the asset side of the balance sheet is the funding that the Fed provided to support AIG and Bear Stearns. While this may seem like traditional lender-of-last-resort activity, remember that AIG was an insurance company not a deposit-taking institution, and not subject to Fed supervision. The Fed's rationale was that the survival of AIG was essential to keep the financial system going.

multiplier fell from 1.6 to 0.86 as the banks increased their desired reserve ratio. Nevertheless, the Fed is very careful to note that if liquidity demands drop it will remove the excess liquidity in the system before it can generate unwanted inflation.

The expansion of the asset side of the balance sheet occurred through a series of innovative and complex arrangements. The overall goal was to increase the supply of liquidity throughout the financial markets—through multiple financial institutions and instruments and across the maturity spectrum. That meant expanding existing programs to accept more types of collateral and to allow a broader range of financial institutions to have access to the programs (See Tools of the Trade: The Remarkable Expanding Balance Sheet). The overall effect is that the Fed now holds a range of MBS, commercial paper, and loans to foreign central banks rather than holding only government debt on its books.

The key message to take away is not the details of individual programs but the extent of the tools that the Fed had in its cupboard or invented on the fly. Truly

Table 23.2    Federal Reserve Balance Sheets

| Assets ($ billions) | | 5 Dec 07 | 29 Apr 09 |
|---|---|---|---|
| Securities | US Treasury | 779.7 | 549 |
| | Agency | | 68.1 |
| | MBS | | 366.1 |
| Commercial Paper | | | 181.8 |
| TALF | | | 6.4 |
| Liquidity | Term Auction Facility | | 403.6 |
| | Discount window | | 45.3 |
| | Currency swap lines | | 249.5 |
| | MMMF | | |
| Support for specific institutions | | | 72.2 |
| Other assets | | 140.7 | 163.5 |
| Total | | 920.4 | 2105.5 |
| | | | |
| Liabilities ($ billions) | | | |
| Currency | | 819.3 | 901.2 |
| Government Accounts | | 5.1 | 237.7 |
| Commercial FI deposits | | 16 | 834.9 |
| Other liabilities | | 80 | 131.7 |
| Total | | 920.4 | 2105.5 |

SOURCE: *Federal Reserve H.4.1, Factors Affecting Reserve Balances; www.federalreserve.gov/releases/H41/. Releases dated December 6, 2007, and April 30, 2009.*

extraordinary steps were taken to keep the financial markets functioning, and remarkable challenges were overcome. But this is uncharted territory. Two clear hurdles remain—will the Fed be able to unwind the liquidity when the crisis is resolved? And will the moral hazard created by the support for institutions in trouble encourage excessive risk taking in the future? The monetary authorities are well aware of both pitfalls. The Fed argues that many of the assets are short-term loans, and that when the loans are no longer needed, the balance sheet will shrink. Alternatively, if the Fed wants to reduce the excess reserve balances in the system without shrinking the asset side of the balance sheet, it can use reverse repos. The moral-hazard issue is a longer-term question, and is part of the broader question of reforming financial system regulation. The issue is not only to offset the lessons of the current policy but also to reduce the likelihood of such a crisis recurring. The lessons of the crisis include the realization that "too big to fail" is a critical determinant of policy, not just an abstract idea, and it is not restricted to depository institutions. Regulation and supervision must encompass all systemically important financial institutions.

## Monetary Policy Response in Canada

The direct effect of the financial crisis was significantly smaller in Canada than in the United States, or indeed most of the world. The indirect effects, however, have been severe as Canada is a small open economy that exports 40 percent of output produced. As we saw in Chapter 19, the reduction in commodity prices in late 2008 caused a dramatic decline in gross domestic income in Canada, and Canada entered a recession in the fourth quarter of 2008.

The smaller impact of the financial crisis meant that the Bank of Canada didn't have to take such large and timely measures as the Fed, although it provided necessary liquidity support as we will describe. However, the severity of the economic downturn did call for aggressive expansionary monetary policy. In Chapters 18 and 19, we described how the central bank implements expansionary monetary policy by lowering the interest rate. However, nominal interest rates cannot go below zero; in early 2009 the interest rate was effectively zero so the Bank had to amend its monetary policy framework to stimulate the economy in the face of that bound.

**Interest Rate Reductions**    As in the United States, you can almost feel the crisis worsening as you look at the path for the target for the overnight rate in Figure 23.5. In July 2007, the Bank of Canada raised the target to 4.5 percent in response to apparent inflationary pressures. Despite the problems in the United States housing market in the fall of 2007, Canadian financial markets were functioning well and no further changes were made until December 2007 when the rate fell by 25 bps. In January there was a further 25 bps reduction. In March and April, following the worsening financial situation, which would now clearly impact the Canadian economy, there were two 50 bps reductions to bring the rate to 3 percent. Then in October the financial crisis became severe and the Bank joined other G7 banks in lowering the official rate by 50 bps then lowered it a further 25 bps on the regular fixed announcement date later that month. The continuing crisis led to reductions of 75 bps in December and 50 more in January and March 2009—bringing the rate to 0.5 percent. Any further reductions in the standard operating band would have reduced the interest rate on reserves to zero, and the Bank altered its operating procedures to prevent this. In April 2009 it reduced the operating band from 50 bps to 25 bps. While the Bank rate was lowered from 75 bps to 50 bps, and the target for the overnight rate was lowered

**Figure 23.5    Canadian Overnight Rate**

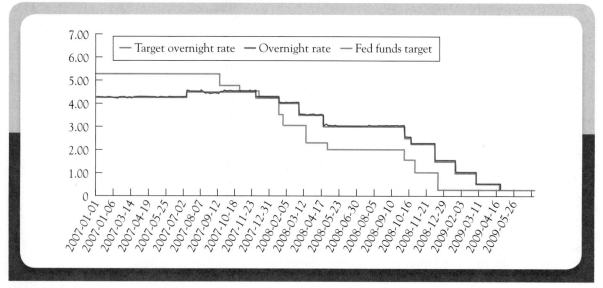

SOURCE: *Bank of Canada. Overnight rate v39050; Target for overnight rate v39079; both from Table 176-0048.*

| Table 23.3 | Bank of Canada Balance Sheets |

|  | Jun 30 2008 | April 30 2009 |
|---|---|---|
| **Assets ($ millions)** | | |
| T Bills | 21,578 | 13,130 |
| Gov't bonds | 29,798 | 32,535 |
| SPRAs | 977 | 29,400 |
| Other Assets | 417 | 251 |
| Total | 52,770 | 75,316 |
| | | |
| **Liabilities ($ millions)** | | |
| Currency | 50,040 | 51,979 |
| Government accounts | 1,443 | 19,122 |
| Commercial FI deposits | 180 | 3,000 |
| Other liabilities | 959 | 1,028 |
| Capital | 148 | 187 |
| Total | 52,770 | 75,316 |

SOURCE: *Bank of Canada, Banking and Financial Statistics (September 2009), Section B1, pages s10–s11.*

to 25 bps, 25 bps was also set as the interest rate on deposits. The Bank argued that it had reached the "effective lower bound" on interest rates, effectively exhausting the scope of this instrument of monetary policy. At the same time, the Bank made a "conditional commitment" to keep the overnight rate at 25 bps until the middle of 2010. From Chapter 7 we know that the expectations hypothesis implies that long-term interest rates are a function of expected future short-term interest rates, so the Bank used the commitment as a way of lowering longer-term interest rates in order to stimulate the economy. The Bank also noted that it has the capacity for quantitative easing (expanding its balance sheet) and credit easing (changing the composition of its balance sheet).

**Changes in the Bank of Canada Balance Sheet**   Again we turn to the central bank balance sheet to see the Bank's response to the crisis (see Table 23.3). First, notice that the expansion of the balance sheet, while striking, is only 50 percent rather than the Fed's doubling of the size of the balance sheet. As in the United States, expansion happened with minimal effect on the notes in circulation, and with a dramatic expansion in government deposits; however, in Canada, there was no significant increase in banking system reserves. In fact, the entire expansion of the balance sheet has been funded by government deposits.

Notice that both the scale and the composition of the asset side of the balance sheet have changed. The Bank of Canada's holdings of government securities are virtually unchanged; all the expansion of the balance sheet is through repos that, remember, are loans to the financial system. The Bank's approach to increasing market liquidity was to increase the range of collateral that it would accept, increase the range of participants that could engage in transactions, and increase the term

Figure 23.6    Interest Rate Spreads

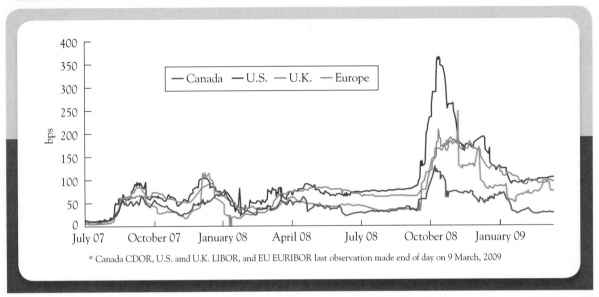

* Canada CDOR, U.S. amd U.K. LIBOR, and EU EURIBOR last observation made end of day on 9 March, 2009

SOURCE: *Bank of Canada. Spreads Between 1-Month Interbank Offered Rates and Overnight Index Swap Rates www.bankofcanada.ca (David Longworth speech 12 March 2009).*

of loans. While the Bank introduced a range of programs, the most durable and popular was the regular-term purchase and resale agreement (i.e., repo) facility.[10] The traditional bank programs allowed primary dealers to participate in PRAs, and the banks (more formally, participants in the large-value clearing system [LVTS]) used the Standing Liquidity Facilities (SLF) for their liquidity needs. But SLF were mainly overnight loans on a narrow range of collateral; the Bank allowed LVTS participants to participate in the Term PRA facility. In expanding the range of collateral, the Bank also allowed the banks to use their Canadian dollar non-mortgage loan portfolios for SLF borrowing (on a temporary basis) and introduced a term loan facility that would also allow LVTS participants to borrow against such loan portfolios.

By March 2009, the money market spreads had decreased (see Figure 23.6), but the Bank observed that secondary bond markets were still not functioning as they had before the crisis. The Bank introduced a term PRA facility for private-sector instruments (e.g., corporate bonds) to enhance the liquidity of that market.

When the target for the overnight was reduced to 25 bps (which the Bank of Canada called the effective lower bound as the rate could not go further without impeding the operations of the system) the Bank lost the ability to use the overnight rate for stimulative monetary policy and switched to other tools to inject monetary stimulus.[11]

[10] Even if a facility is not explicitly used, its existence could provide liquidity. Takeup is not the only evidence for the importance of a liquidity facility. Just knowing that an asset, such as securitized mortgages or credit card debt, could be used as collateral will improve market conditions for those assets without necessarily requiring any takeup of the facility.

[11] The Bank of Canada stated that it could also use credit easing as a stimulative policy, and it could be argued that this is exactly what the Bank has been doing in expanding the liquidity in the economy. In fall 2008, the Bank reduced its holdings of government securities by $13 billion and lent $35 billion through repos. There was both a substitution between asset classes and an increase in the amount of central bank lending.

## YOUR FINANCIAL WORLD
### The Financial Crisis Hits Students

The economic consequences of the financial crisis are likely to persist both because recovery may be slow and because of policies put in place in reaction to the crisis. But the impact of the crisis and its consequences will be uneven. In 2008–9, the impact was felt heavily by those employed in, or earning profits from, natural resource industries and the manufacturing sector, as well as those who were retiring on a defined contribution pension plan (see In the News: Pension Plans Facing a Funding Crisis: Survey on page 292). The employment effects were particularly severe for students. In August 2009 the unemployment rate for students was 16.4 percent, the highest level since Statistics Canada started collecting data in 1977.* The financial situation for students is exacerbated by tighter loan conditions and the general economic decline, which makes parents less able to provide financial support.

Despite the best efforts of policymakers to develop an "exit strategy" that mitigates the negative effects of the very aggressive fiscal and monetary policies implemented to offset the severity of the crisis, there will probably be a lingering aftertaste when the recovery is underway. Stimulative fiscal policies increased the government debt and debt service, which will lead to higher tax rates. Central banks are afraid to pull back too early, which might stall the recovery but if the banks reduce their desired reserves, the excess liquidity may lead to increases in inflation. This is particularly the case in the United States where the money base doubled during the crisis. Recall from Chapter 22 that if inflation is higher in the United States than in Canada, the Canadian dollar will tend to appreciate. The inflationary pressures will test the commitment of the Bank of Canada to its 2 percent inflation target (which is scheduled to be reassessed in 2011). In the face of unstable inflation, the difference between real and nominal values of variables such as interest rates, wages, and exchange rates will carry new significance.

SOURCE: *Statistics Canada, "The Daily," August 7, 2009, http://www.statcan.gc.ca/daily-quotidien/090807/dq090807a-eng.htm.*

Notice that the balance sheet of the Bank of Canada shows that the Bank has neutralized or sterilized the monetary impact of its support for credit markets. (The money stock grew by 11 percent (M2++) or 17 percent (M1+) between December 2007 and April 2009). The Bank could increase the reserves of the banking system either by choosing not to sterilize future repos or by shifting some of the deposits of the government into the financial institutions. The banks could then increase the supply of credit to households and businesses.

## Regulatory Reform

The actions of policymakers in 2008 and 2009 focused on limiting the damage that the financial crisis inflicted on the real economy, but in the longer term the focus will be on reducing the likelihood and severity of future financial crises. As we saw at the beginning of the chapter, financial crises have happened for centuries so their elimination is unlikely; however, policymakers can work toward reducing their frequency and acuteness. The proposals naturally mirror the factors that are seen as the proximate causes of the crisis and we will discuss them briefly in turn. Frequently emphasized principles include alignment of incentives, enhanced transparency, macro-prudential regulation, and international co-operation.

Many proposals emphasize improved regulation of financial institutions—so-called micro-regulation. One feature common to many suggestions is the need to get the incentives right. If CEOs are rewarded (immensely) for short-term gains and not penalized for long-term losses, they may take too many risks; if credit rating agencies get more business when they give high ratings, they will be tempted to inflate ratings; if banks can securitize subprime mortgages and get them off their balance sheets without paying a risk premium, they will issue a lot of subprime mortgages. Proposals to reform regulation attempt to mitigate all theses sources of risk. Other proposals emphasize a need for more transparency in markets. If buyers understood what was in the securitized products they would price them accordingly. There is a need for derivatives to trade on exchanges and through a central counterparty so that the ripple effect is limited if transactions need to be unwound.

The expansion of the Fed's lender-of-last-resort policies to nonbanks has revealed that banks are not the only systemically important financial institutions, and, as we discussed in Chapter 14, if institutions are to be "insured" by the public sector then, to reduce the resulting moral hazard problem, they must be regulated and monitored. Proposals to address the problem that some institutions are too big to fail include taxing large institutions or requiring such institutions to have (continuously updated) break-up plans so that they would never be able to claim they were too big to fail.[12] It remains to be seen whether or not such proposals are implementable.

While monitoring individual institutions is defined as micro-prudential regulation and requires a fine-tuning of existing regulatory institutions and policies, policymakers are also calling for macro-prudential or systemic regulation. Such regulation would recognize explicitly the interdependencies and feedback effects across institutions and sectors of the financial market. The most prominent proposal advocates procyclical capital requirements and addresses the problem that when a financial crisis hits, capital requirements on financial institutions effectively tighten just when capital is hard to raise. For example, risk ratings based on experience during a boom assign low risk to some financial assets and therefore the capital requirements under Basel II are low. When the crisis began in 2007, risks were re-evaluated and the capital requirements rose across all financial institutions. Since capital is hard to raise during a downturn, institutions respond by lowering their loans—the deleveraging process. As many institutions delever at the same time, they drive asset prices down, further eroding bank capital and exacerbating the process. Procyclical capital requirements would force financial institutions to build up a capital buffer in good times that was available in downturns. Again, the practicalities of such a proposal are nontrivial and the need for international co-ordination (when business cycles are not completely in phase) would add to the challenges.

More generally, the globalization of financial markets means that in rewriting the rule book there needs to be international co-operation. First, because if one jurisdiction has tighter rules than another, institutions will headquarter where the rules are lax but they will operate globally. Second, financial institutions are all interconnected: European banks had considerable holdings of U.S. subprime mortgages. The Icelandic banks were funded by Internet deposits from the British. Yet one of the key practical difficulties is finding the appropriate forum or forums for such co-operation— the IMF? the BIS? the World Bank? The G20 leaders met in April and September 2009 to determine which organization has the capacity and the legitimacy to oversee change.

"*Please stand by for a series of tones. The first indicates the official end of the recession, the second indicates prosperity, and the third the return of the recession.*"

[12] The tax is like an insurance premium that would pay for the potential damage if such an institution failed. If size generates economies of scale that are greater than the tax then the institution will pay; if not, they will become many small institutions that are not too big to fail.

# The Great Recession?

The financial crisis began as a liquidity crisis, and turned into a solvency crisis and an economic crisis. The severity of the financial crisis was extreme, indeed similar to the crisis in 1929, and policymakers knew that extreme policy measures were necessary to avoid a repeat of the "Dirty Thirties."[13] In September 2008 global financial markets teetered on the edge of a complete seizure. The Federal Reserve and other central banks stepped in quickly, dramatically lowering interest rates and providing lender-of-last-resort facilities to major financial institutions including some nonbank financial institutions. Their actions stemmed the financial crisis but its economic consequences continued. In mid-2009 it is not clear how long the global economy will take to recover from the crisis, or whether the national and international authorities will develop the tools to ensure the efficient functioning of financial instruments, institutions, and markets. One thing that is clear, however, is the centrality of financial systems in our economy.

[13] In March 2009, Dominique Kahn Strauss, the Managing Director of the IMF, used the term "the Great Recession" to describe the economic situation. It captures very neatly the contrast with "the Great Moderation," but also and more importantly the contrast with "the Great Depression." While the financial collapse and economic crisis are the most severe since the Great Depression, prompt action by monetary and fiscal authorities make it unlikely that the consequences will be as severe.

## Key Terms

deleveraging, 532

macro-prudential
  policy, 548

shadow banking
  system, 532

too big to fail, 534

tranche, 531

zero nominal interest
  bound, 538

## Chapter Summary

1. The crisis of 2007–09 that began in the United States and spread globally came after a long period of macroeconomic stability and was characterized by
   a. A financial crisis comprising a liquidity crisis and a credit crisis.
   b. An economic crisis that led to increased unemployment and negative economic growth.
2. The crisis arose out of a number of factors:
   a. Low interest rates, resulting from U.S. monetary policy, high Chinese savings rates, and low-risk premia, led to an aggressive search for higher yields in the United States.
   b. Rapid spread of new financial instruments and a lack of transparency created greater interconnections and feedbacks in the financial system than regulators realized.
   c. Misaligned incentives in the financial system meant that those taking risks either didn't realize they were taking risks or were not going to have to pay the price if the risk turned out badly.
   d. An excess of leverage and a deficit of liquidity, combined with the vast interconnectedness of the global financial system, turned a problem in a small sector of the U.S. financial market into a global financial crisis.
   e. Canadian banks did not have excessive exposure to subprime housing loans and were well capitalized so that they alone among the G7 countries did not need government support.
3. The Federal Reserve responded by:
   a. Lowering the target for the Federal funds rate to zero (meaning it hit the zero bound on nominal interest rates.
   b. Expanding lender-of-last-resort policies to a wider range of financial institutions and a broader range of collateral.
   c. Expanding the monetary base.

4. The Bank of Canada also lowered its policy interest rate to its effective lower bound and undertook some credit-easing policies.

5. Policymakers (through the G20) committed in principle to a range of international and domestic reforms including:
   a. Greater alignment of incentives—ensuring CEOs are not rewarded for short-term results that reflect risk not return.
   b. Enhanced transparency, particularly in derivative markets.
   c. Macro-prudential supervision that monitors systemic risks.
   d. International co-operation.

## Conceptual Problems

1. Recall from Chapter 16 the traditional *lender of last resort* policy advocated by Walter Bagehot. What policies would Bagehot have recommended that the Fed use, and would that have been a better or worse policy than those of Bernanke?

2. What changes in the financial system had the U.S. regulatory environment not kept pace with?

3. If you were designing a regulatory environment for mortgage markets, which features of subprime mortgages would you keep and which (if any) would you prohibit or regulate?

4. We learned in Chapter 5 that diversification is a good tool to reduce risk. Yet when U.S. financial assets were held by financial institutions around the globe it meant that the financial crisis became a global financial crisis. Does this invalidate our previous conclusion?

5. How are capital requirements a force promoting procyclicality?

6. What are the pros and cons of limiting the compensation of bank CEOs? What limits would you recommend?

7. Are there any circumstances under which nominal interest rates would go below zero?

8. In April 2009 the Bank of Canada committed to holding the target for the overnight rate at 25 bps for one year. Use the expectations hypothesis of the term structure to explain what the Bank would hope to achieve with this announcement.

9. Some economists have argued that all banks should be required to issue subordinated debt. These are bonds that are junior to other claims on the bank and so are repaid only if the bank has enough funds to repay all depositors. Why might the issue of such bonds provide useful signals to regulators?

10. Show how each of the five core principles of the book can inform our analysis of the financial crisis.

## Analytical Problems

11. Some economists have worried that the mounting crisis will bring deflation while others worry about inflation. Using the model we developed in Chapters 18 and 19, what factors make each a valid concern?

12. Suppose the policy interest rate controlled by the central bank and the inflation rate were both zero. Use the aggregate demand–aggregate supply framework to show how the economy could fall into a deflationary spiral if it were hit by a negative aggregate demand shock.

13. Use the aggregate demand–aggregate supply framework to show how a boom in equity prices might affect inflation and output in the short run. In the absence of any policy change by the central bank, what would the long-run impact be on inflation and output?

14. Some economists argue that central banks should monitor asset price bubbles and use contractionary monetary policy to deflate them. Discuss what factors might indicate the presence of a bubble.

15. What implications does the presence of the zero nominal interest rate bound have for the choice of monetary policy target?

# GLOSSARY

## A

**accountability** The idea that central bankers should be held responsible for their policies. (15)

**advances to members of the Canadian Payments Association** Loans under either Standing Liquidity Facilities (SLF) or Emergency Lending Assistance (ELA) to support the functioning of the financial system. (17)

**adverse selection** When the price or quantity in a market is affected by one party having superior information about the products to be traded. (11)

**aggregate expenditure** The total demand for the economy's production; the sum of consumption, investment, government purchases, and net exports. (18)

**American option** An option that can be exercised any time up to the expiration date, in contrast to a *European option*. (9)

**appreciation (of a currency)** A rise in the value of a country's currency relative to that of another country. (10)

**arbitrage** The practice of simultaneously buying and selling financial instruments to benefit from temporary price differences; eliminates a riskless profit opportunity. (9)

**asset** Something of value that can be owned; a financial claim or property that serves as a store of value. (3)

**asset-backed securities** Shares in the returns or payments arising from a specific asset or pool of assets, such as home mortgages or student loans. (3)

**asset-price channel** The channel of the monetary policy transmission mechanism where changes in policy affect consumption and output through their impact on stock prices and the value of real estate. (21)

**asymmetric information** The fact that the two parties to a transaction have unequal knowledge about each other. A borrower, for example, has more information about his or her abilities and prospects than a lender. (11)

**at-the-money option** An option whose strike price equals the current market price for the underlying instrument. (An in-the-money option is one whose strike price is less than the current market price and an out-of-the-money option is one whose strike price is more than the current market price.) (9)

**augmented expectations** Hypothesis of the term structure; the hypothesis that the shape of the yield curve is determined by expectations of future short-term interest rates plus a liquidity premium. (7)

**Automated Clearing and Settlement System (ACSS)** A CPA (Canadian Payments Association) system through which the values of paper-based and electronic payment items are exchanged and the amounts "due to" and "due from" are calculated. (2)

**average** See *expected value*. (5)

## B

**balance sheet** The list of assets and liabilities that shows an individual's or firm's financial position. (12)

**balance-sheet channel** The channel of the monetary policy transmission mechanism where changes in policy affect consumption and output through their impact on household and firm balance sheets. (21)

**bank capital** Bank assets minus bank liabilities; the net worth of the bank; the value of the bank to its owners. (12)

**bank charter** The license authorizing the operation of a bank. (13)

**bank holding company** A company that owns one or more banks and possibly other nonbank subsidiaries. (13)

**Bank of Canada** The central bank of Canada responsible for monetary policy, bank notes, financial system, and funds management. (3)

**bank panic** The simultaneous failure of many banks during a financial crisis. (14)

**bank rate** The Bank Rate is the rate of interest that the Bank of Canada charges on one-day loans to major financial institutions. (17)

**bank run** An event when depositors lose confidence in a bank and make withdrawals, exhausting the bank's reserves. (14)

**bank supervision** Government oversight of commercial banks. (14)

**bank-lending channel** The channel of the monetary policy transmission mechanism in which changes in policy affect consumption and output through their impact on banks' willingness to make loans. (21)

**Basel Accord** An agreement requiring internationally active banks to hold capital equal to or greater than 8 percent of their risk-adjusted assets. (14)

**basis point** (or "beep" or "bp") One one-hundredth of a percentage point. (4)

**benchmark bond** A low-risk bond, usually a government bond, to which the yield on a risky bond is compared to assess its risk. (7)

**benchmark** The performance of a group of experienced investment advisors or money managers. (5)

**Big Mac index** The index used to estimate whether currencies are under- or overvalued; based on the price of the Big Mac in various countries. (10)

**Board of Governors of the Federal Reserve System** The seven-member board that oversees the Federal Reserve System, including participation in both monetary policy and financial regulatory decisions. (16)

**bond market** A financial market in which debt instruments with a maturity of more than one year are traded. (3)

**bond** A financial instrument that promises a series of future payments on specific dates; also known as a fixed-income security. (4)

**branch banking** A banking system that allows a bank to have many branches (compared to a unit banking system, which prohibits branching). (13)

**Bretton Woods system** The international monetary system in place from 1945 to 1971, in which exchange rates were fixed to the U.S. dollar, and the dollar was convertible into gold at $35 per ounce. (22)

**bubble** A persistent and expanding gap between actual stock prices and those warranted by the fundamentals; usually created by mass enthusiasm. (8)

**business cycles** The periodic fluctuations in aggregate economic output. (19)

## C

**call option** A contract that confers the right, but not the obligation, to purchase a financial instrument at a predetermined price on or prior to an agreed-upon date. (9)

**CAMELS** The system used by U.S. bank examiners to summarize their evaluation of a bank's health. The acronym stands for Capital adequacy, Asset quality, Management, Earnings, Liquidity, and Sensitivity to risk. (14)

**Canada Mortgage and Housing Corporation (CMHC)** Canada's national housing agency, which works to enhance housing finance options. (13)

**Canadian dollar effective exchange rate index (CERI)** A weighted average of bilateral exchange rates for the Canadian dollar against the currencies of Canada's major trading partners. (10)

**capital controls** Government-imposed barriers to investment across international boundaries; restrictions on the ability of foreigners to buy and sell domestic assets. (22)

**capital gain** The difference between the price that has been paid for an asset and the higher price at which it is sold; contrasts with a *capital loss*, where the price paid exceeds the price at which the asset is sold. (6)

**capital loss** The difference between the price that has been paid for an asset and the lower price at which it is sold; contrasts with *capital gain*. (6)

**central bank independence** The central bank's freedom from political pressure. (15)

**central bank** The financial institution that manages the government's finances, controls the availability of money and credit in the economy, and serves as the bank to commercial banks. (1, 15)

**central bank's balance sheet** The statement of the assets and liabilities of the central bank. (17)

**centralized exchange** A financial market in which financial instruments are traded in a single physical location. (3)

**cheque** An instruction to the bank to take funds from one account and transfer them to another. (2)

**collateral** Assets pledged to pay for a loan in the event that the borrower doesn't make the required payments. (11)

**commercial paper** Short-term, privately issued zero-coupon debt that is low risk and very liquid and usually has a maturity of fewer than 270 days. (7)

**commodity monies** Precious metals or other items with intrinsic value that are used as money. (2)

**common stock** Ownership shares in a firm; also called just *stock* and *equity*. (8)

**compound interest** The interest on interest as it accumulates over time. (4)

**consol or perpetuity** A coupon bond in which the issuer makes regular interest payments forever, never repaying the principal; a coupon bond with infinite time to maturity. (6)

**consumption smoothing** Choosing a path of consumption spending that is less volatile than income flows. (3)

**consumption** Spending by individuals for items such as food, clothing, housing, transportation, entertainment, and education. (18)

**contagion** When the failure of one bank causes a run on other banks. (14)

**corporate paper** A short-term discount bond issued by a corporation. (7)

**coupon payment** Yearly payment made to the holder of a coupon bond. (4)

**coupon rate** Annual interest rate equal to the yearly coupon payment divided by the face value of a coupon bond. (4)

**covered interest parity condition** A condition that is met when returns on bonds denominated in different currencies are the same assuming that the currency risk is hedged in the forward market. (10)

**credibility** The idea that everyone trusts central bankers to do what they say they are going to do. (15)

**credit card** A promise by a bank to lend the cardholder money in order to make purchases. (2)

**credit default swap** An arrangement in which one party agrees, for a fee, to take the credit risk of an instrument owned by another party. (9)

**credit risk** The probability that a borrower will not repay a loan; see also *default risk*. (12)

**currency board** A fixed-exchange-rate system in which the central bank commits to holding enough foreign currency assets (often dollars) to back domestic currency liabilities at a fixed rate. (22)

**currency** Paper money; for example, dollar bills or euro notes. (2)

**currency-to-deposit ratio** The ratio of publicly held currency to demand deposits held at commercial banks. (20)

**current yield** A bond's yearly coupon payment divided by its current market price. (6)

## D

**debit card** A card that provides instructions to the bank to transfer funds from the cardholder's account directly to a merchant's account. (2)

**debt market** A financial market where bonds, loans, and mortgages are traded. (3)

**debt** A loan obligating the borrower to make payments to the lender. (2)

**default risk** The probability that a borrower will not repay a loan; see also *credit risk*. (6)

**defined-benefit pension plan** A pension plan in which beneficiaries receive a lifetime retirement income based on the number of years they worked at the company and their final salary. (13)

**defined-contribution pension plan** A pension plan in which beneficiaries make payments into an account and then receive the accumulation, plus the investment income, on retirement, at which time they must decide what to do with the funds. The options include accepting a lump sum, removing small amounts at a time, or converting the balance to a fixed monthly payment for life by purchasing an annuity. (13)

**deleveraging** Reducing the ratio of debt to assets; for example, a financial institution can deleverage by selling shares (raising equity) or reducing loans. Households can deleverage by paying down debts. (23)

**demand deposits** Standard chequing accounts that pay no interest; part of M1+. (2)

**demand for dollars** Dollars demanded in the foreign exchange market as a function of the nominal exchange rate. (10)

**demand shock** An unexpected change in aggregate expenditure, such as a rise or fall in consumer confidence, that shifts the dynamic aggregate curve. (19)

**deposit expansion multiplier** The formula for the increase in commercial bank deposits following a one-dollar increase in reserves. (20)

**deposit insurance** The government guarantee that depositors will receive the full value of their accounts should a financial institution fail. (14)

**depository institution** A financial institution that accepts deposits and makes loans. (12)

**depreciation of a currency** The decrease in the value of a country's currency relative to the value of another country's currency. (10)

**derivative instrument** A financial instrument, such as a futures contract or an option, whose value and payoff are "derived from" the behaviour of underlying instruments. (3)

**derivative** See *derivative instrument*. (9)

**diminishing marginal utility** The principle that as you consume more of an object the increase in the benefit from each additional unit declines. (5)

**direct clearer** A member of the Canadian Payments Association that participates directly in the Automated Clearing Settlement System (ACSS) and maintains a settlement account at the Bank of Canada. (2)

**direct finance** Financing in which borrowers sell securities directly to lenders in the financial markets. (3)

**directive** The instruction (in writing) issued by the Minister of Finance to the Governor of the Bank of Canada specifying a change in policy in the event of a profound disagreement between the Bank and the government. (16)

**discount bonds** A security that does not pay interest on a periodic basis, but is initially sold at a discount from its face value and redeemed for the full amount at maturity. (6)

**discount loans** A loan from the Federal Reserve to a commercial bank. (17)

**discount rate** The interest rate at which the Federal Reserve makes discount loans to commercial banks. (16, 17)

**diversification** Splitting wealth among a variety of assets to reduce risk. (5)

**dividend-discount model** The theory that the fundamental value of a stock equals the present value of expected future dividend payments. (8)

**dividends** The payments made to a company's stockholders when the company makes a profit. (8)

**dollarization** One country's formal adoption of the currency of another country for use in all its financial transactions. (22)

**Dow Jones Industrial Average** The best-known index of stock market performance, it measures the average price of a single share in 30 very large and well-known American companies. (8)

**dual banking system** The system in the United States in which banks supervised by federal government and state government authorities coexist. (13)

**dynamic aggregate demand (AD) curve** The graph of the relationship between inflation and the quantity of spending on domestically produced goods and services. (18)

## E

**ECB's Marginal Lending Facility** The facility through which the ECB provides overnight loans to banks; the analogue to the Federal Reserve's primary credit facility. (17)

**economies of scale** When the average cost of producing a good or service falls as the quantity produced increases. (13)

**economies of scope** When the average cost of producing a good or service falls as the number of different types of goods produced increases. (13)

**electronic communications networks (ECNs)** An electronic trading system that automatically matches buy and sell orders, for currencies or stocks, at specified prices. (3)

**electronic funds transfer (EFT)** Movements of funds directly from one account to another over an electronic network. (2)

**Emergency Lending Assistance (ELA)** Bank of Canada facility that provides funding for up to six months to CPA members that are solvent but facing serious and persistent liquidity problems. (17)

**e-money** Private money, as represented by a claim on the issuer, which is (1) stored on an electronic device, (2) issued on receipt of funds, and (3) accepted as a means of payment by persons other than the issuer. (2)

**equation of exchange** The equation stating that nominal income equals the quantity of money times the velocity of money; $MV = PY$. (20)

**equity market** A financial market where stocks are bought and sold. (3)

**equity premium puzzle** The long-run return to owning equities exceeds that to owning bonds by more than standard measures of the risk premium would predict. (8)

**equity** Ownership shares in a firm; also called *stock* and *common stock*. (8)

**euro area** The countries in Europe that use the euro as their common currency. (16)

**euro** The name of the currency used in the countries of the European Monetary Union. (10)

**eurodollars** Dollar-denominated deposits outside the United States. (13)

**European Central Bank (ECB)** The central authority, located in Frankfurt, Germany, which oversees monetary policy in the common currency area. (15, 16)

**European option** An option that can be exercised only on the expiration date, not before, in contrast with an *American option*. (9)

**European System of Central Banks (ESCB)** The European Central Bank plus the National Central Banks of all the countries in the European Union, including those that do not participate in the monetary union. (15, 16)

**Eurosystem** The European Central Bank plus the National Central Banks of participating countries; together, they carry out the tasks of central banking in the euro area. (15, 16)

**exchange-rate channel** The channel of the monetary policy transmission mechanism where changes in policy affect consumption and output through their impact on exchange rates. (21)

**Executive Board of the ECB** The six-member body in Frankfurt that oversees the operation of the European Central Bank and the Eurosystem. (16)

**expansionary output gap** When current output exceeds potential output; the gap puts upward pressure on inflation. (18)

**expectations hypothesis** The proposition that long-term interest rates are the average of expected future short-term interest rates. (7)

**expected return** The probability-weighted sum of possible returns to an investment. (5)

**expected value** The probability-weighted sum of possible values of an investment; also known as the mean or average. (5)

## F

**face value** The final payment made by a bond issuer to the holder of the bond at its maturity; also known as *par value*. (4)

**fallen angel** A low-grade bond that was initially high-grade but whose issuer fell on hard times. (7)

**Fannie Mae** The Federal National Mortgage Association; a U.S. government–sponsored entity that aids in the financing of home mortgages. (13)

**federal funds rate** The interest rate banks charge each other for overnight loans on their excess deposits at the Fed; the interest rate targeted by the FOMC. (16)

**Federal Open Market Committee (FOMC)** The 12-member committee that makes monetary policy decisions in the United States. Members include the seven members of the Board of Governors, the president of the Federal Reserve Bank of New York, and the presidents of four Federal Reserve Banks. (16)

**Federal Reserve Banks** The 12 regional banks in the Federal Reserve System. (1, 16)

**Federal Reserve System** The central bank responsible for monetary policy in the United States. (1, 16)

**fiat money** Currency with no intrinsic value; it has value as a consequence of government decree. (2)

**financial institutions** Firms, such as banks and insurance companies, that provide access to the financial markets, both to savers who wish to purchase financial instruments directly and to borrowers who want to issue them; also known as financial intermediaries. (1, 3)

**financial instrument** The written legal obligation of one party to transfer something of value (usually money) to another party at some future date, under certain conditions. (1, 3)

**financial market** The part of the financial system that allows people to buy and sell financial instruments quickly and cheaply. (1, 3)

**financial system stability** One objective of the central bank is to eliminate financial system volatility, ensuring that it remains stable. (15)

**financial system** The system that allows people to engage in economic transactions. It is composed of five parts: money, financial instruments, financial markets, financial institutions, and central banks. (1)

**fiscal policy** The government's tax and expenditure policies, usually formulated by elected officials. (15)

**fixed-payment loan** A type of loan that requires a fixed number of equal payments at regular intervals; home mortgages and car loans are examples. (4)

**fixed-rate payer** The party to an interest-rate swap that is making fixed payments. (9)

**flight to quality** An increase in the demand for low-risk government bonds, coupled with a decrease in the demand for virtually every risky investment. (7)

**floating-rate payer** The party to an interest-rate swap that is making variable payments. Also called flexible-rate payer. (9)

**foreign exchange intervention** The purchase or sale of foreign exchange by government officials with the intention of moving the nominal exchange rate. (10, 17, 22)

**foreign exchange reserves** Assets of the central bank denominated in foreign currency. (17)

**foreign exchange risk** The risk arising from holding assets denominated in one currency and liabilities denominated in another. (12)

**forward contract** An agreement to exchange an asset for money in the future at a currently agreed-upon price. (9)

**Freddie Mac** A U.S. government organization that buys mortgages on the secondary market, pools them, and then sells them as mortgage-backed securities to investors on the open market (similar to Fannie Mae). (13)

**free rider** Someone who doesn't pay the cost but still gets the benefit of a good or service. (11)

**fundamental value** The present value of the expected future returns to owning an asset, which equals the asset's price in an efficient market. (8)

**future value** The value on some future date of an investment made today. (4)

**futures contract** A standardized agreement specifying the delivery of an underlying asset (commodity or financial instrument) at a given future date for a currently agreed-upon price. (9)

## G

*Glass-Steagall Act* U.S. legislation passed in 1933 that created deposit insurance and separated investment and commercial banking. (13)

**gold standard** A fixed-exchange-rate regime in which the currencies of participating countries are directly convertible into gold. (22)

**Goodhart's law** When a variable is used as a policy instrument, the previous relationship between the variable and the target will break down. (21)

**Governing Council of the Bank of Canada** The Governing Council is the policy-making body of the Bank. It consists of the Governor, Senior Deputy Governor, and four Deputy Governors. It is responsible for monetary policy, decisions aimed at promoting a sound and stable financial system, and the strategic direction of the Bank. (16)

**Governing Council of the ECB** The (currently) 19-member committee that makes monetary policy in the common currency area. (16)

**government purchases** Spending on goods and services by federal, provincial, and municipal governments. (18)

**gross domestic income (GDI)** The purchasing power in the economy; real GDI is measured by deflating nominal GDP by the prices paid by households and businesses. (19)

**gross domestic product (GDP)** The market value of final goods and services produced in the economy during a year. (2)

## H

**hard peg** An exchange-rate system in which the central bank implements an institutional mechanism that ensures its ability to convert a domestic currency into the foreign currency to which it is pegged. (22)

**hedge funds** Private, largely unregulated, investment partnerships that bring together small groups of people who meet certain high-wealth requirements. (13)

**hedging** Reducing overall risk by investing in two assets with opposing payoffs. (5)

**high-powered money** See *monetary base*. (17)

**holding period return** The return from purchasing and selling a bond (applies to bonds sold before or at maturity). (6)

**hyperinflation** Very high inflation; when prices double every two to three months. (15)

## I

**idiosyncratic risk** Risk affecting a small number of people (a specific firm or industry). (5)

**illiquid** The inability to meet immediate payment obligations. For a bank, reserves are insufficient to honour current withdrawal requests. (14)

**index** A measure that aggregates many components and describes their level relative to a baseline. (8)

**indirect clearer** A member of the Canadian Payments Association that participates indirectly in the Automated Clearing Settlement System (ACSS), through using the services of one of the direct clearers to clear and settle accounts. (2)

**indirect finance**  An institution such as a bank stands between the lender and the borrower, borrowing from the lender and providing the funds to the borrower. (3)

**inflation rate**  The measurement of inflation. (2)

**inflation risk**  The risk that the real value of the payments from owning a bond will be different from what was expected; that the real interest rate on a bond will differ from what was expected. (2, 6)

**inflation targeting**  A monetary policy strategy that involves the public announcement of a numerical inflation target, together with a commitment to make price stability the central bank's primary objective to which all other objectives are subordinated. (17)

**inflation**  A sustained rise in the general price level; a situation in which the price of everything goes up more or less at the same time. (2)

**inflation-indexed bonds**  A bond whose yield equals a fixed real interest rate plus realized (as opposed to expected) inflation. (6)

**information costs**  The costs lenders must pay to screen potential borrowers to determine their creditworthiness and monitor how they use the loans. (3)

**information**  A collection of facts. The basis for the third core principle of money and banking: Information is the basis for decisions. (1)

**insolvent**  When the value of a firm's or bank's assets is less than the value of its liabilities; negative net worth. (14)

**interest-rate channel**  The traditional channel of the monetary policy transmission mechanism where changes in policy affect consumption and output through their impact on interest rates. (21)

**interest-rate risk**  1. The risk that the interest rate will change, causing the price of a bond to change with it. (6)

2. The risk that changes in interest rates will affect a financial intermediary's net worth. It arises from a mismatch in the maturity of assets and liabilities. (12)

**interest-rate spread**  1. The difference between the interest rate a bank receives on its assets and the interest rate it pays to obtain liabilities. (12) 2. Can also be used as a synonym for *risk spread*. (7, 12)

**interest-rate swap**  A contract between two counterparties specifying the exchange of interest payments on a series of future dates. (9)

**intermediate targets**  Variables that are not directly under the central bank's control but lie somewhere between the tools policymakers do control and their objectives; the quantity of money is an example. (17)

**internal rate of return**  The interest rate that equates the present value of an investment with its cost. (4)

**inverted yield curve**  When the term structure of interest rates slopes down. (7)

**investment horizon**  The length of time an investor plans on holding an asset. (6)

**investment**  Spending by firms for additions to the physical capital they use to produce goods and services. (18)

## J

**January effect**  A general increase in stock prices in January. (8)

**junk bond**  A bond with a high risk of default. Also called a high-yield bond. (7)

## L

**law of one price**  The principle that two identical goods should sell for the same price regardless of location. (10)

**lender of last resort**  The ultimate source of credit to banks during a panic. A role for the central bank. (14, 17)

**leverage**  Borrowing to finance part of an investment; increases expected return and risk. (5)

**liability**  Something you owe. (3)

**limited liability**  The provision that even if a company fails completely, the maximum amount that shareholders can lose is their initial investment. (8)

**liquidity premium theory of the term structure**  The proposition that long-term interest rates equal the average of expected short-term interest rates plus a risk premium that rises with the time to maturity. (7)

**liquidity risk**  The risk that a financial institution's liability holders will suddenly seek to cash in their claims; for a bank this is the risk that depositors will unexpectedly withdraw deposit balances. (6, 12)

**liquidity**  A measure of the ease with which an asset can be turned into a means of payment. (1, 2, 12)

**loan loss reserves**  A portion of a bank's capital that is set aside to cover potential losses from defaulted loans. (12)

**London Interbank Offered Rate (LIBOR)**  The interest rate at which banks lend eurodollars to other banks. (13)

**long futures position**  The position held by a buyer of a futures contract who has committed to buying the commodity/currency on the settlement date. (9)

**long-run aggregate supply curve (LRAS)**  The quantity of output supplied in the long run at any level of inflation; the LRAS curve is vertical at potential output. (18)

**long-run real interest rate**  The real interest rate that equates aggregate demand with potential output. (18)

**Lucas critique**  Economist Robert Lucas's observation that changes in policymakers' behaviour will change people's expectations, altering their behaviour and the observed relationships among economic variables. (21)

# M

**M1+ gross** The narrowest monetary aggregate, which measures the most liquid means of payment available: currency, travellers' cheques, demand deposits, and other checkable deposits. (2)

**M2++ gross** A commonly used monetary aggregate, it includes M1+ as well as somewhat less liquid financial instruments: small-denomination time deposits, savings deposits, money market deposit accounts, and retail money market mutual fund shares. (2)

**macro-prudential policy** Prudential regulation that aims to reduce risk across the system as a whole—so-called systemic risk. (23)

**margin** 1. A minimum down payment legally required to purchase a stock. 2. A deposit placed by the buyer and seller of a futures contract with the clearing corporation. (9)

**market capitalization** The total market value of a company; the price of a share of stock times the total number of shares outstanding. (8)

**market federal funds rate** The overnight interest rate at which lending between banks takes place in the market; differs from the federal funds rate target set by the FOMC. (17)

**markets** A virtual or physical place where goods, services, and financial instruments are purchased and sold. The basis for the fourth core principle of money and banking: Markets set prices and allocate resources. (1)

**marking to market** Accounting rule in which a financial instrument is repriced and funds transferred from the loser to the winner at the end of every day. (9)

**maturity date** The time to the expiration of a debt instrument; the time until a bond's last promised payment is made. (4)

**maturity mismatch** A balance sheet whose assets and liabilities have different maturities, used especially when liabilities are shorter term than assets. (14)

**mean reversal effect** The theory that profits can be made based on the assumption that stock prices tend to return to their mean. (8)

**mean** See *expected value*. (5)

**means of payment** Something that can be used to purchase goods and services; one of the functions of money. (2)

**minimum bid rate** The minimum interest rate that banks can bid for reserves in the ECB's weekly refinancing operation; the European equivalent of the Fed's target federal funds rate; also known as the target refinancing rate. (17)

**monetary aggregates** Measures of the quantity of money; M1+ and M2++. (2)

**monetary base** The currency in the hands of the public plus reserves in the banking system; the central bank's liabilities. (17)

**monetary policy framework** A structure in which central bankers clearly state their goals and the trade-offs among them. (15)

**monetary policy reaction curve** The relationship between the real interest rate set by the central bank and the level of inflation. (18)

**monetary policy** The central bank's management of money, credit, and interest rates. (15)

**money market mutual fund** A fund that pools the resources of small investors and invests them in short-term marketable debt issued by governments or large corporations. (2)

**money market** A market in which debt instruments with a maturity of less than one year are traded. (3)

**money multiplier** The ratio between the quantity of money and the monetary base; the quantity of money (M) equals the money multiplier ($m$) times the monetary base (MB). $M = m \times MB$. (20)

**money** An asset that is generally accepted as payment for goods and services or repayment of debt, acts as a unit of account, and serves as a store of value. (1, 2)

**moral hazard** The risk that a borrower or someone who is insured will behave in a way that is not in the interest of the lender or insurer; it is caused by asymmetric information. (11)

**multiple deposit creation** Part of the money supply process whereby a $1 increase in the quantity of reserves works its way through the banking system, increasing the quantity of money by more than $1. (20)

**mutual fund** A fund that pools the resources of a large number of small investors and invests them in portfolios of bonds, stocks, and real estate; managed by professional managers. (8)

# N

**Nasdaq Composite Index** The value-weighted index of over 5,000 companies traded on the over-the-counter (OTC) market through the National Association of Securities Dealers Automatic Quotations service; the index is composed mainly of smaller, newer firms and in recent years has been dominated by technology and Internet companies. (8)

**National Central Banks (NCBs)** The central banks of the countries that belong to the European Union. (16)

*National Housing Act* **(NHA)** Canadian legislation to promote housing affordability and the well-being of the housing sector. (13)

**net exports** Exports minus imports; it represents an addition to the demand for domestically produced goods. (18)

**net interest margin** A bank's interest income minus its interest expenses divided by total bank assets; net interest income as a percentage of total bank assets. (12)

**net worth** The difference between a firm's or household's assets and liabilities. (11)

**no-arbitrage condition** A condition that is met if it is not possible to make a profit after expenses by buying in one market and selling in another. (9)

**nominal exchange rate** The value of one unit of a country's currency in terms of another country's currency. (10)

**nominal gross domestic product** The market value of final goods and services produced in the economy during a year measured at current (dollar) prices. (20)

**nominal interest rate** An interest rate expressed in dollar terms; the real interest rate plus expected inflation. (4)

**nondepository institution** A financial intermediary that does not issue deposit liabilities. (12)

**notional principal** The amount upon which the interest payments in an interest-rate swap are based. (9)

**O**

**off-balance-sheet activities** Bank activities, such as trading in derivatives and issuing loan commitments, that are neither assets nor liabilities on the bank's balance sheet. (12)

**Office of the Superintendent of Financial Institutions (OSFI)** The regulator and supervisor of all banks and federally incorporated or registered trust and loan companies and insurance companies; also oversees private pension plans subject to federal oversight supervision, ensuring that financial institutions comply with regulations. (14)

**open market operations** When the central bank buys or sells a security in the open market. (17)

**open market purchase** The purchase of a security by the central bank. (17)

**open market sale** The sale of a security by the central bank. (17)

**operating instruments** The policy instruments that the central bank controls directly; the federal funds rate is an example. (17)

**operational risk** The risk a financial institution faces from computer hardware or software failure, natural disaster, terrorist attacks, and the like. (12)

**output gap** The difference between current output and potential output. (18)

**overnight cash rate** The overnight interest rate on interbank loans in Europe; the European analogue to the overnight rate in Canada. (17)

**overnight rate** The rate at which major participants in the Canadian money market borrow and lend one-day funds to each other. (17)

**over-the-counter (OTC) market** A financial market in which trades occur through networks of dealers connected together electronically. (3)

**overvalued currency** A country's currency when it is worth more than purchasing power parity implies. (10)

**P**

**par value** The final payment made by a bond issuer to the holder of the bond at its maturity; also known as face value. (4)

**payments system** The web of arrangements that allow for the exchange of goods and services, as well as assets, among different people. (2)

**payoff** The amount an investor receives in return for an investment. (5)

**portfolio demand for money** The theory of the demand for money based on the use of money as a store of value; the theory that treats money as an asset analogous to a bond. (20)

**portfolio** A collection or group of investments held by a person or company. (3)

**potential output** What the economy is capable of producing when its resources are used at normal rates; also called sustainable output. (15, 18)

**preauthorized debit (PAD)** A withdrawal from your account at a financial institution (FI) that is initiated by a company or an FI that has your authority to do so. (2)

**precautionary demand for money** The theory of the demand for money based on the idea that people hold money to ensure they have resources when faced with unexpected events. (20)

**present value** The value today (in the present) of a payment that is promised to be made in the future. (4)

**price stability** One objective of the central bank is to keep inflation low so that prices are stable on average. (15)

**price-weighted average** An index based on the average price of a collection of individual stocks. Price-weighted averages give greater weight to shares with higher prices. (8)

**primary credit** The term used to describe short-term, usually overnight, discount loans made by the Federal Reserve to commercial banks. (17)

**primary discount rate** The interest rate charged by the Federal Reserve on primary credit; also known as the discount rate, it is usually 100 basis points above the target federal funds rate. (17)

**primary financial market** A financial market in which a borrower obtains funds from a lender by selling newly issued securities. (3)

**primary market** A financial market in which a borrower obtains funds from a lender by selling newly issued securities. (8)

**principal** The amount borrowed; in the case of a bond, the face value or par value. (4)

**probability** A measure of the likelihood that an event will occur. (5)

**property and casualty insurance** Insurance against damage from events such as automobile accidents, fire, and theft. (13)

**purchase-and-assumption method** Where the Canada Deposit Insurance Corporation finds a firm that is willing to take over a failed bank. (14)

**purchasing power parity (PPP)** The principle that a unit of currency will purchase the same basket of goods anywhere in the world. (10)

**put option** A contract that confers the right, but not the obligation, to sell a financial instrument at a predetermined price on or prior to an agreed-upon date. (9)

**real return bonds** A bond whose yield equals a fixed interest rate plus realized inflation. (6)

## Q

**quantity theory of money** The theory that changes in nominal income are determined by changes in the quantity of money. (20)

## R

**rating downgrade** When a bond-rating agency lowers the rating of a company, signalling that its bonds have an increased risk of default. (7)

**rating upgrade** When a bond-rating agency raises the rating of a company, signalling that its bonds have a reduced risk of default. (7)

**rating** A measure of the default risk associated with a company's debt; normally a series of letters going from AAA for bonds with the lowest risk of default to D for bonds that have defaulted. (7)

**real business-cycle theory** The theory that prices and wages are flexible, so inflation adjusts rapidly, current output always equals potential output, and all business-cycle fluctuations arise from changes in potential output. (19)

**real exchange rate** The exchange rate at which one can exchange the goods and services from one country for goods and services from another country. (10)

**real interest rate** The interest rate measured in terms of constant (real) dollars; the nominal interest rate minus expected inflation. (4)

**recession** A decline in overall economic activity, as defined by Statistics Canada (for Canada) or the National Bureau of Economic Research (U.S.). (19)

**recessionary output gap** When current output is below potential output; the gap puts downward pressure on inflation. (18)

**repurchase agreement (repo)** A short-term collateralized loan in which a security is exchanged for cash, with the agreement that the parties will reverse the transaction on a specific future date, as soon as the next day. (12)

**reputational risk** The risk of an event that would undermine public confidence in an institution or product. (12)

**required reserves** Reserves that a bank must hold to meet the requirements set by regulators in some countries. Canadian banks have no required reserves. (17)

**reserve ratio** The ratio of liquid liabilities of a financial institution (such as retail deposits) to its deposits at the central bank. (20)

**reserves** A bank's vault cash plus the balance in its account at the central bank. (17)

**residual claimant** The final person to be paid. Stockholders are residual claimants; if the company runs into financial trouble, only after all other creditors have been paid will they receive what is left, if anything. (8)

**return on assets (ROA)** Bank net profits after taxes divided by total bank assets; a measure of bank profitability. (12)

**return on equity (ROE)** Bank net profits after taxes divided by bank capital; a measure of the return to the bank's owners. (12)

**risk premium** The expected return minus the risk-free rate of return; the payment to the buyer of an asset for taking on risk. (5)

**risk spread** The yield over and above that of a low-risk bond such as a U.S. Treasury, with the same time to maturity; it is a measure of the compensation investors require for the risk they are bearing. Also called a default risk premium. (7)

**risk structure of interest rates** The relationship among the yields of bonds with the same time to maturity but different levels of risk. (7)

**risk** A measure of uncertainty about the future payoff to an investment, measured over some time horizon and relative to a benchmark. The basis for the second core principle of money and banking: Risk requires compensation. (1, 5)

**risk-averse investor** Someone who prefers an investment with a certain return to one with the same expected return but any amount of uncertainty. (5)

**risk-free asset** An investment whose future value is known with certainty. (5)

**risk-free rate of return** The rate of return on a risk-free asset. (5)

**risk-neutral investor** Someone who is indifferent between investments with different risks but the same expected return. (5)

**rule of 72** The rule that allows you to find out how many years it will take for the value of an investment to double; divide 72 by the annual interest rate. (4)

**Russell 2000** A broad value-weighted index of U.S. stock prices, it is based on the prices of the 2,000 smaller of the 3,000 largest stocks traded in the United States. (8)

## S

**S&P/TSX composite index** A value-weighted index of the largest companies traded on the Toronto stock exchange. (8)

**secondary financial market** A financial market in which previously issued securities are bought and sold. (3)

**secondary market** A financial market in which previously issued securities are bought and sold. (8)

**seignorage revenue** Revenue the central bank earns from the issue of bank notes. (16)

**shadow banking system** Non-depository financial institutions that have low regulation but to which banks and depository institutions may have considerable exposure. (23)

**short futures position** The position held by the seller of a futures contract that has committed to deliver the commodity on the settlement date. (9)

**small-firm effect** The theory that investing in small companies generates higher (risk-adjusted) returns than investing in large companies. (8)

**sovereign risk** The risk that a government will default. (12)

**speculative attack** A crisis in which financial market participants believe the government will become unable to maintain its exchange rate at the current fixed level, so they sell the currency, forcing an immediate devaluation. (22)

**speculator** Someone who takes risks for the purpose of making a profit. (9)

**spot price** The market price paid for immediate delivery of a commodity or financial instrument. (9)

**spread over Government of Canadas** The difference between the interest rate on a bond and a bond of similar maturity issued by the Canadian government. (7)

**spread over Treasuries** The difference between the yield on a bond and that on a U.S. Treasury with the same time to maturity; a measure of the riskiness of the bond. (7)

**spreading risk** Reducing overall risk by investing in assets whose payoffs are unrelated. (5)

**stability** Steady and lacking in variation. The basis for the fifth core principle of money and banking: Stability improves welfare. (1)

**stabilization policy** Monetary and fiscal policies designed to stabilize output and inflation. (19)

**Standard & Poor's** A stock-market index that is based on the value of 500 of the largest firms in the U.S. economy. (7)

**standard deviation** Square root of the variance measure of risk; measures the spread of possible outcomes. (5)

**Standing Liquidity Facilities (SLF)** Bank of Canada facility that provides access to overnight liquidity to direct LVTS participants against eligible collateral. (17)

**sterilized intervention** A foreign exchange intervention that alters the composition of the central bank's assets but leaves the size of its liabilities unchanged. (22)

**stock market** The market where the prices of common stock are determined. (8)

**stock** Ownership shares in a firm; also called *common stock* and *equity*. (3)

**stock-market indexes** Index numbers that provide a sense of whether the value of the stock market is going up or down. (8)

**store of value** Allows movement of purchasing power into the future; one of the functions of money. (2)

**stored-value card** A card that can be used to make purchases after money is transferred from a cardholder's account. (2)

**strike price** The predetermined price at which a call or put option specifies that the underlying asset can be bought (call) or sold (put); also called the exercise price. (9)

**supply of dollars** The number of dollars supplied in the foreign exchange market as a function of the nominal exchange rate. (10)

**supply shock** An unexpected change in the costs of production, such as a rise or fall in oil prices, that shifts the short-run aggregate supply curve. (19)

**sustainable growth** When the economy is growing at the rate dictated by potential output. (15)

**swap spread** The difference between the benchmark interest rate and the swap rate, it is a measure of risk. (9)

**swap** A financial contract obligating one party to exchange one set of payments for a second set of payments made by a counterparty. (9)

**systematic risk** Economywide risk that affects everyone and cannot be diversified. (5)

**Treasury bill (T-bill)** A short-term (one year or less) discount bond issued by a government. (6)

## T

**T-account** A simplified balance sheet in the form of a T that shows the changes in assets on one side and the changes in liabilities on the other. (17)

**target federal funds rate** The Federal Open Market Committee's target for the interest rate at which banks make overnight loans to each other; the FOMC's primary policy instrument. (17)

**Taylor rule** A rule of thumb for explaining movements in the federal funds rate; the monetary policy rule developed by economist John Taylor. (19)

**term life insurance** Insurance that provides a payment to the policyholder's beneficiaries in the event of the insured's death at any time during the policy's term. (13)

**term spread** The difference between yields on long-term and short-term bonds with the same risk characteristics. (7)

**term structure of interest rates** The relationship between yields on bonds with the same risk characteristics but different maturities. (7)

**theory of efficient markets** The notion that the prices of all financial instruments, including stocks, reflect all available information. (8)

**time value (of an option)** The price the buyer of an option pays to the seller that is in excess of the value of the option if it were immediately exercised. (9)

**time** A measurable period during which something can happen. The basis for the first core principle of money and banking: Time has value. (1)

**too-big-to-fail policy** The idea that some financial institutions are so large that government officials cannot allow them to fail because their failure will put the entire financial system at risk. (14, 23)

**trading risk** The risk that traders who work for a bank will create losses on the bank's own account. (12)

**tranche** When shares in a pool of securities are sold they are divided into classes known as tranches with different exposures to risk in the underlying assets. (23)

**transactions costs** The costs, including time, associated with buying and selling financial instruments, as well as goods and services. (3)

**transactions demand for money** The demand for money based on the use of money as a means of payment, for transactions purposes. (20)

**transmission mechanism (of monetary policy)** The channels whereby changes in monetary policy influence the real economy. (21)

**transparency** The central bank's communication of its policy decisions and how they are made clear to the financial markets and the public. (15)

## U

**underlying instrument** A financial instrument used by savers/lenders to transfer resources directly to investors/borrowers; also known as a primitive security. (3)

**undervalued currency** A country's currency when it is worth less than purchasing power parity implies. (10)

**underwriting** The process through which an investment bank guarantees the price of a new security to a corporation and then sells it to the public. (13)

**unit bank** A bank without branches. (13)

**unit of account** The units (like dollars) used to quote prices and other financial quantities; one of the functions of money. (2)

**universal bank** An institution that engages in all aspects of financial intermediation, including banking, insurance, real estate, brokerage services, and investment banking. (13)

**unsecured loan** A loan that is not guaranteed by collateral. (11)

**unsterilized foreign exchange intervention** A foreign exchange intervention that both alters the composition and changes the size of the central bank's balance sheet. (22)

## V

**value at risk** The worst possible loss over a specific time horizon at a given probability; a measure of risk. (5)

**value-weighted index** An index that is based on the value of the firms, such as the S&P/ TSX Composite. Value-weighted indexes give greater weight to larger firms. (8)

**variance** The probability-weighted sum of the squared deviations of the possible outcomes from their expected value. (5)

**vault cash** Currency that is physically held inside a bank's vaults and automated teller machines (ATMs). (17)

**velocity of money** The average number of times each unit of money is used per unit of time. (20)

**vesting** When the contributions your employer has made to the pension plan on your behalf belong to you. (13)

## W

**wealth** The total value of all assets; the net worth of an individual. (2)

**whole life insurance** A combination of term life insurance and a savings account in which a policyholder pays a fixed premium over his or her lifetime in return for a fixed benefit when he or she dies. (13)

**Wilshire 5000** The most broadly based value-weighted stock index in use. It covers the roughly 6,500 publicly traded stocks in the United States. (8)

## Y

**yield curve** A plot showing the yields to maturity of different bonds of the same riskiness against the time to maturity. (7)

**yield to maturity** The yield bondholders receive if they hold the bond to its maturity when the final principal payment is made. (6)

**yield** The interest rate that equates the price of a bond with the present value of its payments. (4)

## Z

**zero nominal-interest-rate bound** The fact that the nominal interest rate cannot fall below zero. (21, 23)

# Photo Credits

# INDEX

# Cecchetti: Money, Banking & Financial Markets

## Commonly Occurring Symbols

| Symbol | Definition | Introduced in: |
|---|---|---|
| M1+ | M1 monetary aggregate | Chapter 2 |
| M2++ | M2 monetary aggregate | Chapter 2 |
| FV | Future Value | Chapter 4 |
| $i$ | Nominal interest rate (usually at an annual rate) | Chapter 4 |
| PV | Present Value | Chapter 4 |
| $FV_n$ | Future Value in $n$ years | Chapter 4 |
| $F$ | Final payment of a bond (principal, face value, par value) | Chapter 4 |
| $P_{BP}$ | Present Value of Bond Principle Payment | Chapter 4 |
| $P_{CP}$ | Present Value of Bond Coupon Payments | Chapter 4 |
| C | Coupon payment | Chapter 4 |
| $P_{CB}$ | Price of a Coupon Bond | Chapter 4 |
| $r$ | Real interest rate | Chapter 4 |
| $\pi_e$ | Expected inflation | Chapter 4 |
| St. Dev. | Standard Deviation | Chapter 5 |
| VaR | Value-at-Risk | Chapter 5 |
| $i_e$ | Expected interest rate | Chapter 7 |
| $i_{nt}$ | Interest rate on a bond with n years to maturity at time $t$ | Chapter 7 |
| $rp_n$ | Risk premium on an n-year bond | Chapter 7 |
| $D$ | Stock dividend payment | Chapter 8 |
| $P$ | Price of a stock | Chapter 8 |
| $g$ | Dividend growth rate | Chapter 8 |
| $rf$ | Risk-free return | Chapter 8 |
| $i_f$ | Foreign interest rate | Chapter 9 |
| ROA | Return on assets | Chapter 12 |
| ROE | Return on equity | Chapter 12 |
| MB | Monetary base | Chapter 17 |
| $\Delta$ | Change in a variable | Chapter 20 |
| $D$ | Chequable Deposits | Chapter 20 |
| $r_D$ | Desired deposit reserve ratio | Chapter 20 |
| $C_D$ | Currency to deposits ratio | Chapter 20 |
| RR | Desired reserves | Chapter 20 |